THE OX

FA

THE OXFORD HANDBOOK OF

FASCISM

Edited by

R. J. B. BOSWORTH

OXFORD

UNIVERSITY PRESS

OXFORD
UNIVERSITY PRESS

Great Clarendon Street, Oxford OX2 6DP

Oxford University Press is a department of the University of Oxford.
It furthers the University's objective of excellence in research, scholarship,
and education by publishing worldwide in

Oxford New York

Auckland Cape Town Dar es Salaam Hong Kong Karachi
Kuala Lumpur Madrid Melbourne Mexico City Nairobi
New Delhi Shanghai Taipei Toronto

With offices in

Argentina Austria Brazil Chile Czech Republic France Greece
Guatemala Hungary Italy Japan Poland Portugal Singapore
South Korea Switzerland Thailand Turkey Ukraine Vietnam

Oxford is a registered trade mark of Oxford University Press
in the UK and in certain other countries

Published in the United States
by Oxford University Press Inc., New York

British Library Cataloguing in Publication Data

Data available

Library of Congress Cataloging in Publication Data

The Oxford handbook of fascism / edited by Richard Bosworth.
p. cm. – (Oxford handbooks in history)
Includes bibliographical references.
ISBN 978-0-19-929131-1
1. Fascism–Europe–History. 2. Fascism–Europe–Historiography.
3. Europe–Politics and government. 4. Europe–Politics and government–Historiography.
I. Bosworth, R. J. B.
D726.5.O96 2009
335.6094–dc22   2008046283

Typeset by SPI Publisher Services, Pondicherry, India
Printed in Great Britain
on acid-free paper by
Ashford Colour Press Ltd, Gosport, Hampshire

ISBN 978–0–19–929131–1 (Hbk.)
ISBN 978–0–19–959478–8 (Pbk.)

2 4 6 8 10 9 7 5 3 1

Contents

PART I   IDEAS AND FORMATIVE EXPERIENCE

PART II   THE FIRST FASCIST NATION

PART III   THE NAZI COMPARISON

PART IV   OTHERS

PART V   REFLECTION AND LEGACIES

ACKNOWLEDGEMENTS

The editor would like to acknowledge the role at OUP of Christopher Wheeler in suggesting this book and of Kate Hind in seeing it through to completion. I am also grateful to Reading University History Department who welcomed an initial workshop of the chapters by most of the contributors in February 2007 and to Samantha Quinn for checking and the index. Elizabeth Stone was a sub-editor of dedication well beyond the call of duty and has proved yet again how crucial good subediting is to quality publication.

LIST OF CONTRIBUTORS

Roger Absalom is Honorary Research Fellow at the Humanities Research Centre, Sheffield Hallam University. His publications include *A Strange Alliance: Aspects of Escape and Survival in Italy 1943–1945* (Florence, 1991); *Italy since 1800: A Nation in the Balance?* (Harlow, 1995); and *Perugia Liberata: documenti anglo-americani sull'occupazione alleata di Perugia (1944–1945)* (Florence, 2001).

Richard Bessel is Professor of Twentieth-Century History at the University of York. His publications include *Germany after the First World War* (Oxford, 1993), *Life after Death: Approaches to a Cultural and Social History of Europe during the 1940s and 1950s* (Cambridge, 2003) (edited with Dirk Schumann), and *Nazism and War* (London, 2004).

Guido Bonsaver is University Lecturer of Italian at Oxford University and Fellow of Pembroke College. His most recent publications include *Censorship and Literature in Fascist Italy* (Toronto, 2007), *Elio Vittorini: letteratura in tensione* (Florence, 2008), and, co-edited with R. Gordon, *Culture, Censorship and the State in 20th Century Italy* (Oxford, 2005).

R. J. B. Bosworth has a joint chair arrangement between the University of Western Australia and Reading University in the UK. His last three books are *Mussolini* (London, 2002), *Mussolini's Italy* (London, 2005), and *Nationalism* (London, 2007). He is working for Yale University Press on a new book to be entitled *Rome and its Histories 1800–2000*.

Anna Cento Bull is Professor of Italian History and Politics at the University of Bath. Her publications include *The Lega Nord and the Northern Question in Italian Politics* (London, 2001) (with M. Gilbert); *Speaking Out and Silencing: Culture, Society and Politics in Italy in the 1970s* (Oxford, 2006) (edited jointly with A. Giorgio), and, most recently, *Italian Neo-fascism: The Strategy of Tension and the Politics of Nonreconciliation* (Oxford, 2007).

H. James Burgwyn is Emeritus Professor of History at West Chester University. His books are *Empire on the Adriatic: Mussolini's Conquest of Yugoslavia 1941–1943* (New York, 2005), *Italian Foreign Policy in the Interwar Period 1918–1940* (Westport, CT, 1997), *The Legend of the Mutilated Victory: Italy, the Great War, and the Paris Peace Conference, 1915–1919* (Westport, CT, 1993).

Mauro Canali is full Professor of Contemporary History in the University of Camerino. His publications include *Il delitto Matteotti* (Bologna, 2004), *Le spie del regime* (Bologna, 2004), and *Mussolini e il petrolio iracheno* (Turin, 2007).

Gustavo Corni is Professor of Contemporary History at the University of Trento, Italy. His most recent publications include *Hitler's Ghettoes: Voices from a Beleaguered Society 1939–1944* (London, 2002); *Il sogno del 'grande spazio': le politiche d'occupazione nell'Europa nazista* (Rome, 2005), and *Hitler* (Bologna, 2007).

Patrizia Dogliani is Professor of Contemporary History at the University of Bologna (Italy). Her publications include *Italia fascista 1922–1940* (Milan, 1999), *Storia dei Giovani* (Milan, 2003), and *Storia sociale del fascismo* (Turin, forthcoming).

Mimmo Franzinelli is an independent scholar who has written a number of important books about Fascism. His study of squadrist violence, *Squadristi: protagonisti e techniche della violenza fascista, 1919-1922*, won the prestigious B. Croce prize in Italy. His most recent books are *Il delitto Rosselli: 9 giugno 1937: anatomia di un omicidio politico* (2007) and *La sottile linea nera: neofascismo e servizi segreti da Piazza Fontana a Piazza della Loggia* (2008).

Robert S. C. Gordon is Reader in Modern Italian Culture at the University of Cambridge and a Fellow of Gonville and Caius College. His publications include *Primo Levi's Ordinary Virtues: From Testimony to Ethics* (Oxford, 2001), *An Introduction to Twentieth-Century Italian Literature: A Difficult Modernity* (London, 2005), and (co-edited with Guido Bonsaver) *Culture, Censorship and the State in 20th-Century Italy* (Oxford, 2005).

Marko Attila Hoare is Senior Research Fellow at Kingston University, London. He is the author of *The History of Bosnia: From the Middle Ages to the Present Day* (London, 2007), *Genocide and Resistance in Hitler's Bosnia: The Partisans and the Chetniks, 1941–1943* (London, 2006), and *How Bosnia Armed* (London, 2004).

Radu Ioanid is the director of the International Archival Programs Division, US Holocaust Memorial Museum, Washington, DC. His publications include *The Holocaust in Romania: The Destruction of Jews and Gypsies under the Antonescu Regime, 1940–1944* (Chicago, 2000), *The Ransom of the Jews: The Story of the Extraordinary Secret Bargain between Romania and Israel* (Chicago, 2005), and *The Sword of the Archangel: Fascist Ideology in Romania* (Boulder, CO, 1990).

Rikki Kersten is Professor of Modern Japanese Political History in the Department of Political and Social Change, Research School of Pacific and Asian Studies, at the Australian National University. She is the editor of and contributor to *The Left in the Shaping of Japanese Democracy* (London: 2006) with D. Williams; and the author of 'The Social Imperative of Pacifism in Postwar Japan', *Critical Asian Studies*, 38/2 (2006); and 'Maruyama Masao and the Dilemma of the Public Intellectual in Postwar Japan', in G. Steunebrink and E. van der Zweerde (eds), *Civil Society, Religion and the Nation* (Amsterdam, 2004).

Alan Kramer is Associate Professor of History at Trinity College Dublin. His publications include *Dynamic of Destruction: Culture and Mass Killing in the First World War* (Oxford, 2007) and *German Atrocities, 1914: A History of Denial* (New Haven, 2001), with John Horne.

Roger D. Markwick is Senior Lecturer in History at the University of Newcastle, Australia. His publications include *Rewriting History in Soviet Russia: The Politics of Revisionist Historiography, 1956–1974* (Houndmills, 2001) and (co-authored) *Russia's Stillborn Democracy? From Gorbachev to Yeltsin* (Oxford, 2000).

Bob Moore is Professor of Twentieth Century European History at the University of Sheffield. His publications include *Victims and Survivors: The Nazi Persecution of the Jews in the Netherlands, 1940–1945* (London, 1997) and *Resistance in Western Europe* (Oxford, 2000). He has recently completed a major study with Martin Thomas and Larry Butler, *Crises of Empire: Decolonization and Europe's Imperial States, 1918–1975* (London, 2008).

Philip Morgan is Senior Lecturer in Contemporary European History at the University of Hull. His published books include *Italian Fascism, 1915–1945* (2nd edn. Basingstoke, 2004), *Fascism in Europe, 1919–1945* (London, 2003), and *The Fall of Mussolini: Italy, the Italians and the Second World War* (Oxford, 2007).

Kevin Passmore is Reader in History at Cardiff University. He is the author of *Fascism: A Very Short Introduction* (Oxford 2006), and 'The Gendered Genealogy of Political Religions Theory', *Gender and History* (2008). He is at present completing *The Right in the French Third Republic*, for Oxford University Press.

Robert O. Paxton is Professor of History Emeritus at Columbia University. His publications include *Vichy France: Old Guard and New Order, 1940–1944* (2nd edn. New York, 2001), *Vichy France and the Jews* (Stanford, CA, 1995), with Michael Marrus, and *The Anatomy of Fascism* (New York, 2004.)

Corinna Peniston-Bird is Senior Lecturer in Cultural History at Lancaster University. Her publications include 'Coffee, Klimt and Climbing: Constructing an Austrian National Identity in Tourist Literature 1918–1938', in J. K. Walton (ed.), *Histories of Tourism: Representation, Identity and Conflict* (Clevedon, 2005), and *Contesting Home Defence: Men, Women and the Home Guard in the Second World War* (Manchester, 2007), with Penny Summerfield.

Mark Pittaway is Senior Lecturer in European Studies at the Open University. His publications include *Eastern Europe, 1939–2000* (London, 2004).

J. F. Pollard is Fellow in History at Trinity Hall, Cambridge, and Emeritus Professor of Modern European History at Anglia Ruskin University. He has published extensively on the history of modern Italy and the papacy, most notably *The Vatican and Italian Fascism, 1929–1932* (Cambridge, 1985), *Money and the Rise of the Modern Papacy: Financing the Vatican, 1850–1950* (Cambridge, 2005), and 'Clerical Fascism: Context, Overview and Conclusion', in M. Feldman and M. Turda (eds), *'Clerical Fascism' in Interwar Europe* (London, 2008).

Martin Pugh was Professor of Modern British History at Newcastle University until 1999 and Research Professor in History at Liverpool John Moores University from 1999 to 2002. He is now a self-employed historian. His publications include *'Hurrah for the Blackshirts!' Fascists and Fascism in Britain between the Wars* (2005), 'The British Union of Fascists and the Olympia Debate', *Historical Journal*, 41 (1998), and 'The Liberal Party and the Popular Front', *English Historical Review*, 121 (2006).

Davide Rodogno is an Academic Fellow at the School of History, University of St Andrews. His publications include *Against Atrocity: Humanitarian Interventions in the Ottoman Empire (1815–1914)* (tentative title, forthcoming), *Fascism's European Empire* (Cambridge, 2006), 'Réflexions liminaires à propos des interventions humanitaires des puissances européennes au dix-neuvième siècle', *Relations internationales*, 131 (2007), and 'La Politique des occupants italiens à l'égard des Juifs en France métropolitaine: humanisme ou pragmatisme?', *Vingtième Siècle*, 93 (January–March 2007).

Glenda Sluga is Professor of International History at the University of Sydney. Her publications include *The Nation, Psychology, and International Politics* (Basingstoke, 2006), *The Problem of Trieste and the Italo-Yugoslav Border: Difference, Identity, and Sovereignty in Twentieth Century Europe* (Albany, NY, 2001), and, with Barbara Caine, *Gendering European History* (Leicester, 2000).

Nathan Stoltzfus, Associate Professor of History, Florida State University, has published numerous articles in general and scholarly journals and is an author or editor of four books including *Resistance of the Heart: Intermarriage and the Rosenstrasse Protest in Nazi Germany* (New York, 1996), *Social Outsiders in Nazi Germany* (Princeton, 2001), and *Courageous Resistance: The Power of Ordinary People* (New York, 2007).

Joan Tumblety is lecturer in modern French history in the University of Southampton. Her publications include 'The Football World Cup of 1938: Politics, Spectacles and *la culture physique* in Inter-war France', *French Historical Studies*, 31/1 (2008), 'Responses to Women's Enfranchisement in France, 1944–1945', *Women's Studies International Forum*, 26/5 (2003); ' "Civil Wars of the Mind": The Commemoration of the 1789 Revolution in the Parisian Press of the Radical Right, 1939', *European History Quarterly*, 30/3 (2000).

Mary Vincent is Professor of Modern European History at the University of Sheffield. Her publications include *Spain 1833–2002: People and State* (Oxford, 2007) and *Catholicism in the Second Spanish Republic: Religion and Politics in Salamanca, 1930–6* (Oxford, 1996).

Bruno De Wever is Associate Professor of History at Ghent University. His publications include *Oostfronters: Vlamingen in het Vlaams Legioen en de Waffen SS* (2nd edn. Tielt-Weesp, 1985), *Staf De Clercq* (Brussels, 1989), and *Greep naar de macht. Vlaams-nationalisme en Nieuwe Orde: Het VNV 1933–1945* (2nd edn. Tielt-Gent, 1995).

Perry Willson is Professor of Modern European History at the University of Dundee. Her publications include *The Clockwork Factory: Women and Work in Fascist Italy* (Oxford, 1993), *Peasant Women and Politics in Fascist Italy: The Massaie Rurali* (London, 2002), and (ed.) *Gender, Family and Sexuality: The Private Sphere in Italy 1860–1945* (Basingstoke, 2004).

INTRODUCTION

R. J. B. BOSWORTH

THE word 'fascism' continues to launch a thousand books. Indeed, of all political concepts of relatively recent times, it, along with the name of the Nazi chief, Adolf Hitler, elicits the most automatically negative reaction in most minds. Its mention at once conjures images of marching automatons, extreme violence, war, and 'genocide', all at the behest of some dictator, armed for a while with a fascinating charisma but, in reality, perverse, brutal, deluded, and, almost certainly, crazed. The fascists, along with Hitler, it is widely assumed, were virtuously beaten in the Second World War, when liberals, democrats and socialists, capitalists and communists, came together, at least from 1941, to resist, to produce, to conquer, and to save humankind. Thereafter, one task of virtue has been to ensure that fascism would not revive. 'Never again' is a slogan to which the vast majority subscribe.

To be sure, almost immediately after 1945 (and even before that), complications surfaced. The wartime alliance did not last long. Very likely, it quickly seemed in the West, communists, with their own 'totalitarian' ambitions, had quite a lot in common with their enemies (whom they called fascists rather than Nazis) and in turn needed to be vanquished in the successive Cold Wars. They were. By the year 2000, the age of statist ideologies seemed over for good. In the new millennium of globalization and the 'end of history', liberal democracy, of some definition, and the market possess hegemony in most places; they therefore ought to be unchallenged.

Yet ours is also an age of fear. And at least part of current trepidation is nourished by the spectre that, with malevolent purposes, 'fundamentalist' rogue states, headed by new 'Hitlers',[1] may toy with again unleashing an updated fascist beast from its lair. Even though it is now more than sixty years since Hitler and his Italian ally, Benito Mussolini, died at the end of the Second World War, the history of fascism, it seems, retains contemporary menace.

There is much that is paradoxical in this situation. After all, the first fascist dictator, in office a decade before Hitler, was Mussolini. The word 'fascism' originated in Italy, as did 'totalitarian'; each term spread from Italian into other languages, with plenty of risks of (mis-)translation. No doubt the two regimes eventually fought the war in an Axis (of evil). Yet, under every conceivable index, the Italians were by 1940 second- or third-rate allies, their nation state in practice already relegated from its accustomed posture as the 'least of the Great Powers'. Just to provide one set of statistics, between 1942 and 1944, Italy produced 6 per cent of the machine guns of its Tripartite alliance with Germany and Japan, 7.8 per cent of its aircraft, 5 per cent of its tanks, and less than 5 per cent of its steel (these tallies ran at about 40 per cent or less of what the United Nations manufactured).[2] Moreover, even if a count of premature deaths caused by the Fascist dictatorship in Italy is expanded to embrace the casualties of its aggressive wars, they still 'only' tally around a million, scarcely competition with the Nazis or the Stalinists or with quite a few liberal imperialists. In seeming scholarly response to this reality, Italian history has rarely won the profile accorded to the German (Russian, British, or even French) past. Italians, for good or bad, seem too lightweight to bear the moral imprint of fascist horror.

Nor in the framing of its series of Handbooks, designed to sum up the latest scholarship on a set of major issues, has Oxford University Press discountenanced this situation. A *Handbook of Modern German History* is in preparation along with this one. What academic space is therefore left to a *Handbook of Fascism*? The answer is doubtless in the pages that follow and the (varied) contributions that they contain from thirty-one historians from three continents and with a number of first languages other than English. But perhaps there is an argument that extremity makes for bad history. Peter Novick has emphasized that there are dangers as well as advantages in focusing on the 'uniqueness' of the Holocaust.[3] Maybe in reviewing the history and histories of European fascisms, it is as helpful to note inadequacy

---

[1] See, for example, the view of one American scholar, before the invasion of Iraq by the United States and its 'coalition of the willing', that 'there will probably never again be a reproduction of the Third Reich, but Saddam Hussein has come closer than any other dictator since 1945'. S. Payne, *A History of Fascism 1914–1945* (Madison: University of Wisconsin Press, 1995), 517. Maybe many would have endured less pain in the aftermath of this invasion had Payne urged instead that Saddam and his Baathists had something of Mussolini and his regime (but by no means everything) about them.

[2] In his recent brilliant survey of the global drive of the Nazis and their ambitions to achieve a double or triple genocide, Adam Tooze scarcely mentions the Italians. See A. Tooze, *The Wages of Destruction: The Making and Breaking of the Nazi Economy* (London: Allen Lane, 2006) (the figures are drawn from his table on 641).

[3] P. Novick, *The Holcaust in American Life* (Boston: Houghton Mifflin, 1999).

and failure, along with the horror. A fascism that is not automatically treated as an absolute 'other' may be worth study and may better purvey those uncertain and treacherous 'lessons' that the discipline of history can offer.

As an editor, I have not sought to impose a party line on my distinguished colleagues. In my editorial chair, I have been a self-consciously 'weak dictator', content to be 'structured' by my contributors and by the literature as much as by my own attitudes and understanding. After all, one of the most positive results of the Second World War and the defeat of Nazi-fascism was the lesson, preached with greater dedication by many historians in the war's aftermath than before, that the discipline of history is best viewed as an 'argument without end', posited on a doctrine of 'criticism, criticism, again criticism and criticism once more'.[4] When they scan this *Handbook of Fascism*, readers will learn quickly enough that the assembled contributors come from different and even rival schools and by no means always or automatically agree with each other.

Yet, however sketchily delineated, certain assumptions do lie behind this book and should no doubt be spelled out in an introduction. Whether the work should be regarded as a 'mere academic exercise' or not, its first point is that this is indeed not a handbook on Nazism. Rather, a third of the chapters focus on Italy, while another third are comparative but with the Italian face of the fascist story taken as fundamental. Mention of Germany, by contrast, is mainly indirect, no more than might anyway be occasioned by Hitler's emphasis that events in Italy had been of major influence in conditioning his approach to power and that 'the march on Rome in 1922 was one of the turning-points of history'.[5] Here is a study where consideration of the finality of Nazism and the oddity of Hitler's behaviour as an executive is at best muted compared with what might be called more everyday fascisms. It is true that the other key interpretations that have threaded the scholarship, notably the arguments that 'fascism' was dreamed up in the *fin de siècle* and especially in pre-1914 France and that fascist totalitarianism was only conceivable after the Bolshevik seizure of power in the Russian empire, are treated where need be by this Handbook's contributors. Yet the thesis survives that, if the history of fascism throughout Europe and the wider world is to be reviewed, then detailed attention to events, achievements, failures, and contradictions in Italy from 1914 to 1945 (and beyond) is essential.

This cascade of nouns alerts readers to another of this book's premises. Any person interested in comparative investigations of fascism that do not focus obsessively on Nazism is unlikely to go far before running into the important work of the Italian historian Emilio Gentile, and that of the British political scientist

---

[4] See the curious wartime career of Pieter Geyl, the author of these aphorisms, as narrated in R. J. B. Bosworth, *Explaining Auschwitz and Hiroshima: History Writing and the Second World War 1945–1990* (London: Routledge, 1993), 11–15.

[5] A. Hitler, *Table Talk 1941–1944*, ed. H. R. Trevor-Roper (London: Weidenfeld and Nicolson, 1953), 10.

Roger Griffin. Over the last two decades they have established themselves as the best and most enduring students of the intellectual history of fascism. They speak clearly. On quite a few occasions, Griffin has preached that a 'new consensus' exists over the meaning of fascism. It can be viewed most succinctly, he is emphatic, as 'palingenetic ultra-nationalism', a force 'ideologically driven' to 'create a new type of post-liberal national community that will be the vehicle for the comprehensive transformation of political, social and aesthetic culture, with the effect of creating an alternative modernity'.[6] Mostly, Griffin's findings have been approved by Gentile with his detailed knowledge of the history of Italian ideas. For Gentile, fascism 'originates from a revolutionary party with an extremist and palingenetic ideology craving a monopoly of power in order to conquer society and transform it according to its conception of men and politics'; its totalitarianism was by its very nature 'a continuous experiment in political domination'. From its active 'laboratory' came an ever more radical 'political religion', aimed at an 'anthropological revolution' and limitless national or racial expansion.[7]

Such conclusions have assisted Griffin's efforts to provide a definition of fascism that will stand the test of time and space. From 1999, a journal entitled *Totalitarian Movements and Political Religions* has become the special vehicle of this intellectual alliance and its contributors have sometimes argued their cause with what might ironically seem semi-religious fervour and quasi-totalitarian intellectual purpose. Griffin may protest too much when he asserts that a vast array of scholars ranging from Ian Kershaw to the political scientist James Gregor, on to the sociologist Michael Mann, and including the historians Kevin Passmore and Robert Paxton among contributors to this Handbook, operate 'a curious form of doublethink in the way that they distance themselves from the new consensus but apply theories plainly consonant with, and even indebted to, many of its tenets'.[8] Gentile has been even more authoritative in writing off the work of any commentators recalcitrant to the view that 'political religion' is the key explanatory device of fascism.

Yet doubters remain. As Martin Blinkhorn argued when he was asked to review contributions to a special issue of *Totalitarian Movements and Political Religions*, 'we continue to be struck more by the "limits of Mussolini's power" than by its extent but also because there had to be a suspicion (to put it mildly) that the limits were due more to factors intrinsic to, if not indeed representative of, Fascism than to extraneous ones which, given time, Fascism might yet have overcome'. The term political religion, Blinkhorn confessed, might be thought even more 'awkward' and unconvincing than totalitarianism. He, for one, remained unconvinced that

---

[6] R. Griffin, 'Introduction: God's Counterfeiters? Investigating the Triad of Fascism, Totalitarianism and (Political) Religion', *Totalitarian Movements and Political Religions*, 5 (2004), 299.

[7] E. Gentile, 'Fascism, Totalitarianism and Political Religion: Definitions and Critical Reflections on Criticism of an Interpretation', *Totalitarian Movements and Political Religions*, 5 (2004), 328, 352.

[8] Griffin, 'Introduction: God's Counterfeiters?', 300, 311.

'a secularisation-induced psychological need has much to do with the actual level of popular support achieved by individual fascist movements'. Maybe some fascists aimed at an 'anthropological revolution' wherein new men and women could be forged. But the purpose was not achieved and, for historians, he concluded, the failure was as interesting, as salutary, and as demanding of research and comment as were the attempt or hope.[9] A year later, John Pollard, a contributor to this Handbook, summed up a further special issue of the journal, this time on clerical fascism, by suggesting that Grifffin and Gentile were seeing the tail and not the dog. 'If Italian Fascism', Pollard contended, 'adopted the trappings of religion—credo, litanies, commandments, and rituals—it was not in order to fill a secular void in Italian society but because it made the movement and the regime more comprehensible and acceptable to the average Italian who was steeped in a living and vibrant *Catholic* culture.'[10]

This division of opinion, however lit up by present academic passion, is not especially new, nor is it confined to the history of fascism. Rather it evinces a variety of approach that has frequently marked historiography. One side is committed to reading (fascist) intellectuals intellectually; the books of fascist theorists are more instructive, it is maintained, than are the behaviour and motivation of a peasant. The other side is more given to reading between the lines and, in so doing, placing fascist thoughts into their social and intellectual context. In this approach, the peasants, being more numerous and perhaps more enduring or anyway possessed of longer and deeper histories than the intellectuals, may well matter the more.

To put the debate another way, for Griffin and Gentile and their supporters, the history of fascism is a single matter. The task of its historians is to assay the fascist past with the intention of unearthing a final pure lode that will identify fascism in a few words or paragraphs. By contrast, as far as their critics are concerned, fascist rule, for all its ambition at control, failed, by definition, to oust the very many histories that coursed through the lives of Italians and others who were living the inter-war crisis. There is no pure fascist history to be teased apart from the rest. Those who were citizens of the Fascist regime in Italy and those who belonged to fascist movements in other European states and societies bore a multitude of attitudes and ideas, and acted in complex and contradictory ways. Their fascisms can be studied but they are most tellingly examined at the interstices of life where individuals make fleeting choices that seem for a while ideal and may be given ideological explanation. Yet, like all ideas, fascism was merely one element in the dynamic functioning of human life. If theorists stop the machine, they may be able to see fascism more clearly and paint it more strikingly. But they simultaneously lose the context in which the fascism lived and upon which, in despite of itself, it was

---

[9] M. Blinkhorn, 'Afterthoughts, Route Maps and Landscapes: Historians, "Fascist Studies" and the Study of Fascism', *Totalitarian Movements and Political Religions*, 5 (2004), 508, 515–17.

[10] J. Pollard, ' "Clerical Fascism": Context, Overview and Conclusions', *Totalitarian Movements and Political Religions*, 6 (2005), 444.

dependent. Even the most fundamentalist fascists were buffeted constantly by their national, local, class, gender, family, religious, and a host of other pasts, presents, and futures. Fundamentalists, too, take time off or, better, find that time takes them off. Not for nothing did most Italian Fascists only wear their uniforms on Saturdays (or when summoned to extra parades). All fascists were in some sense part-time ideological warriors and any serious historical understanding must reckon with that partiality. For those who remain sceptical of Griffin's 'consensus', Paul Corner's plaintive plea 'whatever happened to dictatorship?' (and so his demand for a recognition of the violence, corruption, and caprice, the patronage and clientship, the regional variation of the practice of 'the Italian dictatorship')[11] should not be forgotten.

In sum, the editorial view has been that a *Handbook of Fascism* should cast its net widely. It should be ready to examine social history as much as the history of ideas. It should wonder whether fascism can be so rigorously separated from liberalism or 'democracy' or social Catholicism or socialism as its more ardent followers contended. It should admit that 'events' often condition theory. It should doubt that the past ever offers a single and 'right' answer.

Enough of editorial moralizing. Readers will find that this Handbook is structured in a clear manner. It commences with three chapters collectively devoted to a review of that pre-1914 Europe and, especially, that First World War when the aspiration to totality, and so what has been neatly termed the 'totalitarian seduction', began to afflict the world.[12] A fourth contribution looks instead at the immediate post-war and notes the uneasiness of the Wilsonian solution proffered at the peacemaking with its too easy assumption that liberalism, parliamentary and capitalist, could work seamlessly with nationalism (or 'self-determination').

The book's next segment brings together nine historians of modern Italy, a place conceived as 'the first Fascist nation'. Together these historians appraise what is currently known about a range of topics on Mussolini's dictatorship spanning from war and foreign affairs to local fascist squadrism to the more general role of the secret police, and from the regime's stance towards, and response from, women, youth, and peasants to its relationship with the Church and with lay intellectuals.

Four historians join in the third part of the book, with their task being to think about some comparisons with the Nazi regime in regard to state and society, the position of the dictator, race, and war, but with the emphasis still being rather more on Italian primacy than on German. These contributions are followed by a further eleven chapters, each analysing the fate of fascism or fascisms in places where the relevant movements failed to achieve power, or achieved it, as in Spain, Japan, and,

---

[11] P. Corner, 'Italian Fascism: Whatever Happened to Dictatorship?', *Journal of Modern History*, 74 (2002).

[12] A. Ventrone, *La seduzione totalitaria: guerra, modernità, violenza politica (1914–1918)* (Rome: Donzelli, 2003); in English, cf. O. Bartov, *Mirrors of Destruction: War, Genocide and Modern Identity* (New York: Oxford University Press, 2000).

very briefly, in Romania, in intricate and paradoxical ways, or, in Belgium, the Netherlands, France, Hungary, and Yugoslavia, under Nazi occupation, in Austria before it, and in that British empire that was saved from it. The final part of the book has three varied chapters, one seeking comparisons and definitions in the fascist story, between the wars and, at least potentially, after. This piece is amplified by accounts of the fate of memory in Germany and Italy since 1945 and by a reckoning with the role of post-war neo-fascism.

A glittering array, then, has been assembled. Our purpose, given the restlessness of humankind and the democratic value of debate, has been not to proclaim a new consensus but instead to underline key evidence, especially when freshly unearthed, and to alert readers to some of the disputes that eddy around the history of fascism, broadly understood. This Handbook does not attempt the final solution to the fascist problem, but its contributors rather hope that, from its pages, newly fruitful debates can arise.

It only remains for me to thank my contributors for their promptness and their professionalism in writing and thought, to express my gratitude to my new colleagues at Reading University where much of the book was 'workshopped' in February 2007, and to acknowledge that Christopher Wheeler of OUP was the person who suggested this project and, with his efficient assistants, brought it to publication. My own debts to Michal and the rest of my family, and to that Italy which, mostly with good cheer, has put up with my fascination with it for so long, go without saying.

PART I

IDEAS AND FORMATIVE EXPERIENCE

CHAPTER 1

....

THE IDEOLOGICAL ORIGINS OF FASCISM BEFORE 1914

....

KEVIN PASSMORE

That a new doctrine should use the still vital elements of other doctrines is perfectly logical. No doctrine is born quite new, shining, never before seen. No doctrine can boast of an 'absolute originality'. It is bound, even if only historically, to other doctrines that have been, and to develop into other doctrines that will be.... [B]ut the activity of man reacts upon the doctrine, transforms it, adapts it to new necessities or transcends it.

MUSSOLINI rightly saw fascism as a novel phenomenon, constructed from existing materials that were transformed in the process, as were the men and women who made the new movement.[1] Fascism emerged from the specific context of world war and social and political upheaval. Nonetheless, Mussolini exaggerates. The political landscape did not change completely in 1914–18: some earlier ideologies possessed priorities similar to those of fascism, and they had fitted into the political landscape in similar ways. Populist, ultranationalist ideologies, opposed to Marxism and liberalism, and less systematically to the right, already existed in 1914. Although the

[1] B. Mussolini, 'The Doctrine of Fascism', in M. Oakeshott, *The Social and Political Doctrines of Contemporary Europe* (Cambridge: Cambridge University Press, 1947), 164–79.

cults of violence and paramilitarism were less common in these movements than they would subsequently become, there were significant intellectual prefigurations of fascism.

The only way to identify continuities across geographical and chronological boundaries is to use an ahistorical concept of fascism, for no pre-1914 ideology could have exactly anticipated fascism.[2] Yet we must be aware of the drawbacks of using hindsight. Our model is useful only for our specific purpose. It necessarily obscures the ways in which protagonists made sense of the world. Before 1919, nobody saw her- or himself as 'proto-fascist'. Furthermore, identification of ideologies as pre-fascist does not 'explain' them. We have only illuminated them from our own vantage point. The ideologies and thinkers considered in this chapter were many other things besides harbingers of fascism.

I. FASCISM AS A 'POLITICAL RELIGION'

The fashionable 'political religions' approach to fascism exaggerates the explanatory power of its concepts. According to Emilio Gentile, a 'political religion' emerges when an earthly movement or regime claims sacred status. A secular movement, endowed with the trappings of a religion, endeavours to shape the individual and the masses through an 'anthropological revolution'. Since it sees the world in terms of good and evil, it brooks no opposition.[3] The concept of political religion develops the notion, which originated with theorists of totalitarianism, that fascism had its roots in a messianic, all-encompassing ideology, which was dedicated to the creation of a perfect society.[4] The major strength of political religions theory is that it focuses attention upon what fascists thought.

In spite of its claim to understand fascism from the inside, political religions theory uses extra-historical standards to extract the 'core' meaning of fascism from the plethora of motivations, ideas, and programmes of actually existing fascism. Consequently, it obscures the diversity of pathways by which people came to fascism. Gentile makes the political religion the centre of fascism by attaching it

---

[2] K. Passmore, 'The Essence of Fascism', *Erwägen Wissen Ethik*, 15 (2004), 403–5.

[3] E. Gentile, 'The Sacralisation of Politics: Definitions, Interpretations and Reflections on the Question of Secular Religion and Totalitarianism', *Totalitarian Movements and Political Religions*, 1 (2000), 18–55; idem, *The Sacralization of Politics in Fascist Italy*, trans. K. Botsford (Cambridge, MA: Harvard University Press, 1996).

[4] C. J. Friedrich and Z. Brezinski, *Totalitarian Dictatorship and Autocracy* (Cambridge: Cambridge University Press, 1956).

to laws of historical change and collective psychology.[5] Thus, political religions supposedly emerge when old patterns of thought have decayed under the impact of modernization, without undermining the masses' allegedly innate need for simple explanations of their place in the world. Fascism functions as a secular replacement for revealed religion and thus resolves the anomie of modern life. In discussing the relationship between fascism and its precursors, these assumptions lead Gentile to hesitate between two views. On the one hand, he assumes that since the political religion derives from a functional need, the materials from which it is constructed are merely incidental—the circumstances of its origin give meaning to the ideology. In some of his work, Gentile shows little interest in the origins of the political religion. This approach comes up against a well-known refutation of essentialism and determinism. Since the existence of the political religion depends upon both the need for the religion and the materials from which the religion is constructed, then both are essential to the existence of the phenomenon in question, and one cannot say which is the more important. This point implies that the nature of the religion depends as much upon the circumstances in which it was produced as upon the materials from which it was made, and that in turn makes impossible the notion of an 'essential' similarity between any two objects of study. Similarities certainly exist, but only from one point of view and not another.

On the other hand, in some of his work, Gentile shows greater interest in the origins of the political religion. He distinguishes between full-blown political religions and 'secular religions' which leave some space for individual liberty. Secular religions included, for instance, the republicanism of Mazzini. Notwithstanding this distinction, Gentile tends also to make any pre-1914 secular religion into a forerunner of fascism, while other sources of fascism become 'secondary', or 'circumstantial'.[6] He regards the search for a civil religion as a feature of Italian political culture since the Risorgimento, especially evident in organic nationalism and its spiritual cousin, socialism. Furthermore, like Zeev Sternhell, Gentile takes Mussolini's own account of fascism as a synthesis of spiritual socialism and radical nationalism, both of which he sees as precursors of the political religion, quite seriously. Fascism is a reworking of leftist ideas.[7] Given that there was no equivalent in Nazism of Mussolini's reworking of socialism, Gentile's account of fascist origins cannot be applied directly to Germany. Michael Burleigh is therefore somewhat ambiguous on the question of the origins of Nazism. He argues that Hitler's ideology emerged from a brew of medieval myths of kingship, conventional religion, the writings of Nietzsche and Richard Wagner, and nihilistic art. Nevertheless, he too places special

[5] Like Weberian ideal types, they are supposedly merely descriptive categories because they are related to long-term historical processes.

[6] E. Gentile, 'The Conquest of Modernity: From Modernist Nationalism to Fascism', *Modernism-Modernity*, 1 (1994), 55–87.

[7] Gentile, 'The Sacralisation of Politics'; idem, *The Sacralization of Politics in Fascist Italy*, 1–18. idem, 'Fascism as a Political Religion', *Journal of Contemporary History*, 25 (1990), 229–51.

emphasis on the left-wing origins of political religions, traceable back to the French Revolution, via romantic nationalism.[8]

Fascism, or rather the people who saw themselves as fascists amongst other things, should not be reduced to one of its dimensions. The attempt to do so by relating fascism to a 'fundamental' process of modernization obscures the plethora of historical trends in post-Enlightenment Europe. Fascism was one of several possible developments that emerged from shared roots, leading in multiple directions as contexts changed. Secondly, people's 'need' to explain the world is unproven. When they do seek to explain it, their accounts are shifting, contradictory, and contested. While the sacralization of politics is undoubtedly an important element of fascism, fascists did not always act within its logic and they brought many other agendas to fascism. Insofar as they attempted to create a political religion, they understood it in diverse ways and constructed their utopia from sundry materials.[9] It is also worth noting that the proponents of political religions theory do not see themselves as requiring simple explanations. They therefore endorse implicitly a dichotomous view of the subjective mass and the rational elite, and borrow some of the categories of the collective psychology that was one of the ingredients of fascism.[10]

Fascism is not easily summed up in simple dichotomies such as 'tradition/modernity', 'forward-/backward-looking', or 'reason/unreason'. Fascists certainly used oppositions such as these. However, rather than take them at face value (or deduce their meaning from the movement of history), we must explore what they signified to protagonists. We must also take account of conflict among fascists over the meaning of their ideology. Indeed, fascism was characterized by the dynamic interrelationship of people with different agendas, who nevertheless agreed to work together and oppose, in different ways, rival ideologies. Like all ideologies, fascism defined itself against rivals but also possessed affinities with them. Competing ideologies drew upon and transformed the same intellectual currents. Robert Nye's comments on the history of biomedical thought are relevant to the origins of fascism: no longer can we write a history 'with villains and noble seekers after truth and its narrative tropes of tragedy and ultimate redemption; few unambiguous heroes emerge [from this history]'.[11]

---

[8] M. Mann, *The Dark Side of Democracy: Explaining Ethnic Cleansing* (Cambridge: Cambridge University Press, 2004); M. Burleigh, 'National Socialism as a Political Religion', *Journal of Totalitarian Movements and Political Religions*, 1 (2000), 1–26.

[9] N. Gregor, 'Nazism: A Political Religion?', in idem, *Nazism, War, and Genocide* (Exeter: University of Exeter Press, 2005), 1–21.

[10] K. Passmore, 'The Gendered Genealogy of Political Religions Theory', *Gender and History*, 20/3 (2008), 648–68.

[11] R. Eatwell, *Fascism: A History* (London: Pimlico, 1996), 3–16; H. Lehmann, 'The Germans as a Chosen People: Old Testament Themes in German Nationalism', *German Studies Review*, 14 (1991), 261–73; R. Nye, 'The Rise and Fall of the Eugenics Empire: Recent Perspectives on the Impact of Biomedical Thought in Modern Society', *Historical Journal*, 36 (1993), 687–700.

I shall approach the question of origins by examining some of the ideological materials from which fascists constructed their ideologies, remembering that fascists drew selectively on the ideas they used, and that dichotomous formulae such as 'the revolt against reason' are not very useful. I shall then explore the ways activists began, in the last years of peace, to transform these materials into political ideologies dedicated to the renovation and perhaps conquest of the state.

II. REASON AND UNREASON

Where do we begin? If we regard the religious component of fascism as fundamental, then we might see its earliest precursor in medieval millenarianism. To do so would require indifference to historical actors' self-understanding, to their categories of thought, and to the contexts in which they operated. However, this danger is only an extreme example of a problem inherent in the search for origins. A more important objection is that Aquinas's scholasticism, which deployed reason in the service of faith, anticipated fascist religiosity just as much as millenarianism did. There was more than one religious tradition in Europe.

The late eighteenth century is a more meaningful starting point, since modern political alignments first took shape then. Fascists generally disparaged the Enlightenment tradition, which they saw as the fount of materialist individualism. Yet their stance was complex. On the one hand, fascists believed, like Enlightenment thinkers, that man could create a better world, if only for some. Fascists also agreed that universal laws regulated human societies, even if the laws in question did not lead to universal emancipation. As Gentile and many others before have argued, Fascism owed something also to Jean-Jacques Rousseau, who held that it might be necessary to create a 'civic religion' and to force people to recognize the 'general will'. Yet fascists also had something in common with Rousseau's critic, Gottfried von Herder, for whom national diversity was more valuable than uniformity. However, Herder did not posit the existence of a racial hierarchy.

Notwithstanding, Herder's thought prefigured Romanticism and thus linked with an ideological current that flowed directly into the pool from which fascism emerged. Romanticism rejected rational, classicist, precepts of rationality and balance in favour of individualism and subjectiveness. Like fascism, Romanticism idealized the creative spirit who overturned formal rules. Romantics saw imagination as a gateway to the spiritual truths of national and folk identities. Romanticism also developed the organicist strand evident in anti-Enlightenment thought. This organicism simultaneously provided a bridge to rationalist liberalism, for biological science was attractive to liberal rationalists well before Darwin. Moreover, if the nineteenth-century bourgeoisie abandoned organized religion, it rarely rejected spiritualism. It was prone to regard the contemplation of artistic genius as a means to cultivate the self. Liberals could recognize themselves in the romantic idea of self-realization through struggle against nature and routine.

Romanticism had not entirely disappeared by 1900, when a new wave of artists and writers announced the latest of the many deaths of reason. They had in mind the ultra-materialist positivism typified by Jeremy Bentham, which contended that scientific principles could resolve moral issues. Anti-positivists also attacked the specialist university disciplines as they were then emerging. They saw the sociology of the Durkheimians and the history of the Rankeans as representing the mindless collection of dry facts. Among the critics of the professional academic were figures commonly seen as precursors of fascism. The German Paul Lagarde, the Frenchmen Gustave Le Bon and Georges Sorel, and the Italians Giuseppe Prezzolini and Giovanni Papini all railed against professional academe. In fact, the relationship between university and amateur learning was complex. Those characterized as mere accumulators of facts were just as likely to regard society as an organism, with intrinsic properties, as were their amateur critics. Emile Durkheim respectfully cited Le Bon. As for the rebels, they did not reject science per se. They redefined it.

The rebels rejected positivism for different reasons. Friedrich Nietzsche (1884–1900) is interesting from our perspective because both Mussolini and Hitler wrote positively of him. One can see why fascists should have admired a thinker who idealized fearless individuals, possessed of a will to power, and who rejected universal values for placing intolerable constraints upon individual creativity. Nietzsche envisaged the leadership of an elite, ready to sacrifice untold numbers in the interests of an ideal. Yet his writings are too contradictory to be appropriated by a single ideology. He urged his contemporaries to face the death of god with the creation of new values, and yet he was scathing of any attempt to create new standards. He rejected German nationalism and yet celebrated the national past. He regurgitated crass anti-Semitic stereotypes while abhorring anti-Semites, including, after an initial fascination, Wagner. Furthermore, Nietzsche was a critic of the rational utopia imagined by totalitarians and, in the 1960s, he became an icon for the anarchistic postmodernist Michel Foucault.[12]

Nietzsche's fame extended beyond Germany. French and Italian thinkers read him as a counter to Wagnerian decadentism—Mussolini was among those who did so. Under Nietzsche's influence, Gabriele D'Annunzio's literature moved away from explorations of decadence to the celebration of action, violence, misogyny, and the myth of the superior man. Another Italian follower was Giovanni Gentile, whose idealist philosophy denied the existence of individual minds and of any distinction between theory and practice or subject and object. According to the future Fascist Minister of Education, all such categories were merely mental constructs. Gentile

---

[12] R. S. Wistrich, 'Was Nietzsche a Fascist Thinker?', *Partisan Review*, 68 (2001), 201–17.

saw idealist philosophy as a means of filling the void left by positivism. However, he also believed that traditional religion could participate in this regeneration.[13]

Meanwhile, the French philosopher Henri Bergson rejected Immanuel Kant's view that the mind could know approximations of reality through their impact on the senses. Through intuition, Bergson maintained, one could apprehend the profound life force itself, a state of becoming that, he claimed, was more analogous to cinematic reality than the fixed truth of the photograph. We might read Bergson's critique of positivism as prefiguring the fascist celebration of feeling, but it proved just as suitable to the justification of traditional religion.

Whatever the case, Bergson's thought was rather different from that of the Catholic physicist Pierre Duhem and the mathematician Henri Poincaré, for whom science could not penetrate reality but only produce hypothetical approximations to it (a view actually closer to Kant's). Duhem and Poincaré elaborated an alternative to positivism in the form of a 'provisional' epistemology. Some thinkers combined it with Jamesian pragmatism, according to which knowledge should be judged by its usefulness, not its truth. During the war, some would follow pragmatism to the (not necessarily logical) conclusion that what was useful was true and, indeed, good.

Le Bon, who was cited approvingly by both Hitler and Mussolini, issued from these intellectual currents. He too held that science could discover but not explain, and endorsed pragmatism. However, he refused to draw the conclusion that it was as useful to follow instinct as reason, since that would rehabilitate 'outdated ideas', including religion. Rather, civilization (i.e. progress or modernization for us) meant overcoming instinctual drives. Following Bergson, he argued that instinct and the unconscious could be objects of scientific analysis. In fact, Le Bon made an implicit, but crucially important, distinction between elite and mass. The former, possessed of a proper balance of reason and sentiment, could study and guide the wholly instinctive mass.

Although his political perspectives were initially different, Georges Sorel inhabited the same philosophical world as Le Bon. Sorel is best known for his belief that irrational myths, such as the class war or nation, were capable of inspiring actions that would transform the world. Bringing together his professional training as an engineer and his knowledge of Bergson, he aspired to study these myths scientifically. He criticized socialism because he saw it as deriving from a Rousseauesque superlogical utopia and counterposed to it the practical socialism of the syndicalists.[14] He believed that medieval artisans had reconciled the technical and the artistic. The builders of the Gothic cathedrals had produced beauty without thought of material reward. At about the same time, the German engineer Edward

[13] W. L. Adamson, 'Modernism and Fascism: The Politics of Culture in Italy, 1903–1922', *American Historical Review*, 95 (1990), 372.

[14] R. Nye, 'Two Paths to a Psychology of Social Action: Gustave Le Bon and Georges Sorel', *Journal of Modern History*, 45 (1973), 411–38.

Mayer endeavoured to reconcile technology with a national culture that was traditionally hostile to positivism. In his *Die Technik als Kulturmacht* (1906) he claimed that technical advance stemmed from growing spiritualization.[15]

The rebels rejected the positivist doctrine that general laws explained the behaviour of man, for they believed them to restrict human creativity and spirituality. Yet they often assumed laws of their own. Sorel thought that there were 'regularities' in historical development. He held that each class, later nation, had a unique spirit, which it was the task of heroic leadership to realize. This conclusion connected his thought with theories of national identity, often with a racial component. Racial theories were irrational in the sense that they believed pre-conscious dispositions to determine human behaviour—at least that of the masses. They were rational in that their existence had allegedly been demonstrated scientifically by thinkers informed by Social Darwinism and theories of degeneration. If these ideologies had a religious component, they owed as much to scholasticism as to messianism, for Sorel and others believed that the elite, exempt from the determinations that constrained mass behaviour, could understand and make use of myths for political ends.

Common to most *fin de siècle* thinkers was the belief that only a male, educated elite grasped the principles of social organization. The masses were passive, irrational, implicitly feminine, perhaps foreign and even animal. The distinction has a long history and, at the turn of the century, the discipline of collective psychology gave it a new form. Collective psychology was founded by the Frenchmen Le Bon and Gabriel de Tarde, and by the Italians Scipio Sighele and Pasquale Rossi. Collective psychology took from organicism the notion that the crowd behaved as a primitive organism, and from psychiatry the idea, developed well before Sigmund Freud, that it responded to unconscious motivations and could be influenced by hypnotic suggestion. Collective psychology did not establish a professional presence in the universities before 1914, although it was popular with professionals, journalists, and politicians.[16] In fact, collective psychology was not wholly different from academic sociology. Durkheim, too, rejected positivist inductivism and insisted that the social body was more than the sum of its parts. He agreed that the masses internalized ideas through the repetition of simple images and that unscrupulous elites might exploit this gullibility. Where Durkheim differed from the more right-wing collective psychologists was in his belief that the mass should or could be guided by a democratic elite that would inculcate an (oxymoronic perhaps) 'cult' of reason into the mass through state schools. Collective psychologists were further to the right, although not necessarily of the extreme right, and they were more pessimistic. Le Bon believed that crowds returned to earlier stages of evolution. From there it was a short step to racialization of the mass. D'Annunzio saw the

[15] J. Herf, 'The Engineer as Ideologue: Reactionary Modernists in Weimar and Nazi Germany', *Journal of Contemporary History*, 19 (1984), 631–48.

[16] R. Nye, *The Anti-Democratic Sources of Elite Theory: Pareto, Mosca, Michels* (London: Sage, 1977).

'nobles' and the 'plebs' as two different races. In *Il fuoco*, he recounted the story of an artist-creator who mesmerized, violated, and then discarded the plebeian masses, just as he did women.[17]

Since the Enlightenment, thinkers had assumed that race was a scientific fact, confirmed, notably, by phrenology. Indeed, cranial measurement was not entirely displaced by genetic theories of race—French racial 'experts' used it during the war, for instance. The Comte Arthur de Gobineau's *Essai sur l'inégalité des races* (1853–5) was the culmination of the earlier approach. It contended that history was a struggle between races, in which the dominance of the Aryan race depended on preserving its purity from contamination by the black and yellow races. From the 1860s, Gobineau's theories became influential in Germany, where Wagner and Nietzsche were among their admirers. The latter, in *On the Genealogy of Morals* (1887), depicted socialists and democrats as products of racial regression, and contrasted them with the Aryan elite. By 1900, racial categories were an integral part of intellectual life, and no single political tendency monopolized them. British liberals used them to justify hegemony in Ireland, while reactionary German conservatives invoked them to legitimize German power over Poles.

The novelty of late nineteenth-century racism lay less in the notion of race as a scientific fact than in its marriage with Darwin's theory of natural selection, and in the development of racial *policies*. The master shared the contemporary conflation of sociology and biology, and ambiguities in his work helped ensure that Darwinism would appeal across the political spectrum. Initially, liberals, socialists, and nationalists saw the struggle of species as confirmation of the market, class, and national causes respectively. As liberalism and nationalism shifted to the right and as conservatives overcame (in practice, if not in principle) their religious objections to evolution, Social Darwinism also developed a right-wing version.[18] It was a contested ideology and those who espoused it did so inconsistently. While most non-socialists applied Darwinian categories to the international environment and believed in a hierarchy of nations and races, they less consistently saw struggle as inevitable in the domestic sphere. Some believed that it guaranteed progress. Others felt that success in the international struggle necessitated domestic harmony. Cell theory, which assumed a tendency towards stability in the organism, worked against Darwinism. Fascists would prove to be no clearer in their use of Social Darwinism.

For some, the logic of Social Darwinism seemed to suggest that the 'softness' of modern life, perhaps aggravated by well-meaning social reform, might ensure the survival of the weak, and the degeneration of the race. Medical science underpinned degeneration theory. In France, doctors drew on the Lamarckian alternative to

[17] Adamson, 'Modernism and Fascism', 370.
[18] R. Weikart, 'The Origins of Social Darwinism in Germany', *Journal of the History of Ideas*, 54 (1993), 469–88.

Darwinism. They feared that inherited alcoholism, venereal disease, and unhealthy housing would taint whole populations and disarm the nation in the international struggle for life. Doctors looked to the active element of the population, the elite, to counter the tendency towards degeneration present in the mass. Interventionists regarded social reform as a means to ensure the fitness of the race, not to improve individuals' lives.[19]

Degeneration seemed to provide an explanation for the discontent of the working class, while intervention seemed to offer a remedy for socialism. Thus, Italian criminologists invented methods to identify and segregate southern misfits and expected thereby to cure southern lawlessness and unite the Italian nation. In Britain, France, and Germany, eugenicists focused more upon the dangerous urban poor and the working class. They advocated a variety of measures ranging from improvements in the housing of the proletariat, via methods designed to ensure that only the healthiest reproduced, to the outright killing of the 'unfit'. Darwin's cousin Francis Galton (1822–1911) invented the term 'eugenicist' to designate such policies. He wished to encourage the middle classes to have as many children as possible and to encourage the 'unfit' to emigrate to the land of 'Cantsayanywhere'. In a prize-winning essay, the German Wilhelm Schallmeyer (1857–1919) urged that the weak should be prevented from reproducing. Ernst Haeckel (1834–1919), Professor of Biology at the University of Jena, explicitly advocated killing the sick in the interests of 'humanity'. In France and Italy, few went so far. Catholic teaching on the sanctity of human life was more influential there. Nevertheless, there, too, the health of the race was the measure of the efficacy of social policy.

Fascists built their ideological edifice from diverse materials—the same stock from which opposed ideologies also drew. Fascism did not originate simply in a revolt against reason or in the drive to create a political religion. It was inherently contradictory. It would emphasize both leadership and fulfilment through participation in a crowd. It attacked Enlightenment rationalism as a constraint upon struggle and yet invented its own, ultra-determinist, theories of race and nation, justified with all of the paraphernalia of science. Contradictions such as these (present in any ideology) provided multiple pathways to fascism, from right, left, and centre. Especially widely shared by different political tendencies was the distinction between the supposedly rational elite and the irrational mass. Negative views of the masses did not inevitably lead to fascism, or even to the rejection of liberalism. Much depended upon how the elites were defined. This is an appropriate point at which to explore the ideas described in the political context of pre-1914 Europe.

---

[19] R. Nye, *Masculinity and Male Codes of Honor in Modern France* (Berkeley and Los Angeles: University of California Press, 1998), 75–7; D. Pick, *Faces of Degeneration. A European Disorder, c.1848–c.1918* (Cambridge: Cambridge University Press, 1989).

III. Nationalism

Until the 1860s, nationalism was largely cast as progressive. In the east and south, it sought the reform or destruction of the reactionary tsarist, German, and Austrian empires. In the west, democrats claimed to speak for the nation. Following Rousseau, they believed that each individual was bound to the common good by his [sic] equal share of rights and duties. Democrats condemned aristocracy, monarchy, and the Church for denying the rights of the nation.

There was always an exclusionary potential in democratic nationalism. It derived first from the link between democracy, the people, the indivisible nation, and thence ethnicity. Nationalists took for granted Herder's idea that people and ethnicity coincided or, perhaps more dangerously, that they ought to coincide. They were prone to regard their own nationality as ethically superior to others. The ethnicization of democracy potentially justified moulding the population to the higher good of the nation.[20] As Emilio Gentile argues, the organic conception of the nation often fed into a quasi-religious idealization of the national community.

The dark side of nationalism developed in the inevitable gap between vision and reality. The space was arguably greatest in France, where moderate Republicans seemed unable to regenerate a nation that in 1870–1 had experienced defeat at the hands of Germany and civil war in Paris. France did indeed produce its fair share of pre-fascist thinkers. Nevertheless, I shall concentrate on Italy and Germany because fascism actually came to power there after the Great War.

Italy was united in 1861 to 1870 through diplomacy and war. Popular nationalism played a subordinate role. After unification, the liberal elites set about 'creating Italians'. The regime promoted loyalty to king and country, notably through secularized schools, idealization of the army, sport, parades, and monuments. For some nationalists this was not enough. The obstacles were enormous, for in large parts of Italy, especially the south, 'Italy' meant little more than taxes and police interference in customary ways. Notwithstanding, the followers of the democratic nationalist Giuseppe Mazzini condemned the liberal regime for its unrepresentativeness. They saw the liberals as too concerned with pointless quarrels to bring their policies to fruition and as too elitist to mobilize the masses. Mazzinian nationalists demanded something like a civic religion. In their orbit can be found the criminologist Cesare Lombroso, who claimed that isolation of hereditary criminals—hangovers from an earlier stage of evolution—from the rest of society would benefit the Italian race. Yet Mazzinians also believed that democracy entailed individual rights and the peaceful coexistence of nations. We cannot know how in practice they would have reconciled individual liberty and dedication to the nation. At most, we can say that Mazzinian nationalism was ambiguous and, later, that fascists drew upon elements

[20] Mann, *The Dark Side of Democracy*.

of it. Lombroso's positivist criminology, for instance, influenced the Fascist criminal code of 1930.[21]

By 1914, Italian nationalism had developed a genuinely radical right component. It was rightist in the sense that it was strongly anti-socialist or more particularly anti-Marxist; it was radical in that it held that the creation of a truly united Italy, without the socialists, depended upon the displacement of the old ruling class by a new one. The context for the emergence of this new nationalism was the rise of socialism, anarchist terror, peasant occupations of landed estates, and defeat of the Italian army at Adowa in 1896.

Among the most important of the new nationalist journals was Corradini's *Il Regno*, founded in 1903. Unlike earlier nationalists, Corradini was of conservative background. He incorporated Social Darwinism and pragmatism into a nationalist, anti-socialist, and anti-democratic ideology. He held that Italy must overcome its weakness towards other powers by harnessing the 'iron laws of race', expelling foreign influences, and engaging in an aggressive imperialist policy. Nationalism would incorporate workers into the nation and regenerate the bourgeoisie, forcing it to abandon 'feminine humanitarianism' and degenerate liberalism. Corradini advocated a 'religion of nature and heroes', and a cult of force. If the bourgeoisie did not understand the need to break strikes by force, then socialists would triumph. After 1908, Corradini added syndicalist themes. He likened the struggle of the 'proletarian' Italian nation against the Anglo-Saxons to that of the workers against the bourgeoisie. He admired syndicalism for its violence and for its subordination of the individual to the group. In 1910, Corradini founded the Italian Nationalist Association.[22]

In Germany, right-wing nationalism developed earlier, as liberals bowed to the genius of Bismarck, the aristocratic, conservative, architect of German unity. Wagner's evolution from left to right was symptomatic. The composer initially harnessed his art to the evocation of a socialist and nationalist people's utopia, which he expected to follow from the twilight of the gods—that is, Judeo-Christian religion. There was a messianic element in the operas of a composer who saw himself as a Christlike mediator between the spiritual and material realms. Wagner viewed art as a means to reconcile the individual with the German community, with its past and future. He believed that the Germans were descended from pre-Christian nature-gods and so uniquely placed to apprehend the pure essence of being.[23]

---

[21] Gentile, *The Sacralization of Politics in Fascist Italy*, 7–13; Lehmann, 'The Germans as a Chosen People'; Pick, *Faces of Degeneration*.

[22] A. De Grand, *The Italian Nationalist Association and the Rise of Fascism in Italy* (Lincoln, Nebr.: University of Nebraska Press, 1978); R. Drake, 'The Theory and Practice of Italian Nationalism, 1900–1906 ', *Journal of Modern History*, 53 (1981), 213–41.

[23] M. Brearley, 'Hitler and Wagner: The Leader, the Master and the Jews', *Patterns of Prejudice*, 22 (1988), 3–22.

Wagner was uncertain on the nature of the new Germany. He hesitated between the call for a new national movement free from the Jewish and foreign influences that had allegedly caused the failure of 1848, and the conviction that regeneration would come through art.[24] His conception of his utopia increasingly resembled a comfortable Germany cleansed of divisive elements. By the end of his life, Wagner preached the mutual respect of bourgeois and lord, town and prince within the nation and claimed that the German was essentially conservative. If Wagner's ideas contained religious drives, they were not the only elements, and his putative 'new man' would not have been wholly strange to any 'old man'.[25] Some saw Wagner not as the prophet of a new religion, but as an admirer of Arthur Schopenhauer. The latter regarded suffering as the lot of humanity and political action as absurd.[26] Hitler's Wagnerian fantasies of decadence—he ordered Albert Speer to design buildings that would impress as ruins—were an important ingredient of Nazism. In his final testament, the *Führer* gave full vent to his conviction that the Germans were not worthy of their historic mission.

Wagner's son-in-law Houston Stewart Chamberlain also influenced Hitler. Chamberlain's racism combined Darwinism with mystical idealism derived from *Gestalt* theory. Present-day peoples originated in cross-breeding between different races, followed by careful inbreeding over a long period. Whereas Darwin denied the existence of innate qualities, Chamberlain believed that breeding would lead to the gradual emergence of a perfect form—the expression of a mystical life force. The racial elite would commune with this essence and express it in the arts and religion. The state must preserve the purity of the *Volk*. Although these ideas influenced Hitler, for Chamberlain they legitimized the authority of the Wilhelmine empire.[27]

By 1914, nationalism was so strongly anchored in the German right that its left-wing origins were a distant memory. Nevertheless, the ideas of 1848 survived in the use of categories such as the *Volk*. Conservatives exploited exclusionary potentials long present within nationalism and made it a xenophobic, anti-socialist, authoritarian creed. Paul Lagarde was one of the first to claim the label of radical conservative. As an enemy of positivism, he attacked socialism and democracy for their view that the world was an aggregate of material facts rather than an organic whole. He sought to save Germany by giving it a new religion, inspired by the rituals, but not the dogma, of the Catholic and Protestant Churches. This religion meant striving for a personal relationship with the ideal, through participation in the national community and emulation of an aristocracy of the spirit. Lagarde

[24] Ibid.

[25] R. Wagner, *What Is German?* (Bayreuth: Bayreuther Blätter, 1878; written 1865).

[26] C. Forth, 'Nietzsche, Decadence and Regeneration in France', *Journal of the History of Ideas*, 54 (1993), 99.

[27] M. Woodroffe, 'Racial Theories of History and Politics: The Example of Houston Stewart Chamberlain', in P. Kennedy and A. Nicholls (eds), *Nationalist and Racialist Movements in Britain and Germany before 1914* (London: Macmillan, 1981), 1–22.

rejected the idea of a return to the past, arguing that religion and nation must adapt to changing times. Nevertheless, his definition of the elite was not wholly new. He was a monarchist and opposed the bureaucratic state. He envisaged something like a caste of country gentlemen, mediating between king and people. By the end of his life, he was more favourable to the established churches and wanted to give them control over secondary education. In the domestic sphere, he envisaged harmony and was increasingly willing to allow existing churches a place in his utopia. Internationally, he used Darwinist language, advocating the forceful conquest of lands in the east and the assimilation or driving out of the indigenous populations. Lagarde's racism was not biological but he did preach discrimination against Jews on the grounds that it would encourage assimilation.[28]

IV. THE SOCIALIST ORIGINS OF FASCISM

For much of the nineteenth century, socialists were nationalists. They associated democracy with the triumph of the people and assumed the people to be a nation. They used the terms 'worker' and 'people' interchangeably, thereby enabling broad recruitment, including the petty bourgeoisie and the inevitable bourgeois intellectuals. Socialism had never been free from prejudice, notably towards women and foreign labour. The rise of Marxist socialism, which was theoretically internationalist, secularist, and dedicated to the interests of the industrial proletariat alone, sometimes brought out the exclusionary potential of the older socialist tradition. The French Blanquistes provide an excellent example of this evolution. They espoused a sort of working-class Jacobinism, advocating seizure of power by a revolutionary party on the back of an urban uprising. They were anti-parliamentarian, nationalist, xenophobic, and sometimes anti-Semitic. In 1889, Blanquistes backed the campaign of the political adventurer General Boulanger, in the hope that it might permit them to seize power. This tactic led some of them to accentuate the nationalist and anti-parliamentarian side of their programme. In subsequent years, the Blanquistes split, with one wing launching wholeheartedly into anti-Semitism and nationalism.[29]

Even after the triumph of Marxism in the labour movement, internationalism never entirely replaced nationalism. Marxism, after all, insisted that the triumph

---

[28] F. Stern, *The Politics of Cultural Despair: A Study in the Rise of the Germanic Ideology* (Berkeley and Los Angeles: University of California Press, 1961); V. Viaene, 'Paul De Lagarde: A Nineteenth-Century "Radical" Conservative-and Precursor of National Socialism?', *European History Quarterly*, 26 (1996), 527–57.

[29] P. C. Hutton, *The Cult of the Revolutionary Tradition: The Blanquistes in French Politics* (Berkeley and Los Angeles: University of California Press, 1981).

of the proletariat depended upon a preliminary bourgeois-democratic revolution within the nation. Socialists were as concerned as anyone with the question of leadership and with the creation of an elite, which they implicitly contrasted with the non-elite. Socialists saw the workers both as a potential source of renewal and as lacking in 'consciousness', and vulnerable to 'hypnotization' by rival elites. Some socialists hailed eugenicism as a means to improve the quality of the proletariat and ensure that it proved equal to its destiny. Socialists' predilection for describing capitalists as 'parasites' must be counted among the preconditions of mass murder in the twentieth century. Socialism was no more homogeneous than any other ideology and so there were potentially many affinities with other movements. Some thought socialism less a means of securing political and economic power for the proletariat than a source of idealism that would regenerate a decadent world corrupted by bourgeois materialism.

Some socialists were disenchanted by the cautious practice of organized Marxism. Socialist parties urged their followers to await patiently the working out of the laws of history. Dissidents sought to hasten the revolution. Most often, they turned to the ultra-left but some did not. For certain intellectuals, the Dreyfus Affair was the turning point. In France, Charles Péguy felt that the party had betrayed the idealism of the Dreyfusard cause—claiming that '*mystique* had become *politique*'. Sorel endeavoured to redefine Marxism as 'social poetry'. The sequel of the Affair also disappointed the socialists around the journal *La voce* in Italy. For their leader, Giuseppe Prezzolini, the Dreyfusards had nullified socialism by mobilizing the proletariat against the Church. Typically of the journal's contributors, Benito Mussolini wanted to regenerate Italy through the propagation of new artistic, moral, and social values. *La voce*'s combination of socialism and nationalism prefigured one strand of fascism but the journal did not preach the supremacy of nation or race over the individual.[30]

Syndicalism provided another ingredient in the fascist soup. Syndicalism and radical nationalism shared hostility to liberal democracy. However, for syndicalists to become fascists they had to abandon or modify other beliefs. For Italian syndicalists, the turning point for some was the failure of the strike movement of 1910 and then the debacle triggered by 'Red Week' in July 1914. Some syndicalists concluded that Italy was not yet ripe for socialism and so the most pressing task was to create a modern capitalist state. Some held that parliamentary government had delayed industrialization. The political system, rather than capitalism, became the enemy. Syndicalists also grappled with the old problem of leadership. Embracing a version of collective psychology, the proletariat, they felt, was too immature to embrace the spirit of self-sacrifice that the revolution required of it; the inculcation of such a spirit depended upon revitalization of the elite. The syndicalist Paolo Mantica

---

[30] E. Gentile, 'The Struggle for Modernity: Echoes of the Dreyfus Affair in Italian Political History', *Journal of Contemporary History*, 33 (1998), 497–511.

sought to create a proletarian elite by making trade unions the basis of decentralized self-government. This notion would become an important element of the left wing of Italian Fascism, opposed to Alfredo Rocco's statist version.[31]

Syndicalists did not inevitably become fascists—far from it. For instance, Arturo Labriola argued that alliance with progressive liberals made modernization possible. Nothing better illustrates the dangers of reading intellectual trajectories from their outcome than the case of Mussolini. Like Lenin, the future *Duce* felt that capitalism was unlikely to collapse under the burden of its contradictions. Again like Lenin, he expected an elite to awaken working-class consciousness. Before 1914, he never departed from his revolutionary line. He added a dose of romanticism and a cult of action, reinforced by his reading of Nietzsche and Sorel and by celebration of Marx as a 'man of action'. Mussolini was not the only romantic in European socialism and his ideas surprise us only if we assume that socialist thought was wholly homogeneous and isolated from the general intellectual climate. Neither should Mussolini's admiration of Darwin astonish, nor his view that the party should evict reformists as a living organism expels germs. Mussolini's well-known confusion about nationalism was quite typical of socialists. Whatever the case, Mussolini called for a general strike to halt the 1911–12 Libyan war, and in August 1914 he reaffirmed his conviction that war would profit only the bourgeoisie.[32] Mussolini's conversion to fascism was not predestined. It resulted as much from choices in new contexts as from pre-existing elements in his thought.

V. Liberalism

Some have speculated that in 1904, while in Switzerland, Mussolini attended the lectures of the world-famous political scientist Vilfredo Pareto. He probably did not, and yet the possibility that he did so underlines the extent to which political ideas crossed national and political boundaries. Coupled with the great diversity of fascism, this fact renders it impossible to locate the origins of fascism in a single part of the political spectrum. It makes nonsense, too, of the claim that fascism originated in a coming together of the extremes of romantic socialism and radical nationalism against liberalism. Fascism drew upon centrist ideologies, too.

In the last decades of peace, liberals believed that mass politics was eroding elite leadership. For liberals, too, elites were the progressive element in history and their potential decline would be a manifestation of decadence. Liberals often saw

---

[31] D. D. Roberts, *The Syndicalist Tradition and Italian Fascism* (Chapel Hill, NC: University of North Carolina Press, 1979).

[32] R. J. B. Bosworth, *Mussolini* (Oxford: Oxford University Press, 2002), 56–99.

the market as a Darwinian struggle, in which the elite rose to the top. They were (and are) quietly prepared to sacrifice the humanity, if not the lives, of millions to the imperatives of the 'dismal science' of classical economics. Many liberals felt that the over-democratic parliamentary system excluded 'the best'—those who had demonstrated their worth in the competition of business, professional, or academic life—from public affairs. Parliamentary politics allegedly attracted those who had failed in their professional life, people who saw politics as a means to make a quick penny rather than as public service. Professional politicians were a 'counter-elite', possessed only of a talent for manipulating the impressionable masses. Liberals devised a host of means to ensure that the tide of democracy did not drown the 'best'. These ranged from proportional representation in France through corporatist reform of parliament to strengthening of the executive. The liberal critique of the parliamentary system was not necessarily anti-democratic but it reinforced hostility to politicians.

In France, Hippolyte Taine argued that the inferiority of French elites had caused defeat at the hands of Germany and that democratization threatened to aggravate the problem. In his history of the French Revolution, he drew upon psychiatry to argue that the crowd had been motivated by collective madness. He advocated restrictions on the franchise as the solution to the problem of the elites. Taine influenced the Italian liberal Gaetano Mosca, who held that the elite could not rely on force alone to sustain its power but needed energy and will. If the ruling class conceded suffrage extension, it would forfeit its moral superiority, excite base instincts in the masses, and encourage anarchy. Progress would come from men of genius, who must play upon the quasi-religious proclivities of the masses. Mosca is often bracketed with Pareto. As a Social Darwinist, Pareto worried that socialist protection of the unfit would undermine elite leadership. The elite should abandon humanitarian illusions and refuse to compromise with socialism, for the socialist elites were much better equipped to use demagogic 'illusions' to stir up the masses. Pareto saw nationalism as an alternative myth through which to mobilize the mass. Neither should the elite be afraid to use force. Taine, Mosca, and Pareto may be seen as representing the response of liberal-conservatives to the advent of democracy. Their preoccupations also help to explain why so many liberals joined the fascist coalition.[33]

Mosca and Pareto both cited Le Bon's work on crowd theory as support for their views. Although Mussolini regarded Le Bon as a proto-fascist, in his day he was close to the secular, liberal-conservative and nationalist right. Like Taine, Le Bon held that legislation could be effective only if it accorded with the instinctive constitution of the nation. The elite's job was to understand this natural constitution and govern accordingly. Thus, Le Bon opposed social reform on the grounds that it would inevitably be frustrated by the laws of nature. Nevertheless, he maintained

---

[33] Nye, *The Anti-Democratic Sources of Elite Theory*, 14–20.

that faith, properly controlled by a rational elite, could be a force for renewal. He doubtless had in mind the moderate nationalism of President Raymond Poincaré. If, however, we regard his views ahistorically—as in this essay we must—then they anticipate fascist nationalism in their racism, pragmatism, contempt for the masses, and the 'scholastic' desire to study and channel the irrational. We must also acknowledge that Le Bon did not show great interest in actual techniques of mass manipulation.[34]

In Germany, too, liberalism contained anti-democratic tendencies. Liberals at first embraced Social Darwinism to justify individual freedom and attack aristocratic conservatism. Increasingly, they used it to legitimate social inequality. A key figure in this transition was Haeckel, who urged that 'Passion and selfishness, conscious or unconscious, is everywhere the motive force for life.' In 1878, he claimed that the struggle for existence would not lead to socialism but to a sort of bourgeois aristocracy of talent. With time, German conservatives, too, embraced Social Darwinism. In a book dedicated to Haeckel, published in 1875, Friedrich von Hellwald argued that the struggle for existence would lead to the triumph of the aristocracy. He endorsed militarism, class domination, absolutism, slavery, despotism, and the spiritual yoke of the Church, as 'inventions of men for the purposes of self preservation'. Von Hellwald opposed liberalism as well as socialism, and yet retained a faith in progress, which he saw as the product of violent conflict between individuals, races, and nations, leading to the annihilation of the weak.[35]

In fact, pre-1914 German ultranationalism never lost its liberal component. Heinrich Class's pamphlet 'If I were Kaiser' was transitional between authoritarian liberal-conservatism and fascism in that it appealed to the Kaiser and yet presumed to speak for the nation to him, calling for government by a strong man. Class's themes were similar to those of Pareto. He urged summary justice against strikers, warning against 'half-measures' and 'sentimentality'. He encouraged the government to mobilize popular nationalism, favoured discrimination against Poles and German Jews, and the expulsion from Germany of foreign Jews along with French speakers. Class's ideal Germany was authoritarian and nationalist and yet his ideas may also be situated in the liberal-conservative tradition. He called for the introduction of a class-based voting system in the empire and for 'conversion to a parliamentary system that recognizes the personal accomplishments of the educated and the propertied in the realm of political work'.[36] Like Pareto, Class prefigured the incorporation of conservatives and conservative liberals into fascism. Those liberals who adhered to fascism rarely did so unreservedly. Neither did anyone else, for there was little agreement among fascists about the nature of fascism.

---

[34] G. Le Bon, 'Philosophie et religion', *L'Opinion*, 11 April 1908, 23 May 1908; B. Marpeau, *Gustave Le Bon: parcours d'un intellectuel, 1841–1931* (Paris: CNRS, 2000).

[35] Weikart, 'The Origins of Social Darwinism in Germany', 483.

[36] H. Class, 'If I Were Kaiser' (1912).

VI. CONCLUSION

Fascism was not the product of specific national traditions. Wagner entertained Gobineau at his Venice home; D'Annunzio discovered Nietzsche in French translation in the *Revue blanche*. If fascism crystallized first in Italy, it did so because circumstances permitted, not because it was ideologically predestined to do so: historical analysis is possible only if we think in terms of conditions, not laws. There were proto-fascist tendencies in several European countries in 1914. They were radicalized and brutalized by the war and perpetuated afterwards in the language or reality of civil war. In no country was everyone brutalized. The task of historians' is to explain why the brutalized came to power in some countries and not others.

The fact that fascism was not homogeneous complicates this task. Ultimately, only their decision to belong to the same movement unified fascists. They defined themselves in opposition to rival ideologies, while simultaneously possessing something in common with *all* their opponents. Fascism was a synthesis, perhaps merely an agglomeration, of ideas taken from many different sources. The history of fascism played out through the practices of a disunited movement in varying contexts.

Political-religious impulses were evident in the ideologies we have discussed. They help to explain the violence and exclusionary nature of fascism and its horrifying readiness to use ends to justify means. Yet these impulses were inseparable from other agendas, from the protection of cultural and economic capital in an age of democracy and socialism to the discontent of an intellectual proletariat and workers' resentment of foreign competition in the labour market. Both masses and elites (a loaded distinction that should be historicized) were motivated by a mixture of interests and ideals. Furthermore, a political religion could be conceived in multiple ways. For Filippo Tommaso Marinetti, it involved the celebration of speed and destruction; for Giovanni Gentile it meant the mental pursuit of the ideal. Anyway, the precursors of fascism rarely abandoned *themselves* to religious mysticism. They distanced themselves from the religious phenomena they believed to motivate the mass. Even if they claimed an intuitive relationship with the people and that their ultimate aim was to restore the spiritual, they believed themselves able to study and mould the mass according to the scientific principles of race, nation, gender, and collective psychology.

Ironically, political religions theory reproduces elements of its object of study. The isolation of 'modernization' from the complexities of historical change is little more than an act of faith, while the belief that modernization creates an 'anomie', and potentially the worship of false gods, is the stock-in-trade of modern religions. It is the organizing insight of Michael Burleigh's account of the relationship between politics and religion in the nineteenth century. He cites Durkheim rather than Le Bon as a precedent for this view, perhaps underestimating the ambiguous relationship between Durkheim's sociology of the *conscience collective* and *fin de siècle* collective psychology.[37] Burleigh might also have cited Ferdinand Tönnies, whose account of the allegedly alienating effects of modernization is close to collective psychology theory. Potentially of relevance, too, is Max Weber's notion of charismatic authority, so influential in fascism studies, which emphasizes the magnetic bond between leaders and led, and which also owes something to collective psychology theory. Neither should we forget that Freud developed his theory of unconscious motivation in critical dialogue with Le Bon.[38] Indeed, one might say that political religions theory relies on a collective psychologists' reading of the founding fathers of academic sociology and political science. Thus, Burleigh maintains that the masses are more reluctant than the elites to abandon 'apocalyptic revolutionary illusions' and that the 'uneducated' are vulnerable to manipulation by counter-elites. In other words, political religions theorists define their own rationality in opposition to the unreason of the masses and assume that the masses really are susceptible to manipulation. The argument that political religions work because they meet a need in the masses barely disguises the debt to the notion of the manipulative elite and the manipulable mass.

Moreover, Burleigh amalgamates liberalism and socialism in a manner that would have been familiar to Le Bon. He judges intellectual positions on moral grounds and there is a whiff of decadence in contemporary society as he describes it. Intriguingly, Burleigh writes for 'those who may think atomistic pluralism and multiculturalism have gone too far'. He sees civil religions as more tolerant than political religions and yet fears that pluralism means that anything goes, rather than simply toleration of anything that does not harm others. Burleigh advocates a vaguely defined 'civic religion', which amounts to little more than instrumentalization of the common Christian heritage.[39]

Of course, political religions theory is not proto-fascist. Like its parent, totalitarianism theory, the concept has proved attractive to people of various political persuasions, and theories have to be treated on their merits. To make the transition from any ideology to fascism, one had to abandon convictions previously held dear. Once choice enters the equation and once we remember that fascism shared elements with all other ideologies, it is easier to understand the multiple origins of fascism. Political religions theory rightly encourages socialists to reflect critically upon potential dangers in their beliefs. Nobody is exempt from this obligation.

---

[37] J. C. Filloux, 'Démocratie et société socialiste chez Durkheim', *Revue européenne des sciences sociales*, 25 (1971), 29–48.

[38] Nye, *The Anti-Democratic Sources of Elite Theory*, 36.   [39] Burleigh, *Earthly Powers*, 1–17.

BIBLIOGRAPHY

BOSWORTH, R. J. B., *Mussolini* (Oxford: Oxford University Press, 2002).

BURLEIGH, M., *Earthly Powers: The Conflict between Religion and Politics from the French Revolution to the Great War* (London: Harper Perennial, 2006).

DE GRAND, A., *The Italian Nationalist Association and the Rise of Fascism in Italy.* (Lincoln, NB: University of Nebraska Press, 1978).

GENTILE, E., 'The Sacralisation of Politics: Definitions, Interpretations and Reflections on the Question of Secular Religion and Totalitarianism', *Totalitarian Movements and Political Religions*, 1 (2000).

—— *The Sacralization of Politics in Fascist Italy*, trans. K. Botsford (Cambridge, MA: Harvard University Press, 1996).

GRIFFIN, R., *The Nature of Fascism* (London: Pinter, 1991).

KERSHAW, I., *Hitler: 1889–1936: Hubris* (London: W. W. Norton, 1999).

NYE, R., *The Anti-Democratic Sources of Elite Theory: Pareto, Mosca, Michels* (London: Sage, 1977).

PICK, D., *Faces of Degeneration: A European Disorder, c.1848–c.1918* (Cambridge: Cambridge University Press, 1989).

STERN, F., *The Politics of Cultural Despair: A Study in the Rise of the Germanic Ideology* (Berkeley and Los Angeles: University of California Press, 1961).

STERNHELL, Z., *The Birth of Fascist Ideology: From Cultural Rebellion to Political Revolution* (Princeton: Princeton University Press, 1994).

CHAPTER 2

THE FIRST WORLD WAR AS CULTURAL TRAUMA

ALAN KRAMER

THE title of this chapter incorporates two complex concepts: trauma and culture. Trauma in the original medical sense meant simply a physical injury; it came to mean a state of shock brought on by injury; and in psychoanalysis it means the condition that can result from an emotional shock. Traditionalists might object that trauma is only individual, not collective; there can therefore be no cultural trauma. However, the term 'collective traumatic memory' can justifiably be used in relation to the experience of war, and arguably individuals could sometimes express the traumatic experience of the war in a way that transcended the personal and could symbolize collective experience and mentalities. Nevertheless, we need to be on our guard against the inflationary use of the term trauma which confuses traumatic with non-traumatic experiences and which can even remove the distinction between victims and perpetrators. Culture is also one of those words with several meanings. It is used here both in the narrow sense of 'high culture' (such as literature and art), and in the broad sense of the customs, ideas, and values of a society. To understand the cultural trauma of war we need to explain the enthusiasm for war in certain cultures and sections of societies; what occasioned the trauma and how culture reacted to it.

This chapter is based on my book *Dynamic of Destruction: Culture and Mass Killing in the First World War* (Oxford: Oxford University Press, 2007).

I. Culture and Warfare:
Common Experience, Divergent
Interpretations

There was an intimate link between culture and warfare, in that the First World War was a modern war, fought by societies with mass literacy and a sense of national identity that had developed over the nineteenth century. It was seen by the belligerents as a war to defend their culture; for some, it was even a war to export their culture. Because the war involved the mobilization of the entire nation, not tens of thousands of soldiers but millions, and of almost the entire social, economic, and cultural resources of states, enemy civilians and other non-combatants came to be regarded to a greater or lesser degree as targets of war policy, even as legitimate objects of violence. One of the most important questions, then, is whether there were parallels between nations and where distinctions can be drawn between different cultures and policies.

It is sometimes argued that the war led to the brutalization of politics in Europe, and there is a good deal of evidence to support that contention.[1] Without wartime cultural mobilization it would be impossible to explain the birth of fascism. However, matters were not straightforward. There was no single European political culture: divergent paths of the memory of war were apparent with the pacifist turn in Britain and France by the mid-1920s, and even in Germany there was a majority consensus to reject war for many years after 1918. In Italy and Russia, by contrast, the affirmation of the values of war became state policy in mass violence against the internal foe, which included the destruction of the enemy's culture.

Cultural destruction focused the sense of shock felt by contemporaries at the immense, but as yet unquantified, loss of human life, for cultural destruction is a particularly symbolic transgression—a 'self-mutilation' of humanity.[2] The burning of the university library of Louvain in August 1914 stood as a symbol for warfare that not only demolished cities like Ypres, Péronne, or Treviso but also targeted the culture of the enemy. The news about Louvain made an immediate and deep impact on neutral international opinion. In the Netherlands, the *Nieuwe Rotterdamsche Courant* contrasted the German with the Belgian/British accounts of events and, concluding that the truth might never be told, asked: 'What difference does that make? The fact of the destruction of Louvain remains and this fact...is so terrible that the whole world must have taken note of it with the greatest sadness....It

---

[1] G. L. Mosse, *Fallen Soldiers: Reshaping the Memory of the World Wars* (New York: Oxford University Press, 1990).

[2] D. C. Watt, *How War Came: The Immediate Origins of the Second World War, 1938–1939* (New York: Pantheon, 1989), 5–8.

is a punishment which has affected all western culture.'[3] Louvain, the shelling of Rheims cathedral, and other events described by the Allies as German atrocities played a role in neutral Italy's estrangement from its formal allies Germany and Austria in 1914–15.

The interpretation of cultural destruction therefore varied, according to standpoint in the war. From autumn 1914 the German methods of warfare were taken by the Allies and neutral countries to be characterized by wilful destruction and mass killing of everything and everyone that stood in the path of German war aims. This was an invaluable gift to Allied propaganda. Yet the fundamental principle of German warfare was not questioned by its practitioners. As Colonel Nicolai, chief of German military intelligence and propaganda, told the American journalist John Reed in early 1915, the goal of war was victory, above all else; there were no means a soldier did not have the right to use in its pursuit. If it was a question of terrorizing the civilian population, or shelling undefended towns, to accomplish his aims, he would do it.[4]

Most intellectuals declared their solidarity with the military, notably in the 'Appeal to the World of Culture!' signed by ninety-three of Germany's internationally most respected scientists, scholars, and artists, published internationally on 4 October 1914. This truculently rejected Allied claims that the German military had committed atrocities, especially 'cultural atrocities', and that Germany had started the war; it denied that Germany had wantonly violated Belgian neutrality and that German soldiers had 'brutally devastated Louvain'. It ended by stating the identity of German culture with the army and 'German militarism'. More impressive numerically was the declaration by 4,000 professors (i.e. the vast majority) published on 16 October 1914, initiated by the renowned classicist Ulrich von Wilamowitz-Moellendorf, which announced their solidarity with the army and support for the invasion of Belgium and France.[5]

The shocked reaction in the world of culture outside Germany shows how cultural mobilization was affected not only by the military events but also by the interdependent relationship between European cultures. The Académie Française repudiated the 'Appeal to the World of Culture!', stating: 'In the name of French civilization and human civilization, [the Academy] condemns the violators of Belgian neutrality, the murderers of women and children, the savage destroyers of the noble monuments of the past, the arsonists of Louvain University and Rheims cathedral.'[6] The Académie des Sciences protested against the claim of the 4,000

---

[3] Politisches Archiv des Auswärtigen Amts, Berlin, R 20881, fos. 35, 39.

[4] J. Reed, 'German France', *Metropolitan Magazine* (New York) (March 1915), p. xli, cited in A. Becker, *Oubliés de la Grande Guerre: humanitaire et culture de guerre 1914–1918: populations occupées, déportés civils, prisonniers de guerre* (Paris: Noêsis, 1998), 50–1.

[5] For the text, see K. Böhme (ed.), *Aufrufe und Reden deutscher Professoren im Ersten Weltkrieg* (Stuttgart: Reclam, 1975), 49–50.

[6] References for this and the following paragraph: J. Horne and A. Kramer, *German Atrocities 1914: A History of Denial* (London: Yale University Press, 2001), 283–9.

German university professors that 'the salvation of European civilization lies in the victory of German militarism in solidarity with German culture'. The philosopher Emile Durkheim published a brochure accusing the Germans of corrupting the 'humanitarian morality of the Christianized west' by a Nietzschean drive for world dominance. In occupied Belgium, the 'Appeal to the World of Culture!' caused outrage. Belgium's leading historian, Henri Pirenne, for example, saw the signature of his close friend Karl Lamprecht as a cruel betrayal.

In Britain, *The Times* published a Reply to the 'Appeal', signed by over 100 leading academics, artists, and musicians. Though acknowledging the ties of 'comradeship, of respect and of affection' linking British scholars with their German colleagues, the Reply held Germany solely responsible for the outbreak of the war and contended that German armies alone had deliberately destroyed cultural monuments. It concluded that Germany was 'the common enemy of Europe and of all people which respect the Law of Nations'. The 'Appeal' had a 'disastrous effect' on opinion in neutral Switzerland, as Hermann Sudermann, one of its initiators, discovered when he travelled there in December 1914, and in the academic community in the United States there was widespread disapproval of their German colleagues' uncritical endorsement of the German army.

As the war dragged on and the toll of death and destruction reached new heights, the mood among German intellectuals began to shift and the unanimity of 1914 dissolved. Even before the German intellectual community began to split into a pro-war, ever more extreme nationalist, wing and a reformist one that favoured peace negotiations, there were some who expressed their ambivalence about the war. The historian Max Lehmann, for example, wrote in May 1915 to his colleague Hans Delbrück, condemning 'war psychosis' and maintaining that he, like Delbrück, still believed in the 'unity of the Romance-Germanic nations'. The liberal theologian Ernst Troeltsch wrote openly of the 'European suicide' and refused to subscribe to the general chauvinism of academic pronouncements on the war.[7]

Some, for the first time, publicly announced their opposition to war; others made increasingly raucous declarations in support of belligerence and far-reaching aims for imperialist expansion. Three years after the 'Appeal', in October 1917, eighty-one professors, among them the physicist Albert Einstein, published a declaration calling on the government to adopt the resolution passed by the three parties forming a majority in the Reichstag (Social Democrats, left liberals, and the Catholic Centre) which advocated a 'peace of reconciliation', renouncing all territorial acquisitions. But some 1,100 professors signed declarations against the peace initiative, almost fourteen times as many. Still, the fact that at least two-thirds of the professors now preferred to remain silent indicates a shift by the majority to a more cautious attitude. However, some professors published demands for the removal of Russia

---

[7] K. Schwabe, 'Zur politischen Haltung der deutschen Professoren im Ersten Weltkrieg', *Historische Zeitschrift*, 193 (1961), 606.

from Europe and the creation of vassal states in Eastern Europe, their indigenous populations to be expelled to allow German colonial settlement.

Sigmund Freud, the founder of psychoanalysis, like most intellectuals in Europe, was at first carried away with enthusiasm for the national cause: his 'entire libido', he wrote, belonged to Austria-Hungary. That soon gave way to a growing sense of horror. In November 1915 he described in his essay 'On Transience' how the war had 'robbed the world of its beauties...tarnished the lofty impartiality of our science...[and] revealed our instincts in all their nakedness'.[8] Freud now saw war as a return to something primitive in human nature; violence had been kept under control by the thin veneer of civilization. War was a 'disappointment', as he wrote in *Thoughts for the Times on War and Death* (1915), and Europeans, to his disillusionment, were conducting themselves like barbarians. Not only did the war disregard 'all the restrictions known as International Law', it also threatened to 'cut all the common bonds between the contending peoples, and threatens to leave a legacy of embitterment that will make any renewal of those bonds impossible for a long time to come'.[9]

Freud drew the conclusion that was to influence the subsequent development of psychoanalytic thinking: that human life was not entirely dominated by the sexual drive but by the conflict between that and the death instinct. Judged by our unconscious wishes, he wrote, we are 'like primitive peoples a horde of murderers'.[10] Freud's disillusionment about human nature and his pessimism represented a dramatic shift in his thinking, and while this was no personal trauma, he certainly gave expression to the war as 'cultural trauma'.

II. Culture and the Affirmation of War

Other intellectuals, far from being traumatized by the war, were energized by it. The Italian poet Gabriele D'Annunzio hailed modernity, modern technology, and the potential that the machine age offered to create a new society out of war, ruled by a technocratic aristocracy. D'Annunzio was a leading campaigner for Italian intervention in the war. Invoking the idea of a nation reborn as a united soul, he explicitly provoked violence, encouraging his supporters to launch riots. On 13 May 1915 he announced in Rome, 'If inciting citizens to violence is a crime, I will

---

[8] S. Freud, 'Vergänglichkeit' (On Transience), in idem, *Gesammelte Werke*, ed. A. Freud (Frankfurt: Fischer, 1946–9), x. 360.

[9] *Zeitgemässes über Krieg und Tod* (1915), in S. Freud, *Studienausgabe*, ed. A. Mitscherlich, A. Richards, and J. Strachey (Frankfurt: S. Fischer, 1969–75), ix. 33–60, here 38–9.

[10] Ibid. 57.

boast of this crime, assuming sole responsibility for it.'[11] (Mussolini's speech in 1925 taking responsibility for the murder of the Socialist deputy Matteotti, a key event in the consolidation of fascist rule, contains a striking echo of D'Annunzio's self-inculpation.) The idea of palingenesis, the renewal of all being through fire, later to become a central trope of fascism, runs through D'Annunzio's speeches.

Once Italy was in the war, D'Annunzio joined up and reinvented his persona as the Nietzschean war hero. He flew on well-publicized and dangerous missions to drop propaganda leaflets over enemy territory; he took part in risky naval missions against the Austro-Hungarian fleet, fought on the Isonzo and Carso fronts, and was promoted to captain, later major, and in 1919 to lieutenant-colonel. He redoubled his speaking campaign after Italy's disastrous defeat at Caporetto in 1917 to remobilize the troops. He denounced Italy's victory on 4 November 1918 as incomplete, 'mutilated'. For him the war was not over; according to an acquaintance he said: 'I smell the stink of peace.' D'Annunzio was looking forward to new battles and, while the Paris peace conference was still discussing the new order of Europe, he was demanding the complete fulfilment of the pact of London for territorial expansion in Istria, in anticipation of his symbolic occupation of Fiume.[12]

Another interventionist intellectual, Filippo Tommaso Marinetti, was if possible even more fanatical in demanding war and in linking his cultural programme with violence. He was looking forward to war with fierce joy as early as 1909, in his 'Futurist Manifesto':

We will glorify war—the world's only hygiene—militarism, patriotism, the destructive gesture of freedom-bringers, beautiful ideas worth dying for, and scorn for woman. We will destroy the museums, libraries, academies of every kind, will fight moralism, feminism…

The destruction of past culture would make space for the modern.[13] War would be the key to a glorious future of modern technology, fast cars, air travel, violence, and authoritarianism. Because Marinetti and his movement, Futurism, became so closely associated with fascism, his anticipatory justification and cultural affirmation of war illuminate the dynamics of cultural destruction, mass killing, and the political development of Europe before the First World War to the age of fascism. Marinetti loathed the Italy of his day as the land of museums, professors, tour guides, which he denounced as 'il passatismo', the obsession with the past.

---

[11] G. D'Annunzio, *Per la più grande Italia* (Milan, 1915), cited in P. O'Brien, *Mussolini in the First World War: The Journalist, the Soldier, the Fascist* (Oxford: Berg, 2005), 54.

[12] P. Palumbo, 'D'Annunzio: da Quarto al volo su Vienna', in G. Accame and C. Strinati (eds), *A 90 anni dalla Grande Guerra: arte e memoria* (Rome: Romartificio and Viviani Editore, 2005), 107–12. A summary of D'Annunzio's aerial exploits is in A. Gat, *Fascist and Liberal Visions of War: Fuller, Liddel Hart, Douhet, and Other Modernists* (Oxford: Oxford University Press, 1998), 49–52.

[13] F. T. Marinetti, 'Fondazione e manifesto del Futurismo', in idem, *Teoria e invenzione futurista*, ed. L. De Maria (Milan: Mondarori, 1998; 1st edn. 1968), 10, 11.

Why this revolt against the cultural heritage in Italy, of all places? The Futurists railed against Liberal Italy which they saw as incapable of action; they saw through the new nation state's clumsy attempts to appropriate the past with its invention of national symbols, the monuments of bad taste to King Victor Emmanuel II. The Liberal political establishment, despite its name and its shift to mass politics, was conservative, notorious for corruption, electoral fraud, and intimidation. Secular middle-class intellectuals found a ready outlet for their anger in nationalism and militarism. The violent rhetoric of the Futurists and of the entire interventionist campaign would soon be turned not only outwards, against the enemy abroad, but also against the internal enemy, foreshadowing the violence that destroyed Liberal Italy and its infant democracy.

Like D'Annunzio, Marinetti volunteered for military service and fought with evident relish; he was promoted to lieutenant and company commander. He was much in demand as a speaker to the men and was popular with nationalist officers. Addressing *arditi* officers (elite storm troops) in 1918 he described himself as a patriotic revolutionary, who aimed to rejuvenate Italy (*svecchiarla*, which means also modernize), 'cleanse it, sweep it clean of pedants, priests, cowards, and make it younger, stronger, greater, faster, more intelligent, more modern'.[14] Naturally, the enemy, the cretinous German people, were inferior, lacking in inspiration and mental flexibility, and had no claim to hegemony. Marinetti told the *arditi* officers they were the elite of the Italian 'race', who loved 'our heavenly Italy', urging them to be

proud to feel Italian ... You have become Arditi out of love of violence, of war and the fine heroic gesture ... You are the first, the most worthy. You must be the masters of the new Italy. I love your insolent simplicity of manners. You have every right when you cut the throat of an Austrian!

Marinetti praised the *arditi* in words amounting to an incitement to break the laws of war: 'Few prisoners, many stabbed and the rest kicked down from the conquered summit.' He reminded them of their claim to be the new elite:

'You are not only the best infantry of Italy. You are the new Garibaldians ... You are the new generation of Italy, reckless and brilliant, preparing the magnificent future of Italy.'[15]

Marinetti and D'Annunzio were extreme cases whose post-war careers took them into close alignment with fascism. Yet they were part of a broader stream of nationalist thought. The philosopher Giovanni Gentile was a laicist, a realist in politics, and a patriot, being convinced of the necessity to create Italian national identity. He saw the war as a positive opportunity, although he was neither a warmonger nor a fanatical nationalist; he feared that, if Italy remained neutral and the central powers won the war, they would crush Italy and dominate southern Europe. If Italy, by

---

[14] F. T. Marinetti, 'Discorso agli Arditi', in idem, *Futurismo e fascismo* (Foligno: Campitelli, 1924), 103.

[15] Ibid. 104–6.

remaining neutral, wanted to become one big museum, fossilized in contemplation of its ancient past, its past glories and beauties, then the sacrifice of the patriots of the Risorgimento would have been in vain. War would demonstrate instead that the Italians had become a people ready to defend itself, not merely an unformed mass: it would be a test of nationhood. Citing Heraclitus, he wrote that war was the mother of all things; it was inevitable in history as a principle of nature, and peoples were in a continual struggle for existence.[16] Gentile's thought resembled that of the German sociologist Max Weber in his inaugural lecture of 1895 (where he demanded that newly united Germany should embark on imperialist expansion); this indicates that such ideas were common parlance among the most influential intellectuals in certain cultures where nationalism was soon to become an explosive force.

Futurism and fascism were closely linked after the war. The Futurist Party was founded in November 1918, with a programme that was imperialist, anti-socialist, and anticlerical. It later merged with the *arditi* in the initial *'fasci* di Combattimento'. Mussolini first met Marinetti, to mutual admiration, on three consecutive days in Genoa in July 1918, when they celebrated the Allied victory on the Marne by eating well and ruminating on a post-war Italy ruled by ex-combatants. The periodical *Roma futurista*, founded on 20 September 1918, adopted political positions similar to that of the later *Duce*.

Mussolini himself, despite his admiration for Marinetti and the close organizational bonds between Futurism and the Fascist Party, was no Futurist. His mentality was that of modern soldierly nationalism. Certain key ideas of fascism were present already in the war. Mussolini continued to publish articles in his newspaper *Il popolo d'Italia* during the war, including extracts from his war diary, reinventing himself as heroic soldier and warrior politician: the Mussolini myth. Hinting at the dehumanizing consequences of the war, at Christmas 1916 he noted: 'Today our hearts are as hard as rocks . . . Modern civilization has "mechanized" us. The war has driven the process of mechanization of European society to the extreme.'[17] Before Caporetto, Mussolini had fully absorbed a 'war culture', related to an authoritarian vision of post-war Italy, a state of permanent mobilization under a charismatic leader. After Caporetto, Mussolini portrayed the nation in biological terms, as a being which had suffered 'the most ferocious torture'. Now 'the Nation must be the army, just as the army is the Nation'; on 9 November 1917 he demanded: 'The whole Nation must be militarized.'[18] After the victory, the war would be turned on the internal enemy. This was a revolutionary programme, even if of a very different kind from the revolution proposed by socialists.

[16] D. Coli, 'Croce e Gentile: i filosofi tra neutralità e intervento', in Accame and Strinati (eds), *A 90 anni dalla Grande Guerra*, 101–6.

[17] B. Mussolini, *Mein Kriegstagebuch* (Zurich: Amalthea, 1930; Italian edn. *Il mio diario di guerra* (Milan: PNF, 1923)), 188.

[18] Cited in O'Brien, *Mussolini in the First World War*, 171.

Everywhere in Europe, with the outbreak of war, conventional culture rallied swiftly to the cause of nationalist mobilization. The churches played an important role, justifying war with varying degrees of affirmation and bloodthirstiness. Protestantism in Germany, which since the time of Luther had seen itself as servant of the state, contributed powerful ideological support. Many pastors spoke of Germany's 'holy war', labelling it a 'crusade'; another wrote that this was a war of defence, a 'moral duty and thus a work pleasing to God'. Many stressed the sense of the war as the mission of German Protestantism to spread the gospel throughout the world; it was only logical that they saw Germans as the 'Chosen People'. Sermons declared the enemy nations to be the personification of 'sin', 'evil', the 'forces of darkness', the 'Antichrist', and the 'devil'. It was common to see in the war a sign of the coming day of judgement, an apocalyptic and chiliastic vision, with the expectation that the end of war would bring the second coming of the Messiah and a new epoch of world peace.[19] The mass death of soldiers was interpreted as martyrdom; the blood of the fallen fertilized the field from which the new Germany would arise. Here we can detect the theological roots of the fascist idea of palingenesis.

Despite the 'impartiality' of the Vatican and the repeated condemnations of the war by Pope Benedict XV, the Italian Church and its priests saw no incompatibility between their faith and the bearing of arms. Italian military chaplains were informed that the doctrine of St Augustine, whose teaching on the fundamental distinction between just and unjust war was the highest authority in Christian theology, was not being violated. Italy's subjects thus owed loyalty to the state, even if they did not understand the necessity of the war.

The French Church overcame its hostility towards the Republic which it had recently fought so bitterly over the Dreyfus Affair, control of education, and its entire relationship with the state. In the *union sacrée* both the Republican state, with its universal values of the Rights of Man, and the Catholic Church adopted a form of messianic belief that was not far removed from that of the German Protestant Church. Both parts of French culture agreed on the notion of the war for the defence of civilization: the defeat of France would mean the decline of civilization; victory would mean progress for all mankind. Like the German Protestant theologians, French Catholics saw the French war dead as martyrs who had died in the crusade and for Christ. However, the apocalyptic vision which came to dominate German Protestant war theology did not occupy a central place in the French Catholic interpretation of the war.

The Church of England seldom went beyond identifying with the nation and acting to provide chaplains and spiritual support for the troops. It tended to moderation; since Britain was not waging a war to overturn the balance of power, neither

---

[19] W. Pressel, *Die Kriegspredigt 1914–1918 in der evangelischen Kirche Deutschlands* (Göttingen: Vandenhoeck & Ruprecht, 1967), 108–20, 131–2, 142, 169–71.

the Church nor lay intellectuals engaged much in the violent rhetoric of cultural superiority characteristic of German intellectuals.

It was not only the theologians who saw the war in apocalyptic terms in German culture. The economist Werner Sombart spoke of 'the holy war which Germany is now waging against a world of enemies', a 'war of beliefs'. German modernist artists, such as the Expressionists, who had been rejected by the conservative establishment before 1914, rallied to the support of the nation. The editor of the leading modernist art journal, *Kunst und Künstler*, Karl Scheffler, wrote that war would bring liberation and a 'regeneration of idealism'. Convinced of German intellectual superiority, Scheffler wrote that the issue was 'world rule', which would fall to Germany in due course. 'We must become a master race not just in politics, but also in the spiritual realm.'[20]

III. TRAUMA AND CULTURE

By 1916, however, the interest in the war as theme and as source of inspiration was receding. Most leading writers in Germany who had voiced their enthusiasm in 1914 fell silent so far as the war was concerned. Richard Dehmel, who had written several poems welcoming war in 1914 and glorifying the *Volksgemeinschaft* (the people's community),[21] had changed his attitude. His poem of 1917, 'Hymnus barbaricus', was a grim satire on all nations who rejoiced each time heroic deeds were reported, involving the killing of masses. As Julius Bab, the compiler of a multi-volume collection of war poems, noted in 1919, the emotion expressed in the last two years of the war was ever more frequently horror, no longer pride; poets expressed a sense of human solidarity more strongly than the national unity of 1914, and began to point to the antagonism between rulers and ruled.

The philosopher Adolf Lasson had declared in 1914: 'This war is terrible above all because of the number and the kind of enemies who waylay us and seek to destroy [*vernichten*] us without mercy. If they were to succeed, they would like best to exterminate us [*ausrotten*].'[22] This imputation of the enemy's desire to annihilate Germany was potentially dangerous, not only because it could serve to legitimize

---

[20] W. J. Mommsen, 'German Artists, Writers and Intellectuals and the Meaning of the War, 1914–1918', in J. Horne (ed.), *State, Society and Mobilization during the First World War* (Cambridge: Cambridge University Press, 1997), 25.

[21] E.g. 'Lied an Alle' and 'Predigt ans deutsche Volk in Waffen', in *1914: Der Deutsche Krieg im Deutschen Gedicht*, selected by J. Bab, vol. ii (Berlin: Morawe & Scheffelt, n.d. [probably 1919]); cf. afterword by Bab, written in autumn 1919, 25 and 37.

[22] A. Lasson, 'Deutsche Art und deutsche Bildung', in *Deutsche Reden in schwerer Zeit* (Berlin: Heymann, 1914), 105–6.

unlimited destruction in warfare but also because demonizing the enemy built up a tremendous pressure of apocalyptic expectation. When that failed to materialize, the trauma of defeat remained on the level of the imagination.

Nationalist culture in post-war Germany thus constructed a myth-world around the notion of the Allied will to destroy Germany; for nationalists, the Allied allegation of German 'war guilt' extrapolated this intention into the present and provided the rationale for a cultural campaign of historical revisionism and the preparation of a new war. Thus the collective trauma of hyperinflation, whose cause was the way Germany financed the war and the deliberate ruining of the currency after it in order to demonstrate incapacity to pay reparations, was reinterpreted as the Allied attempt to 'destroy' Germany through reparations and trade restrictions, or the 'system of Versailles'.

The German occupation of Eastern Europe had even longer-term consequences in the history of mentalities, especially for right-wing German political culture which built on the experience of colonial-style rule and racist stereotyping. German troops became accustomed to enforcing obedience from the civilian population through public corporal punishment, also of women, and torture in the prisons. Ruthless exploitation of the natural resources of Eastern Europe and forced labour were intended to improve supplies for Germany. Yet it would be mistaken to see the occupation as a pilot programme for the Third Reich: the occupation in the First World War was colonial and authoritarian; Germany saw itself as a colonial regime with a civilizing mission to transform savages into decent Europeans. In the Second World War occupation in the east was devoted to a programme of brutal ethnic redistribution, enslavement, and genocide. Undoubtedly, here was one crucial link between the First World War and the Second: the German soldiers (two or three million of whom served in the east) returned from the war with a new concept of space: the east they encountered in 1914–18 was a desolate, partly depopulated, disease-ridden, underdeveloped region ready to be colonized.

The experience of the east should also make us wary of inflated claims for the concept of cultural trauma: Germany won a victory in the east and, unlike on the western front, fighting there was often in a war of movement which allowed soldiers to feel they were active agents rather than passive victims of industrialized violence. The Treaty of Versailles forced Germany to give up the dream of vast territorial gains in Eastern Europe. This dented the pride of military leaders and imperialist politicians, and nationalist propaganda never tired of referring to the bleeding wound of the new Polish border, but there is no evidence it was a traumatic experience for German soldiers and society. For radical nationalists the experience of occupation and victory in the east was more like a dream memory than a trauma.

For Germany the cultural trauma of defeat was associated rather with the deeper meaning of the war itself and the hopes attached to it. The Allied governments were not incorrect in their perception that Germany was fighting a war to establish hegemony over the continent. As the German chancellor Theobald von Bethmann Hollweg wrote in late 1914 in a private letter: 'The aim of this war is not to restore the European balance of power, but precisely to eliminate for all time that which has been termed the European balance of power and to lay the foundations for German predominance in Europe.'[23] The government attempted to keep the war aims discussion secret, for fear of alienating neutral countries and disturbing the *Burgfrieden* (peace within the castle) consensus that Germany was fighting a defensive war. That did not stop a very public debate in which nationalist intellectuals and interest groups blurted out the expansionist aims, demanding annexations of enemy territory and world power status. The influential nationalist historian Johannes Haller announced in 1914: 'Thus we are all agreed that we desire nothing less than world rule.' This was a minority view, but the notion of German cultural superiority and the mission to impose German values enjoyed wide support among intellectuals. The words of a poem by an otherwise forgotten mid-century poet, Emanuel Geibel, were inordinately popular in German culture during the war:

> Und es mag am deutschen Wesen
> Einmal noch die Welt genesen.
> (And one day by the German soul
> Shall the world be made whole.)[24]

That cultural mission, as well as the nature of modern warfare, produced a paradoxical response in the war culture of the Allies. French culture did not respond in kind to the German concept of cultural imperialism and made no argument for French hegemony to supplant German hegemonial ambition. In 1917 France's foremost public historian, Ernest Lavisse, addressed to the mayors of all *département* capitals an 'Appel aux Français', where he warned that France must win the war in order to have Germany punished and force it to repair the damage suffered by France; it was returned by most of them with their signatures, thus signifying a national statement about the war. Lavisse warned that Germany would continue to fight for as long as it could and there must be no compromise peace. France, in defending itself, was 'protecting humanity from the hateful yoke' of barbarous Germany.[25] In other words, French intellectuals identified themselves with their nation no less firmly than did their German counterparts but saw their war as defensive and for liberation, not to spread French culture, although the identification of French with universal values held out the potential for expansionism (for which French imperialism had already given ample proof). Moreover, as the war came

---

[23] BA Berlin, N2089/1, Nachlaß Konstantin Freiherr von Gebsattel, Generaloberst v. Kessel, Berlin to Gebsattel, 14 November 1914, citing from a letter from Bethmann.

[24] O. von Gierke, 'Krieg und Kultur', in *Deutsche Reden in schwerer Zeit*, 100.

[25] E. Lavisse, *Pourquoi nous nous battons* (Paris, 1917), cited in G. Krumeich, 'Ernest Lavisse und die Kritik an der deutschen "Kultur", 1914–1918', in W. J. Mommsen with E. Müller-Luckner (eds), *Kultur und Krieg: Die Rolle der Intellektuellen, Künstler und Schriftsteller im Ersten Weltkrieg* (Munich: Oldenbourg, 1996), 152–3.

to an end, the 'defence of civilization' tended to be replaced by ideas of justice, punishment, and vengeance.

French war culture thus gradually shifted to the right over the course of the long war, and to some extent polarized. A racist discourse developed, culminating in the denunciation of the German as the 'entirely vile and evil sub-human...the degenerate boche' in the popular weekly *L'Illustration*.[26] This radicalization, from which the socialist *L'Humanité* in general remained honourably distant, was paralleled in a certain 'brutalization of French politics' where perceived enemies of the state were severely punished, in some cases by execution.[27]

The cultural trauma of the war caused a far deeper polarization in Italy. There, the distortions of political culture had begun even before Italy entered the war. Although the government calculated that going to war would deflate the interventionist street campaign and allow the state to suppress the unrest, the explosive potential of the mixture of left-interventionists and nationalists posed a long-term threat. In an article published under the title 'Down with Parliament!' on 11 May 1915 Mussolini demanded that 'for the health of Italy a few dozen deputies should be shot: I repeat *shot* in the back'.[28] The violence of demonstrations in the *piazze* was a harbinger of the violence that was to re-emerge in Italian politics after 1918.

In Italy, as in several other belligerent states, millenarian visions of future consolation took hold in the last period of the war, offering an escape from the horrors of the present. Frequently, these visions were closely connected with the notion of the apocalypse in which the 'other'—evil in whatever form—would be destroyed. Even the government participated in the spiralling competition, making rash promises that inordinately raised the hopes of the peasant soldiers for the post-war period. The enormous sacrifice had to be worthwhile: about 650,000 Italian soldiers died in the war.[29] This was 11.6 per cent of the mobilized, a similar proportion to that of the United Kingdom but over a shorter period. The contested decision to enter the war and the experience of mass death sharpened the tensions in Italian politics and culture. This nourished the millenarian expectations raised by the war: Prime Minister Vittorio Emanuele Orlando called the war 'the greatest socio-political revolution recorded in history, greater even than the French Revolution'.[30] Italy's war produced a regime of internal repression and built up enormous pressure of utopian

---

[26]   7 April 1917, cited in M. Jeismann, *Das Vaterland der Feinde: Studien zum nationalen Feindbegriff und Selbstverständnis in Deutschland und Frankreich 1792–1918* (Stuttgart: Klett-Cotta, 1992), 358.

[27]   L. V. Smith, S. Audoin-Rouzeau, and A. Becker, *France and the Great War, 1914–1918* (Cambridge: Cambridge University Press, 2003), 59, 142–5.

[28]   O'Brien, *Mussolini in the First World War*, 55.

[29]   M. Isnenghi and G. Rochat, *La Grande Guerra 1914–1918* (Milan: La Nuova Italia, 2000), 228; A. Gibelli, 'Nefaste meraviglie: Grande Guerra e apoteosi della modernità', in R. Romano and C. Vivanti (eds), *Storia d'Italia*, xviii: *Guerra e pace*, ed. W. Barberis (Turin: Einaudi, 2002), 553.

[30]   G. Procacci, *Dalla Rassegnazione alla Rivolta: mentalità e comportamenti popolari nella Grande Guerra* (Rome: Bulzoni, 1999), 143–4.

expectations—whether in the guise of socialism or nationalism or of an entirely new form of mass politics that combined internal war and a state form that expressly continued the wartime regime of national mobilization.

IV. Memory and the Legacy of the War

The nexus between sacrifice, utopian expectations, and the outcome of the war was central to the cultural response to the legacy of war. The rhetoric of patriotic sacrifice was used in every nation to mobilize men and the home front. Yet German and Italian militarist nationalism made it particularly explosive. Werner Sombart expressed a commonly held opinion in German culture when he wrote that duty and sacrifice of the individual were necessary because the existence of the state stood above the life of the individual; indeed, the fate of the individual was to sacrifice himself for this higher life: 'With this belief, indeed only with this belief, the painful dying of thousands gains sense and meaning. The heroic philosophy of life finds its highest consecration in heroic death.'[31] All belligerent states demanded men's obedience in the face of lethal violence and glamorized it as 'sacrifice'; however, the apotheosis of 'painful dying' and 'heroic death' could lead only to massive alienation when the men became aware how senseless the slaughter had been. In Britain and France, the alienation that followed the war took the form of the 'pacifist turn' in culture and politics; in British culture one notable product of this was the literature of disenchantment (of Robert Graves and Siegfried Sassoon). In Germany, with its highly polarized culture between modernists and conservatives, the cultural memory of the war was like a toxic residue.

That difference between Britain and Germany is illustrated by the memory of the battle of the Somme. On what is generally known as the 'first day of the Somme', 1 July 1916, the British had 19,240 men killed and a total of 57,470 casualties, for insignificant territorial gain. Over the entire campaign, July to November 1916, the British lost 420,000, the French 204,000, and the Germans 465,000 to 500,000 men. The Somme is often described as useless slaughter, in which inept generals, above all General Haig, sent brave men to certain death. Commanders are called unimaginative and inflexible in their tactics, continuing to send men in even when it was obvious they would be killed. In popular imagination in the English-speaking world the Somme is reduced to that first day of battle and it remains a symbol of the futility of the First World War. Yet on 1 July the French achieved all their objectives in the southern sector of the Somme, for comparatively light losses

---

[31] W. Sombart, *Händler und Helden: Patriotische Besinnungen* (Munich: Duncker & Humblot, 1915), 89.

(7,000 men).[32] This suggests that the 'first day of the Somme' has become a kind of trauma in British national memory that has obscured the real history of the battle, as Gary Sheffield and other historians have argued. The four-and-a-half-month battle offered a steep learning curve for the British army, at the end of which it had become a highly trained, well-equipped, and effective fighting force which succeeded in taking the initiative away from Germany and restoring mobility to warfare in 1917 and 1918.

In a sense we can see this as a benign response to the trauma of war. It is not the worst historical option to see war as futile catastrophe. Other cultures coped with trauma by reacting in a pathological way. While the majority in Germany after 1918 paralleled (and indeed pre-dated) the pacifist consensus in Britain, militarist nationalism used and distorted the memory of war. That section of society coped with trauma with an obsessive desire to repeat the experience of industrialized violence and mass death; the aim of obtaining a better result second time around was political window-dressing, since ultimately the aims were not important: war was an essential end in itself. In that process shameful traumas had to be repressed or transformed into heroic experiences. German memory of the Somme was thus not the mirror image of the British but its antithesis. The Somme had given the German military leaders a severe shock, with profound consequences. On 7 August 1916, Lieutenant-Colonel Albrecht von Thaer, chief of staff of the IXth Reserve Army Corps, wrote in a letter:

These are *horrendous* days. We have lost some territory, although not very much. Our good IXth Reserve Corps is now 'finished up' after fourteen days of uninterrupted fighting. The infantry have lost about half their men, if not more. Some of those who have survived are no longer human beings, but creatures who are at the end of their tether, no longer *compos mentis*, incapable of any energetic action, let alone attack. Officers whom I know to be *particularly* strong men are reduced to sobbing.[33]

Memories such as these could not be allowed to form part of the national discourse after 1918. In autumn 1916 the Somme battlefield turned into a vast 'primeval mud landscape', an open-air sewer, where men, horses, and vehicles got stuck fast. A German medical officer described:

Everywhere deep shell holes, usually filled to the top with water. One feels one's way past the edge, wading through mud. Then there are tree-trunks, shot to pieces and lying across the ground, which one has to climb over. Then a group of corpses, [the sight of] which makes your flesh creep, about six of them, their bodies torn apart, covered with blood and mud.

---

[32] G. Sheffield, *Forgotten Victory: The First World War: Myths and Realities* (London: Review, 2002; 1st edn. 2001), 168–9.

[33] H. Otto and K. Schmiedel (eds), *Der Erste Weltkrieg: Dokumente* (Berlin: Militärverlag der Deutschen Demokratischen Republik, 1977), 188.

The head of one of them has been half shot away, and some distance away there is a severed leg, and some of the bodies have been so intertwined in the mud that one can no longer distinguish the individual corpses.[34]

The German army never recovered from the serious losses at the Somme, and Erich von Falkenhayn, chief of the army command, was forced to order a return to 'strict defensive' at Verdun as from 11 July and divert forty-two divisions to the Somme.[35] His nerves shattered, he was sacked in August and replaced by Paul von Hindenburg and Erich Ludendorff, who radicalized warfare into a policy of ruthless exploitation of the human and material resources of occupied Europe without regard to civilian well-being, including that of Germans, and squandered even more lives of German soldiers in the last desperate offensive of 1918. Thus the Somme battlefield could never form part of the heroic memory of the war in Germany.

On the other hand, the Somme was the scene for some of the most famous anti-war works of art by Otto Dix, George Grosz, and Max Beckmann. Unlike the writers, painters developed a new aesthetic to express their growing horror of the war. This was true of Germany, France, Britain, and Italy, and in this aspect of culture, unlike others, there was a considerable common ground. Beckmann's unfinished painting *Auferstehung* ('Resurrection', 1918) hints at the erasing of distinction between civilians and soldiers in the war. It holds out no prospect of the Messiah ascending to heaven; equally, there is no sense of the second meaning of 'resurrection', the idea that at the end of the world all the dead will rise up to enjoy everlasting life in a kingdom of peace. It is a vision of despair, where living civilians and almost naked soldiers risen from the dead confront a world of devastation under a black sun. The work he produced in the Weimar period reached an intensity of condemnation of the violence of man that was unsurpassed in its unsparing portrayal of modern suffering. After the war Otto Dix, who alone among the major war artists saw action throughout the war, fighting as machine-gun unit commander, produced a cycle of fifty etchings called *Der Krieg* ('The War') and the painting *Schützengraben* ('Trench'). These are drastic depictions of the consequences of war, filled with injuries, corpses, destroyed landscapes, and civilian victims, aiming to scandalize a post-war society that wished to forget the horror of war.

In Italy, while the Futurists delighted in war as if it were a giant playground for their games, other intellectuals were less convinced that it was good for their health. Gaetano Previati left a memorable anti-war painting, *Gli orrori della guerra (L'esodo)* ('The Horrors of War: The Exodus', 1917–18), which shows women and

[34] H. Natt, cited in G. Hirschfeld, 'Die Somme-Schlacht von 1916', in idem, G. Krumeich, and I. Renz (eds), *Die Deutschen an der Somme 1914–1918: Krieg, Besatzung, verbrannte Erde* (Essen: Klartext, 2006), 86.

[35] H. Afflerbach, *Falkenhayn: Politisches Denken und Handeln im Kaiserreich* (Munich: Oldenbourg, 1994), 419; Sheffield, *Forgotten Victory*, 184.

children escaping, Munch-like terror in their faces. But since the civilians are evidently fleeing from Austrian and German soldiers, Previati, who was known for his pacifism before the war, was not condemning war as such. Similarly, the work of Giulio Aristide Sartorio ranged from objectivist, emotionally neutral depiction of the everyday business of war (for example of troops and horses crossing a river estuary) to the drastic scene of a battlefield strewn with corpses, without a living soul in sight (*Sacile*, 31 October 1917). The interesting thing about Sartorio is how the war changed him. Before the war a symbolist influenced by the English Pre-Raphaelites and by D'Annunzio, with whom he collaborated, during the war Sartorio made use of modern technology—the camera—to produce paintings based on photographs. His subject matter, too, changed from the allegorical to the realistic. His *L'isola dei morti: Fagaré* depicts mass death, with corpses lined up in a desolate landscape. These paintings have a painful intimacy with death, corporality, and contamination absent in Futurism.[36]

British art, too, gave expression to the sense of cultural trauma. C. R. W. Nevinson, who had been the only English follower of Futurism in art, produced works such as *Flooded Trench on the Yser* (1915) which evoke a sense of desolation. *La Mitrailleuse* (1915), despite the Futurism of the geometric lines and the subject matter of the machine gun, does not rejoice in violence; the dead soldier in the picture is completely lacking in heroic aura and the machine gunner and his team are grim-faced, dehumanized beings. William Orpen, who before the war was a society painter, conventional and wealthy, was profoundly affected by the war and his work underwent an aesthetic and political transformation. His *Dead Germans in a Trench* (1918) is free of any sense of triumph or beauty. There is no comforting feature here; even the bright blue sky does not radiate warmth but an unmerciful glare.

Nations and different cultures within nations responded in different ways to the collective trauma of war and its outcome. This affected the post-war history of violence. Comparison across Europe shows that the demarcation lines in political violence did not run between victorious and defeated nations; nation states formed by wars of unification and East European states formed by secession proved to be particularly prone to violence in their political culture and instability after 1918, as opposed to West European nation states created by internal revolution. Such distinctions are arguably more useful than the thesis of a general 'brutalization of politics' following the war or the reductionist model according to which fascism was a response to the Bolshevik Revolution. The different reactions to war had as much to do with culture, including the creation of foundation myths and millenarian visions of the future, as with the actual tally of death, destruction, and economic dislocation.

These differences ran through national cultures. The deeper the emotional investment in the war and/or the war regime, the deeper the trauma at the defeat or,

---

[36] Gibelli, 'Nefaste meraviglie', 581.

in Italy's case, the trauma of shattered expectations of a grand victory. Germany's cultural trauma of defeat was compounded by the collapse of the imperial regime. General Ludendorff had suffered a nervous breakdown when the realization of impending defeat dawned in September 1918. For conservative nationalists the abdication of the Kaiser (on 9 November) was an unbearable emotional blow, worse, in fact, than defeat. General Kar von Einem broke down and wept, suffering temporary aphasia (inability to speak) at the news of the abdication; the shipping magnate Albert Ballin, a friend of the monarch, committed suicide. By contrast, the response of most soldiers, sailors, and workers on 9 November was to demand peace and abolition of the monarchy; with the armistice on 11 November the army of some eight million men melted away, leaving just a hard core of officers and fanatical militarists. Even the pro-war Gustav Noske (Defence Minister, 1918 to 1920) recognized that at the end of the war German workers were filled with hatred of all things military.

Even in relation to the most obvious trauma of war, bereavement, there were differences between and within national cultures, contrary to Jay Winter's thesis of the 'commonality of European cultural life' in the common invocation of the dead through mourning.[37] Bereavement was universal but cultures of mourning differed. France and Britain commemorated the 'unknown soldier', with monuments at the Arc de Triomphe and Westminster Abbey (and also the Cenotaph in Whitehall, literally an empty tomb). The unknown soldier allowed the anonymous masses to enter public memory, rather than the hero, the ordinary man who embodied the nation. He provided 'a means to come to terms with the trauma of war', to 'return to normality…to bury the dead and then go on with life'.[38] Italy, too, constructed a memorial to the 'unknown soldier' in the *Vittoriano*, the monument to Victor Emmanuel II and Italian unification. The Liberal state, caught in the crossfire between left-wing social protest and Fascist violence, sought to use it to underline its legitimization as the rightful owners of Italian unity, but the socialist newspaper *Avanti* claimed the Unknown Soldier as one of its own, a proletarian, and urged its readers: 'Honour him in silence and curse the war!'[39] Germany's path led in a different direction: there was no monument to the unknown soldier. The proposal was debated in Germany but the nationalists rejected it as a pacifist idea invented by the enemy. Russia, meanwhile, had practically no forms of public commemoration of the war dead, since the Revolution displaced all other public memory.

[37] J. Winter, *Sites of Memory, Sites of Mourning: The Great War in European Cultural History* (Cambridge: Cambridge University Press, 1995), 227.

[38] O. Bartov, *Mirrors of Destruction: War, Genocide, and Modern Memory* (New York: Oxford University Press, 2000), 16.

[39] R. Bosworth, *Mussolini's Italy: Life under the Dictatorship 1915–1945* (London: Allen Lane, 2005), 12–13, 36.

In the light of these differences, is there any value in seeing fascist warfare as the response to the trauma of the First World War? Was the Holocaust fascist vengeance for the experience of mass death in 1914–18? The First World War made the unthinkable thinkable. The mass death of thousands in a day, industrialized killing, poison gas, and genocide: these potentials had been shown in 1914–18. The era of the First World War witnessed a decisive step towards total war, as the erosion of the distinction between combatants and non-combatants became more and more visible. Fascist warfare eradicated that distinction. Mussolini's war against Ethiopia, which was both the last war of colonial conquest and the first fascist war in history, was waged with ruthless brutality against the entire population. Between 350,000 and 760,000 Ethiopians were killed, most of them civilians, and the technologically superior Italian forces terrorized the population with air power, bombing, poison gas, and collective punishments for guerrilla resistance. Was there a causal connection between 1915–16, which one Italian soldier at the time called the 'year of the holocaust of the volunteers',[40] and 1935–6 or between the Somme and Auschwitz?

Post hoc does not mean *propter hoc*. Certainly, the fascist regimes arose from their appropriation of the experience of the First World War and in a sense from the extreme pathological variant of the cultural trauma of war. However, that on its own would be an incomplete explanation of fascism. The highly divergent responses to war in Europe reiterate the contingency of history. The cultural trauma of war did not have only one product, as the British and French experience of the war showed; moreover, the cultural trauma of the Second World War produced very different post-war results, both in victorious and defeated nations.

BIBLIOGRAPHY

FREUD, S., *Thoughts for the Times on War and Death* (1915); in *The Standard Edition of the Complete Psychological Works of Sigmund Freud*, ed. James Strachey, Anna Freud, *et al.* (London: Hogarth, 1953–74), vol. xiv (1957).

HORNE, J., and KRAMER, A., *German Atrocities 1914: A History of Denial* (London: Yale University Press, 2001).

ISNENGHI, M., and ROCHAT, G., *La Grande Guerra 1914–1918* (Milan: La Nuova Italia, 2000).

KRAMER, A., *Dynamic of Destruction: Culture and Mass Killing in the First World War* (Oxford: Oxford University Press, 2007).

MOMMSEN, W. J., 'German Artists, Writers and Intellectuals and the Meaning of the War, 1914–1918', in J. Horne (ed.), *State, Society and Mobilization during the First World War* (Cambridge: Cambridge University Press, 1997), 21–38.

[40] Isnenghi and Rochat, *La Grande Guerra*, 169.

MOSSE, G. L., *Fallen Soldiers: Reshaping the Memory of the World Wars* (New York: Oxford University Press, 1990).

SMITH, L. V., AUDOIN-ROUZEAU, S., and BECKER, A., *France and the Great War, 1914–1918* (Cambridge: Cambridge University Press, 2003).

WINTER, J., *Sites of Memory, Sites of Mourning: The Great War in European Cultural History* (Cambridge: Cambridge University Press, 1995).

CHAPTER 3

....

THE FIRST WORLD
WAR AS TOTALITY

....

RICHARD BESSEL

THE word 'total' lies at the heart of our perceptions of the First World War. It was a war that, it was widely believed, involved total mobilization; a war that required total commitment and support from the population, on the home front no less than on the battlefront; a war that led to the total subordination of the economy and society to the needs of the military; a war that saw the total mobilization of the population in a spiritual as well as material sense. The First World War had shown that no aspect of social, economic, cultural, or political life would escape the grip of war; modern war called upon the resources of the whole nation. In July 1917 (when attacking Interior Minister Louis Malvy for weakness with regard to defeatist agitation, and a few months before he became French Prime Minister) Georges Clemenceau expressed with characteristic force his programme for conducting the First World War: 'We present ourselves in the single aim of total war. . . . My foreign policy and my home policy are the same. At home I wage war. Abroad I wage war. . . . I shall go on waging war.'[1] Commitment to war had to be total. This was the apparent lesson of the First World War. Modern war could not be fought with half-measures. War, so the experience of the First World War seemed to have demonstrated, was totality.

  Many of those who fought in the First World War thought either that they had fought a total war or, as Erich Ludendorff sought to convince his public,[2] that in

---

[1] Quoted in M. Ferro, *The Great War 1914–1918* (London: Routledge and Keegan Paul, 1973), 199.
[2] E. Ludendorff, *Kriegführung und Politik* (Berlin: Mittler & Sohn, 1922); idem, *Der Totale Krieg* (Munich: Ludendorff's Verlag, 1935).

order to bring the conflict to a successful conclusion they *should* have fought a total war. The scale of the conflict meant that, in an age of war fought by industrial powers with mass armies, civil society and the economy had to be harnessed completely to the requirements of war and, if necessary, to submit to rule by the military in order to secure victory. Finally, the conduct of the First World War—and, perhaps more important, perceptions of how the First World War was conducted—had a profound effect on what came later. Michael Geyer has noted recently, when considering the destructive and strategically pointless final year of Nazi Germany's war, that 'the seeds for the unending pursuit of war in 1944–45 were sown in World War I'.[3] The lesson of the First World War, it seemed, was that struggle had become total—and should be pursued 'beyond defeat . . . to the point of self-destruction'.[4] The idea of the First World War as totality thus is not only about the extent of fighting and of the social and economic mobilization which it required; it also is about a total conflict, beyond reason and without end.[5] This combination— struggle beyond reason and war without end—became the agenda of fascism.

I. 'WAR ENTHUSIASM' AND 'FRONT GENERATION'

Two sets of imaginations which arose from the First World War, as a total war that swept up entire peoples both body and soul, are of crucial importance here. The first is the imagination of August 1914—of the enthusiasm with which the outbreak of war was greeted across Europe. Certainly there is much truth in this picture, captured in contemporary photographs of cheering crowds and reinforced by statements of men who (as did Adolf Hitler) 'thanked heaven from an overflowing heart that it had granted me the good fortune to be alive at such a time', or who regarded (as did the historian Friedrich Meinecke, writing in 1944) the day when Germany declared war on France in 1914 as 'one of the most beautiful moments of my life'.[6] While the cheering crowds may not have been quite so large as propagandists claimed at the time, men like Hitler, who volunteered for military service when war broke out, also provided evidence of enthusiasm for a great national cause. Across the European continent hundreds of thousands of men volunteered for

[3] M. Geyer, 'Endkampf 1918 and 1945: German Nationalism, Annihilation, and Self-Destruction', in A. Lüdtke and B. Weisbrod (eds), *No Man's Land of Violence: Extreme Wars in the 20th Century* (Göttingen: Wallstein Verlag, 2006), 40.

[4] Ibid. 45.

[5] See M. Eksteins, *Rites of Spring: The Great War and the Birth of the Modern Age* (Boston: Bantam Press, 1989).

[6] H. Strachan, *The First World War*, i: *To Arms* (Oxford: Oxford University Press, 2001), 104.

military service once war had been declared. In Great Britain, where conscription was not introduced until 1916, roughly a quarter of men of eligible age volunteered for military service; by the end of 1915 nearly 2.5 million had enlisted voluntarily (even in Ireland more than 100,000 volunteered to serve 'King and Country').[7] After the often bitter internal conflicts and divisions which had characterized public and political life in the years before 1914—in a France where the divisions which erupted during the Dreyfus Affair were still raw, in a Germany which had seen the growth of the world's largest Marxist political party, in a Russia which had come close to revolution less than a decade before—it finally seemed as though the nation was united in its determination to wage war. The images and sentiments of an all-embracing 'spirit of 1914' would resonate for decades.

More recently, however, historians have cast doubt on the idea that the outbreak of war was greeted so overwhelmingly positively. Instead, as Jean-Jacques Becker has observed of the French, many people reacted 'with much less enthusiasm than has often been alleged, when they read the order for mobilization on 1 August 1914'.[8] We know now that the outbreak of war was greeted with less than total backing both among the urban working classes (who had not been left untouched by the pacifist hopes and anti-war agitation of socialists and social democrats) and among the rural population (who were far from keen to have their sons and horses conscripted, particularly at harvest time).[9] It seems fairly clear that the declaration of war was greeted with considerable fear, resignation, and anxiety among large swathes of the population; that people were at least as likely to engage in the panic buying of food and the withdrawal of their savings from banks as to cheer the declaration of war; that many who enlisted did so more out of a sense of duty or as a result of social pressure than as an expression of genuine war enthusiasm. However, that is not what was reported or photographed at the time. Instead, it was the cheering crowds in the great public spaces of Europe's capitals, on Unter den Linden and the Potsdamer Platz in Berlin, along the northern boulevards

[7] J. Winter, 'Some Aspects of the Problem of Manpower in the Great War: The British Case', in G. Canini (ed.), *Les Fronts invisibles: nourrir—fournir—soigner* (Nancy: Presses Universitaires, 1984), 124; Strachan, *The First World War*, 160.

[8] J.-J. Becker, *The Great War and the French People* (Leamington Spa: Berg, 1985), 3.

[9] See W. Kruse, 'Die Kriegsbegeisterung im Deutschen Reich zu Beginn des Ersten Weltkrieges: Entstehungszusammenhänge, Grenzen und ideologische Strukturen', in M. van der Linden and G. Mergner (eds), *Kriegsbegeisterung und mentale Kriegsvorbereitungen: Interdisziplinäre Studien* (Berlin: Duncter & Humblat, 1991), 73–87; W. Kruse, *Krieg und national Integration: Eine Neuinterpretation des Sozialdemokratischen Burgfriedensschlusses 1914/1915* (Essen, 1993); J. Verhey, *The Spirit of 1914: Militarism, Myth and Mobilization in Germany* (Cambridge: Cambridge University Press, 2000); T. Rohrkrämer, 'August 1914: Kriegsmentalität und ihre Voraussetzungen', in W. Michalka (ed.), *Der Erste Weltkrieg: Wirkung, Wahrnehmung, Analyse* (Munich, 1994), 759–77; R. Bessel, *Germany after the First World War* (Oxford, 1993), 3–4; C. Geinitz, *Kriegsfurcht und Kampfbereitschaft: Das Augusterlebnis in Freiburg: Eine Studie zum Kriegsbeginn 1914* (Essen: Klartext, 1998); N. Ferguson, *The Pity of War* (London: Allen Lane, 1998), 174–211; B. Ziemann, *War Experiences in Rural Germany 1914–1923* (Oxford: Berg, 2007), 15–27.

and at the Gare de l'Est in Paris, and around Trafalgar Square in London, which were captured in the media of the day and which shaped how the beginning of the First World War would be remembered subsequently. Images matter; they may be more important than reality. Whatever the reality, it was the 'spirit of 1914'—the idea of an enthusiastic and total mobilization—which provided inspiration. The famous picture of a crowd celebrating the declaration of war at the Odeonsplatz in Munich—famous because by chance the 25-year-old Adolf Hitler can be seen among the cheering throng—was both a visual record of one aspect of that day and an inspiration for nationalist politics during the inter-war years. The image was of a nation united in war.

The second great imagination was that of the 'front community'—the idea that class divisions evaporated at the front, where all soldiers were united in devotion to the nation and in comradeship with one another. This notion was given powerful impetus at the start of the war when, contrary to expectations in some ruling circles and despite often intense anti-war agitation over previous years, millions of men willingly answered their country's call and joined the armed forces. When the decisive moment arrived, nationalism trumped internationalism. For all the doubts that governments across Europe had had in 1914 about whether men would answer the call to the colours, the numbers who failed to appear were tiny: not just in Germany and France, but also in Russia and Austria-Hungary the overwhelming majority of men called reported for duty.[10] Of course, the awful realities of warfare quickly dented whatever ardour for war there had been among most of the recruits of August 1914, but among the soldiers there often developed a sense of community that transcended civilian divisions. A distance developed between those who had experienced combat and those who had remained at home and, therefore, could not be expected to appreciate or understand what the war really meant. The idea that the soldiers' world was separate from the world behind the lines, and that the combatants of the First World War experienced 'a profound isolation' when they returned home, gained wide acceptance. The common experiences that veterans evoked—sympathetically paraphrased by Jules Maurin in his detailed study of soldiers from Languedoc as 'the camaraderie of the front, the chum helped or rescued, the package from home shared, the tobacco smoked together, the flask making the rounds of the squad, each one swallowing his fill, forgetting the bad character of the one and the grumbling or the scoffing of the other in order to retain nothing but the spirit of fraternity'[11]—set them apart from their fellow citizens who stayed at home and gave the soldiers a special and exclusive sense of community.

No doubt to some extent this was misty-eyed posing, by men who had convinced themselves of the essential truth of their perceptions. Certainly the conviction was widely held among soldiers that the population back home, whatever

[10] Strachan, *The First World War*, 152–9.

[11] J. Maurin, *Armée—guerre—société: soldats languedociens (1889–1919)* (Paris: Publications de la Sorbonne, 1982), 663–78.

belt-tightening and hardships they had to endure, did not understand what men experienced at the front, and this conviction produced deep and widespread resentments on the part of the 'front fighters', which framed public discussion.[12] In contrast to the Second World War, the experiences and the sacrifices of the soldiers of the First World War were overwhelmingly separate from those of the civilian population, who experienced great material hardship but by and large were not subjected to immediate and direct threats to their lives.[13] In their perceived 'isolation' from the civilian world, the soldiers of the First World War could imagine both the exclusivity and the totality of their experience of modern warfare.

This is not to say that the members of the 'front generation' necessarily viewed their war experiences positively. The knowledge of the horror no less than the camaraderie of the trenches was what they had in common. The war also represented the triumph of insanity—a carnage so vast that it overwhelmed all else. On 22 May 1916 the 21-year-old French Second Lieutenant Alfred Joubaire wrote from Verdun in his private diary:

How long is this going to last? Anguish makes me wonder when and how this gigantic, unprecedented struggle will end. There's no resolution in view. I wonder if it won't just finish for lack of men to fight with. It's no longer one nation fighting another. It's two great blocs fighting, two civilizations colliding. The peoples have been touched by the madness of death and destruction. Certainly, humanity has gone mad! It must be mad to do what it's doing. Such slaughter! Such scenes of horror and carnage! I can't find the words to convey them. Hell could not be worse. Men are mad![14]

'Totality' became the totality of slaughter and destruction, of war without end.

The idea of the 'front generation'—of the men who experienced the madness of the Great War, whose immersion into the world of the front set them apart from those who had remained at home—owed a great deal to a number of novel characteristics of the First World War which made that 'generation' ever present in public consciousness during and after the conflict. The first, of course, was the sheer scale of the conflict. Never before had so many men fought in a war and survived to tell the tale. The second was that the overwhelming majority of the soldiers of the First World War, at least in the west, were literate, and could and did write of their experiences in diaries and letters to their wives and parents, siblings, and children, back home. The third is the extensive visual record created of the war: never before had war been so comprehensively photographed, and, for the first time, the results of a major conflict could be captured with cheap hand-held cameras. Of course some photos, in particular of one's own dead, were less likely than others to be

---

[12] For example, for France see S. Audoin-Rouzeau, *National Sentiment and Trench Journalism in France during the First World War* (Providence, RI: Berg, 1992).

[13] R. Koselleck, 'Der Einfluß der beiden Weltkriege auf das soziale Bewußtsein', in W. Wette (ed.), *Der Krieg des kleinen Mannes: Eine Militärgeschichte von unten* (Munich: Piper, 1992), 327–8.

[14] Quoted in I. Ousby, *The Road to Verdun: France, Nationalism and the First World War* (London: Jonathan Cape, 2002), 236–7.

published; however, the visual record of battle-scarred landscapes, of conditions in which the soldiers had to live, of dead men and animals, and of widespread destruction, were widely circulated and came to frame how the environment of 'total' war and the experiences of the front generation were understood.[15] The fourth is the number of men who returned home with evident disabilities. After the First World War, men without arms or legs were a common sight in the former combatant countries, men who became war's 'living memorials'.[16] This situation fed its way into literature, which in turn reinforced the image: as Robert Wohl has observed, 'when we think of the army of returning veterans during the 1920s, we see them through the eyes of Remarque and Hemingway as a generation of men crippled'.[17] And—having been assured during the conflict that the state would care for them (with assurances framed in phrases such as 'You can be sure of the thanks of the Fatherland')—hundreds of thousands of scarred, crippled veterans flocked to organizations formed to represent their interests as members of a 'front generation', and claimed huge proportions of state budgets after the war. In Britain more than 41,000 soldiers had to have limbs amputated due to war injuries, and in the 1930s 220,000 former officers and 419,000 enlisted men were receiving disability pensions.[18] In France about 40 per cent of the 8.4 million men mobilized were wounded at least once during the conflict, 300,000 had been officially designated *mutilés de guerre* by the end of the war, and roughly two million men returned with some form of disability.[19] In Germany the numbers were even greater. According to one estimate, roughly 2.7 million men came back from the war with a permanent disability, and 800,000 received invalidity pensions; the resources devoted to war dependants and the war disabled during the 1920s approached a third of the Reich budget.[20] Never before had descriptions and images of the front been so widely distributed; never before had so many men returned from combat with war-related disabilities and a vital interest in maintaining their identity as members of a 'front generation'.

After the war, many convinced members of the 'front generation' could—and some did—attempt to carry the 'front spirit' with them into the post-war world.

[15] See the contributions to R. Rother (ed.), *Die letzten Tage der Menschheit: Bilder des Ersten Weltkrieges* (Berlin: Ars Nicolai, 1994): B. von Drewitz, 'Zur Geschichte der Kriegsphotographie des Ersten Weltkrieges' (pp. 163–76); J. Carmichael, 'Die Entwicklung der britischen Photographie während des Ersten Weltkrieges' (pp. 177–86); and A. Sayang, ' "Wir sagen Adieu einer ganzen Epoche": Französische Kriegsphotographie' (pp. 187–96).

[16] The phrase comes from Deborah Cohen's excellent study of the war-disabled in Britain and Germany after the First World War, *The War Come Home: Disabled Veterans in Britain and Germany, 1914–1939* (Berkeley and Los Angeles: University of California Press, 2001), 102.

[17] R. Wohl, *The Generation of 1914* (London: Weidenfeld & Nicolson, 1980), 223.

[18] J. Bourke, *Dismembering the Male: Men's Bodies, Britain and the Great War* (London: Reaktion Books, 1996) 33.

[19] L. V. Smith, S. Audoin-Rouzeau, and A. Becker, *France and the Great War 1914–1918* (Cambridge: Cambridge University Press, 2003), 96.

[20] R. W. Whalen, *Bitter Wounds: German Victims of the Great War, 1914–1939* (Ithaca, NY: Cornell University Press, 1984), 95, 157.

This was evident among both the early supporters of Italian Fascism—the ex-servicemen and officers, the *arditi* shock troops—and the tens of thousands of Germans who signed up for the Freikorps units that engaged in anti-revolutionary paramilitary violence in the wake of the First World War. It did not necessarily matter that many who joined Freikorps units themselves were too young to have seen combat during the First World War.[21] The point is that they regarded the imagined experience of war, the myth of the First World War, as something that should put its stamp on the whole of society. It was, George Mosse has posited, a myth of war experience which 'looked back upon the war as a meaningful experience' and 'was designed to mask war and legitimize the war experience; it was meant to displace the reality of war'.[22]

It is well known that for the fascist dictators of the inter-war years, Mussolini and Hitler, the First World War was of central importance. Both served as corporals during the conflict, both experienced combat, and both were wounded; for both it was a people's conflict, that needed to be fought as a 'total war', where those who undermined the war effort should be shown no mercy. The First World War proved a turning point in the lives of both, and provided inspiration for the fascist politics of both. War would give meaning to their existence, to the spirit of their nations; it was something total, beyond rationality, beyond victory or defeat. In *Mein Kampf* Hitler famously referred to his time as a soldier in the First World War as 'the greatest and most unforgettable time of my earthly existence'.[23] For Mussolini, who broke with Italy's socialists over support for joining the conflict, the war was the turning point of his political career. Both Mussolini and Hitler drew the lesson that victory in war was in large measure a matter of will, and that commitment—both material and spiritual—to victory must be total.

Many millions of men shared the experiences that had framed such ideas, even if they did not necessarily reach the same conclusions. The extent and duration of the war meant that the overwhelming majority of young men in the belligerent countries served in the armed forces during the conflict. Subsequently the combatants of the First World War dominated political life across Europe. They may not all have gone off to war with cheerful enthusiasm, but they had gone, and those who survived went on to comprise a huge part of the electorate of their respective countries during the 1920s and 1930s. In Italy, the more than five million men who had seen military service between 1915 and 1918 equalled the number who had gone to the polls in the election of 1913.[24] In Germany, the same was true: the more than 13 million men who served in the German armed forces between 1914 and

---

[21] On the membership of the Freikorps, see H. Schulze, *Freikorps und Republik 1918–1920* (Boppard am Rhein: Harald Boldt, 1969), 36–7.

[22] G. L. Mosse, *Fallen Soldiers: Reshaping the Memory of the World Wars* (New York: Oxford University Press, 1990), 7.

[23] A. Hitler, *Mein Kampf*, trans. R. Mannheim (London: Hutchinson, 1974), 150.

[24] R. Bosworth, *Mussolini* (London: Arnold, 2002), 112.

1918 exceeded in number the 12.2 million who had cast their votes in the Reichstag elections of 1912.[25] Altogether roughly 11 million German soldiers survived the First World War and returned to Germany, and during the 1920s (after women had got the vote) they comprised over a quarter of the electorate of the Weimar Republic.[26] In France altogether 8.4 million men were mobilized during the war—a number almost equal to the nine million votes cast in the legislative elections of 1924 (in what still was an all-male franchise).[27] What is more, many of the people they voted for, the political leaders of subsequent decades, shared experience of combat during the First World War. Not just Benito Mussolini and Adolf Hitler but also Heinrich Brüning (who volunteered for service in 1915 and rose to become an officer in an elite machine-gun unit), Charles de Gaulle (who was wounded three times, and then spent much of the war as a prisoner in Germany), Clement Attlee (who served in the Middle East and in France, and who attained the rank of major), and Harold Macmillan (who was wounded three times, including during the battle of the Somme) had experienced the First World War in uniform—as had Harry Truman (who fought in France in 1918 as a captain in the American Field Artillery). Members of the 'front generation' of the 1914–18 war, quite naturally in the course of things, rose into positions of leadership in the 1930s and 1940s as they reached their thirties and forties. The war experience—real or imagined—was ever present in the politics and public life of the inter-war years (and beyond).

II. Economy and Society at War

The 'total' experience of the First World War was not simply a matter of the men who experienced battle at first hand. The idea of modern, 'total', war also arose from the gigantic levels of organization of societies and economies necessary to sustain the war effort. From the outset, in August 1914, the powers and prerogatives of the state were extended enormously. The realm of the state and the military grew, at the expense of civil society, in all the major combatant powers. States of emergency were declared, censorship was extended, governments were given dictatorial powers, political differences were set aside in the supposed national interest of the nation at war. Unprecedented challenges required unprecedented measures; total war required the total mobilization of society and the economy; modern warfare meant the compression of war and society. This was 'absolute war' which, Michael Howard has observed, 'became possible only when, as happened

[25] G. A. Ritter and M. Niehuss (eds), *Wahlgeschichtliches Arbeitsbuch: Materialien zur Statistik des Kaiserreichs 1871–1918* (Munich: Beck, 1980), 42.

[26] Bessel, *Germany after the First World War*, 270–1.

[27] D. G. Wileman, 'What the Market Will Bear: The French Cartel Elections of 1924', *Journal of Contemporary History*, 29 (1994), 486.

in nineteenth-century Europe, the state acquired the bureaucratic structure, the transportation networks, and the communications systems that gave it the capacity to mobilize its manpower and industrial potential for military purposes, together with the ability, through taxation and loans, to finance a prolonged struggle'.[28] What became possible in the course of the nineteenth century would be realized at beginning of the twentieth.

'Absolute war' required the primacy of military needs over those of civil society. Politics would have to be subordinated to what the military defined as national needs in time of conflict, and the normal political process would have to be suspended. This was apparent from the outset, with the suspension of legal protections and limits on the prerogatives of the state: the demands of war were more important than the strict maintenance of liberal principles or the rule of law. Thus, with the state of siege decreed by French President Raymond Poincaré on 2 August 1914, individual liberties were suspended, publications could be banned, the military could try civilians on security charges, and the army could requisition private property.[29] At the beginning of September, Poincaré signed a decree closing the emergency session of parliament, after which 'for nearly four months the executive was able to govern as a quasi-dictatorship'.[30] Similarly, the state of siege declared in Germany on the day of mobilization (following the Prussian Law of Siege of 4 June 1851) effectively placed civil administration under what was virtually the dictatorial rule of 'Deputy Commanding Generals' in each of the empire's twenty-four army corps districts.[31] Modern war, it seemed, necessitated dictatorial rule (even if the legal basis was rather archaic).

Of course, what actually occurred fell rather short of a total commitment to war. No doubt many agreed with the sentiments expressed by Poincaré when, as France suffered military setbacks in the second half of August 1914, he bemoaned 'the high cost of politics: a relaxing of military discipline, sectarianism overriding the national spirit, humanitarian dreaming'.[32] 'Politics' and 'sectarianism' could not be suppressed easily. As the conflict wore on, Germany's *Burgfrieden* crumbled amid growing divisions about the nature of the country's war aims and growing hardships faced by an increasingly war-weary civilian population; France's *union sacrée* ran up against the crisis of the mutinies of 1917; Russia's wartime unity was shattered under the pressures of military defeat, hardship at home, and, eventually, revolution, where Bolshevik success was due not least to the promise of ending Russian participation in the conflict; and Italy's belated, opportunist, and cynical

---

[28] M. Howard, 'World War One: The Crisis in European History: The Role of the Military Historian', *Journal of Military History*, 57 (1993), 127–38. See also the comments that follow by Michael Geyer, Peter Paret, and Michael Howard, 145–63.

[29] J. F. Godfrey, *Capitalism at War: Industrial Policy and Bureaucracy in France 1914–1918* (Leamington Spa: Berg, 1987), 45.

[30] J. F. V. Keiger, *Raymond Poincaré* (Cambridge: Cambridge University Press, 1997), 201.

[31] See G. D. Feldman, *Army, Industry and Labor in Germany 1914–1918* (Princeton: Princeton University Press, 1966), 31–3.

[32] Quoted in Keiger, *Raymond Poincaré*, 206.

entry into the war rested more on political division than on an Italian *union sacrée* and hardly provided a solid foundation for patriotic consensus. Attempts to harness the economy behind the war effort frequently and inevitably resulted in mismanagement and misallocation of resources and in bitter accusations of war profiteering, which served to exacerbate division and conflict at home. The idea that participation in the First World War was an expression of total commitment was a more an expression of hopes and dreams than a reflection of political realities.

It was not just politics that were to be transcended; the limits imposed by orthodox economics would have to be transcended as well. When war broke out in 1914, however, assumptions had been quite different. On the eve of the First World War it was believed widely that a major war could last only a few weeks or months. In the summer of 1914 general staffs on all sides were united in their conviction that the war would be of short duration. Even the Italian Prime Minister, Antonio Salandra, when he led his country into the conflict in 1915, was 'clinging manfully to his "short-war illusion", well after it had been rejected elsewhere'.[33] Consequently, few regarded it necessary at first to make fundamental changes to the ways in which economic life was organized; as long as war remained limited, total subordination of the civilian economy to military needs would not be required. At the outbreak of the conflict the French General Staff, for example, anticipated no need to increase the number of people employed in war industries, assuming that existing powder stores were sufficient to meet military needs for the entire war. It was not long before the realization dawned that such projections were utterly unrealistic: in the French case, on 20 September 1914 the new Minister of War, Alexandre Millerand, announced that the army's need for artillery shells alone was more than seven and a half times the amounts assumed just two months previously.[34]

The strikingly optimistic military plans which supposedly would deliver speedy victory notwithstanding, it was assumed that limits on resources would put a brake on modern industrial war: stocks would be exhausted quickly and the money necessary to pay for continued fighting soon would run out. Economics, it was believed, would prevent the continued pursuit of battle over an indefinite period. Indeed, before 1914 the belief had been voiced that European powers would be prevented from going to war against one another or, if they did, from sustaining the conflict, because of the economic crisis that would result.[35] Obviously, such assumptions proved to be mistaken. The First World War was of a scale and duration, swallowed up amounts of resources, and caused levels of devastation that had been unimaginable a few years before. And in stark contrast with the global conflict of a century earlier—the Revolutionary and Napoleonic Wars—during the

---

[33] R. Bosworth, *Mussolini's Italy: Life under the Dictatorship 1915–1945* (London: Allen Lane, 2005), 60.

[34] Godfrey, *Capitalism at War*, 45–8.

[35] N. Ferguson, 'How (Not) to Pay for the War: Traditional Finance and "Total" War', in R. Chickering and S. Förster (eds), *Great War, Total War: Combat and Mobilization on the Western Front, 1914–1918* (Cambridge: Cambridge University Press, 2000), 409.

First World War armies were supplied from home rather than being expected to live off the land. This was made possible by breaking the hitherto assumed limits on the resources that could be channelled into the conflict, something which happened very quickly.

Within a few days of the outbreak of war in 1914, the major belligerents (and even neutrals, such as Sweden) suspended the convertibility of their currencies into gold, thus sweeping away the limits on deficit spending that the gold standard had ensured. Governments engaged in deficit spending to an unprecedented degree. Despite steep increases in levels of taxation, tax revenues fell hugely short of the amounts needed to pay for the war, and belligerent governments looked to borrowing: the sale of war loans to the domestic population and, where possible, borrowing internationally. Levels of national debt skyrocketed, as did the amounts of currency in circulation. Rates of taxation were increased and new imposts introduced: in Great Britain the standard rate of income tax was raised progressively during the war from 6.25 per cent to 30 per cent, and all the major belligerent powers introduced excess-profits or war-profits tax.[36] Market mechanisms were suspended to a considerable degree and, increasingly, state control was extended over the supply and distribution of food, raw materials, and labour. In short, previously accepted limitations on economic policy were lifted in the interests of making war. Modern war did not respect the rules of free-market economics; economic orthodoxy could not circumscribe modern war. Over thirty years ago, in his pioneering study of the eastern front during the First World War, Norman Stone observed: 'In the old days, governments under pressure could always make peace before the crisis bit too deep. Now, they had the physical power to carry on the war for a long time, with hundreds of thousands of recruits, the capacity to supply them, and boundless possibilities for joyous arithmetic in paper-money.'[37]

It is not so much the extensions of state and government activity during the First World War per se that are crucial to the argument here, but the assumptions that lay behind them and their consequences for the post-war period. Attempts to exert control over the war economy—for example, the controls exercised by the War Raw Materials Department set up within the Prussian War Ministry in August 1914 under the leadership of Walther Rathenau, and by the various War Raw Materials Corporations it administered in order to control the supply of commodities—may have been regarded in retrospect as models of government control or even as a form of war socialism. In fact they marked less a fundamental departure from conventional capitalist relations of production than an attempt to coordinate the allocation of essential materials that in the event often left a lot to be desired.[38] The capitalist economy remained in place, albeit with an unprecedented degree of state intervention and direction. However, the main effect was neither to transform the

---

[36] G. Hardach, *The First World War 1914–1918* (London: Allen Lane, 1977), 150–69.

[37] N. Stone, *The Eastern Front 1914–1917* (London: Hodder & Stoughton, 1975), 218.

[38] See Hardach, *The First World War*, 58–63.

nature of economic relationships nor to ensure that the war economy functioned smoothly and effectively, but to a greater (in the German case) or lesser (in the British case) extent to focus public criticism on both private enterprise and state control. Roger Chickering has observed of Germany:

By the end of 1915, bureaucratic controls had supplanted the market mechanism; they had encompassed most components and every phase of the food supply, from agricultural production through processing, transportation, storage, and rationed distribution, to consumption. This claim to 'totality' was of dubious value—or validity. Insofar as it associated food shortages with public institutions, it politicized hunger. It also failed to encompass a vast black market in foodstuffs, whose thriving illegality and essential role in feeding the home front derided the legitimacy of these very public institutions.[39]

'Totality' proved illusory. The German case is instructive, as the harder the German military tried to achieve total mobilization of economy and society, the further they receded from their goal. The demands, after Hindenburg and Ludendorff had assumed control of the Supreme Army Command in August 1916, for huge increases in armaments production (the 'Hindenburg Programme') and the call for the total mobilization of labour, including women, juveniles, POWs, and disabled servicemen (the Auxiliary Service Law of December 1916), proved failures. As Michael Geyer has observed of these attempts to increase armaments production and mobilize labour resources to their utmost: 'The War Office administered and organized, but had little influence on what occurred in industry.'[40] Nevertheless, important precedents were set in the quest for a war effort that knew no bounds— not least the use of forced labour and the deportation of workers from Belgium and Poland.[41] Over four decades ago, in his masterful account of Germany's political economy during the First World War, Gerald Feldman described the ascendance of Hindenburg and Ludendorff as having 'represented the triumph . . . of fantasy'.[42] This is an apt description of the 'totality' of the First World War: an idea, a fantasy that would have important effects on the ways in which politics (and, not least, fascist politics) were conceived during the post-war years.

Germany's enemies, too, vastly extended the powers of the state in the attempt to meet the unprecedented requirements of modern warfare. In the United Kingdom the Defence of the Realm Act of 8 August 1914, amended several times subsequently, gave government the power to requisition the output of factories involved in war production, and (from March 1915) to intervene and determine the production of essential factories (which meant that firms such as Armstrong Vickers became subject to government directives); and the public sector was greatly expanded to

[39] R. Chickering, 'World War I and the Theory of Total War: Reflections on the British and German Cases, 1914–1915', in Chickering and Förster (eds), *Great War, Total War*, 51.

[40] M. Geyer, *Deutsche Rüstungspolitik 1860–1980* (Frankfurt am Main: Suhrkamp, 1984), 110.

[41] U. Herbert, *Geschichte der Ausländerbeschäftigung in Deutschland 1880 bis 1980* (Berlin: Dietz Verlag, 1986), 82–99.

[42] Feldman, *Army, Industry and Labor*, 150.

manufacture armaments. Like their German counterpart, the British government (embodied by David Lloyd George at the Ministry of Munitions) toyed with the idea of compulsory labour service for civilians, and like the Germans they backed off from the more extreme proposals.[43] In France, which lost its main areas of industrial production and iron and coal reserves in the north-east during the early months of the war, the government 'became the sole importer and distributor of raw materials...created consortia and omnia to supply the raw materials which industry required'; and Étienne Clémentel, wartime Minister of Commerce and Industry, 'ultimately controlled all non-military industry in France'.[44]

Citing 'the reordering of all domestic priorities to produce guns and ammunition on the enormous scale requisite for military needs' that came with the creation of the Ministry of Munitions under Lloyd George in 1915 and the 'Hindenburg Programme' during the following year, Michael Howard has observed that, 'by the end of 1916 the search for victory on the battlefield was resulting in nothing less than the social and political transformation of the belligerent societies'.[45] Certainly there was huge change, but the total subordination of society and economy to the needs of the military remained an aspiration rather than an achievement. While the Western Allies may have managed things better than did the central powers, nowhere was control of the war economy 'total'—except perhaps in men's minds. Achieving total control over the complex industrial economies of the major belligerents proved impossible, but the attempt massively to extend state controls was of tremendous importance both for the history of the First World War and for structures of state control that were put into place over the following decades. The totalitarian pretences and efforts of Fascist Italy, Nazi Germany, and Vichy France owe a great deal to the vistas that were opened during the First World War. As John Godfrey notes in the conclusion of his study of French industrial policy during the First World War, 'with its stress on industrial concentration and productivity, on state economic planning and management...Vichy had the power and ruthlessness to force through economic measures that Clémentel only dreamt of'.[46] The dreams and fantasies of the 'totality' of economic controls during the First World War were to materialize in horribly mutant form during the Second.

For fascist movements, which advocated and glorified war, the idea that society should be subordinated to the needs of war was central. The First World War as 'totality'—not the reality of that war, with its horrors, social divisions, economic mismanagement and corruption, and divisive pursuit of sectional and economic interests, but the myth of a war in which the whole of society was united behind the national struggle—provided inspiration and a model: for state controls over the economy, for the curtailment of civil liberties in the supposed interest of pursuing

[43] See Hardach, *The First World War*, 77–86.   [44] Godfrey, *Capitalism at War*, 289–91.
[45] Howard, 'World War One: The Crisis in European History', 132.
[46] Godfrey, *Capitalism at War*, 300.

vital national goals, for struggle that supposedly united the whole of society behind the national cause.

Another important facet of how the First World War was perceived has been as a modern, technological war—no matter that the main means of transporting material near the front was the horse, and that across Eastern Europe the fighting generally bore little resemblance to an imagination of industrial warfare, and disease was a considerably greater danger than on the western front.[47] Although in mid-1917 the number of battalions fighting on both sides along the eastern front was roughly equal to those fighting on the western front (although spread out over roughly twice the distance),[48] it is from the latter that ideas of modern, industrial, 'total' war arose; the tank, poison gas, massive artillery barrages, machine guns, and submarine warfare predominate in the images of the First World War. Artistic impressions of the war frequently have emphasized its industrial character; the images associated with the First World War are not of the horse but of the gas mask, the machine gun, and the tank. Men were seen to be at the mercy of machines. Certainly, the fact that so many of the casualties, in particular on the western front, were due to artillery fire, as well as the scale of the industrial resources devoured in the conflict, gave ample ground for believing that this was a modern war that rested on the application of technology to achieve death and destruction. The fact that the reality of how the war was conducted frequently fell short of the rhetoric of modern 'total' war is perhaps beside the point. It was the idea of modern war which transcended all else, which captured the imagination.

The idea of the First World War as a 'total war' also arose from the involvement of non-combatants in the conflict—both the degree to which they were mobilized in the service of war and the fact that they were seen as legitimate targets of deadly force. The first area, mobilization, was not just a matter of organizing and harnessing civilians' labour power and financial resources to an unprecedented degree, but also of seeking to extend their mobilization even to the private, intimate sphere—not only to production but also to reproduction. In theory at least, not just men's bodies (as soldiers) but also women's bodies (as mothers) were to be placed at the disposal of the nation at war. Reproduction was, in the words of Alfred Grotjahn, Professor of Social Hygiene in Berlin and a prominent Social Democrat writing in 1915, 'the only female contribution to war and military power which equals ... men's wartime national service'.[49] Although the state did not actually achieve control over reproductive behaviour, and while the numbers of births plummeted in combatant countries during the conflict, the idea was important: war had claims on the total

[47] V. G. Liulevicius, *War Land on the Eastern Front: Culture, National Identity and German Occupation in World War I* (Cambridge: Cambridge University Press, 2000), 22.

[48] Stone, *The Eastern Front*, 93.

[49] Quoted in C. Usborne, ' "Pregnancy is the Woman's Active Service": Pronatalism in Germany during the First World War', in R. Wall and J. M. Winter (eds), *The Upheaval of War: Family, Work and Welfare in Europe, 1914–1918* (Cambridge: Cambridge University Press, 1988), 389.

being; in a total war there could be no truly private sphere. This was an ambition that was to resonate with fascist regimes, which sought to rule women as well as men, which viewed reproduction as a public concern, and where 'every child-birth...is a battle...for the existence of her people'.[50]

The second area, civilians as targets, also was new in aspiration if not in fact. Civilians always have been on the receiving end of violence in war, but during the First World War there were some novel aspects to this age-old phenomenon. Total war was fought not just by and against soldiers but also by and against civilians, not just between armies but also between societies. War among industrial states involved attacking not only the armed forces of the enemy but also the enemy's productive capacity and the people who produced the goods needed for war. In this regard the First World War saw at least two important innovations—important more for their effects on the imagination than for their contribution to the war effort: the first aerial bombardment of non-combatants and the first use of (unrestricted) submarine warfare which claimed the lives of civilians as well as soldiers. For the first time, aircraft were used to bomb targets far behind the lines: towns, factories, and railways, as well as strictly military targets. Although the effects of this bombing were limited, at least in comparison with the enormous numbers of casualties that were occurring at the front and with the vast amounts of death and destruction caused by bombing during the Second World War a quarter of a century later, it was a start: French and British planes managed to drop roughly 15,700 bombs on Germany killing 740 people, most of whom were civilians. Unrestricted submarine warfare caused greater damage and loss of life (including the 5,249 German sailors who died in the campaign), but it too had its limits.[51] According to Holger Herwig, assessing Germany's programme of unrestricted submarine warfare, 'although the rhetoric was total, the reality was limited'.[52] Shortages of equipment meant that the campaign never met the expectations which had been raised for it. However, it is the aim that is important here: to achieve victory by targeting civilian populations as well as military targets—in this case by indiscriminately targeting all shipping and attacking without warning. It was war as 'totality' in thought, if not quite in deed.

There is a certain irony here, that the First World War should be regarded as 'total' by virtue of the targeting of civilians as well as soldiers, for the First World War is unique among major wars in that the overwhelming majority of its casualties were soldiers, not civilians. Even if one includes high estimates of civilians who died of malnourishment in Germany and the huge numbers of Armenians who died as a result of the brutal expulsions in Turkey, the numbers of civilian dead remained

---

[50] Quoted in ibid. 408.

[51] C. Geinitz, 'The First Air War against Noncombatants: Strategic Bombing of German Cities in World War I', in Chickering and Förster (eds), *Great War, Total War*, 207.

[52] H. H. Herwig, 'Total Rhetoric, Limited War: Germany's U-Boat Campaign, 1917–1918', in Chickering and Förster (eds), *Great War, Total War*, 205.

far below the military dead.[53] During the Second World War, by contrast, the tally of civilian dead approached twice the military dead.[54] Thus the modern war in which casualties were concentrated the most heavily on military personnel provided the benchmark for 'total war', the 'totality' of which consisted among other things of the degree to which civilians as well as soldiers suffered.

Although we have become accustomed to thinking about the First World War as 'total', there had been rather little talk of 'total war' during the conflict itself. The phrase 'total war' gained currency later. What is more, when the term was hatched it was less about the logistics, economics, and strategies of fighting modern wars than it was about the civil–military relationship—about the need to combat the enemy within if one was going to confront successfully the enemy without. It is revealing that the two chief protagonists of the phrase—Léon Daudet, who published a call for national mobilization in France in 1918 under the title *La Guerre totale*, and Erich Ludendorff, whose book *Der totale Krieg* was published in Germany in 1935—both were men of the right: Daudet the co-editor of the journal *L'Action française*, Ludendorff (among other things) Hitler's co-conspirator in the Munich Putsch attempt of 1923.[55] For Ludendorff—always keen to take credit for success and to blame others for failure—Germany's First World War had been lost because it was not 'total', that is, because of the failure to establish a military dictatorship. In this respect, as in so many others, the 'totality' of the First World War was more a way of thinking about it than a description of what actually occurred.

Finally, a thought should be given to the war aims of the power that, in the end, tipped the scales: the United States. The settlement that emerged from the First World War was inspired by ideological goals that were universal, namely the triumph of national and popular sovereignty. This was a far cry from the territorial aims with which the other belligerents had entered the war, whether these were the return to France of Alsace-Lorraine or the annexation by Germany of industrial areas in northern France and Belgium; this was a goal that was total and that fundamentally altered the very nature of politics, both domestic and international. The First World War neither proved to be a 'war to end all wars' nor did it make the world 'safe for democracy', as American President Woodrow Wilson had preached. But it did pave the way for the triumph of demagogic dictatorships which based their supposed legitimacy on popular and national sovereignty and which pro-

[53] According to calculations summarized by Rüdiger Overmans, the total of military dead in the First World War was 8,846,000 and the civilian dead 5,950,000. The latter included 2,000,000 civilians who died in Turkey, the largest number of whom were Armenians. See R. Overmans, 'Kriegsverluste', in G. Hirschfeld, G. Krumeich, and I. Renz (eds), *Enzyklopädie Erster Weltkrieg* (2nd edn, Paderborn: Schöningh, 2004), 664–5.

[54] See the table in I. C. B. Dear and M. R. D. Foot (eds), *The Oxford Companion to the Second World War* (Oxford: Oxford University Press, 1995), 290.

[55] H. Strachan, 'Total War in the Twentieth Century', in A. Marwick, W. Simpson, and C. Emsley (eds), *Total War and Historical Change: Europe 1914–1955* (Buckingham: Open University Press, 2001), 260–1.

ceeded to launch wars of imperialist plunder and genocide in the name of their states and peoples.

III. IMAGINING THE 'TOTALITY' OF WAR

In their recent survey of the historical literature on the First World War, Jay Winter and Antoine Prost have observed how our perspectives on the 1914–18 conflict changed over the course of the twentieth century:

During the interwar period, this conflict was seen as the last war; later on it became for some the first episode of a new Thirty Years War. Now it appears as the very foundation of a short, barbaric twentieth century, and those who survey this war have in mind both the monstrous Nazi genocide against the Jews and the enormity of Stalin's crimes. Was it not the case that the war of 1914–1918 was the first experiment in totalitarian war and mass death? In the interwar years, historians could not pose this question; now historians can not avoid posing it.[56]

Now that the twentieth century is over, we can see that the First World War opened the door to unlimited destruction and death, at least for a limited time. This was a sense in which one can speak of the First World War as 'totality', and of the First World War as a foundation for fascism.

During the inter-war period, the 1914–18 conflict was seen by some but certainly not by everyone as 'the last war'. The idea that war is futile, brings untold suffering, and creates only victims was among the main products of the First World War within European popular opinion and culture, at least in France and Britain, and may be seen as the precursor of attitudes towards war which gained wide currency in the later twentieth century.[57] However, during the inter-war years many people drew quite different conclusions. Those different conclusions—namely that war was something to be welcomed, that war should be fought mercilessly and without limits, that war lay at the heart of human interaction, that men would find their highest purpose in war—found their most effective political expression in the fascist movements of inter-war Europe. Both sets of conclusions assumed that the First World War had been a total war, and rested on the idea that modern war was a totality that necessarily drew everything into it: politics, the economy, society, culture, private life. Some therefore rejected war all the more. Others applauded it all the more loudly.

[56] J. Winter and A. Prost, *The Great War in History: Debates and Controversies, 1914 to the Present* (Cambridge: Cambridge University Press, 2005), 29.

[57] For this argument, see R. Bessel, 'Gewalterfahrung und Opferperspektive: Ein Rückblick auf die beiden Weltkriege des 20. Jahrhunderts in Europa', in F. d'Almeida, J. Echternkamp, and S. Martens (eds), *Der Zweite Weltkrieg in Europa: Erfahrung und Erinnerung:* (Paderborn: Schöningh, 2007), 253–67.

The supposed requirements for 'total war' and the imagination of the First World War as totality formed a basis for fascist ideology and fascist politics during the years that followed. The determination to unite the entire people in bellicose enthusiasm behind the nation, to suppress any internal dissent that might weaken the war-fighting state, to subordinate the economy to the requirements of making war, to embrace the technology of war in the modern age, to forge a nation of modern warriors committed totally to following where their leaders led, links the supposed lessons of the First World War with the terrible success of the fascist movements that followed it. The First World War as totality may not have materialized during the years 1914–18, but it did coalesce in the fascist imagination.

BIBLIOGRAPHY

CHICKERING, R., *The Great War and Urban Life in Germany: Freiburg 1914–1918* (Cambridge: Cambridge University Press, 2007).

—— and FÖRSTER, S. (eds), *Great War, Total War: Combat and Mobilization on the Western Front 1914–1918* (Cambridge: Cambridge University Press, 2000).

FERGUSON, N., *The Pity of War* (London: Allen Lane, 1998).

HARDACH, G., *The First World War 1914–1918* (London: Allen Lane, 1977).

HERWIG, H. H., *The First World War: Germany and Austria/Hungary 1914/1918* (London: Arnold, 1997).

MOSSE, G. L., *Fallen Soldiers: Reshaping the Memory of the World Wars* (New York: Oxford University Press, 1990).

SMITH, L. V., AUDOIN-ROUZEAU, S., and BECKER, A., *France and the Great War, 1914–1918* (Cambridge: Cambridge University Press, 2003).

STRACHAN, H., *The First World War*, i: *To Arms* (Oxford: Oxford University Press, 2001).

THOMPSON, M., *The White War: Life and Death on the Italian Front 1915–1919* (London: Faber & Faber, 2008).

WINTER, J., and PROST, A., *The Great War in History: Debates and Controversies, 1914 to the Present* (Cambridge: Cambridge University Press, 2005).

ZIEMANN, B., *War Experiences and Rural Germany 1914–1923* (Oxford: Berg, 2007).

CHAPTER 4

....

THE AFTERMATH
OF WAR

....

GLENDA SLUGA

Fascism was not everywhere born in the immediate aftermath of the war but it was conceived amid the disorder associated with the transition from war to peace. The war shaped a predilection for the resort to violence, a disrespect for the practices of civil society and for the rule of law. The diplomatic process that was begun in Paris in 1919, raising hopes among progressives for an international solution to the problems of order and the prospects for permanent peace, ultimately exacerbated post-war disillusion. Nascent fascist movements took their crooked vigour from the prospect of a new world order that some viewed as a threat to the primacy of nations, even as it short-changed international idealists.

In the immediate post-war no fascist movement was able to establish a mass base, nor were fascist parties able to assume the government of states through election alone. Historians have argued, however, that the core elements of fascism as a political ideology were a consequence of the war itself and arose out of the climate of intensified militarism and nationalism that predominated after the war's end. For the German historian Ernst Nolte, writing on what he termed 'the three faces of fascism' (French, Italian, and German), '[i]t was the war that made room for a political phenomenon, which was, so to speak, its very own child, a child which by innate law strove in turn to engender yet another war'.[1] But the devil lies in the detail. This chapter revisits the themes of militarism and nationalism in order to consider the variety of ways in which they may have influenced the emergence of

[1] E. Nolte, *The Three Faces of Fascism* (London: Weidenfeld and Nicolson, 1965), 5.

fascist movements, and in order to problematize the place of the aftermath of the war in the story of fascism's rise.

I. Militarism

When the end of the First World War was announced in 1918, jubilation was combined with an enormous sense of loss on all sides. The tally of millions dead and mutilated weighed heavily on populations in all the arenas of war—not only Europe. Among some social groups and individuals it also fuelled expectations regarding the need for change. The Bolshevik Revolution of the previous year had become the aspirational focus across Europe for some of this discontent, at the same time as it was a source of anxiety for the middle classes who feared the spread of the workers' cause.[2] From 1917, the prospect of revolution was in the air everywhere, feeding hopes and fears across the political spectrum and across victor and loser states, and even among intellectuals in European colonies who shared the anticipation of fundamental political change. However, when the war formally ended, there was no easy transition to a peace that might have confirmed the persistence of the old order or the vague possibilities of a new world order. To begin with, there was no *tabula rasa* and no easy abandoning of the culture and memory of war. With the war over, the mood among many soldiers and war veterans had grown even more militant as they faced the reality of readjustment to communities whose features had ostensibly changed. These men brought home bundles of wartime experience and relationships that were not easily adapted to the image of a civilian life at the domestic hearth. One historian's interview with a member of the Erhardt brigade, who had begun fighting in the First World War at the age of 16, brings to our attention the intensity of identification with the war and the difficulty of abandoning its practices:

People told us that the War was over. That made us laugh. We ourselves are the War. Its flame burns strongly in us. It envelops our whole being and fascinates us with the enticing urge to destroy. We obeyed ... and marched into the battlefields of the post-war world just as we had gone into battle on the Western Front: singing, reckless and filled with the joy of adventure as we marched to the attack; silent, deadly, remorseless in battle.[3]

Contemporary literature and memoirs record how, for the professional soldier and for the tens of thousands of men who were unable to find employment, normal civilian life held few attractions. Their alienation was symbolized by the

[2] See Markwick in this volume.
[3] Cited in K. Theweleit, *531 Male Fantasies* (Minneapolis: University of Minnesota Press, 1989).

'feminization' of the domestic 'home front', where, during the war, governments desperate to replace the depleted supplies of men had offered women unprecedented opportunities in the workforce. The demoralized and worn-out returning soldiers perceived the new public roles of women as a further threat to their civilian and domestic status.

In Germany, where the reality of defeat appalled soldier and civilian alike, the displacement of many demobilized soldiers led to massive social and political upheavals that climaxed in October 1918 with the dramatic overthrow of Imperial Germany and the birth of the German Republic. While the new German government stood for the norms and practices of constitutional government, the processes by which it was established chimed with another picture of life in postwar Germany, as a succession of uprisings, insurrections, assassinations, and coups. These included the overthrow of the imperial order by the left in 1918, the attempted seizure of government by the right supported by the Freikorps in 1920 (the so-called Kapp Putsch), and even Hitler's failed Munich Putsch in 1923. A common element in these dramatic events was the willingness of radicals, rebels, groups on the left and right, and elected officials to subvert or sideline the norms of liberal political culture, to challenge the authority of the liberal state, and to resort to arms in order to achieve their political aims. In 1919, the German President, the Social Democratic head of the new liberal republic of Germany, called on the Freikorps—disaffected soldiers who had refused to exchange their comradely military existence for domestic life and, instead, transformed themselves into mercenaries and hit squads—to put down the communist revolutionaries. That same group murdered the communists' leaders, Rosa Luxemburg and Karl Liebknecht. The Freikorps were also given responsibility by regional governments for opposing communist insurrections in Munich. Local governments similarly promoted the creation of civilian armed home guards (*Einwohnerwehren*) as another way of maintaining law and order. In 1919 and 1920, more than one million men in Germany were enrolled in paramilitary groups intended to defend the homeland from the enemy within, namely the revolutionary left and internationalists.[4]

The aftermath of the war saw the rapid radicalization of political movements and allegiances. On the left, a new mass class of workers coming out of the armaments factories as well as the battlefield sought change through an adherence to socialist organizations, some more and some less revolutionary, depending on their specific interpretation of the achievements of the Bolshevik Revolution. In Italy, the Liberal government's awareness of the need to assuage the political ambitions of this class had even led, unexpectedly, to the bestowal of universal male suffrage. Armed with the power of election, many of these new voters gave their support to socialist organizations and parties. For representatives of middle-class, landowning, and

---

[4] P. Fritzsche, *Germans into Nazis* (Cambridge, MA: Harvard University Press, 1998), 122–3.

business interests, this turn of events exaggerated the impression that their own authority and property were at stake. While the details of the rise of the left in Italy are outlined elsewhere in this volume, it is worth noting here that the Italian Socialist Party experienced a nearly tenfold increase in membership, the number of party branches more than doubled, and left-wing union membership stood at around two million men. Socialists saw their number of national parliamentary seats treble, gaining 32.5 per cent of the ballot in the November 1919 elections and winning 63 per cent of the vote in the city of Bologna. In the north, half a million workers in engineering, car manufacture, and metals occupied their factories and set up workers' councils on the Marxist model. In the more rural areas, particularly in Tuscany, there was the phenomenon of land occupations, involving up to half a million rural workers. Many of these peasants had also been conscripted into the war and sought their promised reward of land ownership, often through social and economic disruption. Strikes resulted in lost work-days in the fields as well as in the factories and contributed to the reality of economic instability. They also enhanced a disturbing impression among many observers of general social and political chaos. These were the conflict-ridden immediate post-war years of the *biennio rosso* with its strikes, factory and land occupations, and open clashes between socialist and anti-socialist forces.

It is no coincidence that when, in March 1919, Mussolini founded his Fasci di Combattimento, or battle groups, he deliberately invoked the symbolism of the war, of a trench-ocracy ('*trincerocrazia*') which, he argued, would lead the nation. Newly minted Fascists identified themselves with a war-based culture of masculinity, not unlike that promoted in the past by Futurists and other purveyors of modernity, that would reinvigorate the emasculated society run by old-guard liberals and 'Russian-loving' socialists. They also drew the battle tactics and slogans of war into the ideological confrontations of civilian life. The Fascist gangs that appeared at the same time, known as *squadristi* (or blackshirts), provoked and attacked political opponents as enemies of the nation. Drawing on a range of support, particularly those veterans of the war identified as *arditi* and equating to the German Freikorps, *squadristi* saw their role not only as rooting out any socialists they could find but ensuring the political advance of their cause. During the first post-war Italian elections of 1919, these gangs intimidated local populations in the north-eastern region of Venezia-Giulia, winning the local Fascists their only victory. In 1921 in the Bologna province, when socialists had been especially successful in the regional elections, the tally of agricultural and industrial workers recorded as beaten up or wounded by gunshots ran to 1,936, with nineteen killed. A five-day-long military-style raid launched by Fascists in the province of Arezzo, directed at socialists and their buildings, provoked no opposition from local law-enforcement bodies. Instead, the establishment approved these actions. Roger Absalom records similar events in the countryside, where landowners took the law into their own hands and turned to the *squadristi* to get their message across. Thus in Italy, too, violence and the overthrow of the rule of law were rendered acceptable on the grounds that they were necessary if the nation was to be protected from the spread of bolshevism.

Integral to German fascism was a model of masculinity that intertwined the strands of the chivalric heroic warrior of the past and the aggressive nihilistic technological man of the future. This development was consolidated in the general militarization of public consciousness that continued into (and was even reinforced in) the inter-war period. In the Italian case, George Mosse has described the elevation by the Fascist Party of masculinity to new heights: 'the hopes placed upon it, the importance of manliness as a national symbol and as a living example played a vital role in all fascist regimes.'[5] The emphasis on masculinity in the fascist version of militarist patriotism did not inevitably exclude the interest of women. When Italian Fascism made its formal appearance at Mussolini's meeting in Milan in 1919, nine women were present and involved. They declared their motivation to be anti-bolshevism and national defence. In the German case, historians have explained female interest in fascism through the overlapping identification by women with the victimization of the German nation and with the nationalist oppression of Protestantism by the Catholic French. One of the claimants to the title of the first British fascists, Rotha Lintorn Orman, a royalist and patriot daughter of a military family and the originator of the British Fascists, also claimed to have had anti-Bolshevik and nationalist motivations. It was in the context of perceived threats to national honour and order that Linthorn Orman declared her opposition to two contemporary models of femininity: the 'working woman' and the sexually ambiguous 'new woman'. How ironic, then, that Linthorn Orman, who liked wearing swords and uniforms, was herself ridiculed for being a 'mannish-woman'.[6] Indeed, there was little logic to either the gender ambitions of fascist women or the attacks on women more generally in this period. As some historians have shown, women, regardless of their political persuasion, were accused of letting down the home front. Among those men in whom the war had spurred anti-war feelings, women were even blamed for inciting nationalist militarism. When, in 1919, returning soldiers rioted in England and the fear of sexual attacks on women was rife, newspaper columnists suggested 'that social peace and order would depend upon minimising the provocations of men to anger',[7] that is, by restoring women to their 'traditional' social roles and status, which is precisely the antidote the government resolved upon.

---

[5] G. Mosse, *The Image of Man: The Creation of Modern Masculinity* (New York: Oxford University Press, 1996), 155.

[6] For more discussion of this history, see J. V. Gottlieb, *Feminine Fascism: Women in Britain's Fascist Movement 1923–1945* (London, I.B.Taurus, 2000).

[7] S. K. Kent, *Making Peace: The Reconstruction of Gender in Inter-war Britain* (Princeton: Princeton University Press, 1993), 98–9.

The liberal governments of Britain, France, and Italy responded to the success of the Russian Revolution and the epidemic of strikes and mutinies in factories and armies by promising greater democratization, economic assistance for workers, and more inclusive societies (in Germany, soldiers and workers had forced the creation of a government to bring about those changes). At the same time, these governments rejected the demands made by some women's organizations (liberal as well as socialist) for more rights, exploiting the view of them as symptomatic of the threat of a general disorder and national disarray. In post-war England, where initially only women over the age of 30 were given the vote as a reward for their wartime work, women who had taken on prominent roles in civilian society during the war were forced to retreat. They were made to feel guilty if they refused to accept their 'natural' roles as wives and mothers, and women who persisted in taking up a man's place were made the targets of hatred and intimidation. In Germany, the government of the new liberal republic issued regulations calling for women to be dismissed before men if necessary.

In France, where debate about demographic catastrophe had come to the fore, the aim was the same, although the method was more innovative: offer women bonuses to leave their jobs and return home to have babies for the nation. By the mid-1920s, French women composed a smaller percentage of the national labour force than they had in 1911 and they still had no vote. Instead, the government established medals for motherhood, a practice emulated in both Weimar and Nazi Germany, and in Fascist Italy. In post-war Liberal Italy, commentators from a wide range of political positions emphasized that the war had finally brought to life the latent Italian national spirit and proven that women too could be reliable and enthusiastic patriots at the service of the nation—but such observations did not hasten the vote (much demanded by bourgeois feminists) for Italian women. Where women did gain the vote in the immediate post-war, it was in the Bolshevik governments and the newly constituted states that emerged from the peace process. In all these cases, revision of the economic, social, or political status of women was rarely more than superficial.[8] Instead, the theme of left-wing-inspired gender disorder predominated, adding to the overall impression among those who feared a social revolution was in the offing.

Gender had a peculiar strategic function in the aftermath of the war and in the reinvention of militaristic values in peacetime. Wartime experiences had brutalized men, encouraged nationalism, and fostered a fundamental misogyny. But as George Mosse has noted: 'Fascism was a new political movement but not a movement which invented anything new; it annexed the long familiar and made it a part of its racism and nationalism.'[9] In considering militarism as a force that

[8] B. Caine and G. Sluga, *Gendering European History* (Leicester: Leicester University Press, 2000), ch. 6.

[9] G. Mosse, *The Fascist Revolution: Toward a General Theory of Fascism* (New York: H. Fertig, 1999), p. xvii.

played a crucial role in shaping post-war politics, it is important to remember that, since the late nineteenth century, perceptions of the naturalness of aggressive or physical masculinity occurred across political, class, and national boundaries, encouraged by new theories of biological and social evolution, to the extent that this same model of masculinity was a critical factor in fomenting popular support for war in 1914. The continuum was not only chronological but also ideological. Across the political spectrum, the responses of post-war governments to gender questions were enmeshed in a conventional preference for military masculinity and a masculine nationhood. Elected liberal governments and opposition groups each exploited for their own purposes the rhetorical connections between the figure of the emancipated woman and the internationalist (as anti-nationalist) and the racial other, in particular the 'Jew', and the image of their combined threat to bourgeois respectability and national virility.

II. NATIONALISM

The virulent antagonism towards 'anti-national' enemies historians consider intrinsic to fascism was an attitude that had become acceptable during the war in all European societies, as national identity was defined in 'increasingly populist and racial terms'. It was also fostered as a mainstream approach to politics in the war's aftermath, 'when Nazi Storm Troopers beat up socialists, communists, pacifists and foreigners'.[10] Evocations of national communities at threat and of politics at the service of national defence had a central place in political developments. There are ominous echoes of this kind of nationalism and its focus on the enemy within in the record of one young *fascio* supporter too young to have participated in the war but who felt, now that it was at an end, that 'the great conflict just isn't over. Where there were external enemies, now there are internal foes... On one side real Italians, lovers of their country. On the other, their enemies, the cowards who seek to blow to pieces our national grandeur.... Direct action is needed against them, energetic, decisive and courageous action. And we, the interventionists of the first hour, must accept the sacred task.'[11]

Nationalist rationales for political action were hardly the preserve of the right. On the left, national self-determination, that is the right of nations to political autonomy, was regarded as a respectable political aim, especially after 1917, when Lenin promoted the idea as the proper path to peace, despite its theoretical

---

[10] Fritzsche, *Germans into Nazis*, 4.

[11] Cited in R. J. B. Bosworth, *Mussolini's Italy: Life under the Dictatorship 1915–1945* (London: Allen Lane, 2005).

inconsistency with orthodox Marxism. It was only after the Bolshevik invocation of self-determination for nations as an antidote to imperialism that the liberal governments featured self-determination in their own promotion of post-war ideals, notably in Britain, the United States, and France, each of which had their own empires. There had been a long tradition of pacifist internationalism and support for emancipation among liberal progressives in Europe, the transatlantic world, and its colonial extensions. In the post-war, these liberal internationalist ideals became part of the Wilsonian peace (named after the American President). In their Wilsonian form, national self-determination and liberal internationalism had nothing to do with the view from Moscow and everything to do with averting revolutions on the continent and the wider world, and with consolidating the international authority of the Great Powers. The impact of the peace process that was to regulate the transition to peace for the whole world in the aftermath of the war was complex and is worth examining closely, because of its intended significance for the mitigation of class tensions and militarism, and its exacerbation of contemporary nationalisms and fascist movements, even if unintended.

The peacemaking process that began in 1919 and formally ended the First World War had a number of features that were peculiar to its time: its moral and political legitimacy rested on the democratization of foreign policy making and international relations, and on a scientific approach to territorial disputes. All these aspects of the peace were oriented around 'the principle of nationality'. In theory, territorial sovereignty would no longer be decided by force or by the subjective whims of statesmen but by the determination of a territory's nationality; political borders would be drawn along the lines that separated objectively existing nationalities and result in a fair and democratic settlement. The peacemakers would objectively quantify the national composition of states and scientifically measure according to racial and national criteria the location of national borders on the assumption that the exact identification of nationals with their nations would equate to a democratic outcome. At the same time, it was expected that the legal resolve of the new League of Nations would be used to tame the violent impulses of nations. This version of peace aims was promoted by a wide range of democratic intellectuals, activists, and politicians from Britain and the United States, and, to a lesser extent, France, Italy, and Japan, which seized the prerogative for making a 'new world order'.

There were certainly intentionally progressive aspects to the peacemakers' plans. The League of Nation's Covenant was prefaced by obligations not to resort to war, to conduct open, just, and honourable relations between nations, and to ensure the operation of international law as the basis of conduct among governments. The League's members were obliged to submit any dispute or rupture and to wait for up to three months for the League's report or ruling before even contemplating military action. Where diplomacy could not work, arbitration or judicial settlement was to take place and sanctions and expulsion were to be the operative modes of dealing with contraventions of the League's rules. A disarmament commission was set up within the League to limit the size of navies, reduce the worldwide production of armaments, and thus prevent future wars.

The other international institution created at this time, the International Labour Office (or ILO), was partly the culmination of efforts throughout the late nineteenth century to achieve transnational consensus on labour conditions. Its creation coincided with the demands and expectations that had accompanied the end of the war throughout Europe and the spread of worker grievances. The ILO was to provide an alternative focus for class interests. It encouraged among national governments discussion of international standards for the maximum working week, the prevention of unemployment, a living wage, provisions for old age, sickness, and injury, and protection of children, young people, and women. It could not and did not guarantee these reforms but it did legitimize their discussion in an international forum. In one case, in 1919, an international conference in Washington, organized under the auspices of the ILO, was successful in having European governments accept the general principle of equal pay for equal-value work, although that equation was agreed upon only because of its convenient ambiguity. The peacemakers also agreed to earmark two disputed territories for international status: the port region of Fiume/Rijeka, claimed both by Italy and the new kingdom of Serbs, Croats, and Slovenes, and Danzig/Gdańsk, a port fought over between the new German and Polish states. These territories were to be remade as international or 'free' states exempt from the principle of nationality because of their 'mixed' populations and transnational economic status.

The peace could not deliver on their ideals, partly because they were too ambitious and partly because it was inconsistent. Harold Nicolson's *Peacemaking 1919*—the memoir of a young English diplomat involved in the peace caballing in Paris—makes clear that there was little that was scientific or even procedural about many of the decisions taken. The experts could not agree on what constituted the scientific bases of their tasks, where nations began and races ended, nor how any of these categories were to be measured. Some nations were recognized ('South Slavs', for instance), others were not (Ruthenians, for example), with little accompanying rationalization. The case of the capacity of 'Arabs' for national self-determination might be made on the basis of their impressive masculinity but that of 'the Magyar' according to evidence of a proven national consciousness—an argument that usually legitimized militarist and nationalist values as criteria for statehood.[12]

Where there was no defining conspiracy among the peacemakers, there were also no practised rules. An exclusive group of politicians and diplomats, mainly Wilson, French Prime Minister Georges Clemenceau, British Prime Minister David Lloyd George, and Italian premier Vittorio Emanuele Orlando, scrawled over maps,

---

[12] For more discussion, see G. Sluga, *Nation, Psychology and International Politics* (New York: Palgrave, 2006).

squabbled over dinners, and then made up their minds. From this perspective, the peace did not assert a new order based on objectivity grounded in science and/or law but, as had always been the case in international relations, the random exercise of the relative power of statesmen. The impossibility of establishing a shared perception of the nationality of specific territories merely compounded the more cynical practices of peacemaking and fuelled the post-war discontent within new and old national societies across Europe. This discontent undermined the authority of international procedures and laws and was easily manipulated by right-wing nationalist groups.

The conditions under which the peace conference dragged on in the post-war years, with its contemplation of the reparations and territorial questions on which so many of the events in the troubled regions of Europe hung, were hardly optimal. The peacemaking's outcomes reassured few participants and observers, especially when they appeared to contradict the very principles the peacemakers had established. The first treaty, signed in June 1919 in Versailles, breached the armistice agreements between the Allies and Germany by undermining German sovereignty, despite the weight given to the centrality of national sovereignty in principle. There is no agreement in historical assessments of the peacemakers' treatment of the new German republic but the conditions are easy enough to detail: reparations amounted to £6,000 million, at the same time that around 13 per cent of Germany's inherited territory and 10 per cent of its existing population were excised. Germany 'lost' Alsace-Lorraine (taken from France in 1871), the Polish Corridor (territory that had belonged to Germany but was given to the new Polish state, dividing German East Prussia from Germany proper), and parts of Silesia (territory bordering the new states of Germany, Czechoslovakia, and Poland, populated by a significant number of German speakers, which was not awarded to Germany, despite a plebiscite in its favour). The victors were given the right not only to Germany's territory but also the property of German persons—with no right of compensation—material and colonial possessions, and its mineral resources.

Other loser states suffered less grievously as a result of the peace process but a succession of treaties divided up their territories in a similar high-handed fashion, transforming them into new, albeit radically truncated, political entities and consequently displacing or, at the least, disorienting their populations. The 1920 Treaty of Trianon took from the new state of Hungary 66 per cent of the territory and 40 per cent of the people governed by the old Hungary as part of the Habsburg empire. Where national territories were created or extended, it was always at a cost to some existing state, as in France's reacquisition of Alsace-Lorraine or the carving out of the new states Czechoslovakia, Poland, and Yugoslavia from the territory of the Austrian half of the Habsburg empire or Italy's addition of the Austrian territories of the South Tyrol, Trentino, and Istrian and Dalmatian regions.

Few cynics failed to notice that the redistribution of the colonial possessions of the defeated countries benefited the existing victor states. This occurred even as the term imperialism was being rejected by democratic idealists at the peace, where the creation of 'mandates' as forms of trusteeship rather than colonization and exploitation was being called for. In reality, the mandate system, which applied only to the territories of the losers, took on the gloss of a new, improved, version of empire building, as it allowed France to claim Syria and the new Lebanon and Britain to gain Palestine, Transjordan, and Mesopotamia (Iraq); Italy took some Aegean islands and Greece Smyrna. African and Pacific territories were equally up for grabs and divided as 'mandates' among the victor states, which consequently treated them as their colonial preserves. One did not even have to be particularly cynical to observe that, in 1919, the new world order meant the expansion of colonial possessions for the winners, who had few obligations to report to the newly created League of Nations on the political and social progress towards nationhood of their territorial acquisitions or on the well-being of the populations contained therein.

The history of post-war peacemaking was also a story of war and empire by other means, methods that were often illegal according to new international agreements. The fate of the 'free state' experiments—Fiume was occupied as soon as 1922 by the new Fascist Italian government and Danzig was eventually annexed by Nazi Germany—were only two illustrations that the new world order would not be based on discussion and negotiation alone.

Robert Paxton has observed that the same states and individuals who had taken responsibility for constructing the new world order were also playing an older game, as conservatives 'tried quietly to restore a world in which armed force settled relations among states'.[13] Many examples can be drawn upon in support of this thesis: in 1920 and 1921, when Germany was not able to make its reparations payments, France occupied towns in the Ruhr, Germany's rich industrial area; in 1923, France and Belgium together invaded the Ruhr. Each of these acts was in contravention of the League's rules. In 1919, Czechoslovakian troops moved into a coal-mine region in dispute with Poland (Teschen) and stayed there, despite the League's objections; in 1920 Poland had learned the lesson and occupied for itself the town of Vilnia in dispute with Lithuania. In this last case, the League asked Poland to remove its forces but the governments of Britain and France refused to back the League's demands since they wanted to keep Poland on side as a buffer between the Soviet Union and the rest of Europe. The League had no enforcement powers in the face of these contraventions of its own code, and any legitimacy it had accrued was further diminished by the refusal of the United States to join it. The creation of the League offered, as the historian Sally Marks has described, only an illusion of peace.

In the aftermath of the war, the flouting of the rule of law and the resort to force to win political disputes were a feature of international relations, as well as of national affairs. Force was practised by those governments that were to retain

[13] R. Paxton, *The Anatomy of Fascism* (London: Allen Lane, 2004), 31.

their liberal credentials in the inter-war period, as well as by those that were sooner or later to succumb to fascism. This is nowhere more evident than in the actions against revolutionary Russia taken by Britain, France, and the United States, the key designers of the League of Nations as an instrument for international negotiations. From 1918 to 1920, these states dispatched expeditionary forces into Russia to contain and defeat bolshevism. They employed the disaffected soldier class and newly established paramilitary forces from their own and other countries against Polish communists and nationalists, the Russian Red Army, and Latvian and Estonian nationalists in the Baltic region. These were the same governments that took the initiative in the immediate post-war to usher in a new world order, grounded in the rule of international law and the explicit rejection of force to resolve national disputes and differences of political view. There is a further historical twist to this story. Despite the anti-revolutionary ambitions of the victor states that planned the new world order as a national world order, for many Europeans and interested parties the peace process came to represent just one more example of the encroachments by internationalists and foreigners into terrain that was properly national. As in so many cases in the post-war, impressions were what counted.

III. Militarism, Nationalism, and the History of Fascism

One reason why historians of fascism have focused on nationalism in the post-war is that the defence and promotion of national interests were favoured rhetoric for fascist movements in Europe and beyond. As a result, historians see in nationalism a chief explanation of the support for fascism, describing, for example, the nationalist outrage felt throughout Germany at the loss of territory and resources. This anger is often depicted as the necessary setting for the success of the National Socialist Party, which from its inception in 1920 had two key foreign policy positions: the abolition of the Treaty of Versailles and the unification of all Germans—including the unification of Germany and Austria specifically outlawed by the terms of the peace.

We also see nationalism operating as a historical argument in the Italian case, in descriptions of the domestic reaction to the Treaty of Rapallo. This 1920 treaty gave the Italian state all that had been promised in the 1915 Secret Treaty of London (including German-speaking South Tyrol), except for the territory of Fiume. Even though the port had been added on to the Italian wish-list only at the war's end, on the grounds that it was among those lands that were historically and rightfully Italian and should be 'returned' (*terre irredente*) its 'loss' provoked the popular slogan *vittoria mutilata* or the mutilated victory. To be sure, Fiume offered a telling case study of the extent to which individuals were willing to use force to flout the rule of international law, as the poet-politician Gabriele D'Annunzio gathered a supporting cast of war veterans to march on the city in September 1919. D'Annunzio claimed the town from the inter-Allied (American, British, and French) forces on behalf of Italy, even though the Italian government of the time did not accept his actions. His self-styled state, the Italian Regency of Carnaro, lasted for more than a year, after which the peace terms created the Free State of Fiume, which was then within twelve months annexed militarily by the newly installed Fascist government.

Historical understanding of the impact of the post-First World War peacemaking process on the emergence of fascism throughout Europe has to a significant extent been shaped by arguments regarding the role of nationalism as a psychological and emotional force ripe for fascist manipulation. Thomas A. Row has argued that, in the aftermath of the war, the force of '[t]his generalized nationalist angst, which spread among the middle classes beset by inflation, among returning soldiers, among disaffected intellectuals, and among the many who had hoped that the ordeal of war would produce a "new" Italy, had a powerful impact on Italian political life'.[14] Nationalism constrained the diplomatic manoeuvrability of the Italian government and, according to Row, formed 'one of the ideological underpinnings of Fascism'. In this volume, Paxton states that 'national defeat or humiliation is probably the most important single precondition, and fascists prospered by claiming to be the most uncompromising agents of renewal'. In this same way, other historians have linked the peace treaty to the aggravation of national frustrations and the emergence of fascist movements in Eastern Europe, particularly Hungary. There, it is claimed, the Treaty of Trianon inspired 'stab in the back' legends and victimization mythologies which, in turn, provoked nationalists to organize politically and helped authoritarian elements into power.

In some accounts, the peace itself is directly to blame for the provocation of nationalism by virtue of its failure to fulfil the political promise of the principle of nationality. The problem with the peace process according to Marks is that it preserved economic units at the expense of ethnic coherence.[15] This is evident, for example, in the creation of the Polish Corridor splitting Germany. Marks argues that in general there was no adequate alignment of ethnicity and political borders, so that in Poland, Czechoslovakia, Romania, Hungary, and Yugoslavia, heterogeneity ruled: Poles were mixed with Ukrainians and White Russians, Germans and Jews; Czechs with Magyars, Ruthenes, and Germans. There are a number of problems with this interpretation of the significance to the history of fascism of the

[14] T. A. Row, 'Italy in the International System', in A. Lyttelton (ed.), *Liberal and Fascist Italy* (Oxford: Oxford University Press, 2002), 103.

[15] S. Marks, *The Illusion of Peace: International Relations in Europe, 1918–1933* (2nd edn. Basingstoke: Palgrave, 2003), 24.

aftermath of war and the making of peace. First, it normalizes a form of national or ethnic statehood that hardly mirrors the realities of conditions in the non-fascist states that led the peacemaking. By a 'curious anomaly', as John Dewey described in 1917, in Britain, the United States, and even France, the principle of nationality was never regarded as relevant.[16] These were each 'ethnically' heterogeneous states professing a territorial (*jus soli*) rather than ethnic or blood (*jus sanguinis*) model of nationality.

Secondly, this analysis either agrees with the questionable assumptions held by the peacemakers themselves about the relevance of race to the determination of political borders and the capacity of a people to achieve statehood or it assumes that there was a tidier way of aligning borders and nationalities that the peacemakers and their experts had not been able to delineate and we now know, as if nationality comes down to a question of objective science uncomplicated by subjectivity, by the multiple and dynamic permutations of history and experience. But the experts who were authorized by the victor nations to design these new nations were haunted by the ambiguities of their task. Was a Jew not to be counted as a Pole in the early twentieth century? What was a Ruthene and was his culture of more or less value than that of a Magyar? Did women count as nationals? If we do not accept that nationalism is a natural psychological force or an ahistorical foundational element of state building, then our explanation of the political problems of the post-war cannot stop at the abstract agency of nationalism (any more than it is to be found in the abstract force of fascism). Rather, our attention as historians should focus on the multiple ways in which the assumption that nationalism was a natural force underwrote the principle of nationality and, as a result, emphasize how the primal nature of national instincts and emotions became a powerful rhetorical resource for legitimizing a range of political movements and activities.

This, at least, is an argument made by a few contemporaries critical of the new world order and its political consequences in the aftermath of the peace. John Maynard Keynes, the English economist who resigned in disgust from his position as the official representative of the British Treasury at the Paris peace in June 1919, attacked the manner in which the peacemakers had exalted and dignified 'the divisions of race and nationality above the bonds of trade and culture, and guaranteed frontiers but not happiness'.[17] Keynes went further, arguing that the creation of the League of Nations by the victor states on the basis of the principle of nationality yielded 'the paradox that the first experiment in international government should exert its influence in the direction of intensifying nationalism'. Against the background of the disintegration of the Russian, Ottoman, Habsburg, and German empires into an

---

[16] J. Dewey, 'The Principle of Nationality', *Menorah's Journal*, 3 (1917), 203–8, republished in J. A. Boydston (ed.), *Dewey: The Middle Works 1899–1924* (Carbondale: Southern Illinois University Press, 2008), 286–7.

[17] See J. M. Keynes, *Revision of the Treaty: Being a Sequel to The Economic Consequences of the Peace* (London: Macmillan, 1922), and W. Lippmann, *Public Opinion* (London: Allen and Unwin, 1922).

array of new nation states and the disrepute accumulating around the term imperial (even the British opted for Commonwealth), these new international institutions heightened the political significance of nations. On this counter-view, the peace was responsible for two things: first, for the discontent it aroused among democrats expecting a more just new world order by its masking of business-as-usual tactics; and, second, for legitimizing the forms of racism and nationalism that obscured the extremist potential of fascism itself.

Another way of looking at this same historical problem was provided by the Italian anti-fascist historian Gaetano Salvemini, writing during the Second World War from the perspective of someone who had fled Fascist Italy. Salvemini argued that there was no inevitable relationship between the territorial decisions of the peace and the success of fascist political organizations.[18] He focused instead on what he termed 'the psychological background of "mutilated victory"' and the creation of 'an unprecedented miracle of psychopathic [sic] alchemy'. While no admirer at the time of the post-war treaties, Salvemini now proposed that a critical ingredient in this alchemy was the exploitation by newspapers and politicians of a specific version of peacemaking that was historically important in drawing Italian people into 'a state of morbid irritation', which then led to the political victory of Italian Fascism. To bolster his emphasis on the agency of individuals who should have known better, he argued that, under similar post-war circumstances, France had not succumbed to the forces of fascism. In Italy, by contrast, the crucial factor was 'the poisonous defeatist propaganda to which the Italian people were subjected in 1919'.

Salvemini's comparison with France serves to point up the crucial comparative framework of the history of fascism. Yet he and Keynes, each in his own way, restored the agency of liberals in power, their contribution to flattening out the ideological landscape that should have separated liberalism from fascism and distinguished the liberal states from those that adopted fascism, particularly in their attitudes to and manipulation of national and military values and codes.

Indeed, another critic of the peace process, the American Walter Lippmann, who had been officially involved in the promotion of the Wilsonian peace in 1918–19, complained that the political leaders had brought to the Paris conference deep-seated and prejudiced ways of understanding difference. For example, the French Prime Minister, the radical-socialist Clemenceau, assumed that the 'German mentality' could not conceive of justice in the same way as did the Allied powers. The so-called father of the League, the French republican Léon Bourgeois, also blamed the war on the Teutonic 'mentality' and the instincts of brutality inherent in the 'German race'. Keynes noted 'the anti-Semitism, not far below the surface in such an assemblage as that one', for example when Lloyd George seized an opportunity to poke malevolent fun at the French Finance Minister, Louis Klotz:

---

[18] G. Salvemini, *The Origins of Fascism in Italy* (New York: Harper and Row, 1973; 1st edn. 1942), 24.

[H]e leant forward and with a gesture of his hands indicated to everyone the image of a hideous Jew clutching a money bag. His eyes flashed and the words came out with a contempt so violent that he seemed almost to be spitting at him.... Everyone looked at Klotz with a momentary contempt and hatred; the poor man was bent over his seat, visibly cowering.... Then, turning, [Lloyd George] called on Clemenceau to put a stop to these obstructive tactics, otherwise, he cried, M. Klotz would rank with Lenin and Trotsky among those who had spread Bolshevism in Europe. The Prime Minister ceased. All round the room you could see each one grinning and whispering to his neighbour 'Klotzky'.[19]

To be sure, the implications of the peace process are not simply reductive to the racism or nationalism of the individuals involved. For example, advisers to the peace managed to have the protection of minorities (including Jews) made a part of the work of the League of Nations, and the peacemakers created two international 'Free States', Danzig and Fiume. But when the Japanese, who were among the inner circle of victors at the peace, asked for the inclusion of a clause on racial equality in the League's Covenant, the United States and the United Kingdom and its dominions, most vehemently Australia, refused. (In reflex, the Japanese government of the inter-war merely went more effectively over to the side of nationalism and racism in its own region of the world.) In the aftermath of war, the ambivalent liberal-democratic perspective on race and gender won out and the League became by default the defender of nationalist objectives as much as internationalism and the partisan of the political significance of race, if not of the outright racism to which the world's leaders were inclined.

In the aftermath of the war and even in the creation of new international organizations, little attention was paid to supporting political alternatives that fostered relationships across national or ethnic boundaries, at least partly because those alternatives were associated with the left and the threat of bolshevism that the peace was meant to offset. Instead, the homogeneous virile nation dominated as an ideal and foundation of political organization and the League *of Nations* was designed to protect national sovereignty, not to deny it. As all Western European states and the new states of the Second World pitted nationalism against the bolshevism consolidating in Russia and its surrounds, 'internationalism' became a byword not for political progress but for bolshevism itself.

Nationalism and militarism featured as preoccupations of the post-war world, although not always in the same way or to the same extent. It is significant that, in the more established states such as Britain and even in some of the newer nations such as Czechoslovakia, liberal governments were on the whole able to maintain their position of authority against the efforts of fledgling fascist movements. In other places, political weaknesses evident already in the pre-war period were aggravated and fascist governments took root. In Italy, the parliamentary system seemed to offer no stability, as successive governments and coalitions found themselves

---

[19] J. M. Keynes, 'Two Memoirs', in E. Johnson (ed.), *The Collected Writings of John Maynard Keynes*, x: *Essays in Biography* (London: Macmillan, 1972), 423.

without the authority or ability to rule, and in 1922 Mussolini was invited by the king to form a new government. An unstable political situation also marked the early post-war years in Hungary. In early 1919 the communist government of Béla Kun took over from that of the Liberal Mihály Károlyi which had been inaugurated the year before; 133 days later Kun was overthrown by counter-revolutionary right-wing forces constellating around the military and nationalist appeal of Admiral Miklós Horthy. In both Hungary and Italy, instability was relatively quickly exchanged for authoritarian leadership (only ambiguously fascist in the Hungarian case) that lasted through the inter-war period. While these were both states in which the idea of a mutilated victory had been popularized, we cannot assume that was a decisive factor, since fascism also appeared in Spain, which had remained neutral during the war.

This history of the aftermath of the war returns us then to the question of the political and geographical continuums that aligned many aspects of post-war fascism with post-war liberalism and the points at which they separated. The relative success of fascist organizations was certainly assisted by specific circumstances, including the events that were taking place at an international level, where the overlapping themes of peace and democracy, militarism and nationalism, were being played out at great cost to the future of the world. Across Europe, the disorientation that accompanied the difficult transition for millions of men from the adventure of war to the acceptance of peace was harnessed in the interest of political gain. War and revolution had introduced the idea and possibility that the liberal state could be overcome. It had also nourished more authoritarian practices among governments. Even where revolution remained an apparent threat rather than reality, the wartime experience of military personnel and the language of national defence informed acceptable modes of political response. On the one hand, the war polarized parties and allegiances; on the other hand, the post-war was a flattened ideological landscape, distinguished around issues of class rather than the appearance of nationalism or militarism. Fledgling fascist movements carved out their causes and identities from a terrain of ideas and concepts shared with their opponents and onto which fascists gradually branded their distinctiveness, arguing, and physically asserting, their more effective capacity to meet the social and political challenges of the post-war.

We cannot say that in the states that avoided fascist governments there was a distinctive preference for the rules of civil society—even Woodrow Wilson was tolerant of the resurgence of the Ku Klux Klan in this same period, precisely because of his view of the overlapping menace to American society of bolshevism and subversive 'negroes'. In breaking the very rules of international relations that they had established in the League and legitimizing the use of force to oppose designated internal and external enemies, the liberal governments of Britain, the United States, and France set potent examples for more authoritarian regimes. Their promotion of the principle of nationality elevated the national cause above all other concerns and rendered nationality a principle easily exploited by the new Fascist authorities to justify repression of political and cultural differences within Italian borders and to launch imperial missions in the Balkan east. But these factors alone cannot explain the choices made by individuals who exercised political and popular power. Given the many dimensions of the transnational experience of the war and its aftermath, there is much to be said for historical explanations that emphasize the situated history of politics and agency. On this reading, the First World War and the peace of 1919 constitute the raw ingredients with which men and women made their own histories.

BIBLIOGRAPHY

FRITZSCHE, P., *Germans into Nazis* (Cambridge, MA: Harvard University Press, 1998).

LYTTELTON, A. (ed.), *Liberal and Fascist Italy* (Oxford: Oxford University Press, 2002).

MARKS, S., *The Illusion of Peace: International Relations in Europe, 1918–1933* (2nd edn. Basingstoke: Palgrave, 2003).

MOSSE, G., *The Image of Man: The Creation of Modern Masculinity* (New York: Oxford University Press, 1996).

—— *The Fascist Revolution: Toward a General Theory of Fascism* (New York: H. Fertig, 1999).

NOLTE, E., *The Three Faces of Fascism* (London: Weidenfeld & Nicolson, 1965).

PASSMORE, K. (ed.), *Women, Gender and Fascism in Europe 1919–1945* (Manchester: Manchester University Press, 2003).

PAXTON, R. O., *The Anatomy of Facism* (London: Allen Lane, 2004).

SLUGA, G., *Nation, Psychology and International Politics* (New York: Palgrave, 2006).

THEWELEIT, K., *Male Fantasies* (Minneapolis: University of Minnesota Press, 1989).

PART II

THE FIRST FASCIST NATION

CHAPTER 5

SQUADRISM*

MIMMO FRANZINELLI

SQUADRISM characterized fascism in a decisive manner, furnishing it with a special impulse in its struggle against its political adversaries from its first beginnings until its taking of power. The roots of the squadrists were nourished by the war experience, especially so-called *arditismo*, the spirit that had driven young men who had fought as volunteers in assault units. The initial brigade or *manipolo* of squadrists (since the Roman term 'maniple' was already preferred) was founded in Milan in the winter of 1918–19 by ex-*arditi* officer Ferruccio Vecchi, attracting men who were finding it difficult to resume civilian life. Bound to the charismatic figure of Benito Mussolini, the brigade acted as a bodyguard for the managing editor of the paper *Il popolo d'Italia*, with special fervour in defending the value of the war and in deprecating socialist pacifism. Among the movement's most significant figures was Futurist Filippo Tommaso Marinetti, who, brandishing a revolver, led attacks against what he called 'pro-Bolshevik' rallies; he theorized his taste for provocation as a form of art that counterposed a few brave adventurers against the dully hostile mass. Marinetti, Vecchi, and some others were at Mussolini's side on 11 January 1919 at a noisy contestation of the reformist socialist minister Leonida Bissolati, who, although he had backed the war, was now accused of a 'renunciatory' stance towards possible Italian annexations in Dalmatia and was reduced to silence with volleys of insults.

Well before the official founding of the Fasci di Combattimento, these *arditi* launched raids in various city squares in northern Italy, brawling with both their political adversaries and the police, with the excuse usually being something to do

* Translated by Richard Bosworth.

with foreign policy from a nationalist and chauvinist stance. On 23 March 1919, the first meeting of the *fasci*, in a building facing Piazza San Sepolcro, was chaired by Ferruccio Vecchi, who thereby was elevated to being the commander of the paramilitary force of a political organization. On 15 April, the destruction of the editorial offices and printing works of the main socialist daily, *Avanti!*, at Milan, after the dispersal of thousands of socialist militants who had been protesting against police repression, signalled the opening of an anti-socialist campaign. It spread quickly to Novara, Trieste, and Bologna and invested the left in places where they were currently in the majority politically but yet could not manage to guarantee their right to demonstrate nor the protection of their headquarters. Pietro Nenni, who founded the *fascio* at Bologna, but soon left the movement to become a socialist chief, described the struggles on the squares of Milan in mid-April thus: 'It was the first act of private violence and it was quickly noted that, despite the absolute numerical disproportion of the contending parties, to this violence the proletariat did not reply. Thus, notwithstanding that the strike in Milan produced four dead, in the course of an agitation that swept Italy from top to toe, everything was reduced to the decorous voting of motions and to the collection of funds—more than a million lire—that would in theory allow the proletariat's own newspaper to rise from the ashes.'[1]

The republican and anticlerical thrust of early fascist programmes reflected the views of the squadrists, men who deemed themselves revolutionary nationalists, as determined to fight against state institutions as against the pro-Bolshevik left, and defining themselves as anti-bourgeois and subversive in defence of the symbols of sacrifice in war. Many of the street conflicts were centred around monuments to the fallen, especially if the socialists tried to give the inauguration of such sites a pacifist message. Yet this phase of violence did not become general and was confined to particular situations in certain urban centres. The national wave of socialist maximalism was too powerful to be opposed by a few score men, even if they were armed and ready for anything. Typical in this last regard was the Tuscan Alessandro Carosi, one of those whose war experience had turned him into a mass murderer, who would find fascism offered a convenient outlet for his brutality. By the mid-1920s, he had gone too far in his fondness for killing for purely private reasons and was condemned by the Public Prosecutor as a man who, 'in the Val di Serchio, had terrorized the local population by murder, threatened murder and blackmail. He was always saved from any charge in that regard because of the fear he aroused in witnesses or because he could rely on political amnesty. As a result, although from poor origins, he lived like a lord.'[2]

---

[1] P. Nenni, *Storia di quattro anni* (Rome: Einaudi, 1946), 20.
[2] Procuratore Generale del Represso la R. Corte d'Appello, Florence, to Ministry of Justice, 3 May 1924, Archivio Generale dello Stato (ACS), Ministero di Grazia e Giustizia, Direzione Generale Affari Penali, b. 147, f. 'Firenze'.

The electoral campaign of autumn 1919, disfigured by violence, culminated on 13 November with the massacre of three socialists who, at Lodi, had whistled their disapproval of a meeting favouring the fascist candidate, Enzo Ferrari, later head of the automobile company. After the elections went poorly for the *fasci*, on 17 November there were some thirty arrests for the illegal holding of arms or public riot. Both chiefs and followers landed in jail, commencing with Mussolini (who was almost immediately released at the intercession of Prime Minister Francesco Nitti), Marinetti, and Vecchi. At this time of intense discouragement, facing electoral annihilation, Mussolini found an echoing emptiness around him, except with a few true believers, among whom the group of ex-*arditi* shone most evidently.

After months of relative stasis, squadrism was relaunched, thanks mainly to the evolution of national politics where, by autumn 1920, a settling of accounts with the left became imaginable. The watershed occurred when the new Prime Minister, Giovanni Giolitti, presided over an accord between the employers' organization, Confindustria, and the workers' unions, ending the occupation of the factories and making official the fact that the tide had turned against the socialists. Now the radical right could rejoice in the backing of many students and quite a few *lumpenproletariat*. Together they advanced on a wide front in city and countryside, at their most virulent in Emilia Romagna and Tuscany. The second anniversary of Italy's victory in the war, 4 November, was celebrated with assaults against Socialist Party branches, with the Chamber of Labour at Bologna being purged. There the so-called 'Red Guards' abandoned the field without a contest, surrendering to the victors a quantity of arms. The socialist retreat soon turned into a disastrous defeat under the pressure exerted by paramilitary groups unleashed by big landowners against peasant unions and by great industrialists against their workers. At the head of these squads were men destined for fame in fascist politics: at Bologna, Leandro Arpinati (once an anarchist activist) and Dino Grandi (back from the war as an *alpino*); at Ferrara, Italo Balbo (a republican who had been a lieutenant in the *arditi*); at Rome, Giuseppe Bottai (a volunteer for the *arditi*); at Alessandria, Cesare Maria De Vecchi (a captain in the *arditi*); at Cremona, Roberto Farinacci (an ex-socialist and Freemason); at Carrara, Renato Ricci (a lieutenant in the *arditi*); at Lucca, Carlo Scorza (the same); and in the Trentino, Achille Starace (a captain in the *bersaglieri*).

For such men, the struggle against the 'internal enemy' was conceived as coming in direct line from the war mobilization. The destructive spiral often began from some incautious provocation by the left when the reaction of the squads was enhanced by their access to trucks, a motorization that allowed them to range across a province in their search for recruits and action. Meanwhile 'red' violence, much more likely to be static and unplanned, was typically expressed during strikes or mass demonstrations or, sporadically, in attempted ambushes when shots would be fired against a fascist column. 'Black' violence, by contrast, followed a definite programme and was always paramilitary in nature.

The ruling Liberals left ample space to the blackshirts, believing that they could thereby draw political advantage from the demolition of the socialists' strongholds. In spring 1921, the addition of the fascists to the electoral alliance of the Blocco Nazionale at the behest of Giolitti legitimized squadrism, transforming what had been till then a private militia into a force of order working for the bourgeoisie. The way in which the vote was held, with the distribution of ballots by the parties to their sympathizers, favoured squadrist tactics since they could seize and destroy a huge amount of electoral material and, in some places, ensure that the ballots never reached anti-fascist supporters. Also benefiting from this approach were such leading Liberals as Ivanoe Bonomi, Enrico De Nicola, Vittorio Emanuele Orlando, and Antonio Salandra.

The campaign against the socialist base was matched by similar initiatives against the party leadership. To give but one example, the offensive of March 1921 against the 'subversive redoubt' of Casale Monferrato, in a military style attack, was completed with the exemplary punishment of opposition deputies in that part of Piedmont. As a blackshirt would write ironically: 'The chiefs of the communist and socialist parties sent to Casale the deputies, Belloni from Alessandria and Demichelis from Valenza Po, to stiffen their cowardly comrades. Belloni has been forced to walk through the streets of the town with a tricolour cockade sown into his hair. Demichelis has been conscientiously beaten and sent back marked "urgent".'[3]

The self-taught writer Marcello Gallian, trained in a squadrist atmosphere, depicted the adventurous existence of the blackshirts romantically as giving meaning to the lives of those who, too young to fight in the war, now could deem themselves the agents of epochal change:

The raid was more than war and more than revolution. Among the raiders were only those who felt themselves born body and soul for an atrocious life that went on and on. In all the world, such people did not exist before us. No comparison is of any value in understanding us. Those who donned the black-shirt to go on a raid wherever it need be were those who had utterly rejected any compromise with the enemy, even if they included family members. It was as though they had stripped off their skin and, impelled by their wounds, had put on a new skin. They were born anew, with some to be victims who would sell their lives dearly. To get into the truck, to stay on their feet there for hours and hours, to head into the field of action, alighting armed to 'cleanse' a part of town, meant to accept that it was possible to die without a murmur.[4]

Trips beyond the provincial border became typical of this 'agrarian slavery', as D'Annunzio would critically call the squads who acted in the interest of the great landowners, brimming with violence and certain of their impunity. In 1921–2, the blackshirts of Mantua and Cremona organized strike-breaking in the lower part of the province of Brescia, suffocating the resistance of socialist day labourers; one

---

[3] D. M. Tuninetti, *Squadrismo squadristi piemontesi* (Rome: Pinciana, 1942), 33.

[4] M. Gallian, *Il Ventennale: gli uomini delle squadre nella Rivoluzione delle camicie nere* (Rome: AZ. Lett. Italiana, 1941), 61–2.

after another, the strongholds of the 'red' unions' fell. These acts were accompanied by a further offensive against party branches and local administrations controlled by the left, with a succession of shootings and other attacks on unions and unionists. Against such assaults, the socialist chiefs were powerless, watching immobile as peasants returned to work, now again on the landowners' terms.[5]

Industrialists and landowners proffered their financial backing to the squads in large part out of pleasure at seeing the pro-socialist political and union network demolished. Significant is a communication by the prefect of Milan to the Ministry of the Interior in Rome in mid-May 1921:

I can inform you that the local banks have always been particularly generous in their subventions to the fascist organizations but it is hard to tell the exact amounts involved since such payments come directly and personally from the directorates and are not recorded in the minutes or budgets. It is also true, as is widely known, that not only the banks but also industrialists and businessmen subsidize the fascists' organizations.[6]

In some cases, branches of the *fasci* were directly set up by business circles. So, at Larderello, in the province of Pisa, in May 1920, Prince Piero Ginori-Conti, owner of the Boracifera company, in trouble over a long-running conflict with the union, simply converted the factory security system into a squad. Those who worked for him were enrolled en masse into the Florence *fascio* and, on 16 October, with the dispute with the union now over, a *fascio* was born at Larderello itself, in the prince's living room and sustained by his financial largesse.

The centrality of the squadrists in the early history of the *fasci* ensured that fascism's rise would be accompanied by bitter factional and personal disputes, with frequent conflicts between 'official' fascists and 'dissident' ones in turn ensuring that administration of the movement would prove taxing. In Florence for a while there were two fascist federations, split by wild polemics. This Florentine crucible would temper people destined to stay near to Mussolini for the rest of his life. Among them were Amerigo Dumini, the murderer of the reformist socialist deputy Giacomo Matteotti, Raffaele Manganiello, a key prefect during the Repubblica Sociale Italiana (RSI), Alessandro Pavolini, Minister of Popular Culture and then Secretary of the Republican Fascist Party after 1943, and Tullio Tamburini, then Chief of Police.

In May 1922, Tuscany boasted 51,372 party card holders, grouped into 411 *fasci*, a tally that equalled a fifth of the whole nation. This large force was given impulse by the civil guerrilla conflict that afflicted Italy from 1920 to 1922. But the peculiarity of the Tuscan force was that their members in great part did not come from a reactionary background. Rather, 'almost all those engaged in the intricate making

[5] See R. Chiarini, *L'armonia e l'ardimento: l'ascesa del fascismo nella Brescia di Augusto Turati* (Milan: Franco Angeli, 1988), 323–4.

[6] Prefect of Milan to Ministry of the Interior (Min. Int.), Direzione Generale e Riservati, 16 May 1921 (ACS, PS, 1922, b. 105 f. 'Finanziamento dei Fasci di Combattimento').

and re-making of the Florentine *fascio* belonged to the "left" of some kind, whether from the tradition of Garibaldi or that of Mazzini', near the Republican or Socialist parties, historian Ernesto Ragionieri has underlined.[7] According to the prefect of Florence, in the summer of 1921, about a third of the *fascio*'s members came through squadrism.

The landowners, despite being deluded by the Liberal governments, did not succeed in establishing their own political organization and were poor at cementing ties with sectors of the political world. Rather, anchored by their local interest and understanding, they favoured utilitarian relations with the Fascist movement or, to be more accurate, with the heads of the local squads, who in the countryside were more compact and thrustful than they were in the city. The landowners' chief interest was in the suppression of the two bodies that were their rivals in settling agrarian employment, pay, and conditions, that is, the 'red' unions helping the day labourers and the 'white' or Catholic ones rallying those who held small pieces of land in some sort of rental arrangement. During the *biennio rosso*, or red two years of 1919–20, landowners and some who rented were vexed by the socialists who, with their strikes and boycotts, forced them to pay out considerable sums, and even finance the socialists' class-bound organizations. In the *biennio nero* (black two years) of 1921–2, the fascists drove those who had been the subjects of boycott to denounce their 'extortioners'. Many local union bosses, caught between the hammer of the magistracy and the anvil of the squadrists, were persuaded to refund these sums, even though they had long since been distributed to their followers, by selling the surviving patrimony of their organizations. In a few months local hierarchy was overturned and, in 1921, the countryside fell under the control of fascist unions or syndicates, taking members from the socialist bodies and inheriting the monopoly to decide on conditions for the rural workforce. 'In practice, through 1921, the greater part of the classic zone of socialist dominance across the Po valley was conquered by the fascists.'[8] Figures facing in two directions, like Janus, the squadrist-syndicalists founded institutions designed to replace those of their adversaries, overwhelmed through military force. These new fascist 'representatives of the people' signed rental agreements that were harsher for the workers than those in socialist times, but the day labourers had to keep quiet and accept the new situation.

With these 'militias', Mussolini held ambiguous ties. On the one hand he exploited their applied violence, utilizing politically the weakening of socialist organizations. On the other hand he never ceased to distrust the provincial bosses with their disturbing willingness to embark always and anywhere on the road to violence. The diversity of views became obvious in summer 1921 when the *Duce* negotiated a 'pact of pacification' with the socialists, favoured by Speaker of the House,

---

[7] E. Ragionieri, 'Il partito fascista (appunti per una ricerca)', in *La Toscana nel regime fascista (1922–1939)* (Florence: Olschki, 1971), 62.

[8] L. Preti, *Le lotte agrarie nella valle padana* (Turin: Einaudi, 1955), 461.

De Nicola, and solicited by Prime Minister Bonomi. The agreement, opposed still
by the communists, anarchists, and the self-defence formations of the so-called
Arditi del Popolo, was justified by Mussolini as needed to keep the support of
moderate public opinion: 'An atmosphere of hatred is spreading around fascism.
We must dissipate it. We have erected our fortunes on corpses. We must stay alert
that this situation does not now repeat itself for our adversaries.'[9]

However, the accord signed on 3 August aiming at normalizing the political
situation was denounced by the provincial *ras* (chiefs). Grandi, Farinacci, Balbo,
and their comrades summoned mass meetings, called *adunate* or musters, to set
out an alternative to the proposed pacification. Yet these provincial chiefs could not
constitute a serious national alternative to Mussolini's leadership. At the same time,
the squads did not demobilize, reacting in a provocative manner to government
orders that they be disarmed: '*Me ne frego*' (I don't give a stuff), the Ferrara *fascio*
responded to such a direction from the local prefect.

For a time, a rupture between Mussolini and his paramilitary force seemed possible until, in early November, an accommodation was reached and then confirmed
at the founding congress of the Partito Nazionale Fascista (PNF; National Fascist
Party), held at Rome from 9 to 13 December. Apart from the formal political aspects
of the deal, which, by converting the movement into a party, placed the squads
into a subordinate role, this meeting exposed the curious ties between fascism and
the capital of the kingdom. Rome reacted negatively to the arrival in its streets
of thousands of blackshirts, who responded to the evident coldness by launching
their own provocations, unleashing a urban guerrilla conflict. The Eternal City
was scarred with tension and violence, with one blackshirt and eight opponents
being murdered. With these acts, squadrism, despite the political concessions, was
reconfirmed as an essential element of the Fascist movement.

Following the constitution of the PNF, *Il popolo d'Italia* (the official Fascist organ,
founded by Benito Mussolini and later edited by his brother Arnaldo) declared
the pact of pacification 'dead and buried' in an article published on 15 November
that relaunched the armed offensive in grand style. The clash between Mussolini
and squadrism was now healed and it was clear to all that fascism and squadrism
were twin inseparable parts of the same body. The two forces would now join in
their renewed battle against their adversaries but on the understanding that the
blackshirts would display greater discipline than in the past. Marchese Dino Perrone
Compagni, the political secretary for Tuscany, sent off to his provincial inspectors
and squad commanders a secret circular to bind them to directions from on high:

I must myself acknowledge that some squadrists do not bow to any order and intend to do
what they want, making Fascism into no more than an instrument of violence. But they must
understand, and be made to understand, that today fascism can no longer be compromised
by the actions of individuals. I thus order all the squads in every *fascio* to be summoned

[9] C. Rossi, *Mussolini com'era* (Rome: Ruffolo, 1947), 106.

and told clearly what is set out above. Those who show themselves unwilling to accept the situation must be expelled. Today none of us can view ourselves as arbiters of the situation. We are all executors of the commands of the central committee of the PNF.[10]

In the new political phase, scoured by the behaviour of the Fascist parliamentary deputies who brought into the Chamber the habits of squadrism, the paramilitary forces of the blackshirts continued to inflict severe blows on the left. Now the system of punitive expeditions flooded across the country, with the terrorism involved well exemplified at Roccastrada in the province of Grosseto where, on 24 July 1921, two trucks laden with armed militia fell into an ambush and lost one dead. Such resistance was repaid with the most brutal and indiscriminate vendetta, with the massacre of nine unresisting peasants who had nothing to do with the ambush and were simply rounded up from their labour in the fields.

Among the traditional centres of power of the socialist movement was the capillary diffusion of the party press, whether passed on directly by party militants or sold at *edicole*. A priority of squadrism was to hinder the circulation of 'subversive' material, in particular in those places where the socialists were strong. So, in the province of Reggio Emilia, in the first half of 1921, fifteen or more *edicole* managers reported to the socialist daily *Avanti!* that they had been forced to interrupt their sales. The same was true for another fifteen in the province of Ferrara and for ten in Modena. During the same period, many subscribers, 460 in Reggio Emilia, 320 in Ferrara, and 280 in Modena, wrote to ask for the suspension of their postal arrangement so as not to give a pretext to their enemies. This initial attack on the freedom of the press can be read in very many letters to the editor received by *Avanti!* On 31 March 1921, the subscriber 'C.R.' wrote from Villanova in the province of Ferrara: 'I must regretfully inform you that, not from my own wish, but per force, I must detach myself from the great paper of our faith. We are now become adherents of the Fascio and for this reason they no longer want to see a socialist paper at Villanova.'[11] On 14 April, the comrades of Rio Saliceto in the province of Reggio Emilia signed in great secret a letter of surrender: 'We are all very sad to have to terminate our subscription to our dear paper because of the fascists. But we are forced to do so because otherwise they will come into our homes and beat us to death because it is one of the only papers that sustains and defends the working class. Not content with this, they have already devastated all our party organizations.'[12] From Prato di Correggio, also in Reggio Emilia, 'T.L.' wrote on 10 May: 'I beg you to suspend my subscription to your paper because it is now impossible for me to receive it, given the new fascist movement. When the letter-carrier goes to bring it from the post office, they assault him and, in order not to

---

[10] Circular, 17 November 1921, as transcribed by G. A. Chiurco, *Storia della rivoluzione fascista* (Florence: Vallecchi, 1929), iii. 610–11.

[11] *Avanti!* (ed.), *Fascismo: inchiesta socialista sulle gesta dei fascisti in Italia* (Milan, 1922; repr. 1963), 473.

[12] Ibid. 475.

be beaten up daily, he hands over all the subversive papers.'[13] The Ministry of Posts itself complained to the police that, in some provinces, 'rural letter-carriers have endured Fascist pressure not to distribute such subversive periodicals as *Avanti!*, *Giustizia* and *Contadino*'.[14]

Socialist protests or questioning of officialdom duly received bureaucratic replies, sometimes ones that were involuntarily comic such as the description by the prefect of Modena of an attempt to beat up a distributor of the press: 'On the 8th of this month a Fascist group tried to hinder Umberto Pedrazzi from selling the newspaper *Avanti!* Although he was being protected by the *Carabinieri* and the Royal Guards, Pedrazzi became prey to panic, hurling his papers to the ground and fleeing, not before some Fascists managed to land a blow or two on him without any serious injury.'[15]

After the general elections in May 1921, such boycotting of left-wing journals or of any paper not aligned with fascism spread. If newspapers published 'unpleasant' reports of punitive raids, blackshirts regularly seized copies, otherwise blocked their distribution, or raided the paper's offices 'to give a lesson' to incautious journalists. In such an atmosphere, the protest by the delegate of the National Federation of the Italian Press to Bonomi was faint and, in any practical sense, useless: 'To protect the editorial offices and printing presses from assaults by groups or individuals is something, but it is not all that newspaper workers have the right to expect through the fair and impartial application of state power. The freedom of the press is already made little more than a joke if the ability to distribute the paper is in some way reduced or, worse still, blocked completely.'[16]

In fact, by the end of 1921, the distribution of the daily press was widely conditioned by the power of the blackshirts, who, throughout whole regions, held sway over sellers and readers. The phenomenon was especially evident in Emilia Romagna, where this assessment was made by prefect Cesare Mori (one of the few functionaries to apply the law equally to socialists and fascists and later to be employed by Mussolini in the dictatorship's campaigns against the Mafia): 'The real trouble for the boycotted papers lies in finding places where they can be safely sold. It might be best if they provide their own bodyguards.'[17]

In Carrara, the squadrists gave prior notice to the editor of the daily *La stampa* that they would seize the paper throughout Tuscany in retribution for articles they disapproved of. As the editor dryly informed the Prime Minister: 'Excellency. I believe it is my duty to keep you apprised of this singular event. This editorial

---

[13] Ibid. 473.

[14] Reserved circular of the Ministry of Posts and Telegraphs to the Direzione Generale di Pubblica Sicurezza (DGPS), 30 June 1921, ACS, PS 1922, b. 101, f. 'Fasci di Combattimento', sf. 'Affari generali'.

[15] Telegram, Prefect of Modena to Capo gabinetto, Min. Int., 16 December 1921 (ACS, Gabinetto Bonomi, b. 1, f. 2).

[16] Consigliere delegato, Federazione Nazionale della Stampa Italiana, to Prime Minister, 9 August 1921 (ACS, Gabinetto Bonomi, b. 1, f. 2).

[17] Prefect of Bologna to Prime Minister, 7 December 1921 (ACS, Gabinetto Bonomi, b. 1, f. 2).

office has received from Carrara a despatch signed "Directorate, Carrara *Fascio*" and I enclose the original. As you will see, it entails an unwonted threat made by private citizens to a newspaper by means of a state organisation, the telegraph.'[18] A frequent habit became to seize and burn packets of papers in the public squares of towns where the squadrists were active. According to the prefect of Massa, whom Bonomi had asked for clarification: 'once copies of the paper [*Avanti!*] reached town, the Fascists bought them all from the newsagent, thereupon burning most copies outside their party headquarters.'[19] The prefect was obscuring the truth, given that the squadrists had seized anti-fascist papers by threatening the vendor. He paid for the copies out of his own pocket from a desire not to quarrel publicly with such violent men and expose himself to further attacks.

The prefect of Pisa, the pro-fascist Pietro Frigerio, who was notably fond of the fable of purchase, repeated it even when the local squadrists gave the same treatment to non-socialist papers: 'They went to the agent selling *Il paese* [linked to ex-Prime Minister, Nitti] in that town [Volterra], paying him for all the copies and inviting him simultaneously forthwith to end sales of that journal.'[20] This 'invitation' was so pressing that the newsagent, reassured unconvincingly by the prefect that 'rigorous measures would be applied', agreed 'to cease distribution of that paper', as the prefect solemnly reported in telling proof of an individual's complete lack of faith by that time in government institutions. In a similar case in the adjoining province of Livorno, it was again the free will of the local newsagent that blocked the distribution of *Il paese*: 'At Cecina, the man selling postcards and papers, impressed by the unfortunate incidents that have occurred in other towns, from the end of June informed the editors of *Il paese* that it would be best to stop sending it and he did so without any pressure or open threat made to him by the Fascists.'[21]

Further to ensure the suppression of press freedom, Fascists even took to blocking anti-fascist journalists from getting to work: 'From Bologna the correspondent, Antonio Lorenzini, with a letter of 1 September, reveals that the local telephone office is guarded by a squad armed by heavy sticks who are on the lookout for those who work for *Il paese*. Two days ago, the fascists turned up at Lorenzini's office and not being able to find him, beat up his *portiere* [janitor].'[22] At around the same time, Francesco Ciccotti Scozzese, editor of this paper in Rome, complained to the government about sellers in Umbria who, 'from the end of May, had been unable to resume sales given fascist violence'.[23] Since he himself was protected by a sizeable guard, in vendetta the fascists bashed his son.

---

[18]   Editor of *La stampa* to Prime Minister (ACS, Gabinetto Bonomi, b. 1, f. 2).
[19]   Prefect of Massa and Carrara to Min. Int., 4 August 1921 (ACS, Gabinetto Bonomi, b. 1, f. 2).
[20]   Prefect of Pisa to Capo gabinetto, Min. Int., 28 July 1921 (ACS, Gabinetto Bonomi, b. 1, f. 2).
[21]   Ibid.
[22]   Memorandum from *Il paese*, Rome, 8 September 1921 (ACS, Gabinetto Bonomi, b. 1, f. 2).
[23]   Newsagents in Città di Castello, Norcia, and Umbertide to *Il paese*, 8 September 1921 (ACS, Gabinetto Bonomi, b. 1, f. 2).

Il popolo d'Italia, meanwhile, took open pleasure at the campaign against *Il paese*, reporting that,

for quite some time, it has been the firm intention of the Fascists of Genoa that *Il paese* should not be sold or talked about in our town. This evening, our men, rendered indignant by what that rag had written about events in Rome, decided simply to block all sales. A group of fascists, at eight at night, went down to the station, seized all copies of the paper, carried them into the square and set them on fire. Our men warned the distributors to contact the offices of *Il paese* and say that, from here on, they intend to stop its diffusion by any means.[24]

Such pieces, and there were plenty of other examples, were apologies for crime and an incitement for more, but both government and magistracy turned a blind eye. As a result the boycotting spread further, without the slightest fear of intervention by the public authorities. The resulting impunity allowed one group to write the following letter:

FASCIO ITALIANO DI COMBATTIMENTO CASTIGLIONCELLO (PISA)

18 November 1921

To the Editorial office of the paper *Il paese*,
    We officially inform you that all the copies of your paper sent to Dante Deri here have been seized by this *fascio* because we shall not permit the sale of papers that denigrate our country.
    When you accept the matter, we can return the papers to you by return post at your expense.

The Executive[25]

The culmination of this campaign was that *Il paese* stopped production altogether. Its story is a stark case of how, well before the institution of Mussolini's dictatorship, the squadrists had suppressed a basis of democracy, the freedom of the press.

Back during the government headed by the Liberal Giolitti from 16 June 1920 to 4 July 1921, squadrism had emerged from its localized origins, projecting itself onto the national stage with the connivance of the state authorities. Giolitti's personal responsibility for the matter is aggravated by the fact that he himself held the office of Minister of the Interior, in charge of public order. His closest collaborator and under-secretary, Camillo Corradini, was perfectly aware of the mode of behaviour of the squads, described exactly in a telegram he circulated to his prefects: 'When in a commune there is a disturbance, fascists come in to assist from other communes or from other provinces and they do so through their use of the telegraph.'[26] Yet he did nothing to hinder such incursions.

Giolitti's successor, Bonomi, in office from 4 July 1921 to 26 February 1922, took time to get moving, then concentrated his hopes about normalizing the country on the fascist desire to 'settle down', and thus on the pact of pacification, which,

---

[24] *Il popolo d'Italia*, 15 November 1921, article entitled 'I fascisti genovesi contro il giornale di Nitti'.
[25] ACS, Gabinetto Bonomi, b. 1, f. 2.
[26] Corradini telegram to prefects, 23 May 1921, ACS PS 1921, b. 85.

as noted above, soon came to nothing. Thereafter his main effort was to mediate between that majority of his ministers willing to tolerate fascist violence and a minority urging energetic repression. The radical Luigi Gasparotto was typical of the first category and the reformist ex-Nittian Alberto Beneduce of the second. After many hesitations, Bonomi ended in the camp of those who wanted to avoid hindering the fascists.

The judiciary is in charge of the suppression of crime, but, in practice, judges were highly selective and subjective in their response to misdeeds that had a political air. The faults of the left were punished rigorously and inexorably. Protests against the high cost of living, rural agitation by day labourers, the occupation of the factories, or violence by leftists against their political enemies resulted in a long series of prosecutions, usually involving the early arrest of the accused and the denial thereafter of any provisional liberty. Certain of punishment were efforts at blackmail against landowners or the illegal retention of arms by red guards. A wave of charges pursued men who in the summer of 1920 had acted to defend those workers occupying the factories. Typically, judges arraigned them for joining 'armed groups', engaged in 'precipitating civil war or causing devastation, sacking or murder in the Kingdom'. Lawyers trying to act for the metal-workers' union FIOM (Federazione Metallurgica della Confederazione Generale del Lavoro) put it this way:

Those workers disarming white collar employees who kept revolvers in their offices and did so without the least personal injury had their alleged crime elevated to being 'armed robbery' as defined in article 408 of the Penal Code.

All those involved in occupations that were not entirely pacific found themselves accused under the draconian Crispi Law even when only one or two of them were armed.

The result is that, following the use of articles 252 and 253 of the Penal Code, hundreds of workers have been condemned or can be found waiting in prison or are in hiding, even though they are sure that they have committed no crimes and are only responsible for acts that were shared by at least thirty thousand workers in Turin [who had participated in the occupations].[27]

A year after the period of worker governance of the factories was over, the central committee of FIOM drew the government's attention to the precarious situation of 'workers who still languish in prison following the occupation of the factories back in 1920, when His Excellency, Giovanni Giolitti, then Prime Minister, gave guarantee that no penal prosecutions would be opened'.[28] This petition for mercy was destined to remain a dead letter.

---

[27] Memorandum by lawyers Innocente Perrone and Piero Ollivero to central committee, FIOM, Turin, 12 October 1921 (ACS, Presidenza del Consiglio dei Ministri—PCM, 1921, b. 618, f. 'Grazie sovrane, amnistie').

[28] The central committee of FIOM to the Capo gabinetto, Prime Minister, 18 October 1921 (ACS, PCM, 1921, b. 618, f. 'Grazie sovrane, amnistie').

The variation in approach by state officials was similarly evident in regard to those who engaged in violence. According to the prefect of Siena, this was the natural result of the realities facing those who implemented the law: 'The larger number of [leftist] subversives arrested compared with fascists springs from the fact that the former usually live in the places where the conflicts happened, so being easily traced, while fascists usually arrive from other localities and can readily avoid searches for them.'[29] This situation was seen as explaining the enormous disproportion between those accused and those arrested. In Siena, for example, 112 individuals were arraigned, 106 being fascists and six leftists; of these only the socialists ended up in jail and not one fascist. In sum, a leftist involved in violence was dragged off to prison, while a squadrist, if matters went that far, could rest easy with a denunciation, pursuing his activities without further let or hindrance. Meanwhile, if the judges imposed light penalties or freed citizens accused of violently resisting the fascists, the blackshirts had their own supplementary punishment system, through beatings, arson, or even murder, and did so following the instructions of their provincial federations.

On numerous occasions, *carabinieri*, either in mufti or in uniform, seconded punitive expeditions. In vain, socialists denounced events such as that which happened in the province of Ferrara in the autumn of 1921:

The *carabinieri* escorted the fascists through the city streets and out into the country, singing fascist songs and generally backing the violent raids of this *faction* against the individual and collective interests of the majority of the citizens. We can affirm that the *carabinieri* are not just complicit with the Fascists but are fused with them. Quite a number are formally enrolled in the *fascio*, happy to sport the party badge. In other cases, as happened after the funeral of the fascist, Rino Moretti, they publicly demonstrated their solidarity, with two or three hundred assembling by the windows of the party branch and there singing their songs![30]

The socialist press reported similar events on many occasions. On 16 October 1921, at San Lorenzo a Merse in the province of Siena, a raid saw a man called Pietro Palini battered almost to death with the butt of a rifle. The excuse was the application of public order. As *Avanti!* recorded in a piece headed '*Carabinieri* who beat people up': 'We note that, during *carabinieri* searches, all those found with membership cards of the [socialist] Chamber of Labour must endure any sort of insult.'[31] In part this was retribution for leftist behaviour during their good years of 1919–20 when their zealots had frequently insulted the police, sworn at them, and even on occasion bashed them.

In 1921–2, most *carabinieri* acted in arrangement with the squadrists. Those who instead tried to be impartial found life difficult. The captain of the *carabinieri* at Rimini, for example, was openly abused by fascists for trying to apply the law

---

[29] Prefect of Siena to Min. Int., 2 June 1921 (ACS, PCM, 1921, b. 618, f. 'Grazie sovrane, amnistie').
[30] *Avanti!* (ed.), *Fascismo*, 261.   [31] *Avanti!*, 23 October 1921.

impartially. Fascist parliamentary deputies formally requested his removal in alliance with the prefect of Forlì, who recommended transfer on the grounds that 'Fascist elements who now prevail at Rimini believe him sympathetic with parties hostile to them. For these reasons, and admitting that, in most senses, he is a fine officer, I suggest he soon be moved, using the occasion of his coming promotion to major.'[32] On some occasions the prefects themselves or their officers accompanied the fascists. In Lomellina, a sector of the province of Pavia was dominated by the squads under Cesare Forni and ex-colonel Silvio Magnaghi, who ranged armed from Mortara to Milan and Novara, and were composed of their fascist leaders, *carabinieri*, and other police agents.[33]

Within this general context there were two occasions when the forces of order bloodily suppressed Fascist armed violence—at Sarzana in the province of La Spezia and at Modena. But these were isolated incidents that were duly manipulated by Mussolini to his own ends when he presented his men as victims and blamed the Royal Guards.

The arrest of Renato Ricci, head of the Carrara squad, and his imprisonment at Sarzana prompted the mobilization of hundreds of blackshirts, who, on 21 July 1921, paraded through the Tuscan town urging their chief's liberation. At the station square, the fascists were confronted by *carabinieri*, whose commandant, Guido Jurgens, ordered them to fire when, after he demanded the dissolution of the assembly, his men were insulted and punched by the squadrists. Five fascists fell wounded, with three dying later in hospital. Their comrades fled, hindered by the revenge of socialist peasants who killed another three. Five days later, a fascist muster at Modena was darkened by the shooting of six militants by the local Royal Guard. Both government and judiciary promptly separated themselves from the officials involved in these efforts to restore public order. In Modena, only a few hours after the firing, Commissioner Cammeo was arrested for first-degree murder, along with the Royal Guard Modica, while the policeman Jacobelli was held for culpable wounding.[34] A reconstruction of events, typed out shortly afterwards by Inspector Secchi, qualified the responsibility of the three police involved. Surrounded by hundreds of ebullient Fascists who demanded homage to their standards, they were beaten and then,

Vice-commissioner Jacobelli who stood at the front before the shouts and public threats doffed his hat. Commissioner Cammeo, however, momentarily hesitated and the Fascists thought that he was jamming his hat back on. The most excited and violent now hurled themselves against the police, with sticks raised. The result for an instant was a confused

[32] Prefect of Forlì to Capo gabinetto, Min. Int., 31 July 1921 (ACS, Gabinetto Bonomi, b. 3, f. 'Cesena. Conflitto. Sottoprefetto and Captain of the *carabinieri* of Rimini, Giorgi'.

[33] P. Lombardi, *Il ras e il dissidente: Cesare Forni e il fascismo pavese dallo squadrismo alla dissidenza* (Rome: Bonacci, 1998).

[34] Telegram from Prefect of Modena to DGPS, 27 September 1921 (ACS Gabinetto Bonomi, b. 4, f. 'Conflitti tra fascisti e forza pubblica'.

skirmish with the deputy Vicini hurrying over to calm matters, with cav. Cammeo punched to the ground and another policeman called Izzo also being assaulted. A revolver shot rang out and the Royal Guards, without any direct orders or command, opened fire. On the street now lay seven dead and numerous wounded.[35]

This version of events was unacceptable to the fascists who instituted their own investigating commission under the lawyer Vittorio Arangiu Ruiz, president of the Modena Returned Soldiers group and, in his spare time, a squadrist. He reported courteous behaviour by the blackshirts and a deliberate will to kill on the part of the police:

A fascist with the point of a stick gave a blow under brim of the straw hat of Cammeo that tumbled to the ground. In the meantime around the guards there was a bit of pushing and shoving. Witnesses say, however, that only a few sticks were raised, as were a few arms, but nothing was done to launch the crowd against the police. Commissioner Cammeo put his boater back on in a disrespectful manner, saying: 'Don't be so stupid'. Then it seems again the hat was knocked off with another stroke of a stick. Certainly, while still bare-headed, Cammeo stepped back a little towards the ranks of the guards, bent over as if again to reclaim his headgear but, instead, with his right hand, drew a revolver, pointed it against [the fascist] Carpignani, who tried to make himself safe but was struck and fell prostrate.[36]

Inspector Sechi's version, later endorsed by General Marchetti, blamed the event on the provocation and outright assault of Cammeo and his men, while Arangiu Ruiz painted the Commissioner's behaviour as deliberate murder. (Cammeo spent months in prison as a result, only to be released without being found guilty yet still blamed by public opinion.) At the funeral of the Modena dead, Mussolini, other fascist bosses, and thousands of blackshirts were prominent. In memory of the fallen, a memorial stone was prepared with a text that the new prefect of Modena, Errante (a convinced fascist), believed was inspired by 'noble sentiments', blaming the state authorities, hailing the squadrists as 'innocent bystanders', and ignoring everything else.

The cases of Sarzana and Modena show that isolated local defeats of the fascists were transmuted into clamorous public victories, utilizing a winning strategy of mass communication and the forging of a myth of the fallen. The transformation of reality was not the merit of the squadrists but rather owed to the fascist elite. Each dead squadrist became a martyr, fitted into a cult of the dead whereby the blackshirts took to using a skull as their emblem.

The government headed by Luigi Facta from 26 February 1922 lived a struggling existence, always on the point of collapse and never able to reassert control over public order. The Prime Minister, told about the destructive squadrist raids, which in the countryside were methodically demolishing socialist and Catholic

---

[35] Report of Inspector Secchi to DGPS, 2 October 1921 (ACS Gabinetto Bonomi, b. 4, f. 'Conflitti tra fascisti e forza pubblica').

[36] PNF Federazione Provinciale Modenese, *Relazione della Commissione d'inchiesta sull'eccidio del 26 settembre 1921* (Parma, 1922), 21–2, from a report discussed and approved, 15–8 October 1921.

cooperatives, ordered the prefects to provide some surveillance (defined as 'not merely a pressing need of public order but also an obligation on the highest social interest to stop the destruction of important public goods needed to augment production') and recommended 'severe and prompt repressive counter-measures'.[37] However, the order remained inactive because the state authorities in the periphery, some prefectures apart, no longer raised a finger against Fascism, now accepted as the nation's future, and the government had no means to make its writ run.

While the crisis of the Liberal order was precipitated, the summer of 1922 was dominated by squadrism, its men able to occupy militarily the major cities and liquidate their adversaries' political or union organizations. The final proof was given at the end of May with the march on Bologna with the aim of expelling from the city the prefect, Mori, still the symbol of a steely legalism, besieged for a few days in his prefecture and in the end sacrificed by Facta. Mori's transfer, after a month's stand-off, signalled the complete success of the Fascist attack. In those places where 'red' administrations survived, mayors were now forced to resign, driven to take up residence in far-off places and retire from public life—that is, if they wanted to preserve their lives.

The last gasp of anti-fascism occurred during the 'legalitarian strike', proclaimed on 1 August 1922 to be fought to the bitter end by the pro-socialist Alleanza del Lavoro (Workers' Alliance). The PSI, which, when, perhaps, opposition to Fascism was possible, had counselled passivity, supported the act but lacking any idea where it might lead. The result was an opportunity for the paramilitary right further to sharpen their violence against the last bastions of the workers' movement. On 4 August, militarily equipped brigades seized central Milan, laid waste the head office of *Avanti!* (burned for the fourth time in three years), and camped in the headquarters of the local administration. Similar scenes occurred at Ferrara, Ravenna, Bolzano, and Trento. At the instigation of business elites, the government sacked state employees involved in the strike. The political and union leaders of the left did make an attempt to save their followers' jobs. But the ostensibly committed Liberal Minister of the Interior, Paolino Taddei, told Facta that the socialists were cowed: 'This morning at noon, I talked with [socialist leader] Modigliani. He did not hide his dismay at the sacking of 110 railwaymen. However he left me with the impression that they could do nothing about it given that they recognized their own impotence. Have a good holiday. Cheers.'[38]

Yet Facta's summer vacation would be wrecked by a Fascist offensive. With the socialists routed, the squads turned directly against the Liberal state, advancing towards a seizure of power. In September and October columns of thousands of armed men occupied the major cities of northern and central Italy without meeting any resistance or public disapproval from the Liberal authorities, celebrating the

---

[37] Telegram by Min. Int. to prefects, 28 July 1922 (ACS PS 1922, b. 103, f. 'Cooperative agricole—Danneggiamenti ad opera di fascisti'.
[38] Telegram Taddei to Facta, 18 August 1922 (ACS PCM, 1922, b. 653, f. 'Sciopero generale in Italia'.

demise of the left. Only at Parma did the Arditi del Popolo offer serious counter to the offensive when, for a time, they repelled squads led by Farinacci and Balbo; after days of siege the army took over and the Fascists retreated. The collapse of the Liberal system is well exemplified in Taddei's circular of 7 October: 'Reports and other sources reveal pretty often that the forces of public order, when confronted by violence of a factional kind, do not repress it, even when they have the numbers to do so, avoiding arrests and only collecting information for possible future charges. On their part, the prefects also, despite our request on 29 August, have made no attempt to list the names of those officials who lack energy in their job and fail to do their duty.'[39]

The blatant preparation of a March on Rome allowed Mussolini to negotiate with the leaders of the national political world from a position of strength, even if, in the dealing, 'transformism' was as obvious as 'revolution' and the *Duce*'s arrangement with the liberals and the monarchy left many squadrists embittered. On 29 October, it was King Victor Emmanuel III who appointed Mussolini as Prime Minister, and the arrival of the squads, threatening for some days, was converted into a victory parade for the *Duce*. On 31 October the blackshirts in their thousands marched from the Piazza del Popolo to the *Altare della Patria* in Piazza Venezia. Their route passed by the Quirinal, where they stopped to pay proper respect to the king and to army chief and new Minister of War Armando Diaz. Less formally, ferocious punitive raids purged 'subversives' in the working-class San Lorenzo quarter. And there was a hint of further blackmail when Generals Ceccherini, Fara, and Zamboni marched with the blackshirts, suggesting that, had there been conflict, the king could not have relied on the army.

Once Prime Minister, Mussolini, on 14 January 1923, quickly set up the Milizia Volontaria per la Difesa Nazionale (MVSN; Voluntary Militia for National Defence). Through the decree granting this body charge of public order, Mussolini simultaneously normalized blackshirt activity and demonstrated that party and state were now interdependent. The old squadrist bosses transmogrified into ministers or, if inadequate to the legalist task involved, were inducted into the diplomatic service, through a special law in 1928, and sent abroad. Squadrism assumed a central position in the founding myth of the dictatorship, as was especially made manifest in the Mostra della Rivoluzione Fascista, a museum display which, from 1932, made concrete fascism's usable past, while visited by hundreds of thousands. Those who had allegedly fallen for the revolution were lauded as the regime's saints, with the 425 actual casualties being expanded to 870 (a tally that did not stop the *Duce* from talking blithely about 3,000). In 1939, Mussolini put on another mobilization, in a muster held at the Rome Olympic Stadium on 26 March, with the intent of preparing the nation for war. He pronounced:

---

[39] Min. Int. to prefects, 7 October 1922 (ACS PS 1922, b. 102, f. 'Denunzie e procedimenti penali per reati commesse nei conflitti fra opposte fazioni').

Perhaps there are some who have forgotten the tough early days (the crowd: 'No one!') but the men of the squads have not forgotten them, cannot forget them (the crowd: 'Never'). Perhaps, in the meantime, some have sat down. But the men of the squads are always on their feet, ready to grab their gun, jump on the truck, and raid just like they used to (the crowd: 'Yes! Yes!'). The men of the squads say to those who want to take cover the revolution isn't finished but in personal habits and behaviour, in social view, it has hardly begun. . . . You are not my bodyguard. Above all you are, and you want to be, the bodyguards of the revolution and the fascist regime. . . . That glorious black shirt of yours, with which we fought and shall fight again (The squads: 'Yes! Yes!') glows today with a badge of which you are especially proud. It is a red badge, the colour of that blood that we are ready to spill, our blood and that of others (The squads: 'Yes! Yes!') whenever the interests of Italy and of Fascism are being decided.[40]

Fascism in its own last gasp during the RSI would, in 1943–5, turn back yet again to its 'glorious' squadrist traditions when the PFR secretary, Pavolini, would open ranks of the so-called Brigate Nere (black brigades), reviving the macabre symbol of the whitened skull in a last spiral of violence at a time of German occupation and international and civil war. Fascism cannot be understood without reference to squadrism.

BIBLIOGRAPHY

ALBANESE, G., *La marcia su Roma* (Rome: Laterza, 2006).

FRANZINELLI, M., *Squadristi: protagonisti e tecniche della violenza fascista 1919–1922* (Milan: Mondadori, 2003).

GAGLIANI, D., *Brigate Nere: Mussolini e la militarizzazione del Partito fascista repubblicano* (Turin: Bollati Boringhieri, 1999).

MARINETTI, F. T., *Teoria e invenzione futurista*, ed. Luciano De Maria (Milan: Mondadori, 1968).

MONDINI, M. (ed.), *La politica delle armi: il ruolo dell'esercito nell'avvento del fascismo* (Rome: Laterza, 2006).

ROCHAT, G., *L'esercito italiano da Vittorio Veneto a Mussolini* (Rome: Laterza, 2006).

ROSSI, C., *Mussolini com'era* (Rome: Ruffolo, 1947).

TASCA, A., *Nascita e avvento del fascismo* (Rome: Laterza, 1972).

—— *La nascita del fascismo*, ed. David Bidussa (Turin: Bollati Boringhieri, 2006).

[40] B. Mussolini, *Opera omnia* (Florence: La Fenice, 1959), xxix. 249–53.

CHAPTER 6

....

CULTURE AND
INTELLECTUALS

....

GUIDO BONSAVER

THE relationship between Italy's intellectuals and fascism is a most controversial issue which has generated waves of differing views and many a polemic. To some extent the roots of this controversy go back to the country's return to democracy. Once the dictatorship and the war were over, Italians had to rebuild their identity and relearn the principles of freedom of speech and tolerant cohabitation of different cultures. Benedetto Croce's renowned definition of fascism as a 'moral illness' made the process considerably easier.

Following that logic, the vast majority of Italians had never been sincere fascists, and even the intelligentsia at most had produced culture infected by its sickening virus. Similarly, fascism was described as the negation of culture by another influential philosopher, Norberto Bobbio, according to whom Italian culture had survived in the inter-war years 'attraverso o sotto il fascismo' (through or beneath fascism).[1]

Croce and Bobbio's views are acceptable if the adjective 'democratic' is considered as implicitly attached to the noun 'culture'. It is an assumption which might stand a philosophical argument, but once we move it to the field of historical analysis it quickly becomes impractical. Fascism produced its own culture or, better, a number of different cultures cohabited during the years of the fascist regime, many of which jockeyed for position, aspiring to become synonymous with fascism. However much anti-intellectualism there might have been in the early years of

---

[1] For Benedetto Croce see for example 'Il fascismo come pericolo mondiale', in his *Per la nuova vita dell'Italia: scritti e discorsi 1943–1944* (Naples: Ricciardi, 1944), 13–21. N. Bobbio, 'La cultura e il fascismo', in G. Quazza (ed.), *Fascismo e società italiana* (Turin: Einaudi, 1973), 220.

Mussolini's dictatorship, it is a fact that among its supporters were a number of leading intellectuals, from idealist philosopher Giovanni Gentile to self-appointed national bard Gabriele D'Annunzio, avant-garde artists such as Filippo Tommaso Marinetti and his Futurists, and finally one of the fathers of modernist theatre, Luigi Pirandello, who publicly joined the fascist Party during its darkest hour in the summer of 1924.

As a pragmatist, Benito Mussolini had little time for theoretical discussions and cultural disputes. At the same time, two factors need to be mentioned. First, from his early years of leadership he was advised on cultural matters by a number of influential figures, most prominent of whom were, in his private life, his collaborator and then lover Margherita Sarfatti, and in public office Giovanni Gentile. Second, the *Duce*'s vision of an 'anthropological revolution'—as historian Emilio Gentile calls it—that is, his hope that fascism might forge a generation of 'new men' and 'new women', required the introduction of a number of cultural policies aimed at shaping the image and substance of the Italian people. However unsuccessful and in various cases deserving posthumous derision (fascism's linguistic policies, for example) and disgust (the anti-Semitic legislation), these initiatives were launched in earnest during the regime's second decade in office and were part of a total-itarian project. Their ultimate demise does not pre-empt a number of questions concerning the degree to which Italian intellectuals and artists were attracted by their many-faceted stimulations.[2]

The six short sections of this chapter tackle the central issues related to fascism and culture while trying to add a sense of chronological development over the twenty years of dictatorship. Their limited length does not allow for analysis of both individual cases and historiographical debate. Another missing element is a discussion of the influence of Italy's post-war political history on the study of fascist culture. The 1990s witnessed a resurgence of interest in Italy's fascist past, not all of it free from political reverberations. At the risk of being simplistic, it could be said that, if the early post-war years saw a process of excessive marginalization of the nation's fascist past, in recent times the prominent presence of a former neo-fascist party within the coalition of three Berlusconi governments has caused a momen-tum towards a more lenient revision of those years. The following pages aim at catching the historiographical pendulum at the mid-point of its swinging motion.

I. Fascism and Culture in the 1920s

During the early years of the regime, Mussolini's preoccupation with securing his control over Italy's political body took priority over questions of cultural import.

[2] E. Gentile, 'The Fascist Anthropological Revolution', in G. Bonsaver and R. Gordon (eds), *Culture, Censorship and the State in Twentieth Century Italy* (Oxford: Legenda, 2005), 22–33.

A key role at this stage was played by Giovanni Gentile. Already an established figure as a philosopher and a committed intellectual, his appointment as Minister of Education in Mussolini's first government added scholarly weight and credibility to the regime. His reform of secondary education in 1923, despite its elitist rationale, remained the backbone of Italian state education throughout the rest of the century. But it is in the wake of the crisis following the assassination of Giacomo Matteotti in the summer of 1924 that Gentile's involvement in public affairs took a more militant turn. In order to defend fascism from the accusation of its being an isolated movement with no support among the Italian intelligentsia, Gentile organized a conference in Bologna which took place on 29–30 March 1925. Its planned outcome was the publication of the Manifesto of Fascist Intellectuals.

Published on 21 April (the symbolic birth date of Rome), the manifesto rhetorically presented fascism as a moral and religious movement. Among its signatories were legal philosopher Alfredo Rocco (Minister of Justice 1925–32), historian Gioacchino Volpe, and Futurism's leader, Marinetti. As one of his last public signs of anti-fascism, Benedetto Croce promoted a counter-manifesto, symbolically published on 1 May. Among its signatories were economist Luigi Einaudi, liberal journalist and politician Giovanni Amendola (who was to die in exile the following year after a Fascist beating), and poet Eugenio Montale.[3]

In the same year, Gentile led the project to create an *Enciclopedia nazionale*. This was an important institutional act attempting to establish a monument of national culture following the French and British models. Attempting to bridge the gap between supporters and opponents of the regime, Gentile widened the network of contributors, managing to involve a number of prestigious non-fascists such as Marxist historian Rodolfo Mondolfo and liberal literary scholar Luigi Russo. If the imposing presence of Gentile—in 1925 he became also founder and president of the Istituto Nazionale Fascista di Cultura—acted as a bulwark against the influence of Croce as a potential leader of anti-fascism, the introduction of dictatorial powers allowed the regime quickly to suppress any opposition. Non-fascist intellectuals did not have the organization or the determination to fight back, and many holding moderate and conservative views were prepared to give fascism a chance.

There were a few notable exceptions, among them Croce, who refused to collaborate on the *Enciclopedia italiana* (but did not resign as a Senator, thus occasionally

---

[3] Both manifestos can be found translated into English in J. Schnapp (ed.), *A Primer of Italian Fascism* (Lincoln: University of Nebraska Press, 2000), 297–307. An interesting indication of the still unestablished status of the word 'intellectual', whose introduction in the Italian language dates from the beginning of the century, can be found in the fact that while Gentile's manifesto made confident use of it, Croce preferred to call his manifesto 'A Reply from Italian Writers, Professors, and Journalists'. Within the text, Croce then explained that he understood 'intellectual' as meaning 'i cultori della scienza e dell'arte' (the worshippers of science and of art). On Gentile see G. Turi, *Giovanni Gentile: una biografia* (Florence: Giunti, 1995) and A. J. Gregor, *Giovanni Gentile: Philosopher of Fascism* (New Brunswick, NJ: Transaction, 2001). On Croce see F. Rizi, *Benedetto Croce and Italian Fascism* (Toronto: Toronto University Press, 2003).

voting in favour of Fascist legislation), and the young Turinese journalist and critic Piero Gobetti. The latter's defiant opposition was closely monitored by Mussolini whose orders were instrumental in the police and squadrist clamp down on Gobetti's journalistic and publishing activities.

Among the intelligentsia, a very limited number decided to leave the country as a sign of opposition. The most prominent among them were historian Gaetano Salvemini who was to teach Italian history at Harvard University and the brothers Carlo and Nello Rosselli, founders in Paris of the anti-fascist organization Giustizia e Libertà, both killed by a group of French fascists in June 1937.[4]

Widespread acceptance of the regime was confirmed when, in 1931, the dictatorship required all university lecturers to swear allegiance to fascism. Fewer than twenty out of over a thousand refused to swear, among them mathematician and head of the prestigious Accademia dei Lincei Vito Volterra, philosopher Piero Martinetti, and novelist and critic Giuseppe Antonio Borgese, who avoided the decision by prolonging his visiting professorship abroad. Among those who accepted the imposition, many privately justified it as the only way to guarantee the survival of non-fascist thought within Italian academia.[5]

Another vital stage in the imposition of the fascist regime as a patron of high culture was the creation of the Reale Accademia d'Italia, decreed in 1926 and inaugurated three years later. Mussolini presided over all appointments, using them as an instrument for rewarding both public support and passive acceptance of the regime. Among the scientific community, the appointment and active collaboration of Guglielmo Marconi notably enhanced fascism's international prestige.

With regard to fascism's relationship with contemporary artistic movements, the Futurists, under the leadership of Marinetti, exerted great influence on the regime's self-representation. However, they never managed to monopolize its cultural agenda. Mussolini was careful not to commit fascism to a single school or movement. In this he was advised by Margherita Sarfatti whose sophisticated knowledge of contemporary art and literature, together with her committed support of another artistic movement, the Novecentisti, was instrumental in forging Mussolini's image as an enlightened dictator, eclectically in favour of contemporary art. The simplistic notion behind this position was that avant-garde, groundbreaking artistic movements somehow paralleled fascism's revolutionary shake-up of Italy's outdated political and social structures. Only through such simplification could the work of a modernist author such as Luigi Pirandello be accepted by the

[4] The bibliography in English on Italian anti-fascist culture is rather scarce. See for example the still useful book by F. Rosengarten, *The Italian Anti-Fascist Press, 1919–1945* (Cleveland: Case Western Reserve University Press, 1968), and the recent anthology by S. Pugliese (ed.), *Fascism, Anti-fascism, and the Resistance in Italy: 1919 to the Present* (Lanham, MD: Rowman & Littlefield, 2003).

[5] See H. Goetz, *Il giuramento rifiutato: i docenti universitari e il regime fascista* (Florence: La Nuova Italia, 2000).

fascists, despite the fact that its philosophical relativism was at loggerheads with the certainties of fascist ideology.[6]

II. MYTH AS CULTURE

Gustave Le Bon's and Georges Sorel's ideas of myth as a vehicle for popularizing political ideals were part of Mussolini's intellectual background as a politician. The great myths of Italy's prestigious classical past (its Romanità), of the 'mutilated victory' (following the First World War), and that of the *Duce* as semi-divine leader were vital ingredients of fascist propaganda. Mythical visions were a fundamental part of fascism's self-image. It is therefore reasonable to wonder whether a truly 'fascist' cultural production should have had a mythical vision at its core. Before fascism, nationalist myths had been the creative material of Italy's most celebrated author at the turn of the century, Gabriele D'Annunzio. In this respect, D'Annunzio can rightly be viewed as a predecessor of fascism's cultural propaganda. Italy's Romanità and its divine right to dominate the Mediterranean were already spelled out in such works as *La nave*, of 1909.

Similarly, Italy's tentative colonial adventures were justified and glorified, most conspicuously in the poems supporting the Libyan war, which Liberal Prime Minister Giolitti was forced to censor—they were published in *Corriere della sera*—because of their indiscriminate insults to the European nations opposing Italy's expansion in Africa. Given the great popularity of D'Annunzio's works and deeds—such as the occupation of Fiume in 1919—it is not surprising that many fascists should have looked up to him as the potential leader of their movement. The fact that he never was is the result of both Mussolini's political shrewdness and D'Annunzio's diminishing strength as a public figure and an artist. By the time of the fascists' seizure of power, D'Annunzio's energy and creativity were beginning to wane. From his melancholic retreat on Lake Garda, he remained a powerful icon but somehow failed to become a major presence in fascist society and, more importantly, he could not inspire a new generation of fascist artists.[7]

Nobody was able to fill the shoes of such a global celebrity. But not for lack of trying. Italy at the time was full of aspiring artists and poets of the fascist nation. The ministerial archive for theatrical censorship contains many examples

[6] On Margherita Sarfatti see P. Cannistraro and B. Sullivan, *L'altra donna del Duce: Margherita Sarfatti* (Milan: Mondadori, 1993). On politics and the arts under fascism see M. S. Stone, *The Patron State: Culture and Politics in Fascist Italy* (Princeton: Princeton University Press, 1999).

[7] On D'Annunzio see J. Woodhouse, *Gabriele D'Annunzio: Defiant Archangel* (Oxford: Clarendon Press, 1998).

of embarrassing works designed to eulogize the regime through a number of symbolic representations. Some of them were censored because too counterproductive; others saw some success such as the play *Piave* (1932) by a then young and fascist Vitaliano Brancati. Set in the trenches of the First World War, the final scene featured a towering eighteen-foot-high photograph of Mussolini in a soldier's uniform. The myth of the leader was nurtured through three plays by playwright and filmmaker Giuseppe Forzano, all co-authored by none other than Benito Mussolini (who did little more than provide the initial idea). Dedicated respectively to Napoleon (*Campo di maggio*, 1930, film adaptation 1935), Camillo Benso di Cavour (*Villafranca*, 1932, film adaptation 1933), and Julius Caesar (1939), the plays provide examples of great individuals whose destiny was inextricably linked to that of their nation. In the field of Romanità, a most ambitious and disastrously unsuccessful mythical narrative was Carmine Gallone's film *Scipione l'Africano* (1937). Once more the public was supposed to draw clear parallels between a great historic figure and the *Duce* of Italian Fascism. However, the film's aesthetic flaws destroyed any chance of a mythical epiphany despite the great financial assistance and publicity provided by the Ministry of Popular Culture.[8]

If myth might have provided the key to a genuinely fascist art and literature, no one managed to elevate it to international or even national fame during the entire Ventennio. Curzio Suckert (pseudonym Malaparte), the most literarily gifted of fascist militants, was too Tuscan—as he explained—to detach himself from a realistic and disillusioned vision of his times. Luigi Pirandello's late work addressed myth and collectivity, but it had none of the faith in humanity and institutions that was required for a work of fascist propaganda. If nothing else, his unfinished tragedy, *I giganti della montagna*, can be read as a critique of fascism's cultural policies. Younger generations of authors and film makers were moving away from myth as a narrative mode. By the 1940s, the call for a return to the naturalism of nineteenth-century authors by young director Luchino Visconti and his circle of friends was a clear sign of things to come. Neo-realism was knocking at the door of the Italian narrative arts.

Perhaps a different case can be made in the field of architecture. Fascism's programme of impressive public works benefited from the active involvement of a generation of ground-breaking architects such as Marcello Piacentini, Giuseppe Pagano, Gio Ponti, Giuseppe Terragni, and others. Providing different degrees of fusion between modernist innovation and classical style, they had a considerable

---

[8] On theatrical censorship see L. Zurlo, *Memorie inutili: la censura teatrale nel ventennio* (Rome: Edizioni dell'Ateneo, 1952). On Brancati's *Piave* see G. Bonsaver, *Censorship and Literature in Fascist Italy* (Toronto: Toronto University Press, 2007), 60–2. On Forzano see C. E. J. Griffiths, *The Theatrical Works of Giovacchino Forzano: Drama for Mussolini's Italy* (Lampeter: Edwin Mellen, 2000). On Italian cinema under fascism see J. Reich and P. Garofalo (eds), *Re-viewing Fascism: Italian Cinema, 1922–1943* (Bloomington, IN.: Indiana University Press, 2002).

impact on the image of Italy's major cities. The central station of Florence and other major cities or Rome's La Sapienza University are an immediate example— but, throughout the country, and most evidently in the newly founded cities in the reclaimed marshes such as Sabaudia and Littoria (renamed Latina after the war), the regime managed to project a solid sense of the renewed classicism brought by fascism. Even the cold and geometrical shapes of Rome's (Esposizione Universale: Roma) district, the regime's last and unfinished attempt at symbolic architecture on a massive scale, reached impressive results with examples of modernist Romanità such as the Palazzo della Civiltà Italiana. Those buildings are perhaps the only remaining traces of fascism's dream of a mythical fusion between Italy's prestigious past and the new challenges of the modern era.[9]

III. REVOLUTIONARY FASCISTS

Mention of the 'Tuscan diversity' of Malaparte's Fascism in the previous section introduces another important issue. Among fascist intellectuals and artists, there was a distinctive group who saw fascism as an anti-bourgeois movement aiming at a radical renovation of Italian society. Attached to this was praise of Italy's agricultural, small-town traditions, and of realism as its artistic medium. It was a populist vision that could be interpreted as leaning towards socialism (indeed they were often called 'left-wing fascists'), although their vision was, in a sense, non-Marxist. The term bourgeoisie was understood as an abstract concept encompassing a cultural phenomenon, a spiritual mentality that need not necessarily be identified with those who owned the means of production. The issue was not so much of classist exploitation and unjust social structures, but rather the restoration of order and dignity to the Italian nation after the apathy and decadence caused by pre-fascist bourgeois culture. As Elio Vittorini succinctly put it in an article for the paper of Florence's Fascist Federation, *Il Bargello*, in June 1935: 'anche nell'ultimo degli operai ci può essere un borghese da mettere alla porta' (even within the lowliest worker there might be a bourgeois to be shown the door).[10]

---

[9] On architecture and fascism see R. Etlin, *Modernism in Italian Architecture, 1890–1940* (Cambridge, MA: MIT Press, 1991). In Italian, see C. Cresti, *Architettura e fascismo* (Florence: Vallecchi, 1986) and G. Ciucci, *Gli architetti e il fascismo: architettura e città, 1922–1944* (Turin: Einaudi, 1989).

[10] E. Vittorini, 'Dell'andare verso il popolo', *Il Bargello*, 25 (June 1935), 2; then in R. Rodondi (ed.), *Elio Vittorini: letteratura, arte, società: articoli e interventi 1926–1937* (Turin: Einaudi, 1997), 873.

Fig. 6.1. Palazzo della Civiltà Italiana, EUR district, Rome (1940); by G. Guerrini, E. B. La Padula, and M. Romano

The most important reference point of this group of intellectuals and artists was *Il selvaggio*, a cultural paper initially published in the little Tuscan town of Colle Val d'Elsa. Edited by the gifted artist and satirical writer Mino Maccari, *Il selvaggio* glorified the virtues of provincial Italy. 'Real Italians' were seen— and represented in narrative—as a community of muscular, cynical individualists with strong roots in peasant culture. Such a portrait was supposed to provide a counter to the unappealing reality of bourgeois culture of pre-fascist times, and increasingly to act as a critique of the lack of radical social reforms on the part of the fascist regime. In Florence, a group of aspirant intellectuals took up similar ideals. Berto Ricci, a young mathematician and a passionate political thinker, saw fascism's corporate state as a potential form of non-authoritarian collectivism. In this perspective, the Ethiopian campaign was seen as a chance for the fascist state to give an example of its alternative vision of governance ad social organization.

Mussolini sometimes lent an ear to these radical militants. Some of them, Ricci himself and such others as Romano Bilenchi, were asked to express their ideas on Mussolini's paper, *Il popolo d'Italia*. However, it was a form of 'constructive criticism' which was never allowed to hold any position of power, either political or cultural. Some of these young intellectuals, disillusioned, joined the Italian Communist Party during the last years of the fascist regime, others soon after its fall.[11]

This form of disillusioned radical fascism was not limited to Tuscany and to literary circles. In the world of cinema, mention should be made of the Fascist militancy of Italy's most gifted filmmaker of the inter-war years, Alessandro Blasetti. In his early films, *Sole* (1929) and *Terra madre* (1931), Blasetti attempted a glorification of Italy's rural culture in tune with fascism's call for social solidarity. *Vecchia guardia* (1936) is a formally accomplished portrait of the rise of Fascism in a provincial town. However, despite his involvement with the regime's attempts to create a strong and state-related film industry—he was one of the founders and lecturers of the Centro Sperimentale di Cinematografia—Blasetti's enthusiasm became progressively more lukewarm and disillusioned. His last film under fascism, *La corona di ferro* (1941), delivered a pacifist message in stark contrast with the regime's wartime effort. Nazi Minister of Propaganda Joseph Goebbels was very critical of the film when he saw it at the Venice Film Festival and, according to Blasetti, he declared that any German director would have been shot for making such a film.[12]

---

[11] On revolutionary fascism see the (sympathetic) study by P. Buchignani, *Rivoluzionari in camicia nera* (Milan: Mondadori, 2006).

[12] On Blasetti see L. Verdone, *I film di Alessandro Blasetti* (Rome: Gremese, 1989).

IV. Anti-fascism, Censorship, and the Centralization of Culture

By the second half of the 1920s, the regime had not only established its grip over Italian society: all potential opposition among the intelligentsia had either been silenced or isolated. Among Italian communists, the scholarly voice of Antonio Gramsci was languishing in jail. His work was destined to be influential only once the fascist period was over. More privileged was the case of the great liberal Benedetto Croce. Thanks to constant police surveillance and no lack of eager informants who frequented Croce's house, Mussolini controlled his activities but preferred to allow him limited space for manoeuvre so that the regime could boast about the tolerance of fascism towards dissent. Even as late as 1940, when the newly appointed Minister of Popular Culture, Alessandro Pavolini, attempted to close down Croce's journal *La critica*, with the excuse of paper rationing, the *Duce* intervened in Croce's defence. There is a sense that Mussolini trod carefully whenever he was dealing with renowned figures who could have attracted the attention of the international press. A similar treatment was reserved for Giulio Einaudi's publishing house, founded in 1933. The influence and involvement of Giulio's father, the renowned Liberal economist Luigi Einaudi, was instrumental in convincing Mussolini to keep the young publishing house in business despite its clear anti-fascist drift. The arrest of Einaudi's most prominent editor, Leone Ginzburg, in 1934, followed the year after by a wave of arrests in Turin which hit other members of the publishing house (among them Cesare Pavese), was not enough to convince Mussolini to take resolute action. His correspondence with Luigi Einaudi shows that he was always prepared to show tolerance towards the activities of the Einaudi family (already in 1929 Luigi Einaudi's youngest son Roberto had been arrested while in possession of anti-fascist literature). They were calculated gestures of tolerance. In this respect, Renzo De Felice's comment on Mussolini's involvement in cultural matters seems appropriate: it was not the result of genuine open-mindedness or love of knowledge but rather instrumental to his political aims and, as such, it was deeply illiberal.[13]

Mussolini was inclined towards a system of censorship which would allow for individual exceptions and ad hoc resolutions of delicate cases. However, the creation of a totalitarian society required a progressive centralization of the culture industry. This coexistence of a strong personal imprint and the need for a powerful central organization resulted in a solution which sidelined potential centres of policymaking such as the National Fascist Party or Giuseppe Bottai's Ministry of National

---

[13] R. De Felice, *Mussolini il duce: gli anni del consenso 1929–1936* (Turin: Einaudi, 1974), 107. On Einaudi see G. Turi, *La casa Einaudi: libri uomini, idee oltre il fascismo* (Bologna: Il Mulino, 1990), and L. Mangoni, *Pensare i libri: la casa editrice Einaudi dagli anni trenta agli anni sessanta* (Turin: Bollati Boringhieri, 1999).

Education. Instead, Mussolini allowed his Press Office (Ufficio Stampa del Capo del Governo) to grow to ministerial size, particularly following the appointment of his son-in-law Galeazzo Ciano in the summer of 1933. The following year the Press Office grew into the Under-secretariat for Press and Propaganda (Sottosegretariato per la Stampa e Propaganda) and then became a fully fledged ministry which, as of June 1937, was called Ministero della Cultura Popolare.[14]

In the same years, the debate over fascist art and culture continued. Between 1926 and 1927, following a speech by Mussolini calling for the creation of a fascist art, Bottai's Critica fascista hosted a prolonged exchange of opinions on the issue. In the end no clear consensus was found on what exactly was 'fascist' about contemporary Italian art. Bottai concluded that 'it is impossible to pass judgement on the essence of fascist art', then called for an interventionist approach by the state as a patron, and offered the example of Mussolini as 'the only great artist of the regime'.[15] The appeal of the Decennale—that is, the celebration of ten years of fascism—focused minds again and questioned the success and shape of a supposed 'fascistization' of Italian culture. The Exhibition of the Fascist Revolution (Mostra della Rivoluzione Fascista) in 1932 became a grand exercise in self-representation. Its result, if not a clear definition of culture for the fascists, gave great impetus in the use of culture for displaying the achievements of Fascist Italy. One of its outputs was the film Camicia nera (1933) directed by Giuseppe Forzano, whose script had won a national competition organized as part of the Decennale events. The production and distribution of the film were heavily supported by the regime which coordinated its premiere on the same night in all major European capitals. Through its fusion of narrative and documentary, Camicia nera was supposed to show to both Italians and the world the giant steps made by fascism in the modernization and 'maturation' of Italian society. The film's lack of a cohesive style—a mix of narrative realism, modernist experimentation, and propaganda documentary—is perhaps symbolic of the variety of Italian culture in those years but it nonetheless represented a 'coming of age' of the regime.[16]

Within this perspective, it is possible to argue that the centralization of Italian culture would have proceeded in the mid-1930s with or without the parallel achievements of Hitler's government. At the same time, there is no doubt that the speed and intensity of the 'Nazification' of German culture added momentum and focus to fascism's cultural line. After the spring of 1933, the patronizing attitude with which the Duce had followed the rise of the Führer was replaced by a mixture of admiration and envy. The Nazis implemented their plans of centralization and Nazification of

---

[14] On the development of Mussolini's Press Office into the Ministry of Popular Culture see P. Cannistraro, La fabbrica del consenso: fascismo e mass-media (Bari: Laterza, 1975).

[15] Bottai's conclusion appeared in the 15 February 1927 issue of Critica fascista.

[16] On the Mostra della Rivoluzione Fascista see J. Schnapp, 'Epic Demonstrations: Fascist Modernity and the 1932 Exhibition of the Fascist Revolution', in R. Golsan (ed.), Fascism, Aesthetics and Culture (Hanover, NH: University Press of New England, 1992), 1–32.

German culture with speed and efficiency: Hitler had barely been in power for a few weeks when Joseph Goebbels's new Ministry for Popular Enlightenment and Propaganda (Reichsministerium für Volksaufklärung und Propaganda) began to impose itself on both Germany's government machine and culture industry. The creation of the Reich Chamber of Culture in September 1933 and other legislation passed in the following weeks gave Goebbels's ministry total control over newspapers and publishing houses. Italian Fascism was trailing behind on the cultural front. The appointment of Ciano and the expansion of Mussolini's Press Office were to a great extent a fascist reply to their German counterpart.

The *Duce* and Ciano were well briefed on the composition of Goebbels's Ministry for Popular Enlightenment and Propaganda. The Italian equivalent borrowed not only parts of its name (note that before calling itself Ministry of Popular Culture, it was briefly entitled the Ministry for the Press and Propaganda) but also its overall organization. The six Directorates of Ciano's ministry mirrored those of Goebbels's (which had seven, but the first one was simply a finance department): they covered propaganda, press, radio, film, theatre, and music. Similarly to Goebbels's ministry, Ciano also operated a policy of annexation of national cultural institutions such as the Istituto Luce (a film centre specializing in documentaries), Italy's Tourist Offices, the SIAE (Italy's copyright office for artistic production), and all national opera theatres. The Ministry also created a system that relied on the corruptibility of individuals and institutions. Increasing funds from the secret budgets of the Ministry of the Interior and of the Ministry of Popular Culture were used to ensure either the silence or more often the consensual collaboration of hundreds of journalists, authors, and members of Italy's intelligentsia. In this regard Galeazzo Ciano proved as active as his father-in-law. The costs of implementing such policies provide a measure of the escalating involvement of the Ministry: funds apportioned for financing either individuals or private institutions and enterprises rose from 1,541,517 lira in 1933/4 to 162,831,966 in 1941/2. More particularly, 'incentives' to journalists and authors rose from about 400,000 lira in 1933/4 to 3,613,000 in 1941/2. Publishing houses were equally eager to benefit from government patronage. An early supporter of the regime, Arnoldo Mondadori was always first in line, and his newly founded publishing house owed much to the support of Mussolini's government for its rise to dominance over the whole sector during the inter-war years.[17]

More was to come with the introduction of the anti-Semitic and other legislation in 1938 which will be discussed in the final section of this chapter. By the second half of the 1930s, it will suffice to say that the Ministry of Popular Culture had become a central player in the organization and promotion of a vast array of cultural events. Centralization also meant imposing a national frame to Italy's traditionally

---

[17] On Mondadori see E. Decleva, *Mondadori* (Turin: UTET, 1993). On the patronage of authors and publishing houses see Cannistraro, *La fabbrica del consenso*.

fragmented cultural panorama. Related to this was the attempt to control the local press through a welter of telegraphic directives (famously called 'veline', referring to the carbon copy paper on which they were distributed among staff). The directives varied from the openly censorial to the suggestion of themes and stylistic slants for front-page news.[18]

If a totalitarian production of culture was not achieved (the debate around what amounted to fascist culture went on), the fascists certainly succeeded in subjugating most cultural production either to the vested patronage or to the censorial stick of its Ministry of Popular Culture. A new figure had also emerged in the field of intellectual work, that of—to borrow Mario Isnenghi's expression—'intellettuale funzionario', that is, the intellectual working in state institutions, organizing and delivering the regime's cultural directives. Gherardo Casini is one such figure. A former squadrist from Pisa and a close collaborator of Bottai, in 1936 Casini rose to the position of head of the General Directorate for the Italian Press (Direzione Generale per il Servizio della Stampa Italiana) at the Ministry of Popular Culture (then still called Ministry of Press and Progaganda). Despite a number of departmental reshuffles, he held that position until 1942 and, as such, was a strategic figure in the delivery of government directives and press censorship. In the post-war years he became a publisher himself and his diplomatic and cordial approach as a ministerial *funzionario* was remembered by authors such as Alessandro Bonsanti, co-editor of *Solaria*, who publicly praised him in 1964. By then, the fact that Casini had been an efficient organizer of the regime's anti-Semitic campaign in the publishing industry was a near-forgotten memory.[19]

V. Popular Culture

Many Italians who were children and teenagers during the fascist years still remember that period with a hint of nostalgia and gratitude. In many working-class and peasant families, they were the first generation to enjoy a holiday on the beach or a train journey to the regional capital or even to Rome itself. But to what extent were these happy events the result of fascist policies and not part of the emancipation of the lower classes which, thanks to mass industrial production and socialist-led reformism, was sweeping through Europe and North America during the first

---

[18] The most recent collection of 'veline' can be found in N. Tranfaglia (ed.), *La Stampa del regime 1932–1943: le veline del Minculpop per orientare l'informazione* (Milan: Bompiani, 2005).

[19] M. Isnenghi, *Intellettuali militanti e intellettuali funzionari: appunti sulla cultura fascista* (Turin: Einaudi, 1979). Bonsanti's praise of Casini appeared in the national weekly *L'espresso* on 19 July 1964.

decades of the twentieth century? Already in pre-fascist Italy such developments were, if not in full swing, in motion. Universal male suffrage (for men over 30) was introduced in 1912 by Liberal Prime Minister Giovanni Giolitti, thus opening the door to mass political movements. At the same time, the expansion of the socialist movement was adding momentum to a number of pedagogical initiatives. 'People's' libraries and universities were already mushrooming in many northern and central Italian towns in the years preceding and following the First World War. The initial fascist manifesto of 1919 had nothing to say on these cultural issues but, once established in their dictatorial power, the fascists quickly moved to adopt and exploit this process of emancipation. In November 1925, the director of Milan's Fascist Institute of Culture was put in charge of the National Federation of People's Libraries, and the following year the National Federation of People's Universities was disbanded and partially absorbed by local fascist institutions. Education was no longer supposed to be a step towards political awareness and classist activism. The lower classes had to learn to be law-abiding citizens and active fascists. Ideological correctness inside the classrooms of primary schools was also ensured through the introduction in 1928 of a single prescribed text for all schools.[20]

The regime's own original contribution to this process of acculturization lay in its nationalist and militarist approach. The creation of the Opera Nazionale Balilla (ONB) in April 1926 was supposed to provide all children and teenagers from the age of 8 (later 6) to 18 with the moral and physical indoctrination necessary for Italians to reclaim their rightful place as a world power. Baden-Powell's Scout Movement certainly provided much of the inspiration but the ONB's belligerent, paramilitary fame was directly taken from fascism's squads. 'Libro e moschetto fascista perfetto' (Book and musket make a perfect fascist) was a much repeated motto, and Italian children were often sent to march up and down playgrounds and city high streets, clad in their black shirts and clutching old muskets (replaced by wooden replicas for the youngest). Such activities were a key part of Mussolini's dream of renewing the ethos and stamina of all Italians. It would be simplistic to say that Italy's poor showing on the battlegrounds of the Second World War is the proof of the total failure of fascism's social engineering projects. However, once the regime collapsed, the speed with which Italians happily did without the paraphernalia of fascist militancy is a clear indication that its recipe of militarist nationalism did not penetrate deeply into the Italian soul.

The indoctrination of the younger generations was the area in which fascism found itself in substantial competition with the Vatican. Mussolini wavered between pressure from radical fascists lobbying for a ban on all Catholic youth organizations and the need to respect the Lateran Pacts of 1929 which allowed the Vatican

---

[20] On fascism and education see M. Galfré, *Il regime degli editori: libri, scuola, fascismo* (Bologna: Il Mulino, 2005).

ample space for manoeuvre. The activism of Azione Cattolica Italiana represented a Catholic competitor to the ONB, and young Italians often found themselves split between the preaching of fascist belligerence and Catholic pacifism (or 'pietismo' as it was accusingly called).

As in other areas of friction between fascist totalitarianism and the reality of Italy's cultural diversity, contradictions remained untackled and unresolved. A last example relates to the regime's linguistic policies launched by Mussolini in the summer of 1932. The nation's literary output in dialect was declared unworthy of Fascist Italy and therefore deserved to be banned from public life. It was an absurd attempt in a country whose dialects were the prime medium of communication and, in many cases, of cultural expression. To provide more articulated rules regarding the censorship of dialect literature, Press Office directives distinguished between periodicals and book publications. For the former, all use of dialect was banned, whereas books were allowed to be published provided they contained the work of 'antichi autori' ('old authors'). Italian intellectuals who publicly supported this viewpoint were personally thanked by Mussolini and the then head of the Press Office, Gaetano Polverelli. This happened, for example, when the Tuscan writer and future member of the Reale Accademia d'Italia, Ardengo Soffici, wrote an article attacking dialects in the *Gazzetta del popolo* of 19 January 1933. A sign that this policy was not only controversial but was also a source of embarrassment is implicit in the many exchanges between Polverelli and Italy's prefects. On 18 May 1933 Polverelli ordered the prefect of Bergamo to warn the editor of *L'eco di Bergamo* not to publish any more writings on dialect. Significantly, however, Polverelli required that the warning should be given 'verbalmente e riservatamente' (verbally and confidentially). Such caution was a sign that the battle was hopeless and the policy was constantly ignored. Poems in dialect continued to be published in periodicals and books, and one of the most scholarly defenders of dialects, Filippo Fichera, was successful in defeating the ban in both fields: his periodical *Convivio letterario* continued to publish dialect poetry through the war years; and his propaganda anthology, *Il Duce e il fascismo nei canti dialettali*, despite a first ban in 1934, was later republished with a preface by Marinetti. Equally unsuccessful and a source of derision were the later attempts to impose a 'bonifica linguistica' (linguistic reclamation) comprising the use of 'Voi' in lieu of the polite form and allegedly effeminate 'Lei', and the purge of all foreign expressions. It was not the first time during the regime that a campaign was launched with much publicity and draconian aims, after which the practicalities involved and the actual complexity of the situation on the ground diluted the process and allowed notable pockets of nonconformity to continue to exist.[21]

---

[21] On fascism's linguistic policies see G. Klein, *La politica linguistica del fascismo* (Bologna: Il Mulino, 1986).

VI. ANTI-SEMITISM AND THE FINAL YEARS

The rationale and implementation of the anti-Semitic measures first introduced in the autumn of 1938 are discussed in other chapters of this Handbook. However, within the perspective of this brief outline of Italian culture, they must be mentioned as an important development in Mussolini's attempt to shape the Italian nation. Official anti-Semitism was not the only policy with which Italians suddenly had to conform in 1938. Other, more risible but equally symbolic measures were introduced around the same time such as the already mentioned *bonifica linguistica*, and the introduction of the goosestep for the Italian army in February 1938, just in time for Hitler's official visit to Italy the following May. Its denomination as 'passo romano' (Roman step) awkwardly tried to hide its Nazi derivation. When Mussolini dwelled on these initiatives in his speech to the representatives of the National Fascist Party in October 1938 he addressed them with one of his crude formulae: 'Alla fine dell'anno XVI ho individuato un nemico, un nemico del nostro regime. Questo nemico ha nome "borghesia"' (At the end of year XVI [of the Fascist era], I have identified an enemy, an enemy of our regime. This enemy is called 'bourgeoisie').[22] Within this picture of full-scale 'reformation' of the Italian nation, the Jewish question added a racial element which, given the relatively small dimensions of the Italian Jewish community, promised to be a manageable exercise in the 'purification' of Italian blood. It was the most barbarous among a number of measures which desperately tried to redress the failure of the regime radically to change and shape the ethos of Italian society.

How did the Italian intelligentsia react to this violent act of state racism? On the whole, it passively complied with it. It is difficult not to reach such a conclusion when facing the documented evidence of a widespread lack of condemnation or even public discussion of these policies. In the world of publishing, for example, the regime demanded an act of 'self-reclamation' from the industry. Publishers were supposed to revise their catalogues and exclude all books written, edited, or even translated by a Jew. The process was cumbersome and unevenly implemented, but certainly not opposed, apart from some rare and tolerated exceptions. One concerned the publisher Laterza and, again, Croce. In December 1939, Laterza forwarded to Mussolini a letter in which Croce protested against the madness of expecting a nation to wipe out the presence and influence of Jewish intellectuals and scholars. The letter concluded with the sarcastic comment that if things carried on in that vein one day the government would have had to ban its own racial journal, *La difesa della razza*, because it wrote about the Jews! A couple of weeks later Laterza was summoned to the Ministry of Popular Culture and informed that the seizure of a number of Laterza books written or translated by Jews had been withdrawn. It was

---

[22] Speech delivered at the National Council of the PNF on 25 October 1938, collected in B. Mussolini, *Opera omnia*, vol. xxix (Florence: La Fenice, 1960), 186.

a very discreet and rare exception to the rule. By April 1942, the Ministry of Popular Culture (once more, it must be said, in response to a similar initiative by their Nazi counterpart) published a list of 912 authors who had been banned as 'unwelcome' in Italy. Most were Jews. The shameless acceptance by Italy's intelligentsia of a process which implied the marginalization and professional murder of thousands of teachers, scholars, journalists, and authors is indicative of the degree to which the regime had managed to bend Italian society to its whims and policies, however inhumane.[23]

If, according to De Felice, the years following Italy's invasion of Ethiopia are those that mark the highest tide of popular support for fascism, there is a sense that the introduction of anti-Semitic legislation, however unopposed, inverted the trend and provoked an increasing distance between the regime and its subjects. What became patently clear to Mussolini as much as to such cultural promoters as Bottai (then Minister of National Education) was that the younger generations seemed more and more disillusioned about fascism's promise of a radically new society. Bottai's diary shows that, in the second half of 1940 and throughout 1941, when the Nazi–Fascist Axis seemed destined to rule over continental Europe, the leaders of the regime were preoccupied with the need to counter Nazi Germany's influence in southern Europe. This is the time when Mondadori received large ministerial funds for the diffusion of his illustrated magazine *Tempo*: distributed throughout occupied Europe in eight different languages, it was supposed to provide a worthy competitor to the German magazines *Signal* and *Adler*. However, as Bottai lamented, there seemed to be a lack of enthusiasm and collaborative spirit among young intellectuals. His creation of the cultural journal *Primato*, in 1940, presented by sympathetic historians as a sign of Bottai's open-minded nature, was also part of the regime's last attempt at rallying the support of a disillusioned generation. According to the diaries of another influential *gerarca*, Carlo Ravasio (then Deputy Secretary of the National Fascist Party with the specific mandate to police the morality of the Party), by 1942 Mussolini was enraged at the lack of support for the regime as revealed even in publications sponsored by official youth associations such as the Fascist University Groups (Gruppi Universitari Fascisti).[24]

A symbolic episode was the arrest on 24 December 1942 of young intellectual Mario Alicata, found to be a member of the underground Italian Communist Party. As part of the group of film enthusiasts circling around Vittorio Mussolini's journal *Cinema* (Mussolini's eldest son played an important role in the promotion of cinema in Fascist Italy), as one of the scriptwriters involved in the making of Luchino Visconti's first film, *Ossessione* (1943), and as an influential editor for the Einaudi

---

[23] On anti-Semitism and the publishing industry see the study by G. Fabre, *L'elenco: censura fascista, editoria e autori ebrei* (Turin: Silvio Zamorani Editore, 1998). See also Bonsaver, *Censorship and Literature in Fascist Italy*, chs. 2.3 and 3.1.

[24] Carlo Ravasio's diary of 1942 has been published in G. B. Guerri, *Rapporti al Duce* (Milan: Bompiani, 1978), 307–406.

publishing house (he was in charge of relations with the Ministry of Popular Culture), Alicata was an example of a gifted young intellectual who had turned his back on fascism. His aspirations and ideals were finding a more inspiring home within the communist movement, however dangerous that proved to be. Others followed his path, such as authors Romano Bilenchi and Elio Vittorini, or one of Italy's most gifted painters at the time, Renato Guttuso. Still others stopped collaborating with the regime, such as modernist architect Giuseppe Pagano, who was later to die in a Nazi concentration camp. By 1943, the catastrophic developments in the war had made this situation irreversible. In June 1943, the then Minister of Popular Culture, Gaetano Polverelli, reported to the *Duce* the total lack of support for the regime among intellectuals. By then, opportunism was playing a big part in the mind of many individuals. However, it was equally and unequivocally clear that Mussolini's project of an anthropological revolution was lying in tatters.[25]

BIBLIOGRAPHY

BELARDELLI, G., *Il Ventennio degli intellettuali: cultura, politica, ideologia nell'Italia fascista* (Rome: Laterza, 2005).

BEN-GHIAT, R., *Fascist Modernities: Italy, 1922–1945* (Berkeley and Los Angeles: University of California Press, 2001).

BONSAVER, G., *Censorship and Literature in Fascist Italy* (Toronto: Toronto University Press, 2007).

BOSWORTH, R., *Mussolini's Italy: Life under the Dictatorship* (London: Allen Lane, 2005).

CANNISTRARO, P. V., *La fabbrica del consenso: fascismo e mass-media* (Bari: Laterza, 1975).

GENTILE, E., *The Sacralization of Politics in Fascist Italy* (Cambridge, MA: Harvard University Press, 1996).

GOLSAN, R. (ed.), *Fascism, Aesthetics and Culture* (Hanover, NH: University Press of New England, 1992).

GREGOR, A. J., *Mussolini's Intellectuals: Fascist Social and Political Thought* (Princeton: Princeton University Press, 2005).

STONE, M. S., *The Patron State: Culture and Politics in Fascist Italy* (Princeton: Princeton University Press, 1998).

TURI, G., *Lo Stato educatore: politica e intellettuali nell'Italia fascista* (Rome: Laterza, 2002).

[25] On Alicata, Visconti, and their intellectual milieu see R. Ben-Ghiat, *Fascist Modernities: Italy, 1922–1945* (Berkeley and Los Angeles: University of California Press, 2001), 194–201. Polverelli's report of June 1943 about the lack of support among intellectuals is quoted in E. De Felice, *Mussolini l'alleato*, ii: *Crisi e agonia del regime* (Turin: Einaudi, 1990), 863.

CHAPTER 7

THE PEASANT EXPERIENCE UNDER ITALIAN FASCISM

ROGER ABSALOM

I. GENERAL INTRODUCTION

THE fascist regime was the first system of government in modern Italy to attempt to address the 'peasant question' in a systematic fashion. It not only brought to bear upon it the administrative machinery of the state but also, through its policies and propaganda, attempted to convert the peasantry from a perennial threat to social stability into a positive bulwark of the political system the fascist regime was seeking to consolidate.

A major obstacle to the success of this design was an abiding strength of many groups among the Italian peasantry, a strength that came historically from afar. This was the capacity they had developed at the deepest level of the culture for individual and collective strategies that enabled them to survive with relative success the inroads the state sought to make upon their autonomy, whether through benefits intended to recruit their support, or through compression of their ability to resist and evade its demands. The solidarities that underpinned such strategies varied according to the character of peasant settlement, land tenure, and ingrained local culture. The nature of territory and the long-standing organization of human settlement related to it varied widely, ranging from alpine and Apennine forest and seasonal pasture to artificial water meadows and malarial lowlands, and from scattered single-family dwellings to extensive multi-family farms to dormitory villages housing large numbers of virtually landless day-wage labourers. Each form of land tenure and the associated social structure generated a specific mind- and value-set in those grappling from within it to wrest a living from the land: while some tended more or less indirectly to develop entrepreneurial capacities, others depressed any such tendency, while large-scale intensive capitalistic agriculture tended to generate a militant solidarity particularly open to visceral radicalization.

In most parts of Italy the peasantry had for centuries been perceived both as the foundation of economic life and the main creator of surplus value, and as a dormant volcano of potential social disorder. After unification in 1860, it became, in the perceptions of the elite political class, both the reserve army of clerical (papal-Bourbon royalist) reaction, and—paradoxically—also the hope of radical revolutionaries. As far as the power structure was concerned it had above all to be kept under control. For the first half-century of the new nation's life the relationship between the peasantry and the state was largely repressive and exploitative: the peasants knew 'Italy' only through resented contact with the recruiting sergeant and the tax collector.

The peasantry was of course not always accepting of this situation: sporadic upheavals persisted throughout the period. Open 'banditry' (followed by savage repression verging on planned massacre) was endemic in the southern regions in the first decade after unification. In Emilia-Romagna there was fierce rioting against the imposition of the grist tax. In Sicily during the last decade of the century there was the mass campaign of protests and occupations of land by Sicilian peasants known as the Fasci Siciliani. The founder of revolutionary anarchism, Michael Bakunin, led a failed rebellion in Bologna in 1874 and his Italian followers were the first to have a significant impact on peasant political awareness in the 1880s. Marxist socialists also became influential in the 1890s, and in 1892–3 had some part in organizing the Fasci Siciliani. After these were fiercely repressed by Francesco Crispi's nominally left government, dissidents from the now reformist Socialist Party in the first years of the twentieth century led a powerful Sorelian syndicalist movement that fomented general strikes of agricultural labourers in Lombardy and Emilia Romagna. In Puglia, Calabria, Sicily, and Sardinia, retributive violence at the hands of locally recruited 'enforcers' (variously named and organized but universally brutal gangs of *mazzieri*, *banditi*, *mafiosi*, etc.) was normally directed at anyone who challenged the economic and political control of the landowning elites.

Unrest and violence in the countryside were thus endemic, but the particularities of Italy's countless distinctive patterns of peasant life militated against any overarching or hegemonic movement of protest and rebellion. Indeed, a convergence of interests and perceptions was unlikely between peasants in Sicily, whose supreme ambition was to escape from the feudal residues of the *latifundia*, on the one hand,

and, on the other, the mass rural proletariat of the northern intensively farmed plains resorting to general strikes against capitalist landowners. Naked military or police force had also been a familiar component of the peasant experience in many parts of Italy since the unification of the country, whether in the decade-long campaign to control the 'banditry' of the islands and the southern regions in the 1860s, the repression of the millenarian followers of Davide Lazzaretti in Tuscany, or the ruthless breaking of day labourers' strikes in the northern plains.

Within all the subsystems, however, forms of adaptive clientelism throve, ranging from pre-political subordination to notables, the clergy, and to mafia-type social organizations, and from the quasi-feudal relationship between landowners and their dependants, to more explicitly quasi-political arrangements involving the national and local state and the church, and their institutional expressions at a local level. All these arrangements reflected the reality of the multiplicity of Italies, the modes of exploitation within them, and the ways in which those integrated into their complex networks were able to survive economic pressure and passively resist the inroads of the state.

The fascist attempt to control and direct the centrifugal forces and overcome the inertia present in this mass of historically formed contradictions was itself fraught with mutually conflicting intentions and impulses. A certain haphazard managerial pragmatism was often overlaid by deeply felt but incoherent ideological imperatives. The peripheral and the central were frequently out of sync. Shaky hypotheses were promoted to self-evident truths, and then as quickly relegated to a limbo of unfulfillable commitments. Though the capillary apparatus of the state, largely inherited by the Fascist regime from its predecessor, was generally effective at the level of repression of public dissent or disorder, it was far less pervasive and incisive in dealing with the infinity of webs of clientelism that formed the deep connective tissue of Italian society. The one relatively thought-through initiative, the plan to harness large-scale land reclamation to a wider vision of enlightened resettlement of landless peasants on land they could call their own, was shipwrecked as soon as it conflicted with the vested interests of the great estates of the south, leaving only a hollow rhetorical legacy to the credit of the regime. The failure was emblematic of the outcomes of fascist agricultural policies, particularly those intended to elevate the condition of the peasantry.

II. Framework of Analysis

A review of past and current writing on the subject of Italian peasants in the fascist period (1922–45) reveals a variety of interpretative approaches, none of which accounts for the phenomena entirely satisfactorily, although each has important insights to contribute to a global interpretation. The present article draws in some measure on all of these and attempts to establish a perspective from below as well as from above.

In dealing with the 'peasant question' in Italy, a starting point may usefully be sought in the field of ethnography and cultural anthropology. Peasants exist in time and place in very specific ways: they are deeply aware of their history in the sense that each individual and group is located at the centre of a web of custom and tradition impregnated with powerful symbolisms and largely impervious to the discourse of the 'nation'; equally, they are imbued with a sense of place because the particular territory, in all its complexities, that permits their material survival is ever present to them. For peasants 'the landscape ... is not an object of aesthetic contemplation, but territory socially appropriated, namely, a mosaic of individually owned lots, a clean and ordered landscape to which outsiders should not have access'.[1]

Another critical dimension of analysis of the peasant question is found in the sociology of the family as applied to peasant households. In Italy there was a considerable historical and territorial variation in their structure, closely related to the character of the prevailing land tenure arrangements. While some encouraged the aggregation of adult kinsfolk in one household, others actively discouraged such extended kin units.[2] A factor in the widely varying responses to external political and economic pressures that characterized the Italian peasant population during the fascist period was undoubtedly habituation to household pluriactivity and particularly the increased capacity for economic mobilization of its female members.[3]

Some aspects of political science can also assist the analysis. Italian peasants were by no means a *tabula rasa* on which the messages of ruling elites could simply be imprinted. They had their own clear notions of politics and ideology, although these seldom became part of the 'public transcript' of their relations with the state and its institutions. Their 'hidden transcript' comprised a profound moral critique of the systems of domination to which they were subjected, usually comprising an alternative vision of 'the world turned upside down' that might be located in either the past or the future. In the case of Italy only novelists and oral historians have

---

[1] Cf. J. Stacul, *The Bounded Field: Localism and Local Identity in an Italian Alpine Valley* (New York: Berghahn Books, 2003), 188; cf. also idem, 'Natural Time, Political Time', *Journal of the Royal Anthropological Society*, 11/4 (2005), 819–36.

[2] Cf. D. I. Kertzer, 'European Peasant Household Structure: Some Implications from a 19th Century Italian Community', *Journal of Family History*, 2/4 (1977), 333–49.

[3] Cf. A. Cento Bull, 'Proto-industrialization, Small-Scale Capital Accumulation and Diffused Entrepreneurship: The Case of the Brianza in Lombardy (1860–1950)', *Social History*, 14/2 (1989), 177–200; cf. also F. Ramella, *Terra e telai: sistemi di parentela e manifattura nel biellese dell'Ottocento* (Turin: Einaudi, 1984).

partially represented manifestations of this transcript. As Ignazio Silone's peasants put it in his novel *Fontamara*:

> 'In capo a tutti c'è Dio, padrone del cielo.
> Questo ognuno lo sa.
> Poi viene il principe Torlonia, padrone della terra.
> Poi vengono le guardie del principe.
> Poi vengono i cani delle guardie del principe.
> Poi nulla.
> Poi, ancora nulla.
> Poi, ancora nulla.
> Poi vengono i cafoni.
> E si può dire che è finito'.
> 'Ma le autorità dove le metti?' chiese il forestiero.
> 'Le autorità ... si dividono tra il terzo e il quarto posto.
>   Secondo la paga. Il quarto posto (quello dei cani) è
>   immenso. Questo ognuno lo sa'[4]

('Over everybody there is God, lord of heaven. Everyone knows that. Then comes Prince Torlonia, lord of the earth. Then come the prince's guards. Then come the dogs of the prince's guards. Then nothing. Then more nothing, Then still more nothing. Then come the peasants. And that seems to be the lot.'

'But where do you place the authorities?' asked the stranger. 'The authorities are divided between the third and the fourth place. Depending on their wages. The fourth place (the dogs' place) is huge. Everyone knows that'.)

Finally, the 'dismal science' must also have its say. As James Scott points out, the critical problem of the peasant household is subsistence. The fear of food short-ages explains many otherwise puzzling technical, social, and moral arrangements in peasant society, such as resistance to innovation, the desire to own land even at some cost in terms of income, relationships with other people, and with in-stitutions, including the state. Once the centrality of the subsistence problem is recognized, its effects on notions of economic and political justice can also be seen.[5]

Unfortunately little of the literature regarding the condition of the peasants under fascism directly addresses this issue, being conceived within the narrower framework of economic analysis of policies central to the regime's approach to agriculture.[6] The merit of these works is primarily that they introduce a useful array of statistics drawn from the regular censuses taken by the Italian national

---

[4] I, Silone, *Fontamara* (Milan: Mondadori, 1988; 1st edn. 1933); cf. also S. Colarizi, *L'opinione degli italiani sotto il regime 1929–1943* (Bari: Laterza, 1991); J. C. Scott, *Domination and the Arts of Resistance: Hidden Transcripts* (New Haven: Yale University Press, 1990).

[5] Cf. J. C. Scott, *The Moral Economy of the Peasant: Rebellion and Subsistence in Southeast Asia* (New Haven: Yale University Press, 1976).

[6] Cf. G. Giorgetti, *Contadini e proprietari nell'Italia moderna: rapporti di produzione e contratti agrari dal secolo XVI a oggi* (Turin: Einaudi, 1974); E. Fano, 'Problemi e vicende dell'agricoltura italiana tra le due guerre', *Il mulino*, 29–30 (1975), 468–96. The most readable account remains C. T. Schmidt, *The Corporate State in Action: Italy under Fascism* (London: Victor Gollancz, 1939).

statistical office throughout the years of the regime. With few exceptions they have a more or less Marxian slant and take a denunciatory approach, either dwelling on the compression of living standards that resulted from the regime's efforts to end Italy's 'servitude to foreign wheat' and the revaluation of the currency, or upon the 'scissors effect' whereby the development of heavy industry was a function of the distortions inflicted upon agriculture. Almost no account is, however, taken in this discourse of the importance of peasant self-provisioning and the pervasiveness of its effects in shaping peasant responses to crisis and emergency situations.

It is, nevertheless, impossible, when dealing with the behaviours and attitudes of peasants, to disjoin the material economy from its 'moral' counterpart. The analytical tools just mentioned can only tangentially address the full existential experience of peasants under fascism, and elide the symbolic power of all the relations within it that form the basis for a culture of survival against all odds. This culture came from afar, and it is arguable that it was not extinguished in its essence even by the massive social and economic transformations that occurred in Italy following the Second World War. Inevitably, however, the section of this chapter that attempts to deal with this aspect will be at least as speculative as it is empirical. Before embarking on this risky venture it will be useful to summarize the situation as the fascists found it when they came to power in 1922, and to describe the policies that they then pursued in relation to the agricultural sector of the economy.

III. Starting Point, 1921–1925

The starting point for any historical account focusing on peasants is bound to be arbitrary, but for the purposes of the present analysis the year 1921 appears to be the most logical choice. Elections held with proportional representation in that year as in 1919 had confirmed the destabilization of the political and economic situation in the countryside, with the two largest parties, the Partito Socialista Italiano (PSI) and the Partito Populare Italiano (PPI), able to mobilize an unprecedentedly large number of the rural population in vehement and sometimes violent support of their demands for a radically new deal for those who worked the land. Many, perhaps most, peasant conscripts who had borne the brunt of the fighting in the Great War wanted above all the fulfilment of the promises made to them during the conflict that after victory their age-old dream of owning the land they worked would come true.

In terms of enhanced incomes and ownership of land large numbers of peasant households derived advantage from the conditions prevailing during and immediately after the war. Multiple factors had favoured this: farm subsidies were lavish during the war, while price inflation of agricultural products combined with the wartime freeze on rents increased peasant purchasing power and willingness to incur debt. This coincided with landowners' readiness to sell land at devalued prices after becoming fearful of social disorder and alarmed by the Visocchi reforms of 1919 that appeared to offer state support for the forcible occupation of uncultivated land.

The censuses 1911–21 show a 14 per cent overall rise in total numbers of people active in agriculture, most of which was accounted for by the almost doubling of the numbers of small peasant proprietors, while there was a 10 per cent fall in the number of day-wage labourers, and a much larger decline in the number of leased and tenanted farms (32 per cent fewer). There was no significant change in the number of sharecroppers. During the same period there appears to have been a reduction in the number of absentee landlords.

As soon as the post-war economic boom subsided, however, landowner attitudes, ingrained by centuries of social and economic supremacy, once more came to the fore as they sought to recover their previous position. Demands to the authorities for share, lease, and hire contracts to be restored to their traditional patterns of super-exploitation mounted into a strident campaign. Moreover, Italian landowners had been able to derive considerable profits from low-waged, or unwaged, work by peasants as part of their contracts, without needing to invest capital in improvement of poor land. They had benefited from the deference and insecurity of the peasants and the high level of competition between them for available work. They were also able to exploit their access without payment to peasant supplementary stocks such as eggs and vegetables. Landowner pressure in these respects was less evident during the post-war boom when increased demand for produce and inflation seemed in part to compensate them for the considerable concessions they had made to the peasants in the immediate post-war years, but when the situation changed and their incomes were in danger of being reduced, they demanded restoration also of these quasi-seigneurial rights.

Landowners responded to the new bargaining power of organized labour in the countryside by attacking polemically the 'red' organizations they accused of pursuing the violent overthrow of farm contracts, and the 'white' organizations accused of wishing to convert sharecroppers into tenant farmers, thus allowing them to pay their rents in money devalued by inflation. They attacked the governments of the day that they held responsible for the extension of existing contracts without defending landowner interests. When resort to legal repression was denied them in 1919–21, they rapidly turned to those who could provide it outside the law: the nascent *fasci* in the northern regions. In areas where the peasants had been most militant, growing numbers of landowners switched from the General Confederation of Agriculturalists to support for the fascist counterpart organization.

Fascist *squadre* became the mailed fist of the landowners to violently put down the organized landless peasants, breaking up their *leghe* (unions), removing their leaders by assassination or intimidation, and destroying their premises. On the other hand the *squadre* also adopted the radical rhetoric of Mussolini's project of a 'democracy on the land'. Mussolini's statement was easily susceptible of contradictory interpretations. In fact the radicalism of the early rural fascists was quickly overridden after 1925 when Mussolini in effect reached agreement with the large northern landowners to favour their interests and they then abandoned the radical *squadristi* who had gravitated into the fascists' syndical unions.

The success of the landowners' offensive reflected the growing weakening of peasant militancy due to the financial pressures of post-war economic reconversion, the isolation of the landless labourers whose social demands clashed with the aspirations of the new smallholders, and the lack of a guiding political focus capable of bringing together the differing strands of peasant mobilization into the pursuit of common goals. Within a few months, under the impact of brutal assault and mayhem by the fascist squads, accompanied by several thousand fatal casualties, the peasant movement fell apart.

Meanwhile the early Fascist governments sought politically to restore the power of the landowners. One of their first measures was to rescind the Visocchi reforms and expel the peasants who had occupied and improved the areas of uncultivated land they had taken over on some great estates in the south and in Tuscany. These were returned to their owners without compensation for the improvements made by the committed toil of the occupiers. Everywhere landowners took the opportunity to restore their supremacy in the imposition of terms of tenancy, even going back to rack rents in grain in some areas. At a local level, through the action of their countervailing agricultural syndicates, created ostensibly to defend the interest of the peasants but usually led or otherwise directed by leading local landowning notables, the fascists pursued a policy of 'divide and rule', turning the full force of their rhetorical powers to give the impression that the regime was respectful of the peasantry and ever mindful of its interests, but only within a framework of class collaboration and symbolic incorporation into the 'nation'.

The collapse of their organized trade union movements, both 'red' and 'white', left the peasants defenceless against the enforcement of exploitative contracts of hire or tenancy negotiated on their behalf by the fascist unions, and—in some areas—reversion to payment in kind despite even the fascist syndicate's official stipulation that wages should be in money.

The state's greatest contribution to the process of rolling back the tide of peasant militancy and bargaining power was, however, through economic policy. The violent political attack was quickly compounded by tariff protection for wheat, enshrined in the regime's propaganda, with typically militaristic overtones, as the 'Battle for Grain'. The 'battle' was launched with great fanfare in the summer of 1925. It was envisaged as an all-out effort to expand domestic wheat production in order to end 'the servitude of foreign wheat', but behind this public aim lurked a series of other agendas. Presented as a concrete display of the regime's commitment to rural society, its immediate motivation was to rectify the alarming growth of deficits in the balance of payments that stemmed from the need, despite the fact that agriculture in Italy occupied almost half the active population and still accounted for over a quarter of GDP, to import large quantities of breadstuffs. It was also intended thereby to reduce the rate of devaluation of the Italian currency.[7]

The economically logical step of a devaluation of the lira being, for Mussolini, politically unthinkable, the second economic nail in the coffin of a vision of Italian agriculture based on an independent smallholding peasantry was driven in by the drastic upwards revaluation of the currency to ninety lira per pound sterling, announced with the usual sabre-rattling bombast as the capture of 'Hill 90'. This measure effectively priced Italian small producers out of export markets in which the new peasant proprietors had tended to specialize: market-garden produce, grapes, olives, fruit, and flowers, where family farms could conceal real labour costs and achieve higher productivity than traditional day-labourer-dependent small and medium agricultural capitalists. Those reliant on such specialized production were now forced into fiercely competitive struggle to compensate by entering local niche markets. The wider structural effects of these two policies are discussed at greater length below.

Particularly hard hit by these measures were the mass of day-wage agricultural labourers whose money incomes were reduced by wage cuts and harsher terms of employment now imposed by the landowners, and by growing joblessness in their category. The increase in the price of basic foodstuffs was particularly oner-ous since they had little recourse to the self-provisioning activities normally open to sharecroppers, tenants, and smallholders, who could deploy additional family labour power to food production for domestic use. The general organizational backwardness of Italian agriculture had previously shielded the landless to some extent and this effect was not entirely eliminated, but overall the changes brought about as a result of the policies of the regime subverted the structures of rural society and its way of life. By the end of the 1920s the new small family-owned farms unable to produce large quantities of wheat were being prevented from developing their most promising sectors and, when the general economic crisis eased, they were hindered by the regime's policies favouring forced concentration. The explosive growth of new small farms taken on by temporarily enriched peasants after the Great War was curtailed and then reversed.[8]

---

[7] Cf. Giorgetti, *Contadini e proprietari*, 453–9.

[8] Cf. A. Cadeddu, S. Lepre, and F. Socrate, 'Ristagno e svluppo nel settore agricolo italiano (1918–1939)', *Quaderni storici*, 10/2–3 (1975), 497–518; also S. Salvatici, 'Campagne in crisi: l'Italia rurale negli anni del regime fascista (1927–1935)', *Annali dell'Istituto Alcide Cervi*, 17–18 (1995–6).

IV. Fascist Policies that Affected Agriculture and the Rural Population

When the Fascists came to power more than half the Italian population lived in settlements of fewer than 10,000 inhabitants, and after fifteen years of the regime 47.4 per cent of the Italian population still worked on the land, making Italy comparable more to Hungary than to Germany or Belgium, let alone Great Britain. Agriculture nevertheless accounted for only a quarter of Italy's gross domestic product. Seventenths of the cultivable land belonged to non-farming owners but the average size of farms was only 2.26 hectares and a large number were less than half a hectare in size: 9.5 million people were living on plots of land unable to support them. At the outset there were also some four million wage-earning landless agricultural labourers, a minority permanently contracted to employers, but most hired by the day. The 1936 census recorded their numbers as having fallen to two and a half million, but only by defining as independent smallholders a huge number of people who had no more than a kitchen garden, if that, and who still had to offer their labour to others in order to survive. In the same year the average calorie intake of farm workers was shown to have declined significantly under the regime.[9]

For any government the pattern of Italy's farming would have thus been an obstacle to the forcible economic and social 'modernization' of a country so unevenly developed. The landowning classes were deeply divided in their aims and outlooks and lacked any organic links with the captains of industry. Those in the regions where intensive farming of cash crops was dependent on a low-waged mass labour force and a degree of mechanization differed radically from those in regions where the prevalent mode of agricultural production was structured around specific socioeconomic arrangements such as marginally viable family-run farms, rent-paying tenancies, and sharecropping, or extensive low-yield farming dependent on daywage hired labour capable of partial self-provisioning from tiny plots of land. Any modernizing government would thus have had to deal with the dead weight of a farm sector in the less developed areas of the country (substantially the south and the islands) which existed in an economic time warp inextricably linked to quasi-feudal forms of social control, and structurally incapable of viability in a free domestic market.

Six months after Mussolini had seized power in January 1925 and inaugurated his 'totalitarian state', the first major fascist policy initiative in the field of agricultural economics was launched, primarily to meet the rapidly deteriorating state of the balance of payments: by 1925 more than half the national deficit in the balance of payments was due to grain imports. Landowners and millers were demanding a tariff barrier to protect domestic production. Mussolini proclaimed that a 'Battle

---

[9] Cf. C. F. Helstosky, *Garlic and Oil: Food and Politics in Italy* (New York: Berg, 2006).

for Grain' must now be waged to 'end the servitude of foreign bread', he was merely investing a response to the general economic situation with a strongly 'fascist' overtone.

In quantitative terms over the next decade the 'battle' was crowned with success: while average domestic production of breadstuffs in 1924–8 had been 73 per cent of requirements, by 1938 it was 99 per cent, increasing from 5.0 million to 7.3 million tons. But the combined effect of import tariff barriers and the drastic revaluation of the currency in 1926 rapidly damaged and distorted other forms of agricultural production. Animal husbandry was hit especially hard (reducing available manure and forcing greater use of high-priced industrial fertilizer) but so also were previously thriving exports of niche products (wines, oils, cheeses, fruits, flowers, and early vegetables).

Northern farmers already engaged in large-scale cultivation of the tariff-protected crops (wheat, rice, and beet) extended their areas of cultivation, while those dependent on capital-intensive industrial cash crops such as hemp sought to protect themselves by returning to the practice of paying wages in kind. The new peasant proprietors also suffered. The small family farm, typically growing mixed crops in the traditional pattern of vines interspersed with grain and horticulture, whose only resource was increased exploitation of the captive labour power of the family, increasingly lost its capacity to compete in the new distorted market. Most such households had incurred debts in order to buy their land: the burden of the revalued debt forced many to sell at a time when land values were falling (in Emilia Romagna they fell by 50 per cent between 1927 and 1932). It thus brought a setback to the dream of a dispersion of property, at least in the north of Italy, although, in the south, a new decree dividing up communal lands suitable for cultivation among peasant proprietors did lead to some extension of small property, while the scarcity of credit there meant that southern peasants, unable to contract debt, suffered relatively less.

The 'Battle for Grain' was clearly a propaganda success, and it did achieve higher grain yields per hectare in the north and centre. In the south they fell: 10,000 fewer threshing machines (*trebbiatrici*) were in use in 1931 compared with the previous year, because fewer farms could afford to hire them, although this was offset by higher yields where they were used, confirming the 'scissors effect' between large farms in the north and the quasi-feudal great estates of the south.

As for the great majority of peasants who subsisted as smallholders, share tenants, or sharecroppers on commercially unviable plots, the area they cultivated actually shrank slightly during the depression years 1930–4 despite the strong growth in resident population numbers (including workers expelled from other sectors) and the compression of living standards. This quasi-subsistence sector of Italian agriculture was characterized by an extension of forms of self-provisioning and a restoration of more exploitative relations of production. The number of people engaged in agriculture recorded in the 1936 census was higher than in 1931. This trend remained true even in 1936–9, when the economy was picking up again as a result of the rearmament drive, and can be seen therefore as a sign of the survival of a phenomenon that had marked farming in the main years of the depression.[10]

Mussolini as early as 1921 had seen the agrarian question as an issue Fascism must address urgently on its road to power, defining, with his customary ambiguity, the movement's policy of 'agrarian democracy' as 'the land for those who work it and who make it yield. No socialisation of the land and no state agriculture.... Fascism must not only not oppose, but help the agricultural masses to assuage their ancient and sacred hunger for land.'[11]

Over the next decade his conviction grew that a fundamental project of fascism in power must be to steer economic development towards an integrated mixed economy in which industry and agriculture would have equal weight, and the corrupting trend of development towards the predominance of an urban industrial culture, characterized by the reduced birth rate that he regarded as the 'crisis of western civilization', would be checked, and even reversed.

In 1927 he declared himself to favour henceforth the village over the city and launched an ambitious plan for reclamation of unproductive land which was promulgated as the 'Mussolini Law' for total reclamation (*bonifica integrale*) in December 1928. This was to be the principal strand in an overarching policy aimed at the 'ruralization' of the country, by which it was intended to transform the nature and pattern of economic development of Italy by means of a massive strengthening of agriculture, in terms of area cultivated, numbers of workers, mechanization, investment, and increased production, by restricting the further growth of large-scale industry and encouraging small firms directly serving agriculture, by creating an internal market based on a prosperous agriculture as the basis of a system that would reverse the falling birth rate and thus, since 'numbers are power', enable Italy to wield greater influence in the world: 'In an Italy reclaimed, cultivated, irrigated, disciplined, that is, fascist, there is room and bread for another ten million men. Sixty million Italians will make their weight and their strength felt in the history of the world.'[12] Even Renzo De Felice, Mussolini's generally sympathetic 'revisionist' biographer, felt constrained to describe this programme as 'absurd, anachronistic and unhistorical, a typically petit-bourgeois muddle of ideas and impressions'.[13]

The *bonifica* programme promised far more than it delivered. Here the regime's statistics tend to mislead. By the end of the regime approximately 58 per cent of the announced works had been completed, but in fact only 32 per cent of irrigation necessary to make the reclaimed land fertile had been finished, and of the improved

[10] Cf. G. Corni, 'La politica agraria del fascismo: un confronto fra Italia e Germania', *Studi storici*, 28/2 (1987), 514–15.

[11] B. Mussolini in *Il popolo d'Italia*, 7 January 1921, cited in R. De Felice, *Mussolini il fascista*, i: *La conquista del poetere 1921–1925* (Turin: Einaudi, 1966), 75 ff.

[12] Cited in R. De Felice, *Mussolini il duce: gli anni del consenso 1929–1936* (Turin: Einaudi, 1974), 151.

[13] Ibid. 149–50.

land only 16 per cent involved any break-up of large estates. Much of the investment went to infrastructure works that did not contribute to agriculture, and large sums were paid to unmonitored landowners, a famous example involving a fantastic eight million lira paid to a landowner at Codigoro who did nothing in return for it.[14]

The able and idealistic agricultural expert Arrigo Serpieri, whom Mussolini had originally appointed to carry through the *bonifica* programme, was dismissed in 1934 after a vain attempt to revive the part of the programme that required the landowners to shoulder the costs of preparing reclaimed land for cultivation prior to its redistribution. Thus, almost no private investment was made in the final stage in *bonifica* works, while most resultant new land was rented out, leaving the share-tenants or sharecroppers to complete the improvement at their own expense. In 1935 the funds allocated to *bonifica integrale* were drastically cut, and although Mussolini in 1939–40 relaunched plans to force southern landowners to break up their estates, the billion lira appropriated for it largely ended in the back pockets of the landlords and stewards without producing any results. As the sympathetic De Felice puts it: 'there is no doubt that as far as the "*Duce*" is directly concerned, the downsizing of the original programme of *bonifica integrale*, and the actual results achieved, together wretchedly scuppered his grand design for the ... ruralization of Italy'.[15]

In fact, by 1940 only one-third of the nine million hectares declared suitable for reclamation were being improved with infrastructures and only 1.7 million had been completed, of which less than one million had been fully transformed and distributed, mainly in the north, and mostly to already large farms. Fewer than 20,000 new small farms were created by the programme, of which 12,000 were less than two hectares in extent (and therefore only viable for minimal subsistence farming).

Another key element of fascist ruralization policy aimed at drastically reducing the number of landless agricultural labourers (*sbracciantizzazione*), inducing them to become share-tenants or sharecroppers as a putative step towards independent ownership of land. *Sbracciantizzazione* was in any case bound to meet a mixed response according to the forms of the agricultural labour market prevailing in different areas. Landless labourers in the Po Valley, where social conflict over land had become acute after 1918, were very different from those in the south. Already before the 1915–18 war these northern farmhands had become a self-conscious population of 'land workers' on a par with 'factory workers', strongly unionized and class-conscious. Their main demand was typically for shorter hours and better pay rather than the 'traditional peasant desire' for a piece of land of one's own.

Like the other strands of ruralization, *sbracciantizzazione* was also more apparent than real: the census statistics showing a fall in the number of landless labour-ers from 44 to 28 per cent of the agricultural labour force masked the fact that

---

[14] P. Corner, 'Rapporti tra agricoltura e industria durante il fascismo', in A. Aquarone and M. Vernassa (eds), *Il regime fascista* (Bologna: Il Mulino, 1974), 398–9.

[15] Ibid. 146.

most became share-tenants or sharecroppers through the fragmentation of small family-run farms which declined from 3.42 to 2.73 million between 1921 and 1936. Share-farming did, however, assuage some of the rural discontent by conferring temporarily at least the illusion of autonomy and because its application had been psychologically prepared by the ruralization propaganda.

Even more clamorous a failure was encountered in the attempt to alter the demographic profile of the country by preventing peasants from migrating to the cities and by moving jobless city dwellers to the countryside. Though Mussolini admonished his Minister for Internal Migration that 'we have to ruralize Italy even if takes billions and half-centuries', just the opposite trend established itself throughout the twenty years of the regime: the urban population continued to grow, mainly through migration from the countryside, and the birth rate continued to fall (down from 31.7 per thousand in 1911–14 to 23.6 per thousand in 1936–40). And though almost 1.75 million urban jobless were sent to work outside the cities (mostly on public works projects) they soon drifted back when the funding was cut.

Mussolini was certainly concerned to leave his personal mark on Italian agriculture, with propaganda images frequently showing him begoggled, stripped to the waist, and sweating, helping the peasants on the threshing machine at harvest time. Undoubtedly, too, the propaganda of the *bonifica integrale* was highly valuable to the regime abroad and aroused great, if short-lived, popular enthusiasm at home. 'Ruralization' for him, and for many other Italians, was a myth of a future golden age, but it was also intended in the here and now to reincorporate the peasantry into Italian society to whose margins it had always been relegated, by making peasants at the same time a stabilizing centrepiece of consent to the regime.[16]

According to Giovanni Lorenzoni, the regime's principal publicist in the field of agriculture, some 125,000–130,000 new peasant smallholdings were created in the aftermath of the 1915–18 war, accounting for about 6 per cent of the cultivable area of the country, and there were some 300,000 small farms that acquired extra land.[17] Most such new and expanded small farms were in the Po Valley. The contrast with the fewer than 20,000, often problematic, additional small farms achieved by the *bonifica integrale* of the fascist period speaks for itself.

The praise occasionally voiced for the 'modernizing ruralism' of fascist agrarian policy is scarcely deserved. Outcomes were not in line with objectives because of the resistance of *latifondisti* in the south, the transformation of the *federconsorzi* (landowners' associations) into an arm of the state bureaucracy, and the lack of any credit network serving agriculture. In any case, other major Fascist policies militated against agriculture: the revaluation of the lira at 'Quota 90' in particular more than halved the value of agricultural exports between 1930 and 1934.

---

[16] Cf. Corni, 'La politica agraria del fascismo', 385–421.
[17] G. Lorenzoni, *Inchiesta sulla piccola proprietà coltivatrice formatasi nel dopoguerra: relazione finale* (Rome: Treves Dell 'Ali, 1938).

Behind the façade of defending country folk from the evils of urban culture was hidden the concept of an agriculture that would 'mop up the general social and economic contradictions'.[18] The fascists transferred the costs of the depression onto the fragile budgets of the peasants: 'Work more, consume less, these four words sum up how the depression was dealt with', in the words of a fascist bureaucrat.[19]

Ruralization was intended to keep alive the most backward sectors of agriculture, without reform of obsolete contracts and without correcting the imbalance between north and south. Praise was heaped on sharecropping as the ideal form of small farming and of relations between landowner and peasant farmers, but its conditions were made increasingly oppressive, even in its heartlands of Tuscany and Umbria. They were summed up in the Sharecroppers' Charter of 1934, which in effect gave legal force to protection of landed property incomes by imposing a self-exploitative culture on sharecropper households whose only resource was the labour power of their members, with a particular additional burden being demanded of its female members.[20] Meanwhile, northern capital-intensive farming expanded and prospered: by 1938 in Emilia Romagna, Veneto, and Lombardy alone 42 per cent of national fertilizer output was used, 62 per cent of tractors, 66 per cent of grain silos, they produced 34 per cent of wheat, 62 per cent of maize, 88 per cent of beet, 57 per cent of hemp, and 50 per cent of dairy products of the whole of Italy.

To sum up the nature and impact of fascist ruralization policies, Mussolini's pertinacious biographer must be allowed the last word:

the balance sheet of the ruralization policy ... in relation to the basic aims Mussolini had intended to achieve has to be regarded as a total failure: indeed there is no doubt that the policy of ruralisation did not just fail to transform the basic characteristics and pattern of development of Italian society in the direction desired by Mussolini, but, on the contrary, 'it had this remarkable result: that Italy became an industrial country precisely during the years of fascist ruralization'.[21]

V. Peasant Responses to Fascism, 1920–1945

What peasants thought and said about their lives under fascism is largely absent from the historiography of the period. The first serious attempts at faithful collection and transcription of their utterances only came with the dawn of oral history in the period following the Second World War. Inevitably, evidence collected

---

[18] Corni, 'La politica agraria del fascismo', 403.
[19] Lorenzoni, *Inchiesta sulla piccola proprietà coltivatrice*, cited in Giorgetti, *Contadini e proprietari*.
[20] Cf. Giorgetti, *Contadini e proprietari*.   [21] De Felice, *Mussolini il duce*, 156.

and set down in writing long after the event must be treated with caution, for remembering is always done through the hindsight of a person already influenced by an often radically changed social context, and then transmitted through the filtering assumptions of an interlocutor from another social time and space. Matters are further complicated by the intense focusing of Italian oral history on the experience of specific episodes, groups, and classes, so that the voices of peasants reach us only obliquely, usually through the echo chambers of Resistance history or women's history. This does not annul their significance in their own right but requires a careful scrutiny of how and why they were sought out and dealt with by researchers.

In the literature, the only transcriptions of popular utterances contemporaneous with the fascist period are the few extracted by historians from the confidential intelligence reports on 'Law and Order/Popular Feeling' sent by prefects and provincial fascist authorities to higher authority.[22] They should be assigned to one extreme of the 'public transcript' (the other being the enthusiastic shouting of the crowds at fascist rallies), rather than to the 'hidden transcript', which is not reflected in these reports, since the agents of the state would never be given access to it. Thus, in Vicenza province in 1931, shouts were heard from crowds of protesters: 'We are hungry, give us bread, bread for our children.' 'We have strong arms and don't want to be idle.' 'Give us work if you don't want us to die of consumption.' 'I just ask for work because my little ones are hungry.' In Padua province in the same year threats were heard from the crowd: 'We have the right to work too . . . if you don't put a stop to it we'll come down with our shovels.' And at Messina, an even fiercer voice shouted to his fellow protesters: 'You shouldn't just use your mouth, but sticks, stones and bullets.' No doubt a patient trawl through such official reports for the whole period would throw up other comparable examples, but it is unlikely that there would be any record of sustained peasant discourse referring to conditions under fascism, although beneath the Himalayas of police reports of subversive utterances there might well be many further instances of protest shouted incautiously at night.

One set of observations of the specific existential conditions of the Italian peasantry was produced during the regime. This was a series of 112 in-depth case studies carried out and published by the Istituto Nazionale di Economia Agraria (National Institute of Agrarian Economics) at different dates during the 1930s and published under the title *Monografie di famiglie agricole*, with sections devoted to various geographical areas mainly in the centre and north-east of the country.[23] The studies address, in qualitative terms strongly influenced by the ideal type of peasant family promoted by Fascist propaganda, the microeconomies of peasant families of two

---

[22] Cf. S. Colarizi, *L'opinione degli italiani sotto il regime 1929–1943* (Bari: Laterza, 2000), 46–51.

[23] INEA, *Monografie di famiglie agricole*, 16 vols. (Rome, 1931–9); cf. also S. Salvatici, 'Un mondo in affanno: famiglie agricole nell'Italia fascista', *Passato e presente*, 13 (1995), 36.

categories: smallholders and sharecroppers, the latter forming a large majority of the cases. Another limited study produced in 1932 on the microeconomy of three families of landless labourers in the Bologna area also suffers from a comparable form of stereotyping.[24]

Although these studies are primarily concerned to analyse the household budgets of the subjects involved, distinguishing the forms of income, its proportions from different sources, and, to some extent, the economic contribution to making ends meet made by the different groups comprising the household, they do also provide anecdotal collateral insights into the dimension of intrafamilial sociability and work–life balance. The questionnaire devised by Arrigo Serpieri for the guidance of the fieldworkers producing the *Monografie* was strongly influenced by the work of Frédéric Le Play who, more than seventy years earlier, had laid down the basic criteria for the analysis: means of subsistence, pattern of living, family history, which were all intended to reveal how the family, the basic social unit, fitted into the landscape, describing its many activities and behaviours. Always central to the enquiry, for Serpieri as for Le Play, was the analysis of the family budget. For both men Le Play's axiom ('no feeling or action worth mentioning exists that does not leave a mark in the balance sheet of income and expenditure') was indisputable.[25]

The *Monografie* throw light on the relationship between the labour potential of the rural household and its standard of living, showing that there was little recourse to external capital or mechanization. Families with farms (smallholders, share-tenants, or sharecroppers) under economic pressure sought to maintain, with varying degrees of success, a precarious balance between labour power and land, and between mouths to feed and yields. The methods noted were: a planned division of labour, a faster pace of working, possible hiring of additional hands, and a quest for sources of income outside farming. Changes in household work patterns are shown to be increasingly due to external factors: falling prices and stagnant markets tended to prevent a balance, even precarious, being achieved. At the same time the constant expansion and development of towns altered the town–country relationship through increasing demand for commercialized provisions and changes in patterns of demand, and also offered better chances for marginal or short-term jobs, retail opportunities, and diffuse new models of consumption and behaviour. A recent study appears indeed to demonstrate that, even during the period of maximum downward pressure from fascist policies and the 1929–33 depression, peasant family strategies (particularly recourse to greater marginal self-provisioning, which in the areas of share-farming rarely fell below 50 per cent of food consumption and was often as high as 70 per cent) prevented any significant

---

[24] A. Pagani, *I braccianti della Valle Padana*, ii, Annali dell'Osservatorio di Economia Agraria di Bologna (Piacenza: Tipografia della Federazione Italiana Consorzi Agrari, 1932).

[25] Cf. F. Le Play, *Les Ouvriers européens* (Paris, 1855).

increase in inequality of income compared with the other sectors of the population.[26]

Under fascism, even sharecroppers, the most tenaciously traditionalist class
among peasants, were, according to this analysis, affected more or less directly
by the regime's policies and the economic depression. While, in line with the
stereotype to which Serpieri's observers were working, which placed the dominant
male at the centre of the economic activity of the sharecropping household, a typical
monografia could proclaim:

This farmer feels not only the joy of the family that is his world, his main recreation and
the reward for his toil, but also the need to be succeeded by his sons so that the farm can go
on being worked and provide him with a peaceful old age. His affection goes mainly to his
boys, from whom he can get what he desires, since girls get married and leave home while
the boys stay on with him.[27]

The picture of the male head of household (the *capoccia*) as 'the real motive force of
the farm' was sharply modified in the same monograph by the roles of the daughter-
in-law, who was entirely engaged in the labour of the fields, and the *capoccia*'s wife,
who managed the domestic household, cultivated the vegetable plot, and marketed
its produce.

The study of landless labourers in the intensive farming areas of the Po Valley, moreover, reveals a very different picture: here the family unit was not au-
tonomously able to direct its members' activities in the most economically rational
way, but rather the women, who traditionally supplemented family budgets in ways
that ranged from begging to casual labour in the fields, were increasingly forced to
stay at home while their husbands and brothers were guaranteed a minimum share
of labouring opportunities by the fascist unions.[28]

Although the *Monografie* do provide directly observed evidence about the way
peasants lived under fascism, they do not reproduce, or even represent, either the
public or the hidden transcript of the actual discourse of peasants: they merely
provide materials for inference. What becomes clear from a close reading of them
is that any picture of a virtually unchanging peasant way of life and world view,
even during the counter-historical attempts at social transformation undertaken by
the fascist regime, is profoundly misleading. During Mussolini's twenty-one years
of rule and misrule, the long-term trend of economic development, spasmodic
as it was, moved Italy away from a primarily agrarian social-economic mode to
an industrial-services one. As the economic and social environment was modified

---

[26] Cf. G. Federico, 'Contadini e mercato: tattiche di sopravvivenza', *Società e storia*, 38 (1997),
877–913; N. Rossi *et al.*, 'Is the Kuznets Curve Still Alive? Evidence from Italian Household Budgets,
1881–1961', *Journal of Economic History*, 61/4 (2001), 921–2.

[27] INEA, *Monografie* (1934), 11, cited in Salvatici, 'Un mondo in affanno', 101.

[28] Pagani, *I braccianti della Valle Padana*, 139; Cf. also G. Crainz, 'I braccianti della Valle del Po,
1860–1960', in P. P. D'Attorre and A. De Bernardi (eds), *Studi sull'agricoltura italiana: società rurale e
modernizzazione*, Fondazione Giangiacomo Feltrinelli, 'Annali', 29 (Milan: Feltrinelli, 1994).

so were peasant strategies of survival, partly through increased self-exploitation, where tenurial arrangements permitted, partly through a migration to, and integration with, the cities that not even draconian police measures could do more than vexatiously slow down. The *Monografie* enable us to distinguish the effects of the stronger pull of the home market due to the erection of tariff barriers, the increased possibility of local trading related to the supply needs of the growing city populations, and the changes in food consumption patterns due to replacement of beef by cheaper meats (poultry, rabbit, pigmeat, and vegetables). Though they do not specify quantitatively the effects of the fall in market prices for agricultural produce after the deflation of 1927, they give a clear idea of the qualitative changes that stemmed from it for those living from the land.

At a very different level we can find hints of peasant discourse reflected in some post-war fiction, most of which is, however, focused upon the episodes of Resistance and civil war directly experienced by certain writers.[29] More pertinent here, perhaps, is the documentation of peasant thinking that can, by a freakish accident of history, be found in the vast archive of the Allied Screening Commission, a body set up in June 1944 by the British and American military commands to trace, record, and recompense the hundreds of thousands of Italian civilians who had materially assisted the tens of thousands of Allied prisoners of war who escaped from captivity in the aftermath of Italy's surrender in September 1943, and then scattered to all corners of the Italian countryside and mountains, where they were almost universally incorporated into a 'strange alliance' with peasants of every kind.[30]

In the universe of values shared by most peasants the mass help the rural population of Italy offered the escapers was simply part of its own more ancient struggle to baulk its oppressors. Far from revealing 'the mediocrity of rural life', it disclosed a peasantry capable of accommodating within the cognitive-affective maps of its manifold 'wisdoms' almost any unfamiliar proposition or intrusion, appropriating symbolically both looming disaster and the approaching millennium. To traumas of every kind it had a repertory of practical responses which gave it a better chance of survival than was available to those dependent on the servicing mechanisms of 'modern' urban life. Its understanding of the human predicament was alert and comprehensive, and people in trouble with authority were never regarded as alien. As one helper put it, after the liberation, to those he had sheltered: 'It was nothing, you had nothing to eat and nowhere to sleep and the wicked ones were pursuing you. It was the only thing we could do.'[31]

---

[29] Cf. B. Fenoglio, *Un giorno di fuoco* (Milan: Garzanti, 1964); idem, *La malora* (Turin: Einaudi, 1954); N. Revelli, *Il mondo dei vinti: testimonianze di vita contadina* (Turin: Einaudi, 1977); idem, *L'anello forte, La donna, Storie di vita contadina* (Turin: Einaudi, 1985).

[30] Cf. R. Absalom, *A Strange Alliance: Aspects of Escape and Survival in Italy 1943–1945* (Florence: Leo S. Olschki, 1991).

[31] J. B. Mills, *Waiting for the Sunrise* (Cape Town, n.d. [1946]).

Once symbolically appropriated as kinfolk, the escapers benefited from the peasants' mastery of local space (physical and social) and from their strategies for acquiring, often deviously, the material and cultural margins essential to survival. Escapers benefited greatly from the rejection, by 1943, throughout the peasant population, of previously acknowledged authority. It was most evident in the sharecropping areas, where the traditionally adversarial relationship between landowner and sharecropper provided a permanent training ground for subversive attitudes and practices. Some of the attachments formed, between the escapers and the women who were their main carriers of food and news, blossomed into full-scale romantic involvement, or even marriage. In the majority of cases which did not progress beyond friendship or mild flirtation, the daily contact with the Anglo-American escapers, with their culturally induced litany of 'please' and 'thank you', may have prompted a sense that other destinies might really be available for women no longer accepting of their traditional subordination in the family and community.

Some of the relationships formed between Italian helpers and the men they protected provide examples of a discourse revelatory of basic values: 'He was regarded as more and better than another son to us and when he left we felt his absence as if one of our own family had died, even though we knew he was free and out of danger.'[32] At the deepest level, some of the oldest values resurfaced. An old Abruzzese peasant woman, caught sheltering three wounded Englishmen, explained her actions to her captors as follows:

I am old, they are young. My life is finished, theirs is only beginning. They are not the first I have helped, nor would they be the last if it was possible. I did not help them because they are British but because I am a Christian woman and they too are Christians.[33]

It is clear that in this rare example of genuine peasant discourse 'Christian' does not refer to a specific denomination (Catholic or Protestant), or even to the religious concept of 'Christianity' as a concrete world faith. In the Abruzzi dialectal usage the word *cristiano* denotes simply any human being (it is written without a capital letter). Equally, the formula used, of age and youth, of life ending and beginning, is one of the tropes of an ancient oral tradition of storytelling not peculiar to the Abruzzi, even if certainly well established there. It denotes a cultural matrix that permeates activity and consciousness. The matrix contains 'religion' but is not a mere effect of it. The 'christianity' practised by many peasant helpers of escaped prisoners of war dates from well before St Peter's arrival in Rome. Peasants who harboured or helped an escaper were playing a role, and exercising a power, previously denied them in relation to anyone other than fellow peasants in need. The opportunity to re-enter the millenarian vision that remained at the deepest

---

[32] In ASC Claim Folder No. 11801 in the name of Francesco Cesolani, of Montorio Romano.

[33] Details in ASC Claim Folder 9631, dated 13 September 1944, in the name of Annita Santemarroni; letters from Pte J. W. Leys, who quoted his helper's words, and memoranda from Foreign Office in ASC Correspondence File 7–5.

level of peasant culture informed the simple act of accepting a stranger as a brother
or a son. The experience had no precedent, precisely because it was not part of a
bargain, contract, or relationship expressing peasant subservience.

Memories from that time are not universally grim. Their distinctive Italian peasant flavour, that special mixture of outwitting the devil and practical charity, a trace
Italian peasants have left in popular culture even as they disappear as a class, is
aptly illustrated by the situation in 1944 at a farmhouse in the Friuli region. The
house consisted of three separate dwellings around a common courtyard, in each
of which lived a family providing an evening meal, respectively, for parties of New
Zealand escapers, Italian partisans, and German coastal defence troops. Each family
was aware of what the others were doing (though their guests were not) and the
children were sworn to silence. As the informant, who as a girl was sent on occasion
to warn partisans of German plans to ambush them, and vice versa, explained with
a smile: 'We had to keep the peace, we had to get on with everyone.' And no one
was betrayed on either side.[34]

VI. Legacies and Continuities

As a participant observer of peasant life has remarked: 'The relative universality and
continuity of peasant experience are exceptional to modern history ... How is it that
most people in the world have become exceptional to that world?'[35] The question of
when and how peasants make the transition to a world shaped and managed by and
for the non-peasant minority, and how they can abet or resist the pressure to do so,
remains central to any enquiry into how they have been affected by 'modern' social
and political systems. Where lie the historical roots of their capacity for resilience
under pressure and adaptability in the cause of survival? 'Sopportare e durare' (Put
up with it and last it out) was a wisdom deeply instilled in Italian, as in other peasant
cultures, reflecting an understanding of time and change that was foreign to, or
forgotten by, the urban elites ostensibly in charge of their destinies.[36]

Fascism in Italy represented one of the more extreme forms of the combination
of force and fraud used by states and their political elites to mould the lives and
productive capacity of their peasants, and to harness their energies collectively
and individually to purposes utterly remote from the peasants' own perceptions

[34] Situation at San Gervasio described by Signora Milan, now of Marano Lagunare, interviewed 5
July 1984, who was there.

[35] J. Berger, 'Can Peasant Society Survive?', The Listener, 21 June 1979.

[36] Cf. Revelli, L'anello forte; cf. N. D. Munn, 'The Cultural Anthropology of Time', Annual Review
of Anthropology, 21 (1992), 93–123; J. Stacul, 'Natural Time, Political Time: Contested Histories in
Northern Italy', Journal of the Royal Anthropological Institute, 11/4 (2005), 819–36, ISSN: 1359–0987.

of their interest. An attempt was made, cloaked in a rhetoric of nation building, modernization, and ruralization, to bind almost half of the active population to modes and relations of production inimical to their incorporation into an industry-based economic and social system. Central to the project was a declared intention to increase the national production of cannon fodder as a basis for national aggrandizement.

Such results as were achieved by this project, which engaged the *Duce* and his regime for almost twenty years, were, despite considerable propaganda success at home and abroad, largely ephemeral. The meagre real benefits offered by the regime to sections of the peasantry were never enough to bring more than a fringe to full, enthusiastic support for the project. The vast majority, in all the subsectors described in this article, remained passively recalcitrant, clinging to all the stratagems, inherited from a long past of exploitation, that might enable them to survive materially, and in their existing social niche, all attempts to engineer a full-hearted consensus. When the world was turned upside down in September 1943, with the simultaneous collapse of the regime and the state, they exercised their momentary autonomy by looting all the state property they could reach, and destroying official records about themselves. They coped with the needs of the tide of escapees, refugees, and deserters, and rapidly entrenched their survival in new and largely illegal networks of trade and barter in agricultural products.[37]

Already under Allied occupation in 1943–5, and during the subsequent period of reconstruction, earlier forms of peasant struggle re-emerged: occupation of unused land, and militant demands for new share and employment contracts, accompanied by strikes and demonstrations. Concessions were extracted from authority and landlords, but nothing could prevent Italian agriculture in its traditional forms going into a rapid decline as the 'economic miracle' of the 1950s took hold and the bulk of the rural population became workers in factories, either in the cities or in a newly urbanized countryside, or emigrated abroad. In the 'third Italy' that largely coincides with the areas where sharecropping was predominant, a further socio-economic metamorphosis occurred as families straddled employment on the land and in industry and the more successful found scope for the entrepreneurial skills developed as sharecroppers in the vast mosaic of light industrial development that became the most dynamic sector of the Italian economy from the 1970s.[38]

Prosperity, uneven but real, and mechanization, may have transformed the landscape, and the peasant population may have become urbanized, but—strangely—the attachment to a piece of family land did not decline. Rather it was subsumed in a new pattern of worker–peasant strategies: a week's work on the factory floor being followed by a weekend's work on vineyard and vegetable garden in the original

[37] Cf. G. Becattini and N. Bellanca, 'Economia di guerra e mercato nero', *Italia contemporanea*, 163 (1986), 5–28.
[38] Cf. A. Cento Bull and P. Corner, *From Peasant to Entrepreneur: The Survival of the Family Economy in Italy* (Oxford: Berg, 1993).

family holding. Perhaps this will not continue for another generation, but in itself it denotes the extraordinary energy for household survival generated by the Italian peasant experience.

BIBLIOGRAPHY

AQUARONE, A., and VERNASSA, M. (eds), *Il regime fascista* (Bologna: Il Mulino, 1974).

BECATTINI, G., and BELLANCA, N., 'Economia di guerra e mercato nero', *Italia contempo-ranea*, 163 (1986).

BOSWORTH, R., *Mussolini's Italy: Life under the Dictatorship, 1915–1945* (Harmondsworth: Penguin, 2006).

CENTO BULL, A., and CORNER, P., *From Peasant to Entrepreneur: The Survival of the Family Economy in Italy* (Oxford: Berg, 1993).

COLARIZI, S., *L'opinione degli italiani sotto il regime 1929–1943* (Bari: Laterza, 2000).

D'ATTORRE, P. P., and DE BERNARDI, A. (eds), *Studi sull'agricoltura italiana: società rurale e modernizzazione*, Fondazione Giangiacomo Feltrinelli, 'Annali', 29 (Milan: Feltrinelli, 1994).

DE FELICE, R., *Mussolini il fascista*, i: *La conquista del poetere 1921–1925* (Turin: Einaudi, 1966).

FEDERICO, G., 'Contadini e mercato: tattiche di sopravvivenza', *Società e storia*, 38 (1997).

GIORGETTI, G., *Contadini e proprietari nell'Italia moderna: rapporti di produzione e contratti agrari dal secolo XVI a oggi* (Turin: Einaudi, 1974).

HELSTOSKY, C. F., *Garlic and Oil: Food and Politics in Italy* (New York: Berg, 2006).

INEA, *Monografie di famiglie agricole*, 16 vols (Rome, 1931–9).

LORENZONI, G., *Inchiesta sulla piccola proprietà coltivatrice formatasi nel dopoguerra: re-lazione finale* (Rome, 1938).

RAMELLA, F., *Terra e telai: sistemi di parentela e manifattura nel biellese dell'Ottocento* (Turin: Einaudi, 1984).

REVELLI, N., *Il mondo dei vinti: testimonianze di vita contadina* (Turin: Einaudi, 1977).

—— *L'anello forte, La donna, Storie di vita contadina* (Turin: Einaudi, 1985).

SCHMIDT, C. T., *The Corporate State in Action: Italy under Fascism* (London: Victor Gollancz, 1939).

SCOTT, J. C., *Domination and the Arts of Resistance: Hidden Transcripts* (New Haven: Yale University Press, 1990).

SILONE, I., *Fontamara* (Milan: Mondadori, 1988; 1st edn. 1933).

STACUL, J., *The Bounded Field: Localism and Local Identity in an Italian Alpine Valley* (New York: Berghahn Books, 2003).

CHAPTER 8

....

CORPORATISM
AND THE
ECONOMIC ORDER

PHILIP MORGAN

....

THE 1951 Italian census revealed that, for the first time since the unification of the country in 1860, under half of the economically active population were employed in agriculture. This meant that Italy was, apparently, finally making the transition from being a poor, relatively backward, and mainly agrarian country to having a wealth-creating 'modern', mainly urban and industrial economy. Such an observation may appear to be a strange place to start an analysis of Italian Fascism's economic policies. But it reflects the concerns of the economic historians of Italy, who are trying to uncover and explain long-term cycles of economic growth and development which can make sense of Italy's 'modernization' from 1860 to the so-called 'economic miracle' of the 1950s and early 1960s; and to revisit and enliven the inadequate statistical data which would enable them to model these patterns of development.

These economic histories are clearly worthwhile in their own right. But I wonder if the historian of Italian Fascism should primarily be interested in whether the fascist period was a 'discontinuous interlude in the long-run process of capitalist development',[1] or not. Italian economic historians hardly neglect the role of politics,

[1] J. Cohen and G. Federico, *The Growth of the Italian Economy, 1820–1960* (Cambridge: Cambridge University Press, 2001), 23. See also G. Federico and R. Giannetti, 'Italy: Stalling and Surpassing', in J. Foreman-Peck and G. Federico (eds), *European Industrial Policy: The Twentieth Century Experience* (Oxford: Oxford University Press, 1999), 124–51; G. Federico, 'Italy 1860–1940: A Little-Known Success

or of the state, in the country's economic development. One of their continuing core debates is the extent to which government action was necessary, or instrumental, in overcoming the objective obstacles to Italy's economic growth, which were the lack of indigenous raw materials and energy, and low levels of domestic demand, consumption, and investment. But their basic perspective remains that of explaining the long-term 'modernization' of the country as a politically neutral working out of economic trends.

Locating some of the technological and organizational innovations that made possible the post-war 'economic miracle' in changes to Italian industries in the 1930s[2] leads to interesting, but rather odd, conclusions that the Italian Fascist regime was the conscious, or rather more likely, inadvertent agent of economic 'modernization'. This point has resonance for some historians of Italian Fascism, and is an argument applied, perhaps rather more compellingly, to the outcomes of German Nazism, as well.[3] The American intellectual historian A. J. Gregor has spent a career promoting what is, in my view, a mistaken interpretation of Italian Fascism as a 'developmental dictatorship', the model and precursor for Third World post-colonial dictatorships of all political hues.[4] More subtly, Mussolini's multi-volume biographer, Renzo De Felice, distances a forward-looking, 'modern' Italian Fascism from a regressive, backward-looking German Nazism,[5] which, among other things, supposedly rules out there being any native Italian roots to the regime's late 1930s anti-Semitic laws, and considering fascism as a generic phenomenon of inter-war Europe. Rather too much interpretation has been made to hang on what happened to the Italian economy under Fascism.

That political historians of Italian Fascism, such as myself, ask rather different questions about the Italian economy during the fascist period from economic historians of Italy is evident from their respective treatments of almost every aspect of fascist economic policy. The former see autarky, war, and imperialism as the political essence of fascism; while the latter's judgement on rearmament is that it was 'not the best way to stimulate demand in a backward economy'.[6] The Fascist government's reintroduction of high protective tariffs on wheat imports in 1925 and the ensuing 'Battle for Grain', to increase home-grown production and make Italy independent of grain imports, is seen by the former as an early sign of the autarkic

---

Story', *Economic History Review*, 49/4 (1996), 764–86; N. Rossi and G. Toniolo, 'Catching up or Falling Behind', *Economic History Review*, 45/3 (1992), 537–63.

[2] V. Zamagni, 'Italy: How to Lose the War and Win the Peace', in M. Harrison (ed.), *The Economics of World War II: Six Great Powers in International Comparison* (Cambridge: Cambridge University Press, 1998), 177.

[3] R. Dahrendorf, *Society and Democracy in Germany* (London: Wiedenfeld & Nicolson, 1968).

[4] A. J. Gregor, *The Fascist Persuasion in Radical Politics* (Princeton: Princeton University Press, 1974); idem, *Italian Fascism and Developmental Dictatorship* (Princeton: Princeton University Press, 1979); idem, *Mussolini's Intellectuals: Fascist Social and Political Thought* (Princeton: Princeton University Press, 2005).

[5] R. De Felice, *Intervista sul fascismo*, ed. M. Ledeen (Bari: Laterza, 1975); idem, *Interpretations of Fascism* (Cambridge: MA 1977).

[6] Quoted in Cohen and Federico, *The Growth of the Italian Economy*, 76.

feel and direction given to the national economy by the fascist regime in the 1930s; while for economic historians, it was a seriously dysfunctional move, in 'normal' economic terms, since it protected inefficient domestic producers and inhibited agricultural diversification for export. They are 'right', of course, but Mussolini was not thinking of the post-war 'economic miracle', but of liberating the country from the 'slavery of foreign bread'.[7]

This chapter takes an unashamedly political line on Italian Fascist economic policies, on the grounds that Fascism without the politics is barely Fascism at all. It attempts to outline what was 'Fascist' about the running of the Italian economy during the Fascist era. The concern throughout is to articulate what Fascism's efforts to control the national economy tell us about the nature of Fascism, rather than about the nature of Italian economic development.

It has become something of a truism to say that economics was not central to how fascists understood themselves and their 'revolution'. Indeed, their non-consumerist asceticism was anti-economic, or rather, anti-materialist. The Fascists wanted to make a nation in their own image out of sceptical, individualistic Italians, and transform an aggregate of egoists into a unified collective whose will, power, and energy, mobilized and directed by the Fascist regime, would enable Italy to become a great imperialist power, which Mussolini regarded as the only route to national survival in an inherently competitive and predatory world. However imperfect and faltering in its realization, the point and purpose of the first-ever 'totalitarian' system in Fascist Italy was to equip Italians to be warlike imperialists, capable of conquering, settling, and governing an empire. Fascism's emphasis on inculcating and imposing a transformation of values or consciousness in Italians, changing the way they saw themselves and others, meant that even economic and social initiatives were deliberately infused with the regime's 'spiritual' goals. So, corporatism, where the Fascist state compelled to be brought together, under a single institutional roof, representatives of all those involved in the productive process of a given sector of the economy, workers, employers, managers, technicians, was conceived of as educative, as much as economic, in function. The corporations' job was, under the regime's auspices, to bury for good counter-productive and divisive class conflict, by forcing the various human factors of production to cooperate in the national interest of maximizing economic output.

Even though the Fascist 'revolution' was portrayed as a 'spiritual' one, the Italian Fascist regime had a very clear sense of the place and function of the national economy. It was one of the sources of national power, one of the means of national aggrandizement; it provided the resources and muscle for a strong imperialist nation to assert itself internationally. The economy was not an end in itself, as with capitalism, to gratify consumers' material needs and desires, but a means to strengthen the military capacity of the country, a resource that would enable

---

[7] Quoted in P. Morgan, *Italian Fascism, 1915–1945* (2nd edn, Basingstoke: Palgrave Macmillan, 2004), 116.

the Fascist leadership to realize its political and ideological goals of imperialist expansion. The state drove the economy, not the economy the state. The Marxist historian of Nazi Germany Tim Mason counter-intuitively coined the phrase 'the primacy of politics',[8] and this term can, I think, be used to categorize the economics of both inter-war and wartime fascist regimes.

The 'New Order' thinking and practice of both the Italian Fascist and German Nazi regimes during the 1930s and into the war had important economic dimensions. The concept of 'living space' was as current in late 1930s Fascist Italy (*spazio vitale*) as it was in Nazi Germany (*Lebensraum*), and the geo-political considerations behind it were similar: to match a dynamic, growing population with expanded territory and economic resources. The *Grosswirtschaften*, or 'large economic areas', to be colonized and dominated economically by the Axis powers had different locations: the Mediterranean basin and Indian Ocean hinterland for the Fascists, and Central and Eastern Europe for the Nazis. They were perceived as being complementary and separate, but overlapped in an uneasy condominium of the Balkan and Danubian areas, the source of friction and rivalry in the Axis's actual wartime occupation of these regions.

Partly out of fear of a Nazi domination of Europe, and partly out of a desire to emulate it, the Fascist regime developed a pretty coherent view of Italy's 'living space' and what was to happen within it. Giuseppe Bottai, writing in 1941 when he was still Minister of National Education, anticipated a future economic bloc organized 'fascistically' to ensure Italian dominance within the bloc, around corporations, cartels, a clearing system for intra- and extra-bloc trade, a single currency, the Italian lira, or a 'lira zone'. He summarized the principles of action as 'the superiority of the political sphere over the economy...the subordination of individual interests to collective ones...the state's right to assume economic management of the multiple entities making up the *spazio vitale*...the recognition of private firms and their elevation to public utilities...the collaboration of all classes in the achievement of social order and well-being and a higher level of output'.[9]

Bottai's words encapsulated what the Fascist regime had tried to do in the 1930s, when it had promoted corporatism, the cartelization of Italian industry and agriculture, and experimented with bilateral trade agreements with some central and south-eastern European countries; what it attempted to do against superior Nazi power politics in the Balkan areas Fascist Italy nominally annexed, occupied, or controlled during the war; and what it intended to do in the post-war dawn of a

[8] T. Mason, 'The Primacy of Politics: Politics and Economics in National Socialist Germany', in S. J. Woolf (ed.), *The Nature of Fascism* (London: 1968), 165–95. See also his withering assault on the apolitical character of a 1984 exhibition in Rome on the Italian inter-war economy, in 'The Great Economic History Show', *History Workshop Journal*, 21 (1986), 3–35.

[9] Quoted in D. Rodogno, *Fascism's European Empire: Italian Occupation during the Second World War* (Cambridge: Cambridge University Press, 2006), 48–9.

'new Europe'. For Italians and Europeans devitalized by the materialistic individu-alism of liberal parliamentary and capitalist culture, these elements were to be the economic basis of Italian Fascism's 'new civilization', an alternative 'third way' 'New Order' to bolshevism, which merely accentuated to its statist extremes capitalism's corrosive materialism.

As we shall see, the economic 'system' devised, or improvised, by the fascist regime in the 1930s was characteristically fragmented and competitive, the outcome of sometimes ad hoc initiatives to confront particular issues, problems, and targets. Whatever coherence and consistency the 'system' had were provided by fascism's control of labour and the labour market, and Mussolini's indications as to the direction, if not the definitive shape, of the national economy.

Fascism had become a mass movement in the early 1920s on the back of its violent campaigns against socialist and Catholic workers' organizations in the towns and countryside of north and central Italy. Its control of labour was institutionalized in the structures of the totalitarian state. Free labour unions were suppressed and banned, strikes were made illegal, and monopoly representation of workers passed to fascist unions, or syndicates. Workers' interests were only protected by the syndi-cates at the margins, and were inadequately represented in the fascist corporations when they were formed. The regime's syndical and corporate machinery was the means and channel by which wage and salary cuts were imposed on the workforce, as demonstrated during the lira revaluation crisis of 1926–7, and then during the Great Depression. If coercively depressing wages was one very fascist way of control-ling the labour market, then another, the ban on the internal migration of labour from countryside to town from the early 1930s, was a matter for enforcement by the police.

Fascism's hyper-nationalism was translated economically by Mussolini into au-tarky, war, and empire, all inseparably connected. Autarky, or economic self-sufficiency, was both the outcome of war, and preparation for further wars of imperialist conquest. Autarky was literally unrealizable for both Fascist Italy and Nazi Germany within their current territorial confines, and, hence, its attainment became a self-fulfilling or self-sustaining myth and prophecy. Autarky, for the fascist regimes, was both means and end, a reason for and a product of wars of expansion. The demonstrable fact that neither country could achieve autarky in existing con-ditions and with existing resources was, for the fascist regimes, a further incentive to acquire the territory and resources which would enable autarky to be realized.

The tipping point in the reorientation of the Italian economy towards autarky was war itself, the fascist invasion and conquest of the East African state of Ethiopia in 1935–6, the watershed for the Fascist regime, internally and internationally. League of Nations economic sanctions against Fascist Italy as the aggressor state practically required the regime to make a virtue of necessity of economic self-reliance. Once sanctions were lifted, in the summer of 1936, then, theoretically,

Fascist Italy had the option, or the opportunity, to return to international trade relations, now that countries across the world were beginning to recover from the Great Depression of the early 1930s. The same basic choice between autarky and the global economy was being confronted by Hitler and the Nazi regime in Germany, and at about the same time, if for different reasons.

The choice, if choice there was for fascist regimes, was not a return to international trade, but a stepping up of autarkical preparations for war. This phase, from 1936, was marked by increased military expenditure and rearmament, and higher internal taxation to pay for it; more intense state control of trade, exchange, and currency matters, and of domestic wages and prices; more indigenous production of strategic raw materials and goods at higher than global prices behind government protection and subsidy; and more trade with each other. As a major sanctions-buster, Nazi Germany came to provide 27 per cent of all Italian imports between 1936 and 1938, and 40 per cent by the time of Italy's entry into a general European war in mid-1940. In 1937, Mussolini publicly declared that autarky for war was 'official' Fascist government policy.

Economic historians correctly point to the basic similarities in the emergency measures adopted by all countries, fascist or not, to confront the impact of the global economic crisis, the Great Depression. But in Fascist Italy, these crisis initiatives were not abandoned or dismantled as the depression eased; they were institutionalized, made into national legal entities, and given explicit autarkic and warmongering commissions. Similar economic policies were adopted in very different political and ideological contexts, which make the similarities no more than skin deep. The basic economic choice made by Mussolini in 1936 was the basic political choice of fascism; it was autarky, for war, not international trade, for peace. The same difference in context exposes the equally vapid conclusions on the economic 'continuities' between the Fascist period, ending in 1945, and the post-war era. The retention of some of the economic institutions of fascism by post-war democratic republican governments says little about the legacy, or survival, of fascism in post-war Italy, since the institutions were now made to operate, and were seen to work, in a world of more or less market and free-trading capitalist economies.

The Italian Fascist economic order of the 1930s was a hybrid of Fascist Party and state bodies and, more generally, a symbiosis of the public and private sectors of the economy. Its main components were, first, the regular central state ministries, the economic ministries proper, such as Finance and Agriculture, and the separate armed forces ministries, each responsible for their own armaments and having their own budgets, together with the Foreign Ministry, involved in foreign trade negotiations and agreements; second, the parvenu Fascist Ministry of Corporations and the national and provincial corporate system nominally responsible to it; third, the Institute of Industrial Reconstruction (Istituto di Ricostruzione Industriale; IRI), a state body combining public ownership of industries with their part-public, part-private management; fourth, state economic agencies set up to deal with specific areas of autarky and rearmament, directly answerable to Mussolini as head of government; fifth, cartels, or what effectively were cartels, in industry and agriculture; sixth, Fascist Party bodies which assumed, on an ad hoc basis, important economic and corporative functions; and seventh, near-monopolistic mainly privately run companies, or oligopolies, most of them family-owned business empires, such as Fiat and Pirelli.

We know almost too much about the theory or ideal of corporatism, and about the corporative structures erected by the Fascist state, because corporations were lauded at home and abroad as fascism's distinctive contribution to the resolution of the systemic crisis of capitalism in the Great Depression. The fascist regime organized conferences on corporatism, in which fascist corporative theorists could envisage corporations actually owning the means of production, and set up new university faculties devoted to corporative 'science', the young graduates of which were employed in the syndical and corporative bureaucracies. Corporatism became the 'revolutionary' myth of the regime, and functioned as such in raising both the international and internal profile of fascism, convincing many foreign observers and commentators of the seriousness of its universal mission to change the world, and persuading many university-educated young Italians that the regime, after a decade in power, had not lost its 'revolutionary' élan.

But we know relatively little about how corporative structures operated in practice, and whether, or to what extent, they actually carried out their formal functions, and constituted fascism's new economic and social order. In part, this is down to a lack or unavailability of sources. The files of the most fascist of government ministries, the new Ministry of Corporations, did not survive the fall of the regime. Most of the accessible material on corporations has to be cobbled together from their patchy presence in the files of other ministries and the Fascist Party. It is clear from Gregor's many books on corporatism in theory, though this is not a conclusion which Gregor would accept, that fascist corporatist intellectuals were commenting on a system of economic governance as it developed beneath them on the ground, and providing after-the-event philosophical justifications of what the regime, in the event, had decided to do. So someone needs to write a history of fascist corporatism in theory and practice, though it may prove to be an exercise in futility. Demonstrating that something, after all, did not happen is not much of an inducement to historians.

A certain amount can be deduced from an analysis of the corporative system as it was intended to be, and of contemporary fascist and other generally but not always sympathetic commentary on its operation. The corporations were unlikely to be genuinely educative, class-collaborative organs of economic planning and management, when their rationale and composition simply formalized Fascism's initial and lasting anti-worker-class orientation. The corporations were there to maximize economic production, which involved, among other things, controlling and compressing wages, one of the major costs of production and the most susceptible in a fascist regime to regulation from above. The corporations' 'productivist' rationale meant they allocated the misery of improving the efficiency of production, while not really being concerned with the distribution of the benefits and profits of improved production and productivity among the various factors of production.

Again, the make-up of each and every corporation was unbalanced. The typical composition of the corporation included representatives of the employers, usually managers and technocrats already servicing employers' now 'fascistized' sectoral lobby organizations; representatives of the workers' syndicates, often fascist Party or Ministry of Corporations-nominated state officials; and representatives of the fascist state, nominally the consumers' friend and arbiter of the system in the overriding national interest, who were more of the same. To the extent that the corporations actually made plans for the economic sectors they represented, it was clear that the technical expertise and the sectional interest which would dominate any such planning process were those of the employers.

It is rather odd that the fascist corporate system was put together in such a piecemeal and stretched-out way. The Ministry of Corporations was created in 1926, nominally headed by Mussolini, with the arch-fascist corporatist among the regime's governing elite, Giuseppe Bottai, as its junior, and effective, minister. In a fresh spurt of law making practically imposed on the regime by the onset of the depression and fascism's claim to be resolving the crisis of capitalism, a National Council of Corporations was set up in 1930, composed of seven national groupings of employer and worker syndical organizations covering the main areas of the economy. These representatives met in a general assembly, and were themselves represented on an executive Central Corporative Committee, which did most of the work. But it was still a superstructure without any capillary substructure, a centre without a periphery to manage and coordinate.

Eventually, twenty-two corporations were created in 1934, purportedly to organize the productive cycles of the major branches of industry, agriculture, and the services. Finally, fascism's statist constitutional framework was completed in 1939 with the replacement of the already neutered parliamentary Chamber of Deputies by a Chamber of Fasces and Corporations, a government-nominated legislative body made up of members of the fascist Party's National Council, the National Council of Corporations, and the Fascist Grand Council, the regime's most important collegial organ.

The fascist regime's apparent lack of focus and enthusiasm for putting in place the system which it claimed would supersede both capitalism and bolshevism obviously needs explanation. It is difficult to be absolutely sure about this. But it appeared that the corporate system's stop-go creation was partly down to the stonewalling resistance of the industrial employers, who were suspicious of any potential encroachment on their capacity to manage their businesses as they wanted. They need not have worried that much, of course, at least in respect of the corporations. The lack of any real class-collaborative muscle in the corporative organs that did emerge shows how successful that resistance was.

The process of establishing the corporate system was also hindered by long-running inter-ministerial disputes over areas of jurisdiction and competence. The existing economic ministries were keen to limit the range of action of the parvenu Ministry of Corporations, and its ambitious junior minister, and then full minister, Bottai, who aspired to make his ministry a model of streamlined bureaucracy as a kind of high command of the national economy. The Fascist Party also claimed and, as we shall see, actually enacted a corporative role which arguably was in the remit of the corporate system.

The Ministry of Corporations had a relatively small civil service staffing, corresponding to Bottai's vision of a svelte, dynamic corps of officials, and reflecting the other ministries' determination to hang on to their functions. But it still became what the Fascist Party leader, Augusto Turati, could self-interestedly condemn to Mussolini in 1930, even before the creation of corporations proper, as a 'corpocracy', 'an over-complex complex of organs which justify their existence solely by complicating things'.[10] The rather protracted and cumbersome consultative machinery of the corporate system was ill suited to the crisis management required of the regime during the lira revaluation, and especially in the years of the depression. The result was that the Fascist government improvised its emergency responses to the impact of the depression by creating new bodies which simply supplanted or bypassed the unwieldy corporate structures.

The National Council of Corporations and the corporations were given generic statutory powers to organize and coordinate production in their respective economic sectors. But Fascist Italy was a dictatorship, and it is hardly surprising that corporative organs were deliberately deprived of any capacity for independent initiative and self-regulation. The corporations could fix the prices of goods and services in their sector, for instance. But any such norms were subject to National Council of Corporations (effectively, Central Corporative Committee) approval, and were only binding on the sector once the government had made them law.

The corporate bodies were also, by statute, to be consulted by and to advise the Fascist government on specific and general economic matters. We know that they certainly discussed important issues to do with their specific branches of the economy and the relationship between them, which gave their debates a sense of having a real bearing on the national economy. They seemed to provide a serious semi-public forum for at least the representation of the various economic interests at play. But one is struck by how Antonio Benni, the President of Confindustria, the industrial employers' association, described the handling of a recent crisis in

---

[10] Reproduced in the documentary appendix to A. Aquarone, *L'organizzazione dello stato totalitario* (Turin: Einaudi, 1965), 530–2.

the silk industry, in the parliamentary debate on the law establishing the National Council of Corporations in 1930. His evident intention was to demonstrate that the proposed corporate body was surplus to requirements. The silk makers needed new investment and new bank loans, and fast, explained Benni, and so Mussolini met producers and bankers in his office, with no other intermediaries, and a deal between the two was done, approved later in a meeting of the Council of Ministers, or cabinet, presided over, of course, by Mussolini as head of government.[11] In other words, major decisions about the economy in a personal dictatorship were made at the top, by the few top people, and then endorsed by the organs of government.

In November 1931, the National Council of Corporations discussed the really important issue of trade tariffs. But this did not even amount to consultation, since, two months before, a government decree had raised all protective duties on imports by 15 per cent, and no new measures were taken by the government after the Council meeting.[12] In February 1936, a meeting of the building construction corporation was important enough to be presided over by Mussolini himself. It discussed some contentious and difficult issues facing the sector, the caps and restrictions on private house-building schemes, and the excessive prices for construction materials being charged by the monopolistic industries controlling the production and distribution of cement, plaster, and lime. The evident difficulties facing the private construction industry and its workers were being placed and determined in an autarkic and national economic context. All new building projects required government authorization, in order to ensure that available savings and investment were not soaked up in initiatives which the government determined were unnecessary on 'national' grounds. Mussolini, who was clearly there to ensure that the debate had the required outcomes, effectively killed the discussion by saying that the licensing system for new construction was working really well. Although price fixing was formally on the agenda of the meeting, no motion on the issue was recorded in the minutes. In other words, a decision to do nothing about it had already been taken, no doubt after lobbying by the monopolies, and the meeting was not allowed to change that decision.[13]

If these were representative cases of the corporate organs at work, then it was pretty evident that basic economic decisions to do with planning and management, and, more importantly, with the relations between the economic forces and interests across any given sector of the economy, were being made elsewhere, and in different, uncorporate, but dictatorial ways. Corporate bodies did, however, clearly have some powers of economic control and supervision in the autarkic economy of the 1930s. A law of 1933 made the construction of any new or extended industrial

[11] L. Rosenstock-Franck, *L'Économie corporative fasciste en doctrine et en fait: ses origines historiques et son évolution* (Paris: Librarie Universitaire, 1934), 269–70.

[12] Ibid. 312–14.

[13] L. Rosenstock-Franck, *Les Étapes de l'économie fasciste italienne: du corporatisme à l'économie de guerre* (Paris: Editions du centre, polytechnicien d'études économiques, 1939), 238–9.

plant dependent on the permission of the Ministry of Corporations, and its decisions in the exercise of this power would obviously play their part in regulating the Italian economy, affecting the distribution and allocation of energy, raw materials, and labour resources, and market share, among producers. It was probable that the Ministry of Corporations actually used this power, and in a corporate manner.

For instance, a pig iron and iron alloy manufacturing company located at Porto Marghera, near Venice, one of several special industrial development zones for autarkic production set up or enlarged by the Fascist government in the 1930s, applied to the Ministry of Corporations to expand its production, in 1935. The ministry's decision was even-handed: it allowed more productive capacity in alloys, but banned it for pig iron. It then blocked a further request, later. In making its decisions, the ministry had canvassed or received the objections of other manufacturers producing in the same fields, who had argued, evidently to some effect, that there was already unused productive capacity in the sector as it was. But the point was that the ministry inspectorate had made a technical economic decision which was, at the same time, a politically prioritizing one between autarkic industries. The request was only partially met, and the second request turned down, on the grounds that the expansion of capacity in these areas would mean the diversion of available electricity supply from the aluminium factories operating in the development zone.[14]

Into the provincial gap left by the regime's creation of a Ministry of Corporations without any corporations to administer stepped the single Fascist Party (Partito Nazionale Fascista; PNF) of the Fascist totalitarian state. First at the provincial level, and then nationally, the PNF set up inter-syndical committees in late 1926 and early 1927, only formally wound up in 1937. So, for a decade, the Fascist Party first occupied ground vacated by the corporations, and then, once provincial corporate bodies emerged, successfully competed against the state authorities they were formally subordinated to, to accumulate a set of economic controls over prices, employment, and labour relations. Convened and presided over by the provincial Party leaders, the inter-syndical committees resembled corporations in structure and functions. Composed of representatives of local employers', workers', and commercial syndicates, they investigated and resolved labour disputes in the provinces, helped to draft and then implement provincial collective labour contracts, and controlled and supervised the syndicates. Their major task in 1926–7 was to ratify and execute centrally determined wage cuts as the economy was forced to deflate in the wake of the regime's revaluation of the lira, and then to compensate for the fall in wages by setting and enforcing retail prices for basic items of food consumption. The Party, in effect, was putting together a rudimentary price and incomes policy, and the machinery to implement it.

---

[14] R. Petri, 'Acqua contro carbone: elettrochimica e indipendenza energetica italiana negli anni trenta', *Italia contemporanea*, 168 (1987), 75–6.

The PNF resumed its attempt to control retail pricing through the inter-syndical apparatus in 1934, again, as before, in response to a particular set of circumstances, first of all, to align the cost of living to more wage cuts, and then to restrain an inflationary spiral after the regime finally decided to devalue a heftily overvalued lira in late 1936.

The fact that the PNF found a prices and income regime beyond its powers to manage effectively, since wages always went down faster than prices, was almost beside the point. The Fascist Party, as befitting its totalitarian role in the Fascist state, was the sharp edge of the attempted 'fascistization' of provincial economic life and activity. It became one of the regime's most important, and most 'fascist', instruments to control and regulate the economy at a micro-level.

The Fascist Party did not so much determine economic policy, as implement it, or deal with its impacts on the people. The Party was entrusted with this task because, unlike the non-existent or fledgling corporate apparatus, it was developing a capillary organizational structure which extended its reach into the nooks and crannies of Italian life. The Party's initiatives were a fascist and political manoeuvre, rather than an economic one, since the Party's prices and incomes set-up, for example, was a deliberate effort to bend the 'natural' economic 'laws' of supply and demand to the political will and policies of the fascist regime. The PNF's intervention in the economy was a demonstration that the national economy could be reoriented by political and administrative action, and that Fascist 'will' could not be held back by objective realities.

IRI was the Fascist institution which most engages economic historians concerned with the continuity and process of Italy's economic development, since it survived the fall of fascism in 1945, and was only wound up in the Thatcher-like privatizations of recent decades. Effectively a giant state holding company, IRI was set up in 1933, the final stage of an expediential process during the Great Depression to prevent Italian industries going down with the collapsing banks which financed them and held their shares as collateral for loans. Put simply, IRI bought up the industrial shares held by the failing banks, which made the Fascist state the titular owner or controlling shareholder in the country's steel, ship and locomotive building, engineering, telephone, and electricity industries. The deal was put together rapidly and in secret, which partly explained the success of the manoeuvre, by Mussolini and economic advisers drawn from big business, some already involved in the para-state bodies created earlier to manage the relationship between government, industry, and banks.

There is more than one way of interpreting the significance of IRI, especially in the light of its survival into the post-war and post-fascist period. It was initially seen as a temporary measure made necessary by the impact of the depression on Italy's banks and industries, a safe harbour for industries in crisis which could be reorganized, refinanced, and returned to the private sector as going concerns. Some companies taken over by IRI in 1933 were later reprivatized. But there were signs of

IRI's permanent utility to the Fascist regime even before IRI was made an institution in 1937 with a clear public brief for autarky and war preparation.

The scheme devised to enable IRI to repay the Bank of Italy's funding of the initial salvage operation, and to raise new investment funds for the industries now run by IRI, was the issue of state bonds which, with attractive government-guaranteed interest rates, hoovered up Italians' savings in the mid- and late 1930s. This refinancing could, of course, be seen as making sick businesses healthy enough for eventual reflotation as private companies. But in 1935, the government blocked the sale to the private sector of 'Terni', a major steel manufacturing firm on IRI's books, for reasons which were plain, at the time. The Fascist government had no need, nor desire, to divest itself of war industries; companies owned by IRI could be made to embark on government-funded industrial projects which met autarkic and war preparation needs. IRI's offshoot, Finsider, undertook a planned rationalization and reorganization of the whole iron- and steel-producing sector. The intention was to concentrate productive capacity in a small number of very large companies, which would enable the industry to deliver on Finsider's big decision to convert to an integrated continuous production cycle from iron ore to steel, on electrically powered furnaces supplied by autarkically generated HEP, reducing dependence on imported coal and coke.

Context is all, in evaluating these developments. Finsider's streamlining of the iron and steel sector, started in the late 1930s, probably helped to make the Italian steel industry a strong and internationally competitive player after the war. But this looks like retrospectively making the best of a bad job. The reorganization of the sector was carried out by a fascist government agency, which owned it, with the intention of enlarging the productive capacity of a key industry making arms for war, not civilian products for markets at home or abroad.

The Fascist government's power to intervene in the country's heavy industrial sector and direct its activities towards autarky and war production was based on IRI's major shareholding in the sector. Strategic and day-to-day handling of these publicly owned industries was in the hands of big businessmen and private enterprise managers, whose own interests straddled the public and private sectors. The President of IRI was Alberto Beneduce, who was also a director of electricity, insurance, and chemicals companies: simultaneously, then, a top businessmen and a top state functionary.

Beneduce's profile was replicated many times over among the technocrats heading the quango-like bodies running the Italian economy in the 1930s, as was the 'private sector style management of public enterprise'.[15] Cartels, the formation of which was made obligatory in 1936 and responsible to the Ministry of Corporations, were

---

[15] S. Battente, 'Nation and State Building in Italy: Recent Historiographical Interpretations (1989–1997), II: From Fascism to the Republic', *Journal of Modern Italian Studies*, 6/1 (2001), 101.

usually welcomed by the producers themselves, or at least those already dominant in the sector being legally cartelized. In difficult economic circumstances, cartels enabled the main producers to fix and monopolize a protected domestic market and deter competition. The *ammassi*, a government requisitioning and stockpiling scheme for basic agricultural products, made compulsory in 1938, were run by the big farmers' associations themselves, now the Fascist Confederation of Agricultural Cartels.

As the legally required form for the organization and management of the different branches of the economy, cartelization effectively transformed private into public monopolies, and was certainly a preferable business alternative to the sector being organized in a corporation. So, for instance, the 'Italian Cotton Institute', a voluntary cartel of 'autarkic' cotton producers set up in 1934, had almost identical functions of regulating production to the recently formed corporation in the sector, and was probably designed to pre-empt it.

What we can observe in a national economy being run at the micro-level by a plethora of simultaneously private and public sectoral economic bodies was an almost perfect, mutually beneficial congruence of business and state interests. The fascist regime promoted the organization and enhancement of autarkic cotton production, while cotton producers secured a protected and guaranteed domestic market, in a framework which deliberately bucked the rules of a free-market, capitalist economy. No businessman in his right mind would have attempted to build up an Italian aluminium-manufacturing industry, when its raw materials and energy resource could be imported more cheaply and economically from abroad. But aluminium was defined as a 'national' metal by the fascist regime, a key material in aircraft production, for instance; and so it was the Fascist government that subsidized the construction of factories in designated industrial development zones which, at an uneconomic cost, extracted aluminium from Italian bauxite in a manufacturing process powered by Italian-generated electricity. In IRI, its subsidiaries, and in compulsory cartels, the Fascist regime successfully co-opted and paid for the technical, managerial, and entrepreneurial expertise of the country's business managers, in the pursuit of an autarkic war economy.

That the fascist economic 'system' of the 1930s had so many often competing and overlapping components makes it difficult to discern where and how economic decision-making happened, beyond Mussolini's broad statements that economic policy and initiatives should be aligned to autarky and preparation for war. It did seem likely that the way IRI was created set a kind of pattern, or way of operating, that was appropriately dictatorial. Mussolini, in other words, privately consulted with, or responded to the lobbying of, individual ministers (when these were not Mussolini himself), and leaders of Party, state, and para-state economic bodies, the latter often influential and well-connected businessmen.

Economic policy was almost certainly discussed in the main, supposedly more collegial, forums of the Fascist state, including the Fascist Grand Council, the Council of Ministers, the National Council of Corporations, the Central Corporative Committee, and the corporations themselves. But these seem to have been organs whose members were informed of or consulted about decisions taken behind closed doors by Mussolini and a few advisers.

When a general strategy of autarky and war had so many institutional outlets and outcomes, joined-up thinking and planning was at a premium, and checking up on and accounting for what had been done, or, more likely, not done, ranged from the difficult to the impossible. The regime did have other economic bodies, or committees, with more overarching roles. These were the Supreme Commission for Autarky, apparently responsible for the coordination of autarky projects, and a throwback to the government's organization of the economy during the First World War, the General Commissariat for War Production, to regulate (which was different from coordinate) the arms industry and production. The Supreme Commission of Defence, which met once a year, gathered together under Mussolini's presidency all interested parties in the Italian war economy.

These bodies could arguably have provided much-needed focus and coordination, but, again, we know relatively little about how they operated in the period of 'peacetime' preparation for war in the late 1930s. During the war itself, meetings of these bodies seemed to degenerate into mutually recriminatory slanging matches where people defended their own positions and criticized the performance of the others, an almost predictable evasion of responsibility when the war was not being won.[16]

It is beyond the scope of this chapter to explain how and why this hybrid, multi-faceted economic 'system' strung together by the Fascist regime in the 1930s failed to sustain the country's economic and military effort in a general European war from June 1940. But the hybrid nature of the 'system' and the lack of responsibility and effective coordination of its many components were part of the explanation. If this does not sound too contradictory, the Fascist regime was, in its failure to wage an effective war, being true to itself and its dictatorial system of rule. Bottai, admittedly an eventually jaundiced and embittered observer of Mussolini the dictator at work, recorded Mussolini exploding at a Council of Ministers meeting in August 1940 about the administrative malfunctioning of the war economy after barely two months of the experience of being at war. He attacked a culture of 'imprecise responsibilities' which had created 'this climate of general irresponsibility'. Bottai's comment was that this was a case of 'Mussolini arguing against Mussolini'.[17]

The only conclusion possible may be disappointing to those who still assume that the fascist totalitarian regimes were monolithic enough to ally coherence of political and ideological vision with clarity of execution. What emerged in the course of the 1930s was a fascist economic 'order' which had different priorities from the

[16] A. Raspin, *The Italian War Economy, 1940–1943, with Particular Reference to Italian Relations with Germany* (New York: Garland, 1986), 128.

[17] G. Bottai, *Vent'anni e un giorno* (Milan: Garzanti, 1949), 189.

one which preceded fascism, which operated in different ways from its predecessor before the First World War, primarily in a rolling up of private into public interests, and which was corporate in theory and justification but a-corporative in practice. Indeed, what was needed operationally to create an autarkic economy for war made corporations inoperable. In the end, the fascist economy could not be both warlike and corporate.

BIBLIOGRAPHY

COHEN, J., 'Was Italian Fascism a Developmental Dictatorship? Some Evidence to the Contrary', *Economic History Review*, 41/1 (1988), 95–111.

——and FEDERICO, G., *The Growth of the Italian Economy, 1860–1960* (Cambridge: Cambridge University Press, 2001).

FERRARI, P. (ed.), 'L'industria bellica italiana, 1861–1945: appunti sulla recente storiografia', *Italia contemporanea*, 190/1 (1993), 129–98.

MORGAN, P., *Italian Fascism, 1915–1945* (2nd edn, Basingstoke: Palgrave Macmillan, 2004).

—— 'The Italian Fascist New Order in Europe', in M. L. Smith and P. M. R. Stirk (eds), *Making the New Europe: European Unity and the Second World War* (London: Pinter, 1990), 27–45.

—— '"The Party is Everywhere": The Italian Fascist Party in Economic Life', *English Historical Review*, 114/455 (1999), 85–111.

PRETI, D., *Economia e istitutioni nello stato fascista* (Rome: Riuniti, 1980).

RASPIN, A., *The Italian War Economy, 1940–1943, with Particular Reference to Italian Relations with Germany* (New York: Garland, 1986).

RODOGNO, D., *Fascism's European Empire: Italian Occupation during the Second World War* (Cambridge: Cambridge University Press, 2006).

ROSENSTOCK-FRANCK, L., *L'Économie corporative fasciste en doctrine et en fait: ses origines historiques et son évolution* (Paris: Librarie Universitaire, 1934).

—— *Les Étapes de l'économie fasciste italienne: du corporatisme à l'économie de guerre* (Paris: Editions du centre polytechnicien d'études économiques, 1939).

TONIOLO, G., *L'economia dell'Italia fascista* (Bari: Laterza, 1980).

—— (ed.), *L'economia italiana, 1861–1940* (Bari: Laterza, 1973).

ZAMAGNI, V., *The Economic History of Italy, 1860–1990* (Oxford: Oxford University Press, 1993).

CHAPTER 9

··

FASCISM AND CATHOLICISM

··

J. F. POLLARD

THE first fascist movement to come to power, Italian Fascism, did so in a country which was 99 per cent Catholic and the seat of the papacy, and 'clerical fascist' movements came to power in another two overwhelmingly Catholic countries, the first Slovak Republic and the Croatian Independent State. Fascist movements and regimes in other European countries also entered into relations with the Roman Catholic Church, and in broader terms, many Catholics, individually and collectively, were closely involved with fascist movements and regimes in the inter-war years. The purpose of this chapter, therefore, is to analyse the complex relationships between fascism, the institutional church, and Catholics more generally. What were the initial attitudes of fascist movements to Catholicism/the Catholic Church, what forms did the eventual encounter between fascism and Catholicism take, and what common interests and common enemies brought them together in this encounter? What were the limits of agreement between fascists and Catholics and what circumstances and issues proved insurmountable barriers to further cooperation? How significant, on the other hand, was Catholic *anti-fascism*, the phenomenon of Catholic opposition and resistance to fascism? Finally, were Catholics more prone to accepting fascism and collaborating with it than their Orthodox or Protestant counterparts?

The encounter between fascism and Catholicism most notably took place at the institutional level, between Pope Pius XI and Mussolini, which resulted in the *Conciliazione* of 1929 and what Renzo De Felice described as the 'marriage of convenience' between the papacy and Italian Fascism that endured for most of the 1930s.[1]

[1] R. De Felice, *Mussolini il Fascista: l'organizzazione dello stato Fascista* (Turin: Einaudi, 1968), 432.

A relationship of equal importance was that between Pius XI, Pius XII, and Hitler, which resulted in the *Reichskonkordat* of 1933 but had a very chequered history thereafter. The Vatican had a difficult relationship with the regime established by Msgr Josef Tiso and the Slovakian People's Party after Hitler's dismemberment of Czechoslovakia in March 1939, and Archbishop Alojzije Stepinac of Zagreb had an equally difficult relationship with the Ustasha regime of Ante Pavelić after the latter's proclamation of the Croatian Independent State in 1941. It was almost certainly at the institutional level that the boundaries were clearest, and also that the divergences between Catholicism and various forms of fascism became most pronounced, particularly as the 1930s wore on.

As well as institutional links, the relationship between Fascism and Catholicism meant the participation on an individual basis of Catholics in fascist movements. Men as diverse as Ferenc Szálasi, leader of the Hungarian Arrow Cross movement, Arnold Meyer, Catholic essayist and journalist who founded the Dutch Black Front organization, and Cesare Maria De Vecchi di Val Cismon, 'Fascist of the first hour', one of the *quadumvirs* (organizers) of the March on Rome and later minister and member of the Grand Council of Fascism, all come into this category. More Catholic conservatives were drawn into the Italian Fascist movement as 'agrarian fascism' spread through the countryside and small towns of northern and central Italy in 1920 and 1921. Others, like Stefano Cavazzoni and Egilberto Martire, started their political careers as MPs of the Catholic People's Party, Partito Popolare Italiano (henceforth PPI) and became clerico-fascist 'flankers' of fascism in the early 1920s but went on to become members of the Partito Nazionale Fascista (henceforth PNF).

In other circumstances, we can usefully talk about 'clerico-fascism' or 'clerical fascism', that is movements, currents of ideas in which Catholics predominated, like the Italian Centro Nazionale Italiano, which was essentially a 'flanking' organization of the PNF and one of the intermediaries between it and the Vatican in the years leading up to the Lateran Pacts of 1929, the Slovakian People's Party (henceforth SPP) which combined an essentially clerical and nationalist wing led by Tiso and a more radical one led by Josef Tuka which had clear national socialist proclivities, or the Croatian Ustasha. Arguably another example of clerical fascism would be General Eoin O'Duffy's blueshirts in Ireland.

I. Fascist Anticlericalism and Anti-Catholicism

The two main fascist movements were essentially anticlerical, anti-Christian, or even anti-Catholic in their origins, until they abandoned their prejudices and

'embraced' institutional Catholicism for opportunistic reasons, and then only temporarily. This was certainly true of Italian Fascism, most of whose founders' political past lay either in the anticlerical, socialist left, like Mussolini and Edmondo
Rossoni, or anarchism like Michele Bianchi, or the equally anticlerical movements
of republicanism, like Dino Grandi, or Futurism, like Filippo Marinetti: this last
once wrote that 'the papacy has always defecated on Italy throughout its history'.[2] It
was the Intervention Crisis of 1915, when Italy decided to enter the First World War
on the side of the Entente powers, that brought these disparate groups together for
the first time, and their personal experience of the war was crucial for the fascist
movement that emerged after it. Pope Benedict XV (1914–22) thus attracted the
bitter denunciations of Mussolini and other interventionist 'proto-fascists' for his
Peace Note of August 1917, when he attempted to bring the warring powers to the
negotiating table. The Peace Note was blamed by Mussolini in particular for spreading pacifism and defeatism, especially after Italy's catastrophic defeat at Caporetto
in the late autumn of that year. In his newspaper, *Il popolo d'Italia*, the future *Duce*
of fascism changed the pope's Italian name, Benedetto, meaning literally 'blessed',
to Maledetto, meaning 'accursed', and called him 'Judas'. In November 1919, another
article in *Il popolo d'Italia* declared, 'There is only one possible revision of the Law
of Guarantees [regulating Italy's relations with papacy] and that is its abolition,
followed by a firm invitation to his Holiness to quit Rome.'[3] As the violence of
the fascist squads against socialist and Catholic agrarian organizations spread over
large areas of northern and central Italy from the autumn of 1920 onwards, the
Vatican's authoritative press organ, *L'osservatore romano*, condemned it, and the
cult of war and violence that lay behind it, though it also condemned the rather
more spasmodic violence of militant socialism. So early fascism remained stridently
anticlerical until 1921 when, following the entry of the fascists into parliament,
Mussolini changed his tune.

The Nazi Party (henceforth NSDAP), despite its early and repeated protesta-
tions that it supported Christianity, was strongly anti-Catholic, a judgement which
is not affected by the ongoing debate about the Party's relations with German
Protestantism stirred by Steigman-Gall's book *The Holy Reich*. The late nineteenth-
century Pangerman and *Volkish* precursors of National Socialism were deeply
hostile to Rome, which for them represented the ultimate 'Judaeo-Christian conspiracy'. Well into the 1920s, Erich Ludendorff, German military hero of the First
World War and one of Hitler's companions in the abortive 'beer cellar Putsch', led
the Los von Rom ('Away from Rome') movement decrying Roman Catholicism
as a subversive, anti-German phenomenon. The later National Socialist leaders,
renegade Catholics like Joseph Goebbels, Heinrich Himmler, and Hitler himself,

---

[2] F. T. Marinetti, *L'aeroplano del Papa: romanzo profetico in versi liberi* (Milan: Edizioni Futuriste di
Poesia, 1914), 67.
[3] *Il popolo d'Italia*, 18 November 1919.

not to mention the pagan theorist Alfred Rosenberg, also instinctively viewed Roman Catholicism as the enemy, and some members of the Party, like Artur Dinter, campaigned strongly against the papacy: according to the latter, 'The Roman pope's church is just as terrible an enemy of a *Volkish* Germany as the Jew.'[4] As a result, the Nazis were forced to confront the hostility of many bishops and parochial clergy and competition from the Catholic Centre Party in its strongholds, especially Bavaria.

The Spanish fascist movement, the Falange y JONS of Jose-Antonio Primo de Rivera, was ambivalent in its attitudes towards Catholicism: Primo de Rivera, supported by the other major leader of the Falange, Onesimo Redondo, accepted Catholicism as an intrinsic cultural component of the glorious Spanish tradition, but the Falange's twenty-seven-point programme declared that the church would not be allowed any 'interference or activity that may impair the dignity of the state or national integrity'.[5] Other European fascist movements, like Oswald Mosley's British Union of Fascists or the various minor fascist groups in inter-war France, were not intrinsically anticlerical or anti-Catholic. On the other hand, there were extreme right-wing groups with clear fascist characteristics, like the Slovakian People's Party, the Croatian Ustasha, and the Belgian Rexist movement of Léon Degrelle, which possessed an identifiable Catholic element sufficient to merit their being called 'clerical-fascist'.

II. Italian Fascism, Mussolini, and the Papacy

As new regimes, Italian Fascism and German National Socialism inevitably sought the endorsement of embedded cultural/social forces like the churches, especially in the inter-war years when those forces continued to exercise considerable influence in civil society and politics. This was a part of the wider strategy of courting the support of the established elites in the process of obtaining and consolidating power. Thus Italian Fascism and German National Socialism, and other fascist movements like the Croatian Ustasha, sought approval and support from the churches, Protestant and Catholic, by opportunistic, usually insincere declarations of respect for Christian values as embodying the essential spirit of the nation. Given the absolute, centralized authority that the papacy had established over the Catholic Church

---

[4] As quoted in R. Steigman-Gall, *The Holy Reich: Nazi Conceptions of Christianity, 1919–1945* (Cambridge: Cambridge University Press, 2003).

[5] As quoted in C. Delzell (ed.), *Mediterranean Fascism, 1919–1945* (New York: Walker, 1971), 257–331.

since the mid-nineteenth century, this meant coming to terms with both national hierarchies *and* the Vatican.

In the case of Italy, after the inauspicious beginnings of fascism's relationship with Catholicism, Mussolini saw the light and, like the pre-war Nationalists, the die-hard atheist now recognized that there was no future for an intransigently anticlerical policy in a country like Italy. Just as he had abandoned the initial anti-capitalism and anti-monarchism of early fascism, now he dropped his vocal anticlericalism and in his maiden speech to parliament in May 1921, he claimed that 'Fascism neither preaches nor practises anticlericalism . . . The only universal values that radiate from Rome are those of the Vatican.'[6] This unsubtle wooing cut no ice in the Vatican, but in February 1922 Benedict died and in the pontificate of his successor the Vatican's policy towards fascism changed.

The new Pope, Pius XI, was preoccupied by the communist threat in Italy and hostile to the PPI, not least because it was led by a priest. As the crisis of the Liberal state deepened in the summer of 1922, the Vatican became convinced that a government of 'National Concentration', including the fascists, was the only answer. Mussolini responded by making tangible offers before and after the March on Rome of October which included the reintroduction of religious education into state secondary schools, the restoration of the crucifix to public buildings, an increase in priests' salaries, and in January 1923, in a private meeting with the Cardinal Secretary of State Pietro Gasparri, he guaranteed that his government would salvage the floundering Banco di Roma, in which the Vatican had a substantial stake. Mussolini thus cleverly exploited the Vatican's dissatisfaction with the failing Italian parliamentary system and the PPI, and was able to enter into a direct interlocutory relationship with the papacy.

The Vatican's further support for Mussolini during the debates on the electoral reform law in the summer of 1923 by ordering the leader of the PPI, Luigi Sturzo, to resign and during the Matteotti Crisis of 1924, when Mussolini's government faced collapse following the murder by fascist thugs of the eponymous leader of the Reformist Socialist Party, consolidated the new relationship and led to the opening of negotiations for some sort of resolution of the 'Roman Question', the sixty-year dispute between Italy and the papacy. In February 1929, Gasparri and Mussolini signed the Lateran Pacts which established the state of the Vatican City and restored much of the property and privileges of the church in Italy. For Mussolini this *Conciliazione* (reconciliation) between the papacy and the Italian state constituted a great international diplomatic triumph winning respectability and prestige for Italian Fascism. It also marked the completion of his consolidation of power, putting into the place the last element of the 'Block of Consensus'—monarchy, armed forces, business and agrarian elites, and the church—which would provide the base-line of support for the fascist regime. Though the church

---

[6] As quoted in P. Scoppola, *La Chiesa e il fascismo: documenti e interpretazioni* (Bari: Laterza, 1971).

was now a useful prop to the fascist regime, this did not please all fascists, many of whom, like Roberto Farinacci, remained suspicious and hostile towards Catholicism.

But the church did not completely identify itself with fascism: it was always different, separate, and autonomous, and during the course of the *ventennio* there were clashes between Pius XI and Mussolini in 1929, 1931, and 1938/9 over such issues as the education of youth, Catholic professional associations, the growth of Catholic Action, the lay people's organization, and the introduction of the Racial Laws. Pius XI not only dispensed with the PPI and doomed it to extinction; after 1929 he dropped with equal ruthlessness the clerico-fascist elements whose efforts had helped make the historic agreement with Italy possible. True to its centuries-old strategy, the papacy prepared for an Italy after fascism, by building a network of lay organizations around Catholic Action, including most importantly FUCI and the Movimento Laureato (Catholic graduates) as a possible new Catholic ruling class.

III. Hitler, Nazi Germany, and the Roman Catholic Church

German National Socialism's relationship with Catholicism was inevitably rather different from that between Italian Fascism and the church. Unlike their Italian counterparts, German Catholics constituted a minority (30–35 per cent) of the population, whose episcopal leaders continued to suffer from the defensive attitudes induced by the experience of the *Kulturkampf* of the previous century. Indeed, during the early years of National Socialism, the Catholic authorities were hostile to it, with the result that some bishops continued the ban on Catholics joining the movement until 1932.

After Hitler's accession to power in 1933, the Nazis cannily requested a *Reichskonkordat*, as a means of gaining papal endorsement for their new regime and thus neutralizing Catholic political opposition. This presented Pius XI and his Secretary of State, Cardinal Eugenio Pacelli, with a dilemma. When nuncio in Germany (1917–29), Pacelli had appreciated the dangers of National Socialism but he had also sought and failed to achieve a concordat with the German Reich as opposed to individual states. The Nazi request thus represented a possibly unrepeatable opportunity to obtain juridical guarantees which both Pacelli and the pontiff saw as the best means of safeguarding the German Church. Pacelli has been criticized for being 'overeager' to negotiate the *Reichskonkordat*, and callously sacrificing the

Centre Party, and therefore German democracy, in the bargain.[7] In reality, Pius XI was the driving force in the negotiations, and his sacrifice of the PPI to Mussolini convinced him that he could strike a similarly advantageous deal with Hitler.

National Socialism's powerful anti-Catholic tendencies inevitably led to conflict almost as soon as the *Reichskonkordat* had been signed. Leading Nazis did not change in their hostility to Catholicism after the seizure of power, continuing to view it as 'un-German' and the papacy as a 'foreign power', and, as will be seen, National Socialism's ideological core—Aryan racialism—was more clearly in conflict with Catholic teaching than Italian Fascism. The Nazi regime engaged in wholesale violations of the agreement with the Vatican, such as the closing down of Catholic youth organizations, schools, and newspapers, the confiscation of church property, and the persecution of the clergy, especially members of the religious orders: by 1939 there were hundreds of Catholic priests in prisons and concentration camps. These measures drew increasing protests from the Vatican until, in 1937, the pope issued *Mit Brennender Sorge*, a scathing denunciation of the violations coupled with severe criticism of Nazism's racial, militaristic, and totalitarian tendencies.[8]

IV. 'CATHOLIC FASCISM'?

As well as the concepts of 'clerico-fascism' and 'clerical fascism', some historians have used the concepts of 'Catholic fascism' in their analyses of the phenomenon of Christian relationships with fascism, suggesting an unconditional acceptance of fascism by some Catholics. Fascism certainly did exercise a powerful attraction upon some Catholic movements, especially of youth, even in the most democratic of states, as a result of the apparent bankruptcy of liberal democracy during the Great Depression. Griffiths, for example, argues that in the early to mid-1930s increasing numbers of Catholic intellectuals, especially in Belgium, Britain, and France, looked with benevolence upon fascist movements, especially that in Italy, after Mussolini's *Conciliazione* with the Vatican and the publication in 1931 of *Quadragesimo anno*, which was seen as papal endorsement of corporatist, authoritarian systems. He cites the likes of Douglas Jerrold and the *English Review* in Britain, Robert de Brasillach, Henri Massis, and Emmanuel Mounier in France, and Léon Degrelle and the Rexists in Belgium.[9] To this list could be added elements of the Swiss Conservative People's

---

[7] See J. Cornwell, *Hitler's Pope: The Secret History of Pius XII* (London: Viking, 1999), chapter 8.

[8] For the text of this encyclical and others referred to in this chapter, see C. Carlen (ed.), *The Papal Encyclicals*, 5 vols (Raleigh, NC: Pierian Press, 1990), vol. iii.

[9] R. Griffiths, *The Intelligent Person's Guide to Fascism* (London: Duckworth, 2002), 60–70.

Party, the KVP, which, according to Martin Conway, 'chose to affiliate themselves to the quasi-fascist National Front'.[10] The biographer of Egilberto Martire, a leading Italian clerico-fascist, uses the term 'Catholic fascism' to describe the belief of his subject, and other Italian Catholics, that Fascism could be 'baptized', an illusion cherished by Pius XI but not for as long as Martire.[11]

After the *Conciliazione* and *Quadragesimo anno*, an even more important catalyst of Catholic attitudes towards fascism across Europe was the outbreak of the Spanish Civil War in 1936. This was viewed by most European Catholics as an apocalyptic, titanic struggle between Good and Evil because of the appalling anticlerical violence of some republican forces, the support of anticlerical Mexico and the atheistic Soviet Union for the Republic, and the inevitable lining up of Spanish Catholic forces, including the institutional church, on the side of the Nationalists. In Spain itself, even before the Civil War actually broke out, the Juventudes de Acción Popular, the youth wing of the Catholic, conservative party Confederación de Derechas Autónomas (CEDA), went over en masse to the Falange. More strikingly, the devout Catholic leader of the Belgian Rexists, Léon Degrelle, and some of his followers, moved increasingly towards National Socialism in the late 1930s and early 1940s, and ended up collaborating with the German occupation authorities and fighting in the Waffen SS on the Russian front.

The Spanish Civil War was undoubtedly *the* major moment of encounter between fascists and Catholics, but the looming shadow of the diplomatic and military power of German National Socialism in the late 1930s quickly became a solvent of the phenomenon of 'Catholic fascism'. The emergence of Nazi Germany had originally prompted the Vatican to encourage the formation of a 'Catholic bloc' of powers led by Fascist Italy between Nazi Germany on the one hand and the Soviet Union on the other, in defence of the independence of Catholic Austria. Nazi Germany's subsequent persecution of the church ensured that Vatican diplomacy would tread cautiously in Spain, despite the enthusiasm of Italian Catholics for the cause of the Nationalists, because of Pius XI's fears of Nazi influence in the Iberian peninsula. After Mussolini's acquiescence in the *Anschluss* in 1938 and his increasing alignment with Hitler thereafter, Vatican diplomacy turned towards improving relations with the democratic powers—Britain, France, and the United States.[12] Italian Catholics became increasingly suspicious of Nazi, 'Nordic', influences as the 1930s wore on, seeing Mussolini's introduction of the racial laws in 1938 as their most baleful fruit. The last months of Pius XI's pontificate were darkened by the renewal of conflict with fascism over the laws, in response to which Pius XI commissioned an encyclical, *Humani generis unitas*, as a wholesale condemnation

---

[10]   M. Conway, *Catholic Politics in Europe, 1918–1945* (London: Routledge, 1997), 72.

[11]   D. Sorrentino, *La Conciliazione e il 'fascismo cattolico': i tempi e la figura di Egilberto Martire* (Brescia: La Morcelliana, 1980).

[12]   J. F. Pollard, 'The Papacy in Two World Wars: Benedict XV and Pius XII Compared', in R. Mallett and G. Sorenson (eds), *International Fascism, 1919–1945* (London: Frank Cass, 2002).

of biological racialism, from the American Jesuit John Lafarge.[13] Mussolini was irritated by the pope's protests and he more generally chafed under the limitations imposed on his 'totalitarian' rule by the compromises he had made with the elites during the consolidation of power so that he remarked several times to his son-in-law and Foreign Minister, Galeazzo Ciano, that after a successful war he would settle accounts with the monarchy and cut the papacy down to size.[14]

V. THE SECOND WORLD WAR, GENOCIDES, AND THE PAPACY

While *Humani generis unitas* was prompted by Mussolini's adoption of racial policies there can be no doubt that Pius XI intended it as a blast directed ultimately against Nazi racialism. The decision of his successor, Pius XII, not to publish the encyclical was determined by his desire to seek better relations with both Fascist Italy and Nazi Germany.[15] Throughout 1939, the new pope sought to act as a mediator to prevent the outbreak of war, to no avail. As the Second World War unfolded, Pius was soon faced by diverse fascist genocides, most notably the Holocaust. It is quite impossible to enter here into the complexities of the 'Hitler's Pope' debate, but Pius XII's 'silences' over the Holocaust and other fascist genocides, like the murder by the Ustasha of hundreds of thousands of Gypsies, Jews, and Serbs, were determined more by naive hopes of helping to negotiate a peace, worries about aiding a Soviet victory, and fear of reprisals against Catholics (and even the Vatican itself) than by callous indifference produced by his anti-Semitism.[16] Above all, he was a realist, unwilling to expose the fragility of the church's hold on the allegiance of German Catholics by ordering them to disobey immoral orders in wartime. In this sense, National Socialism triumphed over Catholicism.

Throughout the conflict, the Vatican insisted on neutrality, but its 'special relationship' with Franklin D. Roosevelt, who sent a personal representative to the

[13] For the text, see G. Passelecq and B. Sucheky, *The Hidden Encyclical of Pius XII* (New York: Harcourt Brace, 1997).

[14] Malcolm Muggeridge (ed.), *Ciano's Diary, 1939–1943* (London: Heinemann, 1947), 26, 39–40, 186, 248–9.

[15] For the latest analysis of the mystery surrounding the non-publication of *Humani generis unitas*, see E. Fattorini, *Pio XI, Hitler e Mussolini* (Turin: Einaudi, 2007).

[16] The most dispassionate analyses of Pius XII's motives are to be found in G. Lewy, 'Pius XII, the Jews and the German Catholic Church', in R. P. Ericksen and S. Heschel (eds), *Betrayal: German Churches and the Holocaust* (Minneapolis: Fortress Press, 1999), ch. 7, and J. M. Sanchez, *Pius XII and the Holocaust: Understanding the Controversy* (Washington: Catholic University of America Press, 2002).

Vatican in 1939, and its refusal to endorse the war against the Soviet Union as an anti-Bolshevik crusade, aroused Mussolini's wrath.[17] The Nazi regime treated the Vatican with deep suspicion and hostility during the Second World War and it was placed under close surveillance by German intelligence agencies.[18] Whatever illusions German Catholics might have cherished about their fate in the event of a German victory were dashed by Nazi treatment of the church in the Warthegau, which clearly demonstrated that Hitler meant what he said when he declared that he would eventually eliminate Christianity altogether.[19]

VI. The 'Appeal' of Fascism

Fascism and Catholicism were brought together by common enemies and common interests, and chief among the enemies were liberalism and communism. Indeed, many Christians, Catholic, Orthodox, and Protestant alike, were attracted to fascist-style ideologies, movements, and regimes precisely as a reaction against, and rejection of, liberal parliamentary democracy, which was seen as alien and hostile to the Christian tradition. Liberalism was deemed responsible for secularism and anticlericalism, and the consequent laws which from the French Revolution onwards had restricted the property, privileges, and power of the churches. Associated with liberalism and all its works, including capitalism, were Freemasonry and the Jews.

We shall return to the Jews later, but Freemasonry provoked extreme hostility on the part of both fascism and the Catholic Church. It was suspect for many Italian Fascists and National Socialists because of its secrecy and 'cosmopolitanism', and alleged Jewish influences. Since the French Revolution, continental Masonic movements had usually pursued a secularizing, anticlerical and anti-Catholic, agenda, and in Italy Freemasonry was one of the key institutions of the Liberal conservative ruling class. Hence it was condemned by Pius IX (1864) and Leo XIII (1884) and, according to the Code of Canon Law of 1917, Freemasons were automatically excommunicated. That both Mussolini and Hitler outlawed Freemasonry certainly helped to endear their regimes to Catholics.

The Weimar Republic epitomized to both Catholics and Protestants the worst forms of modernization that the post-1919 triumph of liberal democracy had

---

[17] G. Miccoli, 'La Chiesa e i totalitarismi', in V. Ferrone (ed.), *La Chiesa Cattolica e il totalitarismo: atti del Convegno di Torino, 25–26 ottobre 2001* (Florence: Leo S. Olschki Editore, 2004), 26.

[18] D. Alvarez and R. A. Graham, *Nothing Sacred: Nazi Espionage against the Vatican, 1939–1945* (London: Cass, 1997).

[19] M. Housden, *Resistance and Conformity in the Third Reich* (London: Routledge, 1997), 56–7.

brought—partial emancipation of women, the consequent erosion of Christian-based patriarchy, and the relaxation of legal regulation of public morality. On the other hand, the social policies of the National Socialist movement, leaving aside those tainted by eugenics and racialism, and those of the Italian Fascist regime from the mid-1920s onwards largely converged with Catholic teaching on the question of gender roles, the family, contraception, abortion, and divorce, as reiterated in Pius XI's 1930 encyclical on marriage, *Casti connubi*.[20]

Taking all these factors together, it would be no exaggeration to say that Catholic support for fascism was a major consequence of the 'culture wars' between Catholicism and liberalism that had raged in Europe, and in parts of Latin America, since the early nineteenth century, and that the Spanish Civil War of 1936–9, in which Catholics saw the hand of anticlerical liberalism, Freemasonry, *and* bolshevism, was the last and greatest of Europe's 'culture wars' and had, accordingly, a massive impact on the attitude of European Catholics to fascism.

As a result of the ongoing 'culture wars', one of the major factors that attracted Christians, and the institutional churches, to fascist movements was that they were both engaged in 'palingenetic' projects. If, as Griffin claims, fascism was a form of 'palingenetic, populist, ultra-nationalism', and it is certainly true that fascist movements throughout Europe had national 'rebirth' at the heart of their programmes,[21] Christians, for some of the same reasons, were also seeking a moral and spiritual rebirth of European society. The most explicit and compelling form of this Christian palingenetic project was that which Pius XI embarked upon after his election in 1922. Pius set forth his comprehensive vision of a Christian restoration of a society vitiated by secularism and anticlericalism in his first encyclical, *Ubi arcano Dei* in 1922—'la restaurazione cristiana della societa in sense cattolico' (the Christian restoration of society in a Catholic sense)—and developed it by the institution of the feast of Christ the King in 1925 and through the worldwide development of Catholic Action to mobilize the Catholic faithful in this endeavour. As Jorge Dagnino points out, the commitment to the Christian palingenetic project meant that even in FUCI, the Italian Catholic students' movement whose history has largely been read in an *anti-fascist* key, in the 1930s there was a strong sympathy for fascism's 'spiritual and moral aspirations'.[22]

Despite the shared antipathy towards liberalism, communism seemed the most dangerous common enemy to most fascists and Catholics in the inter-war period. The 1917 Bolshevik Revolution, as well as other attempted revolutions and even short-lived Soviet regimes in Eastern and Central Europe, hung like a shadow over the politics of inter-war Europe. Catholicism obviously opposed the atheistic

---

[20] For the text, see Carlen (ed.), *The Papal Encyclicals*, iii. 225–398.

[21] R. Griffin, *The Nature of Fascism* (London: Routledge, 1993), 32–6.

[22] J. D'Agnino, 'Catholic Modernities in Fascist Italy: The Intellectuals of Azione Cattolica', in M. Feldman and T. Georgescu (eds), *Clerical Fascism in Inter-war Europe* (London: Routledge, 2008), 329–43.

materialism of Soviet communism, but also its economic and social programme. The 'Godless' campaigns of the Soviet governments against all religions, but especially the Orthodox and the Catholic Churches, in the 1920s confirmed its worst fears on this score, though the Vatican stuck in a remarkably tenacious way to a policy of seeking a pragmatic accommodation with the Soviets to protect and advance Catholic interests in Russia until as late as 1929 and did not formally condemn their regime until the 1937 encyclical *Divinis redemptoris*.

Coalitions of forces—church, monarchy, armed forces, and landowners—had cooperated in crushing the threat of Bolshevik revolution in such countries as Hungary and Slovakia, and the authoritarian regimes established in Hungary, in Franco's Spain and Salazar's Portugal (in the latter case, without the monarchy), and also in Austria between 1934 and 1938, were essentially based on such anti-communist coalitions—as arguably Fascist Italy also was. It was in the aftermath of the *biennio rosso* (the red two years from 1918 to 1920), with its upsurge of working-class militancy, that some Catholic politicians and intellectuals abandoned the PPI and rallied to fascism. Given the proliferation of 'clerical', conservative, authoritarian regimes in inter-war Europe, it should be noted that in the 1920s Pius XI and many Catholics saw Italian Fascism as simply a variant of this kind of political system.

Fascism and Catholicism also shared a suspicion of capitalism, even if, in practice, both major fascist regimes usually acquiesced in the workings of a largely capitalist economy. Given the persistence of hostility towards moneylending, not to mention the stereotypical association with the Jews, capitalism was abhorred by many Catholics as 'the evil child of liberalism'. The values it represented—individualism, materialism, profit making, and the brute forces of the market—were regarded as unchristian: they were also not very 'fascist' or *Volkisch* either. Industrialism was a child of capitalism and it produced the twin evils, urbanization and modernization, which eroded the moral values of 'healthy' rural, agrarian societies. In most European countries in the inter-war years, rural, agrarian, small-town society remained the heartland of religion, whether Catholicism, Orthodoxy, or Protestantism, so the rural, agrarian policies of fascist movements and regimes were a natural attraction. Between 1939 and 1945 the SPP ruled a society that, unlike the western part of the former Czechoslovak state, was hardly touched by industrialization and urbanization. And in Italy, the Catholic convergence with fascism manifested itself particularly in the participation of the clergy—bishops and parish priests—in Mussolini's 'Battle for Grain', the unsuccessful attempt to make Fascist Italy self-sufficient in cereals. In broader terms, this was a signal of Catholic support for Mussolini's ideology of *ruralization*, the rationale for an attempt to freeze the balance between rural and urban society as a way of preserving social and political stability. But this was not a purely Catholic phenomenon: in Orthodox Romania, the ideology of the fascist Legion included a romanticization of the 'long-suffering' peasantry who constituted 80 per cent of the population, the

Nazi doctrine of *Blut und Boten* was aimed principally at Protestant farmers, and the Clerical People's Party of Sweden and the Finnish Lapua movement also found their strongest support in rural areas.

In the 1930s, Mussolini translated the ideas of the revolutionary, later national, syndicalists and those of the pre-war Nationalists into the 'Corporate State', the flagship policy of Fascist Italy: Italian Fascism claimed it had invented a 'third way' between capitalism and communism. Corporatism was rather less important in Nazi Germany. The Catholic answer to 'Godless communism' and heartless capitalism, especially during the Great Depression, was also corporatist. Catholic corporatist ideas had first emerged in Austria, Germany, and Italy in the nineteenth century and were at the heart of the Catholic 'social doctrine' enunciated in Pope Leo XIII's encyclical *Rerum novarum* of 1891, in response to European industrialization and the consequent rise of a revolutionary socialist working-class movement.[23] Corporatist theorists elaborated a system of 'mixed' organizations (i.e. representing both capital and labour) that would thus transcend and eliminate class conflict, and Pius XI sanctioned this in his encyclical *Quadragesimo anno* of 1931. Thus the corporatist policies of the fascist regime helped consolidate the support of Italian Catholics for fascism in the 1930s. Yet Pius XI was actually critical of Fascist corporatism in his 1931 encyclical, rightly perceiving that Mussolini's corporative institutions were not Catholic in inspiration and involved rigid regimentation of the workforce and dependence upon the state. This criticism, and Catholic Action's aspirations in the socio-economic field, was one of the causes of the 1931 conflict between the church and fascism.

Nevertheless, inside Italy, Catholic economists, like the later Christian Democratic leader Amintore Fanfani and the Jesuit columnist Fr Angleo Brucculeri, viewed corporatist institutions as an attractive element of fascism. They were also admired by many Catholics outside Italy, were imitated by the regimes in Portugal and Spain, and provoked keen interest among the Catholic circles around the blueshirts in Ireland. Corporative ideas struck a particular chord in Austria; the semi-dictatorial regime constructed by Engelbert Dollfuss after the crushing of 'Socialist Vienna' in 1934 claimed to be 'Christian, Corporative, and German'.

Anti-Semitism was another of the key meeting points between fascist movements and Christianity in the inter-war period, given anti-Semitism's essentially theological roots. In fact, anti-Semitism was an almost universal characteristic of Christian Europe, from Scandinavia to Romania. In the latter, anti-Semitism was at the heart of the beliefs of the Legion of the Archangel Michael: to be a Romanian was to be Christian and anti-Semite. Even in Italy, where anti-Semitism was not on the agenda of fascism until the mid-1930s, in large part because Jews had been well integrated into Italian society since the Risorgimento, there were isolated pockets

---

[23] P. Misner, *Social Catholicism in Europe: From the Onset of Industrialization to the First World War* (London: Dartman, Longman and Todd, 1991), ch. 11.

of virulent anti-Semitism and they were almost always Catholic. One has already been cited: the Jesuits; another was the *Fede e ragione* newspaper in Florence, which represented the most intransigent, *integriste* form of Italian Catholicism. According to Giovanni Miccoli, in the nineteenth century, 'For Catholic anti-Semitism, the Jews became the symbol of the hated modernization which was in train, the inspirers and protagonists of the processes of secularization.'[24] The situation had not changed nearly a century later.

While Cardinals Joseph Van Roey (Malines), Jean Verdier (Paris), and the Patriarch of Lisbon condemned *Kristallnacht* in November 1938, neither of the main German Churches had publicly protested the development of anti-Jewish persecution by the Nazis after 1933. Catholic bishops voted for discriminatory anti-Semitic legislation along with Protestant leaders when it was introduced into the Hungarian parliament in 1938, though they protested against further legislation in 1939 and sought to protect Jews from deportation to Auschwitz in 1944 and 1945. There was no opposition from clerical members, including Bishop Stefan Vojtissak of Spiss, when the Slovak parliament voted in 1942 to legalize the deportation of Slovak Jews to Auschwitz, and the role of Msgr Tiso, Priest-President of the Republic during the actual deportation of Slovakian Jews to the death camps, was equivocal to say the least.

The National Socialist belief in the superiority of the Aryan race was, of course, more than just anti-Semitism, part of a comprehensive doctrine of biological racialism. While many Christians shared anti-Semitic feelings with fascists, only in the context of Protestantism, and more specifically German and Scandinavian Lutheranism, could the encounter between fully developed racial ideas and Christianity evolve into a tightly knit synthesis. According to Richard Steigmann-Gall, the *Deutschen Christen* in Germany, building upon Luther's visceral anti-Semitism, sought to 'Aryanize' Christianity. They 'rejected the Old Testament and contended that Christ was not a Jew', presenting him as an Aryan hero, the archetypal anti-Semitic warrior.[25]

This kind of synthesis between Christian theology and racial ideology was not possible in the Catholic context. 'Catholic' means universal, and whatever forms of racial discrimination, segregation, and repression were actually *practised* by Catholics, the theological essence of Catholicism remained universalistic. Consequently, in the 1920s and 1930s, Pope Pius XI came out repeatedly and strongly

---

[24]   G. Miccoli, 'Santa Sede, questione ebraica e anti-semitismo fra Otto e Novecento', in C. Vivianti (ed.), *Storia d'Italia: annali 11: gli ebrei in Italia* (Turin: Einaudi, 1997), 1367–574.

[25]   Steigmann-Gall, *The Holy Reich*, 33; according to L. Berggren, 'Completing the Lutheran Reformation: Ultra-Nationalism, Christianity, and the Possibility of "Clerical Fascism" in Inter-war Sweden', in Feldman and Georgescu (eds), *Clerical Fascism*, 303–15, the Swedish Lutheran Manhem Society embarked upon a similar project, stripping out the elements in Christianity allegedly the result of Jewish or Catholic 'perversion' and re-presenting it as the cult of 'the Aryan Jesus', Christ as 'an heroic Christian warrior', thus bringing Christianity nearer to Odinism, the Nordic religion.

against all forms of 'exaggerated nationalism' and racialism, as in his condemnation of Charles Maurras and Action Française in 1926, his criticisms of Italian
fascist doctrine in his 1931 encyclical *Non abbiamo bisogno*, his attacks on National
Socialist ideas in *Mit Brennender Sorge* in 1937 and in the decree of the Sacred
Congregation for Seminaries and Universities of April 1938 which condemned the
proposition that: 'human races, by their natural and immutable character are so
different that the humblest among them is furthest from the most elevated than
from the highest animal species'.[26] As has been seen, the encyclical against racialism which he commissioned was not published because of his death in February
1939. But Pius had condemned eugenic theories, especially forcible sterilization,
in *Casti connubi*, in 1930, and euthanasia, which became Nazi policy for the in-
curably ill, the mentally and physically disabled, and the senile in 1939, had long
been condemned as contrary to Catholic doctrine. In the overwhelmingly Catholic
Italian context, it is clear that these stands conditioned the racial policy of Italian
Fascism, discouraging Mussolini from going beyond *Igiene della razza* (largely
public health measures) and adopting compulsory pre-nuptial health tests and
sterilization.

Nevertheless, there was an ambiguous Catholic response to the introduction of
anti-Semitic laws into Italy in 1938. While Pius XI himself spoke out against them,
along with other Italian prelates like Cardinal Ildefonso Schuster, Archbishop of
Milan, leading Catholic intellectual Agostino Gemelli and other Catholics accepted
them: they saw nothing wrong with imposing restrictions upon and discrimination
against Jews, in order to 'protect' Christians.

VII. CATHOLIC ANTI-FASCISM

Though many Catholics succumbed to the 'fascist temptation', and the institutional
church collaborated with it, large numbers of Catholics did oppose fascism, and
some resisted it in peace and war. The parties most resistant to the electoral inroads
of the Nazis between 1930 and 1933, for example, were the Centre Party and its sister
the Bavarian People's Party (BVP): whereas in this period 38 per cent of Protestants
voted for the NSDAP, only 16 per cent of Catholics did. The Catholic party in Italy
was only really put to the test by the PNF in the 1921 elections, but whereas the
PPI won 20 per cent of the vote and was thus the second largest party, fascism won
7 per cent of the seats, and then only on the coat-tails of Prime Minister Giovanni
Giolitti.

---

[26] As quoted in G. Passelecq and B. Suchecky (eds), *The Hidden Encyclical of Pius XII* (New York:
Harcourt, Brace & Co., 1998), 114.

The resistance of Catholic parties to the electoral advances of fascism must be ascribed to the fact that these parties were the political manifestation of a broader ideological and organizational 'subculture'. The defence of the interests of the church, and Catholic values more generally, together with economic and social programmes loosely based on Catholic social teaching, helped cement the parties to an electorate whose Catholic identity and allegiance, especially in rural areas, was reinforced by involvement in economic, social, and cultural institutions like small banks and credit unions, peasant producer and consumer cooperatives, trade unions, newspapers, and sporting associations. This Catholic subculture was even stronger in Belgium, Luxembourg, and in parts of the Netherlands and Switzerland. Only in Belgium were the Rexists able to make significant inroads into the electorate of the traditional Catholic parties, but as a *rival* Catholic political force in a time of economic crisis, and then only briefly.

Speaking of Eastern and southern Europe, Juan Linz has observed that: 'It is no accident that some of the peripheral nationalisms would develop considerable affinity with fascism; that in Eastern Europe integral nationalism would often be fascist or quasi-fascist.'[27] He argues this on the basis of the absence of strong, organized parties of the Christian democratic type in most Eastern European countries. Certainly, the Christian democratic spirit was notably absent from clerical fascist groups such as the SPP, the Croatian Ustasha, and from another clerical fascist group, the Organization of Ukrainian Nationalists in the Polish Ukraine.

After the dissolution of the PPI in 1926, a few Catholic politicians—Sturzo, Guido Donati, Francesco Ferrari, and Guido Miglioli—went into exile but the rest retired into a quiet private life in Italy. Italian Catholic anti-fascism was never significant and the limited Catholic anti-fascist activity at home was largely carried on clandestinely inside the organizations of Italian Catholic Action. The only serious, organized attempt at Italian Catholic anti-fascism during the *ventennio* was that of the Movimento Guelfo D'Azione, whose members were tried and convicted by the Fascist Special Tribunal in 1933. The fundamental problem in Italy was that the *Conciliazione* had effectively ruled out any legitimate form of Catholic anti-fascism. *Afascismo* ('afascism'), rather than anti-fascism, characterized the broad Catholic response to Italian Fascism: most Catholics went their own sweet way, no more committing themselves to the new regime than the bulk of the population.[28]

Active Catholic opposition to National Socialism in Germany was even more exiguous: apart from isolated, scattered incidents like Bishop August Von Galen's protest against euthanasia, and Provost Bernhard Lichtenberg's denunciation of

[27] J. Linz, 'Some Notes towards a Comparative Study of Fascism in Sociological Perspectives', in W. Laqueur (ed.), *Fascism: A Reader's Guide* (London: Wildwood House, 1974), 18.

[28] R. Moro, 'Afascismo e antifascismo nei movimenti intellectually dell'Azione Cattolica dopo il "31"', *Storia contemporanea*, 6/4 (1975), 733–801 and R. J. B. Bosworth, *Mussolini's Italy* (London: Allen Lane, 2005), 256–65.

the Nazi persecution of the Jews, there was little serious Catholic resistance. On the other hand, whereas literally hundreds of Catholic priests ended up in Nazi concentration camps, only a couple of dozen fell foul of the law in Italy, because the fascists never contemplated persecuting the church like their Nazi counterparts.

Catholic anti-fascism reached its high point in the armed resistance movements of Nazi-occupied Europe from roughly 1942–3 onwards. While the Catholic presence was not large in these movements, with the exception of Belgium, it was politically significant in both France and Italy and was accompanied by 'passive' forms of resistance, including the hiding of hundreds of thousands of Jews, partisans, and POWs by both peasants and parochial clergy. The salvation of the former made up in some way for the local church's endorsement of laws against the Jews in the late 1930s and Pius XII's clamorous silences during the Holocaust and other fascist genocides.

VIII. Conclusion

The impact of fascism on Catholicism was determined by the latter's fears of 'modernizing' forces—anticlerical liberalism, Freemasonry, parliamentary democracy and communism, the Jews, and so forth. Initially, the major fascist movements and regimes succeeded in concealing their own fundamental anticlericalism; consequently Catholics were able to believe that fascism offered the best vehicle for the protection and promotion of the interests of Catholicism, including, in the Italian case, the economic and financial interests of the clerico-fascists and the Vatican itself. What Catholics were really looking for was not the radical extremism of fascism but the kind of Catholic, conservative, corporatist, and authoritarian state postulated by Charles Maurras and Action Française for decades before 1914, whose best expression was probably the military dictatorship of Miguel Primo de Rivera in Spain or the Vichy regime of Marshal Henri Pétain in France. And they continued to cherish this ideal even when the growing power and influence of Italian Fascism and German National Socialism had had the effect of 'fascistizing' many Catholic organizations in the mid-1930s. After 1945, Pius XII continued to see Salazar's Portugal and Franco's Spain as the ideal models for post-Fascist Italy. What Catholics actually found was that by allying with fascism they were riding a 'tiger' of extreme nationalism and racialism with anti-Christian tendencies, not only in National Socialism but also in Italian Fascism as it was radicalized in the late 1930s.

It has been argued that the propensity of fascist movements and regimes to 'aestheticize' and 'sacralize' politics, through religious vocabulary and imagery, processions, rituals, and public 'liturgies', filled the spiritual, 'mythopoeic' void created by a secularized society. Emilio Gentile, in particular, has claimed that fascism resacralized an Italian state which had been desacralized.[29] These claims make sense in Germany, where some large cities could arguably be described as 'secularized'. Thus, during the economic and social disruption and political turmoil of late Weimar, and then during the Third Reich itself, the full panoply of Nazi 'sacralized politics' was powerfully effective in giving many Germans a real sense of security, pride, and belonging.

They make less sense for Italy. Apart from the obvious objection to Gentile's claim that the state created in the Risorgimento had *never* been 'sacralized', despite the efforts of its liberal founders, there was no such void in Italy to speak of. Catholics in Italy were attracted to fascism precisely because Mussolini's 'sacralization' of politics made it more comprehensible and acceptable in a country which was steeped in a living and vibrant *religious* culture. Evidence of Italian Fascism's cultural subordination to Catholicism is to be found in the interment of fascist 'martyrs' (killed in the punitive expeditions of the Fascist squads) in the churches of Santa Croce in Florence (1934) and San Domenico (1938) with a ceremonial which was a synthesis of fascist and Catholic ritual, showing that Italian Fascism sought the blessing of the church for its own cult of the dead.[30] There were very similar rituals among the Spanish Falangists after the outbreak of the Spanish Civil War and also among the Romanian legionaries.

There was never much likelihood that fascism would replace Catholicism as a 'national religion' of Italy, despite Mussolini's claims to the contrary. Fascism's attempts to 'remake' Italians, to penetrate Italian society with its values, to 'nationalize' the Italian masses, and to harness their energies in the great military/imperial project failed for many reasons, but chief among them was the resilient presence of the church in Italian society. Even Mussolini's 'cult of the *Duce*' had its rivals, the residual allegiance of armed forces and middle classes to the monarchy but also, more importantly, the peculiarly strong loyalty of the Italian Catholic masses to the person of the pope. The ultimate proof of fascism's failure lies in the fact that during the Second World War a patriotic form of Italian Catholicism, practised by army chaplains, provided one of the strongest supports for the morale of the *Duce*'s soldiers.[31]

---

[29] E. Gentile, *The Sacralization of Politics in Italy* (Cambridge, MA: Harvard University Press, 1996).

[30] R. Valli, 'The Myth of *Squadrismo* in the Fascist Regime', *Journal of Contemporary History*, 35/2 (2000), 131–50, especially 144–6.

[31] D. Rodogno, *Fascism's European Empire: Italian Occupation during the Second World War* (Cambridge: Cambridge University Press, 2006), 154–6.

BIBLIOGRAPHY

BLAMIRES, C. P. (ed.), *Historical Dictionary of World Fascism* (London: ABC Clio, 2006).

BLINKHORN, M. (ed.), *Fascists and Conservatives: The Radical Right and the Establishment in Twentieth Century Europe* (London: Allen Unwin, 1990).

BURLEIGH, M., *Sacred Causes: Religion and Politics from the European Dictators to Al Quaeda* (London: HarperPress, 2006).

CLARK, C., and KAISER, W. (eds), *Culture Wars: Secular-Catholic Conflict in Nineteenth Century Europe* (Cambridge: Cambridge University Press, 2003).

CONWAY, J., *The Nazi Persecution of the Churches* (New York: Basic Books, 1968).

CONWAY, M., *Catholic Politics in Europe, 1918–1945* (London: Routledge, 1997).

CORNWELL, J., *Hitler's Pope: The Secret History of Pius XII* (London: Viking, 1999).

FELDMAN, M., and GEORGESCU, T. (eds), *Clerical Fascism in Inter-war Europe* (London: Routledge, 2008).

——and TURDA, M., 'Clerical Fascism in Interwar Europe: An Introduction', *Totalitarian Movements and Political Religions*, 8/2 (2007), 205–12.

LEWY, G., *The Catholic Church and Nazi Germany* (New York: McGraw-Hill, 1964).

MOLONY, J. N., *The Emergence of Political Catholicism in Italy: Partito Popolare Italiano, 1919–1926* (London: Croom Helm, 1977).

POLLARD, J. F., *The Vatican and Italian Fascism, 1929–1932: A Study in Conflict* (Cambridge: Cambridge University Press, 1985).

SANCHEZ, J. M., *Pius XII and the Holocaust: Understanding the Controversy* (Washington: Catholic University of America Press, 2002).

WEBSTER, R. A., *The Cross and the Fasces: Christian Democracy and Fascism in Italy* (Oxford: Blackwell, 1960).

WOLFF, R., and HOENSCH, J. (eds), *Catholics, the State and the European Radical Right* (New York: Columbia University Press, 1987).

CHAPTER 10

PROPAGANDA AND YOUTH*

PATRIZIA DOGLIANI

Was fascism a generational revolt? Certainly, throughout its history, Italian Fascism emphasized that it was a revolutionary and youthful phenomenon. Moreover, during its rise from 1919 to 1922, the fascist movement, like its communist competitor, was novel in its appeal to youth and in the salient place that youth took in its ranks. Fascism did entail the rejuvenation of the national political class of Liberal days and fostered a social and economic transformation whereby members of a middle class lacking an ancient inheritance of land and professional qualification could take up the reins of power. Most of the fascist leadership under the dictatorship were men born in the mid-1890s, framed by their experience of the First World War as 20-year-olds, animated by their participation in the squadrism of the early days of their movement, and then, if they survived the internal struggles at the time of fascism's installation in government, they found themselves in their forties at the head of their country.[1]

Fascism similarly could count on support from the next generation, sometimes called the 'class of 1899', a group who had only just been old enough to join in the last months of battle or who had missed the war altogether and felt frustrated at their loss. Contemporaries noted their existence: 'the most interesting feature

---

* Translated by Richard Bosworth.
[1] B. Wanrooij, 'The Rise and Fall of Italian Fascism as a Generational Revolt', *Journal of Contemporary History*, 22 (1987), 401–18.

of the uprising that has come with the formation of the Mussolini cabinet is the appearance on the political scene of the very young, adolescents from 15 to 20 who did not serve in the war.'[2] The desire for action, the emulation of elder brothers, accompanied by a profound crisis of family bonds and of adult authority, had pushed adolescents into squadrism. 'The civil war is the war between a generation of the very young who did not experience the last gasp of the war', who willingly placed themselves under the guidance of others still young who had fought the war and who now acted as instructors of their younger brothers, combining to become 'a historic generation'. These youngsters, excluded from the ranks of the Associazione Nazionale dei Combattenti (National Returned Soldiers' Association), adopted rites, rules, symbols, and the black shirts of the fighting elite of the *arditi*. They also expressed themselves in violence, particularly directed against people and property of the left. It was a pattern repeated in the mayhem found in Weimar Germany or Spain of the Second Republic, with radical activity combining with often still confused political objectives. In Italy, local studies, one on Venice for example,[3] can display revolutionary and counter-revolutionary youth groups that are sure in their definition. Only after the March on Rome did the Fascist militia, the Milizia Voluntaria per la Sicurezza Nazionale (MVSN), absorb them, thereby papering over the differences that had existed between D'Annunzians from Fiume, Nationalists, and anarcho-syndicalists. In the light of this experience, the Fascist ruling elite, once from 1925 secure in power, was aware of the need to watch over the younger generation in order to avoid conflict among and with them, and to retain youth as faithful followers of the regime.

I. The New Fascist Cohort

From its beginning the regime was determined to fascistize the new generation. In the so-called corporate order with its plan to organize society through work roles, gender, and ages, the devotion to youth was highly developed and, in most senses, successful. Yet, few historians, whether Italian or not, have focused on the complex organization of the young. The only serious monograph was written more than twenty years ago by Tracy Koon and has never been translated into Italian.[4] A gender approach is even weaker and little has been published on the difficult issue of the fascist organization of girls and young women. Certainly both sexes were

---

[2] 'Grildrind', *Le generazioni nel fascismo* (Turin: Piero Gobetti, 1924).

[3] G. Albanese, *Alle origini del fascismo: la violenza politica a Venezia 1919–1922* (Padua: Il Poligrafo, 2001) and the pieces by A. Lyttelton and J. Petersen in W. J. Mommsen and G. Hirschfeld (eds), *Social Protest, Violence and Terror in 19th and 20th Century Europe* (London: Macmillan, 1982), 257–300.

[4] T. Koon, *Believe Obey Fight: Political Socialization of Youth in Fascist Italy 1922–1943* (Chapel Hill, NC: University of North Carolina Press, 1985).

put through stages of Party instruction, with a steady multiplication of ideological intervention. The youth movement therefore constituted the most evident and perhaps the only genuine mass fascist organization. Key developments in this story occurred in 1926, 1929, and 1937. After the levels of turbulence within the Party prompted a major purge—more than 2,000 leaders and about 140,000 members were expelled—from 1925 membership was expected and to be given mainly to the civil service class. However, from 1927, the procedure became instead that entry occurred when an Italian was between 18 and 20 and depended on previous participation in the Party's youth movements, which therefore became the places of training, selection, and recruitment for the regime's political and administration leadership.

In the troubled immediate post-war, the first Party youth organizations had sprung up mainly in cities and in the north of the country. At Milan on 20 January 1920 an Avanguardia Studentesca (Student Vanguard) was created within the Fasci di Combattimento but, for the moment, the allure of Fiume and D'Annunzio was stronger than that of Mussolini. Further student vanguards, led by the Fiuman 'legionary' Luigi Freddi came into existence in other sectors of the centre-north, notably Liguria and Emilia Romagna. The fascist leadership was suspicious of their independence and, at the Party congress in Rome in March 1921 that saw the birth of the Fascist Party, no youth delegates were admitted. Soon, however, the leadership turned its attention to youth, in December 1921 marshalling boys between the ages of 14 and 17 into the Avanguardia Giovanile Fascista. Later, in March 1923, at Genoa, the Fascist University Groups (Gruppi Universitari Fascisti; GUF) were founded. A month earlier, children and adolescents between the ages of 8 and 14 began to be enrolled into the so-called Balilla, utilizing the name of a boy of the people, who, in that city on 5 December 1746, had allegedly thrown the first stone that unleashed a popular revolt against Austrian occupiers.[5] Yet, in 1924, the number of children who were fascists only tallied 3,000, with 50,000 Avanguardisti. To enhance this situation, the regime would seek both to improve its organization and to destroy its rivals in the field, and this it could only do after the formal cancellation of democratic liberties with the full assumption of dictatorship in 1925.

On 3 April 1926, 'Year IV of the Fascist Revolution', the Opera Nazionale Balilla (ONB) 'for the physical and moral benefit of youth' was instituted by decree. It was to be an autonomous *ente*, with the task of instructing boys, initially from 8 to 18 but gradually extending to younger groups, and from the decree of 30 October 1934 achieving an articulated structure. There were now three categories for boys: Figli della Lupa (Sons of the She-Wolf) from 6 to 8; Balilla proper at 8, and at 11 'Balilla Moschettiere', before an upgrading at 14 to the Avanguardisti (Avanguardisti Moschettieri from 15 to 17). For girls there was an analogous structure, being Figlie

---

[5] G. Oliva, *Balilla*, in M. Isnenghi (ed.), *I luoghi della memoria: simboli e miti dell'Italia unita* (Bari: Laterza, 1996), 391–401.

della Lupa (6 to 8), Piccole Italiane (Little Italians) from 8 to 13, and then Giovani Italiane (Young Italian Women) from 14 to 17 (at first, females were placed under the Fasci Femminili and not the ONB). In 1929, formal control over the movement was passed by the Party to the Ministry of National Education which created an under-secretaryship for physical training and unified both boys and girls under the general school programme. In practice, however, the regime long continued to pay more attention to the physical and political instruction of males rather than of females. The organization was placed under the supervision of provincial committees and given its own rigid command structure, leading down through at least five ranks from the *caposquadra* to a humble cadet.

The transfer of the ONB to the Ministry was an important step given that it spread the movement in a capillary fashion through the entire schooling system and made membership obligatory for all boys and girls in elementary school, from the age of 6 to 11, with the teachers acting as propaganda agents. The perfect-ing of this organization coincided with the banning of any alternative 'free time' groups; the left and the original lay 'Scouts' (with its international connections) were suppressed in 1927, while the Catholic scouting organization, the Esploratori (Explorers), went into 'voluntary' dissolution in 1928. This process left only three Catholic youth organizations surviving—Azione Cattolica (AC; Catholic Action), the Federazione Universitaria Cattolica Italiana (FUCI; Italian Catholic university student federation) and the Movimento Laureati Cattolici (Catholic graduate asso-ciation). The Lateran Pacts between church and state in 1929, in maintaining these bodies, led to further conflict, resolved in 1931 with an accord whereby AC and FUCI were to devote themselves exclusively to the religious needs of their members, while the church took on a major role in the spiritual education of youth in the ONB.[6] Young Catholics thus did retain the potential to opt for a 'double militancy', both in the ONB and in the church groups and, especially, in the university associations. It has been estimated that such young men and women amounted to 15 per cent of those who passed through the regime's youth organizations under the dictatorship.

Although it is true that, until the passing of the *Carta della Scuola* (School Charter) in 1939, it was still technically possible to avoid membership of the ONB, belonging did bring social privileges and economic benefits of considerable signif-icance, especially to the poorer classes. In 1934, a set of special scholarships and entitlements was instituted under direct ONB management, while, from 1929, the organization had taken responsibility for the teaching infrastructure needed in Italian communities abroad, first in the Mediterranean regions and then with a developing interest in other continents, notably the Americas. Furthermore, within Italy, a failure to join the ONB brought down discrimination on errant children,

---

[6] See J. F. Pollard, *The Vatican and Italian Fascism 1929–32: A Study in Conflict* (Cambridge: Cambridge University Press, 1985).

isolating them from the rest of society, ensuring that their family was suspected of anti-fascism, blocking any career in wide strands of the public service, and influencing the territorial placement of a boy when subject to call-up (or having him sent straight to a punishment battalion). By contrast, admission to colleges viewed as elite, notably in the military area (the naval college at Bari or the air force one at Forlì being examples) demanded an ONB background and then offered advantages both in a military career or in the employment structures of the fascist state.

The ONB was built like a pyramid. Teachers and members of the MVSN, assisted by priests and especially military chaplains, concentrated on local and provincial discipline. The provincial branches of the ONB sent members to the national council, chosen by Mussolini and the national secretary of the ONB, and typically combining men from the MVSN, armed services, with the addition of an Inspector General of the clergy. Until 1930, the MVSN had the task of preparing young men for Party membership, essentially through a form of pre-military training, in preparation for military call-up which usually happened after boys turned 21. Young women could move directly into the PNF's women's organizations. Eventually the Party decided to insert another step in the political formation of youth and, in 1931, opened for those aged from 18 to 21 Giovani Fasciste for young women and Fasci Giovanili di Combattimento for young men. Each was granted its own autonomy within the Party and aimed at political, military, and sporting training. Their commander was Carlo Scorza (b. 1895), with a background in Tuscan squadrism. The young people thus marshalled were deemed the new 'cohort' of fascism, the direct heirs of the *arditi* of the Great War and of the 'martyrs' of the Party's rise to power.[7] Eighteen-year-old boys now officially joined the Party's 'new militia', while girls should concentrate on 'the social and family preparation of the fascist woman', under the lead of the Fasci Femminili. From 1930, the weekly *Gioventù fascista* (Fascist Youth), edited by the successive PNF secretaries, Giovanni Giuriati and Achille Starace, was directed at such youth.

In December 1934, military training was made compulsory for the able-bodied male population at the age of 18, while boys from 8 to 14 were now to be trained 'morally and spiritually' for national defence. At 14, they began a special gymnastic and sporting campaign, while those who missed out on the call-up were obliged to take courses in technical-military skills. In 1934, adults, too, were forced to undergo military instruction, notably during the afternoon of the 'Fascist Saturday', allegedly time off granted to the nation by employers.

These courses were widely regarded as boring and useless, devoted to parades and Party flag waving, gymnastics, and other officially choreographed ceremonies. Moreover, where the Party was not particularly active, the young could escape from pre-military training and ideological preaching. Yet, everywhere that they

---

[7] See A. Starace, *Fasci giovanili di combattimento* (Milan: Mondadori, 1933).

were available, sporting and other forms of physical recreation produced by the ONB or the Fasci Giovanili seem to have been crowded and popular. Even the clandestine anti-fascist parties, especially the Communists (PCd'I), admitted that, from 1927–8, 'sport is the means that has given fascism the best results in its ambitions to "neutralize youth"' and was doing so whether through the ONB or the so-called Dopolavoro (OND) or 'after-work organization' which had attracted the voluntary and enthusiastic support of thousands of young from the working class.[8]

Even if much sporting activity remained in practice confined to the elite as is revealed in the elegant pages of the monthly *Lo sport fascista*, where reports of sporting events are interspersed with advertisements about cinema, fashion, and items to be consumed by the upper middle class, the PNF and the national Olympic Committee (CONI) did facilitate sporting activity and bring sporting fame to some young people from poor backgrounds. During the second half of the 1930s, prizes and honours to be won by young athletes multiplied.[9] From 1932, elite university students could participate in the so-called *Littoriali dello sport* (Lictors' sporting games), joined the following year by *Littoriali della cultura e dell'arte*, and from 1938, open to women students, if participating in all arenas separately. From the end of 1939, CONI took authority for the *Littoriali sportivi* (Italy was scheduled to hold the Olympics in 1944) but, with the outbreak of war, they lost purpose and were abolished in 1941. Nonetheless, through the 1930s, sporting activities for women did expand, with the hope of imposing the athletic and healthy image of the fascist 'new woman', as embodied by the 20-year-olds 'Ondina' Valla and Claudia Testoni, who won medals at the 1936 Berlin Olympics. Similarly on the rise were mass alpine and skiing events, especially designed for Avanguardisti and the Fasci Giovanili. Forty-two thousand youth joined in such activities in 1936, almost as if they were another special cohort, and many of these skiers participated in the invasion of France and Greece in June and then October 1940, and in 1941 in the attack on the USSR.[10]

By the middle of the 1930s, then, it was difficult to distinguish sport from military training, with the former embracing marching, wrestling, boxing, various kinds of shooting, and bomb throwing, meant to temper young fascists with a virile and military nature. Not even girls were absent from such pursuits, although, for them, most common were gymnastics of some planned and uniform type, aimed at fostering healthy and courageous mothers, primed to educate their own children in the love of the Nation. The Ministry of Education assisted the distribution through schools of patriotic and fascist literature directed at the young and the

---

[8] Federazione Giovanile Comunista d'Italia, *La lotta della gioventù proletaria contro il Fascismo* (Berlin: Verlag der Jugendintertionale, 1930; repr. Milan: Teti, 1975), 63.

[9] For cases, see P. Dogliani, 'Sport and Fascism', *Journal of Modern Italian Studies*, 5 (2000), 326–43.

[10] For a personal account, see M. Rigoni Stern (b. 1921), *L'ultima partita a carte* (Turin: Einaudi, 2002).

very young—ripping yarns about heroic acts, the biographies of the fighters and *condottieri* from classical Rome through to the present (with Benito Mussolini's own story at the forefront), talk about the 'Famous Italians' who had inspired fascism, 'spiritual breviaries' of a fascist slant, all made up a vast publication enterprise which seconded the already fascistized school textbooks, as available from the first elementary class to *Liceo*.[11]

Nonetheless, the sharing of responsibility for organizing youth did in time prompt dispute between the regime's chiefs, especially the Minister of National Education by the end of the 1930s, Giuseppe Bottai, and Renato Ricci, put by Mussolini in charge of the new ONB in 1926. Ricci, like Scorza, belonged to the 'Fascists of the first hour' as they were called. From a working-class family, he had been a volunteer in 1915, a legionary with D'Annunzio at Fiume, and eventually a squadrist in violently contested Tuscany. He participated in the March on Rome and was enrolled in the leading ranks of the MVSN. In 1924 he won a seat in parliament and, by the time he took over the ONB, was deputy secretary of the PNF. Mussolini believed this ardent and loyal young man, just into his thirties, was the ideal figure to head the new youth movement. For his part, Ricci, despite having no specific training in youth affairs, carried out his task zealously and with faith in his *Duce*. For this reason, despite prompting quite a few rumours about dubious financial dealings and other abuses of power, Ricci was always protected by Mussolini, who had long reflected before entrusting youth training to the Party.[12] The continuing dualism was, however, overcome in October 1937 with the creation of the umbrella organization called the Gioventù Italiana del Littorio (GIL; Italian Lictors' Youth), taking as its motto *Credere, obbedire, combattere* (Believe, Obey, Fight).[13]

Now, although the division by age and gender was preserved, the real novelty consisted in assigning everything to do with children and the young to the direct control of the Party and to its federal and provincial bodies. School retained its privileged position in recruitment. With the attack on Ethiopia in October 1935, the emphasis on military preparation deepened and was reinforced by co-opting into the leadership of GIL officers both from the army and from the MVSN. In June 1940, GIL established select brigades of those too young to join the armed forces. Called the *battaglioni giovani fascisti* (battalions of young fascists), in 1941, under the supervision of GIL while technically qualified as an army regiment, they were sent to fight in North Africa. At the same time, boys in middle school, called

[11] See L. Passerini, *Mussolini immaginario: storia di una biografia 1915–1939* (Bari: Laterza 1991); A. Scotto di Luzio, *L'appropriazione imperfetta: editori, biblioteche e libri per ragazzi durante il fascismo* (Bologna: Il Mulino, 1996).

[12] See the letter by B. Mussolini, 17 September 1937, held in the dossier under Ricci's name. Archivio Centrale dello Stato, Segreteria particolare del Duce, Carteggio riservato 1922–1943, b. 48.

[13] See G. Minucci, *Scuole, asili d'infanzia, scuole all'aperto elementari e medie, Case del balilla, palestre ed impianti sportivi*, preface by the distinguished architect Marcello Piacentini (Milan: Hoepli, 1936).

'aspirant officers', were already being groomed to fill the army's ranks, helped by an intensive training at the so-called *Campi Dux* (*Duce*'s camps), transformed by the war into academies of GIL.

The reorganization of 1937, meant to be definitive and occurring at a time of marked popular consent for the regime, led the way to the peak of enrolment in GIL. The ONB grew from fewer than half a million members in the school year of 1926 to five and half million in 1936–7. In October 1936, the male and female Giovani Fascisti took 874,000 of the young. Given a national population according to the census of 1936 of 42 million, the youth organizations by then included 16 per cent of the total in a country where the birth rate stood between 1921 and 1935 at about 26.7 per thousand, well above the European average of 20 per thousand, and where fascist hostility to migration had ensured that traditional gates of departure were closed. The number enrolled in all sectors of GIL in late 1937 reached 7,532,000 and expanded to 8,830,000 in 1942. In high schools of the varying types, the level of membership augmented from 85.5 per cent in 1931–2 to 99.9 per cent in 1941–2.

For younger children from 6 to 14, the organizations drew more in the north, averaging from 70 per cent to 80 per cent, than in the south, where they was still confined to 30 per cent to 50 per cent. With the passage of the years, some tendencies were confirmed. There was a rise in joining by adolescents and the very young. The prevalence of middle-class children over worker or peasant ones increased as they grew older. Boys outnumbered girls, especially in adolescence and in regard to the south and to the countryside. In 1936, 74.6 per cent of boys had joined the Balilla but 66 per cent of girls were members of the Piccole Italiane. Obligatory school ended when a child turned 11 and was not always observed in the more southern and rural parts of the country. Girls were especially likely to abandon formal education at that moment, with boys staying on. Since they could not take up formal work, banned until they were 14, boys could be attracted to stay in the ONB, even after they had left school, given the opportunities for leisure and for the honing of employment skills offered there.

In other words, the exit from youth organizations by the popular classes coincided with the time when they were no longer eligible for welfare assistance through the ONB or the Opera Nazionale Maternità ed Infanzia (ONMI; Mothers' and Babies' Scheme). By contrast, the bond with the youth organizations remained strong for those who proceeded to further education in high school or beyond, and who were likely to come from the better-off classes and especially their aspirational element. For girls from such social groups, the ONB and GIL were often the only outlet for social life outside the family. For boys, the youth organizations were thought of as offering the chance for rising above the ruck and so securing entry into the leading cadres of the Party and the state, that is, giving opportunity for upward social mobility and distinction in a world where the elite was still a small and narrow group.

Another feature of fascist youth organizations was the great building pro-grammes undertaken in the field by the regime and spread out across the country. Thus the Ministry of National Education and the ONB sponsored the construc-tion of schools, youth hostels, sports stadiums, and holiday camps. Almost every national architect joined in the work. In 1936, the regime's leading figure in that regard, Marcello Piacentini, drafted projects in national territory, Italian colonies, and emigrant communities, notably on the Mediterranean littoral.[14] Along with schools, the commonest construction was of *Case del Balilla* and *Case della Giovane Italiana*, meeting places for boy and girl scouts. These edifices had to follow a set standard which demanded spaciousness and equipment, gyms and showers, places to watch films or to listen to radio, and even prescribed the coloration (so-called 'Pompeian red'). Particular attention was given to sporting equipment. In 1928, PNF secretary Augusto Turati ordered all Party branches to pressure their communes to open a '*campo sportivo del Littorio*' (Lictors' sports field), available both for athletics and football. In 1936 it was estimated that 3,700,000 members of ONB participated in gymnastics and sport in 5,000 centres. Still more active were the Fasci Giovanili; in 1934, according to official figures, 80,000 of them regularly engaged in athletics, 10,000 in cycling, 6,000 in skiing, and 3,000 in swimming.

The activity with the most marked imprint on Italian memory is the summer camps organized for the young and adolescent. Aiming at mass control and the spread of hygiene to improve Italian 'stock' (*stirpe*), the regime developed residen-tial camps for Children of the She-Wolf and for Balilla. From 1926, local Party branches and the provincial insurance banks and then the welfare associations, to which both ONMI and ONB contributed funds and personnel, took charge of these 'colonies'. In 1937, the whole affair was handed over to GIL. Especially after 1932, the dictatorship placed heavy propaganda and organizational emphasis on providing summer camps for every member of the ONB from the age of 6 to 13, with preference being given to the offspring of needy and large families, to war orphans, or to the children of those rendered invalid through national combat. By the mid-1930s, 10 per cent of children in the age category could have a holiday by the sea or in the mountains in thousands of colonies, with stays that were at least a month long. Official figures reckoned 568,680 were thus assisted in 1935 and 806,964 in 1939. The great majority of the children came from the towns and cities of northern Italy. They were joined by the offspring of Italians resident abroad or from the nations' colonies, as organized by the Fasci Italiani all'Estero (15,000 attended summer camps in 1935). To assist this process the regime from the mid-1930s built its own brick structures along the Mediterranean and especially on the northern Adriatic where, between Ravenna and Rimini in the '*Terra del Duce*'

---

[14] See P. Dogliani, 'Colonie di vacanza', in V. De Grazia and S. Luzzatto (eds), *Dizionario del fascismo* (Turin: Einaudi, 2002); S. De Martino and A. Wall (eds), *Cities of Childhood: Italian Colonies of the 1930s* (London: The Architectural Association, 1988); C. Baldoli, 'Le Navi: fascismo e vacanze in una colonia estiva per I figli degli italiani all'estero', *Memoria e ricerca*, 6 (2000), 163–76.

(Mussolini's own land), the dictator's family took bathing vacations. Here in only ten years, twenty-three new camps were constructed, winning profile in Italian and international architectural journals for their innovative style, an example being the 'neofuturist' Colonia XXVIII Ottobre, inaugurated at Cattolica in 1934. Similarly celebrated were the rationalist colonies 'Sandro Mussolini' at Cesenatico and the Montecatini at Cervia.[15]

Avanguardisti, by contrast, spent their summers under canvas. Their camps were not so dissimilar to youth ones in other countries of whatever political system, combining sport and military training, and some instruction for industrial or agricultural employment. In 1929, a *Campo Dux* was established offering a stay of some weeks in the nation's capital with gymnastic and sporting activities. In September 1936, this venue held 25,000 young. Also increasingly welcome in such places were young people from Italian communities and colonies abroad or from such allied or friendly foreign countries as Germany and Austria. From 1937, GIL multiplied its training camps in the provinces, accepting 250,000 young people.[16]

With the expansion of ONB services there also grew the number of paid and voluntary personnel working in its service, or placed there by the welfare and teaching agencies of state and Party. They could come from the army or the militia, while female staff consisted of elementary teachers, nurses, and cadres from the Fasci Femminili, assistants of ONMI, and gymnastics instructors. By the end of the 1930s, four million youths between the ages of 18 and 21 were entrusted to 150,000 militia officials. In 1938, GIL employed 138,000 gymnastic teachers; an elite of them went to the two sporting academies, from 1928 at Rome for boys and, from 1932, at Orvieto for girls, which had tertiary status.[17] Fascism planned that these two schools would forge the mental and physical traits of 'new' men and women and so of a new fascist generation. In parallel and competition with the mystical-pagan Nazi hopes in this regard, GIL aimed to perfect its own model of youth as bearers of a Romano-Catholic, Western civilization and to export the concept to the clerical fascist regimes in Austria, Salazarian Portugal, and, especially, Nationalist Spain.[18]

---

[15] For the international background, see K. Holland, *Youth in European Labor Camps* (Washington: American Council on Education, 1939). Cf. P. Dogliani, 'Jeunesses ouvrières et organisation du social dans l'entre-deux-guerres, en Europe et aux États-Unis', *Le Mouvement social*, 168 (1994), 31–50; P. Dudek, *Erziehung durch Arbeit: Arbeitslagerbewegung und Freiwilliger Arbeitsdienst 1920–1935* (Opladen: Westdeutscher Verlag, 1988).

[16] See ACS, Ministero Cultura Popolare. Gabinetto, b. 84 (Campeggi GIL 1936–1940) and *Lo sport fascista*, September 1936.

[17] L. Motti and M. Rossi Caponeri (eds), *Accademiste a Orvieto: donne ed educazione fisica nell'Italia fascista 1932–1943* (Perugia: Quattroemme, 1996).

[18] See L. Malvano, 'Il mito della giovinezza attraverso l'immagine: il fascismo italiano' and L. Passerini, 'La giovinezza come metafora del cambiamento sociale: due dibattiti sui giovani nell'Italia fascista e negli Stati Uniti degli anni Cinquanta', in G. Levi and J.-C. Schmitt (eds), *Storia dei giovani*, ii: *L'età contemporanea* (Bari: Laterza, 1994), 311–48; 383–459.

II. The Comparison between Fascist
and Nazi Youth Organizations

Nazi youth, as exemplified in the Hitlerjugend (HJ), possessed a clearer dedication and a greater ideological purity than their Italian fellows. Whereas Italian organizations were headed by adults, often as anxious to cut a figure in the Party or state as about anything else, the HJ's entire hierarchy was composed of young people in their twenties and fully focused on their cause. Typical was Baldur von Schirach (b. 1907), the HJ's founder at 24, from 1940 replaced by Artur Axmann, who was then 27. From October 1931, von Schirach was *Reichsjugendführer* in charge of high school and university Nazi groups, as well as those where the children of the middle and working classes assembled. Immediately after he became Chancellor, Hitler could rely on a disciplined youth movement, well penetrated into society and led by a young man utterly committed to the Party and its propaganda. In these circumstances the HJ and its associated bodies (for example, the Bund Deutscher Mädel for girls from 14 to 21) spread rapidly across the national education system, with a leadership that was often only a little older than the membership. Younger children enrolled in the Jungvolk and Jungmädel as 10- to 14-year-olds. Within five years, the youth movement had embraced 77 per cent of children, more than seven million of them, with membership being compulsory for those in educational institutions from 1936. By 1939, the tally reached 82 per cent, plus another 400,000 girls who had places in the work organization, the BDM-Werk Glaube und Schönheit.

Serious comparative investigations are missing from the historiography,[19] but it is clear that each of the regimes sought through their youth organizations to insert the children of the populace into collective life and so 'nationalize' them. Yet both Nazism and fascism were simultaneously systems that promoted the middle classes. In the HJ, 30 per cent of the leadership sprang from the bourgeoisie, being typically from a university and upper high school background or from a new cohort of middle school teachers. Forty-two per cent originated in lower middle-class families of clerks and technicians, while workers in industry or agriculture only tallied 28 per cent. By contrast the membership reflected the national situation: 53 per cent were from a worker or peasant base. Von Schirach and Axmann themselves embodied the rival origins with the former coming from the modern, cosmopolitan financial aristocracy, while the latter was a proletarian seeking to rise up the social ladder.

Another parallel worth examining is the way youth organizations were deployed to control dissent. From 1935, the HJ began a close collaboration with the SS, leading to the signature of a full accord between von Schirach and Himmler to work together for internal security. This agreement foresaw the passage into the

[19] But see V. Gorresio, *I giovani d'Europa* (Milan: Ulrico Hoepli, 1936).

SS of HJ members whose political attitudes and racial stock made them stand out (some were to become Hitler's personal guard or gain similar positions for other regime chiefs). Such youths were also recruited into the Streifendienst (SRD), headed by Heinrich Lüer, himself only just 20, and acting as a sort of youth Gestapo, with the task of providing surveillance over young people's political and moral comprehension of Nazism and of distinguishing those in need of correction and punishment (they would be handed over to the adults in KRIPO—the criminal police). The sexual proclivities of boys and girls were one object of attention, as were their interest in rival bodies to the HJ and their habits in drinking, reading, music, singing, radio listening, and clothing ('un-Germanic' 'extravagance' was especially deplored). With the outbreak of war, a centre to combat youth criminality was established and in 1940 a 'police order for the protection of young people' stiffened the penalties for those who went to the pub too often, broke curfew (no later than 9 p.m. for those under 18), or were too fond of the cinema and theatre. By then, at least 100,000 belonged to the SRD and were encouraged to spy on and denounce their fellows as well as their families and neighbours. As a result, thousands were expelled from the HJ for a range of offences from homosexuality and abortion to violence against property and persons.

Yet, in Germany, there was an apolitical but still radical tendency for young people to express themselves in alternative cultural forms, notably in listening to jazz (that 'degenerate' music originating with 'primitive' black Americans) and in enjoying literature from the Anglo-American world. Youth groups appeared with names like 'Harlem club', 'Charlie gangs', and 'Swingers'. Most were local bands, with the most celebrated being the Edelweisspiraten and the Leipzig gang, composed of adolescents under 18 and not yet called up to work or military service and often workers who had just finished their apprenticeships and were possessed of a marked class and employment solidarity. They enjoyed avoiding the conformism, discipline, and sexual separation of the HJ. Nazi repression of them increased as the war continued, with hundreds of arrests and, in 1944, some executions of Edelweisspiraten at Cologne.

The Italian regime similarly tried to control youth behaviour but never at the same level as in Germany. There was specific legislation directed against youth infractions. Traditional morality was lauded continuously, with much invocation of the Catholic Church, especially in regard to young women. Also effective in a world of surviving scarcity was the removal of privileges that could have an evident punitive effect on the economy of a whole family. Fascism had after all risen at a time of marked social instability, with youth at its forefront, and the memory of these days made the regime perpetually alert to the potential threat of delinquency and indeed any expression of social deviation. It was no accident that juvenile legislation was drafted by the Minister for Justice, the nationalist Alfredo Rocco, at the end of 1929, when the international economic crisis began to make waves in Italy, too. During the 1930s, Starace would underline that the leadership of the Fasci

Giovanili 'must above all prevent any type of deviation, remembering among those from 18 to 21 any act is coloured by passion'.[20] Still influential in such attitudes was the criminological thought associated with Cesare Lombroso from the beginning of the century, with its assumption that the adolescent was a savage, a natural rebel who bore criminal tendencies requiring control and discipline.

In the decade after 1929, fascism deepened its concern with those in the 14 to 18 age range (14 was deemed the moment when criminal responsibility began). 'Special tribunals' were established for minors and a series of institutions grew— re-education centres, reform schools, more directly punitive prisons, with an effort to separate the sexes and adults and minors. In the vocabulary of the period, the young were to be given a 'prophylactic' that would insulate them against any 'moral contagion'. From the early 1930s, minors were sent to correctional institutions on the suggestion of the police and of those with family authority. In the new code elaborated just before Italy entered the war, the authority that had been exercised by father or tutor could be revoked and become subject to that of a Party official. Now a magistrate could deem the family irrelevant if it was not carrying out its duty to educate a minor in fascist faith and Christian principles. ONMI and ONB functionaries could indicate to the judicial authorities those young people whom they thought needed moral re-education or who displayed signs of corruption and 'deviation'. In 1941, the then Minister of Justice, Dino Grandi, defined this policy as *Bonifica umana* (human reclamation), in parallel with the regime's trumpeted programmes to restore swampy and degraded land.[21] The regulations adopted for the various reform schools decreed that the pillars of re-education were the Catholic religion, school, work, gymnastics and other sports, and finally rewards, which, after good conduct, might entail time off on holidays with parents, the presentation of worthy books, enrolment in GIL, or participation at a *Campo Dux*. About 140 youth prisons were opened during the regime, including a model penal colony on the island of Nisida in the gulf of Naples, charged with reforming 350 youths in 1935.

In the comparison between the two regimes one issue was that Italy never introduced a system of obligatory work, one reason being that there was always latent unemployment there. Italy lacked both intense repression and widespread youthful dissent throughout the dictatorship. While youth were corralled quickly, and often forcefully, into the public sphere, the principal novelty and modernity lay in the organization of leisure and the resultant degree of social levelling in a still agricultural country distinguished by massive class difference. In Italy, the stimulation for youth contestation thus did not come from an improvement in the economic and labour situation as in Germany but rather emerged in intellectual and student circles. In that regard, criticism grew of the failure to replace the ruling

[20] A. Starace, *Gioventù italiana del littorio* (Milan, 1939); PNF-GIL, *La Gioventù nella legislazione fascista* (Rome, 1941).

[21] D. Grandi, *La bonifica umana*, 2 vols (Rome: Ministero di Grazia e Giustizia, 1941).

elite, enhanced by a general sense of a regime become senescent and scelerotic, and far from the promised 'youth revolution'. It has long been assumed that a good number of young intellectuals and activists in university groups sponsored a current of rebellion, a so-called Fronde, under fascism. Several elements contributed to this idea, with the first being the publication of the memoirs and letters of such young people as Giaime Pintor, Luigi Preti, and, especially, Ruggero Zangrandi, this last the school friend of Vittorio Mussolini and born in 1915, who already in 1946 spoke for his generation. All were moving slowly from GUF activity to militant anti-fascism, while such of their school friends as Gastone Silvano Spinetti remained fascist, justifying themselves through their service at the front or their experience as prisoners of war.[22]

A second factor can be uncovered in Palmiro Togliatti's *Lectures on Fascism*, delivered at Moscow in 1935. The Communist Party Secretary commented that 'within GUF there are active elements. They do confront the problem of the Fascist dictatorship, and in their discussions...they go beyond what is permitted to reach a withering criticism of the ideological teaching' of the regime.[23] Yet, with few exceptions, until the failures of the war became evident in 1942–3, the greater part of high school and university students, in GUF papers and in their participation of the *Littoriali* games, displayed more dissatisfaction with their country's provincialism and with the failed promises of fascism to renew the nation morally and politically than a clear anti-fascism. It was no mistake that the authority figure for many such young men and women remained the Minister of Education, Giuseppe Bottai, deemed a 'critical fascist', if in fact no less fascist than the rest. By contrast with the blind discipline demanded by Ricci and Starace, Bottai more subtly sought to forge a young leadership elite, who would work together and be ready to deal with the new objectives in domestic and foreign policy that arose with the Nazi alliance. GUF members had the task of enlivening relations with visiting German comrades as part of the New European Order, fascist-style. Between 1940 and 1942, Florence and Weimar, while the war was going well for the Axis, were sites for important cultural displays of Nazi-fascist youth from across the continent.[24] In fact, fascism's effort to cross the generations only happened when the war had degenerated into crisis and the heavy losses on many fronts had undermined popular support. Significant in this regard was the appointment of the national head of the GUF, Aldo Vidussoni, aged only 27, as Secretary of the Party in December 1941.

---

[22] G. Pintor (1919–43), *Il sangue d'Europa, 1939–1943* (Turin: Einaudi, 1950); idem, *Doppio diario 1936–1943* (Turin: Einaudi, 1978); L. Preti, *Giovinezza, giovinezza* (Milan: Mondadori, 1964); R. Zangrandi, *Il lungo viaggio attraverso il fascismo* (Turin: Einaudi, 1946); G. S. Spinetti, *Difesa di una generazione* (Rome: OET, 1946). See also the new biography of Pintor by M. C. Calabri, *Il costante piacere di vivere: vita di Jaime Pintor* (Turin: Utet, 2007).

[23] P. Togliatti, *Lezioni sul fascismo* (Rome: Editori Riuniti, 1974), 71.

[24] ACS, Ministero Cultura Popolare, Gabinetto b. 84, reporting meetings in June 1942 attended by 10,000 young people. Cf. also Pintor, *Il sangue d'Europa*, 133.

III. The Youth War

By 1943 there was a kind of reversal in the situation between Italy and Germany. In Italy youth discontent matured in contact with the anti-fascist forces, leading to acts of open opposition or of convinced adherence to the Resistance. In Germany, by contrast, the lack of any organized anti-Nazi movements and the inculcation of sacrifice and the belonging to a fully united community kept youth in thrall until spring 1945. Both regimes did, as a last throw, appeal to the very young, with the Nazis, from the time of Stalingrad, using teenagers in combat. The SS and Waffen SS had already drawn men from the HJ but, from the spring of 1943, the operation was extended to embrace young men of guaranteed 'Aryan race' across the territory of the Third Reich, including annexed lands, with the slogan *Auch du* (You, too). In 1943 about 60,000 young men born in 1926 were enrolled in that manner, while the Waffen SS took boys born in 1927, 1928, and 1929, including the pupils of NAPOLA (Nationalpolitische Lehranstalt), an elite college for the political training of boys deemed purely Aryan. The campaign was extended to hundreds of girls under 21, most often assigned to communication matters. During the last weeks of the war, it has been calculated that the SS managed to mobilize more than 150,000 adolescents in Panzer divisions and in popular militias aiming to defend German towns from the Allied advance and sent to dig trenches or to engage in guerrilla or sabotage acts. In the final defence of Berlin, 5,000 HJ were in action, with a survival rate of 10 per cent. They were organized by Axmann, who led the last units to their deaths or to capture by the Americans in Bavaria on 1 May.

In Italy the months from autumn 1943 to spring 1945 of German occupation and of the Liberation struggle saw the engagement of young people on both the military and the civil fronts. Claudio Pavone has underlined how, during the Social Repub-lic, the 'long' or surviving generation of squadrists attempted to refurbish the youth myth of their origins and to arouse young people again with the allure of risking all.[25] Just as 'long' was the anti-fascist generation who now guided young resisters. The conflict, spreading across national territory and, in its totality, intruding into the lives of the civilian population in regions occupied by the Nazis, demanded a choice from young people. Especially for 18-year-olds confronted with a call-up into the RSI's (Repubblica Sociale Italiana) armies, a decision was compelling and often had to be made without much in the way of family or institutional advice. After the pervading authoritarianism of the fascist years, the emptiness of authority became all the more striking. Many fathers were away—prisoners in the German camps, disappeared somewhere, or again themselves called to arms. Many schools were unusable or deprived of teachers. The employment market had been pushed awry by compulsory labour service and forced emigration to Germany. In October 1924,

---

[25] C. Pavone, *Una guerra civile: saggio storico sulla moralità nella Resistenza* (Turin: Bollati Boringhieri, 1991), 551–60.

those born in 1925 and in the second and third quarters of 1924 were conscripted. The Graziani Proclamation of 18 February summoned back into service those born in 1922, 1923, and the first quarter of 1924, that is, young men from 19 to 22. At first notice, only about half responded and among those who did there were incidents of protest, flight, and detachment. The simultaneous appeal to soldiers imprisoned in Germany was equally unsuccessful. Out of 60,000 available only 13,000 volunteered, joining the 44,400 who had been conscripted or otherwise picked up for service. This contingent was reorganized, trained, and badly armed into four divisions, kept for the moment inactive in Germany and only employed in battle in the second half of the year. After this failure, the RSI decided to consign its fortunes to more fanatical and professional military bands, including the Guardia Nazionale Repubblicana (GNR, National Guard) and the various autonomous Party groups such as the Brigate Nere (BN; Black Brigades).

In the meantime, the Fascist Party was reconstituted with a new republican identity and placed under Secretary Alessandro Pavolini. However, it attracted only a handful of young people of fighting age. In April 1944, 10 per cent of members were in the 17 to 37 age bracket (47,200 of the Partito Nazionale Repubblicano's tally of 487,000). Nonetheless, in the hope of winning the war and reconquering Italy with Nazi assistance, the Party punted anew on the new generations. Under RSI rule, especially in the cities, the ONB reappeared, still under Ricci, completely faithful to Mussolini and now also become one of the commanders of the GNR. By 1944, ONB claimed to have enrolled 103,200 Figli della Lupa, 231,000 Balilla, 222,500 Piccole Italiane, 43,000 Giovani Italiane, and 47,000 Avanguardisti, once again becoming Fascism's most ample base. From their ranks, the GNR, heir of the MVSN, recruited trainee officers and other recruits. For many this choice followed up their training while very young or occurred after patriotic blackmail from fathers, teachers, and commanders, somehow turned on without any direct orders during the troubled months from July to September 1943.

A proper social survey of the young fighters for Salò is still needed, although memoir accounts suggest that as ever they tended to come from the middle classes, the petty bourgeoisie, white-collar workers, artisans, and small business families from the centre-north and Rome. Among the Avanguardisti Moschettieri, in January 1944 a minimum age of 16 was formally adopted for those fighting in the Fiamme Bianche (White Flames) under the GNR. Many moved from there or directly from the ONB to the BN and, from the summer of that year, worked in the anti-partisan repression. In the autonomous Ettore Muti Legion, inaugurated in March 1944 to work in Piedmont and Lombardy, 38 per cent of legionaries were between 18 and 24 years old and 12 per cent were less than 17. For the Fiamme Bianche some *Campi Dux* were reopened in spring 1944 at various centres in Tuscany, Emilia-Romagna, and the Veneto. By May, 4,000 ONB born in 1929 (and quite a few still younger who had falsified their age) were concentrated at Velo d'Astico in the province of Vicenza and, in August, they were added to the fighting groups of the

Guardia Giovanile Legionaria in anti-aircraft work or to assist in the final defence of the bridges over the Po and Mincio rivers. Quite a few girls were now employed as auxiliaries, after having been trained by former cadets from the Orvieto academy. A first course for such people opened at Noventa Vicentina in April 1944, while six further such courses began in various parts of northern Italy, training thousands of girls born in 1927 and 1928. Many such graduates were to be killed in the last bloody months of the conflict or in the continued mayhem of the first months of civil conflict after liberation.[26]

In 1944, in sum, young people, like Italy itself, were in a state of dissolution, with traditional social and generational hierarchies askew and the formal discipline of the dictatorship in ruins. The young, be they students, workers, or peasants, living in separate zones in the past, now found themselves congregated in partisan forces or in the RSI's bands. Accustomed domestic bonds and protection disappeared as many very young now found themselves engaged in a great adventure and one where past political instruction was of unpredictable effect. The patriotic and nationalist slant of fascism could readily convert to a choice for the Resistance, just as it could for the RSI, favoured to wipe clean the 'dishonour' and 'betrayal' of the armistice and the attempt to change alliances in September 1943. For girls the new freedom often seemed all the fuller, because it was less conditioned by conscription or other age requirements on boys and could be lived as a political and gender emancipation leading on to political involvement during the post-war years. The irregular formations, notably the BN, left much initiative to the young as well as immunity for crimes committed against civilians. As Pavolini announced, here every young man could feel himself at last genuinely 'free'.

In recent times, Carlo Mazzantini and Roberto Vivarelli, born in 1925 and 1929 respectively, have endeavoured to portray this choice for a black shirt as a noble one.[27] In so doing they have provoked a wide debate in Italy about how young people came together in the last stages of the war and what such links at Salò entailed. Not dissimilar is the situation in Germany with Günter Grass (b. 1927) revealing that he had had joined the youth units of the SS and being compared with the rival choice of Joachim Fest (b. 1926).[28] Yet, many questions remain open. They must await subtle historical analysis that can reflect on the array of personal motivations that drove some young people to fight their fellows, to terrorize civilian populations in Nazi-occupied Europe, and convert into fact the propaganda that they had heard because of the fascist determination to win over the new generation.

[26] Associazione Nazionale Famiglie Caduti e Dispersi della RSI, *Fiamme Bianche: adolescenti in Camicia Nera della RSI*, ed. S. Cappelletti and C. Liberati (n.p.: Ultima Crociata, 2003).

[27] C. Mazzantini, *I balilla andarono a Salò* (Venice: Marsilio, 1997); idem, *A cercar la bella morte* (Venice: Marsilio, 1997); R. Vivarelli, *La fine di una stagione: memoria 1943–1945* (Bologna: Il Mulino, 2000).

[28] G. Grass, *Beim Häuten der Zwiebel* (Göttingen: Steidl Verlag, 2006); J. Fest, *Ich nicht: Erinnerungen an eine Kindheit und Jugend* (Reinbek: Rowohlt, 2006).

Bibliography

Addis Saba, M., *Gioventù italiana del Littorio: la stampa dei giovani nella guerra fascista* (Milan: Feltrinelli, 1973).

Charnitzky, J., *Fascismo e scuola: la politica scolastica del regime 1922–1943* (Florence: La Nuova Italia, 1996).

Cutrufelli, R. M., *Piccole italiane* (Milan: Anabasi, 1994).

Dogliani, P., *IL fascismo degli italiani* (Turin: UTET, 2008).

—— *Storia dei giovani* (Milan: Bruno Mondadori, 2003).

Fabrizio, F., *Sport e politica: la politica sportiva del regime 1924–1936* (Florence: Guaraldi, 1976).

Gibelli, A., *Il popolo bambino: infanzia e nazione dalla Grande Guerra a Salò* (Turin: Einaudi, 2005).

Gibson, M., *Born to Crime: Cesare Lombroso and the Origins of Biological Criminology* (Westport, Conn.: Praeger, 2002).

La Rovere, L., *Storia dei GUF: organizzazione, politica e miti della gioventù universitaria fascista 1919–1943* (Turin: Bollati Boringhieri, 2003).

Nello, P., *L'Avanguardismo giovanile alle origini del fascismo* (Bari: Laterza, 1978).

CHAPTER 11

WOMEN IN MUSSOLINI'S ITALY, 1922–1945

PERRY WILLSON

THERE is by now a fairly ample historiography on the role of women in Fascist Italy. It is, however, still somewhat uneven. On some topics, such as the demographic campaign, numerous studies have appeared. On others, particularly the mobilization of women into the Fascist Party and (apart from the Resistance) women's experience during the Second World War, much less has been published. This situation is now, however, changing with some new research in both these areas. This recent wave of interest in some of the more neglected topics is very positive since a due attention to gender can shed much light on the fascist experience in Italy.

The fascist regime paid a good deal of attention to gender and the role of women in its ideology, propaganda, and legislation. The roots of much of this can be traced to the Italian experience in the First World War. The fascists' pervasive emphasis on militaristic values, for example, was clearly in part a product of the great disorientation many men experienced in the aftermath of the confusing events of the war: it owed a great deal to wounded masculine (as well as national) pride after the rout of the Italian troops at Caporetto. Moreover, perceptions of 'gender disorder' (shaped by misleading representations in the press which suggested that large numbers of women had 'invaded'

what were considered male spheres of employment) during the period of hostilities were also important in shaping some of the policies of the blackshirt
regime.[1]

From fascism's early days, a certain conception of manliness (where the ideal
man was a warrior, active, dynamic, and youthful) underpinned a good deal of
the way in which the fascists presented themselves.[2] Attention to gender issues
escalated after the launching of the demographic campaign in 1927, which aimed to
reverse the decline in the nation's birth rate. In this period, fascist propaganda spoke
increasingly of duties not rights, but these duties were to be separate and specific
according to gender: for men this meant bearing arms for the nation, for women it
meant producing many babies. Women's place, as propaganda relentlessly stressed,
was to be in the home, raising large numbers of children. Motherhood was elevated
into a national mission, for a larger population was deemed essential to fascist
projects of imperialism and conquest. 'Numbers', it was said, meant 'strength'.

Nevertheless, as Victoria De Grazia has argued[3] (in contrast to historians like
Piero Meldini who have depicted Italian women in this period as essentially hapless victims of the regime[4]), despite this seemingly backward-looking, misogynist
ideology, some fascist interventions in the lives of women, particularly the attempts
to politically mobilize them, did, in fact, serve to modernize their position. Fascism, moreover, was far from the only force for change in inter-war Italy. Other
influences, such as growing commercialization and new images of women, like the
glamorous, Hollywood starlets of the era, offered alternative role models to that
of the rotund, rural, 'prolific mother' of large numbers of children so frequently
extolled in fascist propaganda.[5] Even the ideology itself was far from simply traditional, for it now elevated what had previously been seen as a private matter,
childbearing, into a public, national duty, and proclaimed women's importance (as
mothers) to the nation.

---

[1] On how representations of female employment in the First World War differed from actual
changes, and the impact of this in the post-war period, see B. Curli, *Italiane al lavoro 1914–1920*
(Venice: Marsilio, 1998).

[2] The history of masculinity is a very new field for Italian historiography. A useful starting point is
S. Bellassai, *La mascolinità contemporanea* (Rome: Carocci, 2004).

[3] V. De Grazia, *How Fascism Ruled Women: Italy 1922–1945* (Berkeley and Los Angeles: University
of California Press, 1992).

[4] P. Meldini, *Sposa e madre esemplare: ideologia e politica della donna e della famiglia durante il
fascismo* (Rimini and Florence: Guaraldi, 1975).

[5] On this question see V. De Grazia, 'Nationalising Women: The Competition between Fascist and
Commercial Models in Mussolini's Italy', in V. De Grazia and E. Furlough (eds), *The Sex of Things:
Gender and Consumption in Historical Perspective* (Berkeley and Los Angeles: University of California
Press, 1996), 337–58.

I. EMPLOYMENT

The question of women's employment is often seen as a key aspect in discussions of women and Italian Fascism and there is no doubt that this was considered important by the fascists themselves. Female employment was often portrayed negatively in ideology and propaganda. Perhaps the best-known example of fascist rhetoric on this topic was Mussolini's 'Macchina e donna' ('Machinery and Women') published in the fascist daily newspaper *Il popolo d'Italia* in 1934, at a time of high unemployment and considerable economic distress. In this article the *Duce* argued that mechanization and women were the two main causes of men's poor employment prospects. Work, according to Mussolini, was essential for men, underpinning their 'great physical and moral virility'. For women, it was a potential danger that could lead to sterility.[6]

The way in which such ideas and rhetoric shaped employment legislation was, however, class specific.[7] Trying to prohibit poorer women from working would have made no sense. Generally, only middle-class male breadwinners could command a 'family wage' in this period and many families would have literally starved if a real attempt had been made suddenly to transform all women into full-time housewives. During the dictatorship, therefore, work of some kind continued to be a normal part of the everyday lives of millions of Italian women, as it had been in Liberal Italy. They were to be found in a wide range of occupations, working, for example, as laundresses, midwives, street sellers, landladies, outworkers, handicraft manufacturers, domestic servants, wet-nurses, seamstresses, and shop assistants. There were also many women employed as factory workers, particularly in textile firms but also in other sectors such as light engineering and tobacco processing. By far the largest number, however, was still to be found on the land. Peasant women were engaged in ceaseless toil at a mixture of farming and domestic tasks. Even some of the non-farming categories of employment just mentioned, including many of those employed in factories where the work was seasonal (such as silk-spinning mills), were carried out by women who worked in agriculture during the rest of the year.[8]

The fascist government made no attempt to ban women from any of the occupations listed. In some cases, however, it did intervene a little in the shape of new

---

[6] B. Mussolini, 'Macchina e donna', *Il popolo d'Italia*, 206, 31 August 1934.

[7] On the history of employment legislation affecting women see, for example, M. V. Ballestrero, 'La protezione concessa e l'uguaglianza negata: il lavoro femminile nella legislazione italiana', in A. Groppi (ed.), *Il lavoro delle donne* (Rome: Laterza, 1996). On the Fascist period specifically see the introduction to P. Willson, *La fabbrica orologio: donne e lavoro alla Magneti Marelli nell'Italia fascista* (Milan: Franco Angeli, 2003).

[8] On the lives of peasant women in fascist Italy see S. Salvatici, *Contadine dell'Italia fascista: presenze, ruoli, immagini* (Turin: Rosenberg & Sellier, 1999).

protective legislation, in particular the law of 1934 regulating certain types of female and child labour. This prohibited women from working at night or underground in mines and from carrying particularly heavy weights. This law also created a new category of 'female minors' (aged over 15 but under 21) who were classified with children and banned from various types of employment deemed too heavy or dangerous for them. Such legislation, however, targeted primarily factory workers (many of whom were, in practice, in precisely the age group now termed 'female minors'). The employment conditions of the vast majority of working women, including the millions employed in agriculture, in domestic service, or working for members of their own families, were excluded from such protection. Moreover, even many factory workers remained unaffected, as the legislation was so frequently ignored by employers.

The real thrust of legislation restricting female employment was aimed at middle-class women, and even this, essentially a product of the anxieties aroused by the First World War, coupled with the extreme difficulties brought by the world economic depression and the background problem of endemic 'intellectual unemployment', served mainly to shore up existing gender hierarchies in the workplace, rather than attempting a wholesale expulsion of women from the labour force. Women could, for example, continue to work as typists or telephonists but they were to be prevented from becoming office managers.

The initial target for gender-specific restrictive legislation was education. From 1923 women were no longer allowed to become headmistresses of middle schools and in 1926 they were banned from teaching what were considered the most prestigious subjects in grammar schools (such as history, literature, philosophy, Latin, and Greek). Other legislation did not actually ban women but, instead, made quota-fixing possible, such as a law of 1928 which allowed the setting of limits on how many women could be recruited as school inspectors. The abolition of fees for male students at teacher training colleges, moreover, was part of an attempt to increase the proportion of men working in what was effectively the only real mass female profession of the time, primary teaching. Female primary teachers were thought by some fascists to be a dangerous influence on young, impressionable boys: too much feminine influence, it was argued, could make boys soft-hearted and unable to be sufficiently warlike and virile.

In the 1930s, other sectors of public employment were targeted. From 1933 the various branches of the state administration were permitted to exclude female candidates from recruitment examinations for new civil service posts or to place quotas on their numbers. In 1938, the attack was extended to the private sector, too, with a law limiting the recruitment of women in both the public and private sectors to only 10 per cent in white-collar jobs. In small businesses, there was to be no female recruitment at all, apart from women working for members of their own families (in practice a substantial category) who were exempt from these restrictions. Moreover, the quotas did not affect quite a few specific occupations, which were considered to be particularly 'suitable' for women, the list of which effectively included many of the main occupations that women actually did in office work, such as shorthand typing. In practice, this legislation was to remain a dead letter, for Europe was on the brink of war: the law was supposed to be implemented over a period of three years, and a mere nine days after Italy's entry into the Second World War the provisions affecting public sector employment were suspended indefinitely.

The impact of these various employment laws is far from easy to gauge. It is clear that there was no wholesale departure of women from the labour force in this period but, given the nature of the legislation, this is hardly surprising. Admittedly, female employment did decline slightly overall during the inter-war period, but this was part of a longer-term trend and very difficult to ascribe specifically to fascist policies or ideology. The fascists may have helped encourage developments but other factors, including the severe crisis in the textile sector, were probably more important. Moreover, at least some of the decline may have been more apparent than real, due to the reclassification, as housewives, of certain groups of women who did, in practice, work. This practice had a great impact, for example, on statistics about the numbers of 'economically active' women in peasant households.[9] Even the census compilers themselves admitted that their figures were frequently far from accurate when it came to females employed in agriculture, commerce, and crafts.[10] Despite the targeting of middle-class employment, women actually managed to advance a little in the professions and, notwithstanding attempts to stem this trend, levels of female education also rose. Numbers of women enrolled at grammar schools and universities, for example, continued to increase in this period.

II. THE FAMILY AND THE
DEMOGRAPHIC CAMPAIGN

Fascism did try to intervene to a degree in the family but not always in a very sustained or even particularly coherent manner. One area where existing legislation was left largely unchanged, for example, was family law, which continued to be

[9] On this question see, for example, O. Vitali, 'I censimenti e la composizione sociale dell'agricoltura italiana', in P. Bevilacqua (ed.), *Storia dell'agricoltura italiana*, ii: *Uomini e classi* (Venice: Marsilio, 1990). See also S. Patriarca, 'Gender Trouble: Women and the Making of Italy's "Active Population" 1861–1936', *Journal of Modern Italian Studies*, 3/2 (1998), 144–63.

[10] E. Noether, 'Italian Women and Fascism: A Re-evaluation', *Italian Quarterly*, 90/22 (1982), 69–80, 72.

governed by the pre-existing civil code, the Pisanelli Code of 1865. This was an extremely patriarchal body of legislation, which the fascists found convenient to retain. They did issue a new code of their own in 1942 but it only tinkered with the existing code and changed little of real substance.[11]

The family was, however, changing in this period. Among some social strata, particularly the urban working class, the trend towards more companionate marriages continued and was enhanced by the fact that, despite anti-migration legislation, the rural–urban shift was far from halted during the years of fascist rule. In rural areas, encroaching forms of modernization, including that brought about by the interventions of the Fascist Party itself, did slightly open up the closed and isolated world of some peasant women. Many, however, continued to live in extremely patriarchal, hierarchical households. Indeed, the fascist policy of *sbracciantizzazione* (decasualization) in agriculture, which aimed to reduce the number of landless farm labourers and increase the numbers of sharecroppers and small landowners, bolstered this kind of family structure, where there was a clearly established gender and age hierarchy. In such households, apart from the *reggitrice*, the most important female, who had authority only over her daughters and daughters-in-law, peasant women had very little power or influence.

Before Mussolini's seizure of power, successive Liberal governments had tended to intervene little in the private sphere, seeing it as a moral rather than political arena and, as such, best left to the Catholic Church. The fascists, by contrast, considered the family an important terrain for intervention, due to their preoccupation both with gender roles and with the declining birth rate.

The fascist focus on the birth rate, which they termed the 'problem of problems', led them to intervene in various ways to attempt to make people have more babies.[12] Some of these interventions promoted early marriage. Others tried to motivate those who were already married to produce greater numbers of children. Bachelors (but not spinsters) were penalized for their failure to wed by the imposition of extra taxes. Families with large numbers of children (usually at least seven or even ten living children were required to qualify) received a range of benefits like free school books, medical care, or priority in certain types of employment. Huge amounts of pro-natalist propaganda were also used. An annual 'Mother and Child Day' was instituted on 24 December in which celebratory events of various kinds were staged all over Italy to honour the nation's 'prolific mothers'. The regime also used coercive methods to stem the decline in the birth rate, banning the

---

[11] On family law in the Liberal and Fascist periods see P. Ungari, *Storia del diritto di famiglia in Italia (1796–1942)* (Bologna: Il Mulino, 1974); D. Vincenzi Amato, 'La famiglia e il diritto', in P. Melograni (ed.), *La famiglia italiana dall'ottocento a oggi* (Rome: Laterza, 1988); C. Saraceno, 'Women, Family, and the Law', *Journal of Family History*, 15/4 (1990), 427–42.

[12] A good deal has been written on the demographic campaign. One of the most useful texts is C. Ipsen, *Dictating Demography: The Problem of Population in Fascist Italy* (Cambridge: Cambridge University Press, 1996).

advertisement of contraceptives and clamping down on abortion. What were seen as 'anti-demographic groups', such as homosexual men and midwives suspected of involvement in illegal terminations, were dealt with firmly, some being sent to *confino politico* (a form of internal exile reserved for those who had committed 'political crimes').[13]

The fascists also intervened in the family through the Opera Nazionale Maternità ed Infanzia (ONMI; National Mother and Child Agency), the regime's organization for maternal and infant welfare. Founded in 1925, before the launching of the pro-natalist campaign, ONMI offered material assistance and instruction in childcare methods to poor mothers, together with a great deal of propaganda. It also gave unmarried mothers the right to claim nursing subsidies to encourage them to keep their babies. This step reversed many centuries of church-led policy towards such mothers, which had encouraged them to abandon their newborn infants in the notorious *ruota* (wheel). Many of the babies abandoned in this manner had perished prematurely in foundling hospitals.[14]

ONMI's effectiveness was constantly hampered by insufficient funding, a problem that was exacerbated by the nursing subsidies for unmarried mothers (the only form of assistance to which women were given an actual right) which virtually bankrupted the organization. As a result, although ONMI did undoubtedly provide useful help to many needy mothers, its provisions were regionally diverse and many women, particularly in rural areas, had no access to its facilities. It is also possible that this organization, with its emphasis on the importance of good mothering, may have actually helped to reduce the birth rate even further by encouraging women to take better care of smaller numbers of children.[15]

By the end of the 1930s, it was clear that the pro-natalist policy was a complete failure, and a new approach was tried with Nazi-style marriage loans for couples with modest incomes who married aged under 26.[16] The debt was progressively cancelled with the birth of successive children. Family allowances, moreover, introduced earlier to offset the worst effects of the economic depression, now

[13] On the treatment of such groups see M. Ebner, 'The Persecution of Homosexual Men under Fascism' and A. Gissi, 'Between Tradition and Profession: Italian Midwives during the Fascist Period', both in P. Willson (ed.), *Gender, Family and Sexuality: The Private Sphere in Italy 1860–1945* (Basingstoke: Palgrave Macmillan, 2004).

[14] On ONMI see, for example, A. Bresci, 'L'Opera Nazionale Maternità ed Infanzia nel ventennio fascista', *Italia contemporanea*, 192 (1993), 421–42; P. Willson, 'Opera Nazionale per la Maternità e l'Infanzia (ONMI)', in V. De Grazia and S. Luzzatto (eds), *Dizionario del fascismo* (Turin: Einaudi, 2003), ii. 273–7. On the previous fate of foundlings and on the reform of provisions for them see, for example, M. S. Quine, *Italy's Social Revolution: Charity and Welfare from Liberalism to Fascism* (Basingstoke: Palgrave Macmillan, 2002); D. Kertzer, *Sacrificed for Honor: Italian Infant Abandonment and the Politics of Reproductive Control* (Boston: Beacon Press, 1993).

[15] On this point see C. Saraceno, 'Constructing Families, Shaping Women's Lives: The Making of Italian Families between Market Economy and State Interventions', in J. R. Gillis, L. Tilly, and D. Levine (eds), *The European Experience of Declining Fertility, 1850–1970* (Oxford: Blackwell, 1992), 260.

[16] On these loans see A. Treves, 'Prestiti matrimoniali', in *Dizionario del fascismo*, ii. 421.

increasingly became seen as part of the pro-natalist campaign. Even these potentially more effective measures, which did offer slightly more substantial financial
incentives, were not, however, enough, and the decline of the birth rate continued.
The real impact of the demographic campaign was, therefore, a more intangible
one. Its impact lay more in how it affected the way in which gender issues were
discussed and in how women were portrayed, rather than in the number of children
they gave birth to.

III. Political Mobilization

Despite its seemingly retrograde gender ideology, the fascist regime created much
that was new in its mass political mobilization of women and girls. This mobilization took place on an unprecedented scale. The balance of the existing historiography gives a somewhat misleading impression of the matter since, perhaps
understandably, there have been many more studies of topics like first-wave feminism, the role of pre-fascist socialist women, and, to a lesser extent, women in
Catholic organizations than there have been of women's activities as members of the
Fascist Party. In reality, however, the fascists mobilized considerably more women.
Only, at most, tens of thousands of women had belonged to feminist groups in pre-
Fascist Italy. Even smaller numbers had enrolled in the Socialist Party. In contrast,
millions joined the Fascist Party. Already in 1929 the Party's sections for women—
the Fasci Femminili (FF; women could not join the Party in any other manner)—
had recruited about 100,000 members. By 1940 this had soared to around 750,000
and to over a million in 1942.[17] Even larger numbers joined the Sezione Massaie
Rurali (Rural Housewives Section) for peasant women.[18] Founded initially in 1933
as a section of the Fascist trade unions with, as its president, the former socialist and
'Fascist of the first hour' Regina Terruzzi, in 1934 this organization was taken over
by the Party to become a section of the FF. Its membership grew rapidly, already
numbering 225,094 in 1935, 895,514 in 1937, nearly one and a half million in 1939,
and reaching over two and a half million by the end of 1942. This tally made it
one of the largest of all the Fascist mass organizations overall. Even the latecomer
Section for Women Workers and Home-Workers (Sezione Operaie e Lavoranti a
Domicilio; SOLD) had signed up an impressive 1,514,860 members by 1942.[19]

[17] On the FF see P. Willson, 'Italy', in K. Passmore (ed.), *Women, Gender and Fascism in Europe
1919–1945* (Manchester: Manchester University Press, 2003).
[18] On this organization see P. Willson, *Peasant Women and Politics in Fascist Italy: The Massaie
Rurali* (London: Routledge, 2002), ch. 1.
[19] On SOLD see P. Willson, 'Sezione operaie e lavoranti a domicilio', in *Dizionario del fascismo*,
ii. 623–4.

The meaning of these enormous membership lists is very controversial and it is clear that many women joined for reasons other than a blind devotion to the *Duce* and the fascist cause. It is true that there were some women who were passionately committed to fascism.[20] For others, however, material incentives, fear, opportunism, or desperation all could play a part too. Some women became members out of simple conformism. Others may have approved of aspects of the regime without committing themselves wholeheartedly to all its ideals and policies.[21]

The role of the three wings of the movement differed according to a strict class hierarchy. The largely middle-class FF served as the organizers for the other sections. The first fascist women's group appeared in March 1920 in Monza (Milan) and was soon followed by others, initially mainly in northern and central urban areas. In the early days, during the rise of fascism, many of the female fascist leaders aspired to a real political role in the new movement. A good number of them had been involved with the feminist movement, mainly, although not exclusively, with more conservative groups like the Consiglio Nazionale delle Donne Italiane. Many were drawn into the nascent fascist movement by their patriotic volunteer work on the home front during the First World War. They were also motivated by the fears and aspirations they shared with males of their class: a desire to unite the nation and thwart a seemingly looming Bolshevik-style revolution. In the early years, such fascist women often spoke in language that mingled feminism with patriotism and they even campaigned for feminist causes like suffrage. In 1924, the Venetian former Red Cross nurse and moderate feminist Elisa Majer Rizzioli was appointed to a new position of National Inspectress of the fascist Women's Groups. By the late 1920s, however, the feminists in the FF had been outwitted by various male hierarchs who strongly opposed the idea that women should have any political influence. The FF soon lost their autonomy and even their leadership: Elisa Majer Rizzioli herself was ousted in January 1926. After her downfall, the FF were placed under the direct control of the Party Secretariat. No woman after Majer Rizzioli was ever given a seat on the Party Directorate.

In the late 1920s, various other troublesome feminist elements in the FF were removed from regional leadership positions. Once this purge had been accomplished, it was deemed safe to expand the women's sections. From 1932, it became compulsory for every local Party branch to have an FF: one was to be automatically created wherever the local Party had at least ten female members over the age of 22. Each local FF was run by a female secretary and she was supervised by a (female) Provincial Fiduciary, who, in turn, answered to the *Federale* (the local male leader).

---

[20] For a portrait of one, particularly fanatical, leader, see P. Willson, ' "The Fairy Tale Witch": Laura Marani Argnani and the Women's *fasci* of Reggio Emilia 1929–1940', *Contemporary European History*, 15/1 (2006), 23–42.

[21] Many of the working-class people (of both sexes) in Turin interviewed by Luisa Passerini, for example, displayed this attitude to the regime and its policies. See L. Passerini, *Torino operaia e fascismo: una storia orale* (Rome: Laterza, 1984).

With the regime firmly in power and the FF safely under the thumb of the male Party hierarchy, fascist women were allowed to play an active role but, rather than making policy, they carried it out. They followed orders but did not issue them. Their task was largely confined to spreading propaganda and engaging in welfare activity of various kinds.

Corralling fascist women primarily into a welfare role was not particularly difficult since various kinds of women active in the public sphere, including many feminists of the 'practical' variety, had tended to do a great deal of welfare work in the years before the rise of fascism. 'Practical feminists', of course, had done such work both in the name of female solidarity and as an activity with the potential to bring female emancipation. Welfare activities, these 'practical feminists' believed, could demonstrate women's organizational capabilities and sense of responsibility and thereby show that they were fit to vote and hold public office.[22] The situation was very different under fascism: now women were addressed in language that focused on duties to the nation not rights and on the importance of hierarchy and obedience. The break with the past was not, however, quite so abrupt as this might suggest, given that already during the First World War many feminists had had a taste of serving the nation in the greater cause of war. The activities of the women's fascist groups must have seemed, to many of their members, little more than a peacetime continuation of what they had done recently on the wartime 'home front'.

Much of this work was done on a shoestring as the FF activities were so poorly funded. A great deal of energy had to be devoted to fund-raising. Despite this distraction, many fascist women were very active in welfare. For example, they were engaged in teaching domestic science, organizing sewing workshops, visiting pregnant women in their homes, assisting at summer holiday camps for needy or sickly children, running nurseries for seasonal olive pickers or rice weeders, setting up employment agencies for domestic servants, and assisting in ONMI's paediatric or obstetric clinics.

The level of activity increased over time, accelerating particularly during the Ethiopian war when the FF were mobilized on the 'home front' to help Italy defy the League of Nations sanctions,[23] mainly by delivering propaganda urging cuts in consumption (for urban women) or raised production (for the peasantry). Eventually the proliferation of activities created a need for some sort of national leadership (albeit still subordinated to the male Party hierarchs). From 1937 onwards, a number of leading female fascists, most of them women who had risen to prominence as provincial leaders, were promoted to a new, salaried, rank of National Inspectress. More employment opportunities opened up soon after for female activists when

---

[22] On 'practical feminism' see, for example, A. Buttafuoco, *Questioni di cittadinanza: donne e diritti sociali nell'Italia liberale* (Siena: Protagon, 1997).

[23] On this mobilization see P. Willson, 'Empire, Gender and the "Home Front" in Fascist Italy', *Women's History Review*, 16/4 (2007), 487–500.

the Party began to recruit 'technical leaders' for the peasant women's sections, trained in the special Party school at Sant'Alessio near Rome, and in 1940 when, for the first time, the FF Provincial Fiduciaries became paid Party officials. Lower-level leaders and those who formed the backbone of the welfare programme, the so-called 'Fascist Home Visitors', however, continued to offer their services for free.

One of the main roles of the FF was to provide welfare assistance to poorer women. Eventually, as part of Party Secretary Achille Starace's policy of 'going to the people' in the 1930s, it was decided to attempt to enrol such beneficiaries of the welfare programme into the Party itself, thereby ensuring that not just the welfare activists but their clients, too, became Party members. Class hierarchies were carefully preserved: poorer women were enrolled into their own separate sections, one for peasants and one for workers, both run by the FF. As the two sections expanded, so did the tasks and responsibilities of the members of the FF, who began to find themselves involved in all sorts of unprecedented activities, including things like inspecting chicken coops for poultry farming competitions (albeit using special forms with boxes to tick which could be filled in even by middle-class FF members with no actual farming expertise).

The peasant women's section offered a considerable amount of training in domestic science, handicraft manufacturing, dairying, vegetable gardening, hygiene, childcare, and the rearing of silkworms, poultry, rabbits, and bees. Much of the training was in the form of weekly lectures or talks (often held straight after mass on Sundays to enable even busy peasant women to attend) but often a competitive element was added to encourage participation (and to create an excuse for prize-giving ceremonies). Attendance was encouraged by incentives like the distribution of free bars of soap or vegetable seeds at meetings and the chance to win numerous small prizes on courses of various types. Peasant women also got the opportunity to participate in leisure excursions and other social activities such as collective radio listening to programmes made especially for them.

SOLD, the workers' section, was founded in 1937. It attempted to recruit all kinds of working-class women, whether employed or not, and particular attention was paid to domestic servants, a category not organized by the fascist corporative bodies and more or less ignored by other fascist organizations. Its main activities were running training courses in subjects like domestic science, childcare, basic literacy, and some professional subjects. SOLD members were also taken on trips and given the opportunity to do sports. In common with the section for peasant women, members were offered various handouts and the chance to buy cut-price goods.

All these activities, in both sections, included a good deal of propaganda. Outings, for example, often had a political flavour, such as trips to war graves, to Mussolini's birthplace in Predappio, or to local or national Party rallies. Indeed, despite the 'technical' air of many activities, the main aim of the Party in setting up these two organizations was to attempt to bring propaganda about the achievements of the regime and about women's domestic mission into even the humblest of Italian homes. Even the members themselves became part of the pomp and ceremony of the regime. The Massaie Rurali, for example, were often paraded at Party rallies dressed in traditional (or, occasionally, invented) regional costumes with, on their heads or tied around their necks, their special kerchiefs decorated with the word *Duce*, the *fascio littorio*, ears of corn, and bunches of wildflowers.

Millions of women were, therefore, drawn into political organizations under fascism. Admittedly, this was a rather diluted form of politics, where women had many duties and virtually no power, but it still should be seen as important, given that it offered a route to the public sphere for many, particularly middle-class, women. Moreover, fascist political mobilization set the scene for the way in which women were to take a political role in the post-war period, both by making women's presence in political parties seem more normal and also by acting as a brake on the future. Fascism set a pattern of female politics (subordinate, with others setting the agenda for their activities, and a pronounced focus on welfare activities) which was later copied by the post-war mass parties. The legacy was, therefore, one of both modernization and conservatism.

IV. The Girls' Organizations

The Fascists also mobilized girls and young women in gender-segregated youth organizations, graded, like the boys' analogous groups, into age-structured ranks.[24] Girls from 8 to 12 years old could join the Piccole Italiane (Young Italian Girls) and those aged 13–18 the Giovani Italiane (Young Female Italians). Initially these groups were run by the FF, but in 1929 they were transferred, together with the boys' groups, under the wing of the Ministry of Education. Unlike their male equivalents whose activities had a military flavour, the girls' groups did a good deal of 'demographic activities', such as domestic science classes and 'doll-drill', where they learned childcare techniques to prepare themselves for their future role as wives and mothers. The older girls also did some welfare activities in parallel with the FF. They were also inevitably subjected to a good deal of propaganda of various kinds. Many of their activities were, however, potentially appealing, such as the opportunity to go on various kinds of excursions and engage in sporting activities. Sports, particularly graceful, artistic forms of gymnastics, were considered suitable for girls to make them healthier for their future maternal role. For many middle-class girls and adolescents, this was really something new, something with the potential to take

---

[24] On the Fascist youth groups see, for example, T. Koon, *Believe, Obey, Fight: Political Socialization of Youth in Fascist Italy, 1922–1943* (Chapel Hill, NC: University of North Carolina Press, 1985).

them out of their families in unprecedented ways. Many got the opportunity, for example, to perform in public at mass, choreographed, Party events.

It was for girls and young women, therefore, that the fascist mobilization should be seen as having had its most modernizing impact. For a few young women, these activities could even lead to careers as sports teachers in schools or in the Party youth organizations. Special training was provided at the elite female sports academy in Orvieto, founded as a female version of the male sports academy in Rome. By 1943, 800 young women had completed the training there.[25]

In 1937 the youth groups for both sexes became part of the Gioventù Italiana del Littorio (GIL; Italian Youth of the Lictors). By this time there were four different age ranks for girls. The Giovani Fasciste (Young Female Fascists), for young women aged 18–21, was effectively a youth section of the FF, involved in many of the same activities. Girls aged 15–17 now joined the Giovani Italiane, those 8–14 the Piccole Italiane, and even the smallest aged 6–7 could sign up in the Figlie della Lupa (Daughters of the She-Wolf).

Membership of the girls' organizations was quite high, at 2,385,060 by October 1936 and 2,698,082 (in the 8–21 age groups) by 1942.[26] This membership, however, was predominantly middle class, particularly in the higher age groups, as generally only school pupils joined and it was still unusual for girls from poor families to stay on for any kind of post-elementary education. After 1939, membership became compulsory for all children at school. Membership levels were higher for girls in northern than southern provinces (something that was also true for the FF and its dependent sections). As with the organizations for adult women, levels of active participation and motivations for membership varied greatly. Some joined out of conformism or because their teachers expected them to sign up. Many others, however, were happy to get involved, attracted particularly by the sports and social events. Such activities were potentially very appealing for middle-class girls, a social group that otherwise led fairly restricted lives as parents tried to protect their 'respectability' until they were safely married. A far greater opening up of this protected world took place, indeed for some it was literally torn apart, during the final years of the Fascist regime, the period of the Second World War, a time both of new opportunities and of great suffering for Italian girls and women.

V. THE SECOND WORLD WAR

Italy joined the Second World War on 10 June 1940, and initially for many women the war seemed far away. The fighting took place abroad and the mobilization of the

[25] On the Orvieto academy see L. Motti and M. Rossi Caponeri, *Accademiste a Orvieto: donne e educazione fisica nell'Italia fascista, 1932–1943* (Ponte San Giovanni-Perugia: Quatroemme, 1996).
[26] Koon, *Believe, Obey, Fight*, 173, 175.

civilian population was half-hearted. Although the experience of the First World War had demonstrated the need to mobilize civilians in modern warfare and plans in this regard had been devised from the early days of the fascist regime, when war broke out, the plans were not implemented.[27] Instead, all that was done was to draw up lists of persons available to be mobilized. The task of registering women aged 18–70 (along with adolescents aged 14–18) was assigned to the Fascist Party, with the Ministry of Corporations listing men. Other than this basic tallying, little was done. This was partly because Italy, lacking essential raw materials, was unable to gear itself up into full-scale war production and partly because victory was thought to be within easy grasp. The need to mobilize all able-bodied adult men into the armed forces was, moreover, considered unlikely, making the forced mobilization of civilians seem a costly, pointless, and potentially unpopular exercise. In the early phase of the war at least, where production did expand, employers could usually meet labour requirements from the ranks of the unemployed. They were also able to retain much of their existing labour force by registering them as key workers to be exempted from military service. By 1941, once it was clear that the war would last longer than expected, greater attempts were made to mobilize civilians, but to little effect.

Nonetheless, many women were employed during the war. Some did new types of work while others saw their existing workloads increase. Many peasant women had much to do as they took over from called-up men. In other sectors, some new opportunities emerged for women, on trams and in post offices, for example, although this phenomenon has yet to be properly studied. Such changes were largely not, however, coordinated by the authorities in any sort of official mobilization. In September 1941, for example, only 73,000 of the six and half million women and children the Fascist Party had registered as available for mobilization were recorded as in employment.[28]

'Civilian mobilization', therefore, largely meant only greater control over existing workforces rather than attempts to train and recruit vast numbers of new workers in a coordinated fashion. By late 1942, moreover, a period of intense bombing, the biggest problem was to keep people at their workplaces, and more and more categories of workers were declared 'mobilized' by decrees of the *Duce*, to prevent them from fleeing from dangerous urban areas. In December of that year all industrial workers were deemed to be 'mobilized': by this time about two million men and half a million women had 'mobilized' status.

From early 1942, it was attempted to force some to work with the creation of the so-called *Servizio del Lavoro* (Work Service) but this obligation tended to be only applied to Jews and to supposedly 'shirking' middle-class men, although,

---

[27] On the various measures taken to mobilize civilians in this period see P. Ferrazza, 'La mobilitazione civile in Italia 1949–1943', *Italia contemporanea*, 214 (1999), 21–42.
[28] Ibid. 31.

in practice, work was found for only a few of them. By late 1942, those doing compulsory work in the Servizio del Lavoro numbered a mere 169,938 men and 10,674 women.[29]

The FF increased their activities in this period but in practice they were mainly limited to more welfare activities and training of various kinds, such as in vegetable gardening to help cultivate the 'gardens of war' that appeared in many urban spaces. Some FF members did volunteer air-raid protection work. In contrast to certain other nations in this conflict, however, there was no attempt to recruit Italian women into the armed forces. As in the First World War, the only female Italians who went to the battlefront were Red Cross nurses.

Despite the rather half-hearted mobilization in terms of employment, everyday life did increasingly change.[30] While in some parts of Italy life went on much as normal in the early part of the war, in others bombing soon began. Air attacks were eventually suffered in many parts of the country, assaults for which very little adequate protection was organized, either in terms of anti-aircraft guns or bomb shelters. Food supplies, moreover, quickly became a serious problem. Rationing was introduced from early on but it functioned poorly because the state proved unable to impose its will on food producers. Many peasants (often with the connivance of local authorities) failed to bring their produce to the *ammassi* (government stockpiles). As a result, much food quickly found its way onto the black market. The simple act of procuring enough food for themselves and their families became a time-consuming and difficult activity for women. Indeed, the hunt for food meant that the war years became a period of unprecedented travel. Urban women began to undertake regular trips to the countryside in search of basic foodstuffs, either to consume or to sell. Peasant women, too, began to move around more than usual, marketing their produce.

The war did, therefore, create some new opportunities for certain women to earn money or simply to play a more active public role. For many women, however, the great conflict marked a time of hunger and grief. Many lost loved ones or suffered in bombing raids. Where evacuation became necessary, it was often chaotic and distressing. After the summer of 1943, the situation worsened for civilians. In this period, after the Allied invasion of the south and the subsequent German occupation of the north, the distinction between the 'home front' and the battlefront became blurred as the rival forces moved gradually up the length of the entire Italian peninsula. For many women, in this complex and often terrifying period, the war literally came to their doorsteps. Some, moreover, actively took part in the 'civil war', either as partisans or as die-hard followers of Mussolini.

[29] Ibid. 40.
[30] Although some scholarly research is currently being done on everyday life for women in the war, a useful starting point is still the very lively and entertaining book by journalist Miriam Mafai, *Pane nero: donne e vita quotidiana nella Seconda Guerra Mondiale* (Milan: Oscar Mondadori, 1987).

This was the period of the Resistance. The historiography on this one topic easily overshadows what has been written about other women's wartime roles.[31] Although for obvious reasons accurate figures do not exist, it is likely that very large numbers of women joined the Resistance (albeit still a minority of all Italian women). Indeed, some estimates put the numbers of women involved as high as two million. Despite this, much early Resistance historiography portrayed it essentially as a male, armed movement. Some more recent writings, however, have begun to acknowledge the importance of women.

Although only a few women shouldered arms to take part in the actual fighting, many acted as spies or transported messages to ensure communications. Women also did the essential work of supplying partisan bands with food and clothing or nursed the sick and wounded. Some risked their lives to hide Jews or partisans. In spite of the secondary importance many Resistance historians have ascribed to such roles, it is clear that, without them, partisan bands could not have operated. Thus the idea that women essentially only 'contributed' to the (male) Resistance is problematic since, as feminist historians have argued, women were an integral part of the Resistance itself. More recently some historians have gone further to argue that, often invoking the notion of 'civilian resistance', many activities hitherto not seen as part of the Resistance per se should, in fact, be counted.[32] Many (although not all) of these activities were female.

Not all Italian women rallied to the Resistance. Even in the final part of the war, there were women who actively defended fascism. Indeed some of them declared themselves willing to lay down their lives for Mussolini and the fascist cause. A few thousand signed up for the Servizio Ausiliario Femminile (SAF; Female Auxiliary Service—instituted on 18 April 1944) to help defend Mussolini's puppet government, the Republic of Salò.[33] Others collaborated in various ways with the Fascists and occupiers, as spies and informants, for example. Some participated far more directly in acts of violence, even torture, behaviour which historians have only very recently begun to explore.[34]

---

[31] On women and the historiography of the Resistance see P. Willson, 'Saints and Heroines: Re-writing the History of Italian Women in the Resistance', in T. Kirk and A. McElligot (eds), *Opposing Fascism: Community, Authority and Resistance in Europe* (Cambridge: Cambridge University Press, 1999).

[32] See, for example, A. Bravo, 'Armed and Unarmed: Struggles without Weapons in Europe and in Italy', *Journal of Modern Italian Studies*, 10/4 (2005), 468–84.

[33] On the SAF, see, for example, M. Fraddosio, 'La mobilitazione femminile: i Gruppi fascisti repubblicani femminili e il SAF', *Annali della Fondazione Luigi Micheletti* (1986); L. Garibaldi, *Le soldatesse di Mussolini* (Milan: Mursia, 1995). In English see M. Fraddosio, 'The Fallen Hero: The Myth of Mussolini and Fascist Women in the Italian Social Republic', *Journal of Contemporary History*, 31 (1996), 99–124.

[34] This theme is a very new one for Italian historiography. For some early findings see M. Firmani, 'Oltre il SAF: storie di collaborazioniste della RSI' and S. Lunadei, 'Donne processate a Roma per collaborazionismo', both in D. Gagliani (ed.), *Guerra, resistenza, politica: storie di donne* (Reggio Emilia: Aliberti, 2006).

Of course, many women in the German-occupied north were neither partisans nor fascist activists. The majority simply tried to survive the war as best they could, forming part of what some historians refer to as the 'grey zone' of those who did not make clear-cut political choices. The failure to take sides, however, was not always sufficient to ensure safety. Italian cities continued to suffer terrible bombing and many civilians died of disease, their immunity weakened by insufficient food and high levels of stress. Living in territories held by occupying armies, moreover, brought numerous violent situations.

For Jewish women the situation was particularly dramatic as now the Holocaust came directly to Italy. Those who were unable to hide were deported to concentration camps. But it was also a dangerous time for many other women. Some died in the terrible massacres of civilians carried out by the Nazis during the occupation, often as reprisals for partisan actions. Others were raped, many, for example, by the occupying German troops.[35] Thousands of others were attacked and violently raped, some of them repeatedly, in 1944 by irregular North African soldiers fighting with the Allied armed forces 'liberating' Italy. These troops ran riot in a number of small villages near Cassino, looting houses, assaulting women of all ages, and killing men who tried to protect their wives and daughters. Their trail of violence continued as they advanced northwards. The victims included children, elderly women, and even nuns. Some died either at the time or later of their wounds. Large numbers were infected with venereal disease.[36]

For many Italian women the 'liberation' by the Allies, which drove the Nazis out of Italy, was a joyful moment to be celebrated for years to come. It was the moment when peace returned and the Fascist dictatorship finally ended. For these rape victims, however, it was the concluding and most horrifying chapter of a terrible war.

On balance it is not possible to see the fascist period as a positive one for female Italians. Although during the *ventennio* there undoubtedly was some modernization of the role of certain, particularly middle-class and urban, women, it also was a period of attacks on women's access to employment and of a deluge of rhetoric stressing that their only real value was as mothers. Even the regime's highly innovative mass political mobilization had an ambivalent impact on the future, both opening up and restricting women's political roles in the post-war years. Finally, fascism's obsession with militarism and war as a trial of national virility led Italy into the great catastrophe of the Second World War, a war that brought tremendous

---

[35] On rapes by Germans and 'repubblichini' see C. Venturoli, 'La violenza taciuta: percorsi di ricerca sugli abusi sessuali fra il passaggio e l'arrestarsi del fronte', in D. Gagliani et al. (eds), *Donne, guerra, politica* (Bologna: CLEUB, 2000).

[36] There has been a certain amount of research on the rapes by Allied troops. See, for example, V. Chiurlotto, 'Donne come noi: Marocchinate 1944–Bosniache 1993', *DWF* 17/1 (1993), 42–67; G. Gribaudi, *Guerra totale: tra bombe alleate e violenze naziste: Napoli e il fronte meridionale 1949–44* (Turin: Bollati Boringhieri, 2005), ch. 10.

suffering and trauma to the civilian population. Fascism, it is clear, governed Italy with a high cost to women.

BIBLIOGRAPHY

DE GRAZIA, V., *How Fascism Ruled Women: Italy, 1922–1945* (Berkeley and Los Angeles: University of California Press, 1992).

DETRIAGACHE, D., 'Il fascismo femminile da San Sepolcro all'affare Matteotti (1919–1925)', *Storia contemporanea*, 14/2 (1983).

GAGLIANI, D. (ed.), *Guerra, resistenza, politica: storie di donne* (Reggio Emilia: Aliberti, 2006).

IPSEN, C., *Dictating Demography: The Problem of Population in Fascist Italy* (Cambridge: Cambridge University Press, 1996).

MAFAI, M., *Pane nero: donne e vita quotidiana nella Seconda Guerra Mondiale* (Milan: Oscar Mondadori, 1987).

MELDINI, P., *Sposa e madre esemplare: ideologia e politica della donna e della famiglia durante il fascismo* (Rimini and Florence: Guaraldi, 1975).

SALVATICI, S., *Contadine dell'Italia fascista: presenze, ruoli, immagini* (Turin: Rosenberg & Sellier, 1999).

WILLSON, P., 'Italy', in K. Passmore (ed.), *Women, Gender and Fascism in Europe 1919–1945* (Manchester: Manchester University Press, 2003).

——*Peasant Women and Politics in Fascist Italy: The Massaie Rurali* (London: Routledge, 2002).

——'Saints and Heroines: Re-writing the History of Italian Women in the Resistance', in T. Kirk and A. McElligot (eds), *Opposing Fascism: Community, Authority and Resistance in Europe* (Cambridge: Cambridge University Press, 1999).

CHAPTER 12

....

CRIME AND REPRESSION*

....

MAURO CANALI

THE availability of new archival evidence is permitting a fuller understanding of the nature of fascist repression. The material is especially helpful in resolving debates about the character of Mussolinian totalitarianism and the issue of an alleged continuity between the policing practices of the Liberal and Fascist regimes. In terms of its repressive techniques, it is clear that the dictatorship did retool instruments and organizations that the Liberal state had forged in its social crisis or under the urgent requirements of running the war after 1915. For almost all combatants, the weakness of opposition to the national war effort meant that policy in regard to domestic security could focus on espionage matters. Only in Italy did government have to deal with active and widespread popular hostility to the conflict, organized and run by 'maximalist' socialists, with their own deep social roots. To confront this threat, the Liberal state yielded to the temptation to impose 'special laws', instituting the so-called Sacchi decree against any public show of 'defeatism'. This measure allowed the internment of anyone deemed a danger to public order and it severely cut into anti-war youth movements.

This recourse to extraordinary legislation laid bare the anomaly of the Liberal system in Italy, demonstrating that the state possessed only a limited level of consent, that it was led by an elite lacking cohesion, and that, unlike in other Western European societies, it was unable to develop a genuine modern liberal party. Rather it still deployed nineteenth-century techniques of rule by notables and

* Translated by Richard Bosworth.

small-scale electoral committees. Simultaneously, it was confronted, unlike other liberal states, by a strong and revolutionary socialist movement, pledged to utilize the 'imperialist' war violently to seize power from a 'warmongering bourgeoisie'. The fears of the Liberal elite in this regard were confirmed by the two international meetings at Kienthal and Zimmerwald, supported by the Italian maximalists who accepted the Leninist and Bolshevik slogan that the real enemy of the working class was to be found at home. It cannot therefore be a surprise to find that the backers of international communism were repaid by the Liberal administration in their own coin, being treated as 'enemies within', to be opposed with the same arms and the same repressive laws that were to be used against spies and saboteurs working for foreign powers.

The fears of the Liberal government and of the bourgeoisie as a whole about the presence of a combative enemy acting as a sort of anti-state in much of Italy were reinforced in the immediate post-war period, when the excited fascination of workers with the Bolshevik triumphs in Russia rendered still harder the divisions that had existed when Italy entered the war. The class struggle between those who had fought the war and those who had at best endured it and had probably rejected it was rendered more acute by events in Russia. The diffuse class hatred reinforced many returning officers, themselves the children of middling people, painted by socialists as guilty for an all but genocidal war, in their visceral anti-socialism, and so drove them into the ranks of rising fascism.

While in Italy the battle between socialism and liberalism radicalized, in the rest of Europe labour's support for the war and participation in the *union sacrée* had rather fostered social reconciliation through the patriotism discovered to exist in every class. While in the West, socialists were now deemed responsible enough to be entrusted with government and so were accepted as pillars of a democratic order, in Italy the violent rhetoric of revolution that continued to mark socialist discourse, despite its impotence, ensured the isolation of its social base from the middle classes who became ever more convinced that fascism would defend the national sacrality of the war, while anti-fascism stood for a complete renunciation of the war's history.

Many later leaders of the dictatorship's police served as junior officers in the war. Typically they were recruited among the forces of order following the reform of the Directorate General for Public Security (DGPS) pushed through by the government of Francesco Saverio Nitti between August and October 1919 at a time when the dramatic events of the *biennio rosso* (red two years) and of the occupation of the factories seemed to confirm the determination of the left to overthrow the state. It was thus no accident that the advent of fascism to power in October 1922 to act as a bulwark against subversion saw not a single voluntary resignation from among police functionaries. In their minds, the struggle of the Fascist state against its foes was simply the continuation of the battle against subversives begun in the war.

In the tense moments following the defeat at Caporetto, the rumour had spread that the military loss had actually amounted to an attempt at social revolution by ordinary soldiers, the so-called *santi maledetti* (holy accursed) as the later fascist writer Curzio Malaparte called them,[1] a coup that only failed because of its lack of political direction. In these extreme circumstances, the government engaged in a severe repression of anti-militarism. In doing so, they exceeded those norms of existing police practice that went back to the social repression of the governments of Francesco Crispi in the 1890s, and notably with the creation of a central body, the Ufficio Riservato (Special Office), that would watch over the various police offices, or *questure*, scattered across the country's provinces. Now the Ufficio Centrale Investigativo (UCI; Central Investigative Branch) was launched to be a more agile force, dependent on the national Chief of Police and possessed of carte blanche to deal with subversion of any kind. To all intents and purposes, the UCI was the progenitor of the Fascist secret police or Organizzazione per la Vigilanza e la Repressione dell' Antifascismo (OVRA). Already in 1917, its culture was illiberal, both in theory and practice, and it foreshadowed the reactionary drift of Italian policing. For UCI officers their foes were composed of dangerous criminals, hoping to be an anti-state, and they must be combated with any means. At the end of the war, the UCI was dissolved but many of its men transferred to a new body called the Divisione Affari Generali e Riservati (DAGR; Division for General and Special Affairs) to which the Nittian reforms assigned political repression. This structure would continue until Mussolini achieved power.

On becoming Prime Minister, Mussolini did not trust ordinary police officials sufficiently to delegate to them the task of repressing anti-fascists. He therefore instituted an extra-legal body, the so-called Fascist 'Ceka', to deploy violence of every kind against the regime's most determined enemies. In this regard, Mussolini was particularly likely to call upon 'Fascists of the first hour' in whom he had full faith. The task of leading the 'Ceka' was given to Cesare Rossi, head of the Prime Minister's Press Office and well known to Mussolini since 1914 as an early collaborator on his newspaper, *Il popolo d'Italia*. Rossi had been one of the founders of the Fasci di Combattimento in 1919 and was a close friend of Amerigo Dumini, to whom he gave the delicate job of carrying out the 'Ceka's' deeds. Among the first to be recruited into its ranks was Albino Volpi, guilty of much of the mayhem perpetrated by fascists in Milan between 1919 and 1922. Emilio De Bono, one of the quadrumvirs of the March on Rome, described him as the *enfant gâté* of Milanese squadrism while Mussolini dubbed him a 'joy to behold'.[2]

Mussolini had explained cynically to Rossi that 'all governments in a state of transition need extra-legal organs in order to set their adversaries to rights'. The creation of a secret police, he ran on, was necessary given that existing legislation was enfeebled by 'the liberal ideals against which fascism had risen' and did not

---

[1] C. Malaparte, *La rivolta dei santi maledetti* (Rome: Rassegna Internazionale, 1921).
[2] ASR, Delitto Matteotti, Esami, from a memorandum by De Bono.

allow the new government 'the means it required to strike down its foes'. In regard to the impunity that members of the 'Ceka' would need, Mussolini assured Rossi that, 'being in charge of government', he and his supporters could 'successfully cloak any illegal violence'.[3] The 'Ceka' could do what it liked because any evidence against it would be suppressed by the Chief of Police, De Bono, another loyal Mussolinian. Indeed, De Bono proved able in this matter, since responsibility for not one of the 'Ceka's' crimes between 1922 and 1924 was ever pinned on an individual.

The 'Ceka' grew slowly, passing through various and distinct phases. In 1923, its actions were entrusted to a number of different fascist chiefs, who then passed matters over to their own loyal clients. On the evening of 29 June 1923, the beating of Alfredo Misuri, an Umbrian 'Fascist of the first hour' who had fallen out with Mussolini, was organized by Italo Balbo, with his agents being some Bolognese squadrists. The first attack on the liberal democrat Giovanni Amendola, in December 1923, was launched by Roman Fascists, acting at the direct behest of De Bono.

From August 1923, when Mussolini could guarantee Rossi secret funds for his underlings, the criminal organization began to be centralized at the Press Office. Now such notorious figures as Dumini, Volpi, and Aldo Putato begin to appear on the pay lists.[4] The first major action by Rossi's team occurred with Dumini's and Volpi's visit to France in September 1923. The two, relying on the complicity of Malaparte who was then stationed in Paris as a Fascist Party inspector, completed a number of provocations among anti-fascist exiles there. In his final report, Dumini urged further terrorist actions against the émigré communist organization and the building of a network of paid informers who could infiltrate the ranks of the so-called *fuorusciti* (those who had left Italy). The next action involved administering a dose of castor oil to the republican member of parliament Ulderico Mazzolani, with curt advice that thereafter he cease publishing articles critical of the Fascist government. There followed in November a second stay in France, when Dumini and Volpi were joined by five other 'Cekists'. On this occasion, however, the mission was foiled when Dumini was mysteriously wounded and driven back to Italy. Another 'Ceka' mission, organized by Rossi in late November with the assistance of Roman Fascists, entailed the devastation of the home of ex-Prime Minister Nitti, who was lucky to escape a lynching. The attack drove Nitti into exile. A few days later, an assault was made on a parade celebrating the anniversary of Italy's victory in the war in order forcibly to expel from its ranks some ex-soldiers who had become members of the moderate Partito Socialista Unitario. This crescendo of violence reached a pinnacle on 12 March 1924 when, at Milan central railway station, a little group of 'Cekists', led by Dumini and Volpi, fell on Cesare Forni, a dissident fascist from Pavia who

---

[3] From a memorandum written by Rossi for investigating magistrates when he was imprisoned over the Matteotti murder. ASR, Delitto Matteotti, Interrogatori.

[4] M. Canali, 'La contabilità di Cesare Rossi, Capo dell'Ufficio Stampa del governo Mussolini (novembre 1922–maggio 1924)', *Storia contemporanea*, 4 (1988), 719–50.

was intending to run in the elections due on 6 April with a ticket opposing the Fascist *listone*. The beating was ferocious and only Forni's strong physique saved him from death.

The last action completed by the 'Ceka' before the murder of Matteotti happened on 3 June was directed against opposition members of parliament while they were leaving the Chamber of Deputies in Rome and who were thereafter pursued through the streets of the capital. It had been approved by Mussolini and Rossi on 31 May and was the direct antecedent to the Matteotti attack. The day before, Matteotti had denounced the corruption and violence of the fascists during the elections. Rossi and Mussolini decided that he had a following that needed to be intimidated. As with the assault on Nitti, Italo Foschi, a leading Rome Fascist, received direct orders from Rossi, who would admit that he in turn had acted at Mussolini's command. Rossi remarked ironically to Foschi that, as in the past action, 'you could not give a public order to assemble two thousand fascists'.[5]

The 'Ceka's' last and most terrible crime was, then, the Matteotti murder.[6] Matteotti was seized virtually outside his home on 10 June 1924 by 'Cekists' led by Dumini and Volpi.[7] The socialist was stabbed, probably by Volpi, in the back seat of the car used for the kidnapping and then buried in a shallow grave not far outside Rome where his corpse was discovered two months later. The resultant political crisis threatened to pull down Mussolini who survived only thanks to divisions in his opposition and because the king feared a 'leap in the dark'. Mussolini continued to deny that the 'Ceka' existed and did so notably in his speech of 3 January 1925 when he otherwise took responsibility for fascist mayhem. As far as he was concerned, he claimed, violence must be 'surgical, intelligent and chivalrous', whereas the 'Ceka' was alleged to have been 'unintelligent, stupid, all over the place'.[8] He therefore implied the need for the creation of an organization that would place all repression directly under his own control.

In Mussolini's ambiguous phrases, he was merely dissociating himself from the lack of skill displayed by the Dumini 'Ceka'. There is plenty of evidence that links Mussolini directly to its acts and to the Matteotti killing. One is a letter written by Rossi to the *Duce* after he had gone underground. Rossi had been sacked by Mussolini and saw himself as a sacrificial victim to squeamish public opinion. He was unwilling, however, to play the *Duce*'s game and so now wrote secretly to say that, 'if the appalling cynicism that you have displayed, added to the troubles that you have brought on yourself, encourage you to plan my physical suppression while I am in hiding or if I should be arrested, you, too, will be destroyed and your fall

---

[5] G. Rossini, *Il delitto Matteotti tra il Viminale e l'Aventino* (Bologna: Il Mulino, 1966), 980.

[6] For full detail, see M. Canali, *Il delitto Matteotti* (Bologna: Il Mulino, 1997). There is an abridged version available (Bologna: Il Mulino, 2004).

[7] The other members of the gang were the Milanese ex-*arditi* Augusto Malacria, Giuseppe Viola, and Amleto Poveromo.

[8] B. Mussolini, *Opera omnia* (Florence: La Fenice, 1956), xxi. 236.

will be accompanied by that of the regime, given that I have made a full and detailed declaration and placed it in the hands of friends on whom I can completely rely'. In this statement, Rossi was alluding to the long list of assaults that the 'Ceka' had perpetrated on Mussolini's direct orders. The tally would reach Giovanni Amendola who published it in *Il mondo* in its last issue in December 1924 and revealed starkly the crude customs of the Fascist Party in regard to political crime.

The second document was from Dumini. In a letter dated 23 July 1925 which he managed to get to his lawyer, Giovanni Vaselli, who had been charged by Mussolini himself to defend the five murderers, Dumini warned off his boss. Dumini had been in prison for a year and began to fear that he would be left there. He now underlined that he had no intention to be a scapegoat and that, if examined, he would confess all. 'We must defend ourselves', he wrote, 'because we do not intend to take a full punishment for a crime that, doubtless, we committed but which was imposed on us and which we, like many others, carried out with a blind discipline and with an absolute guarantee that we would be immune from penalty.'[9] Dumini told Vaselli that the mandate to kill had come directly from Mussolini.

The plain determination of fascism, even in the allegedly 'legalitarian two years' before open dictatorship, to use the 'Ceka' for criminal violence against the opposition also casts historiographical light. The regime's readiness to repress and kill its opponents illuminates the implict and explicit tendency of fascism to become genuinely totalitarian.[10] Failing to examine the 'Ceka' means ignoring an evident characteristic of fascism from its foundation: that is, its willingness to use any form of violence to wipe out every obstacle to its acquisition of complete and unchallenged power. Only by admitting its totalitarianism can it be understood.

In November 1926, Mussolini promulgated the so-called *leggi fascistissime* (thoroughly Fascist laws) which made concrete the construction of a totalitarian state. Now the regime outlawed all other political parties and drafted legislation to suppress any who dared to protest against single party government. The death penalty, long abolished, was now reintroduced for those who made attempts on the life either of the king or of the *Duce* or who threatened state security. The Special Tribunal was established to deal with political crimes, while *confino* (internal exile and internment) was applied against any who could be defined as a public danger. The punishment of *confino* formally replicated the '*domicilio coatto*' (compulsory residence) of the days of Liberal Prime Minister Giovanni Giolitti. For whatever motive, those considered perilous could be relegated to a remote place, even when they had not committed a crime, simply through administrative fiat. In Liberal Italy, the anarchists were almost the only ones to be subjected to such punishment, a practice that could often have terrible effects on the victim and his family. The Fascist regime amplified and perfected the system, aggravating its arbitrariness, since

[9] Canali, *Il delitto Matteotti*, 435.
[10] For important interpretation, see E. Gentile, *La via italiana al totalitarismo: il partito e lo stato nel regime fascista* (Rome: La Nuora Italia Scientifica, 1995).

local Party authorities were often decisive in choosing its victims. For this reason, vendetta or simple personal antipathy could become the real motives for action and there would be no need for serious proof when men and women were dragged before the provincial commission that assigned the penalties. The results could be devastating materially and for the suffering families from whom individuals were now isolated and were likely to remain so. It was widely believed, for example, and the rumour was encouraged by the authorities, that it was dangerous to be friends with, or to employ, anyone who had returned from *confino*.

Moreover, the term of punishment was regularly doubled if a *confinato* displayed any objection or if there was evidence that old political attitudes, hostile to the regime, had not been renounced. From the beginning, the pattern of imprisonment was closely linked to the Special Tribunal. If that body decided to free individuals for lack of proof and the police authorities thought them dangerous, they could still be sent to *confino* for an undetermined time at the behest of the Chief of Police. Similarly, when individuals were reaching the end of their formal terms of imprisonment, rather than being freed, they could be sent anew to *confino*. Quite a number of the most convinced anti-fascists therefore spent the best part of their lives either in prison or in *confino* during the dictatorship. They did not have to be people of fame but could be ordinary men and women, obscure militants, who, out of stubbornness and without flaunting the matter, refused to bend to the regime's demands. Any examination of the regime's repressive system thus must extend beyond the activities of such official bodies as Polpol and OVRA to admit a vaguer, vaster, and equally ruthless general policing of society.

The Divisione Polizia Politica (Polpol; Political Police) had been created to fight and repress political deviancy. If, from June 1924 to November 1926, Mussolini wanted to give the impression of having abandoned plans for a police state, this attitude was merely tactical. The troubles that had arisen during the Matteotti crisis and the danger his career had then confronted counselled that he should not move too hastily. However, the assassination attempt against him at Bologna at the end of October 1926 gave an opportunity that he was not to miss. The genuine public alarm and dismay allowed him to push ahead with the *leggi fascsitissime*, the foundation stones of the totalitarian state. The dictator's partner on this path was the very able Arturo Bocchini, nominated Chief of Police in September 1926 following an assassination effort by the anarchist Gino Lucetti. Bocchini had replaced Francesco Crispo Moncada who, in June 1924, had ousted De Bono. The need to employ a 'specialist' against the regime's most determined foes was enhanced by the recent decision to outlaw all other political parties. In this new world, the old police structure, inherited from the Liberal past, would be inadequate for the dictatorship's totalitarian plans.

The political police with their familiar title of Polpol were founded in November 1926, arising from the First Section of the Directorate of General and Special Affairs and boasting a familiarity with anti-fascist repression through a set of experienced officials and spies. The First Section was left with the lower profile task of coordinating the *questure* with their provincial jurisdictions. Before moving forward with repression, Bocchini sacked men whose faith in fascism had wavered during the Matteotti crisis or who had expressed doubts about the *leggi fascistissime*. The excuse for the purging of various *questori* and inspectors was often said to be 'for serious work matters'; the words meant lack of a secure attachment to the dictatorship.[11]

Polpol was a sleek agency, composed of only a few score officials who yet commanded an extensive network of spies and informers, both within Italy and abroad, where they inserted themselves ably into emigrant communities. Relations between Rome and periphery were maintained through the system of regular reporting expected from the agents. Spies were mostly to be found in the large centres of northern and central Italy and among emigrants and exiles where they kept the centre informed about every move planned in anti-fascist circles and apprised their bosses about attempts to enhance and activate ties between those abroad and their surviving supporters who were still courageously trying to contest the regime's power in Italy. Often the intervention happened at the highest level, with the police being able directly to influence leaders' decisions. In October 1938, for example, Vincenzo Bellavia, the police official in charge of infiltration in Paris, could communicate to Rome with ill-concealed satisfaction that three of his spies, Enrico Brichetti, Alfredo Zanella, and Alvise Nuvoli, had 'the whole of the [liberal democratic] *Giustizia e Libertà* [GL; Liberty and Justice] movement in hand'. Brichetti was so trusted by his GL fellows that, in 1937, when the movement's chief, Carlo Rosselli, was wounded fighting for the Republicans in Spain, Brichetti was nominated to succeed him at the head of the so-called 'Matteotti brigade'. He could therefore provide Polpol with a full list of that force's members. Two other spies had worked themselves into GL ranks, with Antonio Biondi dealing with the movement's correspondence and with any visitors to the Paris office and Giacomo Antonio Antonini, a noted scholar of French and Italian literature and a collaborator on the journal *Solaria*, winning intellectual credit. This latter was another to whom Rosselli gave full trust, so much so that perhaps his last note, written from Bagnoles-de-l'Orne just before his murder, was sent to Antonini.

The killing of Rosselli and his brother Nello was not organized directly by the Fascist police. Rather it was entrusted to the Servizi Militari Informativi Italiani (SIM), the military's spying body, who commissioned members of the French fascist group, the terrorist Cagoule. Yet, in fact, Polpol had participated in the crime, since it had passed over to SIM a huge file of material on Rosselli that had been collected over the previous seven years of determined and constant investigation by its spies in the ranks of GL.

For some months between November 1926 and the summer of 1927, Polpol had functioned as the intelligence wing of the local police. In these circumstances, when

---

[11]   For full details, see M. Canali, *Le spie del regime* (Bologna: Il Mulino, 2004).

Polpol had finished its probing of certain individuals, their cases were passed to the branches of the ordinary police, through the *questure*, for arrest and punishment. However, Bocchini soon decided that the *questure* were too inefficient for his purposes, believing that they were commonly derailed by border wars with rival *questure* and with other police agencies. They therefore were unprepared to cope ruthlessly with the interregional structure that the clandestine Communist Party had established. Bocchini concluded that a new police branch was needed that could act undisturbed by territorial jealousies and disputes about rank, in full secrecy, and across all national territory. He therefore gave life to OVRA.

In time, OVRA extended its control of the nation through eleven zones, the most important being those that ran across northern Italy from Piedmont to the Veneto or centred on the Emilia-Romagna or the one dealing with Puglia. Heading these bodies were such able officials as Francesco Nudi, Tommaso Petrillo, Francesco Peruzzi, Giuseppe D'Andrea, and Andrea Calabrese Aversini. OVRA did at first, from 1927 to 1930, make some effort to extend its activities abroad but it ended by restricting itself to Italy. It had been discouraged by some schemes that had finished badly for its spies and by a fear that it would compromise the existing informers in the various émigré anti-fascist organizations. As once UCI had been able to do, OVRA could act nationally without fear of disturbance. Yet the informers abroad and OVRA at home did collaborate whenever it was necessary. Any missions plotted by anti-fascists to cross the borders were referred to Polpol which almost always thus acquired a full knowledge of the coordinates of the plan. The detail collected by spies thus frequently meant that the unprepared emissary was picked out no sooner than he had entered Italy and that he was thereafter shadowed in his every step, with the result being that the whole network of regime opponents was traced and, when necessary, scooped into police hands. On more than one grotesque occasion, anti-fascist exiles gave the task of entering Italy to men who were themselves spies, one case being in September 1937 with the 'mission' of the informer Secondo Saporetti, who was stationed between Nice and Marseilles. The Fascist police used this escapade to close down what was left after the Rosselli murders of a GL organization in Florence, Bologna, and Cremona.

The surveillance of emissaries from the United States, quite a number of them being anarchists, proved more difficult, since, although *Commissario* Umberto Caradossi, who worked in the New York consulate, could readily provide names identifying individuals on disembarkation in Italy, matters became more complicated if they left their boat at Le Havre or some other foreign port, planning to reach Italy overland. In the first case, the custom became for police officials surreptitiously to board at Gibraltar, the last port of call before Italy, to complete their investigations on the quiet and to identify suspect individuals who could be arrested as they descended the gangplank at Naples or Genoa.

OVRA was guaranteed complete secrecy for its activities, with the *questure*, often enough, not being told what was occurring in their territory. But for Bocchini's tough approach, the *questure* would doubtless have competed against OVRA. The ordinary police were simply ordered to avoid any action that had not received the go-ahead of Polpol, which remained the ultimate supervisory body for all actions. The motives are clear. If, for example, a local police office stopped or arrested someone who was actually under OVRA investigation and did so independently, such a local action could abort a national operation. Bocchini worked to prevent such overlap after a grave mess-up in Milan. Romeo Mangano, a major communist, had been persuaded after his arrest to work with the secret police, and OVRA sent him to Milan to uncover full details about the clandestine communist organization there. But, just after he had initiated his initial contacts, the city *questura*, unaware of the scheme and not knowing that Mangano had been 'converted' and instead deeming him a subversive, arrested him, thus wrecking the entire plot and 'burning' the spy who was thereafter avoided by Party members. After Bocchini's views were known, the *questure* were left to deal with local matters, if, in the biggest cities, they clung to some autonomy, helped by their existing networks of spies and by their lavish budgets. City police chiefs could also remain jealous of OVRA and all its works and resentful of their subordination. Another difficulty could arise from the police role of the Fascist militia, the MVSN, who objected to the rule that, at the final stage of any case, they must hand over the matter to the police officials who had the task of making any actual arrests, and members of the militia continued to try to find ways to enhance and reinforce any autonomy that they had managed to win.

In regard to the network of informers, by the fall of fascism they officially tallied 815, although each was in turn equipped with further spies, quite a few of whom were never fully identified. The total of such agents was therefore between 3,000 and 4,000 men (and some women). The *questure* treasured a further list of their own, of whom the authorities after 1945 managed to identify 1,400,[12] although the archives suggest that these informers were confined to those who acted in that capacity during the last stages of the regime. Thousands have never been named and there must have been at least 5,000 of them. Their labours are the explanation why the regime could regularly decimate any anti-fascist networks that had been initiated, especially in the big cities. When the issue of informing is pursued further, it can be seen to have constituted a widespread activity in many parts of Italy. OVRA was also equipped with special 'regional' spies, making regional reports, and often Polpol itself did not know who they all were, but it is clear that they constituted an effective and pervasive band.

Spies were generally recruited from ex-members of anti-fascist organizations who, after their arrest, had been confronted by a long stretch in jail, now avoided by the signing of a devil's pact with OVRA. It is clear that most of the successful operations against members of the Communist Party were carried out with the

---

[12] See M. Canali, *Le spie del regime*, appendix 5.

crucial help of spies infiltrated into that party's organization. Moreover, a successful raid regularly identified extra communists willing to work for OVRA on further actions. Some 10 per cent of those arrested seem to have been persuaded to collaborate with the secret police and so betray their ex-comrades. The phenomenon became so common that the PCd'I had to resort to emergency measures of counter-espionage leading to the execution or severe wounding of those thought to be spies. Among the more celebrated cases were those of Ardiccio Donegani, shot and killed at Brussels one night, and of Armido Cadente, a leading Florentine communist but also a spy, liquidated by some of his fellows obeying the orders of the Party's foreign command. The body was hidden to allow the killers to get away abroad and only found a year later.

Among those gravely wounded on the charge of being spies were Eros Vecchi, Antonio Quaglia, and Giuseppe Spinelli, all beaten up after leaving Italy, and Alessandro Mileti, assaulted by a man dispatched from France for that purpose. The danger of such punishment did not contain the informing so that the Communist Party in desperation was driven to issue a list of 504 of its members believed either to be fascist spies or to be otherwise compromised with the regime and so to be avoided by loyal comrades. The results could be devastating for those named since quite a few of them had not previously been known to the Fascist police and they were now pitilessly pursued. Detailed research shows that only some sixty were actual collaborators with the dictatorship: about 10 per cent. The rest were either disillusioned communists or people who had drifted away from the Party's organizations for a variety of reasons, many personal. Another prompt came from those who, after arrest, did not simply stay mute as the Party had ordered but instead sought a way out by formal requests for mercy or joined other political groups. This mass 'denunciation' on the part of the Communist Party made sure that those unjustly denounced had the tragic fate of being both boycotted by their friends and suspected by the regime. As a result, they could no longer live an ordinary life and, often enough, turned police informers.

OVRA had been created as a specialist anti-communist force and, until at least 1933, engaged in a bitter battle to stop the PCd'I from doing what had been decided at the Comintern's Tenth Plenary conference in 1929: that is, establish a stable centre in Italy. Between 1930 and 1932, five or six such efforts were frustrated, with Camilla Ravera falling victim to Eros Vecchi and Pietro Secchia and Celso Ghini betrayed by Alessandro Mileti, who was also responsible for the arrest of Giovanni Battista Santhià.

The skill of the secret police is not the sole explanation of the turning of so many communist militants, as can be shown in the case of Vecchi. Going into exile very young, in 1922 he sought sanctuary in Moscow where he remained for four years, attending indoctrination courses and formally signing up for the Red Army. Sent secretly back to Italy and arrested in July 1930, he agreed to work with OVRA, who dispatched him in turn to Paris to report on the 'foreign centre' of the party.

Similar was the case of Giuseppe Marazzi, also ostensibly propagandized by going to Party courses in the USSR and becoming the right-hand man of Pietro Tresso, head of the PCd'I's Sixth Office, its so-called 'illegal office'. No sooner arrested Marazzi showed himself to be one of OVRA's most zealous and effective collaborators. Another such person was Guglielmo Jonna, a railwayman responsible for the national network of Soccorso Rosso (Red Welfare), who commenced work for OVRA, assuming the job as the organization's archivist, thus offering his wide knowledge of the whole communist leadership. He, in a dramatic meeting, was the one to identify the communist Camilla Ravera. Finally, there was the still more controversial case of Secondino Tranquilli, whose pseudonym as a writer was Ignazio Silone. He made a Party career despite being an informer from 1922, if not before.[13] For such people the moment of truth was almost always the arrest when agents subtly contrasted future years or decades in prison, given that OVRA knew everything that needed to be known about the individual, and with hints that they had themselves been betrayed and so should suspect their own comrades. The success rate of OVRA calls into question the PCd'I's skill in tempering its own militants and cadres. After 1945, the myth was spread that the Party was impermeable, its leaders stoic in their dedication, and the membership cunning and determined in their ability to avoid the toils of the dictatorship. But the archives speak differently. Although they confirm that the top leaders did remain tough, they make clear the dramatic reality of a rank and file exposed to informing and to fear of it in a way that communist and fellow-travelling historiography has been most reluctant to admit.

Once its battle with the communist movement was largely won, OVRA switched from being an anti-communist organization to one more generally devoted to the regime's totalitarian plans. In the second half of the 1930s, the recruitment of spies changed tone and purpose, with the regime seeking now to control all aspects of national life. At the same moment, OVRA tended to bureaucratize and to direct its attention to those segments of society that had been thought of as pro-fascist, given that all totalitarian regimes work on the principle that, in the end, no one can be trusted. To make its rule more capillary, OVRA began to designate sub-zones and then sectors, encouraging the paradoxical result that, just to limit discussion to the secret police and to omit other investigative units, in a major centre parallel forces of OVRA and UPI could be found. OVRA developed its own specially paid informers whose identity remained unknown to the heads of the police and Polpol (a situation which allowed quite a number to escape detection after fascism's fall). OVRA spies were likely now to be found wherever working men and women congregated, while the infiltration of the public sector, be it university, business, fascist unions, or party organizations, became ever more invasive. Intellectuals and journalists were subject to rigorous surveillance, since writers and thinkers could influence others,

---

[13] For the author's views on this still controversial case, see D. Biocca and M. Canali, *L'informatore: Silone, la polizia e i comunisti* (Milan: Luni, 2000).

and this process became more pointed from 1937 with the intervention in the Spanish Civil War and the deepening Nazi alliance, both choices that aroused public hostility.

Ironically, the snuffing out of any discordant voice and the absence of any institutional channels that might permit minimal criticism forced the regime, still in tireless pursuit of dissent, to continue to refine its techniques of police control. OVRA was used by the *Duce* to probe mass humour as the war approached and, in the autumn of 1939, Bocchini was told to sound opinion through secret agents and the spies and informers to be found in all ranks of society. The findings were especially disagreeable for Mussolini, since, as Guido Leto[14] and other surviving spymasters would relate, the majority of the country was sharply against the idea of Italy entering the war in short order. After having revealed the matter to the dictator, Bocchini was literally assaulted by Party Secretary Achille Starace, who had given Mussolini triumphalist reports about the passion for war of the Italian people. Now surveillance over the postal system tightened and the interception of telephone converzations became a daily matter. The so-called Servizio Speciale Riservato (SSR; Special Reserve Service), devoted to this end, could listen to thousands of lines simultaneously through linguistically trained staff and expert speed stenographers who worked in the basement of the Palazzo Chigi and there could refer matters directly to the *Duce*. This interception of calls spread to a number of Party chiefs, with the regime believing that their loyalty needed regular checks.

After September 1943, with the constitution of the RSI, OVRA continued to function in its various zones, now sometimes labelled inspectorates, with the same bureaucratic leadership that it had possessed before Mussolini's fall on the night of the Grand Council. But beside these forces with their focus on spying and counterespionage, the so-called 'auxiliary police' were extending their powers. Originally meant to fall under the aegis of Public Security, the 'auxiliary questors' tended to act on their own account and thereby to free their men from formal police supervision. These independent figures were generally resuscitated squadrists, fanatical fascists from the 'first hour', who quickly perceived how developments in the political and military story of the Social Republic could allow them room to manoeuvre to wage their own, often richly rewarded, personal wars against anti-fascism. In the first three months of 1944, the police enrolled 20,000 new auxiliary agents and 300 other supernumerary officials, while, with the toleration of the RSI authorities, 'special squads' proliferated, generally staffed by 'auxiliaries' or irregulars. Often they eventually sought official postings, and the influx into the Republic's police forces became so massive that the Chief of Police, Tullio Tamburini, was forced in May publicly to ban the practice. Many 'auxiliary questors', men such as Eugenio Pennacchio, Mario Finizio, and Dino Castellani, had long been known to Polpol, having been numbered among their most enthusiastic informers. Others, including

---

[14] See his memoirs, G. Leto, *OVRA: fascismo, antifascismo* (Bologna: Cappelli, 1951).

Mario Carità in Florence and Pietro Koch, in Rome and Milan, took their criminality to new depths in the special atmosphere of the RSI.

Among these agents, Finizio had been treated by Bocchini as of absolute trust, while Polpol had utilized his boasted knowledge of Spain and its ambience. During the Civil War, Polpol had encouraged Finizio to set up a covering company with the title Interscambio Spagna (the Spanish Trading Company), of which he became chief executive. In theory its job was simply to engage in bilateral commerce with Nationalists but, in reality, it acted as a branch of the Spanish Fascist Party, the Falange, collecting information about the politically variegated colony of Spanish exiles in Rome. The Roman head office became the agency through which the Fascist government in Italy could send aid to Francisco Franco of any kind. The office was also frequented by Ramon Franco, the brother of the Nationalist *Caudillo*.[15] Finizio's work proved effective when, for example, he succeeded in thwarting a Republican plan for friendly sailors to mutiny on the *Ebro*, a boat carrying a cargo of arms about to leave Genoa for Nationalist Spain, and sink it once it had left Italian territorial waters. Finizio was able to pass news of the plot to Bocchini, who arranged for the vessel to be seized in Sardinia and then replaced the Spanish crew with approved Italian sailors.

After the German occupation, Finizio was active in detecting any communist cells established in Roman factories. Just before the liberation of Rome, he was involved in an affair of great significance for the RSI's exhausted finances. Late in May 1944, to stop the shares of the Società Italiana per le Strade Ferrate Meridionali (Italian Company for Southern Railways), worth ten billion lira, falling into Allied hands, he appropriated the stock by force and transferred it north. He was received with full honours by Mussolini and nominated an 'auxiliary questor'. Thus equipped, he organized in Milan the so-called CIP, Centro Informativo Politico (Political Information Centre), which inflicted major damage on clandestine antifascist organizations. He also engaged successfully in extortion and blackmail, with the scandal of his behaviour reaching such a pitch that, on 5 October, the prefect of the city had him arrested. However, he was soon released after intervention in his favour from the German authorities. In rivalry with other auxiliaries—his conflict with Koch was deep-seated—Finizio and his gang concentrated on two areas: the infiltration of partisan bands and the detailing of the attitude towards the RSI of the world of big business and finance.[16] Finizio's reputation with the Germans was confirmed when he penetrated the communist Moscatelli band, causing them

---

[15] Ramon Bahamonte Franco, until the summer of 1936, kept close ties with Spanish Republicans and with the world of anti-fascism and was close friends with a number of Italian exiles. But, after the Nationalist revolt, he sided with his brother. He died in October 1938 in an aviation accident.

[16] For further details, see the voluminous file on Finizio in ACS, Carte Caserma Campari, SIS, b. 63. After liberation, in June 1946, Finizio was condemned to twenty-nine years in jail by the Corte d'Assise Straordinaria di Milano. He was released shortly after through the so-called 'Togliatti amnesty' of June 1946.

major damage. He had the industrialist Armando Piaggio arrested on accusation of sabotage, handing him over to the Nazis after personally interrogating him to the limits of his endurance.

Another telling case was that of Giuseppe Bernasconi, an early Florentine squadrist, who was expelled from the Party in 1922 because of his fanaticism and his joint fondness for swindling and cocaine. In 1920, he had served with D'Annunzio, already acquiring notoriety for his dissolute behaviour and ostentatiously republican beliefs. He was more than once condemned for theft, money laundering, and fake credit deals. From 1927 to 1930, he took up residence in France, Germany, and Switzerland. His dubious financial dealings and contacts focused the attention of the Fascist police on him, with the suspicion that he was some sort of spy. When he re-entered Italy in July 1931, he was therefore stopped, taken to Florence, and imprisoned. In the summer of 1933, he was recruited by Polpol to spy for them but was sacked in 1934. In November 1935, he was again arrested and sentenced to three years for credit offences. After the establishment of the RSI, he joined the Italian SS at Florence and, after that city's liberation, transferred to Milan, where he founded a 'special squad', soon guilty of an array of crimes.

Eugenio Pennacchio had been another Polpol employee. In June 1944 he came to head the Nucleo Speciale del Servizio Riservato of the Ministry of the Interior and, in August, was given charge of a special police inspectorate, taking the title of ISPA, to pursue partisans. It was based in Brescia where it worked closely with the SS under Erich Priebke. It expanded across a number of regions but its main zone of operation remained the north-west of the country. In October 1944, it numbered 170 men and 250 spies. It became so successful that the special German SS command for the suppression of partisans, under General Willi Tensfeld, urged the closest collaboration with it, given 'the demonstrable utility of *Questore* Pennacchio's force'.[17] Its special task was to catch members of the Committee for National Liberation and of the Garibaldi brigades. When it was constituted, it was officially branded as part of the political police and possessed of that body's privileges. Pennacchio thereby could rely on his 'immediate tie to the Chief of Police and to the Head of its Political branch, dott. Leto, whose direct subordinate he is'.[18] Pennacchio's force was dissolved between December 1944 and January 1945. The investigation that prompted this dissolution had revealed that its members, 'almost all political refugees from Tuscany, the majority ex-squadrists', in a few months of activity had carried out a catalogue of frauds and robberies. The gang had sacked villas and beaten or killed their prey. It might be asked what Leto knew about the matter, since he was in formal charge of ISPA.[19] In 1945, ISPA's ex-members were simply

[17] For documentation, see ACS, SPDCR, RSI, b. 31, f. 238, sf. 11.

[18] Cf. also the names of CIP operatives as listed in 'Organi di polizie speciali in servizio al 25 aprile dell'ex R.S.I.', book 1, 49–50.

[19] In his defence at his trial in 1946, Leto maintained that, 'despite the group's pompous title as the Brigade for the Anti-Partisan struggle, actually it spent its time on systematic rapine of ordinary

distributed around other auxiliary repressive bands. Those who had been based in Piedmont and Lombardy passed with Pennacchio himself under the direct command of Tensfeld and so of the SS for upper western Italy. Among his twelve officers can be found yet another ex-*fiduciario diretto*, Giovanni Cialli Mezzaroma, who, after ISPA's fall, moved on to the Legione Muti of Franco Colombo.[20] Under the occupation, before his move to the north, Cialli Mezzaroma was a close collaborator of the Questor, Caruso, and the Bernasconi gang.

In the north-east of the country a complex situation obtained during German occupation. There an Inspectorate General of Public Security for the Venezia Giulia region had been established in April 1942, with its base at Trieste and headed, except from August to November 1943, by Giuseppe Gueli. The prime task of this body was from its inception political, given the rise of what was viewed as 'Slav irredentism', when Resistance and acts of sabotage spread in the Balkans in reaction to Nazi-fascist occupation. The Inspectorate was to watch over the provinces of Trieste, Udine, Gorizia, Pola, and Fiume. For the Slovenes of the region, 'the inspectorate of the via Bellosguardo' became notorious for the beatings, tortures, and imprisonment that took place there, so much so that, in March 1943, the Bishop of Trieste formally intervened with Under-Secretary of the Interior Guido Buffarini Guidi in Rome to do something to stop this savagery.[21] Reliable testimony recalls the cries of pain that constantly echoed from this grim place. In more local offices, Gueli and his men experimented with even severer tortures, while the treatment of Slovenes was put in the hands of Giuseppe Collotti, described in a police report as 'psychopath of the criminal type'.[22] He tortured people who thereafter were released as entirely innocent of any charge, while some women who fell into his hands suffered irreparable damage to their genitals. Other women suicided by throwing themselves out of the windows of the Inspectorate building rather than let themselves be tortured by the men of the via Bellosguardo.[23] After the war, Gueli and his men were brought to trial and condemned to long prison terms.

A typical case of the repression of local Slovenes and Croats by this gang was that conducted by Alfio Canto in Pola province. He reached the port town in November 1941 and rapidly busied himself in dragging numerous locals before the Special Tribunal. After 25 July 1943, he was so hated by the population that

---

citizens. He remembered ordering one member to go to Bologna in regard to a military emergency only to be told he could not since he had no weapons. This from a body that said it was fighting against the partisans.' ASR, Processo Leto.

[20] Again see 'Organi di polizie speciali in servizio al 25 aprile 1945 dell'ex R.S.I.', book 1, 51. Cialli Mezzaroma had been a socialist *ardito del popolo* who then swung over to fascism. But he was soon expelled from the Party and, in 1930, sentenced to five years *confino*. He was let out after three and then recruited by Polpol, which he subsequently served until fascism's fall. See ACS, confinati politici, fascicoli personali, b. 248, file on Giovanni Cialli Mezzaroma.

[21] For the documentation, see ACS, Personale PS, Versamento 1959, b. 16ter, f. Giuseppe Gueli.

[22] See ibid., report of Chief Commissioner Ottorino Palumbo Vargas.

[23] Ibid., for the details of the sentencing of Gueli.

he had precipitately to flee from Pola to escape the summary justice demanded by the families of those whom he had tortured. After the establishment of the RSI, he returned, however, and pursued a ferocious vendetta against the Slavic people, joining with German troops to deport many of them to Germany.[24]

In the whole delicate frontier Friuli-Julian region, 'special corps' flourished. Apart from Gueli, the questor Saverio Pòlito headed a 'Police Inspectorate for War Services', composed of militarized functionaries from the police, now subject to the Army General Staff. Pòlito's group replicated that of Gueli in hunting down partisans and Slovene irredentists and in directing some 'mobile police squads', unleashed to pursue disbanded soldiers on the Carso plateau, with their reports to go to the OVRA chief at Trieste, Fortunato Lo Castro. The full detail of their actions remains shrouded, with Pòlito being allowed to remain silent about this part of his career after 1945 when he rose to Brigadier General.

How, then, did the post-war magistracy deal with the issue of purging the security police and ridding its ranks of spies? With the decree of 27 July 1944, initially termed the 'Magna Carta' of a purge, a legal base was created that could apply penal and administrative sanctions against those who had been compromised with the dictatorship. The third article promised punishment for those men who, after 3 January 1925, had 'seriously contributed' to keep the regime going, while article five dealt with those who had backed the RSI and then committed 'crimes against the government and military defence of the state, giving aid and nourishment through intelligence ties, correspondence or direct collaboration to the German invader'.[25] From August 1944, Mario Berlinguer, an extraordinary high commissioner in the purging process, adopted a tough line towards those who had worked for Polpol and OVRA, ordering the capture and arrest of all of them, while his communist partner as a commissioner, Mauro Scoccimarro, favoured their immediate sacking.

Yet, some months after these provisions were gazetted, only eight officers had been interned at Padula in Calabria, while thirty-eight were still working for the RSI in the north. The legal base of Berlinguer's policy was made nebulous by the fact that it had to assume that OVRA was not an organism of the state but rather of the Fascist Party, thus allowing its officers to be judged as fascists, not as public servants. Those arraigned had little difficulty in asserting that OVRA was a normal policing agency, composed of officers working for state security. Given this situation, such chiefs as Gesualdo Barletta, Emilio Manganiello, and Leto were soon absolved and their juniors would plainly be treated in the same way. In regard to support of the RSI, it was also accepted that any punitive provisions should be ignored for officers who were forced to serve the Republic or the Germans, if a refusal on their part would have entailed 'mortal danger' to them or their families. Apart from Gueli,

[24] ACS, Personale PS, Versamento 1973, b. 92bis, f. Alfio Canto.
[25] Decreto legislativo lugotenenziale, 159, 27 July 1944, as cited in H. Woller, *I conti con il fascismo* (Bologna: Il Mulino, 1997), 193–205.

therefore, very few were found guilty and those who were generally were freed in the Togliatti amnesty.

The promised purge worked no differently; indeed its legal obstacles were even greater. The original provisions in its regard had envisaged dismissal for those who 'with their participation in fascist political life or with their regular demonstrations of fascist sympathy' or whose 'acceptance of the patronage of the party and its bosses' had rendered themselves unworthy of service in a post-fascist state. Also to lose their posts were those who, 'after 8 September had followed the fascist course and sworn allegiance or otherwise collaborated' with the RSI. In 1945, the initial decree was qualified with release for any who had been 'coerced into service or who had actually worked to damage German rule or that of the government that they ostensibly served', while there would be no purging of men who 'had distinguished themselves in the struggle against the Germans'. These clauses became a life-saving device for public security officials who had worked in the RSI, since almost all could claim that they had joined under some personal or family threat or that they had given subtle aid to partisan formations or, in some further way, undermined the RSI's achievement and purpose. It was therefore quickly established that no one would be purged and, until the 1960s, the police of the new democratic and republican national state would be administered by ex-servants of fascism who, during the dictatorship, had used hateful techniques of repression. At the head of the crucial police office of Rome until 1960, for, example, one able and brutal ex-functionary of OVRA, Barletta, Pòlito, and Arturo Musco, succeeded another. In post-fascist Italy, old policemen did not die and scarcely faded away, while the full history of fascist repression remained shrouded from full narration to, and comprehension by, the Italian people.

BIBLIOGRAPHY

CANALI, M., *Il delitto Matteotti* (Bologna: Il Mulino, 2004).
—— *Le spie del regime* (Bologna: Il Mulino, 2004).
DE FELICE, R., *Mussolini il fascista*, 2 vols. (Turin: Einaudi, 1965).
—— *Mussolini il duce*, 2 vols. (Turin: Einaudi, 1974–81).
FRANZINELLI, M., *I tentacoli dell'Ovra* (Turin: Bollati Boringhieri, 1999).
FUCCI, F., *Le polizie di Mussolini* (Milan: Mursia, 1985).
GENTILE, E., *La via italiana al totalitarismo* (Rome: La Nuova Italia Scientifica, 1995).
GRINER, M., *La 'Banda Koch'* (Turin: Bollati Boringhieri, 2000).
WOLLER, H., *I conti con fascismo* (Bologna: Il Mulino, 1997).

CHAPTER 13

FASCISM AND WAR

DAVIDE RODOGNO

WAR had an essential place in Mussolini's world-view even before he came to power. Like many other Italian nationalists he referred to the mutilated victory in the Great War when Italy was denied an empire in the Adriatic at the expense of the Slavs. After he came to power in 1922, Mussolini showed some realism and opportunism in domestic and foreign policy but he was first and foremost driven by an ultranationalist, racist, militarist, and Social Darwinist world-view that rested on the fundamental assumption that life is a struggle and war the father of all things. In his view history was an endless succession of conflicts between elites, states, or tribes. Mussolini believed the twentieth century to be the century of Italy. If the Italians had faith in the new fascist religion and if they submitted to the *Duce* as he fashioned them into a race of conquerors, they would become the fittest among the elites, ready to subvert the order of Versailles and assert their domination in the Mediterranean. None of these conditions was ever fully verified.[1]

It is important to emphasize that Mussolini failed to assemble his ideas into an all-embracing intellectual system; however, he possessed a sufficiently articulated and coherent world-view whose essence was that the nation would be made through

[1] The reader must be aware that historians' interpretations of fascism as a regime and Mussolini's role as a dictator are divergent. The historiographical debate is ongoing and my views are controversial. I rely upon the studies of MacGregor Knox, Philippe Burrin, Enzo Collotti, Emilio Gentile, Pierre Milza, and of Italian military historians such as Lucio Ceva, Fortunato Minniti, and Giorgio Rochat (see bibliography). Alternative answers to those I provide to the question of why fascism engaged in a number of wars are plausible; they are expressed, for instance, by the editor of this Handbook, Richard Bosworth. See for instance his chapter in this Handbook, his *Mussolini's Italy: Life under the Dictatorship, 1915–1945* (New York; Penguin Books, 2006), his *Mussolini* (London: Arnold, 2002). On the contrary, as far as the account of fascist wars is concerned, I argue that the views expressed in this chapter are not contentious and are generally shared by historians.

war and territorial expansion. This world-view has to be taken seriously for it describes the ideal horizon towards which Mussolini and his regime aimed and allows an appropriate understanding of its failures. Mussolini's myths of revolution and of the nation needed violence to forge a new national community and war to elevate his country's prestige in the world. The domestic revolution Mussolini in vain attempted to realize was to be led by the 'aristocracy of the new civilization' and aimed at the destruction of all rival institutions from Catholic Church to officer corps, from Italian monarchy to the bourgeois way of life. Fascism's national mission was to attain the spiritual and racial unity of all Italians. Racism, which was certainly not imposed by Nazi Germany in the late 1930s, was the most radical part of the fascist project to transform Italians into a warrior race and was also supposed to play an important role in the organization of fascist 'living space' (*spazio vitale*). The ideal type of the new man was to be first and foremost a warrior ready to die for the regime and his *Duce*. He would have been moulded by the PNF youth organizations, would owe loyalty to the *Duce*, not the king and certainly not the pope, he would revel in a martial, violent, fearless, and pitiless universe. Fascism's total war was supposed to result in violent acquisition of a 'living space' wherein the new man would thrive. In this racist 'new order', defeated European, African, and Asian populations would survive in a state of permanent submission which fascism referred to as fascist 'civilization'. Mussolini's fundamental assumption, his myths of the revolution and the nation, revolved around a single, quintessential, catalyst—war. As MacGregor Knox pointed out, under the sign of perpetual struggle, internal and foreign policy, revolution, and war merged. Internal consolidation was a pre-condition for foreign conquest, and foreign conquest was the decisive prerequisite for revolution at home.[2]

During the decade 1922–32 the unconsolidated domestic state of the regime hindered any bellicose plan from being carried out. Indispensable to the survival of Mussolini's regime was a temporary agreement with Italian conservative elites (*compromis autoritaire*, in Philippe Burrin's words): the Vatican and the Italian Church, Italian financial and industrial elites, the monarchy, and the army.[3] This deal jeopardized the *Duce*'s revolutionary aims, and—luckily for the Italians—substantially hindered the degree of fanaticism, decentralization, and movement, violence, and terror which took place in Nazi Germany. The authoritarian compromise did not make of Mussolini a weak dictator nor did it render fascism a disguised Mussolinism. By 1940, Mussolini had accumulated among his offices those of head of government, prime minister, secretary of state, and commander general of the MVSN. He wielded, albeit by proxy, effective powers of command and appropriated the king's prerogatives as commander of the nation's armed forces. Since 1933, he had become chairman of the Supreme Defence Council and Minister of War, the

---

[2] M. Knox, *Common Destiny: Dictatorships, Foreign Policy, and War in Fascist Italy and Nazi Germany* (Cambridge: Cambridge University Press, 2000), 62, 109.

[3] P. Burrin, *Fascisme, nazisme et autoritarisme* (Paris: Seuil, 2000).

Navy, and the Air Force. In March 1938, together with the king, he was elevated to the rank of 'First Marshal of the Empire'.

Although until 1943 the army remained obedient to the regime and to its head, the Italian armed forces were not 'Mussolini's army'.[4] Italian military elites were nationalist, conservative, and monarchist. Italian officers and generals shared nonetheless a number of ideological affinities with the regime such as the experience of the First World War, nationalism, the determination to increase Italy's role in Europe and in the Balkans, the ideas of achieving a mission for the state, of a hierarchical organization of Italian society, and of war as a positive and ineluctable phenomenon in international relations. In order to reach the Great Power status Italy still lacked, they were favourable to the extension of Italy's tiny colonial empire. Italian military elites thought of empire in terms of nineteenth-century European colonial empires, certainly not as racial empire to be established both in Europe and overseas. Italian military elites were beguiled by the same imperialist dream as the Liberal Italian governments while Mussolini attempted, in vain, to pursue a specifically fascist imperialism.

As we shall see, despite having different ideas about empire and colonial rule, and despite the vast failure of the fascistization of the Italian army, Italian military executed the orders emanating from the regime. The nature of the army generals' and officers' consensus on fascism was determined by self-interested reasons such as career advantages offered by the regime; it was also a spontaneous consensus (derived from the above-mentioned affinities) and a dutiful consensus (derived from the allegiance to King Victor Emmanuel III).[5] The generals and some of the army's cadres wavered between loyalty to the king (and therefore bowed to the will of the *Duce*) and the desire to exploit the opportunities for promotion offered by complicity with the regime. The fascistization of the Regio Esercito (which, as the name indicates was the King's Army) never reached the level of Nazification that the Wehrmacht experienced. The rigidity of service promotion procedures and the caste resistance of senior generals, who maintained a traditional gulf between officers and men, inhibited the injection of fresh fascist blood into the higher reaches of the armed forces. Mussolini chose to consolidate his power by numerous 'changes of the guard' rather than by delegating authority to fascistized younger generations. The Italian armed forces lacked the degree of enthusiasm, ambition, initiative, and radicalization which Hitler fostered in every sector of German society, the army and SS included. Revealingly, the MVSN, which incarnated best of other fascist organizations the military spirit of fascism, played a very minor role in all

---

[4] I paraphrase the title of O. Bartov's book *Hitler's Army. Soldiers, Nazis, and War in the Third Reich* (Oxford: Oxford University Press, 1992).

[5] F. Minniti, 'Gli ufficiali di carriera dell'Esercito nella crisi del regime', in A. Ventura (ed.), *Sulla crisi del regime fascista 1938–1943: la società italiana dal 'consenso' alla Resistenza* (Venice: Marsilio, 1996), 75–123.

fascist Italy's wars. The blackshirts were regimented in the army and had no freedom of action.

Mussolini exercised overriding decisional power and control as military leader; he was the pivot of a system as centralized and hierarchical as it was dysfunctional and inefficient. This system enhanced the traditional lack of initiative of Italian military elites; it increased the lack of coordination between the army, the navy, the air force, as well as worsening the pervasive bureaucratic dysfunctions in civilian ministries with military duties (for instance colonial viceroy and governors acted independently from the Minister of the Colonies). In Fascist Italy strategy coincided with the art of warfare typified by the figure of the *condottiere*, who 'drew up plans, made the decisions and carried through the operations'.[6] Conduct of the war was the *Duce*'s political task, with the subservient assistance of a military adviser, the Chief of General Staff, General Pietro Badoglio; conduct of operations was assigned to the general commands of the army, navy, and air force, these being barely and badly coordinated, not commanded, by the Stato Maggiore Generale (SMG; Joint General Staff). Mussolini emptied the SMG of its functions and took over as Minister of War, delegating the ministerial function to the under-secretaries and to the chiefs of the Stato Maggiore (SM; General Staff) of the army, navy, and air force. Their incumbency of government offices meant that they exercised full control over their forces and removed a further portion of power from the chief of the SMG. At the same time it gave the chiefs of the SM privileged access to Mussolini and further strengthened his power. Following his appointment as First Marshal of the Empire, Mussolini—in a clear insult to the monarch—wrested from the king nominal command of the armed forces in the event of war and then arrogated effective power from the chief of SMG, thereby adding strategic-operational military powers to his political-administrative ones. The chief of SMG, which on 20 May 1941 took the name of *Comando Supremo Interforze* (CS; Supreme Inter-Force Command), was an office head charged with the compilation and issue of orders squeezed between Mussolini and the SM of the armed forces.[7] Mussolini's refusal to permit centralization outside his own person was supposed to demonstrate his infallibility as *condottiere*. When, in 1940–1, Fascist Italy started losing important battles in Europe and its African empire, the whole system collapsed, for, among other reasons, the myth of Mussolini's infallibility had allowed the military elites to feel irresponsible for defeats and passively to accept military disasters.

Unsurprisingly, the first truly fascist foreign policy act was the failed aggression to annex the island of Corfu in August 1923. This failure, caused by the opposition of Great Britain, pushed Mussolini to seek appropriate rearmament which would

---

[6] F. Minniti, 'Profili dell'iniziativa strategica italiana dalla non belligeranza alla guerra parallela', *Storia contemporanea*, 23 (1987), 1113–97. G. Rochat, *L'esercito italiano in pace e in guerra* (Milan: Rara, 1991).

[7] The efficiency or otherwise of this arrangement has been dealt exhaustively by Lucio Ceva, MacGregor Knox, and Giorgio Rochat (see bibliography).

allow Fascist Italy to break Italy's alleged encirclement in the Mediterranean Sea. Rearmament began in the 1920s. The gradual increase in the military budget after 1925 financed an air force which, until the mid-1930s, was one of the largest in the world.[8] From the mid-1920s to 1933 Mussolini pursued a peaceful foreign policy of which the 1925 Treaty of Locarno and the 1928 Kellogg–Briand Pact are examples. Through a semi-colonial agreement Albania became the first and last fascist European satellite; it would be annexed in 1939. In 1924 the Italo-Yugoslav friendship pact ratified Italy's annexation of Fiume. The treaty did not put an end to Fascist Italy's ambitions to wage war against Yugoslavia, a country that, to Mussolini, epitomized the loathed spirit of Versailles. As a matter of fact secret projects of aggression kept being discussed between Mussolini and General Badoglio from 1927 on. During the 'verbal pacifism' period the regime had no scruples whatsoever about financing and hosting Croat terrorists responsible for the death of King Alexander of Yugoslavia in 1934. The early 1930s *peso determinante* policy (the decisive factor policy, in Dino Grandi's formula) saw Italy successfully play the role of arbiter in the European balance, which also included a web of alliances with small powers such as Austria or Hungary. It was a policy dictated by the circumstances, most notably Fascist Italy's economic and military weakness and an international order hindering any opportunity for expansion by war.[9] Fascist Italy was buying time, choosing the best moment to act and its indispensable military ally for, even in Mussolini's wildest dreams, fascism could not do without a more powerful partner and aimed at limited territorial conquests; a notable difference from Nazism. In 1933, the international context changed and the road to empire and domestic revolution began to open. When Hitler came to power in Germany, he provided Mussolini with the potential partner to pursue his overambitious, disproportionate, unrealistic, expansionist, and totalitarian aims.

In the colonies, the so-called pacification of Libya, an Italian colony since 1911, represented a test of the regime's colonial ambitions, as well as of the relations between the regime and the armed forces. During and in the aftermath of the First World War, Libyans drove Italian garrisons back to coastal enclaves. The last Liberal government had already begun a brutal occupation which the new regime took over. It was only in 1932 that Mussolini and his faithful general Rodolfo Graziani pacified Libya. Fascist pacification meant the killing or starvation of a third of the population especially in Cyrenaica, where the regime aimed at driving the semi-nomadic tribes out of the most fertile lands of the Gebel and at exercising total political-military control over them. This was part of a broader design to

---

[8] Knox, *Common Destiny*, 120–1.

[9] This interpretation of fascist foreign policy is challenged, among others, by Bosworth who claims that neither in domestic nor in foreign policy did fascism truly innovate. He is sceptical of claims that Mussolini initiated a radical break in Italy's foreign policy and makes a case for the essential continuity of Italian foreign policy from the late nineteenth century through the Fascist decades, of which the *peso determinanate* policy was an expression.

destroy the traditional society of the cattle raisers of the Gebel and convert them into a reserve of low-cost and constantly available labour. General Graziani shared with the Fascist and Liberal political establishment the view of nomad societies as an immanent threat who ought to be eradicated rigorously and permanently for they were enemies of agriculture and progress, as well as potential rebels. Graziani interned civilian populations in concentration camps where living conditions were dire and forcefully expelled many others from the best areas of the Gebel to the pre-desert borderlands. The survivors were condemned to barely subsistence-level living conditions. According to Giorgio Rochat, around 100,000 of them, about 50 per cent of the population, were deported and 50,000 died during the repression.[10] The Italian army used chemical weapons during this campaign as it would later do in the war against Ethiopia. In Libya as well as in Ethiopia after 1935, Italian armed forces (and in some cases, civilians too) did not respect the laws of war and infringed conventions signed by Italy both during the war and in its aftermath when Ethiopian resistance was ruthlessly crushed. Crimes committed by Italian soldiers and officers went unpunished for they took place with the authorization and in presence of clear orders emanating from the political authorities and Mussolini. Forceful deportation of civilians became an ordinary instrument for the maintenance of public and colonial order also in Eritrea and Somalia where the system of incarceration, the installation of a racially discriminatory system, inhuman treatment, lack of respect for persons and property, denial of impartial trial, and torture was systematically enforced by Italian armed forces with the direct responsibility of Mussolini and with the acquiescence of the Italian civilian population living in the colonies.[11] Fascist Italy's rule in Libya and in its other colonies might not have been radically different from other European colonial policy. Some of the plans for the pacification of Libya had been drafted by the Liberal governments and were executed by the Fascist regime. What is specific to fascist imperialism is that victories in the colonies, repression, and the promulgation of discriminatory legislation served the purpose of enhancing revolution at home. Furthermore, contrary to Liberal imperialism, fascist imperialism aimed at conquering European territories, namely in south-eastern Europe, and ruling, directly or indirectly, their white, Christian populations. On this point historiography is again divided. Richard Bosworth argues that such a thing as fascist imperialism did not exist, for Mussolini was beguiled by the same imperialist dream as his Liberal Italian predecessors. He certainly sought an empire, a nineteenth-century colonial empire, not a racial empire similar to the one Hitler and the Nazi regime's experts dreamt of. As far as the achievements of fascist colonial rule are concerned Bosworth's views are certainly correct: Fascism pursued policies initiated by its Liberal predecessors and one can hardly see the difference

---

[10] G. Rochat, *Guerre italiane in Libia e in Etiopia* (Treviso: Pagus, 1991), 5–6, 84–5.

[11] N. Labanca, 'Colonial Rule, Colonial Repression and War Crimes in the Italian Colonies', *Journal of Modern Italian Studies*, 9 (2004), 300–13. A. Del Boca, *Italiani brava gente?* (Vicenza: Neri Pozzi Editore, 2005), 105–228.

between fascist imperialism and other European imperialisms. As far as Fascism's imperialist aims are concerned, they were radically different from Liberal Italy's imperialist objectives: fascism's foreign and imperial conquests were the decisive prerequisite for revolution at home.

In the early 1930s the idea of a war against Ethiopia found enthusiastic supporters in the army, in the foreign and colonial ministries, in the PNF, and also in conservative circles, the monarchy included. As early as 1932, Mussolini encouraged General Emilio De Bono, Minister of the Colonies, to prepare a war of aggression against Ethiopia. In early 1935, it became clear that French politicians who would not tolerate fascist conquests in the Balkans might give Italy a free hand in Africa. Ethiopia represented the first real chance to implement the regime's domestic and foreign revolution. Mussolini did not miss this opportunity. From 1932 to 1935, Italian officers, notably in the air force, battled to get the upper hand in preparing the future war. Italian military's plans did not take into account the political consequences of such an aggression; they had a technical or bureaucratic nature and were not really concerned with empire or the strengthening of the regime. Mussolini allowed his generals and ministers to wage their internecine conflicts and—to paraphrase Ian Kershaw—to 'work towards the *Duce*'; then he decided who, how, when, and for what objectives the war against Ethiopia had to be fought.[12] He ordered the destruction of the Ethiopian armed forces and the total conquest of the country. In early 1935 General Emilio De Bono was in East Africa accompanied by an impressive amount of Italian matériel and units. Mussolini intended not to repeat the shameful defeat of Adwa and to display to the Italians and the whole world fascist military power. Hundreds of thousands of soldiers were hastily dispatched to Ethiopia and the colonial war became national. Badoglio, who replaced De Bono in 1936, marched into Addis Ababa in May. He won the war thanks to the Italian superiority in men, armaments, and matériel. The Ethiopian war was not a typical colonial conflict, fought by a small expeditionary corps, possibly aided by African troops, with very limited military objectives and planned for the long term.[13] Sending so many soldiers was a deliberate attempt to involve Italian cities, towns, and villages, fascist propaganda and mass media, schools, vicars and parishes, and Italian industries. Fascist Italy eventually managed to avenge the 1896 defeat suffered by Liberal Italy against the Ethiopians. Mussolini won a risky gamble thanks only to Great Britain's and France's acquiescence in such a brutal aggression against an extra-European state which was not a possession of theirs.

Mussolini's abrupt change of strategy and of objective vastly raised the cost of war. The conquest of Ethiopia also involved an extremely violent and expensive

---

[12] I. Kershaw, ' "Working towards the Führer": Reflections on the Nature of the Hitler Dictatorship', in I. Kershaw and M. Lewin (eds), *Stalinism and Nazism: Dictatorship in Comparison* (Cambridge: Cambridge University Press, 1998), 80–106.

[13] With two divisions each of 12,500 men, colonial troops especially Eritrean played an important role during the war and during the brutal repression that followed it.

period of pacification during which the repression previously experimented with in Libya was practised on an even larger scale. General Graziani, who executed the orders of Mussolini and the new Minister of the Colonies, Alessandro Lessona, was responsible for the murderous excesses that took place in Ethiopia after 1936. On 1 September 1939, total occupation and vast-scale repression demanded the employment of 200,000 men, a number corresponding to the total of the Italian army in peacetime.[14] One of the most controversial historiographical aspects of the war was the use of chemical weapons, wrongly referred to as gas. According to the two most acknowledged experts on that topic, Angelo Del Boca and Giorgio Rochat, Italian artillery caused the bulk of Ethiopian victims. Mustard gas and phosphorous bombs, launched by the Italian air force—who received undisputedly clear orders from Mussolini, Badoglio, and Graziani—hit both civilian and military objectives. The criminal use of these illegal weapons certainly contributed to the fascist victory, although it was not essential to it.[15]

With the backing of the political and military establishment and an acquiescent monarchy, Mussolini decided on military intervention in the Spanish Civil War. He did not consult the king but obtained a public approval from a marginalized Badoglio. The *Duce* was now seeking the keys to the western Mediterranean. Fascist propaganda played up anti-bolshevism, although the aim of the fascist military enterprise in Spain was mainly expansionist: the Balearic Islands, Ceuta, and converting Franco's Spain into a satellite of Rome. Fascist Italy massively intervened with almost 50,000 men (20,000 from the army and 29,000 from the militia). They were almost all volunteers, attracted less by ideology than by the good money they could make. In March 1937 Republican propaganda successfully portrayed the Italian effort at Guadalajara as a defeat bigger than it was in reality; later, during summer 1937, Italian troops won many significant battles, especially in the Basque region. Franco eventually won the war although Spain never became a satellite of Rome. For an aspirant Great Power like Italy the price paid for the intervention was very high: from 1936 to 1939, 3,266 soldiers died, 11,000 were wounded, and more than six billion lira were spent on war matériel largely lost.

Wars in Africa and in Spain allowed the fascist regime to enhance its schemes of social engineering through drastically racist colonial legislation, the radicalization of the discrimination against national Slav minorities, the eventual promulgation of anti-Semitic laws in 1938, and a related 'war' against the 'bourgeois spirit' of the Italians.[16] Despite the regime's efforts, prior to 1940, the 'stay-at-home preference' (*politica del piede di casa*), perhaps the 'bourgeois spirit', largely prevailed

---

[14] G. Rochat, *Le guerre italiane 1935–1943: dall'impero d'Etiopia alla disfatta* (Turin: Einaudi, 2005), 89.

[15] Rochat, *Guerre italiane in Libia e in Etiopia*; A. Del Boca (ed.), *I gas di Mussolini* (Rome: Editori Riuniti, 1996).

[16] M. Sarfatti, *The Jews in Mussolini's Italy: From Equality to Persecution* (Madison: University of Wisconsin Press, 2006).

over a fascist determination among the population and the majority of the fascist hierarchs. Immediately following Italy's entry into the war, Mussolini was forced to admit that the Italians were far from being the race of conquerors whom he envisioned. The Party, he complained, had failed in the fascistization of Italian society; 'the aristocracy of the new civilization', he conceded, was far from being ready to assume power. The king and the Regio Esercito had not been replaced by a fascist popular army. Nevertheless, the *Duce* did not relinquish his revolutionary and expansionist ambitions but used the King's Army, which he controlled and commanded, to pursue them.

After the victorious war in Ethiopia, Mussolini encouraged the *Anschluss*, pushed for the Rome–Berlin Axis, and risked war in the Czechoslovak crisis of 1938. Since 1938 Berlin had economically and politically penetrated the whole Danube basin which represented the only directly accessible source of raw materials for Italy, with its Austrian communication routes, Romanian oil, Hungarian cereals, and Yugoslav and Bulgarian minerals and timber. Rome was economically and politically excluded from the richest region of its claimed 'living space'. On 15 March 1939 Mussolini issued an ultimatum to King Zog of Albania; then, on a specious pretext, Italian troops occupied Albania, which on 8 April became an Italian protectorate. On the one hand the manoeuvre demonstrated to the Western powers that Rome took its decisions regardless of Germany's wishes and warned Berlin that Fascist Italy had not renounced its expansionist ambitions in the Balkans. On the other hand, as a consequence of the impossibility of competing with Germany in the Balkans, Italy now plainly had to focus on military expansion elsewhere in the Mediterranean, which meant a probable showdown with London and Paris. On 22 May 1939 Italy and Germany signed the Pact of Steel. The Italian Foreign Minister, Galeazzo Ciano, foolishly left the task of drawing up the treaty to the Germans, who contrived for its article 3 to place Italy at the mercy of Germany's decision when war would be declared. When Ciano made it plain that Italy would not be ready to enter the war until 1943 he received only vague reassurances from his counterpart Ribbentrop. No article, nor indeed any clause, of this alliance stipulated that Germany must not act before 1943 when, supposedly, Italy would be ready to wage war in Europe. The objective of the alliance was not stated nor was any formal recognition made of Italy's and Germany's respective spheres of influence. There was no protocol that defined frontiers apart from the declared inviolability of the Brenner, and no jointly defined military strategy. Despite all the risks involved in the alliance, if Fascist Italy looked to gain total mastery of the Mediterranean, Nazi Germany was the only plausible ally.

By the end of 1939 the Ethiopian and Spanish wars had heavily affected the Italian military budget, its reserves of matériel and armament. They drained resources, impossible for Italian industry to replace and needed for the development and modernization of the armed forces. The Italian military elite completely failed to understand the importance of new technology and overestimated Italian matériel and technological capability. Italy's generals imposed a military-technical, tactical, and operational conservatism even more deadening than that of their French counterparts. Until it was too late, the army neglected medium tanks; the navy disdained radar; and the air force opposed the all-metal monoplane fighter. Inadequate training, doctrinal lethargy, administrative disorganization, and the active discouragement of individual creativity produced a junior officer corps with insufficient capacity for command and non-commissioned officers with an almost total absence of initiative.[17] Successes in the fascist wars from 1935 to 1939, as well as the conservatism of the military elites and Mussolini's damaging centralization of all military powers, compromised the preparation for the European conflict to come.

Being a medium-size military power, Italy could have pursued a limited war with limited expansionist objectives. The Italian armies were structured in such a way that they could wage a lightning war (*una guerra di rapido corso*) against a small or medium-size enemy with an equivalent level of equipment and training. Fascist Italy could not open independent war fronts, directly challenge France or Great Britain militarily, or compete with Nazi Germany's economic penetration in Central and south-eastern Europe. Before 1 September 1939, Italy lacked any serious military plan in the event of a war against France or Great Britain (not to mention against the Soviet Union and the United States). Its response to any Anglo-French attack would be the defence of its frontiers combined with an attack against Greece and a probable second offensive against Yugoslavia after fomenting internal uprisings. Thus, any aggression against Italy was to be countered by an offensive against third countries, not against the aggressors themselves: a strategy with a political significance inconsistent with the regime's foreign policy. When, on 23 August 1939, the announcement of a German–Soviet Pact was made, Mussolini informed Hitler that, if the conflict against Poland remained localized, Italy would give Germany the political and economic support that it requested. But if the conflict spread, Italy could not take any military initiative unless Germany delivered the military supplies and raw materials that Italy required to resist an attack by the French and the British. Fabbriguerra (abbreviation for Commissariato Generale per la Fabbricazione di Guerra which procured raw materials and allocated them among factories requisitioned for the war effort) estimated that such resistance would require 17,000 train-loads of materials and supplies, a request Berlin could only refuse. Humiliated at being obliged to acknowledge Italy's lack of preparedness for war, the *Duce* proclaimed Italy's 'non-belligerence'.

Six months of uneasy waiting followed. On 10 March 1940, Mussolini informed Ribbentrop that Italy intended to wage a 'parallel war' in the Mediterranean but it would do so only after Germany's western offensive had begun. On 18 March

---

[17] M. Knox, 'Expansionist Zeal, Fighting Power, and Staying in Power in the Italian and German Dictatorships', in R. Bessel (ed.), *Fascist Italy and Nazi Germany: Comparison and Contrasts* (Cambridge: Cambridge University Press, 1996), 113–33; 120.

Mussolini announced to Hitler that he alone would decide the date of Italy's entry into the war. A secret memorandum circulated by Mussolini on 31 March 1940 confirmed that his policy was one of defence on land (except in Ethiopia and, as regards only air bases, against France in Corsica). The memorandum also outlined the *Duce*'s plans for an offensive in the Balkans, as well as a general maritime offensive, which was wholly incongruous given the lack of terrestrial objectives. This was an indirect strategy by which the threat of war served the purpose of political and diplomatic, more than military, coercion. The German occupation of Denmark, the defeat of Norway, the offensive against Holland and Belgium, and the collapse of France persuaded Mussolini that the time had come for Italy to enter the war. Fascist military engagement was to be above all rapid in its consummation. Fascist Italy's grand objectives increased Italy's military dependence on Germany, for the timing of intervention would be determined by the success of the German offensive—with the added danger (which, in fact, transpired) that Italy's contribution would not be of sufficient magnitude to justify its claims to territory. Mussolini's strategy intended to achieve absolute freedom of action, with the consequence that political considerations took priority over operational ones.

Army commanders ought to have been aware of the risks involved with this choice but raised no objections; reassured by the king's acquiescence, they did as the *Duce* wanted. The doctrine of Italy's absolute freedom of action from Germany was summed up in the notion of the 'parallel war'—independent and brief military action which Italy would wage rapidly and ruthlessly before sitting down at the peace table. It was to be a war which did not overlap or even mesh with the greater and more general conflict. Rather, it was a campaign with its own and specifically Italian objectives, and it had nothing to do with the present adversaries. It was to be fought not for Germany, nor with Germany, but alongside Germany. Parallel war confirmed the gulf between Italy's expansionist ambitions and the instruments available for their accomplishment. Italy rejected any form of strategic collaboration with Berlin, so that the fascists might demonstrate their military prowess to the German ally, to the nation, and to the world. Should this strategy prove successful, Italy could cash it in at the peace table for territorial gains. Should it not, given that Italy's armed forces were very far from war-ready, that the economy was unprepared for long-drawn-out conflict, and that Hitler's real intentions were still unknown, the preconditions for humiliating military defeat were present from the beginning.

On 10 June 1940, Italy declared war against France and Great Britain. After the defeat of France and in view of Britain's difficulties, the regime believed its expansionist ambitions could be easily realized. On 17 June, Hitler announced to Mussolini that France had sued for armistice. The *Duce* reacted by ordering Badoglio to attack France within three days. The Italian military campaign against France started on 20 June and lasted for four days; the French defended themselves exceptionally well against a surprise attack that left more than 600 dead and more than 2,000 wounded on the Italian side. The most 'brilliant' achievement by the Italian troops was the occupation of the town of Menton and of some small communes in the French Alps. On 24 June Italy and France signed the armistice at Villa Incisa (Rome). Italy's 'only' demands were the creation of a 50-kilometre demilitarized zone to the west of Italy's frontier and the military occupation of the communes conquered during the campaign. The Italians also wanted demilitarization of the strongholds and naval bases of Toulon, Bizerte, Ajaccio, and Mers-el-Kebir. The armistice of 24 June heavily conditioned relations between Italy and France. Germany was in no hurry to reach peace with France, because the uncertainty of the armistice made the country easier to control. Mussolini would have liked to impose a harsh armistice and to settle straightaway the territorial question with France. He was in a hurry to reach a conclusion because the passage of time heightened the uncertainty and frailty of his ambitious hopes.[18] Fascist Italy had lost a crucial portion of its Mediterranean 'living space', and the uneasy military victory in the Alps made it impossible for Italy to sit at the peace table as an outright victor.

Fascist Italy was forced to seek its fortune in northern Africa and the Balkans. Only on 13 September did General Graziani attack the British positions in western Egypt and manage to occupy Sidi el-Barrani. But after this first advance—hailed as a 'Roman' triumph by the regime's propaganda machine and by the General himself—the Italians failed to proceed further. If they had accepted the two armoured divisions offered by Hitler, events might have turned out otherwise. But Mussolini rejected Hitler's offer: he wanted an entirely Italian victory and he refused to countenance any deviation from the fundamental principle of the 'parallel war'. By February 1941, which was when the five divisions of the German Afrikakorps arrived in northern Africa under the command of General Erwin Rommel, the Italian troops had lost the whole of Cyrenaica, and the British had captured more than 130,000 soldiers and disabled all the Italians' tanks and 1,000 of their aircraft. In East Africa, on 5 May 1941, the British triumphantly escorted the Emperor Haile Selassie into Addis Ababa; and on 21 May the Duke of Aosta was forced to capitulate. As regards the Balkan theatre of war, Mussolini informed Hitler that Italy was ready to launch an attack against Greece. The latter enjoined his ally not to undertake any military operations there. As absolute master of the economies of the Balkan countries, the Reich was concerned to keep the region out of the war and it had no need—unlike Italy—to assert its hegemony in the concrete form of direct military occupation. Ever more dependent on Germany, Rome received no guarantees from Berlin that it would have access to the supplies—steel, oil, and coal—essential for its prosecution of the war.

The failure of operations against Britain, postponed *sine die* in September 1940, and the German occupation of Romania (on 12 October, and which the Italians

---

[18] E. Collotti, 'L'Italia dall'intervento alla guerra parallela', in *L'Italia nella Seconda Guerra Mondiale e nella Resistenza* (Milan: F. Angeli, 1988), 37.

had known about several weeks beforehand), increased Italian fears that the war was about to conclude with a negotiated peace between London and Berlin from which Rome would be excluded. For this reason, heedless of Hitler's veto of July, Mussolini chanced his hand on achieving rapid victory in Greece. The Italian political and military leaders were perfectly aware of Greece's domestic and international political situation. Reports by the War Ministry depicted the country as anything but poorly armed and nowhere near internal collapse. Nevertheless, at a meeting on 15 October 1940, Mussolini and his closest advisers agreed that the occupation of Greece would be entirely straightforward. The military objective was possession of Greece's western coast, Zante, Cephalonia, Corfu, and Salonika, then to proceed with the complete occupation of the country, an act that would ensure that it would remain within Italy's political-economic space. Italian generals dared not explain to Mussolini that Greece was impossible to defeat with the meagre military means allocated to the campaign (an expeditionary force of 60,000 men) or that the demobilization of 300,000 soldiers (between the end of 1940 and the beginning of 1941) would render any rapid reinforcement of the front in Greece practically impossible. The politicians, too, bore heavy responsibility for the miscalculation, Ciano most of all: for in the hope of increasing his prestige and power and considering Albania some sort of personal fief, he claimed that Italy had the Albanians' support, that the Greeks had little stomach for a fight, and that a pro-Italian faction in Athens was ready to oust the Ioannis Metaxas government. There was not a grain of truth in any of Ciano's assertions and consequently Italy launched an attack against Greece with only five divisions, without the support of the Bulgarians, and without the advantage of surprise. The Greek campaign was an utter disaster. An advance from the Albanian frontier to Epirus while fighting an enemy defending its homeland and during an early and particularly harsh winter was bound to fail. The expeditionary force astonishingly continued to fight but, given the situation, little by little, it disintegrated into a rabble: of its 500,000 soldiers, 32,000 were killed and more than 100,000 wounded. At the same time, the British disabled part of the Italian fleet in the Bay of Taranto (12 November 1940) and regained control over the seaways of the southern Mediterranean. Confronted by such losses, Mussolini thus had to resign himself to accepting Germany military assistance.

By May 1941 Italy's war initiative in Africa and in Europe was over. Germany attacked Yugoslavia and Greece. Between 6 and 23 April, both countries were defeated; armistices were signed, and on 24 April, in Vienna, Yugoslavia was erased from the map of Europe, its territory being militarily occupied or annexed by Germany, Bulgaria, Hungary, Albania, and Italy, while Croatia obtained its independence. When the Italians suggested to the Germans that their respective spheres of influence might be established according to a rigid division of geographical zones (Yugoslavia and Greece to Italy, all the rest to the Germany), the Germans rejected the proposal and obliged their junior partner to accept the principle of each of the two powers' 'prevalence'[19] in a particular zone, so that Germany could maintain a presence in those areas controlled by Italy. However much fascist propaganda might proclaim the priority of Italy's interests in the Balkans, there was no doubt that the Reich had absolute superiority. Since 1941 Berlin could have obliged Rome to place the Italian army under the command of the Germans. Yet Berlin had permitted Italy to occupy large areas of territory and to settle the political question and the boundary dispute with the Croats as it wished. Italy's negligible economic significance but extensive sphere of military occupation gave Nazi propagandists an opportunity to rebut accusations of German hegemony and purvey the idea that the Axis allies were co-participants in the 'new order'. Between May 1941 and July 1943 Italy accepted Germany's real supremacy and the actually demeaning role granted by the ally. With only a narrow margin for initiative, but paradoxically thanks to the magnanimity of the Germans, Italy had gained a nominal foothold in the Balkans.

Italy was now fighting what was—to use Giorgio Rochat's apt expression—a 'subordinate war' as regards its interests. The actual and partial occupation of the 'living space' came about in circumstances that differed entirely from those envisaged by fascist expansionism. Once the Italians gained a foothold in the Balkans and later in metropolitan France, they sought to carve out a broader role for themselves than their ally was willing to grant. The progress of the war, the direct and indirect influence exerted by Germany, Fascist Italy's military weakness, its inability to deal with unexpected situations or to adapt to them, led to the humiliating defeat and ultimate failure of fascism's war. In order that Italy might share in the Axis's eventual victory and true to his promise to march with Hitler 'until the end', in the years that followed Mussolini sent an Italian expeditionary force (Corpo di Spedizione Italiano in Russia, later Armata Italiana in Russia) to the Soviet Union. In 1942 and 1943, around half of the 200,000 Italian soldiers fighting at the Russian front died in battle and many others were lost or taken prisoner. In northern Africa, the defeat at El Alamein in early November 1942 was only a prelude to large-scale advances by the Allies, whose landings in Morocco and Algeria led to the loss of Libya and to headlong retreat by the Axis troops in Tunisia. At the end of 1942 the Axis war effort in the Mediterranean was in disarray, while the capitulation of the German Sixth Army at Stalingrad on 31 January 1943 had marked a turning point in continental Europe as well. The question was no longer whether the Axis would lose the war but when. It was the Allied landings in Africa—these being taken to be a crucial change of circumstances with respect to the armistice of 1940—that induced Germany to occupy the whole of France and invite Italy to join the operations mounted on 11 and 12 November 1942. It was action by the Germans, not Italy's own military initiative, which enabled it to occupy almost all the territory as far as the Rhône originally intended for annexation. The Italian troops, given the task of maintaining

---

[19] In Nazi parlance, 'prevalence' meant that there would be German troops and emissaries in Italian zones; and vice versa, Italian troops and emissaries in German ones.

the order established by the Germans, deployed themselves along the line of the Rhône as well as in Corsica.

Unlike the Germans, who could be and were defeated after their conquests, the Italians were defeated in advance but became conquerors of Greece, vast areas of Yugoslavia, and metropolitan France. It was politically as difficult for the Italians to impose themselves as winners as it was militarily. They could have defended the annexed territories around Menton, Dalmatia, and the Ionian Islands and eventually put down what were still unorganized and uncoordinated resistance movements. The decision to occupy extensive areas of territory required first sending a significant number of men. The soldiers deployed in the Mediterranean territories conquered after 1940 numbered approximately 850,000, which amounted to two-thirds of all troops committed outside Italian borders. The Balkans constantly absorbed 650,000 men and the occupation of southern France and Corsica required a further 200,000. Undoubtedly such a number, as well as those in the ARMIR sent to Soviet Union, weakened the defence of the peninsula. The deployment also required the adjustment of logistics and armaments to the new circumstances. For almost two years Italian armies in occupied Europe fought a guerrilla warfare they were totally unprepared for, despite the experience of the large number of colonial veterans still in armed service. The extremely mobile and logistically agile enemy, who operated in small units and mingled with the civilian population after operations, caused great difficulties for the large Italian units burdened by heavy artillery. The difficulties were worsened by the excessive dispersal of forces in order to defend numerous logistical bases and communication routes, the slowness due to heavy and cumbersome equipment, and the need to ensure that all supply lines were secure. Moreover, the enemy was often well informed about the deployment and movement of the Italian units and the operational intentions of their commanders, while the Servizi Informazioni (where *Informazione* signifies intelligence services), one of the worst among Western European countries, were incapable of furnishing timely and accurate information. With the evolution of the conflict the average size of the Italian battalions, commanded by reservist officers, diminished to around 4,000 men, with weaponry and equipment rarely and inefficiently replaced and increasingly less suited to the manifold requirements of the war.

The military subordination of the Italian occupation forces in Mediterranean Europe deepened with the defeats suffered by the Axis. Until the end of 1942, the Germans left the Italians a semblance of command and a limited margin of autonomy in military decisions which was deemed unacceptable by the generals of the army, resentful of what they regarded as a humiliation. The *Führer*'s Instruction no. 47 of 28 December 1942 put an end to the Italians' scant freedom of manoeuvre in the occupied territories. The German commanders doubted the Italian occupying forces could resist and defend the territories under their control from an Allied landing. After spring 1943 the Italian armies in Greece and Yugoslavia were literally kept under German supervision. As combat continued, an ill-concealed case of rivalry ruled out any possibility of collaboration between the two Axis partners. The psychological impact of Italy's downgrading from equal to junior partner in the Axis provoked resentful defiance of German supremacy. This attitude of both civilian and military elites was irrational because Italy was, by 1941, a de facto satellite of the Reich which, rather than be left with nothing, accepted whatever Germany might concede. Certainly influenced, perhaps befuddled, by fascist ideology, Mussolini and the regime's leadership refused to accept subordination to Germany. They denied to themselves the idea that Italy was in fact Germany's servant and satellite and from 1941 to 1943 they reacted with determination against all German encroachments on Italian sovereignty and interests. This was particularly the case in the occupied territories where Italian civil and military authorities deluded themselves into believing that they controlled what actually was an imaginary fascist 'living space'.

Italian commanders did not sabotage the regime. Until 25 July 1943, and for different reasons under the RSI, with conscientiousness and even stubbornness, they persevered until matters were resolved, working all the while 'towards the *Duce*'. The Italian army showed no reluctance to fight nor any meekness towards their enemies, while its commanders strove to adapt their men and means to guerrilla warfare and to political situations objectively difficult to deal with. They were certainly not defeatists or careless and many of them were convinced of the superiority of the 'Italian race'. In the practice of repression, the Italian army's actions were similar in kind to those of the Wehrmacht, the SS, and the German police. The orders issued by the Italian authorities to crush the partisan bands and to root out support for them in the civilian population envisaged a wide range of measures: hostage taking, the burning of entire villages, reprisals against the families of suspected insurgents, the evacuation of large inhabited areas, the deforestation of zones considered particularly hospitable to partisan formations, the deportation of large groups of civilians, the seizure and killing of livestock—and all these actions with impunity for any excesses that might be committed.[20] The main difference between the two armies concerned their efficiency; in the Italian case, at the end of an operation the number of civilian casualties was generally lower, the uncontrolled impulses were erratic and certainly less fanatical. This brings us to the question of fascism's successful indoctrination of the Italian army (or its fascistization).

Italian commanders were perfectly aware that soldiers were far from being the fascist conquering race and were unprepared to face a long war or military occupations. Italian armies were framed to fight conventional and short military campaigns, not resistance movements and guerrilla warfare. In order to face this situation Italian commanders-in-chief reacted vigorously. Circular note 3C (1 March

---

[20] E. Collotti, 'Sulla politica di repressione italiana nei Balcani', in L. Paggi (ed.), *La memoria del nazismo nell'Europa di oggi* (Florence: La Nuova Italia, 1997), 186–8, 198, 203.

1942) written by General Mario Roatta, commander-in-chief of 2nd Army, is a general instruction explaining the methods of repression as well as a guide to soldiers' attitude towards occupied populations.[21] Roatta ordered his troops always to keep a warlike mentality and to repress all the qualities of the 'good Italian' (*il buon italiano* or *bono'taliano*). Soldiers had to behave fearlessly in all circumstances and harshly fight the enemy. Rebels had to be treated not just according to the saying 'an eye for an eye, a tooth for a tooth', but taking a 'head for a tooth'. Roatta resorted to a simple and not quintessentially fascist psychology, probably because he was aware of the failed attempt to fascistize the Italian army. He threatened harsh punishments for all those disobeying his orders, insulted the enemy, and pushed his troops to be extremely mistrustful about local populations. The general explained to his troops that victorious nations' attitude towards defeated populations was a superior–inferior-based relation. Roatta deliberately attempted to instil into his soldiers' minds the idea that the partisan-enemy as well as civilians supporting the partisans were non-human and uncivilized, barbarians. Hence, it was absolutely forbidden to fraternize with them.[22] General Roatta wrote that Italian soldiers were fighting in the Balkans a colonial kind of war. As in the colonies, it was necessary to deploy massive forces and powerful means even in minor military operations. In annexed Slovenia and Dalmatia massive internment of civilians and a scorched earth policy, analogous to repression methods previously practised in Cyrenaica, were determined by a fascist plan of *sbalcanizzazione* (de-Balkanization), and *bonifica etnica* (ethnic cleansing, as we would say today), and anticipated the Italian colonization of eastern Adriatic territories.

It must be pointed out that Roatta's circular note 3C did not represent an isolated case, and orders having a similar content were promoted also in Greece. Roatta's ideas were not those of a general more fervently fascist than other Italian commanders.[23] Many such high-ranking officers shared the convictions and ideals of the Fascist political establishment and of Mussolini. However, this being the most significant difference from the German soldiers, there is no such evidence with regard to the Italian junior officers and troops in the occupied territories. Many of them executed orders fearing the consequences of a refusal, because of their sense of duty and not for ideological reasons. Yet, on frequent occasions, they were brutal and committed war crimes. If Italian soldiers' crimes—which, for various reasons, were not much brought to light after the war—cannot be directly ascribed to fascist ideology, or to regime propaganda, how are we supposed to explain them? They

---

[21] It has to be emphasized that the document was divulged well before the partisans' military actions undermined the Italian occupation system.

[22] M. Legnani, 'Il ginger del general Roatta, le direttive della II° Armata sulla repressione antipartigiana in Slovenia e Croazia', *Italia contemporanea*, 209–10 (1997–8), 156–74.

[23] D. Rodogno, *Fascism's European Empire: Italian Occupation during the Second World War* (Cambridge: Cambridge University Press, 2006), and L. Santarelli, 'Muted Violence: Italian War Crime in Occupied Greece', *Journal of Modern Italian Studies*, 9 (2004), 280–99.

can certainly be attributed to General Staff orders which succeeded in convincing many Italian soldiers that moral, juridical, and military laws were not in force anymore and the occupiers were entitled to enforce a pitiless vengeance and the most brutal reprisals against civilian populations.[24] As far as the case of the Balkan occupied territories is concerned, they were also the result of a deep-rooted anti-Slav racism widespread among civil servants and officers dispatched to the Balkans. More than any other thing they were determined by the context and condition of the occupation. The violence of repression of partisans and reprisals against civilian populations reflected Fascist Italy's army's substantial weakness. They were the result of an army forced to defend itself against Resistance movements more efficiently equipped, more experienced, and more determined to win a war that, since the end of 1942, was irremediably lost by the Italians.

The Italian army's lamentable performance in 1940–3 derived in part from institutional failure and in part from the backwardness of Italian society compared with that of its ally and enemies. From a military point of view Italian strategies were contradictory and ill conceived: passivity of the CS contrasted with the frantic opening of theatres of war scattering meagre resources from the Channel coast to Ethiopia, from metropolitan France to the Balkans and Soviet Union. The effectiveness of the high command was limited, both because Italian armed forces repeatedly demonstrated its structural and intellectual incapacity in mobile and tactical warfare and because of the structural hierarchy moulded by Mussolini. The regime and military elites showed deference to large industrial combines that produced the least effective, most expensive, and fewest armaments of any major combatant in the Second World War. The regime also failed to decree general mobilization in 1940 as its Liberal predecessor had unhesitatingly done in 1915. Between June 1940 and 8 September 1943 the armed forces condemned to death fewer than 150 men, much fewer than from 1915 to 1918. For the commanding heights of a regime that boasted about modernization, both Mussolini and the Italian generals showed a remarkable incapacity to grasp the importance of technology and resources. The regime failed to rally Italian society, big business, and armed forces to its most important expansionist and revolutionary war, and the willingness to die for the *Duce* diminished rapidly and the home front crumbled after 1940. The effect of the military on fascism was very relevant. The army was a decisive factor in fascism's coming to power in 1922–5 and an inescapable part of its inheritance. During the 1920s the conservative elites restricted Mussolini's war ambitions; the highest ranks in the army and civil service stood firm and avoided a war against Yugoslavia, Turkey, and sweeps into France. After the 1936 victorious war in Ethiopia, the conservative elites were either trapped by the alliance or fully supported the regime.

[24] F. Focardi and L. Klinkhammer, 'The Question of Fascist Italy's War Crimes: The Construction of Self-Acquitting Myth (1943–1948)', *Journal of Modern Italian Studies*, 9 (2004), 330–48, and M. Battini, 'Sins of Memory: Reflections on the Lack of an Italian Nuremberg and the Administration of International Justice after 1945', ibid. 349–62.

Fascistization of the army was a huge failure. However the King's Army shared the responsibility of defeat with Mussolini and the regime and was responsible for war crimes that went and are still unpunished.

When examining how hell-bent fascism was on war and what sort of wars it engaged in and why, it is important to keep in mind the vast discrepancy between fascism's achievements and its foolishly ambitious aims. Fascism came into being as a direct consequence of the First World War and disappeared because of the military defeat during the Second World War. Mussolini and his regime miserably failed to achieve both domestic and expansionist objectives. Despite this failure, fascism's domestic wars resulted in the harsh persecution of its political enemies, innocent Slovene and Croat minorities as well as Italian and foreign Jews. Ideologically driven wars waged by Italian Fascism were murderous and resulted in hundreds of thousands of victims and the premature death of a million people, especially civilians, in the colonies of Libya, Eritrea, and Somalia, in Ethiopia, in Spain, in Albania, in Slovenia, Croatia, Bosnia-Herzegovina, Serbia, Montenegro, Kosovo, and Greece, in metropolitan France, Tunisia, and the ex-Soviet Union. The blood tribute paid by the Italian 'conquerors' was high, too. Hundreds of thousands of Italian soldiers fell for or because of the regime's wars.

BIBLIOGRAPHY

CEVA, L., *Le forze armate* (Turin: Utet, 1981).
—— 'Vertici politici e militari nel 1940–1943: interrogativi e temi d'indagine', *Il politico*, 46/4 (1981), 691–700.
COLLOTTI, E., 'L'Italia dall'intervento alla guerra parallela', in *L'Italia nella Seconda Guerra Mondiale e nella Resistenza* (Milan: Angeli, 1988), 21 ff.
—— 'Sulla politica di repressione italiana nei Balcani', in L. Paggi (ed.), *La memoria del nazismo nell'Europa di oggi* (Florence: La Nuova Italia, 1997), 182–208.
—— and KLINKHAMMER, L., *Il fascismo e l'Italia in guerra: una conversazione fra storia e storiografia* (Rome: Ediesse, 1996).
DE FELICE, R. (ed.), *L'Italia fra tedeschi e alleati* (Bologna: Il Mulino, 1973).
—— *Mussolini l'alleato* (Turin: Einaudi, 1990).
DEL BOCA A., *Gli italiani in Libia*, 2 vols. (Rome: Mondadori, 1986, 1988).
—— *Gli italiani in Africa orientale italiana*, 3 vols (Bari: Laterza, 1979–83).
—— LEGNANI, M., and ROSSI, M. G. (eds), *Il regime fascista* (Bari: Laterza, 1995).
FERRATINI TOSI, F., GRASSI, G., and LEGNANI, M. (eds), *L'Italia nella Seconda Guerra Mondiale e nella Resistenza* (Milan: Angeli, 1988).
GENTILE, E., *La via italiana al totalitarismo* (Rome: NIS, 1995).
KNOX, M., *Mussolini Unleashed, 1939–1941: Politics and Strategy in Fascist Italy's Last War* (Cambridge: Cambridge University Press, 1982).
—— *Common Destiny: Dictatorship, Foreign Policy, and War in Fascist Italy and Nazi Germany* (Cambridge: Cambridge University Press, 2000).

KNOX, M., *Hitler's Italian Allies, Royal Armed Forces, Fascist Regime, and the War of 1940–1943* (Cambridge: Cambridge University Press, 2000).

LABANCA, N., *Oltremare: storia dell'espansione coloniale italiana* (Bologna: Il Mulino, 2002).

LEGNANI, M., 'Il ginger del generale Roatta, le direttive della II Armata sulla repressione antipartigiana in Slovenia e Croazia', *Italia contemporanea*, 209–10 (1997–8), 156–74.

MICHELETTI, B., and POGGIO, P. P. (eds), 'L'Italia in guerra, 1940–1943', *Annali della Fondazione Luigi Micheletti*, 5 (1990–1).

MINNITI, F., 'Profili dell'iniziativa strategica italiana dalla non belligeranza alla guerra parallela', *Storia contemporanea*, 23/6 (1987), 1113–97.

——'Gli ufficiali di carriera dell'esercito nella crisi del regime', in A. Ventura (ed.), *Sulla crisi del regime fascista, 1938–1943: la società italiana dal 'consenso' alla Resistenza* (Venice: Marsilio, 1996), 75–123.

——*Fino alla guerra: strategie e conflitto nella politica di potenza di Mussolini 1923–1940* (Napoli: ESI, 2000).

ROCHAT, G., *Guerre italiane in Libia e in Etiopia* (Treviso: Pagus, 1991).

——'Lo sforzo bellico, 1940–1943: analisi di una sconfitta', *Italia contemporanea*, 160 (1985), 7–24.

——*L'esercito italiano in pace e in guerra* (Milan: Rara, 1991).

SADKOVICH, J. J., 'Fascist Italy at War', *International History Review*, 14/3 (1992), 526–33.

SCHREIBER, G., 'Les Structures stratégiques de la conduite de la guerre de coalition italo-allemande au cours de la Deuxième Guerre Mondiale', *Revue d'histoire de la Deuxième Guerre Mondiale*, 120 (1980), 1–32.

CHAPTER 14

DICTATORS STRONG OR WEAK?

THE MODEL OF BENITO MUSSOLINI

R. J. B. BOSWORTH

IN 1914 Europe was a dictator-free continent. At that time, dictators seemed men whose presence was confined to the comic-opera world of 'fiery' Latin American politics, an arena where, Europeans automatically assumed, the population was passionate and childish, too 'immature' to be taken seriously. Such 'backward' people were in need of a firm hand from one moment to the next simply because they had not reached the European level of civilization. The only other dictators to impress themselves on the European mind of the pre-war era were those who turned up in the pages of Livy. The Roman Republic, a classical education instructed, summoned brave and worthy men to a special form of leadership at some moment of crisis. When it was overcome, the best of them, like Cincinnatus, austere and incorruptible, returned to their farms; only such equivocal figures as Julius Caesar grabbed at greater power (with fatal effects).[1]

Thirty years later, by contrast, every European nation or state outside the narrow western fringe occupied by Britain, Eire, Scandinavia, and the Low Countries had recently endured, or continued to endure, dictatorial rule of some description.

---

[1] For the nineteenth-century Caesar myth, see P. R. Baehr, *Caesar and the Fading of the Roman World: A Study in Republicanism and Caesarism* (New Brunswick, NJ: Transaction Publishers, 1998).

Completely contrary to Marxist doctrine, the Soviet Union had fallen under the sway of Josef Stalin, the new *vozhd'*, and his 'personality cult'. In Germany, the *Führer*, Adolf Hitler, had been jockeyed into power in January 1933 and, from September 1939, led his nation on a crusade known to us as the Second World War, aiming to build a racist and anti-communist dystopia, certainly in Europe and perhaps throughout the world. His chief ally was the *Duce*, Benito Mussolini, Prime Minister of Italy since October 1922 and its dictator from January 1925. In Spain, the *Caudillo*, Francisco Franco, in Romania, the *Conducator*, Ion Antonescu, in Greece, the *Archigos*, Ioannis Metaxas, each in their time generals of their national armies, donned new uniforms and were adorned with new titles cut to fit the moment. In that France which had been so humiliatingly crushed by Nazi armies during the summer of 1940, defeat was similarly countered by dictatorship of a kind. Thereafter, until 1945, Marshal Philippe Pétain stood as the *Chef d'État* of an alleged 'national revolution', based at Vichy. When, looking back in 1966 on the military defeat and political liquidation of Nazi-fascism, historian Elizabeth Wiskemann opted for the title *Europe of the Dictators* for a textbook account of inter-war Europe, her choice was apt.[2]

After the defeat and deaths of Hitler and Mussolini in 1945 (and the demise of Stalin in his bed in 1953), dictators became less omnipresent in Europe, although Portugal's Antonio de Oliveira Salazar, unusual in his trade as tyrant in being originally a pious professor of economics, did not die until 1970, and Franco lasted until 1975, while various communist and post-communist leaders continued to shore up their power pursuing paths where Stalin once had led. Moreover, in the world outside Europe, in Africa, Latin America, the Middle East, and Asia, dictators have become the rule and not the exception. In justifying their pre-emptive war in 2003, American neo-conservatives, their aides and associates, portrayed Saddam Hussein, the dictator of Iraq since 1968, as the 'Hitler of our Time' as George Bush I had called him in 1990.[3] Their reasons for fixing this appellation on Saddam were troubling, given the multitude of candidates in many parts of the globe as the heirs of those tyrants who had disfigured European history fifty years earlier. The fact that our world continues to search for, and locate, (evil) *Führer*-figures suggests the need for scholarship to survey the ideologies, personalities, achievements, and failings of the rash of inter-war dictators, some fascist, some fascistoid, and some not fascist at all, and to ask whether there is a real continuity between the travails of the continent at that time and the wider world today.

To be sure, dictators have had a bad press in those countries that have remained tied to liberal democracy and have endorsed the values and hopes of the Enlightenment. Yet, in much of the rest of society and notably in the celebrated fields of business and sport, 'leadership' is an ever more lauded quality or attainment.

---

[2] E. Wiskemann, *Europe of the Dictators 1919–1945* (London: Collins, 1966).
[3] S. Payne, *A History of Fascism, 1914–1945* (Madison: University of Wisconsin Press, 1995), 516.

Experts purport to teach it; journals record and explain it. Any who cherish liberty, it often seems, must admire the freedom to lead, the freedom to dominate, and, not so far in the shadows, the freedom to dictate. The delight in leadership is especially likely to surface where liberalism tries to convey, or adapt to, populist messages. Deep in the heart of that 'modernizing' liberal 'democracy' which, in 1989, Francis Fukuyama discerned as having achieved the final solution to humankind's political dilemmas,[4] and which our contemporary neo-conservatives have aimed to impose on the Middle East, rests a contradiction.

It was there, after all, from the beginning. No sooner had the *philosophes* dreamed, and the French revolutionaries begun to apply, the new trinity of liberty, equality, and fraternity, than their system fell under the sway of a free individual. Napoleon Bonaparte, a talented and ruthless nobody from Corsica, conquered France, Europe, and more, forging in the process a template for later dictators, even if he eventually crowned himself emperor, spawning what a critical social historian has called the 'gangster dynasty'.[5] Two generations after this Napoleon's overthrow, his nephew assumed the title Napoleon III and governed France, becoming through 'Caesarian democracy' what the pessimistic conservative historian Lewis Namier labelled the 'first mountebank dictator'.[6]

When Namier coined this metaphor after the Second World War, he may well have been reflecting a common attitude by then of those who, to use an American journalist's term, viewed Benito Mussolini as a 'Sawdust Caesar',[7] a leader who had updated the formula of bread and circuses once deployed in that classical Rome which was fading from the noble purity of the republic to the 'degeneration' of the empire. Some dictators, it was agreed, were more mountebank than others. Hitler, the 'madman', the fanatic, what would today be called the 'fundamentalist', the little man who held his people in thrall with what seemed a sorcery beyond human ken, the chief whose total control meant that there was no need for him to address the humdrum tasks of politician and executive since the Germans 'worked towards him' of their own unfree will,[8] was recollected as a figure of stygian mystery and dread (or of a secret, even sexual, allure). The Nazi leader and his elite, along with his fiendishly black-garbed 'praetorian guard', the SS, have an afterlife in the pornography of whips, thigh-high leather boots, and 'nameless' suffering; they, in

---

[4] Later expanded as F. Fukuyama, *The End of History and the Last Man* (London: Hamish Hamilton, 1992).

[5] R. Cobb, *The Police and the People: French Popular Protest 1789–1820* (Oxford: Oxford University Press, 1972), 197.

[6] L. Namier, *Vanished Supremacies: Essays on European History* (New York: Harper and Row, 1963), 54–64.

[7] G. Seldes, *Sawdust Caesar: The Untold History of Mussolini and Fascism* (London: A. Barker, 1936). For a further analysis of the context in 1936, see R. J. B. Bosworth, *Mussolini's Italy: Life under the Dictatorship* (London: Allen Lane, 2005), 396–7.

[8] See the endorsement of this view in the last and best biography of the *Führer*, I. Kershaw, *Hitler* (2 vols, London: Allen Lane, 1998–2000).

popular recollection, are the sadists who turned on the gas. At 'Auschwitz', the world has come to agree, the German dictator carried the world to its historical nadir; Hitler opened the bottommost circle of hell.

Mussolini, by contrast, survives in memory, everywhere except in Italy, as a joke, a ham actor, rolling his eyes, waving his hands and jutting his chin, bellowing, bullying, boasting, blundering. He seems a classic case of all talk and no reality, a dictator certainly, but one who it is hard for any commentator after his death to take seriously. Mussolini's soldiers, despite childish bragging about how, for them, 'making war was like eating a plate of macaroni',[9] ran away when confronted by any serious enemy. Mussolini's regime presided over a country that it was only fair for the Germans to have on their side from June 1940 since Britain, France, Russia, and the United States had had to put up with Italy in the First World War. This dictator was the 'jackal', the back streets' petty killer who specialized in the stab in the back.[10] Whatever the talk about iron-hard personal rule, revolution, and the rest, Fascist Italy was, as a hard-bitten Australian journalist argued cheerfully in 1950, a 'useless Ally—a "Nation of Mandolin-players" and opera-singers who lack warrior stamina. . . . By their sheer incapacity in war, the Italians have earned a reputation unique in the world. They are more dangerous to their allies than to their enemies.'[11]

These two contradictory faces, charted from a common reading of the history of inter-war Europe, are deeply inscribed into current thinking about dictators and dictatorships. Where fear, or its mobilization, predominate, Hitler and his 'lesson of history' command our horrified attention. In more ordinary times, dictators are viewed instead as doubtless malign, but also as bullfrogs, awaiting their inevitable comeuppance. Then, in Charlie Chaplin's superb satirical image in his film *The Great Dictator* (1940), even Hitler is reduced to being an 'Adenoid Hynkel', while Mussolini becomes 'Benzino Napoloni', the 'Dictator of Bacteria', half pyromaniac and half pizza boy.

However hard it is to struggle free from such conditioning stereotypes, scholars doubtless should examine the chiefs of the Fascist and Nazi dictatorships with care and rigour. In such an exercise, it is appropriate to start with Mussolini and not with the grander or more Wagnerian figure of the *Führer*. After all, it was the Italian *Duce* who pioneered the model of modern dictatorship, reaching office a decade

[9] The braggart was Fascist Party Secretary 1931–9, Achille Starace. See C. Senise, *Quando era Capo della Polizia 1940–1943* (Rome: Ruffolo Editore, 1946), 35. There was some irony in the fact that Senise was a Neapolitan and Starace came from Gallipoli, in the province of Lecce, even further south, and 'macaroni' was a dish consumed in the old Kingdom of Naples-Sicily rather than elsewhere in Italy where 'macaroni-eaters' was often used as a pejorative for southerners.

[10] For an exploration of these stereotypes, see R. J. B. Bosworth, 'Mito e linguaggio nella politica estera italiana', in R. J. B. Bosworth and S. Romano (eds), *La politica estera italiana (1860–1985)* (Bologna: Il Mulino, 1991), 35–67.

[11] F. Clune, *All Roads Lead to Rome: A Pilgrimage to the Eternal City, and a Look around War-Torn Europe* (Sydney: Invincible Press, 1950), 27.

ahead of his eventual German partner. Mussolini was neither military man nor monarch. Although he collaborated on a play-script about Napoleon, asserting a half identification of his own story with that of the Corsican conqueror,[12] Mussolini neither led his troops into battle nor ousted King Victor Emmanuel III to claim a royal crown.[13] Doubtless his nationalist allies filled pages of their journals with enthusiasm for an authoritarian and Caesarian monarchy that somehow embodied the people. But Mussolini the *Duce* stepped past the Bonaparte model. He was novel or he was nothing.

The key to Mussolini's new form of tyranny was its basis in ideas, those products of the intelligentsia, a social group who, as modernity spread, everywhere increased in number and preached its own political importance. The *Duce*'s 'dictatorship for the twentieth century' (as regime propaganda soon was calling it) was to spring from a new and 'revolutionary' ideology, from 'fascism' as it was somewhat opaquely called,[14] promising not merely to undergird the institution of dictatorial rule but also actively to mould the lives of subject Italians into 'new men' and 'new women'. This utterly original dictatorship aimed to institute visceral change, in politics and economics, culture and society. Fascist governance would modernize Italy in its own way, different from, and superior to, the modernization that arrived through liberalism or socialism. Mussolini's power would be total. The regime must prove 'totalitarian', a term that first appeared in 1920s Italy among critics of the regime and was then taken over by the *Duce*'s propagandists as a summary of his intention that the population agree automatically that 'All was for the state, nothing outside the state, no one against the state.'[15]

Whereas monarchs had hedged their personal power with the half-apologetic claim that they acted merely as vice-regents of God, and Cincinnatus, with legal propriety, had ruled only while an emergency threatened, this new sort of ruler pledged a new power and a new permanence. His penetration of his subjects'

[12] For an English version, see B. Mussolini and G. Forzano, *Napoleon: The Hundred Days (Adapted from the Italian for the English Stage Version by John Drinkwater)* (London: Sidgwick and Jackson, 1932).

[13] The inter-war dictator who literally followed the Napoleonic model was the curious figure of Ahmed Bey Zogu in Albania. This Italian puppet ruler, having secured Rome's backing, elevated himself to become King Zog I in September 1928, and lasted in that role until Good Friday 1939, when invading fascist armies overthrew his rule and made Albania another part of the Italian empire. Since 1945, Jean-Bédel Bokassa, dictator of the Central African Republic (1966–79, emperor after 1976), has been the only new monarch. In Syria the Assads (with some fascist origin) and in Korea the Kims (Asian 'communists') have provided cases of dictator sons succeeding dictator fathers. Family dynastic inheritance is also, of course, well known in democratic politics, perhaps in an accelerated manner recently as 'product recognition' becomes more important than ideology.

[14] The word boasted a classical derivation and the regime would talk incessantly about its *romanità*, but *fascio* had popped up in past usage all over the Italian political arc, and, at base, meant little more than united group (in favour of the national First World War and its positive history). Cf. Bosworth, *Mussolini's Italy*, 121–2.

[15] The classic account of the legal basis of the tyranny remains A. Aquarone, *L'organizzazione dello stato totalitario* (Turin: Einaudi, 1965).

bodies, minds, and souls must be totally total (and no one must doubt or resent the tautology). In a fascist nation, the population must stand utterly united and cohesive, as the symbol of the *fascio* promised, with its rods bound together and armed with an axe for any who might seek to wriggle free. Fascists must be ready to march triumphantly wherever the dictator guided them. As Futurist painters had half-imagined before 1914 and as a survivor like Fortunato Depero continued to portray as late as 1943, in the modernity forged through the processes of the Industrial Revolution, Mussolini and his followers must literally become steel men, invulnerable to enemy assault.[16] In 1937, the dictator had told a visiting American journalist that he had eliminated from his personal life all 'dispersal of energy and other time-wasting'. His body, he maintained, had become 'a motor, which is under constant review and control and which therefore runs with absolute regularity'.[17] Unlike the ramshackle past, Mussolini's was to be a dictatorship that fired on all cylinders. In the *Duce*'s dynamic power and swirling strength, a fascist dictator would be the prime 'new man' in his country, a Superman indeed, the human epitome of the throbbing power of the machine.

But was Mussolini really a 'strong dictator'? It might seem a paradox, but German historians, a generation ago, debated the issue whether or not there were 'limits to Hitler's power'[18] and the discussion about the possibility of 'weak dictatorship' has recently been extended to Stalin.[19] What happens, then, when a dictator's power is read between the lines and with the flamboyant propaganda and ceaseless deification stilled? Was the Fascist *ventennio* (two decades) from 1922 (or 1925) to 1943 (or 1945) the *Duce*'s? Did Italians then staff a country best summarized as 'Mussolini's Italy'? How, in practice, was power exercised in this dictatorship and with what effect across society?

It is curious that, despite the lingering assumption noted above that Mussolini was little more than a fraud, even the most disdainful historians have maintained that he was nonetheless in charge.[20] So, too, did Renzo De Felice, the increasingly conservative and patriotic author of a massive Italian 'biography' of the *Duce*,[21] which is really no biography at all. So narrow was De Felice's devotion to political and diplomatic history, so stern was his neo-Rankeanism, that his 6,000 and more pages can act as a wonderful mine of factual information about the regime's

---

[16] F. Depero, *A passo romano: lirismo fascista e guerriero programmatico e costruttivo* (Rovereto: Fascio di Trento, 1943), 20–1.

[17] B. Mussolini, *Opera omnia*, ed. E. and D. Susmel (Florence: La Fenice, 1951–62), xxviii. 139.

[18] For the use of this challenging title, see E. N. Peterson, *The Limits of Hitler's Power* (Princeton: Princeton University Press, 1969).

[19] See J. Harris, 'Was Stalin a Weak Dictator?', *Journal of Modern History*, 75 (2003), 375–86.

[20] The prime example in this regard is the English liberal Denis Mack Smith. See his *Mussolini's Roman Empire* (London: Longman, 1976); *Mussolini* (London: Weidenfeld and Nicolson, 1981). For a fuller account of the historiography on the dictator, see R. J. B. Bosworth, *The Italian Dictatorship: Problems and Perspectives in the Interpretation of Mussolini and Fascism* (London: Arnold, 1998).

[21] R. De Felice, *Mussolini* (4 vols. in 8 books, Turin: Einaudi, 1965–97).

doings, and De Felice gives the impression that Mussolini was always in charge. But neither the *Duce*'s personality nor any questioning analysis of the structures and techniques of his personal power emerges from De Felice's turgid prose, curiously dictatorial in its author's certainty that he alone has the answer to the subject under examination.

De Felice so bestrode his field in Italy that those there who objected to his politics or methodology while he was alive or who have worked on fascism after his death in 1996 have mostly been unable to break free from the assumption that, from 1922 to 1945, Mussolini indeed dictated.[22] In the early twenty-first century Silvio Berlusconi summed up the often cosy Italian reading of their country's generation of dictatorship by claiming that 'Mussolini never killed anyone' and by implying that the entire fascist period, like all the past except that disfigured by wicked communists, must now best become a matter of the 'sellebration' of the nation in the contemporary capitalist mode.[23] Given Italians' continued failure to engage in a rigorous examination of their dictator and his world, the most interesting recent biographies of Mussolini have been written by foreigners, whether in French[24] or in English.[25]

What, then, are the key surviving issues about the Italian dictator and his rule?

One prime field is, predictably, that of ideas, and so of the origins, definition, and meaning of fascism. Did Mussolini make his ideology and himself, especially before 1914 when he, another aspirant intellectual from the provinces, was proud to be called *professore* (through his qualifications to teach, first, elementary school and, later, middle school French)? The indefatigable, California-based, political scientist A. James Gregor has never ceased to argue that the young Mussolini possessed a brilliant creative mind.[26] According to Gregor, the youthful *Duce* (he had already acquired the sobriquet before Italy entered the First World War[27]) blended syndicalism and nationalism to pave a path to what would prove a 'developmental dictatorship', promising an Italian catch-up with such patronizing and exploitative

[22] See, for example, A. Campi, *Mussolini* (Bologna: Il Mulino, 2001).

[23] For a critique of this process, not lacking its own cosiness, see S. Luzzatto, *La crisi dell'antifascismo* (Turin: Einaudi, 2004).

[24] See P. Milza, *Mussolini* (Montrouge: Fayard, 1999) and the briefer but more questioning D. Musiedlak, *Mussolini* (Paris: Presses de Sciences Po, 2005).

[25] Compare, for example, a journalist's effort at 'revisionism', N. Farrell, *Mussolini: A New Life* (London: Weidenfeld and Nicolson, 2003), with a professional historian's quizzical account, M. Clark, *Mussolini* (Harlow: Pearson, 2005).

[26] See, among many works, A. J. Gregor, *Young Mussolini and the Intellectual Origins of Fascism* (Berkeley and Los Angeles: University of California Press, 1979); *Italian Fascism and Developmental Dictatorship* (Princeton: Princeton University Press, 1979); and, most recently, *Mussolini's Intellectuals: Fascist Social and Political Thought* (Princeton: Princeton University Press, 2005); *The Search for Neo-fascism: The Use and Abuse of Social Science* (Cambridge: Cambridge University Press, 2006), especially 30–53.

[27] For an account of this matter, see R. J. B. Bosworth, *Mussolini* (London: Arnold, 2002), 97–8. For a history of Mussolini's biography under the regime, cf. L. Passerini, *Mussolini immaginario* (Bari: Laterza, 1991).

winners from early industrialization as Britain and France. Gregor argues further
that the regime in office was largely benign in its effects until, in its decline, it was
trapped into the German alliance and began to practice anti-Semitism. Nonetheless, he adds, the Italian model and its intellectual base became what, somewhere
beneath the rhetoric, drove virtually all modern dictators. Included on his list
are those who claimed, like Stalin, Mao, Castro, and Pol Pot, to be Marxists, and
their regimes, Gregor is sure, were unparalleled in their tyranny, wickedness, and
interfering power.

Gregor's global sweep, allied with his curious defensiveness towards Italian Fascism before 1938 and after 1945 in its neo-fascist version, has by no means achieved
interpretative victory. Rather, it might be agreed that the Benito Mussolini (b. July
1883), who, before the age of 30, was rising from an acceptably educated and not too
poor family in the not totally peripheral Romagna to become, in 1912, the editor of
Avanti!, the chief organ of the Italian socialist party and movement, was a young
man of energy and talent, a personage who, unlike the prim and apparently dim
Hitler (b. 1889), did not need to be 'made possible' by the First World War.[28] With
or without that conflict, by 1914 Mussolini had thrust himself into the attention,
if not reliably of the great world, at least of its fringes. 'Professor' Mussolini, the
socialist journalist, the radical and 'revolutionary', was then already knocking at
the door of power and offering leadership that might be either journalistic (an
Italian Northcliffe, Hearst, or Murdoch potentially in the making) or political or
ideological (while, in the more private realm, it was patriarchally male). For later
analysts, confronted with the stream of Mussolini's writings and initiatives, the
dilemma is whether to winnow them for intellectual consistency or, rather, to
notice that the activity mattered as much, or more, as did the precise meaning of
the words.

A Benito Mussolini may have existed before 1914 and so did not need forging in
the trenches. Yet the Mussolini who became Fascist dictator of Italy was as much a
product of the First World War as was the German *Führer*. During the nine months
intervento in 1914–15, while the Italian government was trying to make up its mind
when to join the war and on which side, Mussolini decided not to be a socialist,
given that Italian socialism was opting for a weak line of non-intervention, a policy
that promised 'neither support nor sabotage' of the national war effort. In helping
to foster the atmosphere in which the Italian leadership entered the war in May
1915, Mussolini decisively abandoned socialism's theoretical internationalism for a
practical nationalism.[29] Thus affirmed as a patriot, from his call-up in September
1915 until his wounding behind the front in March 1917, Mussolini served in the
mountain trenches of Italy's war as an 'ordinary soldier'. His diary about this
experience was published at the time in his newspaper and, after 1922, was sanctified

---

[28] For this conclusion, see Kershaw, *Hitler 1889–1936*, 73.

[29] See further P. O'Brien, *Mussolini in the First World War: The Journalist, the Soldier, the Fascist*
(Oxford: Berg, 2005).

as the key endorsing document of the *Duce's* power.[30] Mussolini the dictator was thereby rendered by his military service into the symbolic holy vehicle of Italy's decidedly idiosyncratic war.

Yet, even at the front, Mussolini was never just a soldier. Rather he remained a journalist, adept at coining a telling phrase, swift to see personal advantage, tough in his dealing with what might seem inefficiency, stubborn in advancing himself in any setting. Dropped in October 1914 from the editorship of *Avanti!*, he had quickly returned with a personal paper, *Il popolo d'Italia*, invoking the people (and so Mazzini) rather than class (and K. Marx; now he renounced that youth when he had edited a paper naively entitled *La lotta di classe*, 'Class Struggle'). In these circumstances, Mussolini's journalism could rely on finance from the French and other Entente secret services and from the commanding heights of national wealth in industry and agriculture.

Yet, Mussolini was not alone in offering himself as a politician of radical or novel appearance who could embody a new age radicalized by war. In 1919, in this regard, he lagged behind such publicity lions as the Futurist F. T. Marinetti and, most notably, the lush poet, airman, war hero, and world's greatest lover (in his own estimation), Gabriele D'Annunzio, in appeal to, or notice from, the best people. But Mussolini was also there; his paper did not go bankrupt. In Milan, Italy's most important modern city, Mussolini was already a man who mattered when, on 23 March 1919, a group assembled in a room, looking out onto the Piazza San Sepolcro in the urban centre and generously lent for the occasion by business groups, to announce the formation of a new political organization called the Fasci di Combattimento (battle groups). For some months, Mussolini had been writing in *Il popolo d'Italia* about the need to make way for the *trincerocrazia* (those from the trenches who had made themselves into the nation's new natural leaders), stressing the duty to favour dynamic 'productivist' elements in the country over tired and flaccid old liberals or deluded, Russian-loving, socialists. Now *fasci* began to spread to other towns, and the aspirant chiefs, among them, most notably that talented wordsmith Mussolini himself, could draft programmes that might win present support and, one day, might turn into action.

In this medley of hopes and ambitions, once again Mussolini was not alone. Before and after his accession to power Mussolini worked with a small group of fellows, such henchmen as Roberto Farinacci, Dino Grandi, Italo Balbo, Giuseppe Bottai, Achille Starace, and others. What is significant about them is that, with the possible exception of the youngest, Bottai (b. 1895), each had found a way to what was to be called fascism before being intimately connected with Mussolini.[31] The nature of 'total war', Italian-style, was making fascists before they knew they were such. The wartime Liberal Italian nation found its society unreliably united,

---

[30] See B. Mussolini, *Il mio diario di guerra (1915–1917)* (Milan: Imperia, 1923).
[31] For development of this theme, see Bosworth, *Mussolini's Italy*, 53–6, 78–82.

its liberalism inadequate when confronted with the requirement to ignite a modern machine economy, its men unreliably ardent in battle.[32] Despite the fact that Italians had been, and would continue to be, among others for all Nazis except Hitler, the butt of racial theory, commentators now took to summoning the national 'blood' in the cause of victory. The interventionist state, fusing capital and workers in what would come to be called corporatism, offering peasants a national role, utilizing modern technology to make its propaganda, demonizing its enemies, especially its socialist ones, the 'traitors' in 1915 who, after 1919, still more deplorably wanted to keep their own different history of the war, dreaming of a time when an adjustment of power politics or imperial gains could make Italy the equal of Britain or Germany, and wondering whether a Strong Man might best lead this new model country, all these themes blossomed as a result of Italy's war. They did not need Mussolini to invent them. Rather, the principles and habits of total war, Italian style, drove forward irresistibly towards a Mussolini, or a Leader of any other name, and could not be blocked in their surge to control the lives of the post-war generation.

Such a conclusion may seem too predetermined. Certainly, much politics was fought out in Italy from March 1919 to the March on Rome on 28 October 1922 with the resultant elevation of Mussolini to the prime ministership of a coalition government. It did not cease when the *Duce* enjoyed a massive electoral victory on 6 April 1924, soon marred, at least potentially, by the murder on 10 June of the moderate socialist leader Giacomo Matteotti by fascists who, at a minimum, were intimates of Mussolini and his friends. A regime was only solidified after Mussolini's speech of 3 January 1925, when he announced the formation of an open dictatorship. During the downs and ups of these years, Mussolini frequently displayed great political astuteness and skill, knowing well when to threaten and when to trim, whom to roll over and whom to ingratiate. This dictator in the making was, at least for the moment, well aware that a week is a long time in politics, that tactics demand as much attention as does strategy, or more, and that history is composed from a fusion of great structures and short-term events.

The rapidity with which 'fascists' moved from being a small and quarrelsome group in a few northern Italian cities to founding a political party, the Partito Nazionale Fascista in 1921, to acquiring power, and then to cementing their regime into place is itself a major factor in any assessment of the birth of dictatorship in Italy and so of the meaning of fascism. In these flurried times, a rough division of labour occurred. Fascists, hierarchically arranged under such local bosses as Farinacci in Cremona or Balbo in Ferrara, enjoyed much local freedom of action. In the fine print of their behaviour, divisions might lurk; a xenophobic nationalism was all the rage in Trieste or Bolzano, a profound hostility to the peasant union Federterra mattered most in the Po Valley and Tuscany (and could occasion either violent

---

[32] See A. Ventrone, *La seduzione totalitaria: guerra, modernità, violenza politica (1914–1918)* (Rome: Donzelli, 2003), 181, 185, for the fears of Bottai among others that a war effort with inadequate thrust implied national emasculation or sodomization.

'squadrist' raiding against socialist redoubts or half-serious, half-opportunist, talk about accommodating fascist peasant and worker unions); further south, old elites sniffed the wind and began to adapt to a fascist victory as, in 1860, they had to the arrival of 'Italy'.

After a half-crisis during the summer of 1921, when he briefly resigned as head of the *fasci*, Mussolini, for the most part, stood above the fascist scrimmage. His job was instead to be a 'national figure', both in crafting words and programmes and in negotiating with any of the old elite who were willing to negotiate with him (almost all were). Before 1922, and then in office leading to the imposition of the 'totalitarian state' after 1925, Mussolini did not automatically hold 'all power', if that term is meant to imply control over the daily thoughts and actions of every fascist. He did not even have to invent the entire paraphernalia, what is sometimes more grandiloquently described as the 'liturgy', of fascism. The starkest of all dictatorial slogans, '*Mussolini ha sempre ragione*' (Mussolini is always right), was not his coinage.[33] Yet, although many a *ras* (local party boss) might retain mutinous thoughts, with every week and certainly with the resolution of the crisis of Christmas–New Year 1924–5, Mussolini became the indispensable chief. As he himself had put it in 1921, he, the *Duce*, alone could 'see the full horizon from the top of the mountain and size up a world that is not Bologna, Venice or Cuneo, but Italy, Europe and the world'.[34] He, alone of his movement, was equipped to confront the globe.

The mechanisms of fascist 'totalitarianism' after 1925 are reviewed in many other chapters in this Handbook. My task is rather to review how the dictator placed himself into this system and with what results.

When such a reckoning is attempted the information it elicits is mixed. In quite a few senses, Mussolini was a highly active and even conscientious ruler, a dictator who dictated, an ideologue whose personal version of fascism overwhelmed any alternatives. In the public circles of authority, he could rely on his underlings, not needing to murder his henchmen as Stalin, Hitler, and quite a few other dictators did, because he had them securely in hand psychologically and practically. On occasion Farinacci, Balbo, or Grandi may have dreamed of a post-Mussolinian Italy backed by the Germans or the British or the Americans, but, except in the muddled sacking of the *Duce* in July 1943, any scheming remained notional.

A great help and comfort in this regard was Mussolini's relationship with his younger brother Arnaldo (until his early death in 1931). Arnaldo, said by the *Duce* to have been the only man whom he ever trusted, was crucial in editing *Il popolo d'Italia*, in measuring the atmosphere in Milan, and in keeping an ear open to many a deal or danger. After Arnaldo's death, Galeazzo Ciano, married to Mussolini's eldest daughter, Edda, filled a different but equally familial role as Minister of Foreign Affairs, fascist dauphin (of an unconvincing and so unthreatening kind),

---

[33] For a more detailed tracking of these matters, see Bosworth, *Mussolini*, 145–6, 210.
[34] Mussolini, *Opera omnia*, xvii. 83.

wit, and intellectual sparring partner. Hitler and Stalin were not familists, but Mussolini, Latin tyrant perhaps, was (even if his graceless sons were no more than annoyances). To be sure, equivocations threaded this matter; Nazis and communists were much more ruthless in their practical and ideological assaults on the traditional family. But Mussolini was, in many senses, the father of his country.

In those realms where the theory of policy was meant to be converted to action, the dictator's authority was enhanced by the useful division between Fascist Party and Italian state, with Mussolini being anxious, especially during his regime's early days, to ensure that 'fascist' radicalism did not get out of hand. Another technique of government, replicated less self-consciously by Hitler, was the palpable, indeed ostentatious, attention to tiny detail. The archives easily show the *Duce* ready to interfere in the minutiae of the urban planning of the national capital and centre of the regime's myths, Rome, for example. His preference was for the lapidary phrase—'*per sbaraccare, occorre baraccare*' (to pull down slums you must erect dwellings)[35]—and for enumerated lists (he absorbed this approach to administration while, as a young emigrant in Switzerland, being taught elementary philosophy by the sophisticated Russian aristocratic revolutionary Angelica Balabanoff).[36] All was best expressed in a militant and military vocabulary, with draconian emphasis and an apparent opting for a precise calendar.

Similarly, in the high policy of the regime, there are plenty of instances where there can be little doubt that it was Mussolini who pushed a chosen line, imposing his will on grumbling or troubled juniors. One case was the choice to rate the lira at ninety to the pound sterling in 1926–7, a policy prompted by fears about the status of the regime and its pretensions to totalitarian revolution. Another was the invasion of Ethiopia in 1935 and the prosecution of the colonial war to brutal (if shallow) victory in May 1936. The use of chemical weapons in Libya and Ethiopia, the swing to active anti-Semitism in 1937–8, and the entry into the European war in June 1940, all were, ostensibly at least, again Mussolinian 'decisions'.

Yet, when examined closely, doubts creep in. A dictator's attention span is not always long: once the triumph in Addis Ababa was celebrated and Mussolini had made his raucous balcony speech about empire returning to the 'fatal hills of Rome', Ethiopia declined as a regime priority. The *Duce* never went there; fascist empire in some senses was governed in a 'fit of absent mind'. Although Mussolini was guilty of deploying weapons of mass destruction on Arabs and blacks, the most immediate initiative for murder[37] came from such generals as Rodolfo Graziani and Pietro Badoglio, and, behind them, the royal family, the old nationalist and Africanist elite, and the newly technologized officers and pilots of the air force. Fascist adventures

---

[35] Segreteria particolare del Duce, Cartegggio ordinario, 5000019/I, 14 March 1933, Mussolini to A. Iraci.

[36] See Bosworth, *Mussolini*, 64–5.

[37] Such killing could shade into genocide. See A. Abdullah Ahmida, 'When the Subaltern Speaks: Memory of Genocide in Colonial Libya 1929 to 1933', *Italian Studies*, 61 (2006), 191–206.

in Africa, with a bloody death toll that reached half a million, were to a degree Fascist and Mussolinian. But they were also Italian, European, 'imperialist', a belated imitation of what Britain, France, Belgium, Germany, and the rest had done long before.

Anti-Semitism was an appalling choice and there is little evidence that it was directly fostered by the regime's Nazi ally. Rather, Mussolini drifted towards the persecution of his nation's patriotic and, in general, socially conservative and pro-fascist Jews, at his own leisure.[38] As a result his dictatorship must accept direct responsibility for the killing of more than 7,000 Jews in the death camps, victims transported there at the behest of the Salò Republic after September 1943. Yet, Italian anti-Semitism had Catholic, elite, and intellectual roots for which the dictator was not the direct cause. When, from 1942, Mussolini from time to time ineffectually tried to suggest to the frighteningly fanatical *Führer* that Operation Barbarossa was proving a mistake, hinting that a separate peace in the East would make more immediate sense and allow a better pursuit of the conflict with the capitalist and liberal West, he was exposing the limits of his own racial fanaticism (and of his 'anti-communism' and anti-Slavism). Moreover, both the *Duce*'s racism and that of his party and subjects mixed with its anti-Semitism currents of hostility to Arabs and blacks, to Eastern Europeans, and to other Italians (especially those from further south in the country). Racism, inter-war Italian style, was not merely a 'war against the Jews'.

Moreover, if power is thought to be located not so much in the daily wave of events, but rather in deeper, structural matters, then Mussolini can often be found not to have dislodged Italian certainties. Constitutionally speaking, at least until September 1943, Italy remained a monarchy. Mussolini's own personality cult and charisma therefore had to put up with ongoing competition, open and, more important, implicit, from the king and the numerous, fertile, and active royal family. A far deeper challenge came from the Pope, and marshalled behind him, the saints, Virgin, and Deity, all bearing histories that were eternal and pervasive in a fashion that neither fascism nor the cult of the *Duce* could hope to match or oppose. In February 1929, the signature of the Lateran Pacts marked a special triumph for the dictatorship and the dictator, who had worked long and hard on the exact phrasing of the agreement (although Mussolini had not originated the deal). This pact between church and state was not a victory but a compromise. Mussolinian governance adapted itself to Italians' (varying) Catholicism and made no serious attempt to purge orthodox religious ideas from Italian minds.

This story of intelligent accommodation and of the Mussolinian and fascist version of history and its processes being added to the slew of other deep matters that coursed through Italian lives rather than a cancellation of the pasts to achieve

---

[38] For a neat study of the matter in Ferrara, see I. Pavan, *Il podestà ebreo: la storia di Renzo Ravenna tra fascismo e le leggi razziali* (Bari: Laterza, 2006).

a fully novel cultural revolution can be repeated in other settings. The survival of the family has already been noted. So, too, this dictator failed fully to conquer the military (not for nothing was Mussolini's replacement after the fall in July 1943 a general, Badoglio, appointed by the king).

Big business was also scarcely cowed; the slogan of Italian industrialists through-out the *ventennio* remained the cynical and double-edged assumption of Giovanni Agnelli that businesspeople were always on the side of government, 'ministerialist by definition'.[39] Despite the totalitarian talk, further down in society patron–client networks flourished and pressure groups remained active, with many Italians being as anxious to see what fascism and its dictator could do for them as they were to offer their service or souls to the regime and its *Duce*. Even the dictator's desire to 'make Italians' proved qualified in practice since every citizen of the country, including Mussolini, clung to a hierarchy of regional attraction and significance as well as to ancient assumptions that the city was more civilized than the country, the north than the south, and the metropolitan than the imperial. Despite the regime's loud but not very original boasting about *romanità*, in practice classical Rome had not bothered to conquer Ethiopia. In return, modern Ethiopia did not fully occupy Fascist Italian minds and destroy the belief that, if you went too far from Rome (or some other northern Italian *città*), then barbarism was all that could be found.

For a myriad of reasons, then, it was not perversity which led me in my biography of Mussolini to argue that, often, he was as ready to 'work towards the Italians' as to expect them mysteriously to read his thoughts before they occurred and so 'work towards him'. On a typical Mussolini day (he performed the executive's job with considerable concentration and, contrary to legend, his speaking tours of the provinces and other oratorical ventures were quite rare), he read the government papers, underlined what he thought mattered, made his succinct and commanding-seeming lists of comments and 'orders', and then let matters happen as bureaucrats or henchmen or others could determine. Providing apparent proof of the dictator's control and caprice were much publicized episodes of 'changing of the guard' at the top. At their *Duce*'s stroke, the henchmen could expect frequently to move from one ministry to the next. Meanwhile, in their obligatory visits to the *Sala del Mappamondo*, where the dictator was ensconced from 1929,[40] they had to endure public hectoring and private cynicism about what drove humankind.

Yet, once again, the dictator's power was incomplete or elusive somewhere be-neath the chat and the bluster. Mussolini did spend a lot of time most mornings and afternoons talking to a stream of visitors, from a variety of fields and social levels (although the most important were the regular updatings the dictator received from his cynical and effective Chief of Police, Arturo Bocchini, until his death in 1940).

---

[39] P. Melograni, *Gli industriali e Mussolini: rapporti tra Confindustria e Fascismo dal 1919 al 1929* (Milan, Longanesi, 1972), 45.

[40] For further context, see Bosworth, *Mussolini*, 242–4.

The long-term purpose and effect of most of these exchanges are hard to determine. Under charismatic rule, minutes were not kept, and a standardized method to convert ideas into practice did not exist. Rather, to quite a degree, Mussolini the dictator, hedged around by the aura of his success and by the ubiquity of his myth, and his country were 'parallels that did not meet', a fact that cheap talk about popular mobilization could not wholly conceal. In the daily administrative system of this dictatorship, 'government', if by that term is meant the considered and consistent implementation of policy, did not always ensue.

Two further dilemmas should be noted. A totalitarian dictator who is always right needs not to make too many obvious blunders as one visitor marches out of his office to be replaced by another. Better, then, very often, if the conversation is kept vague and anodyne. Better, too, unless life is to be made wearisome by endless quarrels, generally to approve in broad terms the enthusiasms of visitors who are certain, after all, to have the immediate details of whatever preoccupies them in hand in a way that is potentially superior to the dictator. Mussolini, as a number of his underlings noticed, was on many occasions anxious to agree with whomever he had last seen. Even after the often smiling and sexy young ruler of the 1920s had given way to the 'granitic' (as propaganda put it) chief of the last decade of fascist rule, Mussolini retained a politician's alertness to atmosphere, implication, and unspoken assumptions and the desire to be admired and loved, despite his curmudgeonly image.

When dictatorial rule is thus reviewed does it mean that this dictator was unable to change his country or even that, at heart, he did not want to? Am I restating the interpretation of a fraudulent *Duce* and suggesting that Mussolini was the weakest of dictators? Only in part, I would want to argue.

The issue is a taxing one, central to any political history and to any effort to appraise human free will. It is absurd not to acknowledge that Mussolini was a fascist dictator. If doubtless not acting alone, he destroyed parliamentary liberalism, banned all rival political parties, liquidated socialist and Catholic unions, infringed the rule of law, pursued economic policies that ended with a desperate protectionism and fostered a corrupt and inefficient corporatism, utilized the secret police to spy on Italians and to persuade neighbours to denounce each other, helped block the advance of women towards equality with men, and launched Italy into a long list of colonial and, eventually, European aggressions, most with a racist intent and culminating in the disasters of Italy's Second World War as the premier ally of Nazi Germany (even if Mussolini himself proved the most inconstant and inadequate of Warlords). Any contemplation of the *Duce*'s 'weakness' must not forget or forgive this black record.

Yet, in the complex weave of his own life and in the survival of many histories under his regime rather than its imposition of a single totalitarianism, Mussolini remains a recognizable human being, as well as a man who indeed acted as a model for the actions and for the failings of many subsequent dictators. Perhaps another matter should be noted. Less than three weeks after the 'March on Rome' that brought Mussolini and his Fascist Party, the Partito Nazionale Fascista or PNF, to national government, Adolfo Tedaldi, an Italian delegate on the Rhine Commission, gave Rome notice of the *Führer*: 'Hittler [*sic*] is the leader of the [German] fascists. He is young. In temperament, voice and gesture he seems more like a Latin than a German. He speaks well, however much with the air of a tribune, and knows how to drag in the crowd. His programme . . . is largely copied from the Italian *Fascio*.'[41] In the history of the Nazi rise to power and then of Hitler's rule after 1933, there were many significant connections with Italy. As Hitler was long willing to acknowledge, Mussolini taught him much that he needed to know in order to become German *Führer*.

There is one crucial difference, however, a matter that remains a basic 'lesson of history' (if contemplation of the past can assist the present). Even Hitler's most thorough biographer has not been able to dispel from the *Führer's* history something inexplicable. For Ian Kershaw, Hitler had 'no real private life'. So extreme was the German dictator's fundamentalism, especially focused into his 'paranoid antisemitism', it must be concluded that he was 'mad'.[42] This dictator remained bohemian in his lifestyle, even after 1933. He seldom read government papers and could rarely be found at his desk. The *Gleichschaltung* or imposition of power owed 'little' to the direct action of its chief. Thereafter Hitler stayed 'largely disengaged from the machinery of government'.[43] When Kershaw discerned that, 'remarkable for a complex modern state, there was no government beyond Hitler and whichever individuals he chose to confer with at a particular time', producing a (non-)system of 'bewildering improvisation, rapid changes of course, uncertainty',[44] there are some parallels with Mussolini. Charismatic rule is meretricious in many senses.

Yet, Mussolini's power (and that of other dictators) was both greater and less than that of the *Führer*. The *Duce* never ceased to work at imposing his domination and, by such labour, to leave open the possibility, even the likelihood, of its limitations. His rule needed daily justification and demonstration. This dictator could not renounce, or rise above, politics in the way that Hitler did with effortless certainty. Indeed, when Mussolini made one of his characteristic misanthropic outbursts about how Italians or the rest of humankind were no more than worms, he was half-admitting that he, too, might be similarly damned. This uneasily aspirant intellectual could not surrender himself to the luxury of assuming that only (fascist) ideas counted. In his contradictions and errors, in the 'spin' as well as the 'meaning' of his ideas and propaganda, in his unrelenting demand for a power that was never quite grasped with full satisfaction or comfort, the *Duce* was indeed the very model of a modern tyrant.

[41] *Documenti diplomatici italiani*, 7th series, i. 131, 17 November 1922, Tedaldi to Mussolini.
[42] I. Kershaw, *Hitler 1889–1936*, pp. xxvi, 64; idem, *Hitler 1936–45*, 92.
[43] Kershaw, *Hitler 1889–1936*, 469, 553.   [44] Kershaw, *Hitler 1936–45*, 227.

BIBLIOGRAPHY

Bosworth, R. J. B., *The Italian Dictatorship: Problems and Perspectives in the Interpretation of Mussolini and Fascism* (London: Arnold, 1999).

——*Mussolini* (London: Arnold, 2002).

——*Mussolini's Italy: Life under the Dictatorship* (London: Allen Lane, 2005).

Clark, M., *Mussolini* (Harlow: Pearson, 2005).

Corner, P., 'Italian Fascism: Whatever Happened to Dictatorship?', *Journal of Modern History*, 74 (2002), 325–51.

Kershaw, I., *Hitler*, 2 vols (London: Allen Lane, 1998–2000).

Passerini, L., *Mussolini immaginario* (Bari: Laterza, 1991).

Preston, P., *Franco: A Biography* (London: Harper Collins, 1993).

PART III

THE NAZI COMPARISON

STATE AND SOCIETY

ITALY AND GERMANY COMPARED*

GUSTAVO CORNI

On 30 January 1933, Adolf Hitler took power at the head of a coalition government where his own followers were in a pronounced minority. This deal resulted from plotting by a small group of conservatives who sought to profit from the political and economic crisis to sweep away the Weimar Republic and its parliamentary institutions. This faction, led by the ambitious Catholic politician Franz von Papen, were convinced that, for the occasion, they could exploit the National Socialist movement and the mass base that they had won and then free themselves from the Nazis at the opportune moment, perhaps then reviving the Hohenzollern monarchy. Hitler's accession to the German chancellorship was therefore based on co-option and followed processes that were in essence legal. In this regard the German story has a major similarity with what had happened in Italy some eleven years before. Nonetheless, two differences should be highlighted between the two stories, matters which would in turn have a great influence on the evolution of the two regimes in office.

* Translated by Richard Bosworth.

At the time of the March on Rome, and still after the successful elections of 1924, the Fascist Party did not possess an unchallengeable level of electoral consent. After all, from its foundation in 1921, it regularly presented itself at the polls with a major number of members from the old liberal ruling classes. It is true that, in 1924, after winning parliamentary support for the Acerbo law, guaranteeing to the party or coalition list that won more than 25 per cent of the vote two-thirds of the seats, Mussolini controlled the so-called *listone* (big list). It duly triumphed electorally assisted by open violence and widespread fraud and it is also plain that, already before October 1922, the Party had signed up more than 320,000 members, a tally never before attained in Italy. Yet a clear electoral tie between Mussolini and the people, or anyway a majority of them, still did not exist.

The situation was not the same in Germany. From 1930, Hitler, displaying great tactical skill and also relying on the capillary paramilitary organization of the 'brownshirts' of the SA, skilfully utilized the grave national economic situation (in the winter of 1932 six million Germans were unemployed) to his advantage. The Nazi Party was, with rising success, able to attract a protest vote and otherwise play on social travail, thereby attracting support from all sectors of society. Already in the poll called ahead of schedule in September 1930, the Nazis unexpectedly garnered 18.3 per cent of the vote and so won 107 seats in the Reichstag. They therefore suddenly became the second largest party grouping and thereafter could decisively influence the unfolding of Weimar politics. Subsequent elections only enhanced Nazi gains, given the continuing worsening of the country's social and economic situation and the evident stasis of the Weimar system.

Unquestionably the *Führer* was a crucial factor in the Nazis' electoral advances, as was further demonstrated in the presidential poll of April 1932 (according to the Weimar constitution, the president was directly elected by universal suffrage). Hitler stood against the existing president, the aged Marshal Paul von Hindenburg, the embodiment of conservative and reactionary Germany. During the campaigning, the Nazis used the slogan 'the *Führer* over Germany' and so were the first party to employ the technological appeal of aviation for political purposes. In the run-off vote Hitler lost but garnered more than thirteen million votes, 37 per cent of the electorate. By contrast with his elderly opponent, Hitler eagerly displayed a modern dynamism, reinforcing his image as the coming man.

In July 1932, there was yet another election. Now the NSDAP became the premier party in the nation, with 230 seats in the parliament and 37.4 per cent of the total poll. The Social Democrats, who had once held the lead position, were now reduced to 133 seats. The Nazis had won support both in the north of Germany and in the south, in rural and in urban areas, among the middle classes, but with quite a penetration of the working class as well. The Nazis had become the first genuine *Volkspartei* in German history. The only sectors of society where the Nazis had not progressed far were those bastions of Catholic Germany still in the hands of the confessional parties, the Centre and the Bavarian People's Party (BVP). The marginal losses suffered by the Nazis in a still further poll in November, one that underlined the overall instability of the system where President Hindenburg continued to nominate minority chancellors who had his approval, did little to alter the situation. Hitler's rise over the next weeks to the chancellorship relied on huge electoral support with a very wide social basis.

In regard to fascism's accession to power in Italy another factor separated it from the Nazi path. Institutionally speaking there were some similarities between the two cases: a constitutional monarchy with a crumbling parliamentary system on the one hand and a parliamentary and democratic republic with its own deepening crisis on the other. Yet, as was noted above, the institutional weakness of the Weimar state was so great and its lack of legitimacy so pervasive that it did not take a great effort on Hitler's part to shake himself free from its surviving toils. Profiting from the confusion provoked by the arson of the Reichstag in Berlin on the night of 27–8 February 1933, Hitler persuaded President Hindenburg to sign and parliament to sanction a list of emergency decrees, which emptied the Republic's institutions of meaning (even though the tension of the moment was not sufficient to give the Nazis an absolute majority in the elections held in March; rather their tally only reached 44 per cent). Despite that check, the new laws meant that legislative power had passed into the hands of the government, civil and political freedoms were suppressed, with the corollary that, soon after, all of the non-Nazi parties were dissolved, many of them at their own behest.

It is true that, after the March on Rome, Mussolini took advantage of a comparably dramatic event—the kidnapping and murder of the reformist socialist deputy Giacomo Matteotti—driving parliament, between 1925 and 1928, to approve a series of provisions labelled the *leggi fascistissime* (the thoroughly Fascist laws), thanks to which he was able to construct his own genuine dictatorship. Yet, these were laws approved by parliament and, more significantly, the fundamental constitutional structure that fascism confronted remained unchanged. King Victor Emmanuel III retained national sovereignty in the full sense of the term. For Hitler, the death of Hindenburg on 2 August 1934 was enough for him to sweep away the last vestiges of constitutional legality. The day before Hindenburg's demise, the government passed a law composed of a few short lines uniting the two positions of president and chancellor, and introducing what thereafter would become the canonical title of *Führer und Reichskanzler* (supreme leader and Chancellor of the Reich). This title implicitly sanctioned the complete elimination of the republican constitution, with the accent now on the novel charismatic power of the leader, on which all institutions would be based. A few days later, this massive affirmation of Hitler's powers was endorsed in a plebiscite, with 89.9 per cent voting in favour.

The *Duce* engaged in a series of attempts to weaken the monarch's power, on 9 December 1928 formally giving the Grand Council of Fascism the right to express a view about the succession and removing from the king the supreme command of the national armed forces at the moment of entry into a war. Yet Mussolini remained pinned down by the constitutional frame of the kingdom of Italy. In July 1943, facing an irreversible military crisis, Victor Emmanuel III finally had the courage to sack the *Duce* and to have him arrested, trusting Marshal Pietro Badoglio (despite his being a major contributor to the impending defeat in the war) with the task of somehow getting Italy out of the conflict.

Notwithstanding some similarities, most blatantly the tactical alliance with sectors of the old ruling elites, there was a profound difference in the acquisition of power between the two regimes. Hitler could always rely on an ample popular consent, hardened by the Nazis' promise of economic recovery and improved social conditions across the classes. In addition, the constitutional set-up in Germany offered less of a block to the new regime's control than did its equivalent in Italy.

I. THE REGIMES AND THEIR INSTITUTIONS

No less than fascism, Nazism was a movement that, during its rapid growth, had assembled a number of groups and grouplets, which, for all their hostility to the Republic, liberal democracy, and communism, nonetheless possessed a range of political visions and ideological concepts.[1] It was only thanks to the weight of his charisma, his oratorical skill and tactical ability to take risks successfully, and his resultant surpassing and removal of his possible challengers that Hitler was able to take full control over the Nazi movement. From 1930, after the Nazi electoral spurt of that time, Hitler became the uncontested *Führer* of the Party. The strength of his position was evidenced when, in the second half of 1932, the Chancellor, General Kurt von Schleicher, tried to win over Gregor Strasser, the head of the political office of the NSDAP and the most prominent figure on the so-called 'left wing' of the Party, with the aim being the formation of a coalition government with some Nazi support but without Hitler's presence. Whatever the temptation, Strasser did not dare to break his bonds with his charismatic chief. Little more than a year later, in the 'Night of the Long Knives', his *Führer* took revenge on this potential mutiny by having Strasser killed.

In other words, the power of Hitler was beyond discussion. Yet, historians have debated the effective authority of the *Führer* within the Nazi regime. Until the 1970s, analysts portrayed a government indeed dominated by the *Führer*, the dynamic force behind all actions which were anyway directed to making concrete Hitler's personal programme, one that had already been elaborated in detail from the early

---

[1] Fundamental still is the study by D. Orlow, *History of the Nazi Party*, 2 vols (Pittsburgh: University of Pittsburgh Press, 1969–73).

1920s.[2] This interpretation treated the *Führer* as a kind of feudal chief. The sovereign leader gave over slices of power to his feudatories who in turn were able to construct their own semi-autonomous zones of power where they, too, could invest sub-feudatories.

Subsequently, however, historians in the main switched the focus on 'Hitlerism' to the so-called polycentric or polycratic line. Following this interpretation, they depicted a *Führer* who held immense decision-making power in certain specific arenas but, in others, either unable or unwilling to impose himself, Hitler operated following the law of *divide et impera*.[3] In this fashion, Hitler was able to consolidate a complete hegemony making use of his skill at arbitrating the innumerable conflicts that ensued between his various henchmen. Some historians went so far as to argue that he was really only a *primus inter pares* in such battles and so was himself entangled in these struggles for power.

In the most recent and at present fundamental biography of Hitler,[4] Ian Kershaw has put forward a new interpretation that promises to end the conflict between 'functionalists' (those who privilege the internal disputation in Nazism, seeing Hitler as a 'weak dictator') and 'intentionalists' (those who believe that the leader decided all).[5] According to Kershaw, the political system that was created in Germany from the first months of 1933, characterized by a chaotic piling up of decision-making potential among the institutions of Party and state, was channelled into a process that can be defined as 'working towards the *Führer*'. Hitler's will, often expressed vaguely or enigmatically, was detected after his zealous followers were already moving into his stance. It was enough for particular policy lines to seem to possess the backing of the charismatic chief for actions to commence to achieve them. These currents in turn accentuated the frenzied Social Darwinism that was so prominent in the institutions of the Third Reich.[6]

The complexity and contradictions in the historiographical debate, added to the now enormous scale of available documentary evidence and of empirical monographs, makes finding a synthesis a vexing task. But there are some undeniable matters that deserve to be underlined. First, Hitler had no intention of clearly fixing the characteristics of the regime he had built. It was for this reason that he opposed an incessant activism to the efforts of his Minister of the Interior, Walther Frick, to design a coherent set of constitutional reforms. Apart from being utterly

---

[2] Typical is E. Jäckel, *Hitlers Herrschaft: Vollzug und Weltanschauung* (Stuttgart: DVA, 1986).

[3] See especially M. Broszat, *The Hitler State. The Foundation and Development of the Internal Structure of the Third Reich* (London: Longman, 1981).

[4] I. Kershaw, *Hitler*, i: *Hubris 1889–1937*, and ii: *Nemesis 1938–1945* (London: Penguin, 1998–2000).

[5] For important historiographical reflection, see G. Hirschfeld and L. Kettenacker (eds), *Der 'Führerstaat': Mythos und Realität. Studien zur Struktur und Politik des Dritten Reiches* (Stuttgart: Klett-Cotta, 1981).

[6] H. Mommsen, *Beamtentum im Dritten Reich* (Stuttgart: DVA, 1966) first portrayed Hitler as a 'weak' dictator. On the historiography, see M. Funke (ed.), *Starker oder schwacher Diktator? Hitlers Herrschaft über d. Deutschen* (Düsseldorf: Droste, 1989).

unimpressed by the importance of the institutional situation, Hitler maintained that such matters could be left for the future, while the present should concentrate on obtaining through war that European and world power which must be the presupposition of any constitutional revolution. One result was that, for Hitler, the actual government lacked significance. From February 1938, he no longer bothered to consult formally with his cabinet, and some ministers were blocked, often for years, from any direct access to the *Führer* through which they might put forward proposals or engage in the review of political issues.

Another certain fact is that Hitler totally lacked administrative experience and, yet, mistrusting experts and disliking calling on them, he preferred to surround himself with people whose cultural level was inferior to his own, a tactic that helped to conceal his dilettantism. Moreover, except for matters where he wished actively to involve himself, notably military strategy and architecture, he was contemptuous of any idea that he should master bureaucratic and administrative detail. These attitudes were in turn confirmed by his erratic work practices and by his emotionalism. For long periods, the *Führer* simply withdrew from the decision-making process, taking refuge in his beloved villa, the Berghof, in the Bavarian Alps. This approach to government sharply distinguished Hitler from his fellow dictators, Mussolini and Stalin, each of whom devoted much time to coping with the vast mass of documents that passed over their desks.

This idiosyncratic Hitlerian style of rule is known mainly indirectly, through the testimony of those in his leadership group. Such witnesses show, too, that, as the years passed, Hitler's habits became more capricious and unpredictable and his refusal to deal with difficult issues or confront unpleasant truths grew. Martin Bormann, initially the deputy of Rudolf Hess in the NSDAP, took over his role after that previously loyal follower of Hitler flew to Scotland in May 1941, perhaps with the aim of finding a peace with those elements in the British government who remained Germanophile. Bormann soon succeeded in winning Hitler over and both took charge of his personal finances and became the all but obligatory filter through which the *Führer* dealt with the external world.

Hitler's lifestyle was yet another matter to complicate bureaucratic process. Still fond of the bohemian habits that he had become accustomed to in Vienna, Hitler liked to be awake at night and slept till late, rarely getting to work before the morning was over. This rhythm meant much trouble for henchmen trying to coordinate the *Führer*'s line with official practice in Berlin.

Yet another oddity in Hitlerian rule was his attitude to the written word. This leader disliked written commitments, preferring to convey his decisions orally. This tendency made it all the more important for ambitious individuals to join the restricted group in his entourage who had the chance to act as 'transmitters' of the *Führer*'s will, as well as being able to choose those granted direct conversation with the dictator. This casual approach ensured that those few who won Hitler's faith had great influence, and they included Bormann and those leading Party chiefs and army generals who managed to talk to Hitler through Bormann.

Talking thereby assumed crucial significance. In his conversations, Hitler often took key decisions, ones that might well overthrow past orders and were prompted by some personal emotion or other chance matter. Given that the regime's structure allowed for great overlapping between Party and state, Hitler often proffered rival answers to specific issues, with his preference frequently being for the solution that he had heard last. On other occasions, Hitler refused to make an open choice, leaving the Nazi potentates to tire themselves in endless skirmishes.

The German dictatorship in this regard was very different from the Italian where Mussolini had an almost pathological desire to control bureaucratic procedure, incessantly annotating the government papers sent to him. It is not by chance that his personal secretariat is still today one of the principal archival sources of the fascist regime. Propaganda maintained that the light in his office in the Palazzo Venezia stayed on all night to prove that the *Duce* laboured unceasingly for his people. Nonetheless, it is true that Mussolini, mistrusting the quality of his henchmen, did place under his own authority a whole list of ministries. Most significantly, he held the Ministry of Internal Affairs uninterruptedly from 1926 until his sacking in July 1943.

Mussolini's centralizing designs accentuated another clear difference between *Duce* and *Führer*. Unlike Hitler, Mussolini was not given the chance to cement his charismatic power before winning office, an event that occurred when fascism was still largely in formation. Before the local strength of the *ras* or Party bosses, so typical of the squadrist phase of the movement, could be subjugated to the *Duce*, he was already his country's leader.[7] And, in the next years, Mussolini had to struggle to make them see reason. A plain demonstration of the matter is given in the fact that, in the aftermath of the March on Rome, more than 100,000 members, many squadrists 'of the first hour' (as they were called), were expelled from the ranks of the PNF. In Germany, except for the cases of Röhm and the rumbustious brownshirts of 1934, it was unimaginable that an extremist *ras* like Roberto Farinacci could exert the pressure he did on Mussolini during the Matteotti crisis[8] or that Italo Balbo could so threaten the dictator that he had to be 'exiled' to govern Libya. When, in 1945, confronted by evident defeat, the two most powerful underlings of Nazi government, Hermann Göring and Heinrich Himmler, dared to rebel against the supreme *Führer*, aiming at secret deals with the Western Powers, they were

---

[7] For investigations of the *ras*, see P. Corner, *Fascism in Ferrara 1915–1925* (Oxford: Oxford University Press, 1973); A. Cardoza, *Agrarian Elites and Italian Fascism: The Province of Bologna 1901–1926* (Princeton: Princeton University Press, 1982).

[8] A comparison of the paramilitary in the two regimes can be found in S. Reichardt, *Faschistische Kampfbünde: Gewalt und Gemeinschaft im italienischen Squadrismus und in der deutschen SA* (Cologne: Böhlau, 2002).

forced to retreat after Hitler, a few days before committing suicide, showed that he was angry with them.

Yet it is also true that a profound ideological difference separated the two regimes. In this regard, the NSDAP was deeply *volkisch*; at its heart stood the idea of the people (*Volk*) or race. This determination owed much to the *Weltanschauung* of Hitler but it also won ample backing in the German extreme right of the era. The quality of the people must be displayed in a naturally expansionist policy. For Hitler, war was an unarguable part of his vision of the world, created through the people's struggle to conquer or to defend their existing territory. The state was no more than an accessory. For fascism, whose ideological roots lay in pre-war nationalism (it has been estimated that, until 1925, one third of members of the PNF came through the Nationalist movement[9]) and whose key subsequent experience had been the First World War, the state was a crucial matter. Furthermore, the matrix of the high philosophy of fascism was the 'spiritualism' of philosopher Giovanni Gentile, who viewed the 'ethical state' as the culmination of human history. An expression like the totalitarian catchphrase 'all for the state, nothing against the state, no one outside the state' was inconceivable in the political discourse of National Socialism.[10]

In regard to foreign policy, which would turn out to be a fundamental matter in the fate of the two regimes, Hitler based his expansionist projects on the conquest of 'living space' for the Germanic people, destined to be brought back to the great Reich in every instance. In effect, this was a simple policy of destabilization embracing extreme violence and full-scale ethnic cleansing. Perhaps he did not really have a 'final' objective, beyond his vague aspiration to rule the continent. Although Mussolini's foreign policy was adventurist in its way, it did have a clear aim: to set Italy firmly in the ranks of the Great Powers and give it military and economic hegemony over a sphere of influence. For the Nazis, the *Volk* was central; for fascism, the state.

Yet there were quite a few similarities in the path whereby the two regimes sought to reinforce their taking of power in wider society. In both cases, the power of the *Duce* or *Führer* was represented in propaganda as absolute, and decision making was meant to occur vertically and in a hierarchical manner. It is true that, given the institutional situation, the legitimization of what was called the *Führerprinzip* reached levels of intricacy that were not paralleled in Italy. This principle, typical of any dictatorship, had been defined by Hitler in *Mein Kampf*:

Our movement is based on the absolute authority of the *Führer*, placing responsibility in his hands, whether in small matters or large. The practical consequences of this principle in the internal functioning of the movement are as follows: the chief of a local group is to be

---

[9] W. Schieder, *Der Strukturwandel der faschistischen Partei Italiens in der Phase der Herrschaftsstabilisierung*, in idem (ed.), *Faschismus als soziale Bewegung* (Hamburg: Hoffmann & Campe, 1976), 69.

[10] See M. Palla (ed.), *Lo Stato fascista* (Florence: La Nuova Italia, 2001).

installed by the leader of rank immediately above him. ... Only the *Führer* of the Party is to be elected and then through the approval of a mass assembly of members. He is the absolute leader of the movement. He both decides and at the same time bears on his shoulders all responsibility.

An example of the matter can be found in the writing of major German jurists in the aftermath of the 'Night of the Long Knives'. The decision of Hitler to have 200 people killed stimulated elaborate legal argumentation. Carl Schmitt wrote about the event:

Confronted by grave violations, the *Führer* preserves the right, when in the moment of danger, to use his supreme authority to be the highest judge. ... The real *Führer* is always simultaneously a judge. Whoever would try to separate these two qualities or to set one against the other, would reduce the judge to an anti-*Führer*. Truly the *Führer's* action was part of his natural jurisdiction, not proceeding through legal forms but in itself of supreme justice. ... The *Führer's* right of judgement springs from the legal fount of every people's law. ... Every law derives from the right of a people to exist.[11]

For his part, the constitutional lawyer Ernst Huber argued that that it was improper any more to speak of 'state power'; now there was only '*Führer's* power'.[12]

Such commentary confirmed that the right of Hitler to take decisions in the name of the German people was absolute and unconditional and that such decisions, if they infringed the law, simply became the law. Hitler held the power of life and death over every one of his compatriots in the name of an alleged identity between his acts and the general interest, and he could delegate similar powers to whomever he nominated. In Schmitt's piece, there is a plain reference to the state of emergency that can justify these juridical powers. In the final analysis, this exceptionality was created by the impossibility of moving from the republican constitution to a new one. At the same time, the precariousness in some sense of Nazism is here made plain; it could never move from its emergency situation to become 'normal'.

In the Italian case, it was harder for legal science to find formal arguments to defend the extraordinary constitutional powers of the *Duce*, who, technically speaking, was simply another head of government in accordance with the rules set out in the Albertine constitution. Only in retrospect, at Salò in 1944, ruling a 'Social Republic', did Mussolini get around to claiming that his ambiguous past relationship with the King had been a 'diarchy'.

Another parallel between the regimes can be found in their proliferation of centres of authority or of organisms that often, with considerable inefficiency, drifted into conflict with each other. 'Both regimes turned over administrative and

[11] C. Schmitt, *Der Führer schützt den Recht: Zur Reichstagsrede Adolf Hitlers vom 13. Juli 1934*, *Deutsche Juristen-Zeitung*, 39 (1934), 954.

[12] Quoted by D. Welch, *Hitler: Profile of a Dictator* (London: Routledge, 2001), 44.

even quasi-legislative powers to new agencies or to economic or political pressure groups.'[13]

Hitler's tendency to duplicate executive power between the agencies of Party and state expressed the fear, common among dictators, that the concentration of authority on an underling or centre will threaten their position. Thus, the delicate area of the police was controlled by the 'normal' state agencies, but considerably infiltrated by Nazis and by the special offices of the SS that, after the Night of the Long Knives, achieved a full autonomy from the SA. Economic policy was shared between the Ministry, headed from 1934 to 1937 by Hjalmar Schacht, a conservative technocrat, and the agencies of the so-called 'Four-Year Plan', founded in 1936 under Göring. In foreign policy, the Ministry was guided until February 1938 by the aristocratic conservative Konstantin von Neurath, and in its ranks career diplomats continued to predominate. Yet Party agencies, each aspiring to occupy a certain sector of international relations, multiplied. In 1934, from one of these emerged the dilettante figure of Joachim von Ribbentrop, who, having won over Hitler, became the *Führer*'s personal adviser on foreign affairs and, in 1938, replaced Neurath.

Similarly in the defence sector, there was an initial attempt to parallel the 'traditionalist' armed forces with the SA. But the risks in this regard were too great and, in the summer of 1934, Röhm's ambitions were brutally liquidated. Only during the war did Himmler's SS become powerful enough to infringe the armed monopoly of the Wehrmacht. It developed a military wing, the Waffen SS, which eventually counted tens of well-armed divisions and hundreds of thousands of soldiers, many volunteers who had enrolled to fight communism from France, Spain, Belgium, Croatia, Italy, and even Russia.

Mostly these alternative centres of authority arose after direct authorization from the *Führer*, thereafter growing and spreading on their own initiative, in accordance with the rules of all bureaucratic systems in the absence of a clear legislative base. It is also worth remembering that Hitler never felt secure enough utterly to sweep away the public service and the other old centres of power, preferring rather to give rein to Party agencies that rivalled the pre-existing authorities.

Furthermore Hitler knew that his movement lacked the technical and professional skills needed to run the state and especially to prepare it for war. It was therefore necessary to keep the state going. Therefore, the few countervailing initiatives, for example the law of 7 April 1933 reordering the bureaucracy, were only marginal in character and devoted to expelling Jews from state employment. The same situation is true of fascism, where Mussolini was even more doubtful about the ability of his followers. Significant evidence about the matter is given in the decree of 5 January 1927 which placed local Party bosses below the prefects who

---

[13] A. J. De Grand, *Fascist Italy and Nazi Germany: The Fascist Style of Rule* (London: Routledge, 1995), 31.

embodied the surviving structure of the Liberal state. In both the regimes there were attempts to forge a new technocracy, combining ideological zeal with professional skills. In Italy this effort had largely failed by the early 1930s despite the Party pressing into the technical realm. In Germany, however, the move did gain ground as was demonstrated in the involvement of technocrats in such delicate policy areas as the governance of occupied territories and the achievement of *Lebensraum*. In both countries, graduates from this technocratic training played an important role after 1945, notably for example in the areas of banking and finance.

In the fascist regime, too, there was a proliferation of centres of activity and power as a result of constant rivalry between the Party bosses. The example of the organizations devoted to the instruction and discipline of youth are proof enough. In 1926, the Opera Nazionale Balilla was created under the Ministry of Education. From 1930, it had a rival in the Fasci Giovanili di Combattimento, founded by Carlo Scorza with a more direct intention to construct a new ruling class for the Party. Yet the character of the two bodies was not really so different; rather the distinction between them was largely personal. The issue continued until 1937 when Mussolini felt obliged to dissolve both to be replaced by the Gioventù Italiana del Littorio, put directly under the aegis of the Party Secretary. As in Germany, where Party agencies like the Reichsnährstand[14] in agriculture and the Four-Year Plan in industry continued to extend their roles, so in Italy, above all in the 1930s, the complex, if at base erratic, apparatus of the corporate state proliferated. In both cases the economic aim was complete self-sufficiency or autarky required for the coming wars. Yet, in Italy, the economic institutions in practice retained major ties with the old state, whereas in Germany the arbitrariness of both Hitler and Göring ensured that they were autonomous.

Some similarities apart, in Italy the tendency was to penetrate the apparatus of the old state and so 'fascistize' it, whereas in Germany this happened little. Yet, paradoxically, the Third Reich could count on widespread support among the bureaucracy, armed forces, and legal fraternity, whether through a lukewarm ideological affiliation or from the more basilar sense of state and of duty. It was typical that, in 1944, the exponents of the military opposition struggled hard to establish the idea that the existing institutions could be overthrown and the dictator, who was head of state, could be killed. Hitler and his regime aimed to build a Party apparatus parallel to that of the state that was thereby formally not infringed. In Italy, by contrast, after years of blocking entry to the PNF for fear that it fall into the hands of opportunists and of demanding that membership be achieved only through service in the youth organizations, from 1932 Achille Starace, PNF Secretary for almost the whole decade, began a loud campaign to drive state officials into Party ranks. At the beginning of the war, the process was extended also to military officers. As a result

---

[14] G. Corni and H. Gies, *Brot—Butter—Kanonen: Ernährungspolitik in Hitlers Deutschland* (Berlin: Akademie Verlag, 1997).

the number of Party members, halted for years at around 800,000, suddenly leaped up to 2.6 million.[15]

II. REGIME AND SOCIETY

It has been established that the two regimes possessed very different ideological bases. This distinction should not be understood, as mostly it has been so far in the historiography, as springing from an ideologically driven Nazism by contrast with a fascism that lacked clarity in this arena, with a Hitler who had allegedly set out a *Weltanschauung* in the 1920s to which he thereafter clung and a Mussolini who was cynical and opportunist. Rather, emphasis should be placed on the fact that each party came from its time and was an assembly of groups and currents, some of them cultural, with many internal divisions. Of course, Nazism did possess clear planks, with racism at the forefront, and the Nazis had a leader who demanded ideological conformity more straightforwardly than did Mussolini in Italy. The Italian dictator was always a tactician, ready to use ideological currents of the most varied kind to reinforce his own power. In other words, it is true that National Socialist policies were the more driven by a strong set of beliefs, even if with rival facets. In Italy, by contrast, fascist ideas could be backed out of conformism or accepted at face value.

This conclusion does not deny that, within fascism, there were currents and groups with powerful ideological impulses, such as the subterranean racism that exploded into light in 1938 through the appalling discriminatory legislation against the Jews. We do now know that this legislative anti-Semitism had native causes, being forged notably in the crucible of the colonial experience during and after the Ethiopian war of 1935–6.

Another example can be given. Historiographically there has been major debate whether the two regimes were modernizing or not.[16] But the sharp distinction made by Renzo De Felice, with his claim that the Fascist dictatorship with its plan for new men and women was modernizing while the Hitlerian regime essentially looked to the past, is now unsustainable.[17] Rather, both regimes possessed modernizing aspects. Each enthused about technology and the machine, in regard to air power,

[15]   A. Aquarone, *L'organizzazione dello Stato totalitario* (Turin: Einaudi, 1965), 186.

[16]   The idea that the Nazi regime was so modernizing as almost to be revolutionary is no longer acceptable. See M. Prinz and R. Zitelmann (eds), *Nationalsozialismus und Modernisierung* (Darmstadt: Wissenschaftliche Buchgesellschaft, 1993). More balanced is J. Herf, *Reactionary Modernism: Technology, Culture and Politics in Weimar and the Third Reich* (Cambridge: Cambridge University Press, 1984).

[17]   R. De Felice, *Intervista sul fascismo*, ed. M. A. Ledeen (Bari: Laterza 1975), 54.

for example. But some differences are significant. In agrarian matters, fascism sought to achieve a detailed plan for *'bonifica integrale'* (the reclamation of the countryside) which embraced demographic, economic, social, and health matters, aiming both to improve the living conditions of rural workers and to modernize production (once again, with the intention of being better prepared for war). In the German case, this sector gives special evidence of ideological intrusion, with the Party apparatus focusing on racial matters. According to the theoretics of Blood and Soil, peasants were the special source of good blood needed to improve the national racial stock. As a result peasants should be protected, and there were those who suggested turning back the historical clock in order to ruralize the whole of German society.[18] In both countries, these schemes were heavily conditioned by propaganda, although they did undoubtedly bring advantages to at least part of the rural sector. In Germany measures to regulate the market and fix prices guaranteed a living return. In Italy the modernization trumpeted in the 'Battle for Grain' plainly did consolidate the most advanced elements of agriculture, if, at the same time, punishing the rest, who were the majority, and reinforcing their economic marginality.

In these circumstances, the modernization thrust of Nazism was racial,[19] while that of Italian Fascism was more broadly agrarian and social. The reason that both schemes were riven by insurmountable difficulties and contradictions is because they were attempted in social, economic, and strategic contexts that could not easily be melded with ideology. It was necessary to produce more and better in order to prepare for war. Yet, especially the Italian case ran up against a social status quo which early fascism had defended, for example in the big estates or *latifundia* of the south, which ought to have been the special target of any serious effort at agricultural modernization.[20]

Nonetheless it is symptomatic of the greater compulsion of Nazi ideology that, during the war, agricultural utopias of Blood and Soil resurfaced, on this occasion through the colonization of the occupied territories of the east. Such plans took for granted the repression and exploitation of the local populace, defined as racial inferiors. The grandiose schemes for expansion and settlement in the east can be read as a modern form of social engineering, containing at the same time pre-modern, perhaps even archaic, elements, with the hope of recreating an ideal peasant world.[21] This chance was never offered to Italian Fascism.

---

[18] See G. Corni, *Hitler and the Peasants: The Agrarian Policy in Nazi Germany* (Oxford: Berg, 1990).

[19] But for the connection between agrarian policy and technocracy, see S. Heim, *Kalorien, Kautschuk, Karrieren: Pflanzenzüchtung und landwirtschaftliche Forschung in Kaiser-Wilhelm-Instituten 1933 bis 1945* (Göttingen: Wallstein, 2003).

[20] There is still no serious study of fascist agrarian policy, but see A. Nützenadel, *Landwirtschaft, Staat und Autarkie: Agrarpolitik im faschistischen Italien (1922–1943)* (Tübingen: Niemeyer, 1997).

[21] See especially G. Aly and S. Heim, *Sozialpolitik und Judenvernichtung: Gibt es eine Ökonomie der Endlösung?* (Berlin: Rotbuch, 1987).

Yet, rather than going too far in presenting a sharp antithesis between the modern and the pre-modern in Germany and Italy, it is worth noting the complexity of social relations, context, and internal structure, where each of the regimes possessed multiple and contradictory aspects. Corporatism can provide a second example. Italian Fascism laid great emphasis on it, presenting it as the regime's 'brand name'. Yet the idea was not new and did entail resolving social conflict under the aegis of the state. In Germany, corporatism, drawing on its own local history, was largely ignored by the Nazi regime in practice. In Italy, a corporate state was formally realized in 1939 with the replacement of the old parliament by a Chamber of Fasces and Corporations. In reality, however, the achievement remained superficial, amounting to little more than the creation of yet another badly functioning bureaucracy, merely consolidating that surviving social structure to which the regime had always been subject. Neither the entrepreneurial class nor factory workers believed in their hearts that corporatism could modify their mutual relations. Despite the delusion of many Fascist intellectuals, corporatism was nonetheless more than a slogan. It had played quite a role in the regime where the debates about it attracted many intellectuals and, while it remained on paper, it could not be wholly ignored.[22]

Another major factor conditioning the ideological impact of the two regimes lay in the huge influence possessed by Catholicism in Italy. Catholic values, the ethical social and behavioural lines the church favoured, and Catholicism's ramified presence in Italian society were crucial matters for Italian Fascism. Mussolini's attempt to reach a compromise with the church in the Lateran Pacts of February 1929, with its ambition to allow the regime predominance in the delicate arena of the mobilization and education of the young, had modest results in practice. As became evident when the regime collapsed, a new ruling elite was primed and ready, and was faithful to the directives of the Vatican. In Germany, Catholicism had always been a minority cause and its influence was further undermined by Nazi pressure. There, by contrast, the Protestant churches were closely bound to the state. It is true that Hitler remained cautious in the religious sphere and held such supporters of neo-paganism as Alfred Rosenberg under tight rein. The dictator thought that the problem of contesting the profound religious attitudes of the populace should be left to a later time.

If the question of each regime's relationship with its intellectuals is considered there is no utterly sharp distinction visible between the two. It is true that fascism was rather more flexible and open in regard to the culture of its time, notably in its most modern elements ranging from Futurism (one of the few artistic currents in the country to be genuinely international and very influential in fascism's early days) to rationalist architecture, than were the Hitlerians. 'Fascism was no monolith, even in culture; it allowed the cohabitation of varied groups.'[23] The Nazi

---

[22] See the recent assessment of G. Santomassimo, *La terza via fascista: il mito del corporativismo* (Rome: Carocci, 2006).

[23] P. Dogliani, *L'Italia fascista 1922–1940* (Florence: Sansoni, 1999), 352.

regime, more aggressively censorious, sought to impose its ideological vision on the role that art or science can play with regard to the state and in assisting the consent being achieved in society. The Fascist regime did use censorship, while also fostering self-censorship by intellectuals in their own immediate interest. The press was rigidly controlled as well as other zones of artistic production. Yet, fascism was never characterized by that deep anti-intellectualism that led the Nazis to burn books and to ban a significant part of the cultural patrimony of the nation. Rather, in Italy, there prevailed what the historian Delio Cantimori (in his time a fascist and then a communist anti-fascist) called 'Nicodemism', that is, the dissimulation of an individual's real political convictions. From the point of view of the functioning of the two regimes, it is nonetheless important that the creation of a Ministry of Propaganda and Enlightenment under Joseph Goebbels in Germany encouraged an analogous institutional change in Italy with the founding of the Ministry of Popular Culture, whereas the more usual story was of the Nazis, who arrived at power a decade after the fascists had set much in concrete, imitating their Italian fellows.

Some basic social details confirm the different contexts facing the two regimes. In Italy in 1921, 54.8 per cent of the population lived in settlements with fewer than 10,000 inhabitants and the figure was still 49.8 per cent ten years later. In Germany at that time the urbanization rate was three times higher than in the peninsula: 35.7 per cent of the population vs. 13.2 per cent. In 1921, in Italy those employed in agriculture tallied almost ten million, more than twice those employed in industry. While, in the 1936 census, agricultural workers had declined to 8,504,000, they still were far more numerous than the five million who worked in the secondary sector. In Germany, the percentage of employed in the primary sector was 25.9 per cent in 1939. At around the same time, the percentage in Italy was still 47.4 per cent—what it had been in Germany forty years before. German society was heavily urbanized, with city populations that were significantly articulated, being possessed of patterns of consumption and other social expectations that, despite the blows inflicted by the depression, were among the highest in Europe. Italian society, by contrast, in very many regards preserved a pre-modern character and was especially backward in the south. In both cases, the pressure of ideology did little to jar these basic social and demographic patterns.[24] The failure of either regime in this field, despite considerable effort to change the birth rate, is proof enough. Another example can be given in the distribution of the population between city and countryside, where the parallel campaigns against urbanization, depicted as causing corruption and decadence, did little to turn around existing processes. Mussolini's order, published on 22 December 1928, to 'empty the cities' did nothing to arrest the drift from rural poverty to cities where a greater prosperity could be hoped for; in the same fashion,

[24] For Italy, see A. Treves, *Le migrazioni interne nell'Italia fascista* (Turin: Einaudi, 1976) and C. Ipsen, *Dictating Demography: The Problem of Population in Fascist Italy* (Cambridge: Cambridge University Press, 1996).

the Nazi campaign for 'ruralization' failed to confine young men and women to the fields when they were allured by the better working and life conditions of the cities.

Both regimes invested enormous intellectual and material resources to build a new society (even when, as in the German case, it retained archaic aspects), and sought profoundly to modify the culture, habits, and mentality of wide strata of society. The fundamental aim was thereby to build a firm and lasting consent for the dictatorships. To achieve this end, there was a massive employment of intellectuals, notably in such modern arenas as radio and film. But here, too, structural differences made an impact. Doubtless the Fascist regime was able in its exploitation of radio as a propaganda and nationalizing force. Yet, by the middle of the 1930s, those who possessed a radio only totalled half a million and they were largely confined to the centre and north of the country. In Germany, five million radios were distributed across the population.

At the same time, both regimes did not hesitate to use their apparatus of police repression, which had some similarities, even if the interventions were much heavier in the Nazi case. In Italy, between 1927 and 1943, the Special Tribunal undertook some 2,000 trials against 5,619 individuals. Of those 4,596 found guilty, the average jail term was about five years. Fewer than twenty received the death penalty.[25] In Germany concentration camps opened in the spring of 1933, at first for the short-term confinement of political opponents, real or alleged, including communists, Catholics, homosexuals, 'asocial' elements, Jehovah's Witnesses, and Gypsies. The police were able to act with ample scope without the law courts intervening. In 1933 alone, about 100,000 Germans passed through the camps. The network of camps was thereafter extended to house tens of thousands of citizens. With the war, the camps grew exponentially, even if the inmates were now generally either Jews or citizens of occupied nations. Those formally condemned to death through court decision, omitting the horrendous 'ordinary' tally of the camps, numbered some 16,650 to 1945, the great majority from the war years. Others fell victim to 'special' 'people's courts'. The limitless terror of Himmler's SS and other police had no serious parallels in the Italian dictatorship.

In conclusion, it should be asked whether the power of the regimes' apparatus lasted not merely because of superficial popular support but because the dictatorships had won the convinced backing and active participation of their populations. Historiography in this regard is uneven. For Germany, there are now a great number of local and regional studies that lay bare, insofar as it is possible for a dictatorship, the changing state of public opinion. In Italy, however, much of the discussion remains generalized or abstract, with the issue often seeming whether a commentator is for or against the work of De Felice, who was the first historian

---

[25] For the figures A. Dal Pont, A. Leonetti, P. Macello, and L. Zocchi, *Aula IV: tutti i processi del Tribunale Speciale fascista* (Rome: ANPPIA, 1961) and G. De Luna, *Donne in oggetto: l'antifascismo nella società italiana 1922–1939* (Turin: Bollati Boringhieri, 1995).

to raise the question of consensus to the regime. Yet, the evidence at hand in both cases illustrates that the people reacted in varied ways to the demands of the centre, and did so thinking of their special interests and within their special contexts. Nonetheless it does seem plausible to argue that the German dictatorship won a more lasting and firm adhesion to the regime and its aims, as was indicated both by a substantial lack of popular dissent and by the rallying of the populace around their *Führer* into the last weeks of the war. In the Italian case, rather, localism, corruption, and the traditional radical breach between state and society were overcome only in an ephemeral and superficial manner by Mussolini's government. In Italy, signs of crisis were apparent before the outbreak of the Second World War.[26] If a successful totalitarianism remains a model which real history can only approach, it is true that the German regime got closer to its dystopian ideal than did the Italian.

BIBLIOGRAPHY

AQUARONE, A., *L'organizzazione dello Stato totalitario* (Turin: Einaudi, 1965).

BROSZAT, M., *Der Staat Hitlers* (Munich: DTV, 1969).

CAPLAN, J., *Government without Administration: State and Civil Service in Weimar and Nazi Germany* (Oxford: Oxford University Press, 1988).

GENTILE, E., *Il culto del Littorio: la sacralizzazione della politica nell'Italia fascista* (Rome: Laterza, 1994).

—— *La via italiana al totalitarismo: il partito e lo stato nel regime fascista* (Rome: La Nuova Italia Scientifica, 1995).

HERF, J., *Reactionary Modernism: Technology, Culture and Politics in Weimar and the Third Reich* (Cambridge: Cambridge University Press, 1984).

HIRSCHFELD, G., and KETTENACKER, L. (eds), *Der 'Führerstaat': Mythos und Realität. Studien zur Struktur und Politik des Dritten Reiches* (Stuttgart: Klett-Cotta, 1981).

MOMMSEN, H., *Beamtentum im Dritten Reich* (Stuttgart: DVA, 1966).

PALLA, M. (ed.), *Lo Stato fascista* (Florence: La Nuova Italia, 2001).

SANTOMASSIMO, G., *La terza via fascista: il mito del corporativismo* (Rome: Carocci, 2006).

---

[26] Cf. R. J. B. Bosworth, *Mussolini's Italy: Life under the Dictatorship 1915–1945* (London: Allen Lane, 2005); P. Corner, 'Everyday Fascism in the 1930s: Centre and Periphery in the Decline of Mussolini's Dictatorship', *Contemporary European History*, 15 (2006), 195–222.

CHAPTER 16

....

RACE

....

ROBERT S. C. GORDON

I. INTRODUCTION

....

IN comparative accounts of Fascist Italy and Nazi Germany, the question of race, both in terms of ideology and of practical politics, has often been adduced as a crucial point of distinction.[1] Whereas Hitler's Germany (1933–45) was centrally structured around a racial or racist ideology—predominantly, a form of 'Aryan' anti-Semitism—Mussolini and the Italy of the *ventennio* (1922–43, and on, in different guise, until 1945) were only marginally and latterly interested in questions of race, and then only for contingent or tactical reasons to do with Italy's political alignment with Nazi Germany. If the former was a 'racial state',[2] the latter—even as it pursued, at times, an aggressive politics of race—was not.

The consequences of this long-held view have been profound and multiple. Three immediately come to mind. First, it has had an impact on general accounts of political, diplomatic, and ideological relations between Nazi Germany and Fascist Italy, pushing a picture of passive subordination of the latter to the former in a way that has tended to weaken any sense of Italian guilt or responsibility for 'Axis' crimes. A similar pattern of attenuation of local responsibility in the shadow of overwhelming Nazi guilt has characterized histories and memories of other Axis

---

[1] See e.g. A. Lyttelton on 'the autonomy and centrality of Nazi anti-Semitism, for which we can find no equivalent in Italian Fascism' (although Lyttelton goes on to talk of 'powerful similarities' in methods, organization, and structures of power), in R. Bessel (ed.), *Fascist Italy and Nazi Germany: Comparisons and Contrasts* (Cambridge: Cambridge University Press, 1996), 12.

[2] Cf. M. Burleigh and W. Wippermann, *The Racial State: Germany 1933–1945* (Cambridge: Cambridge University Press, 1991).

or occupied 'fascist' regimes, such as Ante Pavelic's Croatia or Miklós Horthy's Hungary, occluding many of the complexities of European history of the period. In a related vein, the traditional line has also led to a relative neglect of other forms of virulent racism overshadowed by the overwhelming anti-Semitism of Nazi Germany, but widespread in Italy and elsewhere in Europe and its dominions, of colonial, religious, and ethnic natures. Furthermore, the one-dimensional contrast of a racist Germany to a non-racist Italy has encouraged one-dimensional kinds of historiography. For example, it has promoted agency-led explanations, in which Hitler's personal anti-Semitic obsessions, as opposed to Mussolini's blander and more inconsistent instincts, are taken to explain the actions of two entire regimes and nations. Or it has fostered use of such dubious explanatory categories as national character or collective morality, with Italians labelled as essentially decent folk, sceptical of dogma and immune to racism ('*italiani brava gente*'), and Germans as rigidly programmed to obey the state and deeply engrained with anti-Semitism ('Hitler's willing executioners').[3] These historical perspectives have tended to block out more nuanced and attentive analyses of the state structures and populations of Italy and Germany, their motivations, and levels of active or passive assent, or indeed resistance, to state racism.

Finally, the contrast has had implications for larger questions concerning the nature of twentieth-century totalitarianism (whether fascist or communist), and the existence or otherwise of a single phenomenon—to be seen variously in Italy, Germany, Croatia, and Hungary, but also Japan, Spain, swathes of Latin America, Africa, and the Middle East, down to Saddam Hussein's Iraq and numerous extremist parties in present-day Europe—known as 'fascism'. Theorists of generic fascism are dealt a serious (although not fatal) blow whenever they acknowledge the deep fracture—at the level of race—between the first and, in many ways, model fascist regime, and its most violent and cataclysmically consequential epigone.[4] Certainly, the most influential, although also the most controversial, historian of Fascist Italy, Renzo De Felice, argued that comparisons between Fascist Italy and Nazi Germany which subsumed the two under the single heading of fascism (or 'Nazi-fascism') were invalidated by the core divergences on matters of race.[5]

The historiographical picture has, however, changed dramatically in recent years, especially in the light of the epochal changes around the end of the Cold War. Starting in 1986 in Germany, the *Historikerstreit* (historians' dispute) saw attempts by some historians to relativize Nazi crimes, including genocide, by comparing

---

[3] D. Goldhagen, *Hitler's Willing Executioners: Ordinary Germans and the Holocaust* (New York: Knopf, 1996); D. Bidussa, *Il mito del bravo italiano* (Milan: Il Saggiatore, 1994); A. Del Boca, *Italiani, brava gente?* (Milan: Mondadori, 2006).

[4] On generic fascism, see e.g. R. Griffin, *The Nature of Fascism* (London: Routledge, 1993).

[5] For a summary view, see R. De Felice, 'Foreword', in N. Caracciolo, *Uncertain Refuge: Italy and the Jews during the Holocaust* (Urbana: University of Illinois Press, 1986), pp. xv–xxiii.

them to (prior) Soviet oppression.[6] This form of 'revisionism' was heavily challenged, but others were to follow. The academic and public profile of the Holocaust became ever more prominent and universal in the late twentieth century, replacing the ideological certainties of capitalism and communism with the moral certainty of the 'absolute evil' of the Final Solution. Thereby the Holocaust became less 'German' and more of a European legacy and problem. In Germany itself, more attention has been paid to the parallel persecutions by the Nazis of other races, categories, and communities alongside the Jews; whereas other countries, including Italy, have begun to probe their own role in the Holocaust. In Italy, as the Cold War shape of the national political scene was dramatically punctured in the early 1990s, and categories of 'fascism' and 'anti-fascism' became more unstable than ever, so a positive historical revisionism emerged that paid much closer and more subtle attention to the specific working of race under Fascism. The body of work that resulted has dispelled, or at least qualified, myths of Italian immunity to racism, as well as many assumptions about the subordination of fascist racism to the Nazi racial obsession. One widely read historian, Alexander De Grand, author of a 1995 work of synthesis comparing the two regimes, openly adjusted his views for the second, 2004, edition:

Both Hitler and Mussolini aimed at re-educating their respective societies according to an entirely new set of values that would be a repudiation of the humanitarian and rationalist tradition of the Enlightenment in both its liberal and socialist form. Nowhere is this rupture more apparent than on the issues of creating a new community and racial policy. Since completing the first edition [of this book], I have come to believe that the divergence between Fascism and Nazism on racial policy is not as great as I believed. Both regimes used race partly as an instrument in the realization of a totalitarian state. If this is true, then Italian Fascist racial policies during the late 1930s were not an aberration or an attempt to align Italy with Nazi Germany, but a logical extension of the essential nature of the regime.[7]

De Grand not only recuperates the ideological substance of racial policy under fascism and thereby rejects its exclusively 'Germanic' origins; he also, as a result, talks more widely about the whole fascist project as one of utopian anthropological change, with race at its heart.

This chapter compares Fascist Italy and Nazi Germany on questions of race in the light of such new insights and emphases, offering a snapshot of current thinking about the role of race in the ideology, historical reality, and 'essential nature' of fascism. It looks at the two regimes in parallel, in a sequence moving from origins, to legislation and action once in power, to the extremes of racial violence both reached in their final years.

---

[6] See C. S. Maier, *The Unmasterable Past: History, Holocaust and German National Identity* (Cambridge, MA: Harvard University Press, 1988).

[7] A. De Grand, *Fascist Italy and Nazi Germany* (2nd edn, New York: Routledge, 2004), 2–3.

II. Origins

Whatever the similarities and differences between fascist and Nazi racisms between the 1920s and the 1940s, it is clear that they shared a broad origin in varied discourses on race, and on the Jews in particular, permeating the culture of nineteenth-century and early twentieth-century Europe. Four strands of racist thinking of the period are worth noting. First, there was the millennial tradition of Christian anti-Semitism, centred on the charge of 'deicide'—that the Jews were responsible for the crucifixion of Christ—and on other, long-standing anti-Semitic myths (of child sacrifice and host desecration, for example) and stereotypes (of miserliness, usury, and divided loyalties, for example). Christian anti-Semitism remained a constant substratum underlying attitudes towards the Jews throughout all the changes modernity was to bring, including totalitarian fascism. This was perhaps especially and inevitably the case in Italy, as Wiley Feinstein has argued, given the rooting of its culture in Catholicism and in the power and presence of Rome at its centre.[8] Elsewhere, the anti-Semitic pogroms in nineteenth-century tsarist Russia were in part stirred up by Orthodox Christianity, although also a product of cultural and political scapegoating.

Secondly, the very processes of emancipation and assimilation of the Jews which took place in post-Napoleonic Europe brought with them anxieties about the presence of an alien, Judaic culture within 'host' cultures.[9] Even the enlightened, liberal emancipators of the nineteenth century tended to assume that 'tolerance' of the Jews would pave the way for the disappearance of Jewish rite and culture, merging into the dominant culture, rather than for the coexistence of distinct ethnic or religious identities. Instead, the flourishing successes of many Jewish communities, in France, Germany, and elsewhere, fed both day-to-day anti-Semitism, evident in the Dreyfus Affair in France; and vast conspiracy theories about Jewish control, epitomized in the fake *Protocols of the Elders of Zion* (circulating after 1905). The latter tendency was exacerbated massively by the Bolshevik Revolution of 1917 in Russia, widely perceived as a predominantly 'Jewish' movement. Tellingly, the *Protocols* were first translated into Italian in 1921 by ex-priest and soon-to-be leading fascist anti-Semite Giovanni Preziosi, together with another priest.

Thirdly, the subjugation and administration of vast colonial territories and their populations by European imperial powers were accompanied by racial, even genocidal violence, as well as by elaborate regulations for the social control of indigenous, 'inferior' races. Comparable patterns of colonial race administration

---

[8] W. Feinstein, *The Civilization of the Holocaust in Italy: Poets, Artists, Saints, Anti-Semites* (London: Associated University Presses, 2003). See also D. Kertzer, *Unholy War: The Vatican's Role in the Rise of Modern Anti-Semitism* (London: Macmillan, 2002).

[9] See B. Cheyette and N. Valman (eds), *The Image of the Jew in European Liberal Culture, 1789–1914* (London: Vallentine Mitchell, 2004).

are evident in Italy's role in Libya and Eritrea before and during the fascist era and, in more concerted form, with the establishment of Fascist Italy's African empire following the conquest of Ethiopia in 1936.[10]

Fourthly, and perhaps most importantly for determining the specific nature of fascist notions of race, the nineteenth century saw the rise of a spate of sciences (or pseudo-sciences) and philosophies with distinctive racial dimensions. These fed both into the public administration of nation states and empires, and into the wider culture. They included: the 'eugenics' or Darwinist social engineering of Francis Galton (Darwin's cousin), which became a popular cause, predominantly in leftist, positivist circles across Europe and America; the 'criminal anthropology' of Cesare Lombroso, which identified and classified the physiognomy of deviant or inferior types (criminals, Jews, blacks); the medicine of 'racial hygiene'; the philology of Indo-European languages, Orientalism, and studies in the archaeology and anthropology of non-European cultures, which fed the formation and consolidation of the influential categories of 'Aryan' and other races of origin from which contemporary races and cultures supposedly derived. In philosophical terms, a rhetoric of nation, race, blood, and earth had circulated in German Romantic nationalism from the late eighteenth century; and the elaborations of Wagner on German folk myths and Nietzsche on 'master' and 'slave' moralities and the *Übermensch* (although Nietzsche did not racialize or biologize this concept) were deeply persuasive. Many of these strands were drawn together in work by relatively minor, but retrospectively crucial racist thinkers, such as Joseph-Arthur Gobineau's *Essay on the Inequality of the Human Races* (Paris, 1853–5) and Houston Stewart Chamberlain's *Foundation of the Nineteenth Century* (Munich, 1899).

As Zeev Sternhell has shown,[11] fascist ideology was forged in the crucible of intensely eclectic cultural movements and political philosophies abroad in *fin de siècle* Europe and, although Sternhell did not see racism as a necessary condition of Fascist ideology, these threads of racist thinking and culture were undoubtedly an integral part of this alchemy.

III. RACE AND THE FORMATION
OF MUSSOLINI AND HITLER

Giorgio Fabre has recently argued that the young Mussolini, from his pre-fascist, socialist revolutionary days, was profoundly shaped by the cultures of anti-Semitism

---

[10] See J. Andall and D. Duncan (eds), *Italian Colonialism: Legacy and Memory* (Oxford: Peter Lang, 2005); R. Ben-Ghiat and M. Fuller (eds), *Italian Colonialism* (New York: Palgrave, 2005).

[11] Z. Sternhell, *The Birth of Fascist Ideology* (Princeton: Princeton University Press, 1994).

of his day, especially through his reading of Nietzsche, Sorel, and others.[12] His essays from the period before 1919 are certainly peppered with anti-Semitic asides and gibes, on 'pallid Jews', 'hooked noses', 'the degeneration of the race' caused by 'orientals' or by 'Shylok' [sic].[13] In one 1919 article, he rehashed a series of anti-Semitic (and, incidentally, anti-Christian) tropes:

The great Jewish bankers of London and New York, linked by bonds of race with the Jews of Moscow and of Budapest, are taking their revenge against the Aryan race.... Like does not betray like [razza non tradisce razza]. Christ betrayed Judaism, but, as Nietzsche observed in a wonderfully prophetic passage, only in order to serve Judaism further by overturning the traditional values of Graeco-Roman civilization.[14]

In power after 1922, pragmatic politics would constrain the *Duce* and lead him to distinctly different public positions, at times seeming to support the Jews and even Zionism. Certain Jews would play a significant role in his movement, in his personal life (for example, his mistress Margherita Sarfatti), and in state institutions from an early stage. But the 'racist' assumptions that re-emerged in the 1930s can be seen as latent, if Fabre is correct, from Mussolini's formation.

In Hitler's case, his immersion in the anti-Semitic currents of European thought is more fully established and self-evidently of a piece with his later career. From an early stage, Hitler displayed a pathological obsession with and hatred for the Jews. This pathology found powerful reinforcement and intellectual respectability in the racist sciences and cultures of his day: he drew on Chamberlain, but also on American racist legislation; on anthropological or 'biological' accounts of race; and on currents of eugenics and racial hygiene. He elaborated myths of Jewish control of both world capitalism and Bolshevik communism, of Jews' responsibility for Germany's defeat in 1918 and for the contamination and degeneration of the German race. As elaborated in *Mein Kampf* (1925–6), the notion of a hierarchy of races was narrowed to a blunt opposition: the German-Aryan Master Race (*Herrenvolk*)—creators of culture and civilization, leading the weaker imitator cultures— versus the subhuman, contemptible destroyers of civilization, the Jews.

The psychopathology of Hitler's anti-Semitism has been a source of appalled fascination for many, but it is also a diversion if we seek to contextualize the racial element of the fascist phenomenon. Parallels in the racist intellectual formations of Mussolini and Hitler suggest, more than any eccentric fanaticism, rather the lazily extreme anti-Semitic assumptions which were by no means uncommon in the wider culture of the day. Such assumptions intersected with ease with the exacerbated nationalist politics that were increasingly prevalent before, during, and

---

[12] G. Fabre, *Mussolini razzista* (Milan: Garzanti, 2005); in part in 'Mussolini and the Jews on the Eve of the March on Rome', in J. D. Zimmerman (ed.), *Jews in Italy under Fascist and Nazi Rule, 1922–1945* (Cambridge: Cambridge University Press, 2005), 55–68.

[13] Quoted in Fabre, 'Mussolini and the Jews', 57.

[14] Quoted in M. Sarfatti, *La Shoah in Italia* (Turin: Einaudi, 2005), 73.

after (both cause and effect of) the Great War. It is also worth noting that, in both Hitler and Mussolini, rank prejudice was interwoven with apparently modern, progressive notions of demographics, social engineering, and progress, aimed at the improvement of the national stock or race. Racial persecution and soft and hard forms of demographic control would proceed more often than not hand in hand in fascist states, in their utopian quests to forge a new nation and a 'new man'.

IV. FASCISM IN POWER, 1922–1932

Mussolini's Fascist Party came to power in October 1922, just three years after its foundation as a movement and one year after its transformation into a political party. Within this short time-span, its political ideology had altered radically from a militant, anti-establishment position to a more conservative, authoritarian one; and its nature as a governing force would change sharply again in 1925–6, as Mussolini began to establish a fully-fledged Fascist dictatorship. In keeping with this shifting and inconsistent initial phase, early fascist engagement with issues of race was sporadic or indirect and would remain so until the mid-1930s. Nonetheless groundwork for a racial politics was laid in the 1920s and early 1930s. The Fascist state came to an accommodation with the Catholic Church, culminating in the Lateran Pacts of 1929, which, among other things, officially relegated other religions to a secondary position in Italian schools and in wider society. Mussolini was pro-Zionist in his foreign policy, recognizing some of fascism's own radical nationalism in the Zionist movement and seeing it as a challenge to British imperial influence; but he was deeply suspicious of Zionist allegiances within Italy. Like many other sectors of civil society, the Italian Jewish organization, the 'Union of Italian Jewish Communities', was centralized and 'fascistized' in 1930. Mussolini declared himself a friend to the Jews, telling Emil Ludwig in a famous 1932 interview that 'anti-Semitism does not exist in Italy'; but, as Michele Sarfatti has pointed out, this indulgence was invariably accompanied by a sort of unspoken condition, that the Jews keep out of trouble. As Mussolini wrote in 1920: 'let us hope the Jews of Italy continue to show sufficient intelligence not to provoke any anti-Semitism in the one country where there has never been any'.[15] In fact, throughout this period there were sporadic episodes of anti-Semitic violence carried out by the more extreme fringes of the Fascist movement.

Other forms of racism or racially inflected policies were at work in this early period. African colonial possessions in Libya and Eritrea, inherited from the pre-fascist era, continued to be administered along lines of division and regulation,

---

[15]   Quoted in M. Sarfatti, *La Shoah in Italia* (Turin: Einaudi, 2005), 74.

rooted in assumptions of European 'biological' racial superiority shared by other European colonial administrations. Anxieties over racial mixing between colonizers and colonized, which would be a driving force behind the acceleration of racial policy in Ethiopia in 1935–6, were already prevalent. The need to regulate mixed-race relationships, mostly between Italian colonizers and local concubines—the so-called *madamato*—underlines that these were a relatively common reality.

Control and regulation of national identity were also asserted in the political and cultural borderlands of mainland Italy. This amounted to a form of 'racial' politics, in the cause of the unification, purification, and strengthening of the nation and the forging of an anthropologically 'new fascist man'.[16] Indeed, in the rhetoric of this period, there is frequent semantic slippage between the terms 'nation' (*nazione*), 'stock' (*stirpe*), and 'race' (*razza*). Hence, in the anti-Slav campaigns in the north-eastern territories of Venezia Giulia, bordering on Yugoslavia, and anti-Germanic campaigns in Alto Adige, minorities were forcibly Italianized and discriminated against. Campaigns were launched to 'purify' the Italian language and place names from dialect and foreign infiltration. As early as 1925, official recognition of second languages (German in Bolzano province; French in Aosta; Slovene in Venezia Giulia) was rescinded. Finally, if more ambiguously, fascism's disingenuous but not wholly unsuccessful claim to have 'solved' the historic 'southern question'—the economic, social, and cultural divide between the south and the rest of the nation— through public works and aggressive assaults on the Mafia was also, in its way, part of its unitary discourse of nationhood/race. It was certainly fed, intellectually, by assertions of a Mediterranean racial-cultural identity, through which Italy had become the seedbed of European civilization.

Discourse on race in the early period of the regime was perhaps at its most pronounced, however, in the field of demographics and eugenics. In his Ascension Day speech of May 1927, Mussolini prepared for a major campaign to bolster the 'health of the race' ('*salute della razza*'). The campaign entailed not so much the 'positive' eugenics which would characterize Nazi campaigns to sterilize or elimi-nate 'unhealthy' sectors of the population, as a 'negative' eugenics (also practised by the Nazis), which aimed to improve external factors such as diet, sanitation, the well-being of mothers and babies, through state incentives and regulations. For all that this was a policy of regimented social control, ultimately aimed at bolstering the military and economic efficiency of the nation, it contained clear elements of genuine social reform. Yet, retrospectively, the lines leading from this demographic 'race' campaign to later, more sinister and aggressive racial persecution are several: the very phrase, 'the defence of the race' ('*difesa della razza*'), later adopted by the most virulent of fascist racists in the propaganda magazine of that name (1938–43, edited by Telesio Interlandi), became common currency in fascist discourse at this

[16] E. Gentile, 'The Fascist Anthropological Revolution', in G. Bonsaver and R. S. C. Gordon (eds), *Culture, Censorship and the State in 20th-Century Italy* (Oxford: Legenda, 2005), 22–33.

time; and medic Nicola Pende, one of the key signatories to the 1938 'Manifesto of Racist Scientists'—the document which launched the open persecution of Jews in Italy—was a major influence on the campaign for the 'health of the race'.

V. NAZIS IN POWER, 1933–1940

The Nazis, unlike the fascists, were keen and aggressive legislators on race from their earliest days in power, especially against the country's half-million Jews. Thousands of laws, decrees, and regulations were enacted, starting with the so-called 'Aryan clauses' in the restructuring of the public administration in April 1933, banning all non-Aryan public employees. A boycott of Jewish business was staged on 1 April 1933, although with mixed results. The first concentration camp, for political opponents, but from the start including many Jews, opened at Dachau in March 1933, initiating a network that, by the 1940s and the enactment of the Final Solution, would number in the thousands, including several extermination camps. Jews were forbidden entry to various public places, often on local initiative and well before official state decrees established the practice in law. The so-called Nuremberg Laws, passed on 15 September 1935, excluded Jews from public life, from civil society, and from any position of equality or democratic or human rights. Jews were no longer to be German citizens but subordinate subjects. Intermarriage or sexual relations of any kind between Jews and Aryan Germans was forbidden, as was the employment of Aryans by Jews. Exceptions to earlier rules on Jews practising as state-employed doctors, professors, lawyers, and notaries were cancelled.

The criteria for defining a Jew in law were the cause of intense internal debate within the regime (as also later in Italy). On Hitler's decision, those with three or more Jewish grandparents were defined as Jews; those with one were mixed-race (*Mischlinge*), as were those with two unless they were observant or married to a Jew. Subsequently, 'Jews' were gradually excluded from almost all forms of employment, professional or commercial, from the media, the army, schools and universities, from many public spaces, and from their own property. By the early 1940s, controls were obsessive in their detail, both appalling and absurd: Jews were forced to wear yellow stars, to have a 'J' stamped on their documents, to change their names to Sara or Israel; they were forbidden to own radios, go to the cinema, use public transport, even be out after dark.[17]

The developing legislative programme was accompanied by a mass of anti-Semitic propaganda and rhetoric (such as in Julius Streicher's notorious organ *Der Stürmer*), and by waves of assaults by Nazis, especially the SA brownshirts.

---

[17] De Grand, *Fascist Italy and Nazi Germany*, 69–70.

The street violence, although in part the product of the unruly fringes of the Nazi Party in the early months of the regime and a cause of concern for some in the government, in reality worked tactically to prepare the ground for apparently more controlled and rationalizing legislation. Violence would reach a new peak of intensity with the deaths, the arrests, and the devastation of thousands of Jewish properties on *Kristallnacht*, 9–10 November 1938. All economic activity of any kind by Jews was banned the following day.

The year 1938 also saw the *Anschluss*, the annexation of Austria, which brought with it stringent anti-Semitic legislation and even more extreme violence against the Austrian Jews, as well as the establishment of a forced emigration programme in Vienna, run by Adolf Eichmann. From *Mein Kampf* onwards, even more radical 'solutions' to the 'Jewish question' than the economic, social, and political exclusion seen during the 1930s, including mass emigration but also mass elimination, had been vividly present possibilities to Hitler and to the Nazi hierarchy. As war loomed, in January 1939 Hitler told the Reichstag that, should conflict break out, 'the result would be not the Bolshevization of the Earth and therefore the victory of the Jews, but rather the annihilation of the Jewish people in Europe'.

Alongside the establishment of the anti-Semitic racial state in Nazi Germany after 1933, other racial or related questions, and other radical solutions to them, were also in evidence. Racial discrimination or brute violence in the early phrase of Nazi power was often accompanied and justified by 'eugenic' or 'softer' demographic programmes aimed at forging an improved or 'purified' German race. Thus, for example, mothers were encouraged to reproduce prolifically, so long as they were certified as healthy and Aryan; whereas over 300,000 of them, judged as mentally or physically defective, were programmed for sterilization. Criminals and homosexuals were similarly treated as deviant.[18]

Racial and social persecution ran alongside and often overlapped with other forms of persecution. Born as it had been of a violent struggle with communist forces, the Nazi regime began by imprisoning its political opponents. The majority of the first inmates of Dachau and the other new concentration camps were socialists and communists. Even here, however, a dimension of prejudice was often apparent, for example in the persecution of Christian opponents and Jehovah's Witnesses, quite apart from the common association of communists with Jews.

More directly racial impulses were apparent in the treatment of other cultures and nationalities. Hitler's hierarchy of race placed the Slavic peoples to the east, like the Semitic peoples, as firmly 'inferior'. Slavic territory was the natural target for the expansion of German-Aryan living space (*Lebensraum*) and, military strategy aside, the devastating campaigns against Poland from 1939, and Soviet Russia from 1941, and the murderous violence visited on their (and other eastern) populations,

---

[18] Ibid. 63–74.

always had a distinctly racial, perhaps even genocidal thrust to them. From early on, also, Roma and Sinti communities and rights were targeted for similar reasons.

In terms of connections to the Final Solution and to the particular, horrific *modus operandi* of the extermination camps, the most significant precedent of all was the so-called 'T4' Euthanasia Programme: 70,000 disabled people between 1939 and 1941 (and as many as 200,000 until the end of the war) were murdered by carbon monoxide gas poisoning. Both T4's method and its personnel (including figures such as Franz Stangl) would be instrumental in setting up camps such as Treblinka and Sobibor.

VI. The 'Radicalization' of Race in Fascist Italy, 1933–1943

Robert Paxton has used the term 'radicalization' to describe phases in which fascist regimes, driven towards 'permanent revolution', towards extreme versions of themselves, periodically throw off the compromises of political reality and thrust themselves towards their ultimate (or founding) radical goals.[19] For Paxton, Mussolini and Fascist Italy went through several cycles of radicalization, as was inevitable in a regime lasting for two decades and more. The rush towards a racial reconfiguration of the nation in the mid-1930s marked the start of one such cycle.

In 1938, just as the Nazi state was annexing Austria, and accelerating and qualitatively shifting the ground of its anti-Semitic campaigns, two years after the establishment of the Rome–Berlin Axis (October 1936), and weeks after Hitler's much trumpeted visit to Rome in May 1938, Mussolini unleashed a ferocious anti-Semitic campaign in Italy. July saw the appearance of the 'Manifesto of Racist Scientists' (original title 'Fascism and the Problems of Race'), which enunciated a series of blunt and highly dubious principles, including:

4. *The current population of Italy is Aryan in origin and civilization…*
6. *There is today a pure 'Italian race'…*
7. *It is time for Italians to declare themselves openly racist…*
9. *Jews do not belong to the Italian race.* (italics in the original)

In August, Interlandi's magazine *La difesa della razza* was launched, the 'Demography and Race Office' was founded (led by Guido Landra), and a census of Italy's Jews initiated. These measures were followed in September by the first in a sequence of laws and decrees—known collectively as the Racial Laws—that swiftly reduced the status and rights of Italian Jews in ways comparable to German legislation.

---

[19] R. O. Paxton, *The Anatomy of Fascism* (London: Allen Lane, 2004), 148–71.

As in Germany, once begun, new regulations and laws would accumulate until the fall of the Fascist government in July 1943 (and would be taken up again and extended in the period of the 'Salò Republic' of 1943–5). As in Germany, certain exemptions, such as military service in the Great War or Fascist Party allegiance of long standing, were allowed in the first instance. The laws did not formally remove the status of citizenship from Italian Jews, but they were de facto excluded from the nation, banned from the army, state employment, the Fascist Party, from owning large businesses or land holdings, employing non-Jewish servants, from mixed marriages, even from state schools (a step not fully enforced in Germany until later that year). As in Germany, the impact on intellectual life, in the exclusion and exile of academics, scientists, and writers, was heavy.

The assumption within Italy at the time, as well as for most later historians, was that these orchestrated measures were taken in the service of Italo-German relations.[20] Before 1938, Fascist Italy was not or only very marginally interested in anti-Semitism and race more generally; after 1938, it fell into line with its now dominant northern ally. However, recent research has changed the parameters somewhat, pointing to the contemporary turn to anti-Semitism elsewhere in Europe, for example in Poland or Romania; or to a complex, Italian-specific, and significantly longer-standing racist project. Evidence of an Italian form of racism is clear in Mussolini himself, in other sectors of the Fascist state and Party, and within various academic intellectual circles who had inherited elements of nineteenth-century racial thinking, and were now interacting with the Fascist hierarchy at various levels.

As regards Mussolini himself, if he was dismissive at times of Hitler's obsession with the Jews, he also, in his own way, remained constantly alert to racial questions. Fabre has used the strange story of the Italian translation of Mein Kampf in 1934—surreptitiously paid for by the Fascist state on Mussolini's direct instructions—to show that, as early as 1933, Mussolini was picking up on his racist reading again (Oswald Spengler and others) and beginning a process of purging of Jews from his private and ministerial circles, financial institutions, newspapers, local government offices, and unions.[21] More broadly, the Fascist state entered a phase of concerted renewal and change—or accelerated 'fascistization'—around the tenth anniversary of the March on Rome (1932) and the appointment of Achille Starace as Party Secretary (1931–9). Under Starace's leadership, the totalitarian reach of the Party and state was at its furthest, penetrating to the level of everyday life and language, establishing the mass rites and rituals of what Emilio Gentile has described as the 'civic religion' of Fascism.[22] It was in this period that the cult of the *Duce* was at its strongest, the 'Roman salute' and the Roman version of the goosestep (*passo romano*) were

[20] P. Morgan, *Italian Fascism, 1919–1945* (Basingstoke: Macmillan, 1995), 160.

[21] G. Fabre, *The Contract* (New York: Enigma, 2006).

[22] E. Gentile, *The Sacralization of the Politics in Fascist Italy* (Cambridge, MA: Harvard University Press, 1996).

imposed, and mass gatherings (*adunate*) became regular events. As most religions structure themselves, anthropologically speaking, on the sacrifice of the impure, the scapegoat, so Fascist Italy built its model of the fascist new man to a significant degree on the rejection of the 'other'. In 1937, the enemy in one campaign became the 'bourgeoisie' in its entirety, but the Jew easily came to stand as the 'bourgeois' *par excellence*. From the mid-1930s, anti-Semitic flag-bearers within the Fascist Party such as Interlandi, Preziosi, Roberto Farinacci, or Paolo Orano (author of an influential 1937 work, *The Jews in Italy*) were louder and had much more influence and freedom of movement than previously.

Starace was both a keen anti-Semite and an enthused supporter of (and indeed, murderous participant in) the Ethiopian war of 1935–6. The close coincidence of fascism's anti-Semitic racial turn and its African imperial adventure—the latter a dimension not found in Nazism, or rather channelled into its quest for *Lebensraum* to the east—is of crucial importance. It is now clear that the first and driving impulse to reconceive fascist law and governance in terms of race came from the empire. At a cultural level, there is strong evidence that prejudices against Africans and Jews were tightly interwoven in this period. *La difesa della razza* adopted as its visual logo a triple portrait in profile, which it had used for the full cover of its first issue: a noble Roman, a degenerate Jew, and a 'primitive' African woman, the latter two dramatically cut off from the first by a plunging sword (Figure 16.1). Literary censorship—one of the key areas of accelerated totalitarian control in the mid-1930s—was first tightened and made fully preventive after Mussolini's horrified reaction to a 1934 book cover showing a mixed-race, black and white, African and Italian couple.[23] By 1938, a campaign to cleanse and fascistize Italian books—the so-called 'Book Reclamation' programme, echoing the land reclamations of the 1920s—became, for all intents and purposes, a programme for the elimination of works by Jewish authors, from bookshops, schools, and universities.[24]

Even more significant were the challenges of the war in Africa and the subsequent administration of empire.[25] Paxton notes that war is an inevitable engine of radicalization (just as the Second World War would lead to the ultimate radicalization of Nazi racism, the Holocaust). In Ethiopia, Italy embarked on a programme of 'genocidal' warfare, through its use of chemical weapons and unleashing of colonial violence (following a pattern already established in its activities in Libya in the 1920s).[26] As noted earlier, once the war was won, anxieties over racial mixing swiftly emerged. In 1936, the channels for allowing mixed-race children Italian citizenship were closed and further regulations followed to establish strictly separate living

---

[23] See G. Bonsaver, *Censorship and Literature in Fascist Italy* (Toronto: Toronto University Press, 2007).

[24] Ibid. 186–204.   [25] See n. 10.

[26] See the work of A. Del Boca, from *La guerra d'Abissinia, 1935–1941* (Milan: Feltrinelli, 1965) to *I gas di Mussolini* (Rome: Editori Riuniti, 1996).

Fig. 16.1. *La difesa della razza*, 1, 5 August 1938 (cover)

areas, to abolish the *madamato* and all mixed relations. The rigid separation of the superior European race from the inferior indigenous population was deemed essential. The same principle of racial hierarchy would underpin the 'Manifesto of Racist Scientists' and much of the anti-Semitic turn in fascist government and culture.

It is worth, finally, looking at the intellectual ballast beneath fascist ideas of race. As Fabrizio De Donno has shown, the Italian version of nineteenth-century and early twentieth-century racial thinking fed directly into fascist notions of race.[27] Contradictory and intellectually confused threads ran through fascist racial thinking, and Mussolini (as always) shifted his position more than once. Some, such as Interlandi, propagated a pro-Nazi, biological, Aryan model of race, the model which clearly dominated the 1938 manifesto, but which was subsequently challenged and qualified, especially after a change of heart by Mussolini in February 1939. Others, such as Nicola Pende or Sabato Visco, argued for a more cultural or 'national', Italic-Roman form of racism, where the history of Rome, from empire to Renaissance to fascism, was that of a culturally superior, Mediterranean race which had forged Europe's civilization over millennia. (Pende still signed the manifesto, however.) These positions came to the fore more after 1939. Then there was the esoteric, spiritual-Aryan racism of Julius Evola, on the fringes of the fascist mainstream, but growing in influence as the regime neared its end (and even more influential within post-war neo-fascism).

Between 1938 and 1943—the period of 'persecution of rights' in Italy, as Sarfatti labels it, preceding that of 'persecution of lives' (1943–5)[28]—the Racial Laws were applied throughout the Jewish community with some ferocity. There were regular exceptions and exemptions, and cases of local 'neighbourly' solidarity between non-Jewish Italians and Jews, but the trauma and hardship caused was grave. Most fascist officials fell into line all too quickly with the new position of the regime: thus, Giuseppe Bottai, otherwise credited as a relatively 'enlightened' Fascist minister, was zealous in his application of anti-Semitic principles to the sphere of education, as was the Minister of Popular Culture, Dino Alfieri. Giovanni Gentile's *Enciclopedia italiana*, which contained much impressive, ideologically neutral scholarship, despite its fascist credentials, rewrote its entry on *Razza* in 1938 to reflect the new mood. In the cultural sphere, the ageing Futurist Filippo Tommaso Marinetti is credited with speaking out against the laws, but in reality he was more concerned with defending modernist art from being 'tarnished' by association with the Jews, as had happened with the Nazi campaign against 'degenerate' art.

Italy formally entered the war as an Axis ally in June 1940 and for three years fought, relatively unsuccessfully, in several arenas and occupied territories. Jonathan Steinberg has shown how, in practice, a large number of Fascist officials up to and including Mussolini himself successfully resisted German demands to hand over Italy's and other Italian-administered Jews to Nazi genocide.[29] The reasons for

---

[27] F. De Donno, 'La razza ario-mediterranea: Ideas of Race and Citizenship in Colonial and Fascist Italy, 1885–1941', *Interventions*, 8/3 (2006), 394–412; A. Gillette, *Racial Theories in Fascist Italy* (New York: Routledge. 2002).

[28] Sarfatti, *La Shoah in Italia*, 77–123.

[29] J. Steinberg, *All or Nothing: The Axis and the Holocaust 1941–43* (London: Routledge, 1990).

this filibustering have, however, been assigned too easily to differences in national character, and so to the alleged essential non-racist, human decency of Italians.[30] Fascist occupying forces in regions of Yugoslavia were guilty of violence and killings against local populations to rival that of the German army in the area. Foreign Jews on Italian soil were interned after 1940 in camps such as at Ferramonti di Tarsia in Calabria, and, as David Bidussa has noted, it was only the historical accident of the fall of the regime in 1943 that prevented a wider network of camps being established and frustrated the integration of Italy into the Final Solution.[31] In any case, in bureaucratic terms, the Fascist state had laid all the groundwork necessary for the efficient round-up and deportation of Italy's Jews, which would begin in earnest, in the centre and north of the country, after the fall of Mussolini in July 1943 and the de facto occupation of much of Italy by the Nazis from September of that year.

VII. War and the Nazi Final Solution, 1941–1945

The Nazi Holocaust was, in Paxton's terms, 'the outermost reach of fascist radicalization'.[32] In a sense, however, although it added an entire new level of horror to the annals of inhumanity, it altered little in the ideology of racism. It enacted, literally, the 'exterminationist' rhetoric about the Jews that had circulated in European racial discourse for many years and which had assumed a virulent form in Hitler's vision. Of course, the complexities of how it was enacted and what made it possible are immense, but the coordinates of the Nazi racial state as established before the war, with an obsessive and incessant persecution of the Jews and other groups in law, coupled with persistent violence against them and passive acquiescence from the surrounding population, were altered in scope and degree (to an almost inconceivable extent) during the war period, but not so much in kind.

At some point in late 1941, a number of factors—from decisions taken on high, to responses to complex and evolving on-the-ground realities in occupied territories to the east—converged to allow the formulation of a policy of extermination of Europe's Jews, the 'Final Solution to the Jewish Question' (Göring used the phrase in a document from July 1941). Between the occupation of Poland in September 1939 and 1941, various schemes for the new mass of Eastern European Jews ruled over by

---

[30] Hannah Arendt talked in stereotypical vein of 'the almost automatic general humanity of an old and civilized people' in *Eichmann in Jerusalem* (London: Penguin, 1994 [1963]),170.

[31] Bidussa, *Il mito del bravo italiano*, 103.   [32] Paxton, *The Anatomy of Fascism*, 158.

the Reich were attempted: deportation from country to cities or to special regions (the Lublin reserve); enclosure in appalling urban ghettos; even the reviving of an old plan to deport the Jews to Madagascar. All took place in a context of arbitrary and increasingly fierce violence against the Jews in the eastern territories, overseen by figures such as Reinhard Heydrich and Adolf Eichmann; but insofar as such distinctions are possible and useful, the genocide as such—the mass, systematic process of murder—had not begun. The first steps were taken by the Einsatzgruppen, sections of the SS charged with following behind the invasion force into Russia and eliminating, through shooting on the spot or drowning in mass graves, Jews and communists. The Einsatzgruppen, numbering around 3,000, murdered approximately 800,000 people in the second half of 1941. Crucially, towards the end of that period, they also began to experiment with feeding exhaust gas fumes into closed lorries as a more 'efficient' method of killing.

In January 1942, the practicalities of mass extermination in the east were discussed in detail at the Wannsee conference, presided over by Heydrich and Eichmann. The first extermination camp—at Chelmno—was operational in December 1941; Belzec in March 1942, Sobibor in April, Treblinka in July. These four camps alone, out of the thousands of labour, internment, and concentration camps in the Reich, account for the murder of around 1,700,000 Jews. All were in Polish territory, as was the network of camps at Auschwitz-Birkenau, a hybrid extermination, concentration, and labour camp. The use of the gas Zyklon-B was pioneered by commandant Rudolf Höss at Auschwitz from February 1942. Approximately 1,000,000 Jews were murdered there.

Such was the scale of these camps, and the deportation networks that fed them, that it is impossible to write the history of the Nazi genocide moving directly from gatherings of handfuls of officials, at Wannsee or elsewhere, to the millions of victims. In between, and perhaps crucial for understanding the racist state of mind inculcated by the Nazi state, stand swathes of the ordinary population in Germany and the occupied territories, of ordinary soldiers drafted to do this work, of commerce and industry which supplied the camp system and even cooperated in running it (e.g. IG Farben at Auschwitz). All were corrupted to such an extreme degree by the power of racist rhetoric, and shielded by such euphemisms as Final Solution and 'Special Treatment', to have integrated murderous violence into their own horizon of what was tolerable or necessary. Some of the richest research and debate about the nature of the Nazi phenomenon and its racial ideology have emerged from work on these 'ordinary' bystanders and participants.[33]

The camps accelerated their work, even as the Reich was heading for certain defeat, until the few survivors were liberated by Soviet or Anglo-American forces from

[33] See C. Browning, *Ordinary Men: Reserve Police Battalion 101 and the Final Solution in Poland* (New York: Aaron Asher, 1992).

late 1944 into spring 1945. Somewhere between 5,000,000 and 6,000,000 Jews fell victim to Nazi genocidal violence, as did nearly 2,000,000 non-Jewish Poles, over 3,000,000 Russian soldiers (above and beyond those killed in battle), over 200,000 Roma, around the same number of mentally and physically disabled, and up to 10,000 male homosexuals (the figures for the latter are hard to establish).[34] Stark photo-reportage and newsreel footage from the liberations, as well as dramatic evidence at the Nuremberg Trials begun later in 1945, fixed in the European mind the extraordinary crime perpetrated by the Nazis; although it is remarkable that relatively little emphasis was placed, at that time and for some time to come, on the predominantly Jewish identity of the victims of this devastating horror; that is, on the racial nature of the Nazi crimes.

VIII. Salò and the Holocaust in Italy, 1943–1945

Given the immense scale of the Nazi genocide, in geographical scope, method, and number of victims, the role of fascism in Italy by 1943, and late developments in the nuances of its racial politics, may seem of marginal concern. Certainly, the numbers are of a different, if nevertheless terrible order: of the approximately 40,000 Jews in Italy (and perhaps 10,000 more foreign Jews in Italian territory), between 7,000 and 8,000 lost their lives in the Holocaust.[35] It is worth noting that Fascist Italy killed many times this number of Libyan Arabs and Ethiopians (in the order of hundreds of thousands) in its colonial aggressions. In a sense, however, the Italian role in the Holocaust is all the more significant for being relatively marginal. What was left of the original fascist project of 1919 or of 1922—Hitler's first model—by the time two decades and more, a failing war, and a cataclysmic genocidal violence had overtaken Axis Europe? Or, rather, what was left of fascism within that cataclysmic violence? Can the final throes of Mussolini's career retrospectively enlighten in some way the core nature of the fascist phenomenon and the role of race within it?

The RSI (Italian Social Republic) or the 'Salò' Republic, set up and largely controlled by the Nazis, governed northern and central Italy between September 1943 and April 1945 (although not the north and north-eastern border areas, which were annexed to the Reich and where the concentration camp and gas chamber at the Risiera di San Sabba, outside Trieste, was located). Mussolini was formally head of

---

[34] Figures from United States Holocaust Memorial Museum website: <http://www.ushmm.org/wlc/en/> (accessed 15 Jan 2007).

[35] For precise figures, see L. Picciotto Fargion, *Il libro della memoria: gli ebrei deportati dall'Italia (1943–1945)* (Milan: Mursia, 2002).

state. In Salò, many have seen a fascism of a different order from the fascism of the *ventennio*: a fascism returned to its radical origins, without the compromises of pragmatic government and *Realpolitik* that had previously constrained Mussolini and the Fascist Party and changed their nature into something more conservative than they were designed to be. At the level of anti-Semitic propaganda and rhetoric, Salò certainly returned with renewed fervour to the tropes of nineteenth- and early twentieth-century racism: it insisted more than ever on the 'Judaic-Masonic-Plutocratic' forces threatening Italy and the vocation of fascism as Europe's new supreme religion. Salò's was certainly a Fascism more devoted to violence and radical extremism, born of war, as perhaps the early Fascist movement had been, following the Great War. Its concrete racial policies reflected this grim context.

In late 1943, the Republic produced its constitution, the so-called 'Verona Manifesto', which proclaimed a non-monarchical, one-party state, with an independent judiciary and a social programme of government. It also declared that 'those belonging to the Jewish race are foreigners', to be treated as enemy aliens. On this point at least, the fragile new Republic stuck to its word: on 30 November, the arrest and internment of all Jews was ordered; all Jews' belongings were subsequently made subject to sequestration. Salò militia and officials collaborated in and facilitated the arrests, alongside their Nazi allies, answering to their own internal ministries and to Nazi officials responsible for Jews in Italy (led by Theodor Dannecker and then Friedrich Bosshammer). The 'Black Brigades' hunted down Jews as fervently as they did Resistance partisans. Police forces abetted round-ups—for example, in Rome on 16 October 1943, leading to the deportation of 1,023 Jews—and massacres—notably at the Fosse Ardeatine, near Rome, in 1944, where at least 75 were among the 335 murdered, in reprisal for the killing of 33 German soldiers in via Rasella.[36] Small holding camps were set up in various centres, but the main one was at Fossoli, near Modena in central Italy. Fossoli was run by Italians from December 1943 until February 1944 and then by Germans. Most of its inmates were deported to Auschwitz, where over 90 per cent were to die.

IX. Concluding Remarks

The interweaving of the paths of fascist and Nazi racial policy points to various conclusions. First, the sheer difference in scale, intensity, and outcome of racial violence between the two is, were it necessary, underscored once again. This immense difference cannot and should not be elided. At the same time, however, acknowledging

---

[36] See A. Portelli, *The Order Has Been Carried Out* (New York: Palgrave Macmillan, 2003).

a stronger and broader racial dimension in Italian Fascism—running throughout Mussolini's intellectual formation, starting in earnest several years earlier than 1938, determined by colonial racial questions (including the racial killing of hundreds of thousands of Arabs and Africans), playing its part in propelling several of the total-itarian social measures of the regime, as well as its self-promotion as a civic religion and its anthropological mission to shape a 'new man' in cultural and biological terms—opens up a more flexible field of comparison with Nazi racial conceptions and practices. Similarly, stretching the terms of the Nazi racial state to include persecution of racial groups other than Jews and also measures of social engineering and control has a comparable effect. It suggests that fascism, and perhaps other forms of exacerbated nationalism, need to be analysed as essentially racist in this sense, forged through the exclusion of 'others'. Certainly, post-war fascist move-ments, from early nationalisms down to contemporary anti-immigrant agitators, have all been exclusionary and racist is some form. More widely, recent global syntheses of modern history, such as Tony Judt's *Postwar* and Niall Fergusson's *The War of the World*, have argued, from very different intellectual positions, that vast movements in twentieth-century history, of populations, empires, wars, and ideas, have been the product of racist, monocultural, 'ethnic-cleansing' ideologies and impulses.[37] In this *longue durée* perspective, the problems of moving from the specifics of race within single fascist regimes to a 'fascist common denominator' may fade in comparison with the possibility that racism lies at the core of the modern nation and modernity itself.

BIBLIOGRAPHY

BEN-GHIAT, R., and FULLER, M. (eds), *Italian Colonialism* (New York: Palgrave, 2005).

BESSEL, R. (ed.), *Fascist Italy and Nazi Germany: Comparisons and Contrasts* (Cambridge: Cambridge University Press, 1996).

BURLEIGH, M., and WIPPERMANN, W., *The Racial State: Germany 1933–1945* (Cambridge: Cambridge University Press, 1991).

DE GRAND, A., *Fascist Italy and Nazi Germany* (2nd edn. New York: Routledge, 2004).

FRIEDLANDER, S., *Nazi Germany and the Jews* (London: Weidenfeld and Nicolson, 1997).

GENTILE, E., *The Sacralization of the Politics in Fascist Italy* (Cambridge, MA: Harvard University Press, 1996).

GILLETTE, A., *Racial Theories in Fascist Italy* (New York: Routledge. 2002).

HILBERG, R., *The Destruction of the European Jews* (2nd edn, New York: Holmes and Meier, 1985).

---

[37] N. Fergusson, *The War of the World* (New York: Allen Lane, 2006); T. Judt, *Postwar: A History of Europe since 1945* (New York: Allen Lane, 2005).

PAXTON, R. O., *The Anatomy of Fascism* (London: Allen Lane, 2004).

SARFATTI, M., *La Shoah in Italia: la persecuzione degli ebrei sotto il fascismo* (Turin: Einaudi, 2005).

STEINBERG, J., *All or Nothing: The Axis and the Holocaust 1941–43* (London: Routledge, 1990).

ZIMMERMAN, J. D. (ed.), *Jews in Italy under Fascist and Nazi Rule, 1922–1945* (Cambridge: Cambridge University Press, 2005).

ZUCCOTTI, S., *The Italians and the Holocaust* (London: Peter Halban, 1987).

CHAPTER 17

DIPLOMACY AND WORLD WAR

THE (FIRST) AXIS OF EVIL

H. JAMES BURGWYN

THE *Brutal Friendship*, the arresting title of F. W. Deakin's path-breaking study of the relationship between Mussolini and Hitler, narrates the trials and vicissitudes of two men who endeavoured, and ultimately failed, to bring about an 'Axis New Order'.[1] Both were dreamers who indulged in a mysticism of empire and race. They throve on war and exalted in military reviews and parades. The aura Mussolini and Hitler presented of invincible ruthlessness captured the imagination of people in both countries who were disillusioned with democracy and fearful of the Bolshevik menace. Theirs was a friendship bonded by hate. As consummate misanthropes, they despised humanitarian values and the democratic creed. But were these affinities so irresistible that Fascist Italy and Nazi Germany were predestined to join an Axis of Evil bent on destruction and conquest?

The gifted historian MacGregor Knox, in a variety of articles and books, has driven home the point that a commonality of destiny existed between the two totalitarian regimes. Through a powerful comparative analysis, he points out major similarities between the dictatorships of Hitler and Mussolini. Each regime is found to be genuinely revolutionary, their evil and violent leaders committed to subverting the international system of sovereign states in favour of an Axis New Order

---

[1] F. W. Deakin, *The Brutal Friendship: Mussolini, Hitler and the Fall of Italian Fascism* (Garden City, NY: Anchor Books, 1966).

where racial and ethnic inferiors would be either annihilated or reduced to helots serving barbaric masters. Mussolini, for his part, according to Knox, actively pursued a revolutionary Axis to destroy the colonial hegemony of Britain and France. In the inexorable logic of the Fascist creed, Italy was set on a predetermined imperial programme, a programme crucially contingent upon the political, economic, and military support of a compatible National Socialist regime equally bent on territorial conquest. The Axis powers, which were inextricably bound together by ideological affinity, were fated to wage war together. The *Duce* mocked *Realpolitik* as a tiresome and silly game whose rules were set by old-fashioned and decrepit status-quo statesmen heading effete and decaying empires. The time had come for the young and vigorous totalitarian movements to overturn the cramped power balances of a bygone age.[2]

A dominant nationalist school of thought in Italy holds quite a contrary view. Its master, Renzo De Felice, believes that Mussolini's Fascist foreign policy was anything but a tightly defined catechism; it was rather a loose and shifting combination of biases and historical resentments. Behind a veil of imperturbability, Mussolini constantly backslid, temporized, or swaggered—behaviour hardly dictated by fundamentalist ideological principle, beyond his desire to achieve glory through war. Although, as De Felice concedes, Mussolini's foreign policy was imbued with aggressive language and a Social Darwinist philosophy of international relations, it was informed by no *Mein Kampf* or *Secret Book*, and therefore was not propelled by any particular Fascist dynamic. In spite of his personal idiosyncrasies, Mussolini was essentially a pragmatist.

In the main, according to De Felice, Mussolini, in seeking 'equidistance' between the chief European states, aimed to utilize Nazi Germany as leverage to extract colonial concessions from the Western Powers. Only for propagandistic reasons did Mussolini applaud Hitler as he marched into the Rhineland, Austria, the Sudetenland, and Poland. His frequent gestures of solidarity to the Rome–Berlin Axis are judged by De Felice as a cover by a 'realistic' power broker striving to contain the Germanic menace in continental Europe. His student Rosaria Quartararo goes further: Mussolini tried hard to consummate a general accord with the Western Powers but was thwarted by their essentially anti-Italian prejudice and predisposition to appease Hitler. Faced by Western intransigence, the *Duce* was left with no choice but to come down in Hitler's camp.[3]

---

[2] M. Knox, 'The Fascist Regime, its Foreign Policy and its Wars: An "Anti-Anti-Fascist" Orthodoxy?', *Contemporary European History*, 4/3 (1995), 347–65; idem, *Mussolini Unleashed, 1939–1941: Politics and Strategy in Fascist Italy's Last War* (Cambridge: Cambridge University Press, 1982); idem, 'L'ultima guerra dell'Italia fascista', in B. Micheletti and P. P. Poggio (eds), *L'Italia in guerra 1940–1943* (Brescia: La Fondazione 'Luigi Micheletti', 1991), 17–32.
[3] R. Quartararo, *Roma fra Londra e Berlino: la politica estera fascista dal 1931 al 1940* (Milan: Bonacci, 1980).

The *Duce*'s relationship to Hitler, avers De Felice, was riddled with ambiguity, a kind of love/fear relationship. Quite contrary to any ideological pull, according to De Felice, Mussolini's drift into Hitler's embrace resulted from his fear of Nazi vengeance and the conviction that a betrayal of the alliance would provoke the end of Fascism. Further, Mussolini's decision to take Italy into the Second World War was not based on a desire to build a Nazi-Fascist new world order but was guided principally by the shifting tides of war that seemed, in June 1940, unquestionably to favour the Third Reich. Led by De Felice, Italy's nationalist historians think that accommodation between Germany and Italy was the fruit of *Realpolitik* and reflected the pursuit of traditional national interests rather than being the product of ideological similarity or dictatorial will.[4]

I. THE ESSENCE OF MUSSOLINI'S FOREIGN POLICY

In seeking to broaden our understanding of Mussolini's part in 'The Brutal Friendship', and to stake out areas for further research in the field of Fascist Italy's foreign policy, we need first to provide a brief chronology of events.

When Mussolini came to power in 1922, he had a rough idea of what he intended to accomplish: spheres of influence in the Balkans and Danube region and an expanded Italian empire in Africa. First on his agenda was to carve out an Italian *spazio vitale* in the Balkans. But France and its allies in the Little Entente stood in Italy's way. Though dreaming of replacing France as the dominant influence in south-eastern Europe, by force if need be, Mussolini was aware that his military was not up to the task of war against the 'Latin Sister'. Hence, he fell back on a stratagem—a *revisionismo fascista*—by joining up with the defeated powers of the Great War to disrupt the status quo established by the victorious powers at the Paris Peace Conference in 1919. Specifically, by promoting insurrection, Mussolini intended to destroy Yugoslavia. But, burdened by economic and military weakness, his terrorist probes were merely a nuisance.

When Hitler arrived on the scene in January 1933, Mussolini rejoiced over the establishment of a radical regime in Berlin, which, he thought, opened up expansionist vistas for Italy. But Hitler's immediate interest in effecting an annexation of Austria sent a chill down the *Duce*'s spine. A loss of Austria to Germany would place Nazis at the Brenner frontier and imperil Italy's hold over the

[4] R. De Felice, *L'organizzazione dello stato fascista, 1925–1929: Mussolini il duce*, i: *Gli anni del consenso, 1929–1936*; ii: *Lo stato totalitario, 1936–1940*; idem, *Mussolini l'alleato 1940–1945*, i: *L'Italia in Guerra 1940–1943*; ii: *La guerra civile 1943–1945* (Turin: Einaudi, 1968–97).

South Tyrol, a German-populated area annexed by Italy at the end of the Great War. To shore up Austria's independence, Mussolini befriended a fellow authoritarian in Vienna, Engelbert Dollfuss, and fathered the creation of a Rome Protocols bloc consisting of Austria, Hungary, and Italy, to check a German expansion south-eastward.

At the end of 1934 Mussolini fixed on the conquest of Ethiopia. Faced by lacklustre opposition on the part of the Western Powers, Mussolini tossed aside the League of Nations and marched to a quick victory over the poorly armed Ethiopians, flung against his Italian legions. He proudly proclaimed an Italian empire from the balcony on the Palazzo Venezia before cheering throngs in May 1936.

Mussolini had arrived at a crossroads. Contemporary observers asked: would he undertake a rapprochement with the Western Powers offended by fascist aggression or gravitate toward an alliance with Hitler? The chance opening of the Spanish Civil War and Mussolini's decision to aid a fellow would-be dictator, Francisco Franco, propelled Italy into the arms of Nazi Germany. Mussolini meekly accepted the *Anschluss* in March 1938 and signed the Pact of Steel with Hitler in May of the following year. The more Mussolini became entangled with the Third Reich, the more his mind was cluttered with ideological prejudice. When Britain and France allowed German rearmament and appeased Hitler at Munich in March 1938 by forcing Czechoslovakia to hand over the Sudetenland areas to him, Mussolini took such capitulation as proof positive that they were decadent democracies in hopeless decline.

One can easily imagine the impotent frustration Mussolini felt when Hitler unleashed the Second World War by attacking Poland in September 1939. Since wars in Ethiopia and Spain had reduced Italy to a military and economic paraplegic, he was forced to take a grandstand seat on the German side of the field as a non-belligerent.

Although itching to join the fray, Mussolini never lost sight of battlefield realities. With Machiavellian logic he watched and waited before making any irreversible move. The choice was either continued non-belligerency or war on the side of Hitler—but at the time most profitable for Italy. The French collapse ended Mussolini's internal debate. He would not let Hitler be the sole arbiter of Europe. If there had been stalemate on the western front, there is no telling what Mussolini might have done. Perhaps he would have squirmed endlessly on the sidelines, or, if the two sides appeared to have reached mutual exhaustion, he might have convened an Italian 'Munich' from a position of relative strength, handed victory to Hitler, and picked up spoils from the losers as the 'mediator' of a 'lenient' peace.

One wonders why Mussolini thought he could move a battered two-bit power of 1922 to a war that would win imperial glory and the respect of the world. Was this ambition forged in the crucible of the fascist creed, or did it germinate during the period from the founding of the nation in 1860 to the outbreak of the First World War?

Richard Bosworth, the most prolific and thought-provoking writer on Fascist Italy today, plumbs Italian history from the Risorgimento to the fascist period and finds continuity. There is no real difference in aim between the policies of Liberal and Fascist Italy, he asserts, only in method. In the drive for empire, Mussolini's foreign policy was not new, 'totalitarian', or 'fascist', but 'old, traditional, and nationalist'. In a probing phrase reminiscent of the provocative and brilliant English historian A. J. P. Taylor, Bosworth writes:

> It is at least arguable that, whatever his rhetoric, Mussolini waited longer and displayed more scruples in 1940 than did Salandra and Sonnino in 1915. It is equally arguable that no imaginable Italian leader, who accepted the myths around which Italian society had been organized since the Risorgimento, would not have entered a Great Power war at a time when it seemed plain that one side had won a total victory. Because of the myths of the Risorgimento any Italian leader would have declared war on Germany's side in June 1940 because it was by then the only step that could possibly lead to the survival of Italy's pretensions to be a Great Power.[5]

There is wisdom in this passage; still, one wonders. Would a traditional monarchist like Sidney Sonnino, who wore his cuffs and stiff collar proudly, and who felt a deep nostalgia for the defunct Habsburg empire, have ever gone to war on the side of plebeian Nazis? Was there not a real clash of standards and habit between the Old World and the Axis New Order?

The 'intentionalist' theory runs counter to the continuous-flow-of-history views propounded by Bosworth. The intentionalists hold that Mussolini was, in truth, 'one man alone', an inveterate and deranged warmonger who had committed Italy to the German alliance and undertook a war of aggression hand in hand with the Third Reich. Outspoken anti-Fascist critics like Gaetano Salvemini saw the *Duce* as 'always an irresponsible improviser, half madman, half criminal, gifted only in the arts of propaganda and mystification'.[6] The English historian Denis Mack Smith, mocking the *Duce*'s flamboyance, notes that he 'deliberately steered his fascist movement into imperialism and into a succession of wars that left Italy prostrate'.[7]

From quite another perspective, Italian nationalist historians, led by Benedetto Croce, argue that fascist-style expansionism was but a parenthesis in history, an aberration that ran counter to the traditional aspirations of the House of Savoy. The boundless ambition of Mussolini, in their view, defied accredited diplomatic practice, which means, it would seem, that Fascist Italy collapsed into the arms of the mighty instead of selling itself dearly in the hours of great crises to the highest bidder as was the habit of Liberal Italy's prudent Machiavellians.

---

[5] R. J. B. Bosworth, 'Italian Foreign Policy and its Historiography', in R. Bosworth and G. Rizzo (eds), *Altro Polo: Intellectuals and their Ideas in Contemporary Italy* (Sydney: F. May Foundation, 1983), 78.

[6] G. Salvemini, *Prelude to World War II* (London: Gollancz, 1953).

[7] D. Mack Smith, *Mussolini's Roman Empire* (London: Longman, 1976), p. v.

Knox is an intentionalist historian *à outrance*. War occurred, he posits, because a violent Mussolini willed an ideological, fascist, and totalitarian war of revenge on the Italian establishment—the monarchy and church—and against the Western Powers to acquire a fascist empire. In creating a nation through bloodshed, Knox avers that Mussolini aimed to craft the spiritual unity of all Italians. The pattern went: drug the enemy by soothing words and distract him with interminable negotiations. Empire was not a means to material profit, but to national regeneration. Since fascists worshipped strength, this meant siding with the strongest power. Symptomatic of Mussolini's subservience to Hitler, Knox points out, was Italy's adoption of racism in 1938. During his time as *Duce*, Mussolini searched for every possible opening to wage war abroad to resurrect the Roman imperium conquered by a hardened nation of warriors.[8]

It could be that the single most potent factor in the foreign policy of Italy from the Risorgimento through fascism was resentment—resentment against powerful neighbours aiming to undo unification and resentment of Italy's leaders over their failure to win any glittering prizes in the colonial scramble. Mussolini nimbly exploited the nation's most burning grievance, which originated at the Paris Peace Conference of 1919. Instead of receiving handsome imperialist prizes from grateful alliance partners for a gallant contribution to the victory at a tremendous cost in lives and resources, Italy was treated as a grasping and belligerent Balkan state that had fought selfishly—'Sonnino's war'. If Gabriele D'Annunzio originally captured the public mood with the slogan 'the mutilated victory', no one knew better than Mussolini how to work this legend into national fury. Italy would avenge itself against its erstwhile allies by taking up the 'revisionist' cause hand in hand with the treaty breaker par excellence, Germany.

Italy certainly did appear addicted to egoistic and petty intrigue. A number of famous English historians have poked fun at 'the Least of the Great Powers'. A. J. P. Taylor once expressed it this way: 'In international affairs there was nothing wrong with Mussolini except that he was an Italian.'[9] One can be excused for reading behind such witty asides an Anglo-Saxon sense of moral superiority.

Objectivity is similarly muddied by the sudden intrusion at the Paris Peace Conference of Wilsonian principles and a League of Nations infused with an American exceptionalist morality that frowned on warmongers, empires, and war. The Western Powers shook censorious fingers at Italy over its territorial greed and imperial inexperience, while portraying themselves as enlightened advisers assisting the unseasoned peoples residing in League 'mandates' to reach a civilized nationhood. There was hypocrisy in this, for while bringing Italy up to speed on Wilsonian principles, Lloyd George and Clemenceau pointedly ignored the

---

[8] M. Knox, *Common Destiny: Dictatorship, Foreign Policy, and War in Fascist Italy and Nazi Germany* (Cambridge: Cambridge University Press, 2000), 53–147.

[9] Cited in R. J. B. Bosworth, *Benito Mussolini and the Fascist Destruction of Liberal Italy, 1900–1945* (Adelaide: Rigby, 1973), 36.

patronizing American President by refusing to disavow wartime agreements that partitioned the Middle East between them. Worse still, as a majority of Italians saw it, the Western Powers declined even to throw scraps from a rich hoard of colonial real estate to their wartime ally. Underneath the platitudes, *Realpolitik* ruled.

In the effort to sort out bias in our search for explanations of Fascist Italy's foreign policy, let us expand our discussion by analysing the system of independent and sovereign states in which Italy participated that prevailed in Europe from approximately the 1648 Treaty of Westphalia to the bipolarity of the Cold War. In this arena every sovereign state acted unreliably and irresponsibly toward each other and to the world community at large. Of necessity, each head of state, whether democratic, communist, or fascist, considered its main duty to be defending national interest (if this elusive term can ever be pinned down), by force if necessary. In this law of the jungle, if one country aims at security by building up a predominance of weapons, all the others are bound to read this as intent to commit aggression. Since no power wishes to feel exposed to attack, it must arm at least to a level of deterrence against the most powerful, which, not surprisingly, gives rise to an arms race. War and the threat of war are part and parcel of each state's behaviour; alliances and alignments are forged to correct an adverse power balance or to tip the scales in one's favour. Oddly, in the struggle for power between 1815 and 1914, no major war occurred among the players in an essentially immoral system. One can even reasonably argue that none of the Great Powers willed a general war in the lead-up to 1914.

Although it is indisputable that Hitler personified evil, and that Mussolini was an international gangster, we must not overlook the fact that both dictators conducted policy in an essentially immoral structure of power politics in which war was considered as an acceptable instrument of coercion. The League of Nations and the idea of collective security were smokescreens put up by the status quo powers, the Great War victors, that hid this essential reality.

Still, it is unsatisfactory and incomplete to excuse Mussolini's warmongering as typical behaviour in the above-described 'realist' and 'amoral' system of power politics. Moreover, his major imperialist aims were not just irritable mental gestures but powered by real ideological imperatives. Many of these were appropriated from the nationalists' creed or borrowed from European disseminators of the 'culture of despair'. Living in a lawless world, Italy must be among the fittest to survive and compete for power. 'Expand or die' in Fascist Italy translated into a radicalized struggle between incompatible political regimes. The 'Decline of the West' was taken as the decline of France and England, which, according to the fascists, had lapsed into corruption and degeneration in the post-war era, as proven by their desire for peace and penchant for diplomatic solutions and appeasement. Overcoming these democratic countries, infested with feckless politicians of a bygone era, would be a cakewalk for the resurgent modern-day Sparta.

It is relatively easy to describe the ideological components of fascist foreign policy. Far more difficult is to pursue the absolutely vital line of enquiry that Richard Bosworth exhorts us to undertake: discovery of the linkages between domestic affairs and fascist foreign policy. For all its pretensions to totalitarian uniformity, was the fascist system in practice fractured by personal, practical, and ideological conflicts that the *Duce* was powerless to keep under control? A 'functional' analysis is here required to see how self-interest, bureaucratism, and other structures enduring over the years meshed together to produce fascist policy.[10]

Of particular importance in our search for the essence of fascist foreign policy is the extent to which Mussolini was able to fascistize the Foreign Ministry. What did such an effort imply? After the resignation of the nationalist Salvatore Contarini as under-secretary in 1926, we can discern many of Mussolini's personal emissaries as well as old-guard diplomats beginning to employ fascist language and prejudices in their reports, which gave them a real *tono fascista*. For example, their memoranda were peppered with such colourful phrases as the 'atavistic impulses' of Serbs, the 'social-democratic, Masonic, Jewish internationalist plot', and the occult influences of 'Grand Orient masonry and its funds'. Was this an example of 'working toward the *Duce*' that was becoming the norm in the Italian bureaucracy?

Mussolini's youthful son-in-law Galeazzo Ciano supposedly endeavoured to complete fascistization when he became Foreign Minister in 1936. As helmsman of policy, he did take bold initiatives in leading his country toward the Axis. To what extent was Ciano able to brainwash his underlings to be ardent advocates of the Axis? Did he have to do this? A more intensive content analysis of Italy's diplomatic correspondence, coupled with an in-depth study of the decision-making process in the Italian Foreign Ministry, might tell us more about the kind of fascist/nationalist that resided there.

With this background, let us revisit specific eras of fascist foreign policy in more detail. In the first period, Mussolini's 'early diplomacy', we should both avoid analysis in a fascist vacuum and steer clear of the Italian nationalist proclivity for portraying *revisionismo fascista* as a justified Italian response to a 'mutilated victory'. A wider framework is suggested: Mussolini's penchant for terrorist diplomacy in the 1920s (he never was 'a good European') should be judged in conjunction with British and French determination to dominate international finances, Eastern Europe, and the colonial world.

Resenting the image of Italy as European intriguer, Mussolini vowed that war and war alone could assuage the national inferiority complex and make the nation whole. The Fascist Lords of the Trenches (*trincerocrazia*) would teach the supercilious foreigner that Italy was no longer the land 'of travelling storytellers, of peddlers of statuettes, of Calabrian *banditi*'.[11] The insecurity of a 'great power'

[10] R. J. B. Bosworth, *The Italian Dictatorship: Problems and Perspectives in the Interpretation of Mussolini and Fascism* (London: Arnold, 1998).

[11] Knox, *Common Destiny*, 61–2.

lacking greatness gave fascist policy a neurotic tone, which only partially answers the question why the 'mutilated victory' held so many Italians in thrall, and why they were so unwilling to notice that, in fact, Italy's power position had been significantly improved. Austria-Hungary had disintegrated, the northern frontier extended to the Brenner, and the Yugoslav successor state could neither challenge Italy at sea nor threaten it on land.

The *Anschluss* question showcases many themes in fascist foreign policy. Since Austria formed the linchpin of Italian security in Europe, simple prudence required that Italy uphold the independence of the hapless truncated state to avoid a flanking movement by any German *Drang nach Südosten*. Ideology seemed to reinforce *Realpolitik* when Engelbert Dollfuss became Austria's Chancellor in May 1932. For now an authoritarian was installed in Vienna who, like Mussolini, hated democracy and socialism. Dollfuss, flaunting his Austrian patriotism, made no secret of his desire to fend off pan-Germanism.

When Hitler openly declared that *Anschluss* was a top priority, the *Duce* quickly moved to defend Austria, but in a Fascist way, by spinning an alliance between Dollfuss and the Italian-financed paramilitary Heimwehr. But first essential business had to be taken care of by 'smoking out' the hated internal enemy, the Social Democrats, from their stronghold in 'Red' Vienna. The idea was that a kin Fatherland Front would be able to stand against both Nazis and Austro-Marxists. But Social Democracy was the strongest pillar holding up Austria's independence against Nazi Germany, and its demise, much to the *Duce*'s surprise, opened the door wide for a Nazi assassination of Dollfuss on 25 July 1934. Mussolini replied by rushing troops to the Brenner to keep Germany's legions at bay. At the same time he sent a favourite, Eugenio Morreale, to Vienna as press attaché, armed with money and agents, to build cultural ties between the two countries as a counter to the local National Socialist movement. Was this effort half-hearted, half-baked, or was it fully supported? Eventually, since Mussolini never hit it off with a far less savvy and *simpatico* Kurt Schuschnigg as Chancellor, his interest in manning guard on the Brenner began almost immediately to dry up. When Hitler ordered the *Einmarsch* into Austria in March 1938, Mussolini shut his eyes as if averting a punishing nightmare come true.

The Italian nationalist school holds that Britain and France, by showing no interest in Austria, were co-conspirators in its demise. Certainly there is something to this. But what might have discouraged Mussolini the most were Schuschnigg's pan-German predilections and reports coming into Rome that Italians were universally hated in Austria.

In our effort to comprehend fascist influences on Italian foreign policy, the above bare-boned description of this vitally important Austrian phase raises important questions. Did Mussolini, in his fierce hatred of socialism, defeat his own purpose of defending Austria's independence? If one concedes that the *Duce* felt a greater camaraderie with Dollfuss, the clerical-fascist, than he did with Hitler, the Nazi, were the regimes in Rome and Berlin really destined for each other? What if Dollfuss had lived?

De Felice feels the pulse of the Italian body politic after Mussolini's declaration of empire in May 1936 and concludes that he had achieved a 'masterpiece' by forging a national consensus behind the war of imperial conquest. Women rushed breathlessly to deliver their wedding rings to the national treasury, the Catholic hierarchy and the Pope bestowed their blessings, the middle classes, and even workers and peasants, swaggered in newly found national pride. De Felice happily reports that finally a dream of every nationalist since the Risorgimento had come true: a conscious national unity hewn from the diverse regions of the country.

De Felice goes on to add that Mussolini also conducted *Realpolitik* superbly well. Furnished by his secret service with purloined British reports, Mussolini was fairly certain that his exposed supply lines would not be disrupted by the British navy. And provisioned by American oil, the *Duce* scoffed at talk of oil sanctions by the Western Powers. His daring will had prevailed over feckless opponents.

Although Mussolini clearly proclaimed on 30 June 1934 that Italy's mission was to destroy the Ethiopian armed forces and effect the total conquest of the country, De Felice still argues that had the League of Nations stood firmly against Italian aggression, Mussolini might well have settled for a diplomatic solution that granted him less than the conquest he sought. Only after the British and French came up short did he opt for a 'totalitarian solution'. But Renato Mori's view, that the dictator did his best throughout the Ethiopian crisis to sabotage, not seek, any settlement denying him a 'violent solution', is more convincing.[12]

From quite a different angle, Alan Cassels writes: 'By the mid-1930s whatever social reforming zeal Italian fascism had initially possessed was exhausted.... The function of Fascism had become essentially conservative. Only the cult of the *Duce* remained, but its voracious appetite required constant feeding.' In a sense, military imperialism supplanted social change as the *raison d'être* of Italian Fascism.[13]

In proceeding stubbornly toward war against Ethiopia, Mussolini brushed aside the reservations about the impending invasion. King Victor Emmanuel III and old-line diplomats worried that the invasion of Ethiopia would undermine Italy's friendship with England. High military officers of the armed forces also opposed the *Duce*'s war plan because it weakened Italy's military presence in Europe. Can we describe Mussolini's co-opting the nation in the war of aggression against Ethiopia as a domestic virtuoso performance and his alone? There is important evidence to indicate that perhaps the army did not need to be cajoled, and that the navy did not share the dire predictions of military disaster predicted by some of Mussolini's entourage. Perhaps the conquest of Ethiopia was not only Mussolini's *capolavoro*

---

[12] R. Mori, *Mussolini e la conquista dell'Etiopia* (Florence: Le Monnier, 1978).

[13] A. Cassels, 'Switching Partners: Italy in A. J. P. Taylor's *Origins of the Second World War*', in G. Martel (ed.), *The Origins of the Second World War Reconsidered: The A. J. P. Taylor Debate after Twenty Years* (Boston: Allen & Unwin, 1986), 80.

but also one shared by the *classe dirigente*. In any event, the whole question of consensus needs to be revisited.

Italy's colonial war was besmirched by the use of poison gas against practically defenceless Ethiopians. When Mussolini hurried to pass laws against miscegenation, Italy's imperial war looked not much different from Nazi racial conflict. Richard Bosworth, on the other hand, argues that Mussolini in East Africa was still seeking 'Glory, God, and Gold', just as his predecessors in other European countries had done in the world beyond their continent during earlier centuries. What of Prime Minister Giovanni Giolitti's attack on Ottoman 'Libya' in 1911–12?[14] If no toxic gases were used, butchery of natives by bullets and knives abounded. Do we not have here similar barbaric methods and the same end result of mass slaughter?

Soon after reaching this lofty pinnacle of power, Mussolini ended speculation that he would align Italy with the Western democracies to check Hitler by intervening in the Spanish Civil War in summer 1936. At the outset, however, it was not clear that this decision would drive Mussolini inexorably into an Axis with the Third Reich. For one thing Italy's involvement occurred largely by accident and in the belief that a victory over Spain's weak Republican forces would be speedily won. In taking no heed of the historical lesson that intervention in civil wars is like stepping into quicksand, Mussolini paid a heavy price. Franco was anything but grateful, and fascism's fragile prestige suffered a body blow when the Garibaldi Brigade of expatriate anti-fascist Italians contributed to the defeat of blackshirt units at Guadalajara in March 1937.

Did Mussolini hope to forge a tie with, and eventually a patronage over, a kin Spanish authoritarian movement? Perhaps he was mainly moved by the twin strategic purposes of forestalling a Popular Front encirclement of Italy in the Mediterranean and of acquiring the Balearic Islands as a way-station to hegemony in the Mediterranean. As the conflict in Spain dragged on, Mussolini posed as a crusader at the head of a larger ideological struggle that pitted European fascism and its allies against the international forces of democracy and bolshevism.

Historians have for long grappled with these issues,[15] but there is one not yet carefully explored angle. Was the Italian intervention in Spain a classic example of a hand-to-mouth decision-making process on the part of a ramshackle regime that took no stock of the economic and political costs involved? Was Mussolini subjected to adverse criticism by other institutional forces besides the king and military which advised against any escalation of Italy's ongoing farrago of madness?

This brings us to the threshold of the Second World War. There is no doubt that Mussolini had a programme of conquest in mind, and that in full-throated rhetoric he preached war and the establishment of a totalitarian state. It should be noted that he consulted neither his cabinet nor the Fascist Grand Council on

---

[14] R. J. B. Bosworth, *Mussolini* (London: Arnold, 2002), 297.

[15] The standard work still remains J. F. Coverdale, *Italian Intervention in the Spanish Civil War* (Princeton: Princeton University Press, 1975).

these matters. But it is not unusual in Italian history for such important diplomatic decisions to be made secretly. Salandra and Sonnino did the same in easing Italy from neutrality to war in 1915. And why was there no 'blood, toil, tears and sweat' asked of his country in making what was supposed to be something more strenuous than a mere phantom war? Was Mussolini afraid that Italians would rise up against him if he demanded major sacrifices?

Perhaps, in preparing the public to expect Olympian deeds from the regime through such means as overwrought journalism, the *Duce* set a trap for himself. According to a popular determinist notion, Mussolini did indeed fall victim to the cycle of violence he preached and to the immense pressure of expectations he had built up in large cross-sections of the Italian people. If the *Duce* failed to walk the talk, he would lose face and fascism would die out. Thus, according to this theory, he had brought about the ineluctable necessity to make war.[16]

No different from their forebears, the Italian people in 1940, from the *classe dirigente* on down, had mixed feelings over a big war for additional patches of empire. More unambiguously they distrusted Germans, felt ill at ease with Italy's racial laws, disliked the Pact of Steel, and feared Hitler and his Apocalypse Now. If Italians felt trapped in the Pact of Steel, why did the upper classes, fascist moderates, senior military authorities, business CEOs, and particularly the lower middle classes follow the *Duce* into war apparently without protest? Were the Italians, in spite of fascism, a people exemplifying 'the banality of good' who either tripped into the war as if by accident or were simply duped by the *Duce*?

These are murky issues that need to be clarified by a comprehensive study that breaks Italians down by class and institution. Was Italy's entry into the war mainly due to the manipulations of *il Duce* that ran counter to Italian history and public opinion? Or did war occur as a natural outgrowth of a history enshrined in nationalist myths since the Risorgimento?[17]

Perhaps Mussolini had reached a summit of fleeting popularity on 10 June 1940 because his timing was shrewd and it seemed to many that he had played his cards cleverly, even for a country as ill prepared as Italy. Who could question the *Duce*'s calculation that England, after the debacle of Dunkirk, would not be able to stand

[16] G. Schreiber, Part I: 'Political and Military Development in the Mediterranean Area, 1939–1940', in G. Schreiber, B. Stegemann, and D. Vogel (eds), *Germany and the Second World War* (Oxford: Clarendon Press, 1995), 5–179; J. Petersen, 'Die Außenpolitik des faschistischen Italien als historisches Problem', *Vierteljahreshefte für Zeitgeschichte*, 22 (1974), 417–57; idem, 'Gesellschaftssystem, Ideologie und Interesse in der Außenpolitik des faschistischen Italien', *Quellen und Forschungen aus italienischen Archiven und Bibliotheken*, 54 (1974), 428–70.

[17] Two recent surveys of Italy's approach to the Second World War squarely in the intentionalist school are R. M. Salerno, *Vital Crossroads: Mediterranean Origins of the Second World War, 1935–1940* (Ithaca, NY: Cornell University Press, 2002), and G. B. Strang, *On the Fiery March: Mussolini Prepares for War* (Westport, CT: Praeger, 2003). While both these books, based on a vast array of military and political archival materials, convincingly argue that Mussolini had a coherent programme of imperialist expansion and was bent on war against the Western Powers to achieve it, neither attempts to weave into his account any kind of structural analysis of Italian domestic institutions and classes.

alone against the full fury of Hitler's wrath? After a short but sharp and victorious fight, in a war that Hitler supposedly had already won, Italy would co-author a rearrangement of power in the Mediterranean. The idea that America and the Soviet Union would eventually join in a crusade against the dictators was at that point unimaginable.

What kind of ally did Mussolini intend to be? Reminiscent of the old Liberal refrains of 'l'Italia farà da sè', or of 'Sonnino's war', Italy would fight a 'parallel war': not with Germany, not for Germany, but for Italy on the side of Germany. This formula revealed both a decided fear of Teutonic supremacy and Mussolini's awareness that none of Italy's imperialist ambitions could ever be realized without Hitler's victories against Britain or against his will. Nor was there to be any joint military planning. The woebegone parallel-war idea, added to the lack of any joint Axis military planning, hardly represented Fascist Italy's commitment to a blood brotherhood with Nazi Germany.

II. Italy in the Second World War

No one will dispute the obvious, that Italy's performance in the war was one of unrelieved mishaps and failure. Mussolini's troops attacking the French in the Alps quickly bogged down and those in the Libyan desert got no traction. He was unwilling to induce Franco to join in the war that would have facilitated capture of the Suez Canal and failed to get an immediate peace treaty from France to give Italy full measure on its claims to Tunis, Corsica, and Djibouti. The *Duce*'s life's dream to lead a triumphal march through Cairo to the edge of the Suez Canal, mounted on a white charger and brandishing the sword of Islam, miscarried dismally because his navy remained anchored at port and because his chief desert general, Rodolfo Graziani, trembled at the very idea of staging offensive warfare against the skeleton British forces arrayed against him on the Libyan frontier.

In the absence of military initiatives, Mussolini engaged in a juggler's act, hoping to time an offensive in the desert with a German landing in England—Operation Sealion. When Hitler cancelled the invasion plan later that month, it put an end to Mussolini's calculation that England would soon be knocked out of the war. While the Italian army in Libya stagnated under the burning summer sun, the British utilized the breathing space to build up their forces for a counterattack that was successfully launched on 9 December 1940. Still, Mussolini rejected much-needed armour until crushing Italian military defeats left him lost in African sand. To avert a complete collapse, he finally sought German aid. Once the Desert Fox arrived in February 1941 to take command of the Afrika Korps, Italy's 'parallel war' was over.

Without consulting his German allies, Mussolini had launched an attack on Greece on 28 October 1940, but gave his military practically no time to prepare a well-drilled and equipped invasion force. The Greek campaign turned out to be a masterpiece of ineptitude that verged on rank humiliation when the Greek army won a series of major victories. Disaster nearly struck when a valiant offensive by the Greeks drove the Italians back into Albania. An Albanian Dunkirk loomed. Finally reinforcements poured in to stiffen the Italian defences. Stalemate ensued. The Germans broke the logjam by knifing through the Balkans to crush the exhausted Greeks in April 1941. The Axis powers divided the country and, as usual, the Germans gave themselves the lion's share of the plunder. In possession of efficient machinery of destruction, they also outdid their Axis partner in cruelty visited on the native Greek population.

Mussolini's long-held dream to break up Yugoslavia finally came to fruition after the German air force had reduced Belgrade to rubble on 6 April 1941. The *Duce* rode into the defeated country on Hitler's coat-tails and impotently obeyed a German *diktat* on the allocation of conquered territories that robbed Italy of its Balkan *spazio vitale*. When the Italian Second Army arrived to take up occupation duties, it was welcomed by chaos. Ante Pavelić, Mussolini's terrorist henchman, set up a regime in Zagreb to preside over an elephantine Croatia. But instead of ruling as a faithful Italian puppet, he promptly initiated a vicious genocide of Orthodox Serbs, Jews, and Gypsies. To the dismay of Rome, Zagreb, and Berlin, the Second Army gave refuge to the persecuted peoples and tolerated—and eventually befriended—'Chetnik' bands that the harried Orthodox had spontaneously organized to defend their communities from Ustasha outrages.

In the annexed territories of Dalmatia and Slovenia, the story turned out differently. When the Croats and Slovenes of these provinces failed to welcome the Italian conqueror, the fascist civilian rulers immediately launched Italianization programmes as their method of assimilating a 'culturally inferior' people into a 'civilized' Roman imperium of their imagination. Rather than comply, the captive peoples rose up in a communist-inspired resistance. General Mario Roatta, the commander of the Italian Second Army, took over the police powers from ineffectual fascist administrators and applied a brutish counter-insurgency programme on 1 March 1942 that eventually backfired, fanning ever-greater hatred of Italy on the part of the persecuted Slavs. Encountering tough partisan resistance and determined German rivalry, the engine of Italian imperialism frequently sputtered and eventually burned out, leaving behind many enemies and few heroes to honour at home. By the end of the year, it had become patently clear that the war against the partisans was a fool's errand.

As 1943 turned, everyone in Italy knew that the war had been lost, which placed Mussolini on the shakiest limb of his rule. Presiding over a demoralized army as bantam commander, he had nothing left in his arsenal of weapons save diplomacy. He tried to pull Hitler from Armageddon by urging him to sign a separate peace with the Soviet Union on the eastern front, an idea derisively dismissed in Berlin. A few limp overtures were made to London for a separate peace, but these came to nothing. The Allied offensive rolled on. After a tough fight, in one of the few instances that the Italians fought well and bravely, the Axis powers laid down their arms in Tunisia on 13 May. The Allies landed on Sicily on 10 July practically unopposed. On the 25th the sand in the fascist hourglass ran out when Mussolini was removed from power.

Many aspects of Italy's war have been exhaustively covered. Knox has devastatingly dissected the mismanagement, backwardness, and lack of preparation in all phases of Fascist military planning.[18] A battery of writers has exhaustively critiqued Italy's poor military performance in the North African desert and on the Mediterranean sea.[19] Italy's infamous invasion of Greece and the ensuing battlefield catastrophes provide comic-strip amusement on one of the most absurdly planned wars in modern times.[20]

Less well known has been Italy's occupation of conquered territories. Davide Rodogno has written a path-breaking study on Mussolini's conception of the 'New Mediterranean Order' in which he details vicious fascist occupation policies in Greece, France, and Yugoslavia. He discusses the notion posited by the Italian mass media in the post-war era that there is a clear difference between Italy and Germany with respect to their policies in countries they occupied. Thus the image of '*cattivo tedesco*', a fanatical warrior capable of any wickedness, is contrasted with '*bravo italiano*', the Italian 'good guy'.[21]

Rodogno has no truck with such distinctions; Germans and Italians all behaved badly. He proves beyond doubt that Italian generals, army ranks, *carabinieri*, and the rogue fascist militias implemented harsh counter-insurgency programmes that turned out to be open war on Italy's occupied peoples—Slovenes, Greeks, and Albanians. By resorting to internments, destruction of houses and villages, and hostage-taking, many Italians committed war crimes. Rodogno goes one step further by arguing that Italy's many war crimes were provoked, and committed, by signature fascists, who, in lock step, 'worked toward the *Duce*'. But is it not inevitable that occupiers undertaking counter-insurgency against a hostile population imprison, torture, blow up houses, and shoot innocent victims? Examples are legion of countries doing abominable things that are imperialist but not necessarily fascist: the British in Malaya, the French in Algeria, the Americans in Iraq.

---

[18] M. Knox, *Hitler's Italian Allies: Royal Armed Forces, Fascist Regime, and the War of 1940–1943* (Cambridge: Cambridge University Press, 2000).

[19] The best writer on Italy's North African campaign is Lucio Ceva. See his *Africa settentrionale 1940–1943* (Rome: Bonacci, 1982), and *Guerra mondiale: strategie e industria bellica 1939–1945* (Milan: FrancoAngeli, 2000).

[20] M. Cervi, *The Hollow Legions: Mussolini's Blunder in Greece 1940–1941* (New York: Doubleday, 1971).

[21] D. Rodogno, *Il nuovo ordine mediterraneo: le politiche di occupazione dell'Italia fascista in Europa (1940–1943)* (Turin: Bollati Boringhieri, 2003).

In my own research on the subject of Italy's conquest of Yugoslavia, I have arrived at the following preliminary conclusions: Italy's occupation was anything but monolithic; terror was not applied systematically; nor was there a linear or coherent Italian occupation policy given the grim reality of omnipresent ethnic violence and the crazy-quilt pattern of the Italian presence. Furthermore, Mussolini was hardly a micromanager of imperialism, and the Second Army acted like a loose cannon in its freelance scheming with the officially declared 'Chetnik' enemy. And yes, many Italians—military, *carabinieri*, and rogue militia—committed heinous war crimes. Finally, I suggest that, in the absence of clear directives from the top, the Italian imperial machinery of government was shredded by internecine rivalries. Once set into motion by Mussolini's decision to invade Yugoslavia, it lurched into a final *Götterdämmerung* with the Axis ally.[22]

Italy tottered into the war sclerotic and hidebound, and during hostilities 'fascist totalitarianism' appeared to be only a sad replica of the *Führer* state. When Italy's 'parallel war' ended in winter 1940–1, Mussolini lost the prestige, and the power, if he ever had it, to undertake radical revolution. Untouched by fascist 'commissars', the military continued to be a gnarled law unto itself, more loyal to the king than to the *Duce*. The party had never replaced the civil service, and the ardour of leading fascist hierarchs had been smothered by ministerial appointments in a bureaucracy where the Italian arts of obfuscation and delay worked against any 'totalitarian' reform. Nor had Mussolini created an SS apparatus to bring terror directly to region, village, and family, which, beyond lip-service obedience to the regime, still clung to tribal loyalties. As Germany's subaltern, the Fascist state staggered to the end lifeless and emasculated.

Who, in fact, can be held responsible for Italy's many dark deeds in the Second World War? No doubt Mussolini wins this race to infamy handily, but we need more study to determine how widely the net should be cast to catch accomplices. Here we must try to define who deserves the epithet fascist. Certainly *squadristi* and active Party members were true believers. How many of these retainers were actually involved in important Italian decision making during the war? A cursory look at the diaries and memoirs of those industrialists and diplomats exercising power in Mussolini's dictatorship reveals essentially moderate fascists, and often German-haters, who might better be described as ambitious traditional nationalists following Mussolini as long as he respected the authority of crown and church. Many of these men stayed loyal to fascism till the end out of fear of communism and social disorder at home should the regime collapse.

Having set a high value on heroism and fighting, Mussolini, his following, and the Italian right as a whole, despite their fear and dislike of Nazi Germany, were drawn to it by qualities that they shared with Hindenburg and Hitler: individual

---

[22] H. J. Burgwyn, *Empire on the Adriatic: Mussolini's Conquest of Yugoslavia 1941–1943* (New York: Enigma Books, 2005).

discipline, community spirit, and self-sacrifice. Like their German counterparts, they instinctively hated liberalism and communism and vowed to destroy them, in alliance with the Axis ally if need be. But when the true Nazi spirit emerged gradually from the conservative and reactionary matrix into blatant nihilistic reality during the war, many of these same Italians hurried to dissociate themselves from the Third Reich and drew up reasons why they had been fooled. Their original image of Nazism had been distorted. Nazism was not the legacy or prolongation of pan-Germanism, as they had once understood, but an unprecedented form of racist imperialism that had caught them by surprise.

Is it true, as many fascist fellow-travellers and their nationalist apologists still argue to this day, that they had not the vaguest idea of the real nature of German dynamism? Is it possible to figure out with any degree of accuracy what the various classes of Italian people really thought about German Nazism as opposed to what Mussolini through his monopoly on the mass media told them to believe? Is it enough to rely on police and prefecture reports that might have distorted reality by reflecting what they thought the *Duce* wanted to hear?

Having reviewed important themes in Fascist foreign policy and indicated areas requiring additional research, perhaps we can venture a judgement on the nature of the 'Brutal Friendship' during the Second World War.

Although Mussolini and Hitler firmly believed their shared values to constitute a blood vow of solidarity, Hitler, though esteeming the *Duce*, lied to him, while Mussolini, since he was mesmerized by Nazi power and was totally reliant on the Third Reich to carry out his programme of conquest, swallowed his contempt and fear of the *Führer*. Mussolini ultimately chose to link Italy's fate with Germany from a position of weakness. Driven by precepts of war and empire building, he ignored national interests that required a foreign policy of limited aims consonant with Italy's paucity of natural resources and an underdeveloped industry incapable of supplying the armed forces with the sinews of modern warfare. Hitler, on the other hand, dealt with Mussolini from a position of overwhelming strength; he did not need Italy as an ally. With a mighty war machine and a militarized nation at his disposal, he enjoyed having the *Duce* on board for sentimental reasons, for his fellow dictator once had been an inspiration and beacon of light. No matter what the power disparities were between their two countries, Mussolini and Hitler were attracted to each other by a shared fascination for war, a common antipathy toward the Western democracies, and a relentless urge to dominate.

Although both *Führer* and *Duce* wrote new and terrible chapters in the handbook of imperial conquest, they envisioned the Axis New Order somewhat differently. In his goal of annihilating 'inferior' races, Hitler made a successful beginning, but did not have time to settle conquered territory with the master race. Mussolini stopped short of systematic mass killing—except for Africans—but frequently talked about clearing out native peoples for Italian settlement. People died en masse from malnutrition and unsanitary conditions in Italy's camps, but not from Nazi-style torture and gassing. While the single-minded Hitler demonstrated a savage capacity for evil, Mussolini's lapses in morality and cheap theatrics made him appear by comparison a dabbler in wickedness.

Yet, as Rodogno suggests, it is most likely that Mussolini, if he had been given his druthers, would have implemented a nasty 'New Mediterranean World', a euphemism for an imperial asylum of racist oppression and economic plunder. But he could have done so only under the cover of Hitler. On the other hand, if Italy had truly been a Great Power, there might have been no Axis. Mussolini would have barred Germany from the annexation of Austria, avenged himself against the Western democracies, and enlarged the Italian empire.

These 'ifs' and speculations have been provided to show that there are unexplained ambiguities in the 'Brutal Friendship' that continue to taunt us. Before the symbiotic relationship between Mussolini and Hitler can be better understood, a gifted historian is needed to provide us with a comprehensive study of Italy in the Second World War that weaves together, by means of a structural analysis, the domestic scene, foreign policy, and war and occupation.

BIBLIOGRAPHY

BOSWORTH, R. J. B., *Benito Mussolini and the Fascist Destruction of Liberal Italy, 1900–1945* (Adelaide: Rigby, 1973).
—— 'Italian Foreign Policy and its Historiography', in R. Bosworth and G. Rizzo (eds), *Altro Polo: Intellectuals and their Ideas in Contemporary Italy* (Sydney: F. May Foundation, 1983).
—— *Mussolini* (London: Arnold, 2002).
—— *The Italian Dictatorship: Problems and Perspectives in the Interpretation of Mussolini and Fascism* (London: Arnold, 1998).
BURGWYN, H. J., *Empire on the Adriatic: Mussolini's Conquest of Yugoslavia 1941–1943* (New York: Enigma Books, 2005).
CASSELS, A., 'Switching Partners: Italy, in A. J. P. Taylor's *Origins of the Second World War*', in G. Martel (ed.), *The Origins of the Second World War Reconsidered: The A. J. P. Taylor Debate after Twenty Years* (Boston: Allen & Unwin, 1986).
CEVA, L., *Africa settentrionale 1940–1943* (Rome: Bonacci, 1982).
—— *Strategie e industria bellica 1939–1945* (Milan: FrancoAngeli, 2000).
COVERDALE, J. F., *Italian Intervention in the Spanish Civil War* (Princeton: Princeton University Press, 1975).
DEAKIN, F. W., *The Brutal Friendship: Mussolini, Hitler and the Fall of Italian Fascism* (Garden City, NY: Anchor Books, 1966).
DE FELICE, R., *Mussolini il fascista*, i: *La conquista del potere 1921–5*, ii: *L'organizzazione dello stato fascista, 1925–1929*; *Mussolini il duce*, i: *Gli anni del consenso, 1929–1936*, ii: *Lo stato totalitario 1936–1940*; *Mussolini l'alleato 1940–1945*, i: *L'Italia in guerra 1940–1943*, ii: *La Guerra civile 1943–1945* (Turin: Einaudi, 1968–97).

KNOX, M., *Common Destiny: Dictatorship, Foreign Policy, and War in Fascist Italy and Nazi Germany* (Cambridge: Cambridge University Press, 2000).

——*Hitler's Italian Allies: Royal Armed Forces, Fascist Regime, and the War of 1940–1943* (Cambridge: Cambridge University Press, 2000).

——'L'ultima guerra dell'Italia fascista', in B. Micheletti and P. P. Poggio (eds), *L'Italia in guerra 1940–1943* (Brescia: Fondiazione 'Luigi Micheletti', 1991).

——*Mussolini Unleashed, 1939–1941: Politics and Strategy in Fascist Italy's Last War* (Cambridge: Cambridge University Press, 1982).

——'The Fascist Regime, its Foreign Policy and its Wars: An "Anti-Anti-Fascist" Orthodoxy?', *Contemporary European History*, 4 (1995), 347–65.

MORI, R., *Mussolini e la conquista dell'Etiopia* (Florence: Le Monnier, 1978).

PETERSEN, J., 'Die Außenpolitik des faschistischen Italien als historisches Problem', *Vierteljahrshefte für Zeitgeschichte*, 22 (1974), 417–57.

—— 'Gesellschaftssystem, Ideologie und Interesse in der Außenpolitik des faschistischen Italien', *Quellen und Forschungen aus italienischen Archiven und Bibliotheken*, 54 (1974), 428–70.

QUARTARARO, R., *Roma fra Londra e Berlino: la politica estera fascista dal 1931 al 1940* (Milan: Bonacci, 1980).

RODOGNO, D., *Il nuovo ordine mediterraneo: le politiche di occupazione dell'Italia fascista in Europa (1940–1943)* (Turin: Bollati Boringhieri, 2003).

SALVEMINI, G., *Prelude to World War II* (London: Gollancz, 1953).

SCHREIBER, G., Part I: 'Political and Military Developments in the Mediterranean Area, 1939–1940', in G. Schreiber, B. Stegemann, and D. Vogel (eds), *Germany and the Second World War* (Oxford: Clarendon Press, 1995).

PART IV

OTHERS

CHAPTER 18

COMMUNISM

FASCISM'S 'OTHER'?

ROGER D. MARKWICK

At first sight, there seems much to commend in the view not only that Soviet communism and Italian Fascism were close 'totalitarian' cousins, if not twins like Stalinism and Nazism, but also that the threat of communism begat fascism in its Italian, German, and other European guises. 'Totalitarianism', a concept proudly endorsed by Mussolini in his definition of Fascism in 1932, which became common currency among Western scholars during the Cold War, has usually been identified with what Hannah Arendt called the 'radical evil' of Hitler and Stalin rather than that of Mussolini.[1] The latter part of this essay, however, primarily compares Stalin's Soviet Union with Mussolini's Fascist Italy, with occasional asides on Fascist Germany. Close inspection of Italian Fascism and Soviet communism, on a historical basis rather than abstract, political science principles, suggests that their similarities were more apparent than real. Viewed through the totality of their social, economic, and political structures, functions, and consequences, and their place in relation to the 'capitalist world-system', to invoke Immanuel Wallerstein,[2] rather than exclusively through the narrow prism of Party-state institutions and practices, Fascist Italy and the USSR are revealed essentially as antonyms. That is not to say that there were no similarities or symbiosis between them. On the

[1] J. Kohn, 'Arendt's Concept and Description of Totalitarianism', *Social Research*, 69/2 (2002), 621–57.

[2] I. Wallerstein, *World-Systems Analysis: An Introduction* (Durham, NC: Duke University Press, 2004).

contrary, the rise of fascism in its Italian and other European manifestations was, in good part, a response to the Bolshevik Revolution in Russia and its shock waves in Europe after the First World War. But fascism, like communism, was also a radical reaction to the crises that racked European states and societies in the aftermath of that traumatic, total, war. Fascism's victories, especially in Italy and Germany, arose from the failure of socialist revolution to resolve those crises. But to win, fascism had to appropriate much of communism's revolutionary, mass appeal to traumatized European societies. This appropriation goes a long way towards explaining the outward similarities of radical European left and right in the inter-war years.

I. Fascism: Reaction to Bolshevism?

Communism as a movement certainly preceded fascism. The former could be dated at least from 1848 in Europe and, in the case of Russia, from 1898. Fascism as an organized political movement in Italy was not established until 1921, as the Partito Nazionale Fascista (PNF; National Fascist Party). But immediate precursors to fascism in the twentieth century were to be found in tsarist Russia. After the defeat of the 1905 Russian Revolution, the Black Hundreds, viciously anti-Semitic gangs, unleashed pogroms with the connivance of tsarist authorities against the remnants of the revolutionary movement. When Mussolini's Fascist movement first erupted onto the scene, Lenin likened it to Italian 'Black Hundreds': by implication, a creature of the Italian state, with a purely reactionary ideology. Counter-revolutionary fascism was, but also more; it was a primarily middle-class mass movement with a dynamic independent of the Italian state and with an ideology that fused progress and reaction.

Fascism simultaneously repudiated the revolutionary movement—demonized as 'bolshevism'—and mimicked its organization and its tactics. But, far from simply appropriating 'bolshevism', it parodied it. Mass politics was key to both; but where communism, at least in its Leninist phase, in the context of war and revolution, advanced internationalist, anti-war demands designed to win working-class and peasant support to challenge the economic basis of capitalism as a system, fascism indulged in a populist demagoguery that played on middle-class nationalist fears and prejudices, while attacking only capitalist excesses such as war profiteers and those who lived off interest. Where communists sought power through armed insurrection against the semi-feudal states of East Central Europe, fascists and their allies colluded with these tottering militarist states against the left and labour movements. In the case of Italy, in October 1922 the PNF and its blackshirts indulged in a theatrical 'March on Rome', crucially acquiesced in by monarchist, military, business, and church interests. Far from being Italy's 'October Revolution', a seizure of state power by armed insurrection, the March was a semi-constitutional victory that handed Mussolini the prime ministership and legitimized the place of fascism in the new political order as a bulwark against any further left-wing threats to the status quo.

From its inception, Italian Fascism defined itself in opposition to 'bolshevism', particularly in its indigenous incarnations, although it was more ambivalent about Russian bolshevism, which it viewed simultaneously as an Asiatic enemy and as inspiration for revolutionary modernization. However, fascism was not simply a radical nationalist reaction to the rising tide of revolution towards the end of the First World War. Fascism was also an expression of the weakness of Italian parliamentary liberalism, of Italy as a nation state, and of the Italian bourgeoisie as bearer of modernization. The shock troops of fascism, the *squadristi*, were not merely violently anti-Bolshevik; they also saw themselves as revolutionary nationalists, intent on replacing a listless Italian parliamentarism with a dynamic, authoritarian 'new Italy'. As Mussolini himself put it on the eve of the March on Rome, fascism was consummating the Risorgimento.[3]

In short, fascism expressed the crisis of a late developing Italian capitalism and its weak state apparatus, caught between an already established world capitalist system, dominated by a few imperial powers such as Britain and France, and increasingly militant working-class and peasant movements. In these respects, Italy had much in common with tsarist Russia, where an even deeper crisis demanded either a decisive break with the past, through socialist revolution, or a return to it, through massive military-fascist repression. Ultimately, the failure of the Italian left to resolve Italy's crisis as the Bolsheviks had done in Russia, by seizing political power and breaking out of the world capitalist system, allowed fascism to step into the breach. Destroying the labour and peasant movements as a whole, under the banner of smashing bolshevism, was an essential component of resolving the crisis of Italian capitalism in the name of a dynamic, 'new Italy'. In short, both Italian revolutionary socialism and pseudo-revolutionary Italian Fascism were products of the very same crisis of state and society; hence their seeming symmetry; hence too, their antonymic solutions to that crisis. One could only flourish at the expense of the other: there was no 'third way'.

Fascism was thus both an expression and a cause of the crisis of the Italian Liberal state.[4] In the modern era of mass politics, political stability depended on creating mass support for the state, not only to maintain the status quo but as a counterweight to radical forces from the left, which could no longer be contained by the traditional measures of police and military repression, as in the 1890s, or by

---

[3] Cited in R. Griffin (ed.), *Fascism* (Oxford: Oxford University Press, 1995), 39–41.

[4] See G. Eley, 'Fascism as the Product of "Crisis"', in A. A. Kallis (ed.), *The Fascism Reader* (London: Routledge, 2003), 133–4.

integrating them into the Liberal parliamentary state, as had occurred under Prime Minister Giolitti (1901–14). Exacerbated by the outbreak of European war, this crisis of Italian Liberalism reached a crescendo in the so-called 'red years' of 1919–20 when bolshevism, in reality working-class and peasant militancy, seemingly threatened to engulf the entire country.

Violent anti-bolshevism, based on a hatred of Marxism's class-based revolutionary internationalism, was certainly at the core of the Fascist movement from its inception in 1919. But in Italy the infant Partito Communista Italiano (PCd'I; Communist Party of Italy), not formally established until 1921, was not its primary target; rather, it was the nominally revolutionary Partito Socialista Italiano (PSI; Italian Socialist Party). Nevertheless, the spectre of bolshevism and the role of fascism in combating it were essential to its *raison d'être*. Speaking at the founding conference of the Fasci di Combattimento in Milan on 23 March 1919, Mussolini reasserted the movement's 'revolutionary' nature, but simultaneously repudiated Russian bolshevism and Italian socialism, which he depicted as synonymous. Equating bolshevism with economic ruin, 'famine and hunger', and 'ferocious dictatorship', he rejected it because it was a 'Russian phenomenon', and therefore alien to 'Western civilization'. Accordingly, he declared 'war on socialism . . . because it has opposed nationalism', whereas fascism was based 'on the war and the victory'. Likewise, the Fascist Agrarian Programme (adopted January 1921), was stridently anti-communist and anti-socialist, warning the Italian peasantry against the 'pitiless' 'Soviet Commissars' who 'shot the *muzhiks*' and the 'collectivist transformation of all Italy into single administrative *latifondo*'.[5]

By March 1920, by which time the northern industrial triangle and the Po Valley were aflame with labour and peasant league militancy, Mussolini, the ex-PSI militant who had proclaimed in 1915 that 'Socialism is in my very blood', was preparing to spill the blood of his former comrades. Now proud of the title 'reactionary' and hailing 'freedom of the individual', he denounced the socialist state as a 'Moloch' and more barbaric than 'cannibals', a verbal threat that the future *Duce* was prepared to back with armed force.[6] As socialist support surged in urban and rural northern Italy, at the second Fascist congress Mussolini denounced the socialists for being 'un-Italian'. Amid the turbulent, two-million strong, occupation of the factories in August–September 1920, Mussolini was in full flight, denouncing 'class struggle' in favour of production: 'Our principles have been and remain these: to defend the national war effort, to enhance the existing victory, strenuously to oppose the imitation of revolutionary Russia indulged in by our home-grown socialists.' In the face of the factory occupations, he boasted that 'a million sheep will always be dispersed by the roar of one lion'. Only the fascist lion, alone among the anti-socialist parties, had the courage to act. In short, Mussolini was forging a new

---

[5] 'The Birth of Fascist Movement' and 'Program of the Italian Fascist Movement', in C. F. Delzell (ed.), *Mediterranean Fascism 1919–1945* (London: Macmillan, 1971), 7–21.

[6] R. J. B. Bosworth, *Mussolini* (London: Arnold, 2002), 138–9.

weapon that the Italian state could wield against the labour movement: a political party that, mimicking the labour movement itself, was organized along military lines for extra-parliamentary, violent mass action.

II. FASCIST ANTI-COMMUNIST VIOLENCE

Violent action against the labour movement was inherent in the Fascist movement, which prided itself on action rather than words. The political crisis of 1919–20 was accompanied by an upsurge in 'private political violence' unleashed by the incipient Fascist movement against the socialists, starting with the torching of the *Avanti!* offices in May 1919. By mid-1920, after the farce of D'Annunzio's Fiume expedition, *squadrismo* metamorphosed from a radical-nationalist, *putschist* movement to one that, under the banner of 'anti-bolshevism', exclusively targeted the labour movement. Here lay the novel, lethal effectiveness of fascism: a mass political party organized along military lines to grind down the mass labour and peasant movements.

Colluding with the coercive arms of the state—the police and the army— *squadrismo* acted as an extra-legal arm of the state unleashed against Socialist Party and union organizations. *Squadrismo* terror operated according to a set formula: intimidating, hysterically patriotic, propaganda campaigns were followed by physical assaults on socialist clubs and offices and the decimation of peasant league organizations, which were replaced by employers' unions.[7] In 1921 virtual civil war reigned. In that year alone, extra-parliamentary *squadristi* and police violence took the lives of 1,500 workers and peasants; 700 workers' organizations were destroyed. In 1922 the Fascist *squadristi* again took the offensive against the left. In a 'night of terror' in July, they scorched Mussolini's home region of Romagna, 'determined to finish for ever Red terror'.[8] By November 1924 PCd'I leader, Antonio Gramsci, who would die in a fascist jail, despairingly acknowledged that sustained *squadristi* violence had 'reduced the working class to "a disconnected, fragmented, scattered mass" with no energy or purpose', a conclusion that contradicted his accompanying conclusion that 'fascism and liberal democracy were "objectively alike" ' and the subsequent consolidation of the Fascist dictatorship in January 1925. The murder of Socialist deputy Matteotti in 1924 and subsequently of a Fascist deputy triggered a 'second wave' of *squadristi* violence, again justified as anti-communist. The radical *ras* Roberto Farinacci called for vengeance: 'The land of Dante and Mazzini must

[7] A. Lyttelton, *The Seizure of Power: Fascism in Italy 1919–1929* (2nd edn, London: Weidenfeld and Nicolson, 1987), 35, 52–4, 147.
[8] Bosworth, *Mussolini*, 164.

not be consigned to Lenin.'[9] This was a rhetorical justification for repression; by this time there was little threat from the left. It was precisely the violent grinding down of an already defeated working class and the paralysis of the PSI, not the threat of Bolshevik revolution, that had facilitated the consolidation of self-styled fascist 'totalitarianism'.

III. Other Fascisms' Anti-Communism

Violent anti-communism lay at the core of all fascisms. Amid the turmoil following the First World War, East Central Europe was awash with ferocious, fascistic movements. Finland's White Guards under General Mannerheim, and Hungary's 'White Terror' under Admiral Horthy, were primarily military regimes accompanied by what would nowadays be called 'death squads'. Fiercely anti-communist, they unleashed lethal 'White Terror', usually on the pretext of Bolshevik 'Red Terror'. Some 27,000 'Reds' died under Mannerheim in the wake of his victory in the Finnish Civil War (1918), most executed or in concentration camps; an estimated 5,000 died under Horthy following the overthrow of Bela Kun's communist government in 1919. These were the forerunners of a series of savagely repressive, anti-communist, governments and movements that emerged in East Central Europe during the decade after the war, notably the Tsankov regime in Bulgaria (1923–6), Marshal Pilsudski's dictatorship in Poland (1926–39), and the Iron Guard movement in Romania, established in 1927. If not strictly fascist, all of these regimes or movements combined to varying degrees military and religious reaction and violent plebeian support; and all were fuelled by fiercely patriotic anti-communism, often combined with anti-Semitism.

Fascism, however, in the sense of a mass plebeian movement, was to assume a particularly virulent form in crisis-ridden Germany in the aftermath of military defeat and the collapse of the monarchy in 1918. Again, like Italy and Russia before it, this was a crisis of a later-industrializing state and society, caught between the anvil of an already established world capitalist system and the hammer of a powerful, politicized working class. But in the case of Germany, the crisis and the fascist response was even more dramatic than in Italy, not only due to the near collapse of the traditional state in the wake of military defeat, but also to the strength of the contending domestic interests: a powerful industrial-commercial sector aligned with a military-feudal state; a strong, increasingly radical, workers' movement; and, not least, a large urbanized middle class (unlike Italy) which could provide a reservoir for mass fascism.

---

[9] Bosworth, *Mussolini*, 200–1.

Vicious manifestations of German anti-communism surfaced in the wake of the abortive November 1918 revolution. The 'Union for the Struggle against Bolshevism', formed at the end of that year with the support of conservative business and state figures, targeted Rosa Luxemburg's and Karl Liebknecht's Spartacist Union not only as the cause of domestic upheaval, but also as an agent of Russian bolshevism, often luridly depicted in political propaganda as black wolves from the east drowning Europe in blood. The infamous Freikorps volunteers, akin to the *squadristi*, fought alongside the Whites in the Baltics; turning their murderous skills to eliminating Luxemburg and Liebknecht and hundreds of other communists in the period 1918–23, many eventually found their place in the Nazi movement.

While the anti-Semitic Hitler initially paid limited attention to bolshevism or the Soviet Union, as the NSDAP began to take shape in 1922–4, he increasingly viewed bolshevism as the modern manifestation of the Jewish conspiracy against European civilization and the Soviet Union as Germany's real enemy, destruction of which would open the way to German *Lebensraum* in the Slav east, as he threatened in *Mein Kampf*. In the Weimar Republic, German fascism fed on a diet of traditional fear of Russia, of Bolshevik revolution and anti-Semitism; Weimar's liberal cultural trends were construed as the 'culture of bolshevism'.[10]

Although, in general, 'Judeo-bolshevism' was the primary target of Nazi venom and Storm Trooper (SA) violence, on the road to power, indeed up to *Kristallnacht* 1938, it was politicide against domestic communism and warmongering against its alleged citadel, the USSR, rather than genocide against the Jews, that defined Nazi politics. As Goebbels's Propaganda Ministry decreed in 1935–6, the 'German people' have to be shown that 'they have been saved by Adolf Hitler' from 'bolshevism' their 'mortal enemy' that threatens them 'with the help of the Jews'.[11] As was the case with Italian Fascism, Nazism's crushing of the entire labour movement, not just the Communist Party of Germany, was the precondition for 'totalitarian' dictatorship and eventually 'total' war, in Germany's case against Soviet 'Judeo-bolshevism'.

IV. Italian Fascism and Soviet Communism

Italian Fascism certainly had no truck with home-grown communism. However, communism in Soviet Russia was, until the mid-1930s, viewed ambivalently and,

[10] G. Camphausen and P. Jahn (eds), *Museum Berlin-Karlshorst* [Exhibition and Guide] (Berlin, 2005), 8.

[11] 'Antikommunist Propagandafeldzug im Inland', 1935–6 Bundesarchiv, Museum Berlin-Karlshorst [Exhibition].

by some fascists, sympathetically. Mussolini carefully distinguished between bol-shevism as an ideology and the Soviet Union as a state. Russian bolshevism was depicted by Mussolini as the bastard child of Asiatic, Russian backwardness and the bearer of 'extreme, aggressive, and expansionist pan-Slavism', a perspective that derived from traditional Italian nationalist phobias about 'the East'. By severing the 1917 revolution, which Mussolini called a 'deceit', arguing that it had estab-lished a centralized state not socialism, from bolshevism, which he derided as a 'Russian myth', Mussolini effectively 'denied the universality of the Red October'; an ideological weapon he wielded against Italian communism as 'anti-nation'.[12] Accordingly, the early Soviet Union was seen not so much as fascism's arch enemy, as Nazism and other rightists saw it, but rather as a revolutionary rival, doomed to fail due to its abolition of private property and lack of the Fascist spirit, seemingly confirmed by Lenin's retreat to the New Economic Policy (NEP) in 1921. Despite Mussolini's vehement anti-bolshevism, he preferred coexistence to confrontation with Moscow; among his first acts as Prime Minister in 1922 was to recognize the Soviet Union, thereby laying the groundwork for harmonious diplomatic and commercial relations for more than a decade.

Mussolini could tolerate the Soviet Union, provided it did not try to extend international revolution; the suppression of Comintern activity in Italy in 1923–6 provided the necessary reassurance. Moreover Mussolini, like many other fascists, saw significant 'intellectual', if not 'political', affinities between Soviet communism and Italian Fascism. Indeed, the first Italian comparative study appeared in 1924: written by Mussolini's old socialist admirer turned Fascist Torquato Nanni, it ar-gued that bolshevism and fascism had common roots. The decade from 1925 to 1935 saw unprecedented interest in the Soviet experiment as a possible model, facilitated by numerous fascist visitors and quality translations of Soviet publications, includ-ing the writings of Trotsky. *Critica Fascista*, published by Minister for Corporations Giuseppe Bottai, became the vehicle for Mussolini himself to keep abreast of Soviet developments in law and economic planning.

At the beginning of the 1930s, however, fascist perceptions of the USSR began to shift. Crucial factors were Stalin's turn to force-marched industrialization in 1929 and Mussolini's Lateran Pacts with the Vatican, signed in February that same year. While fascist advocates of corporatism were fascinated by the Soviets' Five-Year Plan 'programmatic economy' and the 'new', 'collective man', the Pacts endorsed the Vatican's more militant anti-communism, to which Mussolini's regime began to revert.[13] The accession of a rival, fiercely anti-communist, fascism in Berlin in 1933 also helped to drive a wedge between Rome and Moscow, as Mussolini reasserted his fascist credentials.

---

[12] G. Petracchi, 'Bolshevism in the Fascist Mirror (1)', *Telos*, 133 (2006), 45–7.   [13] Ibid. 50–4.

Symptomatic of the growing divide was the publication in 1935 of *Empire of Forced Labour*, which depicted bolshevism as a substitute tsarist serfdom.[14] Other Fascist ideologues rightly discerned profound changes under Stalin—the enormous, state-driven industrialization coupled with the resurgence of patriotic, traditional culture—but wrongly assumed that the Soviet Union was on the road to becoming 'fascist'.[15] Mussolini's intervention along with Hitler in support of Franco in the Spanish Civil War (1936–9) hitched Fascist Italy's wagon firmly to Hitler's anti-communist crusade, formalized in the 'Rome–Berlin Axis' of October 1936 and the 1937 'Anti-Comintern Pact', which also included militarist Japan.

The road to fascist war against the USSR was now being paved. Within both Italy and Germany, anti-Soviet propaganda was to the fore. In Germany, it had taken a qualitative leap forward after 1933, when the Reich Ministry of Propaganda unleashed a torrent of anti-Soviet press releases, books, exhibitions, and films, a campaign which peaked with the Nuremberg Nazi Party rallies of 1935–8. Meanwhile in Italy, 'bolshevism stopped being fascism's ideological mirror and became the target of its propaganda'.[16] In 1937 a Centro di Studi Anti-Comunisti was established to study Soviet politics, which, fuelled by the Stalin purges, were now being likened to those of a bloodthirsty Asian despotism. Mussolini was aghast when the August 1939 Ribbentrop–Molotov Non-Aggression Pact was signed, fearing that it would facilitate Bolshevik penetration of East Central Europe. But within months Hitler was planning to unleash his final crusade against 'Judeo-bolshevism'—a fateful decision that would ultimately be the downfall of both Italian and German fascism.

V. THE STALINIST STATE

Soviet communism, particularly in its Stalinist guise, clearly constituted both Italian and German fascisms' 'other', if to varying degrees. But was Stalin's state merely the Janus face of fascist totalitarianism as so many commentators have suggested, although usually with Nazism in mind? Certainly, as we saw above, in the 1930s some Italian Fascists believed that Stalin's Soviet Union was heading towards fascism. They were not alone. Recognition that Stalinism mirrored many fascist values came also from the Russian extreme right. Under the influence of fascism, Nicholai Ustryalov, a former Propaganda Minister in Admiral Kolchak's anti-Bolshevik, civil

---

[14] L. Barzini, *L'impero del lavoro forzato*, in S. G. Payne, 'Soviet Anti-Fascism: Theory and Practice, 1921–45', *Totalitarian Movements and Religions*, 4/2 (2003), 19.

[15] R. Bertoni, *Il trionfo del nell'URSS* (1934) and *Russia: Trionfo del fascismo* (1937), in Payne, 'Soviet Anti-Fascism', 20.

[16] Petracchi, 'Bolshevism in the Fascist Mirror (1)', 59.

war government (1918–19), concluded that neo-Slavophil, étatist 'National bolshevism' was the best guarantor of Russian statehood. Ustryalov welcomed Stalin's doctrine of 'Socialism in One Country', with its authoritarian, autarchic industrialization and its increasing embrace of Russian nationalism. Nikolai Bukharin, a former Stalin ally turned oppositionist, feared Ustryalov's support for Stalin was an omen of 'fascist Caesarism' emerging on the basis of capitalist restoration.[17]

In the post-war era, Western Sovietology also discerned convergences between fascism and communism. The Cold War, which set in almost immediately after the Soviet defeat of Nazi Germany, saw the paradigm of 'totalitarianism' shift from fascism, more precisely Nazism, to Soviet communism. The criteria for the classical 'model' of 'totalitarian dictatorship' advanced by Carl J. Friedrich and Zbigniew K. Brzezinski in 1956 included:

1. 'a single mass party typically led by one man, the "dictator" ';
2. 'central control and direction of the entire economy';
3. 'a system of terror ... effected through party and secret-police';
4. 'near-complete monopoly ... of all means of effective mass communication';
5. 'an elaborate ideology'.[18]

First applied to Fascist Italy by Friedrich's student Dante Germino in 1959,[19] these alleged totalitarian 'traits' provide a useful if not sufficient basis for comparing Mussolini's Italy and Stalin's Soviet Union. The discussion that follows also includes comparative considerations on political discourse and aesthetics, women and the family, and colonialism and war. It also has a different starting point. Friedrich and Brzezinski's criteria focused almost exclusively on the functions of the state. However, any discussion of Stalinism must locate it in the political economy of the Soviet revolution.

VI. THE STALIN DICTATORSHIP

The starting point for any serious comparative analysis between fascism and Stalinism must be that Stalin's rise to power in the 1920s was not the result of combining *piazza* demagoguery with opportunist electoral overtures to established monarchy, military, and church, as Mussolini did, but a gradual accretion of power within

---

[17] T. Krausz, *Sovietskii Termidor: Dukhovnye predposylki stalinskogo povorota (1917–28)* (Budapest: Vengerskii institut rusistiki, 1997), 87, 92, 99, 128–9.

[18] C. J. Friedrich and Z. K. Brzezinski, ' "Totalitarian Dictatorship" and Fascism', in Kallis (ed.), *The Fascism Reader*, 259.

[19] D. L. Germino, *The Italian Fascist Party in Power: A Study in Totalitarian Rule* (Minneapolis: University of Minnesota Press, 1959).

the bureaucratic structures of a non-capitalist Soviet state that had issued from the revolution of October 1917. Before Stalin rose to political pre-eminence, the political power of the tsarist autocracy, a triumvirate of monarchy, military, and Orthodox Church, had already been broken by the end of the civil war (1918–20). Although the Soviet NEP (1922–9) saw the resurgence of market relations in the countryside, the 'commanding heights' of the economy, as Lenin put it, were firmly in the hands of the Soviet state, which, while awaiting socialist revolution in Europe, particularly Germany, set itself on a course of non-capitalist development under siege from an economically and militarily hostile capitalist world.

VII. Stalin's 'Cult of Personality'

As the Soviet revolution found a 'breathing space' in the NEP, Stalin, elected Communist Party General Secretary in March 1922, quietly consolidated his power by virtue of his control over key appointments to the Party and state apparatuses. After Stalin vanquished his oppositionist rivals, first Leon Trotsky then Bukharin, from 1929 on a 'cult of the personality' was cultivated around Stalin as the *vozhd'* (the leader) that was to grow especially strong in the wake of Soviet victory in the 'Great Patriotic War', 1941–5. In many respects, the Stalin cult was little removed from that which surrounded Mussolini and Hitler. Like them, Stalin became the personification of the regime. In doing so, he promoted a cult around Lenin that had emerged as early as 1918, despite the latter's wishes. After Lenin's death, Stalin virtually deified him, beginning by mummifying his body in the marble mausoleum on Red Square. Stalin then proceeded to depict himself as Lenin's successor. Exalted as 'Lenin's closest friend and disciple', the 'greatest genius of all time', and 'the father of the peoples', Stalin was immortalized in monumental statues, operas, paintings, films, print, and, not least, in 'Stalin city': Stalingrad. Above all, official histories wrote Stalin into a pivotal place in the October Revolution and civil war, while his doomed Bolshevik rivals were erased from the historical record.

Yet Stalin's leadership style was also distinct from that of his fascist peers. As Party General Secretary, Stalin became, in Trotsky's words, 'the personification of the bureaucracy'.[20] Stalin's bureaucratic style was to be reflected by his falsely modest public image, even at the height of his cult. As supreme Soviet bureaucrat, Stalin was no 'weak ruler' in the sense that Hitler was, at least until wartime: distant from the daily affairs of state. In this respect Stalin had much in common with Mussolini,

---

[20] L. Trotsky, *The Revolution Betrayed: What is the Soviet Union and Where is it Going* (New York: Pathfinder Press, 1973; 1st pub. 1937), 277.

who was also an 'assiduous bureaucrat'.[21] But while the *vozhd'* was the people's tsar, to whom ordinary men and women wrote to solve their problems with housing or the local NKVD (secret police), Stalin was no spellbinding, charismatic orator, haranguing crowds about the superiority of Slav civilization. On the contrary, he was the laconic, plainly attired, avuncular figure who eschewed crowds and public oratory, more comfortable with the ordered mutual applause of the Communist Party congress or orchestrated adulation on Red Square. Unlike any of the fascist leaders, he did not project militarist masculinity or strut in uniform; Stalin was not given to displays of bare-chested virility, unlike Mussolini. Rather, Stalin was the bureaucratic 'grey blur', in Trotsky's expression; the bland chief executive, albeit a ruthless one, of a highly bureaucratized 'command' economy.

VIII. Command Economy

Centralized control of the entire economy, based on a series of five-year plans, rested at the core of the Stalinist economic model. But it was qualitatively different from the fascist economies. It eclipsed either fascism's attempts in 1931 to bring key sectors of industry under state control through the Institute for Industrial Reconstruction or Nazism's imposition of state controls from 1936 on as it geared for war. In the case of both Italy and Germany, key sectors of the economy remained in private, profit-driven, hands. In this respect there was no comparison with Stalin's 'command' economy, in which the industrial and agricultural resources were monopolized by the state and investment decisions made on the basis of five-year plans, however chaotic in reality.

Further, Stalin's political pre-eminence coincided with this state monopolization of the economy, and it did so at a quite different stage of economic development from that of fascism. In 1929 Stalin unleashed his 'Socialist Offensive' to collectivize agriculture that was to provide the surplus to fuel a semi-autarkic, forced-march industrialization that outstripped anything achieved by either Mussolini or Hitler. While Italian fascism certainly hastened Italy's shift to modern cartelized capitalism, the same cannot be said for Nazism: Germany was already the most industrial-ized society in Europe. Further, exactly when depression and mass unemployment rocked fascism and spurred the growth of Nazism, Stalin's 'Socialist Offensive' unleashed industrial expansion that created unprecedented demand for labour. This crash industrialization was primarily to resolve the profound disparity be-tween Soviet industrial and agricultural development, but it was also driven by a feared threat from the capitalist world, at this time assumed to be led by Britain

---

[21] R. J. B. Bosworth, *Mussolini's Italy: Life under the Dictatorship* (London: Allen Lane, 2005), 352.

and France rather than Italy or Germany. As Stalin presciently declared in 1931: 'We are fifty to a hundred years behind the advanced countries. We must cover this distance in ten years. Either we do this or they will crush us.'[22] This hyper-industrialization objective fuelled Stalin's veritable 'revolution from above' that in a decade would transform the Soviet Union into an industrial-military power capable ultimately of crushing its real enemy: Fascist Germany, and its crusade against 'Judeo-bolshevism'.

Forced collectivization and the associated campaigns to 'eliminate the kulaks [rich peasants] as a class', through exile, execution, and starvation, a veritable declaration of war on the countryside, which resulted in 5 million dead, largely in the Ukraine, are often cited as prototypes for Nazi death camps and genocide: 'classist' as opposed to 'racist' genocide.[23] But this conflation of Auschwitz with the Gulag is untenable. Despite the monstrous human suffering and mass death, the 1931–2 *Holmodor* (murder by hunger) was not a genocidal project directed specifically at ethnic Ukrainians. Rather, it was a combination of calamitous environmental conditions, crop failure, limited draft power, and excessive grain procurement, in the context of forced-march modernization; the peasantry had to be forced to surrender their grain both to feed the cities and to sell on the world market to finance industrialization.[24] As in all industrializations, the countryside would also provide the new, urban workforce; coercing millions of peasants into urban-industrial workers. Stalinism oversaw this brutal, 'primitive socialist accumulation', as oppositionist Yevgeni Preobrazhensky termed it. None of the European fascisms, least of all Nazism, was a means to achieve the 'primitive accumulation of capital', which Italy and Germany had largely completed by the turn of the twentieth century. On the contrary, fascism came into power at time when Italian and German capital accumulation was already constrained by their belated arrival on the world scene as would-be, expanding, colonial powers.

IX. STALIN'S TERROR

The telescoping of Soviet industrialization into a decade, and the accompanying extension of state control over economy and society, generated extraordinary social and political tensions that could only be contained by draconian police repression. Stalin made an extreme virtue out of Bolshevik necessity, on the way substituting

[22] 'Stalin's 1931 Speech to Industrial Managers', in D. Christian, *Imperial Power and Soviet Russia: Power, Privilege and the Challenge of Modernity* (2nd edn, Melbourne: Longman Cheshire, 1994), 267.

[23] Payne, 'Soviet Anti-Fascism', 3.

[24] M. B. Tauger, 'Natural Disaster and Human Actions in the Soviet Famine of 1931–33', *The Carl Beck Papers in Russian and East European Studies*, No. 1056, June 2001.

internationalist ideals for Soviet, nation state, *Realpolitik*. Where the early Bolsheviks had imposed terror, a one-party state, and censorship largely through force of circumstances, and partially and voluntarily relinquished them, which Fascism did not do; during the NEP Stalin reverted to a permanent state of 'war communism'.

Stalinism, far more 'totalitarian' in terms of the societal reach of the coercive state than Italian Fascism and even Nazism, simultaneously continued the original Leninist project of non-capitalist development while largely repudiating its internationalist, class-based, democratic ideals. Nevertheless, despite Stalin's abandonment of many Bolshevik dreams, and eventually killing off the old Bolsheviks themselves, there was no abandonment of the objective of building Soviet socialism, if only in 'one country' and by draconian means.

Mass terror and murder were the means by which Stalin eventually established his personal police state, in which he ruled above party, state, and law. In doing so, he certainly exceeded Mussolini's political repression and even Hitler's murderous excesses, at least until war was unleashed on the eastern front in June 1941.[25] The assassination of Leningrad Party leader and Stalin's rival Sergei Kirov, in December 1934, like that of Matteotti in June 1924 and the Reichstag fire in March 1933, provided the pretext for decreeing 'extraordinary law' and eventually unleashing, in 1936, NKVD terror for the first time against the Communist Party itself.

Party membership provided no protection. The accused were denied defence; interrogations, often under torture, were conducted post haste; and execution could follow immediately. Peaking in 1937–8, Stalin's 'Great Purge' saw 680,000 'enemies of the people' executed and 1.3 million condemned to Gulag slave labour and often death. The result of this frenzied *auto-da-fé* was the subordination of all political and social institutions to Stalin and his secret police. The Communist Party, the government, youth organizations, trade unions, cultural organizations, the military, and even the NKVD themselves, twice subject to purges, were all brought under Stalin's steel heel.

In terms of the techniques and the number of victims, Stalin's Great Purge easily eclipsed Mussolini's and even Hitler's initial political repression; but Stalinism added additional, distinctive ingredients redolent of a medieval witch hunt— purges, mock trials, and public confessions. The 'medieval methods' of this 'infernal machine', to quote one of its most prominent victims, Bukharin, were the product not only of a revolution from above consuming its own elites but of one taking place amid a superstitious peasant culture that enveloped Stalinist elites and masses alike. If scapegoating is a feature of fascism, then Stalin's Great Purges had it in large doses. 'Trotskyite-wreckers', hidden 'enemies of the people' who conspired with 'white guard pygmies' and 'fascists', were everywhere, especially in the Party. They needed to be unmasked and 'shot', like 'mad dogs'.

---

[25] S. Wheatcroft, 'The Scale and Nature of German and Soviet Repression and Mass Killings, 1930–1945', *Europe-Asia Studies*, 48/8 (1996), 1319–44.

If one were to judge Stalinism by terror alone, it would seem more fascist than the fascists. Trotsky himself accused Stalin of resorting to fascist methods, even if his regime had different socio-economic foundations. Certainly Italian Fascism saw nothing like the political convulsions or paranoid hysteria of Stalin's terror, although, when Mussolini's regime began to sour in the early 1930s, the so-called 'fourth wave of Fascism' intensified the cult around the *Duce*, anti-communism took on renewed vigour, and, under pressure from Nazi Germany, Italy's minuscule Jewish population was targeted for persecution. Nazism, however, though an expression of the crisis of the most modern society in Europe, produced its own witch hunts against Judeo-bolshevism, culminating in *Kristallnacht*, the anti-Soviet crusade on the eastern front, and the Holocaust.

On a political level, however, Stalin's consolidation of his power has some precursors in, and parallels with, Mussolini's consolidation of power and even more so Hitler's. The defeat and final destruction of the old Bolsheviks in 1937–8, the taming of Farinacci in 1925, the 'Night of the Long Knives' against the SA in 1934: in each case state stability was being consolidated through the taming of radicals who threatened the interests of economic and political elites. But the parallels, in terms of social content and consequences, stop there. Where Stalinism imposed a fundamental 'revolution from above', fascism imposed an illusion of revolution; to quote from *The Leopard*: 'For things to remain the same, everything had to change.'

In Italy and Germany, fascism secured the interests of well-established elites. In the Soviet Union, Stalinism was part of a tortuous process of forging newly emergent, bureaucratic elites. Massive expansion of the state and economy in the 1930s and the 'Great Purges' opened the way for personal and political advancement for the *vydvizhentsy*: the upwardly mobile, technocratically educated, scions of the urbanized peasantry cum proletariat, catapulted into millions of administrative positions. The *vydvizhentsy* formed the new *nomenklatura* bureaucratic elite that would govern the Soviet system until the end of the Brezhnev era.[26] It was also part of the process of the USSR accommodating the world capitalist system as a 'normal', if non-capitalist, state, that began with the enunciation of 'Socialism in One Country' in 1924 and would end, nearly seventy years later, with the USSR's demise and reintegration into the world system.

X. Mass Communication and Ideology

Stalinism established a monopoly of media control and censorship without parallel in Fascist Italy. Although in the 1930s the Fascist regime made real attempts

[26] S. Fitzpatrick, 'Stalin and the Making of a New Elite, 1928–1939', *Slavic Review*, 38/3 (1979), 377–402.

to censor literature, press, and film and to produce fascist propaganda, through such agencies as the National Fascist Institute of Culture and the Secretariat for Press and Propaganda, there was nothing like Stalin's draconian intellectual and propaganda regime. As part of his so-called 'socialist offensive' at the beginning of the 1930s, the one-party state moved to consolidate its already formidable controls over intellectual life. State censorship by *Glavlit* (established 1922) and Party-state monopoly of print publications were reinforced by ruthless campaigns to impose Marxist-Leninist orthodoxy in all spheres of cultural and intellectual production, including education. The establishment in 1932 of the Union of Writers and the imposition of Socialist Realism strictly controlled literary life. Academic disciplines, publications, and institutions were required, in the militarist discourse of Stalinism, to adhere to 'party spirit' on the appropriate 'Front'.

Both Stalinism and fascism justified their actions in the light of holistic doctrines: Marxism-Leninism and Fascist 'totalitarianism'. But they were not doctrines of the same order. For all Stalin's willingness to manipulate Marxism in the interests of his personality cult, the Soviet Union still adhered to, and was guided by, a body of thought that aspired to rigorous scientific status; codified by the statement on historical materialism in Stalin's *Short Course History of the Party* (1938), which governed not only history and politics but also scientific and cultural endeavour. Fascist doctrine, however, when it was finally formulated by Mussolini in 1932, was little more than a mystical statement about the nature of the fascist state, revolution, and totalitarianism, short on content and programmatic intentions. It could not be otherwise, since fascism offered no more than the mirage of a revolution, shimmering in the rhetorical desert of the *Duce*'s grand promises to rebuild a Roman empire.

Furthermore, Stalin's crude, deterministic *Short Course* codification of Marxism avowed a secular commitment to human equality based on ending class exploitation through socialism, which the Soviet constitution boasted had been achieved in 1936. Soviet reality certainly fell far short of these claims, but there was none of the racist Social Darwinism espoused by Mussolini that he invoked in his war to 'civilize' the tribes of Ethiopia by gassing them, let alone Hitler's sinister rhetoric about the superiority of the so-called Aryan races.

XI. STALINIST CULTURE

Similar distinctions can be made between the respective discourses, rituals, and iconography of Stalinism and fascism and the public values they inculcated. While both certainly 'aestheticized politics',[27] the Soviets did it earlier, with different classes, in different circumstances, and to different ends. Communism aimed to mobilize and politicize a tiny working class and a vast, illiterate peasantry to make a socialist revolution. Accordingly, up to the early 1930s, the Communist Party set about generating a new revolutionary, popular culture, although there were vigorous debates about the degree to which bourgeois culture should be retained. Fascism, pitched primarily at urban, aspirant middle classes, used spectacle as an antidote to bolshevism and a surrogate for actual social revolution.

Stalin, Mussolini, and Hitler attempted to harness artistic culture to their regimes. But Stalin and Hitler did it far more prescriptively than Mussolini, and took it in a different direction. Where fascism had been allied from its inception with the avant-garde Futurists, in the early 1930s Stalinism, as part of the 'Great Retreat',[28] turned its back on the cultural experiments of the NEP years and the Cultural Revolution (1928–31). Artists were required to be Stalin's 'engineers of the soul'. 'Proletarian' music, art, and literature succumbed to demands for didactic genres that incorporated national, parochial, popular, and classical traditions. In literature, 'Socialist Realism' demanded realistic, sentimentally romantic, hyper-heroic works that celebrated the socialist future. Soviet puritanism outlawed modernist art, which fascism prized, as 'decadent', 'coarse', 'depraved', and tainted by sexual deviance. Despite their shared, nationalistic politicization of culture, Stalinist and fascist culture reflected different regime roots, objectives, and values. Stalinism sentimentalized traditional, folkloric, peasant culture to ward off Western culture contaminating its autarkic, socialist project, especially after its victory over Nazism. Fascism, however, hailed modernism's celebration of industrial aesthetics, especially the aesthetics of the ultimate instrument of modern warfare the aeroplane, which promised conquest of peoples and colonies. Nothing in Stalinism's folk culture celebrated colonial war or conquest.

XII. Propaganda and Public Discourse

Nevertheless, it is true that Stalinism, like Leninism before it, militarized political discourse. 'Class warfare' was innate to Marxism and Leninism, but where they envisaged the demise of class struggle with the development of socialism, Stalin, in 1933, proclaimed its 'intensification' the more 'socialist' the Soviet state became.

---

[27] Payne, 'Soviet Anti-Fascism', 3.

[28] N. Timasheff, *The Great Retreat: The Growth and Decline of Communism in Russia* (New York: Dutton, 1946).

Likewise, the building of Soviet socialism was a military project: Stalin declared 1929 'The Year of the Great Breakthrough'. The struggle for socialism was to be carried out on numerous 'fronts', with victory assured by a Stalinist variant of 'triumph of the will': 'There are no fortresses that the Bolsheviks cannot storm!' he proclaimed in February 1931. In the tempestuous years between two total wars, it should come as no surprise that Europe's fascisms, direct offshoots of the militarism of the First World War, should similarly employ militarist language and slogans to justify its wars, not only against bolshevism and Stalinism, but also of conquest. Stalinism's combative rhetoric was primarily directed against internal enemies, including former Bolsheviks, and invoked for the crash building of an industrial state. Further, where fascism, and even more so Nazism, openly hailed the virile virtues of war, in its international and diplomatic policies Stalinism increasingly invoked the rhetoric of 'peace' and the diplomacy of 'collective security', not militant class struggle or revolution, as its antidote to the threat of fascist war.

The modern state is a propaganda state, not least when it is at war. Both Stalinism and fascism, the former a state under siege, the latter a state girding for colonial war, excelled at this. Soviet festivals sacralized politics, striving to displace the Orthodox Church as the focus of popular belief. The anniversaries of the October Revolution, International Women's Day, and Red Army Day were celebrated by military parades, gymnastics displays, and serried rows of Communist Party youth hailing Soviet achievements and paying homage to the 'Great Father of the Peoples' standing on the dais above the Lenin mausoleum on Red Square. Like the Great French Revolution, the Soviet order legitimized itself with new symbols, liturgies, and rituals affirming the new proletarian and peasant state.

Mussolini's state, like Stalin's and Hitler's, made mass propaganda and mass rituals an art, if not always a fine one. Radio and film were quickly recognized by both Stalinism and fascism as powerful means for disseminating verbal and visual imagery in the era of mass politics. But even here there were distinctions. Goebbels's Ministry of Propaganda controlled every aspect of film production, from script to circulation. No film, even the most Hollywood influenced or escapist, was immune from Nazi ideology. However, film under Mussolini and Stalin was not just propaganda. Some 700 films produced under fascism, aided by Mussolini's Experimental Centre for Cinematography founded in 1935, laid the basis for the much-vaunted, post-war, Italian neo-realism. Likewise, despite the dead hand of Socialist Realism, Soviet cinematography, like that developed by Sergei Eisenstein's workshop in the Institute of Cinematography, rested on a sophisticated film theory that had a powerful impact on cinema worldwide, not least Italian film which was influenced by Soviet montage techniques. *Jazz Comedy*, directed by Eisenstein's colleague Grigory Aleksandrov, triumphed at the newly inaugurated Venice International Film Festival in 1934.

XIII. Mass Mobilization

Mass participation, or at least the illusion of it, was pivotal to both the Stalinist and fascist 'revolutions'. Stalin's rise to bureaucratic power had been facilitated by the demise of popular participation in the revolution, particularly through the marginalization of the Soviets—the network of councils that had sprung up in 1917, which had no fascist equivalent but were echoed in the Italian factory committees in the 'Red Years', 1919–20—and through the increasing concentration of power in the hands of the party *apparat*. Nevertheless, carefully orchestrated mass campaigns remained a crucial element not only of the early years of the revolution but also during Stalin's industrializing 'revolution from above'. There were real commitment, substance, and achievements, as well as costs, in these campaigns. Mass literacy campaigns, entailing thousands of young communist volunteers going to the countryside, had been a feature of the NEP and continued under Stalin. Forced collectivization too mobilized the 'twenty-five thousanders'—young communist militants who went to the furthest, bleakest reaches of the country to enforce collectivization, in the face of fierce resistance. The very process of industrialization entailed the mobilization of millions of workers who genuinely embraced the Soviet idea, epitomized by the 'Stakhanovite' worker movement launched in 1935, driven by mass enthusiasm and the promise of scarce consumer goods.

There were no comparable mass movements under fascism. Mussolini's 1925 'Battle for Grain', which saw the *Duce* ostentatiously leading the harvest by example and urging peasants to increase their output in the interests of agricultural self-sufficiency, entailed no real mass mobilization. Of course, there were the ritualized expressions of mass support, such as the *Duce* addressing the throng in the piazzas and the rallies on 'fascist Saturdays'. But the only substantive social objectives for which fascism mobilized its supporters were preparing boys for war, through sport and quasi-military activities of such organizations as the Avanguardisti, and metaphorically mobilizing women to engage in the 'battle for births'.

XIV. Women and the Family

The Stalinist and Fascist states were patriarchal states. Pro-natalism was high on the agenda of both, a feature they had in common not only with Nazism but with the European states in general. Nevertheless, the issue of gender was one of the great divides between Soviet socialism, even in its Stalinist form, and Italian

Fascism. Women's emancipation had been high on the agenda of the October Revolution—confirming the worst fears of fascism that bolshevism was the scourge of family and femininity. In the first few years of the revolution, the Women's Section of the Communist Party, Zhenotdel, oversaw a radical programme which established equality of the sexes, eliminated male proprietary rights over women, decriminalized abortion and adultery, and introduced civil marriages. Stalin's 'Great Retreat', anticipated by the abolition of Zhenotdel in 1930, reversed many of the earlier advances of women: divorce and abortion were once again out-lawed, marriage, family, and motherhood were idealized, and distinct gender roles reasserted.

Nevertheless, unlike fascism, Stalinism did not try, even rhetorically, to force women out of the public domain back into the family. Quite the opposite: as part of its drive for industrial accumulation, millions of women were forced by hunger, poverty or enthusiasm out of the home and countryside into the factories. In the 1930s a veritable 'regendering' of the workforce took place as women took on previously male-dominated occupations, including heavy industry.[29] By the end of the Second World War women were more than 50 per cent of the industrial workforce. Soviet women were nurturers and the givers of life; but they were also producers: workers and peasants.

Unlike fascism, the Soviet Communist Party adhered to a Marxist conviction, albeit a crude, deterministic one, that socio-economic development, not biology, was the key to equality between the sexes. Although a tendency towards biological determinism justified re-emphasis on the family and mothering from the mid-1930s on, Stalin's super-industrializing regime could not only actively promote the role of women in production, it could also urge them to acquire military skills—a triple burden.

Mussolini, however, like all fascists, believed that war was exclusively men's busi-ness; but his pro-natalist designs for women were not far removed from those of Stalin. Fascism set out to 'nationalize Italian women', consigning them to 'home and hearth' and 'bearing babies'.[30] Fascism's inherently anti-egalitarian doctrines depicted gender as biologically determined and immutable. Masculinity pervaded fascist discourse, not least that of the *Duce*. For Mussolini, liberalism and democ-racy were weak, soft, and feminine; the crowd passive and open to manipulation by a 'virile' leader, such as himself: 'Mine is the armed love, not the tearful and unwarlike love, but severe and virile.' After 1935, a concerted attempt was made to drive women back into domestic and maternal servitude; but it failed, thwarted by the needs of a modernizing capitalist economy and war.

---

[29] W. Z. Goldman, *Women at the Gates: Gender and Industry in Stalin's Russia* (Cambridge: Cambridge University Press, 2002).

[30] V. De Grazia, *How Fascism Ruled Women: Italy, 1922–1945* (Berkeley and Los Angeles: University of California Press, 1992), 1, 6.

XV. War

Aggressive, expansionist, colonial war drove fascism, in both its Italian and its more lethal, genocidal, German variants; the former aspiring to a Mediterranean and African empire; the latter, to the conquest of Slav Russia and Eastern Europe. Here was the fundamental difference between Stalinism and fascism. Authoritarian hyper-industrialization was at the heart of Stalinism, which, with the defeat of European socialism at the hands of fascism, necessarily had to develop a massive, economically draining, military apparatus to defend its semi-autarkic, socialist project against what it saw as predatory capitalism, in the first place that of non-fascist France and Britain, a misunderstanding of the nature of German Fascism that would cost the Soviet Union dearly.

Stalin never had a clear understanding of fascism and its relationship to war. In the main his impoverished theorizations of fascism were dictated by the diplomatic needs of the Soviet state, increasingly the prism through which the *Vozhd'* viewed world affairs. His first and most disastrous foray into the question was his infamous declaration in 1924 that fascism and social democracy were 'not antipodes', they were 'twins'. This formula subsequently governed the German Communist Party's suicidal unwillingness to enter into a united front with the German Social Democratic Party (SPD) against their common foe: Nazism. Stalin feared that an SPD government would effect a rapprochement with the Versailles victors, Britain and France, which he believed, virtually until Hitler unleashed Barbarossa in June 1941, the most likely instigators of war against the Soviets. For Stalin, monopoly finance capitalism, irrespective of its political regimes, was the source of war. Even after the Comintern adopted the formula in 1935 that fascism represented 'the open terrorist dictatorship of the most reactionary, chauvinistic, and most imperialist elements of finance capital', Stalin made no qualitative distinction between democratic and fascist capitalism, nor between Fascist Italy and Nazi Germany. He refused to recognize that Nazi Germany, alone of all the European fascisms, had the capacity and the intent to unleash war of annihilation against the Soviet state. Stalin's illusions in state diplomacy and the willingness of Hitler to adhere to their August 1939 Non-Aggression Pact proved near fatal for the Soviet Union in 1941–2.

The different approaches of Stalinism and fascism to war were reflected in their foreign policies. Whereas, after Hitler came to power, Stalin sought and achieved admission to the League of Nations and encouraged the formation of Popular Front governments in the hope that they would thwart fascism and befriend the Soviet Union as part of his quest for collective security, Mussolini and Hitler defied the League and geared themselves for war. The essentially defensive militarization of Soviet society on the one hand, and the aggressive militarization of Italy and Germany on the other, derived from the distinct dynamics of a non-capitalist state, in which planning determined investments, and capitalist states, in which commercial and industrial capital stood to benefit from military expenditure and colonial conquest. From its inception, fascism valorized masculinist, martial values, as it strove to militarize civil and political society; and military conquest of *Lebensraum* in Russia had been on Hitler's agenda since *Mein Kampf*. War was perceived by both fascist regimes as the highest test and objective of nationhood, manhood, and race. Despite Stalin's symbolic importance for the millions of soldiers who fought and died, many with the official battle cry of '*Za rodinu! Za Stalina!*' (For the Motherland! For Stalin!) on their lips, militarism was never elevated to a virtue in Soviet society. The deaths of an estimated 27 million Soviet citizens at the hands of German fascism and its allies cemented that anti-war sentiment, long after Stalin was gone.

XVI. Conclusion

The victory of the Soviet Union at extraordinary human cost over its fascist opponents, German and Italian, and their fascistic Finnish, Hungarian, and Romanian allies, fundamentally challenges the notion that Stalinism was simply the mirror image, let alone the prototype, for fascist totalitarianism. The evisceration of Nazism by the Red Army, while the Soviets' allies in the Grand Alliance baulked at opening a second front, confirms that, despite the ruthlessness of the Stalin regime, nevertheless the fundamental structures and values of Soviet state and society and fascism were mutually exclusive. The aftermath of Soviet victory and fascist defeat confirms this: the fascist regimes could only be destroyed by exogenous, military means; but de-Stalinization would be driven by endogenous reform from above, dramatized by Nikita Khrushchev's 'Secret Speech' at the 1956 Twentieth Communist Party Congress.

Bolshevism was certainly the fascisms' other, but there were degrees of this. For fascism, bolshevism also provided a mirror for its development, but for Nazism it was the ultimate enemy from day one. The seeming symmetry of fascism and communism derived from the fact that they were antithetical responses to the cataclysm of the First World War, as the Second World War would brutally confirm. But this antithesis has long been masked by the concept of totalitarianism.

Bibliography

Evans, R., *The Dictators: Hitler's Germany, Stalin's Russia* (London: Allen Lane, 2004).
Fitzpatrick, S., *The Russian Revolution* (New York: Oxford University Press, 2001).

GETTY, J. A., and MANNING, R. T. (eds), *Stalinist Terror: New Perspectives* (Cambridge: Cambridge University Press, 1993).

GLEASON, A., *'Totalitarianism': The Inner History of the Cold War* (New York: Oxford University Press, 1995).

GRIFFIN, R. (ed.), *Fascism* (Oxford: Oxford University Press, 1995).

ILIC, M. (ed.), *Women in the Stalin Era* (Basingstoke: Palgrave Macmillan, 2001).

KALLIS, A. A. (ed.), *The Fascism Reader* (London: Routledge, 2003).

KERSHAW, I., and LEWIN, M. (eds), *Stalinism and Nazism: Dictatorships in Comparison* (Cambridge: Cambridge University Press, 1997).

LYTTELTON, A., *The Seizure of Power: Fascism in Italy 1919–1929* (2nd edn, London: Weidenfeld and Nicolson, 1987).

PAYNE, S. G., 'Soviet Anti-Fascism: Theory and Practice, 1921–45', *Totalitarian Movements and Religions*, 4/2 (2003), 1–62.

PETRACCHI, G., 'Bolshevism in the Fascist Mirror (1)', *Telos*, 133 (2006), 45–74.

SIEGELBAUM, L., 'Building Stalinism, 1929–1941', in G. Freeze (ed.), *Russia: A History* (2nd edn. London: Oxford University Press, 2002).

SUNY, R. G., *The Soviet Experiment* (New York: Oxford University Press, 1998).

WARD, C., *Stalin's Russia* (2nd edn, London: Arnold, 1999).

CHAPTER 19

·····························

SPAIN

·····························

MARY VINCENT

ON 29 October 1933, the Falange Española held its founding meeting at the Teatro Comedia in Madrid. The Falange would become the most clearly identifiable expression of fascism in Spain, but in 1933 there was little to distinguish it from the numerous other *grupusculos* thrown up by the radical right. Indeed, there was little to distinguish the 29 October meeting from other political rallies: the theatre was full, though the lack of uniforms or any obvious fascist aesthetic 'disappointed those attending'.[1] The emerging leader of the party, José Antonio Primo de Rivera, returned the Roman salute but deliberately avoided the words 'fascist' or 'fascism'. Nonetheless, this was a genuine beginning for fascism in Spain, and José Antonio— as he would come to be known—was a genuine asset. Son of the deposed dictator General Miguel Primo de Rivera, who had ruled Spain from 1923 to 1930, José Antonio represented both the wider authoritarian origins of the Spanish right and the generation that would change its nature for ever.

Some early work on Spanish fascism—particularly that produced by scholars with no particularly Spanish expertise—questioned the very existence of a Spanish fascism. The Falange was too elitist and above all too Catholic to be seen as a true fascist party, and José Antonio's initial equivocation as to the use of the label was cited as testimony to this. In contrast, however, the seminal work of Stanley Payne firmly established the Falange as a European fascist party.[2] A separate

---

[1] D. Jato, *La rebellion de los estudiantes (apuntes para una historia del alegre SEU)* (Madrid: CIES, 1953), 59.

[2] S. G. Payne, *Falange: A History of Spanish Fascism* (Stanford, CA: Stanford University Press, 1961); idem, 'Spanish Fascism in Comparative Perspective', in H. A. Turner (ed.), *Reappraisals of Fascism* (New York: New Viewpoints, 1975).

historiographical trend then developed: the Falange was admitted to the fascist club but as its only Spanish member. The terms 'fascist' and 'Falangist' became coterminous, often to the exclusion of any wider interpretation. In several respects, such a tendency has proved long-lasting. Histories of Spanish fascism have often taken the form of organizational studies or 'organigrams', while even purportedly comparative works may actually present parallel studies of discrete movements.[3] Such approaches are not uncommon in histories of fascism and, in this particular context, were encouraged by the taxonomic approaches favoured by both Payne and Juan Linz.

The early work on Spanish fascism was carried out under the shadow of the Franco regime which, in marked contrast to any other fascist, fascistizing, or quasi-fascist regime, survived well past the Second World War until the dictator died in his bed in November 1975. There have been numerous attempts to categorize the Franco regime—some of them recapitulated in the previous sentence—but none has been as influential as Linz's taxonomy of authoritarian regimes. First published in 1964, this categorically distinguished the Francoist regime from totalitarian ones.[4] The effect was to establish a difference between Francoism and fascism and so reduce Spanish fascism to a particular historical moment: that is, the outbreak of civil war. The Falange's fleeting moment of political influence came only at the breakdown of the Second Republic and the right's mobilization for war. The beneficiary of circumstances, the Falange had its relative lack of autonomous strength exacerbated by the deaths of all its leaders during the first few months of war and it was unable to resist the Francoist encroachments that resulted in the party's rapid domestication by the regime. Echoes of this argument may still be heard today. Michael Mann's comparative study of fascist movements, for example, uses Spain as a counter-example of a regime where fascism was always the junior partner. Indeed, the term 'domestication' is used in his work.[5]

During the 1970s, however, the tendency to equate Spanish fascism with the Falange—and only with the Falange—led to a contrary impulse. As the Franco regime drew to a close, scholars both in and outside Spain began to consider its origins in terms of the crisis of the 1930s.[6] The specific challenge mounted by a reforming Republic to Spain's established elites had led to a last-ditch reaction as entrenched elites took up arms rather than submit to the Republican legislative project. The Civil War was thus brought about by the right's willingness to forge

---

[3] See e.g. J. Tusell, E. Gentile, and G. Di Febo (eds), *Fascismo y franquismo: cara a cara* (Madrid: Biblioteca Nueva, 2004).

[4] 'An Authoritarian Regime: Spain', in E. Allardt and Y. Littunen (eds), *Cleavages, Ideologies and Party Systems: Contributions to Comparative Political Sociology* (Helsinki: The Academic Bookstore, 1964). Reproduced in S. G. Payne (ed.), *Politics and Society in Twentieth-Century Spain* (New York: Franklin Watts, 1976), 160–207.

[5] M. Mann, *Fascists* (Cambridge: Cambridge University Press, 2004).

[6] For example, J. Jiménez Campo, *El fascismo en la crisis de la Segunda República* (Madrid: Centro de Investigaciones Sociológicas, 1979).

violent alliances with fascist partners. The key to defining fascism lay, not in style or ideology, but in its 'social and economic function'. Such interpretations had a specifically theoretically input, whether that was provided by structural Marxism or, as in the case of Paul Preston, by Barrington Moore's conception of a 'reactionary coalition'.[7]

The functionalist models these scholars espouse have not worn well. From the vantage point of the early twenty-first century—so shaped by the 'linguistic turn' and the apparently impregnable prominence of culture—determinism is viewed with suspicion even when it is not dismissed as irredeemably teleological. As those who favoured functionalist arguments tended to regard fascist ideology and style as superficial epiphenomena, a wider problem developed. For, if style is dismissed and socio-economic 'function' left to one side, then little is left of the Franco regime's 'fascism' other than its violence. There are, of course, many more brutal regimes than there are fascist ones, yet the point about the crisis of the 1930s remains salient. The Spanish right had developed in ways that were remarkably similar to 'pre-fascism', not least in the elaboration of a hyper-nationalist discourse. The rapid politicization that Spain experienced during the Second Republic provided a new breeding ground for fascism as the right both mobilized and radicalized. However, these relationships between fascists and others on the right have been obscured by a historiography that has long emphasized fascism's unique and radical character.[8] While the understanding of this uniqueness has changed, for example from fascism as the 'third way' between capitalism and socialism to fascism as 'political religion', the emphasis on fascist difference remains. In Spain, where fascism clearly originated on the right, such an emphasis is often misleading.

Over recent years, historical scholarship has firmly established the nature of Spanish fascism. Local studies have revealed a wealth of empirical material, tracing not only the origins of the local parties but also their relationship to other groups on the right and the role they played in cementing the power of the early Franco regime.[9] In contrast to work being done outside Spain, which is dominated by generic fascism,[10] regional studies stressed the density of political life, its accommodations and compromises, above all in times of civil conflict and state building. As the links and overlaps between old and new right became more and more apparent,

---

[7] P. Preston, 'Spain', in S. J. Woolf (ed.), *Fascism in Europe* (London: Methuen, 1981); idem, *The Politics of Revenge: Fascism and the Military in Twentieth-Century Spain* (London: Routledge, 1990), 3–29.

[8] See, however, M. Blinkhorn (ed.), *Fascists and Conservatives: The Radical Right and the Establishment in Twentieth-Century Europe* (London: Unwin Hyman, 1990).

[9] See, for example the work on Aragón: A. Cenarro Lagunas, *Cruzados y camisas azules: los orígenes del franquismo en Aragón, 1936–1945* (Zaragoza: Prensas Universitarias de Zaragoza, 1997); J. Casanova et al., *El pasado oculto: fascismo y violencia en Aragón (1936–1939)* (Madrid: Siglo Veintiuno, 1992).

[10] The most significant example is, of course, the work of Stanley Payne. See, in particular, his *Fascism in Spain, 1923–1977* (Madison: University of Wisconsin Press, 1999).

an old concept—that of fascistization—was given new life. Influenced in part by current work on Vichy France, in part by the local history he had himself been involved in writing, Ismael Saz argued that fascistization was a process that, under the impact of mass politics, led certain groups on the Spanish right to adopt clearly fascist characteristics. The result of this two-way process was a hybrid phenomenon, 'neither fascism in the strict sense nor a right that was the same as it had been before its confrontation—dialectic, even—with fascism'.[11]

The relationship between fascism and other groups and creeds on the Spanish right has thus become central to investigations of the Falange. What mattered was not what distinguished the party from other members of the Nationalist alliance but rather the alliance itself. Spanish fascism was thus situated once again in a wider spectrum of reactionary, nationalist politics. Certainly, in cultural terms, Spanish fascists shared the same intellectual roots as both conservatives and reactionaries, positioning themselves within a spectrum of both radical and conservative thought. José Antonio, for instance, was versed in left-wing theorists, including Marx and Lenin, as well as Spengler and Sorel, but he was also widely read in Catholic doctrine. His personal taste was for poetry—Kipling's 'If' had pride of place on his office wall—and his most sustained cultural influences were Spanish, notably Regenerationist literature and Ortega y Gasset's philosophical elitism.[12] In both intellectual and emotional terms, his inheritance was that of a hard-edged conservatism. Although profoundly influenced by Italian Fascism, José Antonio and his close-knit circle of friends remained wedded to that particularly Spanish vision of regeneration that served as a national counter-revolutionary tradition.[13]

Both José Antonio's politics and his background therefore placed him squarely in the mainstream of conservative Spanish politics, in contrast to the early experimental initiatives that characterized the Falange's forerunners. Such initial positions were radical and often idiosyncratic, marked by aesthetic innovation and an experimental internationalism that contrasted sharply with the later hyper-nationalism of the Falange. The first significant convert to the new Italian model of mass politics was Ernesto Giménez Caballero, one of many reactionary figures who made inter-war modernism such a politically ambivalent idiom. Memorably referred to as 'fascism's Groucho Marx', 'GeCé' was a self-conscious member of the avant-garde, publishing both Lorca and Buñuel in his pluri-nationalist *La Gaceta Literaria*. He cherished dreams of uniting the political and intellectual vanguards of all Latin cultures—including the Catalan—in a Mediterranean vision of dynamic

---

[11] I. Saz Campos, *Fascismo y franquismo* (Valencia: Universitat de València, 2004), 84–90 at 86. See also idem, 'Fascism, Fascistization and Developmentalism in Franco's Dictatorship', *Social History*, 29/3 (2004), 342–57.

[12] J. Gil Pecharromán, *José Antonio Primo de Rivera: retrato de un visionario* (Madrid: Temas de Hoy, 2003), 69, 77–9.

[13] On this 'pre-fascist' tradition see I. Saz Campos, *España contra España: los nacionalismos franquistas* (Madrid: Marcial Pons, 2003), 59–99.

modernity.[14] Indeed, his personal commitment to Latin destiny led to marriage with the daughter of the Italian consul in Strasbourg. Yet, it was his recognition of Catalan culture that gave a radical edge to Giménez Caballero's vision of a southern Europeanism within which Spain's national 'genius' would be rediscovered. To conservatives, Spain's national destiny would be revealed only in opposition to Catalonia, which was simply a region, ready to be reincorporated into the single unity of Spain.

A self-declared fascist by 1924, Giménez Caballero remained an eccentric figure, though his key work, *Genio de España* (1932), was well received by many on both the conservative and the radical right. He had a profound influence on a studious young Germanophile Ramiro Ledesma Ramos, who founded Spain's first stable fascist political grouping. Ledesma used the columns of his paper, *La Conquista del Estado*, to elaborate his Nietzschean vision of national 'regeneration' in which the confederal nature of Giménez Caballero's Hispanic imperialism was reinvented as a conventional centralist and Castilian *imperio*.[15] This search for a 'Spanish formula'—which would create a new fascism and not simply mimic the Italian version—led Ledesma to hyper-nationalism and a rejection of any sense that Catalan identities could shape Spain's destiny or that they had any purchase within Spanish fascism. In response, Giménez Caballero abandoned the *Conquista del Estado*, a paper that was soon drawing comparisons with *Libertad*, another self-styled fascist publication established in the Castilian city of Valladolid in 1931, the same year Ledesma's mouthpiece began publication in Madrid.

In October, the tiny groups around each title merged to become the Juntas Ofensivas Nacional-Sindicalistas (JONS). The unwieldy title suited the Madrid group better than its comrades in Valladolid. Ledesma—who hoped to publish *Mein Kampf* in Spanish—advocated an uncompromisingly statist and economically radical fascism. In contrast, the Valladolid leader, Onésimo Redondo, was a devout and passionate Catholic whose dreams for regeneration centred on the rural heartlands of Castile, the 'cradle of Spain'. His personal faith was such that, as his Jesuit confessor remembered, he would tremble as he took communion, and, while he also admired Nazism, his initial followers came from the same pious circles as he did himself. Redondo was clearly the more reactionary of the two JONS leaders and also by far the more anti-Semitic, defending Nazi policies against the Jews as 'a Christian and national reaction' to conspiratorial plans for world domination.[16]

---

[14] E. Ucelay Da Cal, 'Vanguardia, fascismo y la interacción entre nacionalismo español y catalan', in J. G. Beramendi and R. Máiz (eds), *Los nacionalismos en la España de la II República* (Madrid: Siglo XXI, 1991), 39–95. The Groucho Marx epithet was coined by the writer Franciso Umbral (quoted M. Carbajosa and P. Carbajosa, *La corte literaria de José Antonio: la primera generación cultural de la Falange* (Barcelona: Crítica, 2003), 83).

[15] Ucelay Da Cal, 'Vanguardia, fascismo y la interacción entre nacionalismo español y catalan', 43–52; Saz Campos, *Fascismo y franquismo*, 39–45 and *España contra España*, 122–8.

[16] G. Alvarez Chillida, *El antisemitismo en España: la imagen del judío, 1812–2002* (Madrid: Marcial Pons, 2002), 340–1.

Such a reliance on the well-worn falsehoods of the *Protocols of the Elders of Zion*—which were to be serialized yet again in Redondo's paper—were found most commonly among the monarchist and reactionary right, notably Carlism. In Spain at least, anti-Semitic discourses owed more to Catholicism than to biological racism, and they ran through all variants of Catholic politics, highlighting the connection between fascism and the wider right.

Redondo and Ledesma held many beliefs in common—the death of 'old' politics, the need for a youthful fascist dynamic, the purgative and constructive power of violence—but the profound differences between them ensured that their followers remained distinct groups, albeit contained within a single party. This sense of separation was exaggerated by the new party's tiny size: when Ledesma lectured in the Madrid Atheneum he was accompanied by a mere twenty-five comrades in an auditorium 'full of enemies'.[17] Factionalism remained embedded in the early variants of fascism, though the sharpest difference between the Madrid and Valladolid *jonsistas* was not necessarily religion. For all the intensity of his faith, Redondo was clear that any fascist project had to be secular, not least because of its totalitarian nature. Nation took primacy over religion, he argued, and the totalitarian state would only be achieved through violence. The opposition between the secular and revolutionary nationalism of Ledesma and Redondo's Catholic (and therefore reactionary) fascism should thus not be exaggerated.[18]

The Spanish fascist project, in all its manifestations, was essentially secular. For perhaps the first time on the Spanish right, fascism offered a radical break with the past. The reliance on religion—which had for some time defined the essential difference between left and right in Spain—was reworked to make Catholicism a national attribute. As part of the Spanish character and 'essence', Catholicism was necessarily incorporated into the palingenetic vision, but it was now a function of Spanish identity and an expression of national greatness rather than the motor force of history. But, just as anti-Catalan feeling, which sharpened under the Second Republic as the region gained autonomous status in 1932, had created common ground between Ledesma and Redondo, so the accommodation with Catholicism became more pronounced after the JONS merged with the Falange to create the Falange Española y de las JONS in February 1934.

The new name—justifiably described by Stanley Payne as 'the most peculiar and long-winded ... of any fascist party in Europe'—was created by a simple process of addition.[19] This also accurately reflected the processes of merger, with a resulting lack of clarity or ideological precision. Yet, merger brought clear advantages to all. The first of these was size: the party was still small but numbers rose as public attention focused on the new party, whose first rally was a full-scale fascist affair,

---

[17] R. Ledesma Ramos, *¿Fascismo en España?* (Madrid, 1988), 71.

[18] Saz Campos, *España contra España*, 137–8; M. Vincent, *Catholicism in the Second Spanish Republic: Religion and Politics in Salamanca, 1930–36* (Oxford: Oxford University Press, 1996), 220–2.

[19] Payne, *Fascism in Spain*, 99.

marked by banners, insignia, and Roman salutes. The street brawls that followed the meeting not only made plain the Falange's commitment to political violence, but also led to the death of the party's first 'martyr'. Now visibly distinct from other far-right political options in Spain, the Falange's radicalism was apparent on a wider stage than had ever been possible while the JONS remained a few close-knit circles around Ledesma Ramos in Madrid. The merged Falange developed a truly theatrical sense of style, adopting the eponymous blue shirt to replace the imitative black shirts previously worn—sometimes with a red tie—by the JONS.[20] The *jonsistas*' revolutionary dialectic also survived, as did their red-and-black flag, yoke and arrows emblem, and Ledesma's slogan '*España, Una Grande, y Libre*'. There was thus now a clear fascist option within Spain, and the existence of this option redefined understandings of the term itself, putting a marked distance between the new party and monarchist and reactionary groups. Dr Albiñana's 'legionaries', for example, may have masqueraded as 'fascists' but their politics obviously belonged to an earlier age.[21]

Nevertheless, despite the radicalism and fascist style of the Falange Española y de las JONS, the party was born on the political right with none of the socialist influences that characterized British or, more significantly, early Italian fascism. The radical discourse of the Falange placed it at the extreme but it was still recognizably part of wider right-wing discourses in Spain. Indeed, although merger marked a hardening of the fascist position, the inclusion of José Antonio Primo de Rivera in the party's leadership, alongside his fellow Falangist Julio Ruíz de Alda, tipped the ideological balance away from Ledesma, whose national-syndicalist theories became increasingly downplayed. The hard fact was that Spanish fascism benefited from a general anti-Republican impetus that both propelled the new movement and diluted it. Indeed, without such mobilization against the Second Republic, the new party would have got nowhere. Fascism may have despised liberal politics but it was born into a liberal polity, and an accommodation with the concerns and *mores* of the wider right was inevitable as anti-Republican mobilization led to a rapid process of radicalization among all sectors on the right and, indeed, on the left.

For some of the fascist leaders, there may also have been less tension between the non-fascist and fascist positions than might have appeared. José Antonio's class background and personal religious faith contributed to a change in tone for the Falange, as the hardened spiritualism of Redondo's hyper-nationalism was reinforced at the expense of Ledesma's redistributive totalitarianism. Despite the essential secularism of the early fascist project, Catholicism became a more explicit component of the Falange's ideology and rhetoric (as is quite apparent in, for

[20] M. Vincent, '*Camisas nuevas*: Style and Uniformity in the Falange Española, 1933–43', in W. Parkin (ed.), *Fashioning the Body Politic: Dress, Gender, Citizenship* (Oxford: Berg, 2002), 167–71.

[21] J. Gil Pecharromán, '*Sobre España inmortal, solo Dios': José María Albiñana y el Partido Nacionalista Española, 1930–37* (Madrid: UNED, 2000).

example, the twenty-seven points). This shift was exacerbated by Ledesma Ramos's increasing isolation. His differences with José Antonio, which were both personal and ideological, became increasingly apparent and, in early 1936, Ledesma was expelled from the party along with a mere two dozen followers.

Inevitably, such a evolution brought the Falange closer to reactionary, traditional, and conservative groups on the right, a position Redondo's party had always enjoyed. In Spain all these groups were heirs to some form of monarchist tradition, and the proclamation of the Second Republic in April 1931 had knocked them sideways. Though temporarily derailed, the right regrouped remarkably rapidly, abandoning all ostensibly monarchist loyalties and throwing themselves wholeheartedly into a whirlwind of mobilization and modernization.[22] The result was a new political organization, Acción Popular (AP), which looked to mobilize as broad a spectrum of Catholic, conservative, and right-wing opinion as possible. The structures, networks, and press outlets provided by Catholic organizations—including newspapers, agrarian syndicates, parish organizations, and women's groups—proved essential to this process, which saw the distinction between the traditional and radical right become ever more blurred.

A new style had developed on the political right during the 1920s, under the dictatorship of José Antonio's father General Miguel Primo de Rivera. Under a regime famously categorized by Shlomo Ben-Ami (1983) as 'fascism from above', Spain had experienced its first single party (Unión Patriótica; UP), a national militia, and, most importantly, a consistent and systematic attempt to remake—or regenerate—the nation. Under Primo, male citizens took up arms in the defence of order while all citizens demonstrated their loyalty to the fatherland, parading under national symbols, not least during the international expositions mounted in Seville and Barcelona. Some rightists—notably Albiñana—continued to see Primo's dictatorship as the model for future self-styled 'fascist' solutions. But fascism is not instituted 'from above', at least not in peacetime, and, as a model for the future, Primo's experiment was fatally undermined by failure. Under the Republic, the right built on its experience in the UP, but nevertheless recognized that it was entering a new and much more uncertain phase.

The crisis of conservatism that Spain experienced in the 1930s, while a genuine reflection of a wider European travail, was essentially that of mass politics. Primo's great innovation had been to recognize the fact of mass politics and consciously to begin to broaden the basis of political activity and construct an active citizenship intended to incorporate loyal subjects into the nation. But the failure of his project meant that the right remained much more accustomed to the politics of oligarchy. Only after April 1931 did the right abandon the language and values of monarchism,

[22] P. Preston, *The Coming of the Spanish Civil War: Reform, Reaction and Revolution in the Second Republic* (London: Macmillan, 1978); R. Valls, *La Derecha Regional Valenciana, 1930–36* (Valencia: Alfons el Magnànim, 1992); L. Alvarez Rey, *La derecha en la II República: Sevilla, 1931–1936* (Seville: Ayuntamiento de Sevilla, 1993); Vincent, *Catholicism in the Second Spanish Republic*.

and while they had few scruples over ditching the king, the common currency of monarchist values—order, hierarchy, elites—remained embedded in an ostensibly republican discourse. But even if the right's preference was for a traditional social order and elite leadership, it could not ignore the rapid and unstoppable transformation of ordinary people into political actors. The solution was, of course, to mobilize the masses. But, in doing so, the fragility of the anti-republican right became all too apparent. Essentially, there was no strong conservative presence to act as a bulwark against fascism and the entire anti-republican project careered rapidly towards the (radical) right.

This was recognized by Ledesma Ramos, when he asked:

Who are the fascistized? It is easy and simple work to point them out and list their names: Calvo Sotelo and his Bloque Nacional. Gil Robles and his forces; above all those who belong to the JAP. Primo de Rivera and his groups, today still orbiting around the two previous groups, but surely not [doing so] tomorrow. Without forgetting, naturally, part of the Army.[23]

The quotation reveals not only the right's profound intoxication with fascism but also its search for charismatic leaders. Though warnings against putting one's faith in a 'providential man' were not infrequent, particularly among more Catholic sectors, one of the first effects of fascistization was the leader cults that developed around a series of figures, among them José Antonio, whose good looks, elegant bearing, and impassioned rhetoric made him a plausible candidate for charismatic leadership. Indeed, José María de Ariezla, who financed some of Spain's early fascist initiatives, claimed Primo de Rivera had the *'physique du role*, the visible and external signs of a great political leader'.[24] His competitors were not as prepossessing. A less convincing cult developed around José Calvo Sotelo, whose Bloque Nacional was a clear attempt at an authoritarian intervention in Spanish politics. Both these men, though, were dwarfed by the AP leader, José María Gil Robles. This should not be taken literally—Gil Robles was rather short and distinctly portly. Indeed, in physical terms this bourgeois lawyer from Salamanca seemed as unlikely a candidate for charismatic leadership as the nerdish Ledesma Ramos. But a pronounced leader cult developed around Gil Robles, and, while it was most prominent in the party's youth movement, the Juventudes de Acción Popular (JAP), it was by no means confined to them.

AP had been conceived as a vehicle for mobilization and, early in 1933, it changed both its name and its constitution, becoming the Confederación de Derechas Autónomas. The CEDA, whose name was nearly as unwieldy as that of the FE de las JONS, did not, in fact, have the structure or organization of a political party, though

---

[23]   Quoted Jiménez Campo, *Fascismo en la crisis de la Segunda República*, 45.

[24]   Quoted Payne, *Fascism in Spain*, 125. See also Gil Pecharromán, *José Antonio Primo de Rivera*; P. Preston, *¡Comrades! Portraits from the Spanish Civil War* (London: HarperCollins, 1999), 74–108.

it functioned and campaigned as one.[25] Rather, the CEDA was a confederation of ad hoc local alliances: in Sevilla, for example *cedistas* talked to the Falange, though in other provinces they were partners with conservative republicans and, in places like Salamanca, had a firm alliance with the Carlists. After all, they shared a distrust of the language of party, an insistence on 'organic' social and political groupings, and a deep antipathy to democratic pluralism. Thus, while the CEDA's federal structure might have been expected to enhance the republican elements of the party—which undoubtedly existed—it actually encouraged the party's rightward swerve. Essentially the party remained a means of mobilizing as much of the right as possible. Its central organization was weak—'conglomeration' is in many ways a more apt description than 'confederation'—and the leader cult reflected both the emphasis on electioneering and the lack of other unifying elements.

In terms of presenting an uncompromising, immediately identifiable message to a mass audience, leadership cults had much to recommend them. The size of the CEDA guaranteed that people would listen to Gil Robles when, for example, he addressed the nation via the new medium of radio during the final half-hour of the 1933 electoral campaign. Internal tensions and ambiguities in policy could be referred back to the leader, covered up by slogans such as 'the *jefes* are never wrong' or 'our *jefe* never makes mistakes'. The term *jefe*, which is both more spontaneous and more commonly used in Spanish than the grandiose *caudillo*, was adopted with most enthusiasm by the JAP, among whom the leader cult was pronounced. During 1934, the JAP held a series of mass rallies at symbolic sites such as Covadonga, mythologized as the battleground where the 'reconquering' Christian kings first defeated the Arab invaders, and El Escorial, where Philip II built his monastery-palace as the spiritual heart of Spain's empire.[26] Following a visit to Nuremberg, Gil Robles had originally planned to mark the El Escorial rally by taking the salute at a march past. This plan was abandoned, but the rally was still characterized by precisely the same kind of orchestrated, quasi-liturgical, participative spectacle that might lead to the label of 'political religion' had it not been for the presence of Christian liturgy, including an open-air mass, in the same ceremony.

As the only centralized element in the CEDA party structure, the JAP saw itself as the vanguard, even the shock troops, of the main party. Unlike the women's organizations, which were locally organized, the (male) youth movement radiated out from Madrid. The JAP was the CEDA's most radical component, inaugurating its newspaper under the banner headline 'we want a new state'. Quickly affected by the 'vertigo of fascism', *japistas* espoused a fascist 'style', adopting khaki shirts and a quasi-Roman salute and volunteering for 'police duties' during the general strike and insurrection of October 1934. Unsurprisingly, rivalry with the Falange

---

[25] J. R. Montero, *La CEDA: el catolicismo social y político en la II República*, 2 vols (Madrid: Revista de Trabajo, 1977).
[26] For Covadonga, see C. Boyd, 'The Second Battle of Covadonga: The Politics of Commemoration in Modern Span', *History and Memory*, 14/1–2 (2002), 37–64.

was intense. Neither group was averse to violence, but the JAP did not court it in the same way as did the Falange: both groups commemorated their victims (and in remarkably similar ways) but the JAP produced fewer killers. Nevertheless, it was clear that the two groups were recruiting among the same social milieux—university students and the Catholic middle classes, above all in provincial towns—and that their political aims at least coincided. They were effectively operating within the same political space and the much greater success of the JAP severely confined any possibility of success for the Falange.[27]

This rapid political polarization that characterized the Second Republic ensured that, by the time of the February 1936 elections, the only division that mattered was left/right, that is, republican/anti-republican. This meant that, when the CEDA lost, albeit by a narrow margin, its brilliant career collapsed. The party had staked everything on winning an absolute parliamentary majority that would allow them to dismantle the Republic and create a corporate state. Before the election, the *jefe* had erected a gigantic poster of himself in Madrid's Puerta de Sol, showing his head against a background of marching troops and the words 'These are my powers'. Now he had failed and his party had lost. As large sections of the right's political leadership moved from electioneering to conspiracy, the CEDA imploded and many members of the JAP moved to the Falange. This was probably not the immediate mass exodus depicted in much of the literature; many, perhaps most, erstwhile *cedistas* and *japistas* bided their time, waiting to see what would happen next. And, as the Popular Front government soon rounded up the Falange, jailing its leaders and closing its premises, membership was not for the faint-hearted.

This period of clandestinity transformed the Falange. Not only did it mark the beginning of real political influence but it also changed the movement's character, giving the embryonic women's section a new-found importance. The Women's Section, led by José Antonio's sister Pilar, only existed because of some girls' insistence that they be allowed to join. The *jefe* himself had opposed female membership as incompatible with the party's violence. Yet, the Sección Feminina (SF) would become the only branch of the Spanish party to rival its Italian counterpart. Like the party itself, it expanded during the Civil War, with approximately 580,000 members by the end of the conflict.[28] War work was the key to this success. Female Falangists ran laundries and clothing depots, as well as staffing hospitals, soup kitchens, and orphanages. The SF thus created a completely new public role for

---

[27]   M. Blinkhorn, 'The Iberian States', in D. Mühlberger (ed.), *The Social Basis of European Fascist Movements* (London: Croom Helm, 1987), 320–48; idem, 'Conservatism, Traditionalism and Fascism in Spain, 1898–1937', in idem (ed.), *Fascists and Conservatives* (London: Unwin Hyman, 1990), 118–37.

[28]   Payne, *Fascism in Spain*, 301. In July 1936, the SF had branches in 18 provinces with *c*.2,500 members: K. Richmond, *Women and Spanish Fascism: The Women's Section of the Falange, 1934–1959* (London: Routledge, 2003), 7. This pattern was similar to that of the Fasci Femminili during the Second World War, though the FF reached 1 million members in 1942: P. Willson, 'Italy', in K. Passmore (ed.), *Women, Gender and Fascism in Europe, 1919–45* (Manchester: Manchester University Press, 203), 27.

Spanish women. Their sphere of action may still have been traditionally defined—welfare, the provision of food and clothing—but they worked independently and in uniform. Their freshly created institutions also provided a secular, political alternative to the Christian charity that otherwise dominated welfare and hospital relief.

This new public role had its origins in party's period of illegality during spring 1936. With the men in jail, women became indispensable. Still largely composed of sisters and girlfriends of the original Falangistas, or *camisas viejas* ('old shirts'), the SF acted as envoys and messengers, keeping the Falangist leadership apprised of what was happening on the streets and in contact with the military and monarchist conspirators plotting against the Republic. Their role was that of heroism *in extremis*, and this continued into the Civil War when, as well as providing practical home front support, SF members established escape networks, known as Auxilio Azul, for those trapped in Republican cities. Those who died were commemorated after the war as both martyrs and heroines, for the militarism of the Falange was a genuine option and, while its women never bore arms, they too were determined on war.

In 1934, José Antonio had sounded a note of caution against the military when he called on the army to participate in the rebellion that would bring the Falange to power but made it clear that both vision and leadership belonged to the party. In spring 1936, he simply called on the army to stage a coup: the destruction of the Republic was a political imperative, and one that united an otherwise disparate right.[29] This was, if anything, even more apparent at local level, particularly in the *pueblos*, where the affiliation of the local leader would often determine that of the village rightists. And many of these *jefecillos* were moving to the Falange, because they, like the Carlists, were actively preparing for war, principally by collecting arms and organizing militias. Despite their own robust identity, the Carlists were not immune from the intoxication of fascism.[30] And, in contrast to the JAP, they were elated, rather than traumatized, by February's electoral defeat. During spring 1936, the Falange and the Carlists, together with important sections of the army and significant members of the erstwhile CEDA leadership, prepared for the coming coup.

When the coup finally occurred, on 18 July 1936, it failed. After a weekend's bitter fighting, all of Spain's major cities and most of its territory and population remained under Republican control. The rebels' dire situation was only retrieved when both Italy and Germany agreed to send military aid, a turning point, not only in the Civil War, but also in the fortunes of the Falange. Mussolini had been aiding the Falange financially since April 1935, though his regime had earlier funded the

---

[29] *José Antonio Primo de Rivera: Selected Writings*, ed. H. Thomas (London: Jonathan Cape, 1972), 238–43.

[30] On Carlist mobilization, see J. Ugarte Tellería, *La nueva Covadonga insurgente* (Madrid: Biblioteca Nueva, 1998).

conspiratorial activities of both Alfonsist and Carlist monarchist groups, and had also provided training facilities for the Carlist militias. The point was not that Italian military aid would automatically favour the Falange but that civil war favoured the growth of fascism. Certainly, the decision to send transport planes to Franco's Army of Africa, stranded in Morocco after naval mutinies foiled the officers' plans to join the rebellion, was taken separately from any earlier involvement in Spanish affairs. Similarly the decision to intervene must be distinguished from the later escalation of Italian aid, a process that ended with Mussolini fighting the Spanish Republic more or less head on.[31] In contrast, German aid, while both crucial and carefully targeted, remained limited for the duration of the war.

On 18 July 1936, however, all this was unforeseeable. Franco's frantic appeals for aid to both Mussolini and Hitler were testimony to the ill-thought-out nature of the coup. Rather than the immediate success that they had assumed, the rebels encountered stiff resistance, not only from the organized working class but also from loyal army and police forces, who were crucial to defeating the rising in both Madrid and Barcelona. The rebellion was a relatively impromptu affair, at least in strategic terms, and the original rebels were a motley crew of counter-revolutionaries. Many of the prime conspirators on the mainland were aristocratic monarchists, looking for a return to the *status quo ante*. But this was never a realistic, or realizable, option and the contribution of the Falangist and Carlist militias, combined with aid from the Axis powers, would soon make it impossible. The Carlists and Falangists were the radical political outriders of the conspiracy but, while Carlist ideology was proudly traditional and essentially reactionary, the Falange offered the prospect of modernity and dynamism. They did not, though, have the strength to command the movement, particularly as, once the troops were over the Straits of Gibraltar, there was no doubt of the military might wielded by General Franco's *africanista* troops. As experienced colonial soldiers, used to policing the recalcitrant and restive Moroccan highlands, the *africanistas* had long assimilated a racialized discourse and were well used to the violent suppression of local dissent.[32]

Both the Carlists and the Falange expanded under conditions of war, though so too, of course, did the army. The Falange, however, grew exponentially, transformed during the first year of the Civil War from a small, tightly knit group into a genuinely mass party. Among all the party groupings on the right, the Falange was best equipped to take advantage of the popular dynamic unleashed by the war, though this was also exploited to some extent by the Carlists. Falangist organizations and particularly its militias attracted myriad recruits, even if some, among them many *japistas*, abandoned all party options and chose to join the army instead.[33] The

[31] P. Preston, 'Italy and Spain in Civil War and World War, 1936–45', in S. Balfour and P. Preston (eds), *Spain and the Great Powers in the Twentieth Century* (London: Routledge, 1999), 151–84.

[32] S. Balfour, *Deadly Embrace: Morocco and the Road to the Spanish Civil War* (Oxford: Oxford University Press, 2002).

[33] For a discussion of the numbers involved, see Payne, *Fascism in Spain*, 244–5.

rapid and sustained expansion of the Falange Española came at the expense of conservative options, finally eclipsing them but only at the price of its own dilution. The Falange was transformed from a small vanguard party of committed activists, essentially formed from among coteries of friends and cousins, into a vehicle for mobilization behind the Nationalist war effort. The key to Falangist success was thus armed anti-republicanism; like Carlism under the Second Republic, fascism had broadened its appeal but only as a 'counter-revolutionary amalgam'.[34] The 'new shirts' that flocked to the movement after February 1936 were prepared to risk their lives against the Republic, but they were not necessarily as committed to the redistributionary programme of the radical right.

Franco's rise to prominence was equally rapid—he was commander-in-chief of the armed forces by August and head of state in September—but it would be some time before he would be sufficiently powerful to dictate the terms under which his New State would be constructed. Indeed, while his dictatorship would provide the original model for the idea of authoritarian rule as distinct from fascism,[35] had it not been for the fascist movement, it would never have existed in the first place. An example of this is the leader cult which quickly grew up around the unlikely figure of the *Caudillo*: he was just as short as Gil Robles, if not as podgy, and his voice had an unnerving tendency to break into falsetto at moments of stress. Military uniform suited him, and was indeed his preferred form of dress, but he looked ridiculous in the blue shirt of the Falange. Yet, he was the subject of a genuine leader cult, the object of real adulation, including among Falangists. What mattered was the idea of leadership; the actual leader was incidental. The Spanish right had already invented the *jefe*: they simply needed a plausible figure to occupy that imaginary space.

Fascism and Francoism were thus intimately and inextricably combined, and while the dictator's image as a consummate manipulator with an acute sense of political brinkmanship has proved long-lasting, it is clearly an insufficient explanation of the regime's development. Like the Mussolini regime before it, Franco's New State represented an alliance between the radical and conservative right. This symbiotic relationship was demonstrated most acutely in April 1939 when Falange and Carlists were merged into a single party and their militias incorporated into the regular army. The intention was clearly to instrumentalize the party—now known as the Falange Española Tradicionalista y de las JONS—both by subordinating it to the military hierarchy and by recreating it as a vehicle for state-building. As both commander in chief and head of state, Franco was at the apex of both pyramids: the power of the *jefe* was finally confirmed.[36] He was therefore also the new party's leader for, as the party statutes put it, 'As author of the Era of History when Spain

[34] J. Canal, *El carlismo* (Madrid: Alianza, 2000), 273–341.

[35] J. J. Linz, 'An Authoritarian Regime: Spain', in S. Payne (ed.), *Politics and Society in Twentieth Century Spain* (New York: New Viewpoints, 1979); idem, *Totalitarian and Authoritarian Regimes* (Boulder, CO: Lynne Rienner, 2000).

[36] P. Preston, *Franco* (London, Harper Collins, 1993), 248–74.

achieved the possibility of realising its destiny, and with it the desires of the Movement [i.e. the combined party], the Head assumes fully and completely the most absolute authority.' There is thus a real sense in which unification represented the subordination, or 'domestication', of Spanish fascism. However, unification would not have been possible, and certainly would not have been successful, had it not been for a pre-existing sense of purpose that united the Francoist camp around the common goals of winning the war and reconstructing Spain.

The moment of unification is often taken as signifying the emasculation of the Falange and so the end of any true fascist option in Spain. Yet, if fascism was, in Michael Mann's words, an 'extreme version of nation-statism' then even its distinctive style and paramilitarism could not disguise the commonalties shared by the fascist and non-fascist right.[37] Nation-statism was 'the dominant political ideology' of the era and it was never more pronounced than in times of war. The 'moment of history' defined by the Civil War was understood as the occasion for national rebirth, an unparalleled opportunity brought about by Providence. The advantage unification brought to the Falange was thus not simply that it acknowledged the Falangist present at the heart of the regime, or that it established the fascist aesthetic as that of the New State.[38] Rather, the palingenetic vision that lay at the heart of fascism had suddenly become common currency on the Francoist right. Admittedly, the vision had been modified by the admission of divine purpose but, as *Genio de España* had shown as early as 1932, that had not come from nowhere. The circumstances of the Civil War, in particular the anticlerical massacres in the Republican zone, had given Catholicism a purchase it had not had before, not even in Spain. Indeed, this transfer between Catholicism and fascism, religion and politics, was part of the process of fascistization.

The position of the Falange was, though, enhanced over that of other political groups because of their attitude to the nation state. Falangist attitudes towards the state were far less ambivalent than those held by Carlists or, indeed, any confessional grouping. The Catholic Church proclaimed the primacy of both church and family vis-à-vis the state; totalitarian Falangists admitted neither. The 'democracy' of the public square already allowed Franco to legitimize his rule by acclamation and the massed presence of blue-shirted crowds in various forms of political spectacle. The Falange thus became the acknowledged agent of mobilization and active citizenship and, as the main constituent of the single party, a clear vehicle for state-building. As Franco drove on towards complete victory, the consolidation of power demanded a more robust state, with more direct control over its people. The process of fascistization was thus apparent within the construction of the New State itself: the Falange peopled the New State, quite literally embedding itself within it. In the

---

[37] Mann, *Fascists*, 2, 3.

[38] S. Ellwood, 'Falange Española and the Creation of the Francoist "New State"', *European History Quarterly*, 20 (1990), 209–22.

aftermath of civil war, the purpose of the single party became the reconstruction of the social basis of the Francoist alliance.

In the aftermath of victory, the various institutions and mechanisms of state power established on a contingent basis during the war—purge commissions, party offices, loyal *ayuntamientos*—had to be brought within a single orbit. Forming an official party had created 'a new power-allocating system' and though local rivalries, such as those between radical 'old shirts' and conservative 'new shirts' or between Falangists and Carlists, were common, they are easily overstated.[39] 'Fascistization' had the paradoxical effect of making the Falange less fascist, even as it fascistized conservative members of the Francoist alliance. Throughout Spain, party members filled more and more government posts and local council places, creating coordinated charitable institutions and a state-run system of labour representation. The Women's Section was essential in providing a fund of labour for these projects and also took the party into girls' schools, where the SF was responsible for both political and physical education. The welfare work begun during the war under the guise of Auxilio Social continued with volunteers and nurses providing rudimentary welfare services, notably vaccination programmes. The presumption of six months' voluntary social service for women aged between 17 and 35, which again originated during the war, thus also continued into the post-war.[40]

The work of the SF brought women into the state on a scale unseen before in Spain.[41] Party workers were essential in creating a state apparatus that touched the lives of all of Spain's citizens—a new relationship symbolized by the introduction of identity cards in 1941. The Falange thus peopled the regime, but the division between party and state became increasingly hard to see. Spanish fascism appeared to be becoming an adjunct, a 'domesticated' component of an authoritarian regime. Yet, at least in the early years of the post-war, a period commonly known as the 'first Francoism', this continuing blue-shirted presence indicated that, as a political project, fascism was not entirely dead. The potential for an autonomous Falange still existed as, indeed, did the dictator's suspicion of it.

For most of Franco's supporters, victory in the Civil War had been a sufficient end in itself: they had looked to the extirpation of republicanism and that had been achieved. But many of the *camisas viejas* still harboured palingenetic ambitions, and the circumstances of the Second World War enhanced both their authority and their ambitions. Victory for the Axis would result in a fascist Europe and, within this context, a specifically Falangist vision of a regenerated Spain could be achieved. Never did this seem more tangible than during 1940–1, as Nazi troops

---

[39] A. Cenarro, 'Elite, Party Church: Pillars of the Francoist "New State" in Aragon, 1936–45', *European History Quarterly*, 28/4 (1998), 461–86.

[40] A. Cenarro, *La sonrisa del la Falange: Auxilio Social en la guerra civil y en la posguerra* (Barcelona: Crítica, 2006).

[41] H. Graham, 'Gender and the State: Women in the 1940s', in H. Graham and J. Labanyi (eds), *Spanish Cultural Studies: An Introduction* (Oxford: Oxford University Press, 1995), 182–95.

swept through Europe and Axis prospects of victory seemed assured. The Falange began to flex its muscles, looking for more influence within the state and more ideological autonomy against the encroaching hegemony of 'national-catholicism'. For dedicated Falangists, absolute victory in the Civil War was only a beginning: they now looked to (re)incorporate the defeated into the national body. The purging that so profoundly marked the first years of Francoism, and in which the Falange was intimately involved, was in ideological terms a catharsis. For the regime, however, it was a process of consolidating victory and building state power.

This was essentially the difference between passivity and dynamism, 'anaesthetization' and mobilization. The political crisis of May 1941 was provoked by the resignations of several high-ranking Falangists, including Pilar Primo de Rivera, who wrote that she could no longer work to convince people that this party was the Falange 'when in reality it is not'.[42] The *camisas viejas* were once again bidding to conquer the state, as was made clear by their most powerful member, Franco's brother-in-law, Ramón Serrano Suñer. Their ambitions were obvious, their failure absolute. The Falange came out of the crisis with more cabinet posts but less influence: the only power confirmed by the crisis was that of the *Caudillo*. His difficulties with recalcitrant ideologues were lessened when Germany declared war on the Soviet Union. A volunteer battalion, the Blue Legion, was formed to fight with the Wehrmacht on the eastern front. Many of the most dedicated Falangists volunteered to fight while the party threw itself, once again, into war work. Yet the discourse created around this new anti-communist crusade was as Catholic as it was fascist and more patriotic than either. Hyper-nationalism remained as important to the Francoist project as it had been to the fascist one; now, however, the nation state was not only an ideological imperative but an increasingly powerful reality.

The Falange lost the power struggles of 1941. It was a junior partner in the regime even before the tide turned against the Axis in the Second World War. The key to this defeat was the enhanced power and capacity of the state that emerged from the Civil War rather than the political cunning of the *Caudillo*. As absolute ruler, Franco had access to more direct power than any previous Spanish government, and not all of that power came out of the barrel of a gun. The rhetoric and, to some extent, the apparatus of fascism survived in Franco's New State, but its political ambitions were curbed. Fascism had, indeed, been domesticated by a wider authoritarian alliance. This is not, though, to say that the dictatorship that emerged from the Civil War was simply 'authoritarian'. After victory had been made secure by a brutal repression, the regime was consolidated as a conservative, hierarchical military dictatorship, emphasizing public order and social 'peace'. Fascism became either an oppositional current, in the case of the *camisas viejas*, or a badge of office, worn by some as Francoists both during the dictatorship and, as conspiratorial groups, into

---

[42] There is a clear account of the crisis in J. M. Thomàs, *La Falange de Franco: el proyecto fascista del Régimen* (Barcelona: Plaza y Janés, 2001), 264–76; quote at 269.

the democracy that succeeded it.[43] But the prospect of consolidation—of turning a brutal military victory into a stable regime—would never have existed without either fascism or the Falange.

Francoism, as its name suggests, was a hybrid, the result of a profound dialectic that existed between the all sections of the anti-republican right during the 1930s. Fascism provided the dynamism, rhetoric, and mobilizing force that proved to be invaluable assets during the Civil War while the Falange peopled Franco's New State, as soldiers, killers, leaders, and officials. Falangism always existed within a wider and more general right-wing discourse and ideology which may have eventually undermined an identifiable fascism but which had also brought it into existence in the first place. To call the New State 'fascistized' may be to state the obvious, but it is a far closer approximation of its real nature than either 'authoritarian' or 'fascist'.

BIBLIOGRAPHY

ALVAREZ CHILLIDA, G., *El antisemitismo en España: la imagen del judío, 1812–2002* (Madrid: Marcial Pons, 2002).

BLINKHORN, M. (ed.), *Fascists and Conservatives: The Radical Right and the Establishment in Twentieth-Century Europe* (London: Unwin Hyman, 1990).

CANAL, J., *El Carlismo* (Madrid: Alianza, 2000).

PAYNE, S., *Fascism in Spain, 1923–1977* (Madison: University of Wisconsin Press, 1999).

PRESTON, P., *Franco: A Biography* (London: HarperCollins, 1993).

RODRÍGUEZ JIMÉNEZ, J. L., *Raccionarios y golpistas: la extreme derecha en España del tardofranquismo a la consolidación de la democracia, 1967–82* (Madrid: CSIC, 1994).

SAZ CAMPOS, I., *España contra España: los nacionalismos franquistas* (Madrid: Marcial Pons, 2003).

—— *Fascismo y franquismo* (Valencia: Universitat de València, 2004).

THOMÀS, J. M., *La Falange de Franco: el proyecto fascista del Régimen* (Barcelona: Plaza y Janés, 2001).

VINCENT, MARY, 'Spain', in K. Passmore (ed.), *Women, Gender and Fascism in Europe, 1919–45* (Manchester: University of Manchester Press, 2003).

[43] J. L. Rodríguez Jiménez, *Raccionarios y golpistas: la extreme derecha en España del tardofranquismo a la consolidación de la democracia, 1967–82* (Madrid: CSIC, 1994).

C H A P T E R 20

HUNGARY

MARK PITTAWAY

HISTORICAL interpretation of Hungarian fascism has been shaped by the political divisions that followed its fall in 1945. Almost from the moment of the war's end, Hungary's left-wing political parties used their anti-fascist credentials to legitimize their political project for Hungary's future. They sought to emphasize not only how they distinguished themselves from the country's national socialist parties—especially the Arrow Cross Party (Nyilaskeresztes Párt), which briefly held office during the last tragic months of the war—but also attempted to tar Hungary's authoritarian inter-war regime with the brush of fascism. From the end of the Second World War, through most of the socialist era, politics in the era of Admiral Miklós Horthy, from 1919 until 1944, was described as 'Horthy fascism'; its pursuit of territorial revision and institutionalized anti-Semitism held responsible for the tragedies of Hungary's painful entanglement in the Second World War and the murder of the majority of the country's Jewish population. Since the 1970s, and more overtly since 1989, the historiography of the inter-war period has emphasized the distance between fascism, and the authoritarian and conservative practice of politics during the Horthy era, based as it was on an oligarchic parliamentarianism, which as much harked back to the political system of the dualist era as looked forward to the political practices of Fascist Italy or Nazi Germany.

While Hungary's radical national socialist parties defined themselves as radical nationalist opponents of the country's inter-war political system, it is impossible to explore Hungarian fascism without considering its relationship to the dominant 'neo-conservatism' of the inter-war years. This is so, principally because Hungarian fascist movements in the 1930s existed in a symbiotic relationship to the structures and patterns of social support for the dominant inter-war regime; in many respects the National Socialism that emerged during the decade was a radical variant of the neo-conservatism to which most of Hungary's ruling elite subscribed. The boundaries between the neo-conservative governing elite and the radical right had been fluid from the beginnings of the Horthy era in 1919. Counter-revolutionary governments of the early 1920s had drawn considerable support from the radical right within both the military and the country as a whole; the consolidation of their political authority relied on the development of a symbiotic relationship between the aristocratic governing elite and counter-revolutionary paramilitarism. While, during Prime Minister István Bethlen's period of office between 1921 and 1931, the influence of the radical right on the political system was contained and governing practice instead resembled the authoritarian liberalism of the pre-war years, the depression radicalized political opinion. During the early 1930s public opinion moved sharply to the right, associating increasingly not only democratic ideas with a 'foreign' and 'liberal' spirit, but also the political practices of the Bethlen era.

Explicit fascism and National Socialism were the most radical manifestations of this shift, and this process goes some way to explain some of its peculiarities in the Hungarian context. By the turn of the 1940s, National Socialism had achieved a considerable popularity, resting on a cross-class coalition which stretched from army officers, public officials, small businessmen, the poorer segments of the agrarian population, and even sections of the industrial working class. It was, however, kept out of power at that point only by a combination of the selective use of state power against the movement and the appeasement of anti-Semitic and irredentist opinion by governments. Its medium- and long-term fortunes were tied to the prestige and popularity of German National Socialism within Hungary. For this reason, hampered by its own political mistakes, the Hungarian far right found that the unpopularity of the Second World War led to an evaporation of support. When it finally came to power, as a result of a German-backed coup in October 1944, Hungarian National Socialism was considerably weaker in terms of the backing that it enjoyed than four years previously. Its association with the period in late 1944 and April 1945 when Hungary was the theatre of bloody military conflict between the Soviet Union and retreating Axis forces, and its own violence and extremism in power left it profoundly discredited. While the early post-war years were marked by isolated acts of anti-Semitic violence, Hungary's various post-war regimes closed off the political space into which neo-fascist organizations might have emerged. During the years of socialist dictatorship from 1948 'the struggle against fascism' became a central aspect of the regime's ideological armoury. While the re-emergence of political pluralism since 1989 has seen the appearance of some radical right-wing movements and parties and, indeed, acts of protest, these hark back more to the broader radical right of the inter-war years than solely to those movements, which can be characterized unproblematically as fascist.

The roots of both Hungarian fascism and the dominant neo-conservative ideology of the inter-war years lay in a polarization of politics that began in the 1890s, when conservative intellectuals responded to the growing mobilization of the left in the country's industrial centres and a greater assertiveness from non-Magyar speakers, who composed half of pre-war Hungary's population. They argued that the dominant liberal oligarchy, which ruled Hungary throughout the pre-war years, had allowed society to become dominated by an 'alien spirit', which they associated with the country's Jews, who they asserted had become powerful beneficiaries of the development of capitalism during the last third of the nineteenth century. Their apparent 'power', an emergent labour movement, and the growing influence of democratic ideas, based on notions of individual rights, were, according to this view, threatening the territorial integrity and character of a 'Christian', 'historic' Hungary. 'National Christian' neo-conservative ideas were strengthened during the First World War and mixed with other, more explicitly racist, intellectual currents. With the onset of the crisis of Hungary's variant of authoritarian, oligarchic liberal nationalism, the ideas of this late nineteenth-century new right came to dominate hegemonic discourses of national identity, thus shaping both inter-war Hungarian conservatism and, indeed, later, fascism.

The political crisis of liberalism, to which 'National Christian' neo-conservatism was a response, culminated in the collapse of the Austro-Hungarian monarchy. Mobilization among the kingdom's minorities, especially on the country's geographical periphery, among Romanians in Transylvania, southern Slav groups along the southern border, Slovaks in northern Hungary, and Germans in western Transdanubia, shattered Hungary geographically. The designs of neighbouring states such as Romania and newly created Austria, the alternative Yugoslav and Czechoslovak national projects, as well as the interests of the victorious powers, interacted to shape a post-war settlement which dismantled the kingdom of Hungary. Because of centrality of notions of the 'permanent' and 'God-given' nature of statehood to notions of 'National Christian' neo-conservatism, such a settlement—institutionalized through the Treaty of Trianon in 1920—was utterly unacceptable to Hungarian conservatives and, more generally, to the bulk of Hungarian opinion. As the state fragmented, society and politics polarized on class lines. The strains of the war economy stimulated increasing protest in industrial areas, which generated the social revolutionary pressure leading to bourgeois revolution in the autumn of 1918 and then the creation of a brief Soviet Republic in 1919. Revolution produced counter-revolutionary reaction, aided by neighbouring states that emerged victorious to shape the contours of Hungary's inter-war regime. Consolidated by the early 1920s, this regime was institutionally far from fascist; instead it reproduced many of the practices of the pre-war liberal polity. Hungary remained a monarchy, though one presided over by a regent, Admiral Miklós Horthy, and one which rejected the attempts of Károly IV, king until 1918, to reclaim his throne in 1921. Inter-war Hungary retained a parliamentary system but from 1922 with an ever more restricted franchise; it also remained a multi-party system and, while elections were competitive, they were far from free or fair; the ruling party, which existed in several incarnations until 1944, acted as an arm of the administration, and for this reason its power was never seriously threatened. Communist parties were banned and organizations considered subversive, like the legal Social Democratic Party and its unions, were subject to official harassment and police supervision.

Hungary's inter-war regime broke more radically with the practice of the pre-war years in several important respects of central relevance to the later development of fascism. The first was the role of paramilitarism within both the political system and culture of inter-war Hungary. With defeat in autumn 1918 the Austro-Hungarian military collapsed. The army fragmented; a fragmentation exacerbated by the deep-seated political polarization of which the revolutionary moment was a part. Those who refused to accept either the democratic or later the Soviet Revolution formed themselves into a number of paramilitary societies, most of which adopted radical nationalist, anti-socialist, and anti-Semitic political programmes. Many of these offered their support to the counter-revolutionary forces that crystallized around the Anti-Bolshevik Committee in Vienna and then, later, the anti-communist government based in the south-eastern city of Szeged. The military defeat of the Soviet Republic and the consolidation of the power of the counter-revolutionary government in 1919 countrywide were accompanied by a wave of paramilitary violence. Paramilitary groups engaged in murder of those whom they accused of supporting and serving the Soviet Republic but often targeted anyone they believed sympathetic to the aims of the labour movement. Motivated by a clearly anti-Semitic ideology, many of the groups extended this violence to Jews, especially in provincial western Hungary in the immediate aftermath of the Soviet Republic's collapse. Right-wing paramilitary actions in late 1919 are believed to have claimed as many as 2,000 lives.

While the wave of paramilitary bloodshed abated, it was often selectively condoned by the emergent regime as it consolidated its authority. In 1921, Hungarian paramilitary violence erupted in those parts of western Hungary awarded to Austria, when the Austrian gendarmerie occupied them in August. This carnage, dubbed officially in Hungary the 'Western Hungarian Uprising', was backed by the Hungarian authorities who used it to force a referendum on the drawing of the border around the city of Sopron. Often there existed a fluid boundary between paramilitaries and the regular army, since the former could be used to shore up the regime when the latter proved unreliable, as during Károly IV's final attempt to reclaim the Hungarian throne in October 1921. His march on Budapest to remove Horthy, supported by legitimist sections of the army, was repulsed on the outskirts of the capital at Budaőrs, by a force organized by the prominent paramilitary and later radical right politician Gyula Gömbös, who ensured that the ranks of pro-Horthy soldiers were bolstered by paramilitaries and armed members of radical right student organizations. Even when the inter-war regime was consolidated during the 1920s when István Bethlen sought to place distance between his government and the radical right, forcing some like Gömbös into opposition, paramilitarism preserved a presence within Hungarian society and political culture. Prominent political organizations with their origins in the counter-revolutionary paramilitarism of 1919, like MOVE (Magyar Országos Véderő Egylet, or the Hungarian National Defence Association), retained a presence in local society and politics, in some areas compensating for the fact that the governing party lacked its own mass-membership organization in much of the country prior to 1932.

If paramilitarism was one element of the inter-war Hungarian political scene relevant to the later emergence of fascism, then anti-liberalism and the hegemony of National Christian ideas within the political culture of inter-war Hungary constituted another. Cultural and political commentators during the 1920s defined the regime in opposition to the 'liberalism' of the dualist era which, it was maintained, had led to the incursion of 'alien elements' that had led the country to catastrophe in the aftermath of the First World War. Such attitudes generated forms of political discourse that stressed the unified and eternal nature of the Hungarian nation, its fundamentally 'Christian' character, and emphasized that political leaders had a duty to 'defend' Magyars from their 'alien' enemies. In turn such opinions led to a growing interest in *völkisch* ideas of 'race' and 'racial defence' and their translation into a Hungarian context during the 1920s, inspiring political movements that stressed the apparent Turanian origins of Magyars, which embedded themselves in radical right-wing rhetoric. The most disturbing aspect of anti-liberal, National Christian conservatism was its political anti-Semitism, which prompted legislation limiting the proportion of Jews admitted to universities from 1921. While during the 1920s this law was unevenly implemented, anti-Semitism played a central role in public discourse. It was often married to an anti-capitalism in which 'Jewish international capitalism' was asserted to be undermining the position of Hungary's 'Christian' population, especially at moments of economic dislocation, such as during the hyper-inflation between 1922 and 1924, and the period of economic restriction that brought it to an end. Right-wing radicals argued that measures to destroy the economic influence of Jews provided the key to integrating marginal groups, like the working class, into their proposed 'national community'. While they maintained that they were not opposed to capitalism as such, those like Gyula Gömbös maintained that 'A capitalism which is not national, which is not Christian, which does not take into account higher national considerations, but which is simply selfish, I hate and see as dangerous.'[1]

The notion of the creation of a 'Christian Hungary' was allied to the Hungarian regime's core policy goal of reversing the territorial losses institutionalized by the Treaty of Trianon and regaining as much of the territory of pre-1918 Hungary as possible. Irredentism was an article of faith across most of the political spectrum, including the far right, and infused official and popular political culture. Belief

---

[1] 'Beszéd a Nemzetgyűlés Indemintási Vitájában Kül- és Belpolitikai Kérdésekről, a Külföldi Kölcsönről', in J. Vonyó (ed.), *Gömbös Gyula: Válogatott Politikai Beszédek és Írások* (Budapest: Osiris Kiadó, 2004), 225.

in Christianity and irredentism was equated, as anti-Trianon propaganda invited Magyars to 'believe in one God, to believe in one homeland'. Given the circumstances in which 'historic Hungary' had been dismantled, the dominant ideology of the inter-war era was characterized by an aggressive anti-socialism, which not only blamed communism for the 'tragedy' that was said to have befallen the nation in 1919, but attacked Hungary's legal Social Democratic Party, too. Official rhetoric condemned the labour movement in all its manifestations, maintaining that it had played a role in delivering Hungary into the arms of 'foreigners', because it had concentrated on a politics of class to the exclusion of nation; it should 'not have forgotten, that a Hungarian worker is not just a worker, but a Hungarian too'.[2]

While these notions were hegemonic, political actors committed to radical right-wing policies were successfully marginalized under István Bethlen during the second half of the 1920s. This position changed as a result of the depression, which brought severe economic dislocation that affected social attitudes and the nature of the political system. The political change brought about by the depression occurred simultaneously at both elite and popular levels. The first element was a crisis at governmental level causing the fall of Bethlen in 1931, and then, following a brief interregnum under Gyula Károlyi, Horthy appointed Gyula Gömbös, paramilitary-turned-politician, admirer of Mussolini, and Hungary's most prominent advocate of radical right politics, as Prime Minister in 1932. His term of office, which ended with his death in October 1936, proved to be a disappointment to supporters of his policies. His attempts to transform the political system within the constraints of the inter-war settlement to create a 'purposeful national state', underpinned by an attack on the autonomy of the labour movement, a more protectionist, *dirigiste* economic policy, and social reform were frustrated by those members of the governing elite suspicious of his intentions. While disappointment in his government generated the space for explicitly fascist mobilization, some of the reforms he did implement bolstered the later radicalization of the political system. Among his first acts was to transform the governing party into a mass-membership organization—the NEP (Nemzeti Egység Pártja, or National Unity Party). In organizing the party, Gömbös's radical right supporters were given key positions. Furthermore, in part because of the opportunities for political protection in a clientelist political system, the NEP quickly became a mass party, attracting members from sections of the population who had previously not been politically active and permitting transitions of power at local level, where the membership were able to restrict the ability of local elites to secure influence over the political system. Within the army, Gömbös also conducted a purge of senior officers, which removed many supportive of conservative positions, replacing them with sympathizers with the radical right. This step would prove especially fateful during the Second World War.

---

[2] 'Munkásvédelem: politika nélkül', *Soproni Hírlap* (18 May 1939), 1.

The depression led not merely to a shift in the balance of forces within the ruling elite of the inter-war regime but brought about considerable social dislocation. The international crash led to severe falls in the world market prices of agricultural goods, which, in an economy so based on agriculture, caused a serious crisis. Given the enormous inequalities of land ownership, and the numbers dependent on casual seasonal employment on the country's *latifundia*, the social crisis of Hungary's agrarian poor—both propertied and landless—sharpened considerably. Industrial dislocation led to widespread urban employment, while budgetary restriction caused job losses among the state bureaucracy, severely affecting the middle classes. This social crisis placed social reform firmly on the political agenda; while some who advocated radical change could be identified as being on the left, they were a minority. The impact of the depression radicalized right-wing opinion, both among backers of the radical right and neo-conservative camps within the governing elite, and among intellectuals in a way that undercut the attempts of those supportive of the regime, like Bethlen, who wished to pursue a more conservative-liberal course.

Furthermore, Hungary looked to the countries to its west, particularly Germany, for political models. While Italian Fascism had been widely admired among radical right-wing politicians like Gömbös, the rise to power of the National Socialists in Germany interacted with domestic pressures within Hungary to precipitate a number of explicitly fascist formations during the first half of the 1930s. These early movements, like the Scythe Cross Movement, founded by Zoltán Böszörmény in 1931, demanded social transformation underpinned by radical anti-Semitic measures aiming at removing Jews from economic life. Hungarian National Socialism was far from a homogeneous movement, however. Böszörmény's attempts to build a mass movement among the seasonally employed agrarian proletariat on Hungary's Great Plain were quickly eclipsed by other parties that sought to organize in conservative western Hungary. Analysis of the votes cast for national socialist candidates in the 1935 parliamentary elections revealed considerable support for their combination of land reform, radical anti-Semitism, and ultranationalism that was concentrated among poorer smallholders in western Hungary, whose incomes and, therefore, economic independence had been threatened by the downturn and the slow process of recovery in agriculture.

The coalition of ultranationalism, demands for social transformation in the interests of poorer Magyars, combined with the radical anti-Semitism that emerged in Hungary's earliest phase of national socialist mobilization, characterized the Hungarist, or Arrow Cross, movement. As a consequence of at times uneven mobilization and official harassment, it existed as a series of different parties; yet after 1935 it quickly emerged as the dominant national socialist movement in the country. The movement was closely associated with its founder, Ferenc Szálasi, an army officer who, in view of his exceptional abilities, had been promoted to the Hungarian General Staff on the completion of his studies in 1925. Despite the connections he established to leading officers within the army and to certain politicians, including Gyula Gömbös, Szálasi became increasingly active politically, openly advocating a restructuring of the Hungarian state along fascist lines. As a consequence of this political activism, he was pensioned out of the General Staff in 1935 to emerge as leader of a new party, the Party of National Will (Nemzet Akaratának Pártja). This body was the first of several institutional incarnations of Hungarism, while it rapidly grew to reach its peak of support between 1938 and 1940.

Hungarism was, in terms of its own self-presentation, no straightforward copy of German National Socialism but its adaptation to specifically Hungarian conditions and concerns. As far as Szálasi himself was concerned, 'Hungarism is the Hungarian practice of the National Socialist world view and *Zeitgeist*.'[3] The party presented itself as the most enthusiastic advocate of 'National Christian' ideas and concepts of the nation, sharing with the neo-conservatism of the ruling elite a desire to overthrow the 'unjust' Treaty of Trianon and to 'restore' the borders of Hungary to those of the 'lands of the Holy Crown'.[4] Hungarism expressed itself as being in agreement with the dominant Christian nationalism of the inter-war ruling elite; in the words of the 1938 programme of its second institutional incarnation, the National Socialist Hungarian Party–Hungarist Movement (A Nemzeti Szocialista Magyar Párt–Hungarista Mozgalom), it rested on 'the moral and religious views of Christianity and the fundamentals of the thousand years of Hungarian constitu-tionalism'.[5] It commitment to Christian politics was closely tied to its nationalism— for Szálasi 'true love of God and true love of Christ leads only to true love of the nation and love of the homeland'; yet at the same time this stance was combined paradoxically with an anticlerical streak, as it strongly condemned the role of the established Christian Churches as political partners of the neo-conservative regime.[6] Its commitment to radical Christian nationalism fused with national socialist influence from abroad to shape Hungarism's radical anti-Semitism; while its belief in a 'Christian' Hungary was deployed to justify its belief in the necessity of solving 'the Jewish question', the movement's definition of Jewishness was racial and not religious: 'Jewry is a race, not a religious group. We regard someone as of Jewish race, if they have more than one Jewish grandparent.' They argued that 'a person who is of Jewish race may not exercise the full rights of a Hungarian citizen', and sought the separation of Jews and Christians and active, radical economic discrimination.[7]

Radical anti-Semitism operated as a consequence of Hungarism's commitment to radical Christian nationalism but also formed a means through which the

[3] F. Szálasi, 'Út és Cél', repr. in idem, *Hungarizmus*, i: *A Cél* (Budapest: Gede Testvérek, 2004), 104.
[4] Ibid. 105.
[5] 'A Nemzeti Szocialista Magyar Párt: Hungarista mozgalom programja', repr. in J. Gergely, F. Glatz, and F. Pölöskei (eds), *Magyarországi Pártprogramok (1919–1944)* (Budapest: ELTE: Eötvös Kiadó, 2003), 372.
[6] Szálasi, 'Út és Cél', 110–11.
[7] 'A Nemzeti Szocialista Magyar Párt: Hungarista mozgalom programja', 375.

movement sought to realize its goal of an organic national community based around peasant and worker. Within Hungarist conceptions of the national community, 'the peasant is the sustainer of the nation…the worker is the builder of the nation'.[8] This conclusion provided the ideological foundation of a radical social programme which promised to free subordinate social groups from the 'service of Jewish big capital' through the creation of what it termed 'a Hungarian work-based state' that would 'secure the greatest earnings possibilities for…those who want to work and are capable of work…workers, tillers of the land, farmers, and artisans alike'.[9] Its concentration on an egalitarian Magyar national community purged of 'Jewish' influence would, as far as Hungarism was concerned, allow Magyars to recover their role as 'a leading people' within the 'living space of the Carpathians and the Danube'.[10] Yet Hungarism at the same time recognized the ethnic pluralism of the territory of the pre-Trianon Hungary it sought to restore, arguing that all non-Jewish and non-Roma ethnic groups could be united behind one national border under Hungarian leadership, while at the same time being given cultural autonomy. For Szálasi, 'according to our Hungarist view the maintenance of the mother tongue and a particular folk culture is not in contradiction with loyalty to the homeland'.[11]

During the second half of the 1930s, Hungarism grew in influence and by the end of the decade it had sufficient public support to mount a serious challenge to the hegemony of the country's ruling elite. Its growth was closely tied to the way pent-up desire within Hungary for social reform, especially agrarian reform, interacted with the increasing prestige of Nazi Germany. Germany's armaments-based economic boom came to be seen as a positive model for Hungary, given its slower process of recovery. Large sections of Hungarian opinion drew the conclusion that a similar economic programme, combined with more radical anti-Semitic measures, held the key to national economic recovery. While many within the governing elite held these opinions—indeed, Prime Minister Kálmán Dáranyi increasingly moved in this direction during 1937 and 1938—its effect on subordinate social groups was to produce an upsurge in support for Hungarism. In 1937 and 1938 many Hungarian agricultural labourers worked on seasonal employment contracts in Germany to plug labour shortages; their experiences of wages that were substantially higher than in Hungary served to enhance the prestige of Nazi Germany and National Socialist ideas at home. The incorporation of Austria into National Socialist Germany further increased this prestige, because it raised the possibility that an alliance with Germany would allow Hungary to achieve its own territorial goals. More immediately, however, the impact of incorporation on the former

---

[8] Szálasi, 'Út és Cél', 140.

[9] 'A Nyilaskeresztes Párt programja', in Gergely, Glatz, and Pölöskei (eds), *Magyarországi Pártprogramok*, 426.

[10] F. Szálasi, 'Nagytér, Élettér, Vezetőnép', repr. in Szálasi, *Hungarizmus*, i: *A Cél*, 230–2.

[11] Szálasi, 'Út és Cél', 156.

Austrian province of Burgenland, which lay immediately adjacent to Hungary, into the Third Reich, where the new rulers forcibly expelled most of the region's Jews in spring 1938 and immediately introduced discriminatory measures against the Roma population, was marked. These actions, combined with the rapid elimination of unemployment there, represented a further demonstration, for many in western Hungary, that racist measures combined with an assertive programme of social reform could solve the economic problems of subordinate social groups. The high tide for national socialist and Hungarist positions coincided with parliamentary elections in May 1939, when such parties polled almost a quarter of the vote. Due to the restricted franchise and the considerable obstacles the pro-government public administration placed in the way of these parties, their actual level was almost certainly higher.

There is little more than fragmentary evidence as to the social base of Hungarist and national socialist movements. In November 1938, the National Socialist Hungarian Party, Hungarism's second institutional manifestation, claimed a public membership of 240,000. Because of bans on public servants and army officers— among whom it maintained it had considerable backing—joining the party, it claimed a further 300,000 secret members.[12] Its successor, the Arrow Cross Party, founded in March 1939 after its predecessor was banned, claimed 400,000 open members and a further 100,000 who belonged in secret.[13] In the absence of archival sources it is very difficult to check the reliability of such figures; it is similarly impossible to reconstruct properly the social composition of the membership. From the fragmentary evidence available on the state of the movement at local level, the figures given above seem not to be unrealistic: in the north-western town of Magyaróvár in 1938 the local police estimated a membership of around 1,000—just short of 10 per cent of the local population—concentrated among its artisans and skilled workers.[14]

The 1939 election results provide a better, though still partial, guide to the extent of national socialist support. Analysis of these results is suggestive of the broad movement's strength in those parts of rural, western Transdanubia, where national socialism had made substantial inroads among the propertied smallholder population in 1935. Yet, it performed especially well in all those areas where a poor, smallholder population was on especially significant element of local society, not merely in the far west of the country. A second significant trend was its success in industrial areas, among working-class voters. In the industrial towns adjacent to Budapest, regarded as strongholds of the labour movement, it outpolled the Social Democrats in 1939. While the election results themselves were an imperfect guide, due to the shortcomings of the election process, a number of conclusions

---

[12] ÖStA/AdR, 'Bürckel' Materie, Zl.1575/2, Kt.12, Die Hungaristische Bewegung in Ungarn, 1.

[13] M. Szöllösi-Janze, *Die Pfeilkreuzlerbewegung in Ungarn: Historischer Kontext, Entwicklung und Herrschaft* (Munich: R. Oldenbourg Verlag, 1989), 128.

[14] GyMS.GyL, IVf.B.451a, A m.kir.rendőrség magyaróvári kapitánysága.

can be drawn from these results. First, national socialist support was frequently a reaction to ethnic tension and it attracted considerable backing from Magyars in regions characterized by diversity. In regions with large ethnic German populations in the 1939 elections, the key to defeating Arrow Cross challengers was to persuade German populations to back pro-government candidates. Where this was not done successfully, in areas like Mosonmagyaróvár along the German border, where many German voters spoilt their ballots by drawing swastikas across them, the far right's mobilization of the local Magyar minority led to the victory of a national socialist candidate.[15] Likewise the movement profited from increased anti-Semitism during the late 1930s: in much of rural western Hungary the organization of the Arrow Cross was accompanied by violence against the property of Jewish businessmen and a growing willingness to denounce local Jews, for offences both real and imagined, to the local gendarmerie.

While it profited from increased ethnic conflict—even when its cause, paradoxically, was the politicization of the German minority as a result of the increased prestige of Nazi Germany, from which Hungarists themselves gained—the most notable aspect of its social base was its plebeian nature. It owed most of its support to its credibility as an agent of radical social change and, at the turn of the 1940s, successfully articulated popular desire for reform. Its open advocacy of radical land reform allowed it not merely to expand the support it had won among poorer smallholders during the mid-1930s but extended to manorial servants and other agricultural labourers, attracted by its promises of creating 'a peasant state' and breaking the power of large landowners. Perhaps the most notable elements of this plebeian social base were reflected in the movement's success in securing votes among the industrial working class, winning, in 1939, relative majorities in working-class districts, especially surrounding Budapest and especially among sections of the labour movement not well integrated into the left-wing political structures of social democracy; in Greater Budapest's machine plants, for example, Arrow Cross support was concentrated among the young, who had become adults amid the right-wing climate of the 1930s, while their elders remained loyal to the political left. Most significant was the poll Hungarism picked up among coal miners, as a consequence of the unpopularity of the moderate left-wing mineworkers' union and its weakness in the face of employers. During 1940, the Arrow Cross built on the base they had won in mining areas the previous year to organize mineworkers and led a national miners' strike in 1940, where they sought to arrest declining living standards that had set in as a consequence of accelerating inflation. While, after an initial and unsuccessful recourse to repression, the strike was bought off through a generalized wage settlement, it represented the peak of Hungarist organization of the industrial working class.

[15] BA, R1501/3332, 78.

The ruling elite responded to the challenge of Hungarism in a way that transformed their rule. Publicly, representatives of the governing parties presented their National Socialist rivals as 'extremists', akin to Bolshevik revolutionaries in 1919, with their demands to overturn the existing order. Yet the challenge of Hungarism, combined with the changing international context within which Hungary operated, served to transform the practices of the governing elite. Thus fascism played a central role in reshaping the governing practice of the ruling party. This was not an uncontested process within the governing elite; one faction wished to emulate closely the radical right, associated with Béla Imrédy, the Prime Minister between 1938 and 1939. Imrédy and his allies sought to reconstitute the ruling party as a 'movement' that would serve as the basis for an explicitly dictatorial form of rule, while driving forward with anti-Semitic measures that were designed to curtail 'Jewish economic influence'. Imrédy's politics generated distrust from more conservative segments of the ruling elite who had the ear of Horthy, and they succeeded in removing him from power by revealing his alleged 'Jewish origins'. While Imrédy left the ruling party, forming his own radical right-wing party in 1940, conservatives within the elite failed to prevent its rightward drift.

The most marked sign of the shift in the practice of Hungary's ruling elite under the influence of the challenge of fascism was the country's transformation at the turn of the 1940s into an explicitly racist state. The most striking marker of this change was the passage of a series of anti-Jewish laws between 1938 and 1942. Initially, the Hungarian state sought to remove those it defined as Jews from intellectual occupations, by first employing a religious definition, which shifted in 1941 to an explicitly racial one based on ancestry. In 1939, it then moved to restrict the political rights of Jews and their rights to engage in commercial and business activities. During the early 1940s, mixed marriages were banned; Jews were to serve in the military as members of 'labour service battalions', while any agricultural land they owned was progressively confiscated. The demotion of Jews to the status of second-class citizens was accompanied by the dominance of anti-Semitism within public discourse and a further layer of discrimination introduced by those local authorities that fell under the influence of radical right ideas. They also intensified their stigmatization of and discrimination against the Roma population. Although this policy was far less obvious and more uneven than the measures directed against Jews, it, too, represented one way in which the governing elite sought to restrict the rights of social groups it saw as being outside the boundaries of the 'nation'.

The second major consequence was the Hungarian state's growing, if uneven, willingness to work with Nazi Germany in terms of the achievement of its territorial goals against the neighbouring states. While Hungary refused to support Germany's invasion of Poland in 1939, it increasingly moved closer to Berlin, regaining southern Slovakia in November 1938, Carpathian Ruthenia in March 1939, and northern

Transylvania in September 1940. Hungary's support for Germany's invasion of Yugoslavia in April 1941, which prompted the suicide of the Prime Minister Pál Teleki, led to the reannexation of a substantial part of former Yugoslav territory, including the Vojvodina and the Prekmurje region of Slovenia. While these territorial changes were celebrated as the winning of Hungarian national goals, they came at the cost of a growing militarization of Hungarian society. Furthermore, the Hungarian army in the new territories killed civilians, frequently motivated by nationalist and racist ideas. The reoccupation of northern Transylvania was accompanied by violence on the part of Hungarian troops against Romanian civilians. In Vojvodina Hungarian forces were embroiled in a brutal guerrilla war against local partisans and they responded with a series of raids in January 1942, in which several thousand civilians, including a substantial number of Serbs and Jews, were murdered by Hungarian forces. This step set the stage for Hungary's entanglement in Hitler's war against the Soviet Union from late June 1941 and the further complicity of the Hungarian military and political authorities in a number of atrocities, the most serious of which was the deportation of 16,000 stateless Jews from Hungary, who were murdered by German and Ukrainian troops at Kamjanec'-Podil's'kij in 1941.

While Hungarism and National Socialism had helped drive the regime to the right and thus assisted in entangling the country in Nazism's racist war of conquest against the Soviet Union, the unpopularity of the conflict at home undermined support for the movement. The Arrow Cross in parliament had been damaged by individual political errors, most notably when two of its members of parliament, Kálmán Hubay and Pál Vágó, proposed a bill to realize the party's programme of cultural autonomy for ethnic minorities within Hungary in 1940, and were accused of 'treason' by the government. More fundamentally Arrow Cross support had rested on the prestige of National Socialist Germany and on their credibility as a party that could improve the position of the poor, both of which were eroded by the impact of the war on the home front. Among poorer smallholders the spread of conscription was highly unpopular, given the lack of adequate material compensation for absent family members who would have worked on their farms. The impact of the introduction of war economy, which brought more despotic practice in industry, compulsory deliveries and high taxation in agriculture, and cuts in real incomes, intensified this unpopularity. The mounting human costs of the conflict, especially after the destruction of the Second Hungarian Army on the Don in early 1943, undercut support for the war effort further. As the likelihood that the Soviet Union would overrun Hungary increased and the Hungarian government sought a way out of the war, society became more fearful and polarized. By the time the Germans occupied a Hungary that they were worried would switch sides and join the Allies in March 1944, the Arrow Cross Party was a shadow of the organization that it had been four years previously. In western Hungary, police reports suggested that in spring 1944 the party's membership was only a quarter of the level of four years previously.[16]

Thus, when the party finally took power as the result of a coup supported by the German occupation authorities in October 1944, in response to Horthy's attempt to take Hungary out of the war, the party was effectively well past its peak. The pro-German government of Prime Minister Döme Sztójay, in power between March and August 1944, had already implemented much of the programme of the radical right. The labour movement had been disbanded, while, most significantly, 437, 402 Jews from all over the country, save the city of Budapest, were deported, with the overwhelming majority murdered at Auschwitz. Horthy dismissed Sztójay in August and began to negotiate Hungary's exit from the war. Soviet troops crossed Hungary's border in the following month and the country became a direct theatre of military conflict. When the Arrow Cross was brought to power, with Szálasi combining the roles of head of government and head of state, proclaiming himself *Nemzetvezető* (leader of the nation), his support rested on the most militant sections of the army, state bureaucracy, and those among the population who believed the very survival of 'Christian Hungary' was threatened by the 'Bolshevik menace'. His control over the country quickly ebbed; by Christmas 1944 Budapest was surrounded and Soviet troops were advancing across western Hungary.

Szálasi, however, was determined that Hungary should fight until the end, and, despite the weakness of his regime, it was actively terroristic. In order to guarantee its power in Budapest and other cities that remained under its control, it armed party activists, giving them powers equivalent to the police. This was done in order to bypass regular police forces and a public administration that the Arrow Cross regarded as too compromised by the previous system to provide effective support to the German and Hungarian armies in reversing the war situation. In urban centres these militants became the face of the regime and gained a reputation for arbitrary violence, torture, and murder, directed especially against any Jews who remained, political opponents, and even those they suspected of avoiding the call-up into the army as the Soviets approached. Budapest's Jews, who had avoided deportation earlier in the year, were the primary focus of the wave of terror launched by the Arrow Cross regime. In order to meet German demands for forced labour to construct defences on the German border and prevent Soviet troops from crossing into the Reich, some tens of thousands of Budapest Jews—most estimates suggest 76,000 of them—of working age were rounded up and force-marched the 220 kilometres from the capital to the western border. Following the encirclement of Budapest, Arrow Cross party activists determined to kill all Jews who remained in the city, by whatever means were open. Despite the attempts of diplomats from those neutral states who continued to operate in Budapest to save Jewish lives, an estimated

---

[16] GyMSMGy.L., IVf.451.B.35d., A m.kir.rendőrség mosonmagyaróvári kapitánysága.

15,000 Jews were murdered in the Hungarian capital between October 1944 and February 1945. While Hungary's remaining Jews were the primary targets of the Arrow Cross's attentions, the country's Roma were also targeted, albeit sporadically, by the regime's policies of extermination.

Terrorism and racist murder were tied to Szálasi's policies of the total mobilization of the population in the interests of the war effort and the enforced evacuation of plant, and of those among the population who could not be mobilized, to Germany in the face of the Soviet advance. As the regime was restricted during early 1945 to a narrow portion of western Transdanubia, the population became ever more difficult to mobilize. The attempts of many among the population to avoid conscription, believing that further participation in the war was senseless, were met with arbitrary violence and even murder by militant local Arrow Cross activists determined to 'fight to the end'. Few among the civilian population were enthusiastic about evacuation to Germany, even though war had brought near starvation conditions in many communities; in Mosonmagyaróvár locals expressed their opposition to evacuation, maintaining that 'here we are starving and freezing, and if we have to starve and freeze, at least we are at home'.[17] Much of the population was terrified by the prospect of eventual Soviet occupation; popular anti-communism interacted with news of atrocities committed against civilians by Soviet troops further east, which served to intensify this climate of fear. This situation was exacerbated by the presence of substantial numbers of refugees from parts of Hungary that had already fallen to the Red Army; some western cities reported that their populations had swollen to three times that of their peacetime level, placing severe strain on food supplies.

With Hungary's 'liberation' complete in April 1945, the new Soviet-backed regime, a popular front coalition of anti-fascist parties in which the Communist Party was first among equals, defined itself by its anti-fascism. 'Fascism' was blamed for the war and the consequent devastation that had overtaken the country. The 'new' state set out on a course of anti-fascist retribution; those it identified as war criminals, who had fled west, were arraigned by specially constituted People's Courts. Many who had played leading roles on the radical right, including Szálasi and Imrédy, were brought to trial and executed. Many others, including registered members of the Arrow Cross, were interned; others were prevented from returning to their pre-war jobs; while institutions, like the gendarmerie, that were seen to have supported the occupation and anti-Jewish measures were simply disbanded. Left-wing anti-fascism was shaped to define the 'new' state against the practice of the entire inter-war regime, which was blamed for the Second World War and the material destruction that resulted. The whole of the Hungarian people were said to be the victims of this system, subsuming the Holocaust within a generalized narrative of

---

[17] GyMSM.Gy.L., IVf.B.451a., 2d., M.kir.rendőrség politikai rendészeti osztálya szombathelyi kirendeltsége. 7/1945 pol.rend.biz., 5.

national victimhood. This set the pattern for the whole of the period until 1989. Yet, at the same time, the post-war state and especially the Hungarian Communist Party sought to appease those whom it regarded as 'little Arrow Crossists', who had sympathized with Hungarism because of its promise of social reform. With the relaxation of regulations concerning internment in 1946, many 'little Arrow Crossists' were freed from the camps. During the late 1940s large numbers of those who supported Hungarism's radical programme of reform joined or supported the Communist Party; indeed, one Communist journalist admitted that Communist-voting poor peasants in Fejér county had transferred their allegiances because in the 1930s 'the far right represented a revolutionary promise'. Often the Communists' class-based rhetoric directed against 'speculators' and 'reactionaries', in the climate of post-war penury, fused with anti-Semitism. As far as the same peasants were concerned 'the Jews are reactionaries, who squeeze the poor'.[18]

In the hyper-inflation of the immediate post-war years, heightened social tension fed popular anti-Semitism that occasionally erupted into open violence, as it did with two pogroms in Miskolc and Kunmadaras in 1946. This wave of popular anti-Semitism subsided, as socialist dictatorship was built. While fragmented opposition to the dictatorship during its early, Stalinist phase in the early 1950s betrayed traces of the dominant political attitudes of the Horthy era, the expression of right-wing opinion was firmly suppressed throughout the early part of the decade. During the 1956 Revolution there were a small number of serious, albeit isolated, incidences of anti-Semitic violence. For the rest of the socialist era, opinions incompatible with the official 'anti-fascist' stance of the regime were driven underground. After Hungary's 'change of system' in 1989, radical right-wing movements began to re-emerge. Though Hungarist movements have only won a negligible following, a significant radical right has emerged displaying notable continuities with that of the inter-war years. The first free elections were won in 1990 by a coalition of centre-right parties, led by the Hungarian Democratic Forum (Magyar Demokrata Fórum), who formed a government led by József Antall. His politics were based on a synthesis of post-war Western European centre-right ideals and some springing from the liberal-conservative wing of the governing elite of inter-war years. All three of the parties who supported his government were, however, loose coalitions and some of their component parts supported more radical right positions. The coalition fractured under the pressure of political disputes over the degree to which the new Hungarian state would be based on radical anti-communism and issues of the restitution of property. The latter issue led to the takeover of one of the junior partners in the coalition, the Independent Smallholders' Party, by the right-wing populist demagogue József Torgyán. Antall's government was forced to deal with economic crisis that led to high inflation, a difficult fiscal position, a deep recession, and tremendous social polarization. The consequence of economic

[18]   A. Sándor, Övék a föld (Budapest: Szikra, 1948), 55–8.

difficulties, combined with considerable government unpopularity, led to a split within the Hungarian Democratic Forum. Right-wing radicals were led by István Csurka, a senior member of the party, who advocated an explicitly anti-Semitic course reminiscent of the right-wing radicalism of the inter-war years. Thrown out of the Democratic Forum, Csurka founded the Hungarian Justice and Life Party (Magyar Igazság és Élet Pártja) in 1993—to date Hungary's most successful party to sit openly on the radical right since the 'change of system'. While it has only entered parliament once—in 1998 with 5.47 per cent of the vote—its social base differed substantially from that of the inter-war far right, attracting disproportionate support from elderly, middle-class, urban voters, especially those living in the wealthy Buda districts of the Hungarian capital. Ideologically, the party harked back more to the political positions of the radical right of the inter-war governing elite than to Hungarists; indeed its name contains echoes of the Hungarian Life Party (Magyar Élet Pártja), the ruling party between 1939 and 1944. Its self-identification as 'a Christian and Hungarian party', its desire to overthrow the Treaty of Trianon, and its anti-Semitism made it a focal point for the far right throughout the 1990s.

While Csurka and his party have had to compete with other groups for leadership on the radical right—during the 1990s most notably with Torgyán's Smallholders and, since 2000, with a range of far right groups composed of younger activists more prepared to engage in direct action, sometimes violent direct action, than in formal electoral politics—one notable feature of the post-socialist radical right has been its symbiotic relationship with the mainstream right, a reproduction under post-socialist conditions of similar links during the inter-war years. This process began with the return to power of the ruling party of the state socialist years, re-constituted as the Hungarian Socialist Party (Magyar Szocialista Párt), in coalition with the liberal wing of the former opposition, in 1994. This act began a process of polarization between right and left, since many right-wingers refused to accept that a party they regarded as 'Communist' had any legitimate role in the political system. The result was a realignment on the mainstream right, under the leadership of the FIDESZ party, originally a youth group that adopted increasingly conservative positions. Through its period in office under Prime Minister Viktor Orbán between 1998 and 2002, it sought the unification of the whole right under its banner. Following its narrow defeat in the 2002 elections at the hands of the Socialists, FIDESZ moved to integrate the radical right into its electoral coalition and became itself rhetorically more radical, casting itself as the sole legitimate representative of the nation, thus denying legitimacy to its political opponents. This process culminated following its second consecutive electoral defeat in 2006, when following revelations that Prime Minister Ferenc Gyurcsány lied to voters about the state of the economy in order to win the elections, violent protest erupted. Radical right-wing activists stormed and briefly occupied the headquarters of state television in September 2006 before being evicted by police; the following month—on the fiftieth anniversary of the

1956 Revolution—serious violence again erupted in the capital, initiated by radical right protestors, who demanded the overthrow of the government and a change of system. While FIDESZ as the official opposition did not openly back the radical right-wing protesters, they did not distance themselves from them either, blaming the October violence, to which a rally they had called contributed, on excessive police brutality and arguing that the government, which they described as 'legal, but not legitimate', should resign. In a climate of intense political polarization between right and left and a situation where the mainstream right has been unprepared to distance itself from the more radical of the demonstrators, the radical right has grown in confidence. Its past may be complicated, but, at the time of writing, it does seem likely to have a future.

Bibliography

Gerlach, C., and Aly, G., *Das letzte Kapitel: Der Mord an den ungarischen Juden, 1944–1945* (Frankfurt am Main: Fischer Taschenbuch Verlag, 2004).

Hanebrink, P. A., *In Defense of Christian Hungary: Religion, Nationalism and Antisemitism, 1890–1944* (Ithaca, NY: Cornell University Press, 2006).

Katzburg, N., *Hungary and the Jews: Policy and Legislation, 1920–1943* (Ramat-Gan: Bar-Ilan University Press, 1981).

Lackó, M., *Arrow-Cross Men, National Socialists, 1935–1944* (Budapest: Akadémiai Kiadó, 1969).

Macartney, C. A., *October Fifteenth: A History of Modern Hungary, 1929–1945* (2nd edn, parts I and II, Edinburgh: Edinburgh University Press, 1961).

Pelle, J., *Sowing the Seeds of Hatred: Anti-Jewish Laws and Hungarian Public Opinion, 1938–1944* (Boulder, CO: East European Monographs, 2004).

Szöllösi-Janze, M., *Die Pfeilkreuzlerbewegung in Ungarn: Historischer Kontext, Entwicklung und Herrschaft* (Munich: R. Oldenbourg Verlag, 1989).

....

CHAPTER 21

ROMANIA

....

RADU IOANID

THE modern Romanian state was born in the nineteenth century, as a result of the struggle for the independence and unity of its intellectual and political elites in a fragile and shifting equilibrium between the Great Powers. Its political functioning remained troubled.

Before the First World War the Romanian Assembly of Deputies was elected by four electoral colleges, based on income of the delegate. The electoral tax was higher in Romania than in other European countries. Even after the revision of the constitution, from 1884 about five million Romanian peasants could send only thirty-eight delegates, one-fifth of the number of parliamentary members. Between the two world wars, governmental majorities never cooperated with the opposition even though their programmes were not very different. The mechanism of assuming power in Romania did not follow the classic scheme of elections that declare as winner a party which, after the electoral process is over, starts to rule. Instead the sovereign dismissed the prime minister—the leader of the party previously in power—and named a new prime minister, chosen from the heads of the opposition parties. Several months later, the new party in power organized elections, thereby inevitably gaining an overwhelming majority, while the newly defined opposition went crashing to a spectacular defeat.

Electoral fraud and electoral premiums—the winner obtained an extra number of seats in order to ensure its majority—characterized the inter-war Romanian electoral process. The comparison of the electoral results obtained at the polls by the largest political parties during the period is telling. For example, in 1920 the

The views presented in this article are those of the author and do not necessarily reflect those of the United States Holocaust Memorial Museum.

National Liberal Party, then in the opposition, won 6.8 per cent of the votes; in 1922 when it came to power, it garnered 60.3 per cent; while in 1926, back in the opposition again, its tally was 7.3 per cent. A year later it returned to power and now won 61.7 per cent of the vote. In 1928 its share of the votes dropped to 6.5 per cent, only to rise to 47.5 per cent in 1931 when it, in what is now a predicted rhythm, was again in charge of the government. In 1932, again part of the opposition, its support fell to 13.6 per cent of the vote; while in 1933 in power once more, it won 51 per cent.

In this see-saw political world, nationalism was the main slogan of the political class. In the Romanian parliament between the two world wars almost all the parties wanted to be perceived as being 'national' and duly named themselves the National Liberal Party, the National Peasant Party, the Nation's Party, the National Christian Party, or the Nationalist Party of the People. For an embattled nation, 'leaders' often seemed essential. Romanian fascists were not the only politicians who came out in favour of a dictatorship designed to suppress democratic liberties and the parliament before the command of a 'providential' political leader whose appearance was encouraged by such mainstream politicians as Alexandru Vaida-Voevod, Constantin Argetoianu, or George Bratianu. The best example in this case is perhaps the one of King Carol II, who sought to oppose Romanian fascism by manipulating one branch of it against the other and ending up by establishing his own brand of a totalitarian right-wing movement with unmistakable fascist features.

Romanian fascism was—and proclaimed itself to be—the spiritual heir of the nineteenth- and early twentieth-century native strains of conservatism and xenophobia. The most powerful component of this xenophobia was anti-Semitism, which from the nineteenth century expressed itself in economic, social religious, and political models. Basically most of the founding fathers of the Romanian modern state who took on any major role in politics, economics, social sciences, philosophy, or literature were anti-Semites. This characteristic applies to such politicians as Ion Bratianu and Vasile Kogalniceanu, to poets like Mihail Eminescu and Vasile Alecsandri, to philosophers and economists Vasile Conta, Dionisie Pop Martian, and Stefan Zeletin, to such linguists as Bogdan Petriceicu Hasdeu, and to many others. Of course there were exceptions to this dominant trend: Alexandru Ioan Cuza, the first prince of the freshly united Walachia and Moldova, and Nicolae Balcescu, a prominent leader of the 1948 failed revolution and a gifted historian, were not anti-Semites.

Yet, the anti-Semitic intellectual and political elites fought a hard and successful battle against article 44 of the Congress of Berlin (1878) which tried to impose on the newly established nation state the naturalization of the Jews who composed 4.3 per cent of the Romanian population, who lived from crafts, trade, and liberal professions and who were perceived as therefore offering a menacing competition to the emerging Romanian middle class. Most of the Romanian Jews gained equal rights, at least officially speaking, after the First World War and then only because of the renewed pressure of the Western Powers. Article 44 of the Congress of Berlin remained an anathema for Romanian nationalists and fascists until the end of the Second World War.

Although the best known and the most powerful, the Iron Guard (also known as the Legion of the Archangel Michael) was not the only Romanian fascist movement. The League of the National Christian Defence (LANC), which later became the National Christian Party (PNC), as well as other smaller organizations fit into this category, too. Similarly, although it governed from January 1941 without the support of the Iron Guard, the regime of General (later Marshal) Ion Antonescu shared the ideology of the main Romanian fascist movements, the Iron Guard and LANC.

The political programmes of the Romanian fascist parties were in general very sketchy. A. C. Cuza, the founder of LANC whose ideas are too often reduced to his rabid anti-Semitic statements, urged between 1929 and 1931 the need for his movement once in power to govern 'solely by decree laws', proclaiming that 'the dictatorship of LANC has to be imposed in the face of the proven bankruptcy of the parties'.[1] LANC's programme advocated 'harmonizing capitalist interests and those of the workers' through 'the patriotic and religious education of the worker'. At the same time, A. C. Cuza and LANC promised to support the 'preservation of the monarchy', the 'solution of the Jewish problem through a *numerus clausus*', the return of the cities to the Romanians, and the nationalization of all foreign businesses with the exception of an otherwise undefined 'constructive foreign capital'.[2]

In 1935 the LANC and the National Agrarian Party of the Transylvanian poet politician Octavian Goga amalgamated, forming the PNC, whose programme called for modifications in the structure of the legislative bodies (lowering the number of deputies and nominating senators in accordance with the principles of corporatism), the introduction of anti-Semitism as state policy, the arming of the country, the simultaneous satisfaction of all social claims through the establishment of harmony between classes, the pre-eminence of the Orthodox Church in the life of the state, and restrictions on the freedom of the press.[3]

Compared with the Iron Guard, LANC and PNC were more inclined to accommodate at least for a while with the Romanian parliamentary system. Equally, both LANC and its successor the PNC were more willing than the legionaries to accept the prominent role of King Carol II in the Romanian parliamentary system. As Paul Shapiro has underlined:

---

[1] *Apararea Nationala*, Arad No. 39, 6 October 1929, and Nos. 30–5, 9 August 1930, in G. T. Pop, *Caracterul antinational si antipopular al activitatii Partidului National Crestin* (Cluj Napoca: Dacia, 1978), 71–2.

[2] *Programul Ligii Apararii National Crestine de AC Cuza* (Cluj: Tipografia National SA, 1934).

[3] Pop, *Caracterul antinational si antipopular al activitatii Partidului National Crestin*, 124–8.

The swastika, the distinctive emblem of LANC, became the official PNC parading and propaganda symbol, though the party's founders felt constrained to emphasize again and again that the use of the symbol did not indicate any association with Hitler since Cuza had begun using it as a sign of his anti-Semitism before 1910.... Despite their disclaimer of association with Hitler, the head of PNC Octavian Goga and AC Cuza were quick to adopt fascist trappings and to associate the PNC with international fascist causes. Cuza commanded blue-shirted elite paramilitary units as well as an elite party militia called the *lancieri*. Between 1935 and 1937 these were responsible for Jew-baiting and brutality that rivalled that of the Iron Guard. Imitating Hitler and Mussolini and in a competitive way the Iron Guard, Goga and Cuza organized massive displays of disciplined manpower. For example they assembled 200,000 uniformed men in Bucharest on November 8, 1936 on the occasion of the PNC congress.[4]

After its foundation by Cuza in 1923, LANC remained for only four years the main fascist political party in Romania. In 1927 the leader of the LANC's youth organization, Corneliu Zelea Codreanu, split from his mentor to establish the League of the Archangel Michael.

Like other Romanian and foreign fascist movements, the legionary movement (which over the years, successively called itself the Legion of the Archangel Michael (from 1927), the Iron Guard (1930), All for the Country (1937), and, from 1940, the Iron Guard again) pretended to speak for the whole nation: 'we were five, we are a million, we will be the whole country'.[5] Such populism meant that it could avoid framing a detailed and coherent programme and opt instead for broadly phrased promises addressed to all categories of Romanian society. Occasionally Codreanu made such specific programmatic statements as 'I see the future form of the Romanian state taking its course in corporatism,'[6] or 'within 48 hours after the victory of the legionary movement, Romania will be allied with Rome and Berlin'.[7]

However, more often the leader of the Iron Guard and the ideologues of his movement focused rather on a 'spiritual revolution', proclaiming the need to create a new man. In this regard, C. Z. Codreanu stated: 'My programme refers above all to the virtue of man. It is on the basis of this new moral foundation that we can proceed to the redemption of our race and to the establishment of new relations with the other races that populate the Romanian territory.'[8] An Iron Guard publicist, Dan Botta, defined the new man as ignorant and illiterate: 'the new man will stand forward against knowledge and schools, against all that culture [privileges].... Ignorance which anchors us to the most admirable land in the world, [is] a mystical guarantee of wisdom, of energy, of victory... In the present

[4] P. A. Shapiro, 'Prelude to Dictatorship in Romania: The National Christian Party in Power December 1937–February 1938', *Canadian-American Slavic Studies*, 8 (1974), 50–1.
[5] *Buna Vestire*, 23 December 1937.
[6] C. Z. Codreanu, interview, *Buna Vestire*, 26 January 1938.
[7] C. Z. Codreanu, interview, *Buna Vestire*, 30 November 1937.
[8] Codreanu, interview, *Buna Vestire*, 26 January 1938.

day conditions let a country of illiteracy be an ideal for us.'[9] A pre-eminent Iron Guard ideologist, Mircea Eliade, later famous as a philosopher of religion, enthused about the same ideal: 'When the centre of gravity of the new man becomes salvation and spiritual accomplishment, then the man becomes free.... Furthermore, virility and sincerity, the great legionary virtues, will soon be changing the image of the country.'[10]

Both LANC and the Iron Guard had connections in Berlin. Initially it was LANC and the PNC who the Nazis favoured as their special friends in Romania. As Paul Shapiro has noted: 'the SS had some ties with the Iron Guard but these were not significant enough in the mid-1930s to worry the Romanian government. In contrast the PNC's ties with German officials provoked repeated Romanian diplomatic protests against German intervention in Romania's domestic affairs.'[11]

In spite of the fogginess of the programmes of the Romanian fascist parties, their ideological features can be delineated accurately enough. 'The main characteristic features of Romanian fascism are: nationalism, anti-Semitism and racism, negation of the democratic system, the cult of the supreme leader and of its elite, mysticism, the social diversion and finally anticommunism. These features define the Romanian fascist movement and its political parties and determine both its originality as well its resemblance to other fascist movements.'[12] In their work, the theoreticians of LANC and of the Iron Guard movement made respectful reference to Maurice Barrès, Charles Maurras, Oswald Spengler, H. S. Chamberlain, Friedrich Nietzsche, but above all to Mussolini, Hitler, Goebbels, and Alfred Rosenberg. However, as Michael Mann has remarked, the ideology of 'the Romanian variant of Fascism was essentially home-grown, though it borrowed a little from both Nazism and Italian Fascism'.[13]

The adoption by the Romanian fascists of doctrinal and ideological views from outside their country was carried out within certain limits. Fascists from all over Europe had in common the cult of the supreme leader, a penchant for violence, a special commitment to propaganda, and the proclamation of a wish to build a 'new world'. The affinities between various brands of fascism were limited by the difficulties of coexistence between the various chauvinist brands of nationalism advocated by these movements. In the texts of Romanian fascists the influence of such doctrinaire racists such as Arthur De Gobineau and Houston Stewart Chamberlain can be traced along with the more obvious names listed above. In the early 1920s a series of ephemeral groups of local fascists were directly influenced by Italian Fascism. This was the case of the National Italo-Romanian Fascist Movement (Miscarea Nationala Fascista Italo-Romana) and of the Romanian National Fascio

---

[9] D. Botta, 'Tara analfabeta', *Buna Vestire*, 28 February 1938.

[10] M. Eliade, *Sinzana*, 1/16 (1938).   [11] Shapiro, 'Prelude to Dictatorship in Romania', 53–4.

[12] R. Ioanid, 'The Sacralised Politics of the Iron Guard', in R. Griffin (ed.), *Totalitarian Movements and Political Religions*, Special Issue: *Fascism as a Political Religion*, 5 (2004), 419.

[13] M. Mann, *Fascists* (Cambridge: Cambridge University Press, 2004), 265.

(Fascia Nationala Romana). LANC and its leader, by contrast, always vehemently denied their subjection to any foreign fascist influence. However, during 1932 and 1933, close ties were forged with the NSDAP. George Cuza, the son of A. C. Cuza, visited Adolf Hitler, who donated to LANC a large amount of propaganda material. Coincidentally or not, in 1932 LANC proclaimed the Romanian people as being Aryan. Perhaps as a result, until the late 1930s, the Nazis considered LANC and its successor, the PNC, as being the closest political party in Romania to the Nazi ideology.

Iron Guard ideologists used on occasion to quote Mussolini, Hitler, Goebbels, and Alfred Rosenberg, but an extreme nationalism and xenophobia rejecting everything foreign in general dominated Iron Guard writings. Between 1935 and 1937, nonetheless, the sympathies of the Romanian extreme right covered a galaxy embracing Josef Pilsudski, Hitler, Mussolini, Franco, Primo de Rivera, Salazar, Jacques Doriot, La Roque, Léon Degrelle, Oswald Mosley, in other words everyone in the political world who could be identified with dictatorship and fascism and whose naming might promise significance and achievement. Once in power the Iron Guards moved to a closer identification with Nazi ideology. Emil Cioran, the Iron Guard ideologist, who later became a well-known French philosopher and regretted his youthful political affiliations, wrote in 1941 that the legionaries, 'even at the risk of being accused of [submitting to foreign] influence, must learn from Germany the conscious cult of force, the unlimited obsession with power, [an] organized megalomania',[14] and Leon Topa proclaimed in the Iron Guard daily *Cuvantul* in 1940 that '*Mein Kampf* must remain an eternal value for every nation'.[15]

The nationalism of the Romanian fascists was grounded in a series of bombastic, racially tainted assertions. In A. C. Cuza's view, the nation was composed of 'the totality of individuals of the same blood who occupy the same territory and constitute the same collective being',[16] specifying further that 'any given territory must serve the development of a single nationality'.[17] Along the same line, C. Z. Codreanu argued that the nation possessed from the very beginning a 'patrimony both physical and biological in nature, namely flesh and blood',[18] and was constituted by the Romanians who were alive, those to be born, the souls of the dead and the tombs of the ancestors. A fanatical follower of Codreanu and one of the main Iron Guard ideologists, Mircea Eliade, hoped even more grandiloquently for a 'nationalist Romania, frenzied and chauvinistic, armed and vigorous, pitiless and vengeful'.[19]

---

[14] E. Cioran, *Schimbarea la fata a Romaniei* (Bucharest: Vremea, 1941), 273.
[15] L. Topa, 'Puterea cuvantului', *Cuvintul*, 22 November 1940.
[16] A. C. Cuza, 'Nationalist', *Buna Vestire*, 27 March 1937.
[17] A. C. Cuza, *Nationalitate in arta* (Bucharest: Ed. Minerva, 1908), 72.
[18] C. Z. Codreanu, *Pentru legionari* (Sibiu: Ed. Totul pentru Tara, 1936), i. 426.
[19] M. Eliade, 'Elogiul Transilvaniei', *Vremea*, 29 November 1936.

In the perspective of Nicolae Rosu, a legionary theoretician, culture ought to be based on nationalism and race. Rosu, who theorized about the 'biology of culture', defined legionary nationalism in the following way: 'First of all, an essential point must be made: nationalism does not aim to discover, to build up or to propagate ideas. Nationalism is a fluid that takes its source from the very substance of natural things and is realized in concrete facts.'[20] For his part, Iron Guard leader Alexandru Cantacuzino proposed a similar characterization of legionary nationalism but he placed the accent on the necessity of separating legionary spirituality and material needs: 'We are forging a superior species of humanity in accordance with Christian concepts, and [we shall create] a new philosophy of life, conceived as a permanent effort, an irrational and pertinent impulse, to free ourselves from material needs in order to serve God and the legionary nation.'[21] While evincing some hesitation about the atheism of Hitler and Mussolini, Cantacuzino wanted to fuse legionary ideology with orthodox theology: 'Christianity is specific to us because, once its seeds have been sown in the legionary soil, it bears specific fruits.'[22]

What, then, were the expectations of Iron Guard ideologists about a future Romania? Along the same lines as Mircea Eliade, Emil Cioran proposed a Romania with 'the population of China and the destiny of France',[23] 'a Romania in delirium'.[24] 'We don't want a logical, ordered, dutiful and well-behaved Romania, but a Romania that is agitated, contradictory, furious and menacing.'[25] A similar notion was applauded by Alexandru Cantacuzino, when he affirmed that 'our nationalism will accept nothing but the superman and the super-nation elected by the grace of God'.[26]

Iron Guard nationalism went hand in hand with xenophobia. Obsessed by the so-called 'denationalization of the cities' of the country, Eliade urged in 1935 that 'Bucharest, bloodied and intoxicated, must realize the destinies of our race.'[27] Becoming more and more chauvinistic, the next year Eliade described the Hungarians as 'the most imbecile people that ever existed in history, after the Bulgarians'.[28] In 1938 he regretted that 'the Bulgarian element in Dobrogea [had not been] cruelly destroyed', while deploring that, in 'Maramures, Bukovina and Bessarabia, Yiddish is spoken', bewailing the alleged fact that the 'Jews have invaded the villages of Maramures, Bukovina, and Bessarabia', and affirming that 'I do not get angry when I hear the Jews cry: "anti-Semitism", "fascism", "Hitlerism". . . . It would be absurd to expect the Jews to resign themselves to being a minority with certain rights and many obligations, after having tasted the honey of power and having won the positions of command to such an extent.'[29]

---

[20] N. Rosu, *Dialectica nationalismului* (Bucharest: Cultura Naţională, 1935), 341–2.
[21] A. Cantacuzino, *Romanismul nostru* (Bucharest, 1936), 8.   [22] Ibid. 5.
[23] Cioran, *Schimbarea la fata a Romaniei*, 115.
[24] G. Calinescu, *Istoria literaturii romane* (Bucharest, 1941), 368.
[25] Cioran, *Schimbarea la fata a Romaniei*, 281.   [26] Cantacuzino, *Romanismul nostru*, 10.
[27] M. Eliade, 'Bucuresti centru viril', *Vremea*, 12 May 1937.   [28] Eliade, 'Elogiu Transilvaniei'.
[29] M. Eliade, 'Pilotii orbi', *Vremea*, 19 September 1937.

Similarly, in Cuza's eyes, the Jews represented a foreign body, a source of the country's economic difficulties, an 'alteration', an 'inferior race because of their crossbreeding'. Another founding father of the LANC, Nicolae Costache Paulescu, was even more direct than Cuza, stating: 'our most terrible enemy is the kike who acts like a mole in the darkness of the hidden society of Freemasons.'[30] When it comes to the anti-Semitism of the Iron Guard, as Michael Mann has noted,

there was already much racial antisemitism among the country's intelligentsia, who often saw the Jew and the Romanian nation as diametrically opposed. The distinction between the Romanian 'productive classes' and the 'dirty business world', dominated by 'usurious', 'banking', 'vagabond' Jewish capital, was common, as was the solution—a Romania 'disburdened' or 'disinfected' of Jews. The legion borrowed all this, but gave antisemitism a place in a broader national struggle against Soviet communism and western exploitation.[31]

Mann adds that 'Codreanu himself demanded "desperate defence" against Jewish "invasion" and "infiltration". "A dirty Jewish nest" dominated the cities, spreading "an infection of Judaic culture and caricature". This defence involved spreading "death and mercy" to the "Jewish wasp nests". The language was often violent involving demands for cleansing, especially of deportation: "Jews to Palestine".'[32]

Racism was another profound element of Romanian fascist ideology. A. C. Cuza exalted a 'vigorous Romanian race' which he never defined. Rosu argued that 'only works that draw upon tradition, with roots that run deep into the race and the past can aspire to permanence. Tradition in culture always remains a matter of race.'[33] An Iron Guard author, Ion Foti, argued that the Romanian race is characterized by 'clarity and precision of expression, seriousness, devotion to God and to the nation, nostalgia for life to the point of enjoying the pleasure of death, the pride of an imperial people whose race has been kept pure, the safeguard of the light of Christ, the pious preservation of tradition.'[34] Iron Guards such as sociologist Traian Herseni advocated the 'purification of the Romanian race', quoting as their inspiration Adolf Hitler and his eugenic practices and arguing for 'the sterilization of certain categories of human beings [which] is to be envisaged, not in a stupid manner as a violation of human dignity, but as a tribute to beauty, to morality and in general to perfection.'[35] Another Romanian fascist who advocated eugenics was Petru Tiparescu who wrote fearfully about the impact of 'racial maladies' and their countering through a 'rapid and intense eugenic activity'.[36]

---

[30] N. C. Paulescu, *Coplot jidano-francmasonic impotriva neamului romanesc* (Cartea Medicala, 1924), 1.

[31] Mann, *Fascists*, 277.   [32] Ibid. 271.

[33] N. Rosu, 'Biologia culturii', *Cuvintul*, 10 January 1941.

[34] I. Foti, *Conceptia eroica asupra rasei* (Bucharest: Biblioteca Generatia Noua, 1936), 155.

[35] T. Herseni, 'Mitul singelui', *Cuvintul*, 23 November 1940; T. Herseni, 'Rasa si destin national', *Cuvintul*, 16 January 1941.

[36] P. Tiparescu, *Rasa si degenerare* (Bucharest: Tipografia Bucovina, IR Toroutiu, 1941), 8.

Romanian fascism relied heavily on the cult of its autochthonous elites and of the supreme leader, distancing itself simultaneously from capitalist elites and the masses. The legionary theory of the elites was based on the notions of order, discipline, and hierarchy, on absolute submission to the leader, as well as on a boundless contempt for the masses. In his fascist phase, Cioran for one pronounced that 'the parliamentary system is a British present which confused the world for many decades',[37] concluding as a result that 'democracy must be destroyed'.[38]

Despite its proclaimed Christian orthodox character, Iron Guard mysticism did not simply mean the total assimilation of orthodox theology by a fascist political movement, but rather entailed an attempt to subordinate and transform that theology into a political instrument. In their flaunted reverence for 'blood and soil', the legionaries went around villages and towns, organizing special religious services, kissing the soil, filling little bags with earth then hung around their necks, and asking villagers and town inhabitants to swear allegiance to their movement. In theory, as Eliade wrote, the goal of the Iron Guard was to give birth to a Christian revolution through the redemption of the whole nation. Eliade enthused about Codreanu's intention to mediate between Romania and God: 'A political leader of youth said that the goal of his movement was to "reconcile Romania with God". Here', he added fervently, 'is a messianic formula that does not appeal to the class struggle, nor to political interests, nor the bestial instinct in man.'[39] Yet, it must be acknowledged that legionary mysticism did not set up itself as a Christian Orthodox mysticism in the pure state. Rather traditional religion was adapted to materialize in the attempts to canonize certain saints chosen from the 'legionary martyrs', or in the intense cult of death used especially for the preparation of those whose job it was to achieve the physical liquidation of the legion's adversaries. Despite its formal Orthodoxy, legionary mysticism did not simply mean the total assimilation of Christian theology by a fascist political movement, but rather was an attempt at subordinating and transforming that theology into a political instrument. In this ideological exaltation, all the legion's adversaries became at the same time adversaries of God, the church, and Christ. Although Codreanu complained on occasion that the majority of the Orthodox priests were hostile to the legion, his organization was able to make major inroads into the ranks of the Orthodox hierarchy. During the 1937 elections, out of 103 candidates of the All for the Country party (another name for the Iron Guard), 33 were priests.

Codreanu stated that the legionary elite was required to show the following qualities: 'purity of soul, capacity for work and creation, courage, ability to lead a hard life and engage in permanent combat against the chains enslaving the nation, poverty meaning voluntary renunciation of the accumulation of the riches, belief

---

[37] E. Cioran, *Schimbarea la fata a Romaniei* (Bucharest: Humanitas, 1990), 33.   [38] Ibid. 168.
[39] M. Eliade, 'Un popor fara misiune', *Vremea*, 1 December 1936; see also M. Eliade, 'Cele doua Romania', *Vremea*, 4 October 1936.

in God [and] love.[40] When it came to the cult of their elite the Romanian fascists successively (and somewhat promiscuously) adulated A. C. Cuza, Octavian Goga, King Carol II, Codreanu, and military dictator Ion Antonescu. According to Eliade, those who composed the elites more generally represented a 'new aristocracy' which had as its main mission the resurrection of the Romanian Middle Ages,[41] while Iron Guard journalist Constantin Noica, later a renowned Romanian philosopher, provided a quantitative evaluation of the Iron Guard elites, asserting that their number should not exceed 10,000 individuals, adding that women could not achieve such elevation.[42] The authority of the fascist chief was not to be questioned or questionable. The leader of a Romanian fascist party was not to be elected and his authority was supposed to be total.

The cult of the dead, common to several fascist movements, occupied a privileged position in the legionary mystique. The main goal of this mystique was to raise to the rank of 'martyrs' the dead leaders of the movement. Horatiu Comaniciu, one of the leaders of the Iron Guard, wrote typically about Codreanu, also known in the legionary writings as the 'Captain' (after his murder—shot 'while trying to escape'— at the behest of King Carol in November 1938): 'And above our heads, from the Dniester to the Tisza our Captain passes in flight. Tears of joy gleam in his steely eyes, while his holy lips murmur: the Fatherland! the Fatherland! the Fatherland!'[43] The legionaries' cult of the dead occupied a privileged place in Constantin Noica's writings, too. According to him (with somewhat troubling gender implications), Codreanu was a reincarnation of Joan of Arc,[44] and a colleague, Nae Ionescu, was 'the man who had paid so that God and Life might descend upon our nation'.[45] Even the insignificant intriguer Horia Sima, successor of Codreanu as supreme leader of the Iron Guard with the cynical blessing of the king, took on special virtues in Noica's eyes: 'at this moment when the divine breath is upon us, Horia Sima does not demand taxes on income, he gets the souls moving.'[46] For Noica, the future would be happily garrisoned by the rule of the Iron Guard phantoms: 'the day of the terrifying domination of the ghosts approaches.'[47] Eliade similarly believed that the 'ghosts of Ion Mota and Vasile Marin [Iron Guard leaders killed in the Spanish Civil War while fighting alongside Franco's troops] are going to reign for a time', until Romanians 'construct a country like the saintly sun of the sky',[48] the latter formula being a common slogan of the legion. The theme of 'Holy Iron Guard

---

[40] Codreanu, *Pentru legionari*, 420.

[41] M. Eliade, 'Noua aristocratie legionara', *Vremea*, 23 January 1938.

[42] C. Noica, '10001', *Buna Vestire*, 20 September 1940; idem, 'Electra sau femeia legionara', *Buna Vestire*, 9 October 1940.

[43] H. Comaniciu, 'Se reface sufletul tarii', *Buna Vestire*, 18 September 1940.

[44] C. Noica, 'Procesul Ioanei d'Arc', *Buna Vestire*, 26 September 1940.

[45] C. Noica in *Buna Vestire*, 21 September 1940.

[46] C. Noica, 'Sinteti sub har', *Buna Vestire*, 4 October 1940.

[47] C. Noica, 'Cumplita lor calatorie', *Buna Vestire*, 12 September 1940.

[48] M. Eliade, 'Strigoi', *Cuvintul*, 21 January 1938.

spirit' similarly recurs in the writings of Traian Herseni, who argued that 'the spirit of the Captain leads the nation to victory'.[49] In this vein there was a significant attempt made to enrich the orthodox calendar by adding new legionary 'saints' or 'prophets'. As if to contradict Cioran, who affirmed that 'Romania is a country without prophets',[50] Pertre P. Panaitescu wrote: 'The greatest prophet of the nation, however, has been the Captain.'[51]

With regard to the arguments, for raising Mota and Marin to the rank of martyrs and saints of the nation, Eliade came straight out and labelled the death of the two legionaries the birth of a Christian revolution: 'Those who had dedicated their youth to the legion, that is, to prisons and persecution, did not hesitate to sacrifice their life in order to hasten the redemption of the whole nation. This death has born fruit. It has set the seal on the meaning of life and of creation for our generation. The climate of the spirit against the climate of the temporal, in which the preceding generations have believed. And they have indicated to us what remained to be built from this ephemeral human life. A Christian revolution.'[52]

As was true of fascism in other countries, the Romanian version proclaimed the ideas of social solidarity and of harmony between social groups as the only solution that could achieve the prosperity of the nation. If the Romanian fascists condemned capitalism in their writings, they almost always did so by identifying it with the Jews. The Romanian fascist parties and especially the Iron Guard basically asked the Romanian mainstream political elite to concede power to fascist political parties whose members, through a redistribution of the national wealth and through economic corporatism and political dictatorship, could alone guarantee their economic survival endangered by the communist and Jewish menace. The Iron Guard was willing to strike this deal at a certain price: the old elites were supposed to renounce their fondness for parliamentarism, liberal ideals, and, above all, their tolerance of ethnic minorities and especially of the Jews. Indeed, when briefly in power in 1940, the Iron Guards limited their 'anti-capitalist' measures to the massive confiscation of Jewish properties, big or small, individual or communal.

A typical fascist programme of government resembled that written by Nichifor Crainic, a writer and journalist, who had drafted the PNC programme called the 'doctrine of the ethnocratic state', advocating national 'Christian legislation', based on 'private property for every Romanian worker, proportional [political] representation for all professions, suppression of the middlemen between the producer and the consumer and the destruction of the Jewish parasitism'.[53] The Iron Guard doctrine, which very often called the middle class 'petty bourgeoisie', favoured 'the

---

[49] T. Herseni, 'Duhul Capitanului', *Cuvintul*, September 1940.

[50] Cioran, *Schimbarea la fata a Romaniei*, 8.

[51] P. P. Panaitescu, 'Profetii neamului', *Cuvintul*, 1 December 1940.

[52] M. Eliade in *Buna Vestire*, 14 January 1938.

[53] N. Crainic, 'Programul statului etnocratic', *Sfarma Piatra*, 27 May 1937.

creation of the middle class of tradesmen and manufacturers, thanks to the legal support of the state and the encouragement of active Romanian energies'.[54] P. P. Panaitescu, a historian and an Iron Guard ideologist, explained: 'the legionary doctrine foresees the constitution of a petty bourgeoisie on the basis of workers made wealthy, and of artisans and tradesmen with workshops and stores, rather than protecting a large industry based on capitalism.'[55] Nicolae Rosu was more specific about the practical way this process was to be accomplished. It would be enough 'to show that, by cancelling the licences of tobacco and liquor stores belonging to the Jews, many jobs would be made available for occupation by Romanians who come precisely from the petty bourgeoisie'.[56]

Romanian fascism and especially the Iron Guard seemed to have a special relationship with the peasantry. The forms taken by the Romanian Iron Guard propaganda in the rural areas have led sometimes to the conclusion that in Romania a form of 'peasant fascism', even of revolutionary peasant fascism, did exist. In reality the legionary movement remained a political organization with general objectives, among which the agrarian was rarely spelled out precisely. In spite of its solid support in the rural world, the Iron Guard remained an urban political movement. As Lucretiu Patrascanu (one the very few intellectual leaders of the Romanian Communist Party to be executed in the Stalinist purges from the early 1950s) argued, the Iron Guard represented mostly the urban middle class, a part of the intelligentsia, and the *lumpenproletariat*.[57] It was true that the legionaries argued that the Romanian village represented ethnicity in the pure state as opposed to the cosmopolitan city. Equally legionary ideologists recommended that the social and governmental organization find its inspiration in the Romanian village taken as a model, praising the traditional mode of rural life, while taking a stand against the penetration of capitalism into villages. In the eyes of the legionaries the peasant supposedly refused all the progress of civilization. In the Iron Guard vision the peasant refused to become a learned human being in order to keep his 'purity' and traditions. Yet, somewhere beneath the rhetorical exaltation, such a frozen figure, deprived of education, superstitious, and often illiterate, suited legionary chiefs, for he was easier to manipulate. When legionary propaganda dedicated to the peasantry made use of folkloric element and superficial promises, as well as the cult of agricultural toil in which the whole nation was supposed to take part, and promised the peasantry the family vote and above all land, in keeping with the slogan 'to every man his half-hectare', political manipulation was evidently present.

[54] *Legiunea Arhanghelului Mihail-Garda de Fier-Pogramul si caracterul general* (Cluj: Cartea Romaneasca, 1931), 5.

[55] P. P. Panaitescu, 'Orasele noastre', *Cuvintul*, 14 December 1940.

[56] N. Rosu, 'Soarta marii burghezii', *Cuvintul*, 12 January 1941.

[57] L. Patrascanu, *Problemele de baza ale Romaniei* (Bucharest: Socec, 1944), 250–1.

Whatever the political orientation of the moment, fascist ideology denied legitimacy to all ideologies except its own. In spite of the fact that during the inter-war period the Romanian Communist Party (RCP) never reached a membership higher than 1,000 people, anti-communism was one of the main planks of the Romanian fascist movement. When it came to communists, Iron Guards often heaped them together with Jews and Freemasons, while attributing the most satanic characteristics to this combination. By invoking a supposed incompatibility between communism and the Romanian nation, fascist ideologists were trying to stop the spread of Marxist ideology in a country with major social problems. Furthermore Romanian fascist anti-communism was fuelled by the strong patriotic resentment generated by the annexation of Bessarabia by the Soviet state in 1918. Yet, serious analysis of Marxism was in the main eschewed. The anti-communism of Romanian fascism in general did not rise above the level of invective, falsification, and incitement to violence. Romanian fascists often presented communism as being predominantly Jewish but they also applied the opprobrious term 'communist' to all their political adversaries or to any cultural figures whom they disliked.

At the same time Romanian fascists represented themselves as extreme conservatives, anti-liberals, and anti-modernists. Their ideologists violently attacked not just foreign and domestic communists but also such authors as Dostoevsky, Gide, Freud, Proust, and Bergson and such artists as Brancusi, Kokoschka, and Picasso. A deliberately chosen amalgam of politicians, writers, poets, painters, and scholars was used by the Romanian fascist ideologues to inculcate into their audience fear in the face of modernity, novelty, and a supposed state of disorder, all allegedly the benighted products of democracy.

Its line won many converts. The impact of Romanian fascism on the local intelligentsia was very strong, as the internationally distinguished playwright Eugene Ionescu noted: 'They were very few who opposed the fascist dementia, few who took the side of democracy. So few that we were asking ourselves if the truth is on our side, if a lonely individual could be right, in spite of the majority.'[58]

On 20 December 1937 the PNC won 281,167 votes (9.15 per cent) and the Iron Guard 478,368 votes (15.58 per cent). Together the most important Romanian fascist parties attained 25 per cent of the national tally, being represented in parliament by 105 deputies (66 belonging to the Iron Guards and 39 to the PNC). While the PNC remained a regional political party, obtaining its votes mostly from the north-east of the country, the Iron Guard was more evenly represented, alluring voters throughout the country. Certainly, as Shapiro has maintained, 'PNC and Guardist support was "geographically complementary" and not "overlapping".'[59]

---

[58] Z. Ornea, *Anii Treizeci: extrema dreapta romaneasca* (Bucharest: Editura Fundatiei Culturale Romane, 1996), 189.
[59] Shapiro, 'Prelude to Dictatorship in Romania', 65.

Faced with this political situation, at the very end of December 1937 King Carol II appointed Octavian Goga, the leader of the PNC, to be Prime Minister. Goga was to head a short-lived, virulently anti-Semitic government—over 200,000 Romanian Jews were immediately deprived of their citizenship—which lasted only until February 1938, and, in that time, was greeted with apprehension by the western liberal democracies and with jubilation by Berlin and Rome. Shapiro has explained: 'The PNC government...burned the country's bridges to the Western powers and turned her toward Germany. Attempts between 1938 and 1940 to reconstruct the bridges came to naught. King Carol's dictatorial regime proved no more capable of solving Romania's problems than its Goga-Cuzist predecessor. And while the PNC regime had been a prelude to dictatorship, Carol's was a precursor of disaster.'[60]

Now followed a spiral of trouble, with the king's dictatorship, and then the adoption in July and August 1940 by the Gigurtu government of sharply anti-Semitic legislation. Finally, with the coming to power in September 1940 of General Antonescu allied with the legionary movement, Romania definitively tipped into the fascist camp. On 6 September Romania was formally proclaimed a 'national-legionary state' and the legionary movement became the only political movement recognized under the new regime. General Antonescu was made the new head of state and so he, not Sima, the notional Guardist chief, commanded the legionary regime. The alliance between General Antonescu and the Iron Guards was short-lived, however, lasting only until January 1941 when Antonescu, supported by Hitler and the OKW, crushed an Iron Guard rebellion supported by the SS and SD; not before the Iron Guard had murdered 121 Jews in a pogrom in Bucharest where over a thousand Jewish homes, stores, and synagogues were looted and destroyed. Although a fascist in his convictions and behaviour, Antonescu found that his military disposition forbade him to approve the administrative and economic disorder brought on by the legionaries, whose greed and incompetence sowed confusion and difficulties everywhere in the country's economy. There were no major differences in terms of ideology between the Antonescu–Iron Guard regime that collapsed in January 1941, and the subsequent government by General (later Marshal) Antonescu lasting until August 1944, except the fact that in the post-Iron Guard period Antonescu ruled without a fascist political party backing him. During his time of command, Antonescu presided over the killing of at least 280,000 Romanian and Ukrainian Jews. All Jews who survived under his administration were heavily discriminated against, and tens of thousands of them were sent to forced labour. Pogroms, deportations, transit camps, and ghettos marked the fate of the Jews ruled by the Antonescu regime, which also deported to Transnistria 25,000 Roma, of whom fewer than half survived the war.

[60] Ibid. 88.

While the historiography of the Romanian fascism and its intellectual followers has developed in a spectacular way during the last twenty years the contemporary impact of Romanian fascism should not be limited to the academic world. After the fall of the Romanian Communist regime, a campaign aiming to rehabilitate both Antonescu and the Iron Guards was waged by Romanian extremist political parties and organizations. Extreme right and left political parties, many of whose members were unreformed and nostalgic elements from the former Securitate, the feared secret police of the communist administration, newly adopted xenophobic and anti-Semitic programmes.

Sadly, however, the nationalist myths of a Romania always victim of 'foreigners' (be they from inside or outside the country) are not merely the monopoly of extremists. The attempt to rehabilitate the Iron Guards and the Antonescu regime made highly successful inroads in the Romanian mainstream post-Communist political class and intelligentsia, too. As Mihai Dinu Gheorghiu has underlined, today's Romania is facing 'a double extremist discourse, one of an ordinary fascism, and one of an elitism which pretends to be non-political and sometimes liberal or pro-Western'.[61] One of the causes of this phenomenon lies in what Vladimir Tismaneanu has described as 'the peculiarity of the Romanian situation', where 'intellectuals of both liberal and radical populist persuasion tend to cherish the same anti-Western, deeply nationalist, and communitarian ideas of the proto-existentialists Emil Cioran, Mircea Eliade, Constantin Noica, and Nae Ionescu. The need for self-esteem among the country's intelligentsia seems to be intimately linked to the unthinking, fervid glorification of these apostles of political irresponsibility.'[62] In the twenty-first century, Romania has still not fully confronted its fascist legacy.

BIBLIOGRAPHY

CARP, M., *Cartea Neagra* (Bucharest: Diogene, 1996).
GENTILE, E., *Qu'est-ce que le fascisme: histoire et interpretation* (Paris: Gallimard, 2004).
IOANID, R., *The Sword of the Archangel: Fascist Ideology in Romania* (Boulder, CO: East European Monographs, 1990).
—— *The Holocaust in Romania: The Destruction of Jews and Gypsies under the Antonescu Regime, 1940–1944* (Chicago: Ivan R. Dee, 2000).

[61] M. D. Gheorghiu, *Intelectualii in campul puterii: morfologii si traiectorii sociale* (Iasi: Polirom, 2007), 330.

[62] V. Tismaneanu, 'Fascism, Antisemitism, and Mythmaking in East Central Europe: The Case of Romania', in R. L. Braham (ed.), *The Destruction of Romanian and Ukrainian Jews during the Antonescu Era*, Social Sciences Monographs (Boulder, CO: Distributed by Columbia University Press, 1997), 329.

LAIGNEL-LAVASTINE, A., *Cioran, Elieade, Ionescu: l'oubli du fascisme* (Paris: PUF, 2002).

MANN, M., *Fascists* (Cambridge: Cambridge University Press, 2004).

ORNEA, Z., *Anii Treizeci: extrema dreapta romaneasca* (Bucharest: Editura Fundatiei Culturale Romane, 1996).

PAYNE, S. G., *A History of Fascism* (Madison: University of Wisconsin Press, 1995).

SHAPIRO, P. A., 'Prelude to Dictatorship in Romania: The National Christian Party in Power December 1937–February 1938', *Canadian-American Slavic Studies*, 8 (1974).

VOLOVICI, L., *Ideologia nationalista si 'problema evreiasca' in Romania anilor '30* (Bucharest: Humanitas, 1995).

CHAPTER 22

YUGOSLAVIA AND ITS SUCCESSOR STATES

MARKO ATTILA HOARE

YUGOSLAVIA and its successor states have produced a myriad of regimes and movements that were 'fascist' in one sense or another. Under the inter-war Yugoslav
kingdom (1918–41), regimes and movements appeared that were inspired by or
resembled the Nazi and Italian Fascist regimes and movements. They reached their
apogee in the Second World War under the umbrella of the Axis powers which
occupied Yugoslavia in 1941. Following the Second World War defeat of the pro-Axis
and collaborationist forces by the Communist-led Partisan resistance, Yugoslavia
was under Communist rule until 1990. The fall of communism permitted new
regimes and movements to emerge that either objectively resembled fascist regimes
and movements in their ideological and organizational character, or that self-
consciously modelled themselves on the fascist or Axis-collaborationist movements
of the Second World War. The best way to understand this myriad is to examine
them chronologically, against the backdrop of the historical periods in which they
appeared. Scholars disagree over the definition of 'fascism'; the present author
defines it briefly as 'revolutionary anti-liberal chauvinism': that is, as the ideology
and practice of mobilizing chauvinism on a popular basis in order to assault liberal
values, bring down a liberal order, cement in power an authoritarian regime, and/or
territorially expand.

'Yugoslavia' was born as the 'Kingdom of Serbs, Croats, and Slovenes' on 1 December 1918, through the union of most of the South Slav territories of the former Austria-Hungary (most of present-day Slovenia, Croatia, Bosnia-Herzegovina, and Vojvodina and part of contemporary Montenegro) with the kingdom of Serbia. This last had conquered present-day Macedonia and Kosovo in the Balkan Wars of 1912–13 and united with the kingdom of Montenegro immediately prior to Yugoslavia's birth. Yugoslavia therefore comprised diverse lands and peoples with different histories and political traditions. The idea of 'Yugoslavia'—the land of the South Slavs—was a product of modern, nineteenth-century national ideology, not of any genuine sense of Yugoslav identity on the part of most ordinary 'Yugoslavs'. Rather, with the formation of the new kingdom, the 'Yugoslav' national idea was imposed on the older, organic national identities of its constituent peoples. In practice, however, Yugoslav politics would be dominated by the narrower national ideologies of its constituent peoples. On 28 June 1921, the Constituent Assembly, dominated by the Serbian parties, promulgated a constitution based on the principle of a unitarist Yugoslav state, disregarding the wishes of the Croats and Slovenes for a federation and consigning the new state to perpetual conflict.

The centralist Yugoslav order rested upon coercion, and proponents of integral Yugoslav nationalism pioneered fascist-style behaviour. Serb politics were dominated by two parties in particular: the populist Serb nationalist 'People's Radical Party' and the integral Yugoslav nationalist 'Democratic Party'. The powerful Democratic Party politician and Yugoslav Interior Minister Svetozar Pribičević, a committed opponent of Croatian autonomy, established in 1921 a paramilitary organization that soon adopted the name 'Organization of Yugoslav Nationalists' (ORJUNA), for the purpose of terrorizing Croats and other opponents at the local level. ORJUNA's leaders came to be openly sympathetic to Italian Fascism and, subsequently, German Nazism.[1] ORJUNA's activities provoked the emergence of paramilitary rivals linked to other parties, while Serbian army veterans formed their own paramilitary, or 'Chetnik', organizations. The activities of these groups helped push Yugoslavia toward civil war by the late 1920s. Stjepan Radić, leader of the principal Croat party, the 'Croat Peasant Party' (HSS), was shot by a Serb terrorist on 20 June 1928 and died six weeks later, after which Yugoslav King Aleksandar took advantage of the political turmoil to establish a dictatorship on 6 January 1929.

Aleksandar's Karađorđević dynasty had been brought to power in Serbia in 1903 by a coup carried out by a group of Serbian army officers, which in 1911 spawned the organization 'Unification or Death' or 'Black Hand', which bore some similarities to a proto-fascist organization. It favoured the unification of all 'Serb lands' in a single state, to be achieved through a combination of revolutionary agitation in

---

[1] N. Šehić, *Četništvo u Bosni i Hercegovini (1918–1941)* (Sarajevo: ANUBiH, 1971), 122–5.

the Austro-Hungarian and Ottoman lands with military conquest by Serbia, whose officials and public were to be coerced to pursue these aims. It comprised a disciplined core under a 'Central Executive Committee' and a wider membership that may have reached into the thousands, and it acted as a state within a state in Serbia. Nevertheless, the Black Hand was not ideologically committed to overthrowing parliamentarism, but focused its revolutionary activities outside Serbia's borders.[2] Through its involvement in the assassination of Archduke Franz Ferdinand, it was instrumental in plunging Serbia and Europe into war in 1914. Aleksandar, then Crown Prince, challenged the power of the Black Hand by cultivating a dissident minority within its ranks that became known as the 'White Hand', under General Petar Živković. The Black Hand's power was then broken in the Salonika Trial of 1917, leading to the execution of its strongman Dragutin Dimitrijević ('Apis'). Yet it was Aleksandar, with Živković's assistance, who twelve years later would attempt the most radical experiment in authoritarian national engineering that the Yugoslav kingdom experienced.

The dictatorship of King Aleksandar, with Živković as Prime Minister, dissolved the Yugoslav parliament and suppressed all political parties and trade unions. The kingdom of Serbs, Croats, and Slovenes was renamed 'Kingdom of Yugoslavia' on 3 October 1929, and the internal map of the country was redrawn with the aim of destroying the traditional regional identities of the Yugoslav lands in favour of a homogeneous Yugoslav nation and state. Aleksandar's dictatorship has been termed by some Yugoslav historians 'monarcho-fascist', though it did not see itself in such terms. In 1931, Aleksandar moderated the form of his dictatorship by restoring a semblance of constitutional rule and political pluralism. He promulgated a new constitution and established a ruling party, initially called the 'Yugoslav Radical Peasant Democracy'—an amalgam of the names of the three most important old parties—and subsequently the 'Yugoslav National Party'. A 'Yugoslav National Workers' Union' was established, supposedly to protect the interests of the working class. Other political parties were permitted to function, but only on the basis of electoral lists covering the entire country—parties based on a single nationality or region were disallowed.

The unwillingness of the politicians of the older, still-banned parties to participate in what was effectively a controlled parliamentarism led Aleksandar to found puppet opposition parties to maintain the semblance of pluralism. Part of the ruling party thus separated to form the 'Yugoslav People's Party' which, under Svetislav Hođer, would develop consciously along Nazi-inspired lines, with its members dressing in a blue-shirted uniform. In foreign affairs, Aleksandar attempted to build good relations with Italy and Germany. Though Mussolini proved unreceptive, Hitler was friendly. On 1 May 1934 Germany and Yugoslavia signed a commercial

---

[2] D. MacKenzie, *The 'Black Hand' on Trial: Salonika, 1917* (Boulder, CO: East European Monographs, 1995), 38–42.

treaty—the first of a series of agreements that would during the 1930s turn Yugoslavia into an economic satellite of the Reich.[3]

By smashing the old Yugoslav party system and engaging in an apparently revolutionary experiment in nation building, Aleksandar inspired the enthusiasm of certain members of the radical right while raising them to prominence in place of the ousted traditional politicians. Some of these individuals and groups then moved into opposition to a regime which did not seem sufficiently radical, marking the birth in Yugoslavia of fascist politics proper. The early 1930s therefore witnessed the appearance of Velibor Jonić's 'Yugoslav Action', which advocated a 'total state' and directed its agitation against the Croatian-centred federalist opposition, but also against the ruling Yugoslav National Party; the 'Association of Fighters of Yugoslavia', organized by Yugoslav-nationalist Slovenes, which saw itself as a 'link in a chain of Associations of warriors for a whole state'; and 'Zbor' in Herzegovina under Ratko Parežanin and Radmilo Grćić. The name 'Zbor' ('Assembly') was chosen on the grounds of the importance of people's assemblies in Serb tradition, but also because the letters of the word 'Zbor' formed an acronym whose initials stood for 'Cooperative Fighting Organization of Work'.

The most important member of these groups was Dimitrije Ljotić. Aleksandar relied upon loyalists of his Karađorđević dynasty to staff his dictatorship, and Ljotić was one such, appointed Minister of Justice in 1931. Ljotić then went into loyal opposition and, with Aleksandar's blessing, arranged the formal fusion of the small fascist groups under his leadership on 6 January 1935—symbolically, the anniversary of the establishment of the dictatorship. The new party, retaining the name 'Zbor', called itself the 'Yugoslav National Movement—Assembly'. It combined an integral Yugoslav nationalism of a Serb flavour inspired by Orthodox Christian mysticism and anti-materialism, advocating an organic state and society on a non-democratic, non-parliamentary basis. It was strongly anti-Semitic, anti-Western, and anti-capitalist in its rhetoric, and favoured a planned economy. Zbor's symbol was a shield displaying a head of corn emblem, behind which was a sword.[4] Zbor competed in subsequent elections, but failed to attract more than a tiny proportion of the electorate.

The Alexandrine dictatorship also inspired fascists negatively. The principal Croat fascist movement grew out of the 'Croatian Party of Right' (HSP), also known as the 'Pure Party of Right', founded by Josip Frank (1844–1911), which under Austria-Hungary had been *kaisertreu*, directing its nationalism not against Croatia's foreign overlords but against the Serb minority. Croatia was until 1918 under the Hungarian Crown, and the Hungarians, employing a strategy of divide and rule, privileged the Serb minority in Croatia. The resulting anti-Serb sentiment provided the principal *raison d'être* for eventual Croat fascism. The HSP was

---

[3] W. S. Grenzebach, Jr, *Germany's Informal Empire in East Central Europe* (Stuttgart: Franz Steiner Wiesbaden GMBH, 1988), 44, 68, 171–2.

[4] M. Stefanović, *Zbor Dimitrije Ljotiča* (Belgrade: Narodna knjiga, 1984), 11–34.

originally a conservative, Catholic party opposing the break-up of Austria-Hungary and Croatia's inclusion within Yugoslavia. The establishment of the Alexandrine dictatorship drove many of its members into exile, above all in Hungary and Italy, states that aspired to portions of Yugoslav territory and therefore aided such anti-Yugoslav separatists.

The most important exile was Ante Pavelić, who began evolving along more radical lines from the late 1920s, under the impact of the brutality of Yugoslav politics. Basing himself on the youth wing of the HSP, Pavelić founded the 'Croatian Home Guard' in October 1928. Following the establishment of the dictatorship, he installed his group of Croat exiles in Italy as the 'Ustasha [Insurgent]—Croatian Revolutionary Organization', which mimicked the fascism of its Italian hosts. The Ustashas favoured in principle a totally independent Croatia that would include all the allegedly historical and ethnic Croat lands—Croatia-Slavonia, Dalmatia, Bosnia-Herzegovina, and parts of contemporary Montenegro and Serbia. The Ustasha symbol was the letter 'U'.[5]

The Ustashas turned to terrorism in response to the Alexandrine dictatorship's brutality, and training camps were set up in Italy. Ustasha terrorism was, however, limited by meagre popular support—Croats overwhelmingly still backed the HSS. The Ustashas nevertheless succeeded in building a working alliance with another group of anti-Yugoslav terrorists—the Internal Macedonian Revolutionary Organization (VMRO), based in Yugoslav Macedonia. The VMRO was an inspiration for the Ustashas, and the latter used a VMRO gunman when they accomplished their most spectacular terrorist act: the assassination of King Aleksandar on 9 October 1934.

Aleksandar's death led to a loosening of the regime without, however, a return to full parliamentary democracy. Power passed to a regency headed by Prince Pavle Karađorđević, who appointed Milan Stojadinović as Prime Minister in June 1935. Stojadinović was a politician of the People's Radical Party and therefore, in contrast to Aleksandar, a more traditional Serb nationalist. Stojadinović responded to declining French influence and rising German fortunes by continuing Aleksandar's reorientation of Belgrade's foreign policy toward Berlin and Rome. On 25 March 1937 Italy and Yugoslavia signed a treaty of friendship and non-aggression, requiring Italy to suppress the Ustasha movement on its soil. In January 1938, Stojadinović visited Berlin and received Hitler's guarantee of Yugoslav territorial integrity in return for Yugoslav acquiescence in the *Anschluss* with Austria.[6] Stojadinović in January 1939 discussed with the Italians the possibility of partitioning Albania, and encouraged Italian expansionist ambitions toward French territory.[7]

At home, Stojadinović established a regime party of his own: the 'Yugoslav Radical Union', a fusion of elements of the People's Radical Party with the 'Yugoslav

---

[5] M. Jareb, *Ustaško-domobranski pokret* (Zagreb: Školska knjiga, 2006), 47–163.

[6] M. Stojadinovic, *Ni rat ni pakt* (Rijeka: Otokar Keršovani, 1970), 454–7.

[7] Milan; H. Gibson (ed.), *The Ciano Diaries 1939–1943* (Garden City, NY: Doubleday, 1946), 12–14.

Muslim Organization' and 'Slovene People's Party'—the principal Muslim and Slovene parties respectively. Stojadinović increasingly mimicked the fascist regimes: he organized mass rallies of green-shirted followers, who saluted him as '*Vođa*' (Leader). Stojadinović adopted the slogan 'One king, one nation, one state', an old Radical slogan that mirrored the Nazis' '*Ein Volk, ein Reich, ein Führer*'. His government established a regime 'Yugoslav Workers' Union', inspired by the official workers' associations of Fascist Italy and Nazi Germany. Stojadinović competed with Ljotić for the fascist constituency, and in late 1937 he appointed several senior former members of Zbor to official positions.[8]

Stojadinović was, however, forced to operate within a semi-free parliamentary system, and after his party fared badly in a general election in December 1938, he was ousted in February 1939 by Prince Pavle, who now took over the Yugoslav Radical Union through his cipher, the new Prime Minister Dragiša Cvetković. Under British pressure, Pavle moved to resolve the long-standing constitutional conflict with the Croats, through a '*Sporazum*' ('agreement') with the leadership of the HSS that resulted formally on 26 August 1939 in the establishment within Yugoslavia of an autonomous Croatia incorporating over a quarter of Bosnia-Herzegovina.

Zbor denounced the autonomy granted to the Croats; Ljotić in February 1940 called for a military coup directed against them, and for exclusive Serb control of the Yugoslav army (presaging the politics of Slobodan Milošević a half-century later). The Ustashas likewise denounced the Sporazum, as a betrayal of the cause of complete Croatian independence, and because it partitioned Bosnia-Herzegovina rather than giving the whole to Croatia. The Sporazum was opposed by all the Serbian parties. Other than Zbor and the Ustashas, its fiercest opponents came from the ranks of another extreme nationalist organization: the 'Serb Cultural Club' (SKK). This was established in 1937 by Slobodan Jovanović, a former mouthpiece of the Alexandrine dictatorship, and other eminent Serb intellectuals who lamented the loss of Serb unity and purpose within Yugoslavia. The SKK agitated under the slogan 'Strong Serbia—Strong Yugoslavia !', in favour of a centralized Yugoslavia under Serb domination. It spearheaded 'Serbs Assemble!', an anti-Sporazum Serb mass movement and a precursor to the wartime Chetniks. The SKK enjoyed warm relations with Zbor.

Hitler supported a united Yugoslavia as a desirable partner for the Reich. Elements within the Yugoslav ruling elite—especially Foreign Minister Aleksandar Cincar-Marković and Defence Minister Milan Nedić, an army general and former supporter of King Aleksandar and Stojadinović—were pro-German, but the pro-British Pavle attempted to steer a middle course between Axis and Allies. In autumn 1940 his government enacted anti-Semitic legislation, restricting Jewish rights in education and business, but also banned Zbor and sacked Nedić for his extreme pro-

---

[8] P. J. Cohen, *Serbia's Secret War* (College Station, TX: Texas A&M University Press, 1996), 16–17.

German views. Berlin nevertheless coerced Yugoslavia into joining the Tripartite Pact on 25 March 1941, against widespread popular opposition.

Serb-nationalist air force and army officers reacted by staging a putsch that ousted Pavle on 26–7 March. The putschists were reacting against the regency's marginalization of the traditional Serbian political classes and its concessions to the Croats; they immediately assured Berlin of their loyalty to the Pact. Hitler nevertheless treated the putsch as a personal affront and his Yugoslav policy turned around 180 degrees. On 6 April 1941, German forces attacked and, with token assistance from Italy and Hungary, rapidly defeated and dismembered Yugoslavia. This enabled the Ustashas, Zbor, and other extremist groups to seize control as Axis puppets. Parts of Yugoslavia were simply annexed by the Axis powers, but in the core Yugoslav lands of Serbia, Croatia, and Bosnia-Herzegovina, the Nazis established two genuinely fascist regimes.

Serbia, including the Banat (eastern Vojvodina) and part of Kosovo, fell under exclusive German occupation. The Banat formed an autonomous region under joint Serbian and *Volksdeutsche* (local ethnic German) control, with the participation of the Hungarian and Romanian minorities. But in Serbia proper, the Germans established a 'Commissars' Administration' on 30 April 1941, headed by Milan Aćimović, formerly Stojadinović's Minister of the Interior. The Germans banned all political parties except Zbor, but most of the pre-war parties, including the Radicals and the Democrats, were represented in the Commissars' Administration.

Germany's tight control over Serbia was loosened slightly following the Partisan uprising in July. Hitler was impressed by the zeal with which members of the Serbian elite mobilized behind the Germans to crush the uprising, and permitted Serbia greater autonomy. On 29 August, the Commissars' Administration was replaced by a 'Government of National Salvation' under Nedić. This was permitted its own relatively small armed forces, the Serbian State Guard, which peaked at approximately 37,000 men. The Nazis permitted a second Serbian collaborationist force to be formed under Kosta Pećanac, who had headed a Chetnik organization before the war.

Ljotić played a central role first in organizing the Commissars' Administration and then in helping the Germans to select his relative Nedić to be Prime Minister. Although Ljotić had himself been considered as a possible Serbian quisling leader, he was a religious zealot without great personal ambition, who recognized that he did not enjoy sufficiently high standing among the Serbian people, and that the eminent General Nedić would receive more widespread acceptance. Ljotić received Serbia's former medieval capital of Smederevo—his home town, where he enjoyed genuine popular support—as his personal fiefdom. Nevertheless, Zbor's members assumed prominent positions in Nedić's government, including Jonić, former general secretary of Yugoslav Action, who served as Minister of Education from October. Also prominently represented in Nedić's governments were Stojadinović's former supporters (Stojadinović himself spent the war under British internment).

Rivalry between the followers of Ljotić and Stojadinović was a feature of Serbian quisling government politics.

On 15 September, Zbor created an elite military formation of its own, subsequently named the 'Serbian Volunteer Corps', of 3,500, eventually expanded and diluted to perhaps 10,000. It engaged in combat against the Partisans and Chetniks and rounded up hostages for execution by the Germans in anti-guerrilla reprisals—most notoriously in October 1941 at the city of Kragujevac, when over 2,000 people were massacred. The Volunteers' symbol was an image of St George slaying a dragon representing communism. During the Nazi and quisling retreat from Serbia in autumn 1944, the Volunteers came under the command of, and formally joined, the SS.[9]

Nedić's Serbia subscribed to a Nazi-style ideology in which Serbs were viewed as members of the 'Aryan race'. Jews were removed from all walks of public life and segregated from the rest of the population; the Serbian police rounded them up and delivered them to the Nazis. Anti-communism was a central motivation; Ljotić lamented the failure of Serbian units to participate in Hitler's campaign against the Soviet Union. Thousands of suspected Communists were incarcerated in concentration camps, most notoriously the Banjica camp in Belgrade and—after its Jewish inmates had been exterminated by the Nazis—the Sajmište camp on the capital's outskirts. Thousands of these were killed.

Nedić and his ministers invoked a 'new Serbia' that supposedly arose from the defeat of April 1941 under the Reich's protection, and a 'peasant state', celebrating the peasantry as the essence of the Serb nation. This focus on Serbia's agrarian character dovetailed with Nazi plans to exploit East European lands as captive agricultural producers for the Reich. The Nedić regime set up a 'National Work Service' to rejuvenate Serbia and indoctrinate youth, and a 'Serbian Union of Work', equivalent to the Nazis' German Labour Front. Commissars were attached to schools and universities to ensure that education was conducted according to the regime's ideology.

Although Nedić portrayed his role as protector of the Serbian heartland following the catastrophe of defeat, he harboured ambitions to establish a 'Great Serbia' under the Nazi umbrella. This was supported by Ljotić, who abandoned his prior commitment to a centralized Yugoslavia—much as Milošević would a half-century later. Nedić attempted to negotiate with the Germans for the transfer of parts of Bosnia-Herzegovina and Montenegro to Serbia, and he armed and supplied Chetnik units in these areas. Some German officials were sympathetic to these Serbian requests. Nedić himself met Hitler on 18 September to request the annexation of Montenegro, the Sanjak, East Bosnia, Srem, and Kosovo-Metohija. Hitler opposed this, seeing a strong Serbia as a potential obstruction to German control of the

---

[9] J. Tomasevich, *War and Revolution in Yugoslavia, 1941–1945: Occupation and Collaboration* (Stanford, CA: Stanford University Press, 2001), 187–94; Stefanović, *Zbor Dimitrije Ljotića*, 301.

Balkans, but his opposition weakened as the Reich's military position crumbled during 1944. Nedić claimed after the war that had it not been for the German collapse, Hitler would have established a Great Serbia.[10]

Hitler was for strategic and economic reasons fundamentally less interested in Croatia than in Serbia. After resolving to destroy Yugoslavia, he offered Croatia to Hungary. When Hungary's Miklós Horthy rejected this, Hitler opted to establish a Croatian puppet state as an Italo-German buffer state or condominium. The 'Independent State of Croatia' (NDH) was proclaimed on 10 April 1941 by the Ustashas' Slavko Kvaternik, on SS prompting, in the name of Pavelić as *Poglavnik* (*Führer*). The Germans initially suspected Pavelić as an Italian puppet, but Pavelić rapidly transferred his loyalty from Mussolini to Hitler. Unlike quisling Serbia, quisling Croatia was formally recognized by the Axis powers as an 'independent state', and was permitted a greater degree of autonomy and much larger armed forces, peaking at around 250,000. The NDH was also granted much more generous borders, including the whole of Bosnia-Herzegovina.

The NDH was organized as a fascist state along lines inspired by Italy and Germany. All political parties but the Ustashas were banned. Under the Poglavnik, the top body of the ruling Ustasha party was a 'General Ustasha Headquarters', equivalent to the Fascist Grand Council in Italy. Beneath this were Ustasha agencies at the county, district, municipal, and village levels. Pavelić formally established an unelected puppet parliament, which met twelve times from February 1942, before ceasing to function at the end of the year. The NDH armed forces were divided into three wings: a regular army, or 'Home Guard'; the 'Ustasha Militia'; and the gendarmerie. The division between the Home Guard and Ustasha Militia corresponded roughly to that between the Wehrmacht and the SS, although in terms of morale and fighting ability, the Home Guard was more similar to the Italian than the German army. The 'Ustasha Surveillance Service' incorporated the secret police and concentration camp network.

The NDH was formally organized on a corporative model, with 'communities' set up for each branch of the economy to act as intermediaries between the state and the producers. All material goods in the state were declared the property of the Croatian people; the peasantry was portrayed as the 'foundation and source of all life' and the 'carrier of all political power in the Croatian state'; while ownership of agricultural land was to be limited to peasant households that worked the land themselves. In addition, the regime established State Business Centres to manage national assets, a policy that served as window dressing for a regime that was economically incompetent, corrupt, and unprincipled.[11]

The NDH's 'independence' was illusory. Pavelić had to acknowledge Italy's Duke of Spoleto as 'King of Croatia', though the latter never actually visited the country.

---

[10] M. Borković, *Milan Nedić* (Zagreb: Centar za informacije i publicitet, 1985), 268–80.

[11] F. Jelić-Butić, *Ustaše i Nezavisna Država Hrvatska 1941–1945* (Zagreb: Sveučilišna naklada Liber, 1978), 99–134.

On 18 May, the NDH was forced to accept the Italian annexation of a large part of Dalmatia, including the capital, Split, and most of the islands. In autumn 1941, the Italians reoccupied their zone of the NDH; they expelled Croatian military forces, took over civilian government, and co-opted Serb Chetnik bands as auxiliaries, partly to prevent the consolidation of the NDH and with the long-term aim of further territorial annexations. The Italians and particularly the Germans ruthlessly plundered the NDH's economic resources, including the mass exploitation of Croatian labour power in the Reich, in conditions approaching or reaching slavery. Like quisling Serbia, the NDH was forced to bear the cost of German and Italian occupation forces on its territory.

The NDH was absolutely subservient to the Axis in international affairs. Following the Japanese attack on Pearl Harbor, the Croatian government announced on 14 December that, in light of 'the blatant endeavours of the United States of America' to 'establish for itself a hegemonic position, on the basis of which it would in ever greater measure impose its plutocratic domination on all other nations', Croatia was declaring war on the United States and Britain.[12] As the war progressed, the Wehrmacht in Croatia acquired command over the NDH's armed forces in its zone of the country, followed by the right to alter Croatian legislation at will, prompting Eugen Dido Kvaternik, head of the Ustasha Surveillance Service, to admit later that there remained nothing 'independent' about the NDH except the 'N' in its name.[13]

The Ustashas claimed Croatia as the exclusive homeland of the Croat nation, which they pronounced not Slavic but descended from the Goths, therefore part of the 'Aryan race'. Ustasha propaganda stressed Croatia's alleged historic role as the 'wall of Christendom', now reinterpreted as a bastion against the Orthodox rather than the Islamic East. The Ustashas were, at one level, aggressively Catholic in a sectarian manner: many clergymen participated in the movement, and there were efforts forcibly to convert part of the NDH's Serb population to Catholicism. Nevertheless, the regime's relationship with the church was uneasy: some leading clergymen, such as Zagreb's Archbishop Alojzije Stepinac, who initially welcomed the regime came increasingly to denounce its atrocities and sheltered Jews and other victims. Unlike quisling Serbia, however, quisling Croatia had a highly heterogeneous population, only about half of which was Croat, while about a third was Serb. The Ustashas embarked on a genocidal policy aimed at creating a nationally homogeneous state. The Ustashas, in conjunction with the Nazis, exterminated most of the NDH's Jews and Gypsies, condemned as distinct and unassimilable races, though an Ustasha innovation was to designate certain Jews as 'honorary Aryans', thereby exempt from anti-Jewish measures.

The largest and most problematic 'alien' national minority, from the Ustashas' perspective, was the Serbs, who comprised a third of the NDH's population. The

---

[12] B. Krizman, *Pavelić između Hitlera i Mussolinija* (Zagreb: Globus, 1980), 243.
[13] E. D. Kvaternik, *Sjećanja i zapažanja 1925–1945* (Zagreb: Prilozi za hrvatsku povijest, 1995), 61–2.

Ustashas did not formally view the Serbs as a distinct racial group, but they rejected the existence of a Serb nationality on Croatian territory and attempted to eradicate it through a combination of extermination, expulsion, and forced assimilation. The Ustasha genocide, in conjunction with the Nazi Holocaust with which it overlapped, claimed the lives of at least 30,000 Jews, a similar number of Gypsies, and, perhaps, nearly 300,000 Serbs. At the notorious Ustasha death camp at Jasenovac, modelled on the Nazi camps, approximately 90,000 people of all nationalities were killed, including thousands of anti-Ustasha Croats. The combined German-Ustasha operation at Kozara in north-west Bosnia in June–July 1942 cost the lives of approximately 25,000 Serbs, mostly in concentration camps.[14]

In keeping with traditional integral Croat nationalism, the Ustashas attempted to claim the Bosnian Muslims as 'Croats of the Islamic faith'. A minority of Muslims, who in the 1930s had formed the 'Muslim Branch of the Croat Peasant Party', became enthusiastic Ustashas; others joined the regime for more opportunistic or pragmatic reasons, including Džafer Kulenović, leader of the Yugoslav Muslim Organization, whom Pavelić appointed Deputy Prime Minister. But generally, the Bosnian Muslim elite and population rejected the Ustashas, though more were ready to collaborate with the Germans. Autonomous Muslim collaborationist forces were formed, including the 'Volunteer Home Guard Regiment' of Muhamed-aga Hadžiefendić and the 'Green Forces' of Nešad Topčić.

On 1 November 1942, a group of leading Muslim politicians headed by Uzeir-aga Hadžihasanović, the *éminence grise* of the former Yugoslav Muslim Organization, and going by the name of the 'National Committee', presented a Memorandum to Hitler, or 'Our Fuhrer!', as it enthusiastically addressed him. It announced that the Bosnian Muslims were Gothic in origin, applauded the destruction of the Jews, and requested that an autonomous Bosnia be set up under Hitler's direct and personal authority, which would be granted independence following the Nazi victory.[15] Although Hitler rejected this proposal, he approved in February 1943 the establishment of an SS division made up of Bosnian Muslims, which was established as the '13th SS Volunteer Bosnian-Hercegovinian Division (Croatia)', more commonly known as the 'Handschar Division'.[16] Its formation was supported by some members of the Muslim elite, who hoped it could be used to establish an autonomous Bosnia-Herzegovina, separate from Croatia.

The 'Yugoslav Army in the Fatherland' under Draža Mihailović, commonly known as the 'Chetniks', was not properly a fascist movement, and did not ideologically identify with fascism or the Axis, but bore similarities through its extreme nationalism, authoritarianism, anti-Semitism, and its close collaboration with the

[14] M. A. Hoare, *Genocide and Resistance in Hitler's Bosnia: The Partisans and the Chetniks, 1941–1943* (London: Oxford University Press, 2006), 19–28.

[15] V. Dedijer and A. Miletić (eds), *Genocid nad Muslimanima, 1941–1945* (Sarajevo: Svjetlost, 1990), 250–64.

[16] G. Lepre, *Himmler's Bosnian Division* (Atglen: Schiffer Military History, 1997), 17–60.

occupiers and quislings. As developed by ideologue Stevan Moljević, formerly of the SKK, the Chetnik programme envisaged a greatly enlarged Serbia as the dominant element in a restored, tripartite Yugoslavia consisting also of Slovene and Croatian units. Serbia's population was to be made ethnically homogeneous, a programme the Chetniks attempted to implement through a genocide of Muslims, Croats, and other non-Serbs that claimed tens of thousands of lives, in particular in East Bosnia and the Sanjak. The Chetniks were viciously anti-Semitic, identifying communism with the Jews, and frequently murdered Jews or handed them over to the Nazis. In the NDH, from mid-1942, Chetnik units were legalized by the Italians as the 'Volunteer Anti-Communist Militia', while Chetnik commanders signed pacts with the NDH. Mihailović's officers frequently served as the auxiliaries also of the Nedić regime, which supplied them with weapons and munitions. Following the Italian capitulation, the Germans themselves began systematically to collaborate with the Chetniks against the Partisans.[17]

The territory of the NDH was the scene of the most bitter fighting and great-est bloodshed during the Second World War, but collaborationist formations also operated in the peripheral regions of occupied Yugoslavia. These included 'Slovene Action' and the 'Legion of Death' in Italian-held Slovenia; the Greens, Chetniks, and the 'Montenegrin Volunteer Corps' in Montenegro; the 'Second League of Prizren for the Defence of Kosovo' and '21st SS Volunteer Mountain Division "Skanderbeg"' among the Kosovo Albanians; the remnants of the VMRO in Bulgarian-held Macedonia; and the '7th SS Division "Prinz Eugen"', composed largely of *Volksdeutsche* from the Banat.

The Partisans under Josip Broz Tito emerged victorious by 1945 in their struggle with the Axis, quisling, and collaborationist forces, and established a new Yugoslavia as a federation of six republics: Slovenia, Croatia, Bosnia-Herzegovina, Serbia, Montenegro, and Macedonia, with Kosovo and Vojvodina as autonomous entities within Serbia. Remnants of the anti-communist bands continued to resist the new regime until well into the 1950s. Some anti-communists who succeeded in fleeing abroad established émigré organizations to continue the struggle, involving not just agitation and propaganda but, in some cases, terrorism. The most serious attack occurred in June 1972, when nineteen members of an émigré group called the 'Croatian Revolutionary Brotherhood' entered the Bugojno region of Bosnia; they were all killed or captured within six weeks, but at the cost of thirteen dead and fifteen wounded members of the Bosnian security forces.

The most serious opposition to the Titoist order came, however, not from the émigrés, but increasingly from dissident communists and other public figures in the country. As the regime decayed in the years following Tito's death in 1980, intellectuals among the various Yugoslav nationalities began to challenge its official interpretation of history, and there were moves toward more positive evaluations

---

[17] Hoare, *Genocide and Resistance in Hitler's Bosnia*, 156–62.

of some of the collaborationist and quisling groups of the Second World War. In Serbia, Croatia, and Bosnia-Herzegovina in the late 1980s and early 1990s, authoritarian former communists seeking new bases for their power and legitimacy came together with dissident nationalist opponents of the Titoist order to produce regimes that were arguably, to a greater or lesser degree, fascist or semi-fascist. Above all, the regime of Slobodan Milošević in Serbia was fascist in practice, if not in self-identification.[18]

Serbia's position under Titoism resembled Germany's under the Weimar Republic. First, at the end of the Second World War, Serbia was forced to accept a territorial settlement involving both the 'loss' of lands that it had effectively annexed before the war (Montenegro, Macedonia, nearly three-quarters of Bosnia-Herzegovina), and Vojvodina's and Kosovo's establishment as autonomous entities. Then, as Yugoslavia liberalized and decentralized from the late 1960s, Serbia lost both its de facto position of first among equals in the Federation, and almost all control over Vojvodina and Kosovo. These factors—above all the increasing transfer of power in Kosovo from Serbs to Albanians—created the basis for a *revanchist* Serbian nationalist backlash against the Titoist order. The intellectual father of this backlash was Dobrica Ćosić, a former hard-line communist ousted from the Serbian leadership in 1968. Ćosić wrote in 1982 that 'the Serbs are ruined, assimilated, persecuted and brought to the position of an oppressed nation'. He called for a 'spiritual and political revolution' to destroy the 'spiritual trash-heap' of the Titoist system, one that would involve 'Burning all the books, all the texts and newspapers written by the Communists and under their government'.[19] Ćosić would become President of Milošević's 'Federal Republic of Yugoslavia' in 1992.

Milošević began, like earlier fascists and proto-fascists such as Georges Sorel and Mussolini, as a radical socialist who decided that nationalism provided a better weapon than the class struggle and internationalism with which to overthrow the liberal (in this case, quasi-liberal) order. He centred all power in Serbia in his own hands and proceeded to tear up the Titoist settlement of the national question, much as Hitler had torn up the Versailles settlement. As President of the League of Communists of Serbia, he effectively seized power against his Communist rivals in September 1987. He consolidated it by using Serbian party, police, and media organs to carry out a mass nationalist mobilization of the Serbian population, above all over the Kosovo issue. Post-Titoist Yugoslavia was governed by a quasi-pluralist system, with power divided between different institutions and individuals, and it was this system that Milošević's 'anti-bureaucratic revolution' brought down. A

[18] Stanley Payne describes the Milošević regime as a 'violent, militarist, and expansionist nationalist regime that has acquired aspects of fascist style in its mass atrocities and "ethnic cleansing"' (S. G. Payne, *A History of Fascism, 1914–1945* (Madison: University of Wisconsin Press, 1995), 519). Robert J. Paxton describes it as the 'functional equivalent' of a fascist regime (R. J. Paxton, *The Anatomy of Fascism* (London: Allen Lane, 2004)).

[19] D. Ćosić, *Promene* (Novi Sad: Dnevnik, 1992), 65, 69–70.

series of mass nationalist rallies between October 1988 and February 1989 overthrew the governments of Vojvodina and Montenegro, replacing them with ones loyal to Milošević, and pressurized the Yugoslav Federal leadership first to pass legislation restoring Serbian control over Kosovo and Vojvodina, then to deploy the Yugoslav People's Army (JNA) against the Kosovo Albanians. These rallies were Milošević's 'March on Rome', establishing his power through crowds and intimidation. Milošević became President of Serbia on 28 May 1989.

This mass nationalist mobilization used to consolidate power flowed seamlessly into ill-conceived wars of conquest. Until spring 1990, the Milošević regime fought to establish a recentralized Yugoslav Federation under Serbian leadership. When this definitely failed, with the collapse of the Yugoslav Communist organization and the emergence of non-communist regimes in Slovenia and Croatia, Milošević and his allies in the top Serbian party and Yugoslav military bodies switched to a policy of dismembering Yugoslavia and redrawing the borders of the republics to create a Great Serbia, with boundaries similar to those proposed by Moljević half a century earlier—though this Great Serbia would officially still be called 'Yugoslavia'.

In July 1990, Milošević established the 'Socialist Party of Serbia' (SPS) as his new ruling instrument, abandoning the concept of an all-Yugoslav party. After promulgating a new Serbian constitution on 28 September 1990, declaring the Republic of Serbia's 'sovereignty' and 'independence', Milošević effectively seceded from Yugoslavia on 16 March 1991 when he announced that Serbia no longer recognized the authority of the Yugoslav presidency.[20] On that day, he gave a speech to Serbia's municipal leaders in which he proclaimed that 'if we do not know so well how to work and to earn, at least we know well how to fight'. Furthermore: 'We have to ensure that we have unity in Serbia if we want, as the Republic that is biggest, that is most numerous, to dictate the further course of events. These are questions of borders, therefore fundamental, state questions. And borders, as you know, are always dictated by the strong, never by the weak. Consequently, what is essential is that we have to be strong.'[21] This was immediately followed by the launch of terrorist actions by Serb extremists in Croatia, initiating a war of conquest for new Serbian borders that escalated in the summer of 1991 following Croatia's declaration of independence on 25 June, and that was subsequently extended to Bosnia-Herzegovina, continuing until late 1995.

Serbian forces—the Serbian-controlled JNA and Croatian Serb and Bosnian Serb militias—engaged in systematic massacres and forced expulsions of Croats, Muslims, and other non-Serbs in Croatia and Bosnia-Herzegovina. This involved concentration camps, most notoriously at Omarska, Keraterm, and Trnopolje in north-west Bosnia. In July 1995, Bosnian Serb forces conquered the East Bosnian town of Srebrenica and massacred 8,000 Muslim civilians, an act that constituted

[20] M. A. Hoare, 'Slobodan Milošević's Place in Serbian History', *European History Quarterly*, 36/3 (2006).

[21] *NIN*, Belgrade, 12 April 1991, 40–1.

genocide according to the International Court of Justice. By the war's end in late 1995, the territory of the self-proclaimed 'Serb Republic' in occupied Bosnia-Herzegovina, under the leadership of Radovan Karadžić and Ratko Mladić, had been almost wholly emptied of the roughly 50 per cent non-Serb part of its population. Yet Serbian military defeats combined with international reluctance to recognize forced border changes left Milošević in formal control only of his new 'Federal Republic of Yugoslavia', proclaimed on 27 April 1992 and comprising only Serbia and Montenegro.

Milošević's domestic system of government has been accurately described as a 'soft dictatorship'.[22] The SPS was established through the merger of the League of Communists of Serbia with the Socialist Alliance of Working People of Serbia, the Communists' 'mass' front organization that had formed the counterpart of the 'elite' League. This merger gave the SPS a more powerful institutional dominance over Serbian life than even the League of Communists had held. The first multi-party elections in Serbia took place in conditions in which the regime enjoyed absolute dominance in the media and state institutions, and which were consequently far from free. Although a multi-party parliamentary system continued formally to operate, this was a 'hollow shell' masking the ruling party's absolute dominance of the state, economy, and public life.[23] Members of the regime who fell out of favour were frequently assassinated; the murders invariably remained unsolved. The opposition parties themselves were tamed through their infiltration by the secret services, and where necessary by beatings and assassination attempts. The regime's manipulation of elections provoked repeated popular protests, continuing until October 2000, when Milošević's refusal to recognize electoral defeat resulted in his overthrow in a popular revolution.

At the height of his power, Milošević's control over his country's political life was probably greater than the pre-Salò Mussolini's had ever been; unlike Mussolini, his power was unconstrained by king, church, or army, and he could not be removed constitutionally but had to be overthrown. His grip, however, was gradually weakened by military defeat, economic collapse, and, eventually, active US support for the opposition. Ironically, one of the major reasons for Milošević's loss of legitimacy was his promotion of a second regime party, his wife Mira Marković's 'Yugoslav Left', parallel to the SPS. The Yugoslav Left accumulated great power despite its almost complete absence of electoral support, earning the hatred not only of much of the population, but also of senior SPS politicians. Ultimately, however, Milošević fell because, like Hitler and Mussolini, he could not stop the boulder of nationalist mobilization that he had set in motion from rolling; he could never rest on his laurels, but needed continuously to provoke crises and pick fights with ever-stronger opponents until he destroyed himself. This culminated in Serbia's war with

[22] L. J. Cohen, *Serpent in the Bosom: The Rise and Fall of Slobodan Milošević* (Boulder, CO: Westview Press, 2002), pp. xiv–xv.

[23] R. Thomas, *Serbia under Milošević* (London: C. Hurst and Co., 1999), 422–3.

NATO over Kosovo in spring 1999, involving the attempted expulsion of 800,000 Albanians and the killing of thousands more, but ending inevitably in military defeat, paving the way for Milošević's overthrow the following year.

For all the close similarities of the SPS regime with classical fascist regimes, it made no attempt to rehabilitate elements of the Serbian quisling or Nazi-collaborationist legacies. Yet the SPS did at various times form coalition governments with other parties that openly identified with the Chetnik movement: the 'Serbian Renewal Movement' of Vuk Drašković' and the 'Serbian Radical Party' of Vojislav Šešelj. Drašković was a pioneer of the Serbian nationalist renaissance of the 1980s; his novel *The Knife* (1982) stirred passions with its depiction of Muslim persecution of Serbs during the Second World War, and he formed a militia to fight in Bosnia. Yet Drašković's idolization of the Chetniks was essentially quixotic, and he periodically condemned Milošević's warmongering policies.

Šešelj, by contrast, was a genuine ultranationalist rabble-rouser; an ally of France's Jean-Marie Le Pen and Russia's Vladimir Zhirinovsky, he gained notoriety in 1991 with his televised call for the slaughtering of Croats 'with a rusty spoon, to make [their suffering] last longer and to be sure that if they don't die on the spot, they are susceptible to infection'.[24] The Serbian Radical Party's thugs terrorized the Croat minority in its fiefdom at Zemun on the outskirts of Belgrade. The party continues to this day to claim Bosnia-Herzegovina and large parts of Croatia for Serbia. Šešelj's 'Chetnik' militia, and another neo-fascist paramilitary force, the 'Serbian Volunteer Guard' or 'Tigers' of Željko Ražnatović ('Arkan'), fought under JNA command during the Bosnian war, and were centrally engaged in the killing and expelling of Muslim civilians. However, Arkan and the Tigers, unlike Šešelj and the Chetniks, were compliant tools of Milošević: with the latter's acquiescence, Arkan ruled a powerful crime empire in Serbia until his assassination in January 2000.

The regime of Franjo Tuđman and the 'Croatian Democratic Community' (HDZ) in Croatia, in power from 1990 until 1999–2000, also had some affinities with fascism. Tuđman was a former Partisan general and hard-line orthodox communist who had begun his evolution into an anti-Yugoslav Croat nationalist through his work as a historian. He had attempted to evaluate Croatia's Second World War history more positively: this involved emphasizing Croatia's contribution to the Partisans, but also downplaying the Serb death toll in the Ustasha genocide, in particular at Jasenovac. Although Tuđman correctly claimed that the widely accepted figure of several hundred thousand dead at Jasenovac was a gross exaggeration, his own estimate of 30,000–40,000 was somewhat lower than realistic estimates of the actual figure, which the Holocaust Memorial Museum in Washington today places at 56,000–97,000. Dismissed as director of a

[24] O. Pribičević, 'Changing Fortunes of the Serbian Radical Right', in S. Ramet, *The Radical Right in Central and Eastern Europe since 1989* (University Park: Pennsylvania State University Press, 1999), 193–211.

historical institute and expelled from the League of Communists for his 'nation-alist deviations', Tuđman, like Ćosić in Serbia, reinvented himself as a nationalist 'dissident'. In 1989, Tuđman published his controversial book *Wastelands of Histor-ical Truth*, a study of mass violence throughout history, which did not deny the Holocaust, but relativized it and downplayed the suffering of the victims. Tuđman suggested that the figure of six million Jewish dead was unreliable; that Jewish inmates at Jasenovac had enjoyed privileged treatment; and that Israeli treatment of the Palestinians was similar to the Holocaust.[25]

Tuđman and the HDZ came to power in free elections in the spring of 1990, bankrolled by right-wing and pro-Ustasha sections of the Croatian emigration. Tuđman saw himself as 'father of the Croat nation', and his task as healing the Second World War divide between the former Partisans and Ustashas. The new constitution promulgated by the Croatian parliament in December 1990 formally upheld the legacy of the Partisans while rejecting that of the NDH. In selecting a version of the traditional Croatian chequerboard emblem as official state symbol, the HDZ regime chose the version used by the inter-war Yugoslav kingdom, with the red squares at the corners, rather than the version favoured by the Ustashas, with the white squares at the corners (Titoist Yugoslavia had employed both versions).[26] This did not prevent Serbian propaganda from misrepresenting the chequerboard as an 'Ustasha symbol'.

Yet while Tuđman formally upheld the Titoist legacy, he sought also to incorpo-rate elements of the Ustasha legacy in his stated goal of 'national reconciliation'. The Croatian currency was renamed from the Yugoslav 'dinar' to 'kuna', as the NDH's had been. Tuđman prominently stated: 'The Independent State of Croatia was not merely a quisling creation and a fascist crime, but also an expression of the historical aspirations of the Croatian people for an independent state of their own.' The HDZ politician Stipe Mesić, who served as Croatia's last representative on the Yugoslav presidency and speaker of the Croatian parliament before breaking with Tuđman's nationalist policies and eventually succeeding him as President, stated in 1991 that 'we won on 10 April [1941] when the Axis powers recognized Croatia and we won after the war, when we again found ourselves with the victors, at the victors' table'. In this respect, Tuđman and the HDZ were readier than Milošević and the SPS to appropriate elements of the Second World War fascist heritage.

Tuđman and the HDZ waged their own war of conquest in Bosnia-Herzegovina, directed primarily against the Muslims and involving massacres and expulsions of both Muslims and Serbs and the establishment of concentration camps, particularly at Dretelj near Čapljina. Tuđman's principal executor of this policy was his Defence

[25] F. Tuđman, *Bespuća povijesne zbiljnosti: rasprava o povijesti i filozofija zlosilja* (2nd edn, Zagreb: Matica Hrvatska, 1989), 156–60, 316–17.

[26] M. A. Hoare, 'Whose is the Partisan Movement ? Serbs, Croats and the Legacy of a Shared Resistance', *Journal of Slavic Military Studies*, 15/4 (2002), 24–41.

Minister Gojko Šušak, a former émigré from Canada and member of a pro-Ustasha Bosnian Croat family. Croatian army operations against Serb-occupied areas, particularly at the Medak pocket in September 1993 and Operation Storm in August 1995, were marked by large-scale atrocities against Serb civilians. Tuđman's style was autocratic; he turned Croatian television into a propaganda outlet for the regime, harassed independent newspapers, and manipulated or repudiated election results, most notably following the opposition victory in the Zagreb mayoral election of autumn 1995. Initially a heterogeneous coalition containing liberal, conservative, and neo-Ustasha currents, the HDZ rapidly mutated into a monolithic authoritarian-nationalist party.

Nevertheless, Tuđman's Croatian regime was ultimately less fascistic than its Serbian counterpart. Tuđman was a quieter and more conservative figure than Milošević. He did not come to power through mass nationalist mobilization in a fascist manner, aimed at bending the existing institutions, but through a traditional electoral campaign. His use of violence against domestic opponents was much less than Milošević's. His territorial expansionism was also on a smaller scale and did not flow from nationalist mobilization and rhetoric, but was covert and underhand: Tuđman sought to partition Bosnia-Herzegovina through a 'gentleman's agreement' with Milošević, modelled on the Sporazum of 1939. Despite its anti-Serb and anti-Yugoslav rhetoric, Tuđman's policy was collaborationist in relationship to Milošević and the JNA, with whom he sincerely hoped to avoid war; he defused Croatian resistance activities in 1990–2 to the point where he clashed with Croatia's own Defence Minister and almost provoked his own overthrow.[27] The difference in political character may explain the divergent fates of the two despots: unlike Milošević, Tuđman did not overextend himself; he died quietly in office, after which his HDZ was peacefully voted out of power.

The principal Serb and Croat nationalist parties in Bosnia, the 'Serb Democratic Party' (SDS) and the Bosnian wing of the HDZ, which took power in the free elections of November–December 1990, identified more openly than the Milošević and Tuđman regimes with the Second World War quislings and collaborators. Karadžić's Bosnian SDS and its successors at the helm of the Serb Republic identified with the Chetniks. In 1998, Serb Republic President Biljana Plavšić, formerly Vice President under Karadžić, bestowed an honorary award on the exiled former Chetnik warlord Momčilo Đujić, who had fought on the side of the Nazis and Ustashas. The Bosnian HDZ under Mate Boban, which headed the separatist 'Croat Republic of Herceg-Bosna', named units of its militia, the 'Croat Council of Defence', after the Ustasha commanders Slavko Kvaternik and Jure Francetić. Paradoxically, however, the Bosnian HDZ's collaboration with the SDS in partitioning Bosnia led it to reverse Pavelić's policy, and to ally with the Serbs in exterminating Muslims.

[27] L. Silber and A. Little, *The Death of Yugoslavia* (London: Penguin, 1995), 169–89.

A second, still more overtly neo-Ustasha Croat militia was the black-uniformed 'Croatian Armed Forces', the paramilitary wing of Dobroslav Paraga's 'Croatian Party of Right'. The party's insistence that the Muslims were Croats and that Bosnia was a Croatian land that must remain united ironically meant that it rejected Tuđman's aggression against Bosnia, bringing it into disfavour with the Tuđman and Boban regimes. In a military ambush on 9 August 1992, the Croat Council of Defence wiped out the staff of the Croatian armed forces, after which the latter was forcibly incorporated into the former.

The Muslim 'Party of Democratic Action', which under President Alija Izetbegović held power in Bosnia during the war, was authoritarian and nationalist but, unlike its Bosnian Serb and Croat counterparts, not neo-fascist or overtly chauvinist in its rhetoric, though some right-wing party members identified with the SS division 'Handschar' of the Second World War. Yet all three sides in the Bosnian war attracted volunteers and mercenaries from extreme right-wing groups from abroad: Russian and Greek fascists fought on the Serb side; fascists from Catholic Europe fought on the Croat side; and Islamists, some with links to al-Qaeda, fought on the Bosnian side.

The principal reason for the rise of fascist-style regimes and movements in Yugoslavia, both in the inter-war and post-Tito periods, was the inherently repressive character of successive Yugoslav regimes and the reaction this generated, combined with the unresolved conflict between the rival national movements of the country's constituent peoples. State repression and national conflict in the 1920s culminated in the Alexandrine dictatorship, which served as incubator of authentic fascist movements among Serbs, Croats, and others. Although these attracted very little popular support, they enjoyed a false dawn in 1941, when the Axis conquest of Yugoslavia brought them to power. The popular reaction to their terror, in turn, helped bring about the Communist victory in 1945 and the negation of their politics. Yet the Communists' own repression, their suppression of nationalism, and in particular their overturning of Serbian hegemony, created the basis for a backlash against the Titoist order among the Serbs, and to a lesser extent among other Yugoslavs, that found expression in the autocracies of Milošević, Tuđman, and Karadžić and their wars of conquest and mass killing. Yet with the defeat of Serbian and Croatian expansionism, the overthrow of these autocracies, and the ongoing incorporation of the former Yugoslav states into Euro-Atlantic institutions, neo-fascist politics are increasingly on the wane in the former Yugoslavia.

BIBLIOGRAPHY

CIGAR, N., *Genocide in Bosnia: The Policy of 'Ethnic Cleansing'* (College Station: Texas A&M University Press, 1995).

COHEN, P. J., *Serbia's Secret War: Propaganda and the Deceit of History* (College Station: Texas A&M University Press, 1996).

DULIĆ, T., *Utopias of Nation: Local Mass Killings in Bosnia-Hercegovina* (Stockholm: Uppsala University, 2005).

HOARE, M. A., *Genocide and Resistance in Hitler's Bosnia: The Partisans and the Chetniks, 1941–1943* (London: Oxford University Press, 2006).

HUDELIST, D., *Tuđman: biografija* (Zagreb: Profil international, 2004).

JAREB, M., *Ustaško-domobranski pokret od nastanka do travnja 1941* (Zagreb: Školska knjiga, 2006).

JELIĆ-BUTIĆ, F., *Ustaše i Nezavisna Država Hrvatska 1941–1945* (Zagreb: Sveučilišna naklada Liber, 1978).

LEPRE, G., *Himmler's Bosnian Division: The Waffen SS Handschar Division 1943–1945* (Atglen: Schiffer Military History, 1997), pp. 59–60

REDŽIĆ, E., *Bosnia and Herzegovina in the Second World War* (London and New York: Frank Cass, 2005).

SILBER, L. AND LITTLE, A., *The Death of Yugoslavia* (London: Penguin, 1995).

STEFANOVIĆ, M., *Zbor Dimitrije Ljotića, 1934–1945* (Belgrade: Narodna knjiga, 1984).

THOMAS, R., *Serbia under Milošević: Politics in the 1990s* (London: C. Hurst and Co., 1999).

TOMASEVICH, J., *War and Revolution in Yugoslavia, 1941–1945: Occupation and Collaboration* (Stanford, CA: Stanford University Press, 2001).

CHAPTER 23

······································

AUSTRIA

······································

CORINNA PENISTON-BIRD

In the twenty-year lifespan of the First Republic, there were three contenders for the label of fascist: the Austrian Nazi Party, the Heimwehr (also Heimatschutz, Heimwehren, variants on Home Defence/Guard), and the Corporate State (1934–8). In Austria, therefore, one is not only comparing Austrian fascism with parallel movements in other countries, but also with variants within the same country. One is not comparing like with like, however: the Heimwehr and the Austrian Nazis constituted movements which existed from the outset of the new republic, the Nazis with origins reaching back to the turn of the century. The Corporate State, on the other hand, was a short-lived regime ushered in from above and which incorporated and reacted to (and against) these movements. One can best compare the opening phases of fascism in the case of the Heimwehr and the Nazis: the Heimwehr only accrued partial power, and was ultimately dissolved and incorporated into the Corporate State, and the ultimate Nazi victory in 1938 was ambiguous given that it was under German party leadership. The Corporate State did not follow a conventional pattern of creation, party formation, and acquisition of power, and existed for only four years. The relationship between the three was complex—sometimes antagonistic, sometimes cooperative—and their fortunes waxed and waned, dependent on both the national and international context. Their existence reflected a society deeply divided as to the best way forward following defeat and the end of the monarchy.

The independent democratic Republic of German-Austria was proclaimed on 12 November 1918, following the dissolution of the Habsburg empire. 'Independent' was to prove a relative term, since throughout its existence the country was played as a pawn in international affairs by the victors of the First World War, the League of Nations, and by its more powerful neighbours with a vested inter-est in Austrian affairs. The first half of the hyphenated compound name for the country ('German-') was prohibited by the victors, wary of fuelling demands for a union of German-speaking peoples that would have meant a defeated Germany of greater area than the country had occupied before the war: German-Austria was renamed the Republic of Austria (21 October 1919). The new Republic was nationally homogeneous, encompassing much of the German-speaking parts of the Habsburg empire, but it lost territory and one-third of the Empire's German-speaking nationals to Czechoslovakia, Italy, Poland, and Yugoslavia, which gave impetus to the Heimwehr in the conflicted border regions. The Heimwehr began in the opening years of the Republic when numerous provincial voluntary local defence units sprang up. These were gradually assembled into a paramilitary orga-nization which sought to defend Austria not only against foreign enemies, such as the Yugoslavs in Carinthia, or the Italians in the Tyrol, but also against domestic enemies, in particular Marxists. In 1921, the Heimwehr numbered from 2,200 men in Vorarlberg to 23,000 in Upper Austria.[1] Its membership was drawn from agricul-tural workers and farmers, the impoverished middle classes, and disaffected nobles. It had both Christian Social and pan-German support (predominantly in northern Styria and Carinthia) and found financial help from big business, particularly in Styria, which sought in the Heimwehr a counter-force to labour organizations.

Unlike the other successor states, Austria and Hungary were treated as the de-feated enemy in the peacemaking. In the Treaty of Saint-Germain (1919; part III, article 88), the independence of Austria was deemed 'inalienable' other than with the consent of the Council of the League of Nations (an escape clause which left hopes for a revision alive). Austria's dislocated economy encouraged the belief that the new 'rump state' was unviable, a judgement underpinned by the chronic unemployment rate, which seldom fell beneath 10 per cent. From that perspective the depression did not create dramatic change in the nation's economic fortunes. Austrian history in the inter-war period must be understood against this backdrop of defeat, economic dislocation, and the widespread sense among its population that Austria had been poorly treated by the Entente; condemned to exist yet denied the prerequisites to do so. Hopes for Austria's survival were pinned on union, most popularly (at least until 1933) with Germany, or, alternatively, in a Danubian Federation reviving (and revising) the Habsburg empire. The *Anschluss* ideal (union with Germany) was a common theme across the political camps, but at different times and with contradictory motivations. It was consistently thwarted until 1938 but remained an impetus in the development of Austrian Fascism both as a goal and as a fate to be resisted. However, on 13 March 1938, five years after Hitler came to power, and with no international intervention, German troops crossed the

---

[1] F. L. Carsten, *Fascist Movements in Austria: From Schönerer to Hitler* (London: Sage, 1977), 52.

border and Austria was demoted to the '*Ostmark*' (Eastern March) of the German Reich.

The fascist credentials of the Austrian Nazis, the Heimwehr, and the Corporate State have provoked much argument among historians. Initially, differences in opinion could be explained through the political sensitivities of a nation in whose interest it was to be represented as the first victim of the Third Reich, and whose political structure continues to be defined by three *Lager* (camps). James Miller argued that 'If you ask an Austrian whether Engelbert Dollfuss was a fascist or an anti-fascist, the answer you get will be a fairly accurate predictor of the person's political orientation.'[2] The debate is also not aided by the all-too-frequent absence of an explicit definition, with movements being labelled 'fascist', 'proto-fascist', or neither, with little justification for inclusion or exclusion. There are thus three areas of contention: whether these organizations constitute distinct forms of fascism (given internal divisions, more numerous than the organizations themselves); whether they in fact constitute separate strands of an 'Austro-Fascism' (itself a contentious term); or whether they can be labelled as fascist at all.

Robert Paxton suggests in this volume that the key characteristics of fascism include, among others, a sense of victimhood, the identification and attempted suppression of enemies, and a rejection of liberalism and socialism. One problem of analysing fascism in Austria, however, is not only that some of the characteristics of fascism were missing, for example a strong sense of a Darwinian struggle among peoples, but that others were overly abundant. Extreme antagonism to the left, visions for an alternative order to liberalism, veneration of (invented) tradition, willingness to resort to violence, and distrust of civil liberties and parliamentary democracy did not distinguish fascism in the inter-war period. Austria suffered similar problems to other defeated nations in the First World War adapting to democracy, and the history of the Republic was marked by political instability. Between 30 October 1918 and 25 July 1934 Austria had twenty-three governments under twelve heads. The most popular chancellor was Ignaz Seipel, theologian, priest, and politician, who led five governments, followed by Johann Schober, the Chief of Police of Vienna (who led three). Despite some fluidity within and between groupings, the Republic's political situation was marked by a threefold division between antagonistic *Lager* with incompatible visions: the labour movement on the left (of which the strongest party were the Social Democrats, who became the largest in the country by 1930); the Catholic conservatives (dominated by the Christian Social Party); and the multiple smaller National/Liberal parties. When coalition government ended in 1920, the Christian Socials could not command an absolute majority. They were therefore dependent on coalition

---

[2] J. W. Miller, '*Bauerndemokratie* in Practice: Dollfuss and the Austrian Agricultural Health Insurance System', *German Studies Review*, 11/3 (1988), 405. For continued contemporary discussion, see for example the discussion site 3H-Galerien on <http://www.3h-galerien.com/forum/9/2570/seite_10.html>.

with smaller parties such as the Großdeutsche Volkspartei (the Greater German People's Party) and the Landbund (Agricultural League). Despite their ideological differences, the right-wing camps had in common deep-seated antipathy to Social Democracy and the Austro-Marxists. In broad outline, while Social Democrat support was based predominantly on industrial workers, Christian Social backing was less sociologically homogeneous, drawn from farmers, small businesses and tradesmen, the self-employed, civil servants, monarchists, and the Catholic Church; German nationalist movements relied on Germans in Bohemia, Moravia, and Silesia, as well as the anticlerical and anti-Semitic sectors of the middle classes in Austria, and especially students (although the Christian Socialis made some inroads among that constituency). Austrian politics was marked by a lack of belief in the efficacy of liberal democracy to resolve the problems facing the state, a resistance to break political deadlock or respond to international vulnerability through cooperation or coalition between the polarized parties, and a widening schism between popular political identities. Conservative elites, banks, industry, and landowners proved willing to cooperate with and subsidize extremist movements.

The tripartite structure can be linked to the increasing radicalization of Austrian politics in the inter-war period, as each of the *Lager* sought to coexist with a more radical wing. Communism was successfully contained within the Social Democratic Party, but with the consequence that radical ideology and rhetoric detracted from the party's moderate pragmatism. The party's political opponents could use such rhetoric as that found in the Linz Programme of 1926, which elucidated the '*Befreiungskampf der Arbeiterklasse*' (battle for the liberation of the working class) to stir up fears of a party that was in practice supportive of Austrian parliamentary democracy, despite its unwillingness to enter coalition government after 1920. The Heimwehr's greatest domestic enemy was the Vaterländische Schutzbund, the paramilitary organization of the Social Democrats which had developed out of the factory guard units. Provocative demonstrations were staged by both sides, with resultant casualties deepening the animosity between the groups. The first ominous domestic upheaval of the First Republic was the consequence of a clash between the Schutzbund and the right-wing paramilitary organizations in the Burgenland. In January 1927 two rival parades were staged in Schattendorf. As the Schutzbund marched out of the village, shots were fired. A veteran and a child straggling at the back of the marchers were killed and four were wounded. When the *Frontkämpfer* held responsible for the shots were acquitted, on the following day, 15 July, disorganized fighting broke out in Vienna and the Palace of Justice was set on fire in protest (largely because of its name). In the riots, seven policemen and seventy-seven demonstrators were killed, and many more wounded. The transport strike called by the Social Democrats brought various areas to a standstill, but Seipel's government did not fall, and the Heimwehr acted as an auxiliary police force. This conflict had two significant consequences for the fate of Austrian democracy. The first was that the failure of the general strike marked a decline in Social Democrat power. Ironically, however, events appeared to provide evidence that the threat from the left had not been exaggerated. The Heimwehr gained both financial support from banks and industry and increasing political influence as well as popular support. The state had turned to the Heimwehr to help its attempts to crush the left: it would do so again in the civil war of 1934.

The provincial character of the new Republic was highly significant for the development of fascism in Austria. The population was distributed across eight provinces: Upper and Lower Austria, Carinthia, Salzburg, Styria, the Tyrol and Vorarlberg, and the Burgenland (German West Hungary) was gained by Austria. On 29 December 1921, the capital Vienna was also granted provincial status. While Vienna was a huge industrial and multicultural city where just under a third of the population resided (*c*.1.9 million), the rest of Austria was predominantly agrarian, with individual manufacturing islands, such as Graz. Political divisions reflected the divergent economic interests of country and city, exacerbated by the fears surrounding urban modernity. Individual provinces were not committed to being part of the new republic: although it came to nothing, in April 1921, for example, 98.5 per cent of the citizens of North Tyrol voted to join Germany. The strength of provincial over national loyalties explains why, despite the abundance of the conditions encouraging the growth of fascism across Europe, no convincing mass movement emerged in Austria. Many local branches were only committed to regional affairs and did not celebrate youth or action for themselves. Provincial rivalries also explain why no unifying leader emerged from the ranks of the Heimwehr or the National Socialists. There were individual reasons why the appeal of some Austrian leaders was limited, such as their social class or poor public speaking skills. But the history of both movements is of ideological schisms and bitter infighting rooted in provincial rivalries.

Throughout its existence the Heimwehr maintained a marked provincial character and suffered from organizational weaknesses, poor leadership, and ideological rifts and confusions, despite attempts to unify it behind an ideology based on more than opposition to Social Democracy or democracy. These ideological divides would prove difficult to overcome given, for example, the challenge of reconciling pro-Catholic and pan-German loyalties. The commonality in Heimwehr ideology, its opposition to the left, encouraged contact with foreign movements which had identified the same enemy, including the anti-Bolshevik and anti-Semitic Bavarian defence units united by Georg Escherich in 'Orgesch', later dissolved at the demand of the Entente. The Heimwehr also provoked the interest of Hungary and Italy, although the claims to the Burgenland and Italian policies in South Tyrol complicated relations. The Heimwehr in Carinthia and the Tyrol developed close ties with Italian fascism, while the Styrian units gained financial support from Berlin, and were more explicit about their commitment to *völkisch* and racial ideology, particularly after the Nazi seizure of government in Germany. Carsten concludes that 'the story of the Austrian fascist movements is really a story of their failure to achieve power by their own efforts'.[3]

Despite the undeniable influence from Italy, the Heimwehr is the main contender for constituting an indigenous Austrian fascist movement: Ludwig Jedlicka is adamant that it was 'the sole repository of authoritarian and fascist thought' in inter-war Austria.[4] The emphasis on Heimwehr fascism suggests a ready differentiation between the (fascist) Heimwehr and the (conservative) Christian Socials. Metaphorical descriptions of the relationship are popular in the historiography: Ernst Hanisch used the term '*Kettenhund*' (literally, a chained dog; guard-dog) to describe the role the Christian Socials had designated for the force, while Edmondson calls it a 'bludgeon'.[5] If the distinction is drawn too strictly, however, it erodes the overlap in both membership and sympathies. In May 1930, the Tyrolean Heimwehr leader, Richard Steidle, tried to unite the movement, calling a meeting in Korneuburg where he introduced the so-called Korneuburger Oath. The intention was to establish a firmly fascist direction for the movement, and to elicit an unambiguous commitment to an authoritarian future from the Christian Social membership and functionaries. In the constitutional reform in 1929, the Heimwehr had sought to introduce a parliament based on Estates and to strengthen the power of the president: their goals had been unfulfilled and were reiterated in Korneuburg. As this oath is a primary piece of evidence put forward to substantiate the fascism of the Heimwehr, I translate it in its entirety here. Written by the sociologist and economist Walter Heinrich, whose book *Staat und Wirtschaft* (State and Economy, 1929) was to provide a theoretical foundation for the Corporate State, the oath read:

We want to renew Austria from its foundations!
We want [to create] the *Volksstaat* of the *Heimatschutz*
We demand of every comrade:
   unshrinking belief in the Fatherland,
   unceasing zeal for the collaborative effort
   and passionate love of the Homeland.
We want to seize power in the state and to reshape it and the economy in the interests of the whole *Volk*.
   We must forget our own advantage, must subordinate all party ties and interests to the goals of our struggle, for we wish to serve the community of the German *Volk*.
   We reject western democratic parliamentarianism and the party state!

---

[3] Carsten, *Fascist Movements*, 334.

[4] L. Jedlicka, 'The Austrian Heimwehr', *Journal of Contemporary History*, 1/1 (1966).

[5] E. Hanisch, *Der Lange Schatten des Staates: Österreichische Gesellschaftsgeschichte im 20. Jahrhundert* (Vienna: Ueberreuter, 1994), 286. Martin Kitchen suggests that the Heimwehr was 'a sorcerer's apprentice' to the parties who sought to use it. M. Kitchen, review of W. Witschegg's *Die Heimwehr: Eine unwiderstehliche Volksbewegung?*, *American Historical Review*, 94/2 (1989), 485.

In their place we want to put the self-administering corporations (*Stände*) and a strong leadership, which emerges not from party representatives, but from the leading individuals of the large corporations, and from the men of our movement who have proved to be the most competent and trustworthy.

We are fighting against the corrosion of our *Volk* through the Marxist class struggle and the organization of the economy by liberal capitalism.

We want to implement the independent development of the economy on the basis of corporations.

We shall overcome class struggle and establish social dignity and justice.

We want to raise the prosperity of our Volk through an autochthonal economy administered for the common public interest.

The State is the embodiment of the whole *Volk*, and its power and leadership serve to ensure that the corporations remain subordinate to the needs of the *Volksgemeinschaft*.

May every comrade feel and profess himself to be responsible for the new German sense of state, be prepared to commit his possessions and blood and recognize only three powers: Faith in God, his own unshakeable belief, and the commands of his leaders [*Führer*]!

The ideological posturing of the Korneuburger Oath revealed the intertwining of patriotic Austrian, German-nationalist, and fascist ideas. The emphasis on corporations could be seen as inspired by the Italian model, but equally possessed German nationalist origins. The Austrian academic Othmar Spann envisaged in his *Der wahre Staat* (The True State) of 1921 a new structure of society based on Estates or Corporations, reminiscent of medieval guilds. This idea had a long tradition: as early as the beginning of the nineteenth century, for example, Adam Müller had presented a similarly glorified vision of corporations, based on a medieval ideal. Spann suggested that the population be organized and represented according to their occupations (from manual workers and entrepreneurs, to members of the army or clergy, to intellectuals and educators). The great appeal of the corporate vision was that it appeared to offer an alternative to discredited party politics: indeed political parties and traditional class structures would be rendered obsolete. National Socialists were wary of the potential impact of the corporations on the *Volkgemeinschaft*, but were most critical of the lack of emphasis on race and anti-Semitism in the oath. It also demanded loyalty to the leaders (not leader) of the new order.

The Korneuburger Oath failed completely to unite the Heimwehr behind one ideology and rather deepened the existing schisms. In the Tyrol and Vorarlberg, the Heimwehr had had since its foundation the support of the provincial governments, who envisaged it as functioning as an auxiliary police force. Members who served on the provincial governments proved hesitant to commit to an ideology seeking to undermine the state they had sworn to serve. Otto Ender, the influential *Landeshauptmann* of Vorarlberg, thus rejected the oath as anti-constitutional. Similarly, the leaders of the Landbund were adamant that the oath could not be reconciled with holding a mandate in an elective assembly, a stance born from the fear that any dictatorship would give stronger economic groupings than the Landbund the upper hand. Other critics did not trust Steidle's *post hoc* emphasis on German nationalism, detecting Italian Fascist influence. Distancing himself from the oath, Ernst Rüdiger Starhemberg, the regional leader in Upper Austria, replaced Steidle as the leader of the Heimwehr on 2 September 1930. Despite such opposition, however, the oath reveals the trend towards fascist ideals within the movement and elements of the Christian Social Party, and marks the growing influence of Mussolini.

Hitler's influence in Austria should also not be forgotten. The Nazis were the most radical of the German nationalists, and were the party with the longest history. The Deutsche National-Sozialistische Arbeiterpartei (DNSAP) of 1918 was the renamed Deutsche Arbeiterpartei (DAP; German Workers' Party), which had been founded in 1903/4 from Bohemia, Brno, Graz, and Klagenfurt. The DAP had drawn its membership from trade unions, industrial workers, and the petty bourgeoisie spurred by anti-Semitism, pan-Germanism, and the sense of threat from the rise of, in particular, Czech nationalism. It combined radical national and socialist demands with a veneration of the German race and culture but, in 1918, alongside anti-Semitic and nationalist demands, the party included democratic and social reforms among its goals: it cannot be termed fascist at this point of its existence. With the dismemberment of the empire, the DNSAP split in two, with the smaller half remaining in Austria, attracting only 23,000 votes (0.78 per cent) in 1919.[6] The loss of northern Bohemia altered the social composition of the party, with trade union membership declining but students and civil servants rising. In the next twenty years, its membership varied greatly depending on the period under discussion, but encompassed public and private salaried employees, the self-employed, and students. Industrial and agricultural workers remained under-represented. The party's growth was impeded not only by the strength of the two major parties but also by the number of competing organizations: the Heimwehr and the paramilitary Frontkämpfervereinigung (Front Fighters' Association) founded by Colonel Hermann Hiltl, to name but two.

The Austrian Nazis were led until 1923 by Walter Riehl, a lawyer and government attorney, who had joined in 1908. But from 1923, the Austrian Nazi Party was marked by a series of leadership disputes and factionalism, and a deepening divide between those members who wished to preserve their party's autonomy and those who sought increasingly radical and violent means to achieve its goals. By 1926, the DNSAP split into two irreconcilable parts, one group coming under the more moderate Karl Schulz, the other which accepted Hitler as their *Führer*. Hitler gave this group the name 'NSDAP Österreichs (Hitlerbewegung)' (Hitler movement). The great split lay between older and younger members, both in terms of the date of joining, and age. Younger members were more likely to be attracted to Hitler and his willingness to use force: they were also more prepared to accept Hitler's

---

[6] G. Botz, 'Arbeiter und andere Lohnabhängige im Nationalsozialismus', International Conference of Labour and Social History (Linz, 14–17 September 2006), <http://www.lbihs.at/BotzArbeiterNS.pdf>, 4.

pro-Italian stance on South Tyrol. Gerhard Botz draws attention to the age profile of National Socialist supporters, whose mean stood at *c*.32 years of age between 1926 and 1933.[7] The age profile had a pronounced generational character: the party exerted a particular fascination for men born between 1894 and 1903, and 1904 and 1913, that is those who saw service in the First World War, and those who were just young enough to have missed it, but still hankered after the perceived camaraderie of the front (*Fronterlebnis*).

Despite attempts to reunite the two groups, the Austrian Nazis remained divided until 1935 when the 'Schulz Nazis' were dissolved. Until 1935, however, there was bitter infighting between the two groups, with the Hitlerbewegung benefiting from Hitler's successes in Germany. Bruce Pauley argues the Schulz Nazis sacrificed political success to ideological purity and lacked the fanaticism, expansionist programme, hierarchy, and the leadership of a fascist movement.[8] Even the Hitlerbewegung suffered the tension between their theoretical commitment to a unified German *Volk* and their practical desire to safeguard the autonomy of the Austrian Nazi Party and a distinct Austrian state. Their first real successes were not until after the failed Heimwehr Pfrimer Putsch (see below): in the regional elections of April 1932, the party became the third greatest political force in Austria. This result reflected their ability to attract former national-liberal middle-class voters, as well as German-nationalist supporters of the Großdeutsche Volkspartei and the Landbund. They made few inroads into the Social Democrat supporters, or those of the Christian Social Party, except in regions where these were weak (largely in urban areas for the Christian Socials and rural for the Social Democrats): the Nazis proved adept at adapting their appeal according to the specific province and rural and urban regional differences. The party gained 41.1 per cent in the local elections in Innsbruck on 23 April 1933: the next national poll (had there been one) would have been likely to repeat these successes.

Nonetheless, no Nazi *Landesleiter* could unify the local leaders behind him, as the rapid turnover in that position suggests.[9] The (deliberate) lack of effective intervention from Germany, particularly between 1926 and 1931, thus had significant consequences for the movement: regional leaders, such as Alfred E. Frauenfeld in Vienna, or Walter Oberhaidacher of Styria, retained considerable influence, and power struggles within the regions continued. It also meant that the Hitler Jugend, the Sturmabteilung (SA), and, later, the Schutzstaffel (SS) invested their energies in competing within the party for power, rather than focusing on its external enemies. This concentration was obvious in the failed Putsch of July 1934 when the SA (who led the revolt in the provinces) refused to cooperate with the SS (who attacked the Federal Chancellery in Vienna). Setting aside the historical debate on the

---

[7] Ibid. 9.

[8] B. F. Pauley, *Hitler and the Forgotten Nazis: A History of Austrian National Socialism* (Chapel Hill, NC: University of North Carolina Press, 1981), 49.

[9] See ibid. 53.

important distinctions between fascism and National Socialism, the Hitlerbewegung's German orientation places doubt on the extent to which the movement can
be representative of *Austro*-fascism.

Both the Nazis and the Heimwehr had in common a rejection of liberal democracy, parliamentarianism, Marxism, and capitalism. They sought a society free from
class conflict, looking to corporatism to inaugurate national harmony, though with
a difference in emphasis depending on whether the goal was a *Volksgemeinschaft*
or the Christian (for which read Catholic) *Ständestaat*. These ideological common-
alities encouraged cooperation between the movements: in Carinthia, Lower and
Upper Austria, and Salzburg, the Nazis and the Heimwehr were drawn together
by their common antagonism to the left and to parliamentary democracy. But
cooperation born from shared marginality lasted only as long as neither side could
seize the advantage.

Despite the Heimwehr leader Richard Steidle's cynical reiteration that fascism
'was not an article for export',[10] and despite Hitler's disdain for the Austrian Nazis, it
would be difficult to overemphasize the importance of the example set from abroad,
and the practical support offered to the Heimwehr, the Nazis, and the Corporate
State by Austria's neighbours. The links with foreign movements proved a blessing
and curse. Although Italian financial support was fundamental to the Heimwehr,
the close ties prevented the Heimwehr from taking an unambiguous stance on the
Anschluss question and required renunciation of any claim on the highly emotive
issue of South Tyrol. Since 1927, the Italian government had given financial backing
and weapons to the Heimwehr on condition that it sought to overcome internal
rifts and developed beyond a paramilitary organization into a political one. Domestic financial supporters from both industry and banking, including the Alpine
Montangesellschaft (the largest iron and steel conglomerate and a major Styrian
employer) and the Central Association of Bankers, exerted similar pressure. In the
1930 elections, the history of the Heimwehr entered a new phase when it put forward
its own candidates for parliament in the *Heimatblock* under Starhemberg, gaining
6 per cent of the votes, double that for the Nazis, but was still too low to prevent
a further fracturing of the Heimwehr antagonizing those against any involvement
in the parliamentary system and encouraging a shift towards the extremist fringes
of the movement. The abortive putsch by the Styrian Heimwehr leader Walter
Pfrimer in September 1931 illustrates this disillusionment; the lack of support from
other Heimwehr units (and outright opposition in the Upper and Lower Austrian
sections) revealing its lack of unity. The Pfrimer Putsch did little to improve the
credibility of the Heimwehr and provided an impetus to the National Socialists
alert to the possibilities of exploiting the disaffection among former Heimwehr
supporters. The Heimwehr increasingly broke into different ideological positions:
some, following Starhemberg, aligning themselves with the Christian Social Party

---

[10] Steidle quoted in Carsten, *Fascist Movements*, 172.

and a patriotic Austrian stance; others, notably the Styrian Heimwehr, moving closer to National Socialism. A number of prominent Heimwehr leaders were given commands in the SS following the *Anschluss*.

In 1932 Chancellor Engelbert Dollfuss invited the *Heimatblock* members of parliament to join the coalition government to strengthen its one-vote majority. Over the next four years individual members of the Heimwehr took a variety of significant posts in government: Starhemberg served as Vice Chancellor under Dollfuss and as Minister of the Interior under Schuschnigg until excluded in 1936; F. Hueber became the Minister for Justice; while in 1932, Emil Fey, leader of the Viennese Heimwehr, became Secretary of State and organized the Heimwehr into an armed auxiliary police force.[11] The close links between Mussolini and the Heimwehr provided the *Duce* with a conduit through which to exert further pressure on the Austrian government, with the greatest impact in 1934. Jill Lewis nonetheless suggests that the Heimwehr must be seen as supporting the Christian Social leadership rather than as a competing or dominant force.[12] It certainly had a chequered history in terms of its relationship with the Großdeutsche Volkspartei and the Christian Social Party, which themselves differed on key ideological issues. The Chancellor Ignaz Seipel represented the Heimwehr as a force protecting democracy and had hoped that it, alongside other right-wing organizations, could be mobilized in domestic conflicts and against foreign intervention, but he was wary of according them too much political power at the expense of Christian Socials. The more radical wings of the Heimwehr (in Carinthia, Vienna, and parts of Styria) opposed any alliance with the Christian Socials, whom they viewed, with some justification, as monarchist and reactionary. In Lower Austria and the Burgenland in particular, the relationship between the Heimwehr and the Christian Social Party was close, and too intimate a drawing together with Italian Fascist or German nationalist theories was resisted.

Comparisons with the foreign paradigms have provided one way of ascertaining whether and which movements in Austria can be labelled fascist. Walther Wiltschegg, a former member of the Heimwehr who wrote an apologetic history of the force, queried whether the movement could be termed fascist when it merely mimicked uncritically the Italian paradigm, from which it differed, however, in too many key ways for the epithet to be accurate.[13] Comparisons dependent upon correlations are misleading, however, because they place too great an emphasis

---

[11] In May 1936 Starhemberg sent a telegram of congratulation to Mussolini following the Italian occupation of Addis Ababa, where Starhemberg spoke of the 'close bonds of sympathy which involve me as a Fascist in the destiny of Fascist Italy'. See E. Wiskemann, *Fascism in Italy: Its Development and Influence* (London: Macmillan, 1970), 107 for the full text of the translation. She argues that Austria was still too dependent on the League of Nations for Schuschnigg to be able to countenance this.

[12] J. Lewis, 'Conservatives and Fascists in Austria, 1918–34', in M. Blinkhorn (ed.), *Fascists and Conservatives: The Radical Right and the Establishment in Twentieth-Century Europe* (London: Unwin Hyman, 1990), 104.

[13] W. Wiltschegg, *Die Heimwehr: Eine unwiderstehliche Volksbewegung?* (Vienna: 1985).

on the 'master copies' at the expense of national variants, and emphasize fascism as an import rather than seeking its indigenous foundations and appeal. The German model is more problematic than the Italian in this context because the common language, while it certainly permitted easy cross-fertilization between the two countries, can lead to an emphasis on similarity (Spann was widely read in both countries, for example) at the expense of difference, such as religious belief. Most significantly, nationalist feeling had developed in different ways in the two countries: in a monarchy of multiple nations and nationalities, the Austrian understanding of the meaning and value of the nation state took a different path from Germany's: the *Kulturnation* was not assumed to find natural fulfilment in coterminous boundaries with the *Staatsnation*.

One of the main differences between Austria, Italy, and Germany is the absence of a militarist expansionist policy in Austria, or aggressively favouring autarky at any stage. The desire for union with Germany or a revived Danubian Federation reflected the search to overcome the boundaries imposed by the peace treaties which had purportedly rendered Austria unviable, but these projects were not accompanied by nationalist military planning, and a whole host of solutions to Austria's economic troubles were sought. Lewis provides a compelling argument for the importance of understanding national variations when she notes that the Austrian economy was 'small, structurally weak, relied heavily on foreign capital and trade, and lacked the diversity which would have allowed a policy of economic autarky'. She concludes, however, that 'rather than ruling out the possibility of fascism, this simply suggests that an Austrian fascist regime would adopt other economic politics in an attempt to promote domestic capital'.[14] Furthermore, just because the corporate economy never became fully functional, or because the Austrian movements were less successful at galvanizing popular support than their Italian or German counterparts, does not necessarily preclude them from being fascist: being successful is not a compulsory element of any definition of fascism.

The history of the democratic Republic came to an end in 1933: it was followed by a year of authoritarian rule followed by four of the Corporate State, a phase often labelled as 'Austro-fascist'. In response to a railway strike threatened by the transport union, on 4 March Karl Renner resigned his post as President of the Nationalrat in order to be able to cast his vote against the government. His two fellow speakers of the house followed suit. Exploiting the confusion that followed, and rejecting any constitutional solution, Chancellor Engelbert Dollfuss claimed that parliament had dissolved itself (*sich selbst ausgeschaltet*), suspended the Nationalrat and the constitution indefinitely, and, until May 1934, ruled by decree through the War Economy Emergency Powers Act of 24 July 1917. Any attempt to use this situation to strengthen the government's negotiating position to press constitutional change

---

[14] Lewis, 'Conservatives and Fascists', 102.

on the opposition was abandoned in favour of a *Staatsstreich auf Raten* (a coup by instalments): the first acts being to suspend freedom of speech, the press, demonstration, and strike. It was thus the Christian Social Party which ushered in the authoritarian state by a coup from above, in what was only the last step against parliamentary democracy. Although the Heimwehr had sought the elimination of the parliamentary system and the establishment of a corporate state, it had never been in a position to achieve these goals other than by acting as an auxiliary force to the government.

The final contender for the label 'fascist', this regime has not found a single uncontentious descriptor. One reason is that there was little time to do more than lay the foundations of a future order, although the regime's priorities (the destruction of the left and the reform of the school curriculum) were telling. Its characteristics could be termed either traditionally authoritarian or potentially fascist: the destruction of parliamentary democracy, the (attempted) elimination of political opposition. Dollfuss moved swiftly against the perceived enemies of the state, suspending the Constitutional Court and establishing concentration camps. The Schutzbund received a country-wide ban on 31 March 1933, followed by the outlawing of the Communist Party on 26 May. On 19 June 1933, the Styrian Heimatschutz and the Austrian Nazi Party were also banned by the government. In the same year the Social Democrats provoked further antagonism from Mussolini when they revealed that he was sending military equipment to the Austrian arms factory at Hirtenberg, intended for both the Heimwehr and Hungary. In February 1934, the ensuing mounting provocation of the Social Democrats erupted into civil war, the authorities reacting swiftly and harshly to put down SD resistance. Henceforward the party, the trade unions, and all other SD organizations were banned. The state thus forfeited the possibility of reconciliation with the socialists and seriously compromised the plausibility of its claim that it sought to unify the population behind a distinctively Austrian national identity. Nor did the crushing of the left rob the Nazis of their impetus. After an initial drop when the party was banned, membership began to rise again, from 87,000 members in 1934 to 164,000 in 1938, reflecting German successes and the increasing intervention of Hitler in Austria's domestic affairs. A wave of bombings by Nazis in the early months of 1934 escalated into a countrywide terror campaign leading to widespread arrests of those Nazis too slow to flee to Germany to join the Österreichische Legion (Austrian legion) founded in July 1933.

It was in this beleaguered context that the new constitution was introduced: in its final session, a rump parliament adopted a constitution which, in effect, abolished democracy. Historical opinion is divided whether this had always been his intention, or whether Dollfuss became increasingly radical once in power. But his impatience with both democracy and consultative processes is well documented. The regime had to walk a rocky path between the Heimwehr and Italian pressure on the one hand, and the Nazis, inside and outside Austria, on the other. However the regime's attempts at appeasement should not detract from the point that it placed greater priority on destroying Social Democracy than defending Austria's independence.

The strength of foreign influences should also not mask the peculiarly Austrian dimensions exhibited by the regime, many roots of which can be traced to Christian Social political thought and tradition.[15] Austria was henceforth defined as an authoritarian Social, Christian, German state based on corporations—a State of Estates. Six councils (state, culture, the economy, and the provinces, as well as a federal diet and assembly) replaced parliament. Membership in all except the federal diet was nominated, not elected. Seven corporations were envisaged: for industry, trade and communication, small enterprises, banks and insurance, the professions, agriculture, and the public services: only the latter two were founded. The estates encompassed both employers and employees, but in practice favoured employers as workers had no right to their own unions. Although the *Ständestaat* (Corporate State) was the official title for the Austrian state between 1934 and 1938, this designation is misleading given that restructuring of society into corporations remained more theory than practice.

In the *Trabrennplatz* (a race course) speech (11 September 1933) Dollfuss had declared Austria to be a German state. But Austria was also to function to preserve and represent German values that were being warped and betrayed abroad. Catholicism was a vital component of this Austro-German character, and the clearest feature to distinguish it from German Protestantism. The promise and appeal of a single communal faith that would supersede all societal division was a long-standing component of right-wing utopian thought.[16] In Austria, religious faith was a more significant component of that vision than in Germany. Alongside belief in the self and the leader, 'Faith in God' had featured in the Korneuburger Oath. Declaring Austria to be a 'Christian State' gave the concordat that had been reached with the Vatican in 1933 legal status. This had abolished the supremacy of the state in church matters and secured the latter's legal status, religious education in schools, the church's right to its own schools, church weddings, and religious holidays, as well as its property and financial presence. Financial support for Catholic education was promised when economic conditions improved. The role of the Catholic Church was one of the most Austrian features of Austro-fascism.

The most recent inspiration for the corporate structure came from the 1931 papal encyclical *Quadragesimo anno*, itself inspired by the fortieth anniversary of Leo XIII's encyclical of 1891, *Rerum novarum*. *Quadragesimo anno* envisaged a class-free corporate state where the conflicts of contemporary society would be replaced by an organic community working together for the greater good. This inspiration for

---

[15] Lewis, 'Conservatives and Fascists', 104.

[16] See T. Rohkrämer, *A Single Communal Faith? The German Right from Conservatism to National Socialism* (Oxford: Berghahn, 2007). I'd also like to express my gratitude to Thomas for his insightful comments on the penultimate draft of this chapter.

a 'third way' found support also in Portugal, Poland, and Spain, and differentiated the Austrian 'Catholic' Corporate State from earlier fascist corporative structures in Italy and (to a much lesser extent) Germany. It could even be construed as an attempt to erect a defence against the increasing influence of the latter. Unlike the encyclical, however, the new constitution did not allow for free associations or choice of government. Tálos hence denounces the claim that Austria's corporate structure was based on the encyclical as entirely farcical and Wiltschegg argues that the estates structure in Austria owed more to Nazi ideas than either Spann or Catholic theoreticians, interpretations which place doubt whether the new regime truly constituted an alternative to the Italian or German paths.[17]

On 25 July 1934, Dollfuss was assassinated in what F. L. Carsten describes as 'the only attempt ever made by any National Socialist organization to overthrow the existing government by military means'.[18] The plot involved seizing key members of the government and replacing Dollfuss with Anton Rintelin, instigating a Nazi revolt across the country. In practice, having been tipped off, most government officials had already left the Federal Chancellery. Dollfuss was one of the few who remained, and he was shot trying to escape. The refusal to permit him a priest for the last rites as he bled to death underpinned his subsequent elevation to martyr. The Nazi insurgents were suppressed by the Austrian army and the Heimwehr after three days of bitter fighting. Another reason the putsch did not escalate as planned was because of the mobilization of Yugoslavian troops and Mussolini's mobilization of troops on the Brenner frontier. Dollfuss was succeeded by the less charismatic Kurt (von) Schuschnigg, who struggled to hold together the multiple factions upon which the regime depended.

The organization of the new order was the Vaterländische Front (VF; Fatherland Front), proclaimed in May 1933 and represented as a non-partisan mass organization of all Austrians, intervening in labour disputes and organizing public demonstrations and social programmes, from tourism to welfare. The VF was a highly hierarchical organization, led by Dollfuss who adopted the title *Führer*, and emulating foreign theatricality with uniforms, flags, parades, etc. It was not conceptualized as a party and demanded loyalty to authoritarian German Austria, but otherwise permitted 'full freedom of conscience', thus avoiding a fascist claim for a full monopoly of authority. Nor was it accepted without resistance: Dollfuss had not held a leading post in the Christian Social Party (before becoming Chancellor of the coalition government in 1932 he had served as Minister of Agriculture and Forestry), and the increasingly authoritarian direction taken by Dollfuss and his Heimwehr allies was met with resistance from other party members: Karl Vaugoin, who was *Obmann* of the party from 1930, resigned in November.

---

[17] See E. Talos, 'Das austrofaschistische Herrschaftssystem 1933–1938', in W. Maderthaner and M. Maier (eds), *Der Führer bin ich selbst: Engelbert Dollfuss–Benito Mussolini, Briefwechsel* (Vienna, 1984), 116.

[18] Carsten, *Fascist Movements*, 266.

The development of a national vision certainly mirrored the appeal of a fascist vision promising national harmony. But although the VF had the external signifiers of a fascist movement (the adoption of the *Kräckenkreuz*—cross potent—for example, public demonstrations, multiple sub-organizations intended to cater to youth, motherhood, as well as recreational organizations), it failed to exert any genuine appeal. VF membership was based on the absorption of organizations and individual pragmatism related to employment practices: although its membership stood at two million by 1936, the degree to which it could muster committed public support remains highly questionable. Karl Renner (the first Chancellor of both the First and the Second Republic) offers the following (probably specious, but nonetheless telling) contemporary anecdote which suggests such scepticism is appropriate: it describes the experience of a VF official who is visiting a locality where he asks where the locals' loyalties lie. He is told that half of them are brown [Nazi] and the rest are red [Socialist]. In horror he asks how many, then, can be in the VF? The response is immediate: 'Oh, all of us!'

Despite a sincere desire to foster an Austrian national identity that was distinct from the German (a challenge, given that nationalism in Austria was associated with German nationalism), a genuine but misguided effort to defend Austrian sovereignty, and various attempts to create enthusiastic servants of the state, the authoritarian state remained ambivalent toward the notion of popular support in the sense of involvement rather than acquiescence. It proved more committed to destroying any potentially hostile groups whose integration might have bettered its chances of survival and whose exclusion could only ever be a mixed blessing at best and fatal at worst. Despite the VF's continued resistance to the wooing of the Nazis, the quashing of the Social Democrats damaged irreparably one such bulwark and the attempts at reconciliation in 1938 were too late to have any chance of success.

The likelihood of defending Austria's independence worsened following Italy's invasion of Ethiopia and the subsequent drawing together of Germany and Italy. The remaining months of Austria's independent existence were marked by attempts to appease foreign governments and come to an arrangement with Germany that would protect Austria's sovereignty. In 1936, the Chancellor dissolved the Heimwehr in an attempt to curry favour with Germany and the liberal democratic powers: its paramilitary units were incorporated into the VF in the *Frontmiliz*. Their final dissolution was partially caused by falling financial support from Italy. In the July Agreement with Germany of 1936, Austria was defined as a second German state, although its sovereignty was recognized. In return for German rhetoric, Austria had to offer practical measures: charged and sentenced Nazis were granted an amnesty, and representatives of the 'national opposition' (Edmund Glaise-Horstenau and Guido Schmidt) were given positions in the new cabinet. The July Agreement did not go far enough for Hitler, and was followed by the Berchtesgaden Agreement in February 1938 whereby Arthur Seyss-Inquart became Minister of the Interior and Security, Schmidt Foreign Minister, and Glaise-Horstenau remained a member of cabinet. Nazi agitation in Austria continued. When on 9 March Schuschnigg announced a referendum on 13 March 'for an independent and social, a Christian, German, and united Austria', Hitler demanded it be cancelled. When Schuschnigg refused, German troops entered Austria on 12 March, encountering no resistance. The corporate experiment was at an end. The Corporate State can be viewed as a sincere but desperate attempt to mobilize an Austrian sense of national identity that could stand firm against increasing pressure from Nazi Germany or, alternatively, as paving the way for the popular acceptance of the Nazi takeover in 1938 and collusion with the regime thereafter.

The regime was famously labelled clerico-fascist in Charles A. Gulick's *Austria from Habsburg to Hitler* (1948), reflecting the intertwining of fascism with Catholic clericalism.[19] Over 90 per cent of the population of the Republic was (nominally) Catholic, and the church had a firm presence in Austrian politics throughout the inter-war period, reflecting the contradictory traditions of both authoritarianism (for example, Seipel's vision of a single-party Catholic state which laid ideological foundations for Dollfuss and Schuschnigg) and strong party-political representation in the Christian Social Party. However, despite explicitly supporting and legitimizing the regime, the Catholic Church retained internal autonomy and acted as a barrier against increasing radicalization. Laura Gellot questions the clerical dimension of 'clerico-fascist', arguing that this label misleads more than it illuminates: 'the dominant feature of church–state relations in this period, despite the surface rhetoric indicating harmony, was a continuation of longstanding rivalries between church and state, intensified, not diminished by the government's claim that it was a Christian state, and by the state's attempt to exercise influence in areas traditionally addressed by the Church.'[20] Carla Esden-Tempska agrees: while the Catholic Church bolstered the authoritarian state with its emphasis on obedience to a higher authority, its influence also ensured the exclusion of features emphasized abroad, such as Social Darwinism and the glorification of violence.[21]

If the 'clerico' label can be challenged in descriptions of the state between 1934 and 1938, so, too, should the post-hyphen 'fascism' whether in 'Clerico-' or 'Austro-' fascism. Historians as diverse as Jedlicka, Edmondson, Botz, and Kirk agree that the Corporate State is most helpfully understood as a mixture of authoritarian and conservative ideas, ideologies, and tendencies rather than as fascist. While both

---

[19] C. A. Gulick, *Austria: From Habsburg to Hitler*, vols. i and ii (Berkeley and Los Angeles: University of California Press, 1948).

[20] L. S. Gellott, 'The Catholic Church and the Authoritarian Regime in Austria, 1933–1938' (University of Wisconsin-Madison, PhD thesis, 1982), 27. These areas included youth organizations, educational and recreational programmes, and interventions in family life.

[21] C. Esden-Tempska, 'Civil Education in Authoritarian Austria, 1934–1938', *History of Education Quarterly*, 30/2 (1990), 189.

imported and indigenous fascist elements of the regime are readily identifiable, few historians are prepared to bestow the fascist label without adding qualifications. In the historiography of Austrian fascism, fascism is partial, not absolute, as reflected in the modifiers 'proto-' 'semi-', or 'pseudo-' fascism to describe the Austrian variants. Roger Griffin coined the phrase 'parafascism' to define the Dollfuss/ Schuschnigg regimes: 'a form of authoritarian and ultranationalist conservatism which adopts the external trappings of fascism while rejecting its call for genuine social and ethical revolution.'[22] These multiple terminologies represent an attempt to negotiate difference and pursue descriptive accuracy. Given that eclecticism is one of fascism's defining traits, the debate over the extent to which Austria's movement can be labelled fascist easily becomes sterile: more productively it points to the existence of a spectrum ranging from conservatism through authoritarianism to fascism, with the unsurprising consequence that there are many different positions on that spectrum. Edmondson offers the most convincing summary why Austria did not produce a successful native fascist state or movements: 'postwar Austria was too new, too small, too dependent, too Catholic.'[23] The historiography is evidence of the enduring slipperiness of the term fascism, the differing resultant conclusions depending on whether the emphasis is on ideology or on revelation through action, and the challenges of comparative history. The Austrian variants of fascism pale into insignificance if the focus is on the destructive impact of those of its more powerful neighbours. Such relativism has proved a hindrance to *Vergangenheitsbewältigung* (confronting and coming to terms with the past), and enduring fascist sympathies remain a significant element of contemporary Austrian politics. It is perhaps here that we find stronger parallels with Italian Fascism than with German National Socialism.

BIBLIOGRAPHY

BISCHOF, G., PELINKA, A., and LASSNER, A. (eds), *The Dollfuss/Schuschnigg Era in Austria: A Reassessment*, Contemporary Austrian Studies Series (New Brunswick, NJ: Transaction, 2003).

CARSTEN, F. L., *Fascist Movements in Austria: From Schönerer to Hitler* (London, 1977).

EDMONSON, C. E., *The* Heimwehr *and Austrian Politics, 1918–1936* (Athens, GA, 1978).

JEDLICKA, L., 'The Austrian Heimwehr', *Journal of Contemporary History*, 1 (1966).

KIRK, T., 'Fascism and Austro-Fascism', *Contemporary Austrian Studies*, 11 (2003).

KITCHEN, M., *The Coming of Austrian Fascism* (London: Routledge, 1980).

KLINGENSTEIN, G., 'Bemerkungen zum Problem des Faschismus in Österreich', *Österreich in Geschichte und Literatur*, 14 (1970).

[22] R. Griffin, *The Nature of Fascism* (London, 1991), 240.
[23] C. E. Edmonson, *The Heimwehr and Austrian Politics, 1918–1936* (Athens, GA., 1978), 7.

PAULEY, B. F., *Hitler and the Forgotten Nazis: A History of Austrian National Socialism* (Chapel Hill, NC: University of North Carolina Press, 1981).

RATH, J. R., 'The First Austrian Republic: Totalitarian, Fascist, Authoritarian or What?', in R. Neck and A. Wandruszka (eds), *Beiträge zur Zeitgeschichte: Festschrift Ludwig Jedlicka zum 60. Geburtstag* (St Pölten, 1976).

SIEGFRIED, K.-J., *Klerikalfascismus: Zur Entstehung und sozialen Funnktion des Dollfuß-Regimes in Oesterreich. Ein Beitrag zur Faschismusdiskussion* (Frankfurt am Main, 1979).

TÁLOS, E., and NEUGEBAUER, W., *Austrofascismus* (Vienna, 2005).

CHAPTER 24

THE NETHERLANDS

BOB MOORE

THERE is a general consensus among historians and political scientists that fascism has never had much popular appeal in the Netherlands, and that the various manifestations of what might be categorized as such have been largely confined to the margins of politics and society. The reasons put forward for this view have themselves varied over time, but centre on the stability of a Dutch political system epitomized by relatively unchanging voter allegiances and cabinet formation through coalitions of two or more parties. Traditionally, these allegiances were defined primarily by confessional or established ideological positions: Roman Catholicism, Orthodox Calvinism, liberalism, and Social Democracy. These 'pillars' of Dutch society extended beyond the realm of politics and created separate milieux that framed many aspects of everyday life. Thus there was little room for right-wing authoritarian or fascist-inspired groups to build any real constituency. What support there was for a fascist alternative came from those whose anti-democratic sentiments went beyond the margins of right-wing parliamentary politics, and those whose greatest fear was the growth of the Social Democratic and Communist Parties. More recently, a fear of immigrants and of an increased presence of Islamic culture has helped spawn movements that, if not openly fascist, certainly contain some of the attributes associated with mainstream fascism.

The first forms of fascism emerged in the Netherlands during the 1920s, inspired by a small minority who were motivated by admiration for what Mussolini had achieved in Italy. Thus, for example, the priest and publicist Wouter Lutkie expounded the ideas of a traditional Christianity combined with the youthful dynamism of fascism as an alternative to the democratic state, a line given an increased importance after the Lateran Treaties between the Vatican and the Italian state in

1929, and his journal *Aristo-* brought together a small group of similarly minded adherents. There were other right-wing authoritarian and fascist groups in this period, such as the Nieuw Verbond van Nationalisten and the Nationale Unie. There was also Nationaal Herstel, an elitist organization whose journal had five professors, a senator, a lieutenant-general, and a baron on its editorial board. Another impetus came from Austro-German Roman Catholic social critics; yet most of these groups were extremely small, had little popular appeal, and seldom lasted long. The first overtly fascist newspaper aimed at a popular audience, *De Bezem*, had appeared in 1927. Edited by the 21-year-old student Hugues Alexandre Sinclair de Rochemont and inspired by the Hegelian teachings of the professor of philosophy at Leiden, G. J. P. J. Bolland, the publication was funded by Alfred A. Haighton, an heir to a family insurance company whose sole object was the pursuit of political power. With Sinclair de Rochemont, Haighton had previously formed and funded the Verbond van Actualisten, which had stood in the 1925 general election but had garnered only 0.08 per cent of the popular vote. These organizations all had their origins before the electoral success of National Socialism in Germany and took most of their intellectual and organizational ideas from Italian fascism. Indeed, even after Hitler's success at the polls, Lutkie rejected the ideas of National Socialism as being too German-Imperialist—a view shared by many others who saw an imperially minded Germany as a direct threat to Dutch independence and its own imperial destiny.

In 1932, one group from the *Bezem* circle split to form the Algemene Nederlandse Fascisten Bond (General Dutch Fascist Association). Led by Jan Baars, it was an attempt to unite various strands of fascist thought and organizations in the Netherlands, but it made little or no impact on Dutch politics and was all but dead by the later 1930s. In 1934 Arnold Meijer, a Roman Catholic essayist and journalist, brought various activists from these groups together to form the Zwarte Front. This was a shadowy organization that remained the main overtly fascist organization in the Netherlands until 1940, espousing a virulent anti-Semitism and *dietse* (greater Dutch) ideas of union of all Dutch-speaking peoples. Yet even the effects of the economic depression after 1929 failed to give organized fascism any real popular base in the Netherlands, and people remained wedded to their existing religious and political milieux. In the 1939 general election, Meijer's Zwarte Front polled only 8,179 (0.2 per cent) votes, of which more than a fifth came from his home town. This lack of right-wing radicalism was matched, and perhaps partly explained, by a similar lack of left-wing radicalism: the Dutch Communist Party had also failed to make any real impact in electoral or popular politics.

The 1930s also saw the growth of two even more marginal groups, the imitative organizations both known as the Nationaal-Socialistische Nederlandse Arbeiderspartij (NSNAP). The first was founded in The Hague in December 1931 and led by a triumvirate of Dr Ernst Herman ridder van Rappard, Adalbert Smit, and Albert de Joode van Waterland. A triumvirate was an unusual structure for a fascist organization and it soon collapsed as van Rappard alienated and then marginalized his colleagues by claiming that the only way forward for the Netherlands was through union with Germany. Van Rappard had studied in Berlin, Munich, and Vienna, but was described as a poor organizer, poor speaker, and doctrinaire weakling who was totally under the thumb of his German wife. He continued as the leader of the NSNAP (Hitler-Movement) throughout the 1930s while both Smit and de Joode had brief but unsuccessful political dealings with Haighton. A second NSNAP was founded by the former colonial soldier Majoor C. J. A. Kruyt. He had shifted from liberalism to fascism in the later 1920s and spoke out against the influence of the Jews. However, the NSNAP-Kruyt managed only 1,000 votes in 1937 and some of its membership came from Dutch citizens living inside Germany. Finally there was the Verbond van Dietse Nationaal-Solidaristen (Verdinaso), originally founded by the Flemish nationalist Joris van Severen who championed the union of Flanders with the Netherlands but excluding Friesland. This group, together with the other small parties, were united in their hatred of disorder, humanitarianism, socialism, and communism, and united in an anti-democratic and authoritarian mindset. Hitler, Mussolini, and Salazar became the adopted role models for these would-be political leaders, although their espousal of doctrines of dictatorship ran aground on the bedrock of the unwavering popular support for the monarchy that was a feature of the Netherlands in this period.

If fascism in the Netherlands began largely as an intellectual movement, radical right-wing politics was transformed by the electoral success of the NSDAP in Germany in 1930. A Dutch Nationaal-Socialistische Beweging (NSB) was founded as a political party the following year. Mirroring the organizational and structural innovations of its German sister party, and led by the respectable engineer Anton Mussert, the NSB proved far more successful in mobilizing popular support in the first half of the 1930s. A combination of anti-Marxism and anti-liberalism, coupled with a continuing and deep economic recession addressed by deflationary government policies, created circumstances where the movement was able to garner nearly 8 per cent of the popular vote in the 1935 provincial elections. While nowhere near a major electoral breakthrough, this tally nevertheless represented a substantial shift in the usually staid patterns of Dutch voting behaviour. Local studies suggested that support was strongest in the main cities and among certain hard-pressed petty-bourgeois circles and independent small farmers in the provinces, but individual hot-spots of support could often be explained by specific local factors. Pre-war party membership reached a peak in 1936 with 52,000 adherents.

In the interim, the NSB had been included on a list of political organizations deemed incompatible with government service—a list that also included the Communists, revolutionary Socialists, and Social Democrats, as well as such fringe right-wing groups as the Zwarte Front. After 1935, NSB fortunes declined as the movement adopted a more openly anti-Semitic attitude—again aping its German neighbour—and also suffered from sanctions imposed by the major churches on adherents who were members or gave it 'important support'. The more radical posture seems to have come from newer members and increasing German influence rather than from any deliberate decisions from the leadership. A moderate economic recovery also had some impact in drawing voters back to more mainstream political allegiances. Whatever the precise reasons, the NSB vote fell to 4.2 per cent in the general election of 1937 and 3.9 per cent in the provincial elections of 1939.

In some respects, the NSB suffered from the same problems as other fascist and neo-fascist groups, namely that its leader, Mussert, possessed few of the charismatic or oratorical qualities of a Mussolini or a Hitler. He had wanted to become a naval officer, but had been rejected on health grounds. Qualifying as an engineer in 1918, he had built a successful career and was head of the Waterstaat (Department of Building and Roads) for the province of Utrecht by his thirty-third year, but his family life was somewhat more controversial. In 1917 he had married Maria Witlam, a woman eighteen years his senior who also happened to be his aunt, and a special royal dispensation had to be granted to override the legal proscription of such a marriage. The union was less than fruitful; producing no children, and also no political gains for Mussert. His wife was loyal, but far from intelligent, and she saw her role as purely to look after her husband and to keep house. Thus she took no part in her husband's political life and did not even join the party he led. Nevertheless, the initial success enjoyed by Mussert and the NSB in comparison with the other fascist groups of the period does need to be explained. His skills as an organizer and his understanding of propaganda were key elements, as was his good name as a successful civil servant. His nationalist credentials were also impeccable as he had been active in opposing the treaty with the Belgians on the Scheldt issue during the 1920s. His respectable background made him much more appealing as a political leader for the disaffected lower middle-class Netherlanders than the bohemians and other dubious characters that inhabited the fascist world in the Netherlands. Although his National Socialism remained abhorrent to most Dutch voters, he could nevertheless be seen by a disaffected minority as championing law, order, and decent, middle-class values.

Two notable characteristics of the NSB were, first, the fact that ideological leadership was split within the movement. The bourgeois, nationalist, and respectable Mussert was challenged by M. M. Rost van Tonningen who had joined the party in 1936, held a parliamentary seat in the Second Chamber, and edited the party newspaper *Het Nationale Dagblad*. His line was more radically racist and advocated union with Nazi Germany. The rivalry between the two men transcended the shock of 1940, although neither benefited greatly from German preferment during the occupation. The second, and perhaps unique, feature of Dutch National Socialism was its support in the empire. The movement boasted 5,000 members in the East Indies in 1935—the same year Mussert toured Java and was received by the then Governor-General B. C. De Jonge—but this was to fall to around 1,800 by 1939. At the same time, the party's fortunes in the metropole showed no signs of improvement, with a declining popular vote in the 1939 provincial elections and a falling membership. This decline was largely attributed to the perception that the radicalized but still supposedly nationalist NSB was becoming increasingly pro-German and therefore 'un-Dutch'.

After the German invasion, Mussert and the leaders of the other small fascist and National Socialist movements imagined that they would find favour with the occupiers, but these ambitions went largely unfulfilled. After the departure of the royal family, Mussert envisaged himself as head of state under German tutelage, but his Dutch nationalism and ideas for a Greater Netherlands were at odds with German ambitions that the Dutch and Flemish peoples were 'Aryans' and therefore candidates for annexation to the Reich. His party owed its ideology more to Italian Fascism than to German National Socialism in that it preached 'strong government, national self-respect, discipline, order, and solidarity of all classes of the population and the precedence of the national interest over that of groups'.[1] Ostensibly the party retained its nationalist beliefs and recognized Christianity as one of the foundations of Dutch national existence. During the occupation, the split between Mussert and the more *völkisch* elements within the movement led by Rost van Tonningen became increasingly marked and many members were prepared to defy their own leadership and put German interests above those of the Dutch, by operating as Gestapo informers and by assisting in the persecution of the Jews. The party nevertheless generally supported German actions and membership reached a peak of around 50,000 by the end of 1940 with perhaps another 50,000 registered 'sympathizers', but there was also a high turnover of members. These numbers hardly represented the basis for a major mass movement even in the most propitious of circumstances, and undoubtedly included many political opportunists who had little or no ideological commitment to the principles laid down by Mussert. One bonus to the movement was the support given by Generalkommissar Fritz Schmidt in appointing NSB members to vacant mayoralities and other civil service posts as a means of Nazifying Dutch society. However, apart from producing a wave of NSB appointments to lower-ranking administrative posts, it did little to improve the movement's public position.

The second characteristic was the creation and expansion of its paramilitary elements, and especially the Weerafdeling (WA), which became compulsory for all male members of the NSB between the ages of 18 and 40. Mussert also sponsored the creation of the Nederlandse SS, which recruited some 3,000 members, some of whom eventually fought on the eastern front. A home defence formation, the Landwacht, was formed in 1943 to protect the party leadership, but was almost immediately converted into an auxiliary police force by Generalkommissar

[1] W. Warmbrunn, *The Dutch under German Occupation, 1940–1945* (Stanford, CA: Stanford University Press, 1963), 86, cites *Volk en Vaderland*, 24 May 1940, 7.

Hanns Albin Rauter, head of police and security under Reichskommissar Arthur Seyss-Inquart. There were also other armed units created under the aegis of the NSB, namely a Vrijwilligerslegioen Nederland (Netherlands Volunteer Legion) whose members were incorporated into the Waffen SS and the Landstorm (Home Guard). Estimates of the numbers of Dutchmen involved in military service vary, but they probably totalled around 25,000, of whom 10,000 may have perished. How many of them were motivated to join by allegiance to fascism and National Socialism rather than to a fear of bolshevism or just a spirit of adventure will probably never be known.

In spite of four personal meetings, Mussert was unable to persuade Hitler to make him head of state in the Netherlands. The best he was offered was an appointment as '*Führer* of the Dutch people' and head of a National Political Secretariat that would advise the Reichskommissar. For Mussert this recognition signalled that he was on the way to a takeover of the Dutch state machinery, but popular discontent and a failure of the German authorities to concede that anything had really changed put an end to such aspirations and his influence waned after the summer of 1943 as his support in German circles collapsed, increasing demands for forced labour were made on the country, and the movement was implicated in the ever more brutal tactics of the occupying Germans. The movement came to an abrupt end when the BBC erroneously reported the fall of the city of Breda in September and 30,000 NSB members and their families fled across the border to Germany. Mussert remained at his post and was ultimately arrested in his office in The Hague at the liberation on 7 May 1945. Tried and condemned to death by a special court, he was executed exactly one year later.

Other elements within the NSB were even more wedded to the German cause than Mussert. Rost van Tonningen was considered by both Himmler and Rauter as far more suitable as a leader for the Dutch but he failed to gain any mass support. Appointed as Secretary-General for Financial Affairs and President of the Nederlandse Bank in 1941, he continued to oppose Mussert and champion outright German integration of the Netherlands. He also differed from his party leader in opposing the idea of an authoritarian government bound by law and freedom of religion in favour of Himmler's ideas of subordinating law and government to the biological imperative of improving the superior race. Unable to unseat Mussert, Rost van Tonningen first joined the Landstorm and then returned to civilian life. Arrested after the liberation, he apparently committed suicide in Scheveningen prison on 9 June 1945.

The other would-be Dutch *Führers* fared little better. Arnold Meijer and his Zwarte Front, with their uncritical support for Mussolini and Hitler and virulent anti-Semitism, were in some ways a better match for the Nazis but were considered suspect because of their links to Catholicism and support for *dietse* ideas. The party was banned on 13 December 1941. The two NSNAP organizations became increasingly oriented towards Germany, both demanding immediate incorporation of the

Netherlands into the Greater German Reich. However, even this slavish following of German ideas did not save them. From the summer of 1940, Reichskommissar Seyss-Inquart encouraged members of the NSNAP-Kruyt to cease operations and join the NSB. The NSNAP-van Rappard, which had grown to around 10,000 members, was kept on by the Germans as a counterweight to the NSB but was itself disbanded in January 1942. The arrival of these radicals in the ranks of the NSB only served to strengthen the opposition to Mussert from within his own party, but widespread popular support for any of the National Socialist or fascist political variants remained elusive and increasingly unlikely as the war turned against Hitler's Germany and the Nazis made increasing economic and ideological demands on the Dutch people. Of the NSNAP leaders, Kruyt died in March 1945 and van Rappard was sentenced to life imprisonment in 1949. Meijer was also arrested after the war but sentenced to only four years in jail as the Germans had banned his movement during the occupation. Freed in 1947, he settled in Oisterwijk where he ran a hotel until his death in 1965.

The defeat of Germany drove all public manifestations of fascism and national socialism deep underground as over 100,000–120,000 former adherents and collaborators were put on trial or purged for their conduct during the occupation. These included the *politieke deliquenten*, those convicted of political offences against Dutch interests. Most received only short terms of imprisonment and by 1950 many were back on the streets, albeit condemned to the margins of society as 'foute Nederlanders'. While many eschewed politics altogether, a few small self-help groups for these political offenders began to emerge at the end of the 1940s and gave rise to the first post-war organization, the Stichting Oud Politieke Deliquenten (SOPD). The organization had to tread a very fine line—ostensibly confining itself largely to charitable work—but such preoccupations did not prevent it being banned in 1952 as dangerous to public order under the legislation for the dissolution of treasonable organizations. Certainly some of its members saw its outward manifestations as a cloak for an increased political activity. The SOPD championed the idea of a rest home for invalid SS men—to be called the 'Anton Mussert Home'—and also planned a remembrance ceremony at Ysselstein, the major German war cemetery in the Netherlands, during November 1952. All these plans met with storms of protest and a flurry of parliamentary questions. It was also possible, although never confirmed, that SOPD activists masterminded the escape of seven Dutch war criminals from Breda jail on Boxing Day 1952.[2]

In early 1953, the jurist Jan Aksel Wolthuis and bank clerk Jan Hartman, both of whom had been active in the SOPD, then teamed up with a former SS man, Paul van Tienen, to create a formal political party, the Nationaal Europese Sociale

---

[2] These Dutch war criminals included Herbertus Bikker (b. 1916), Klaas Karel Faber (b. 1922), Sander Borgers (1917–85), Toon Soetebier (b. 1921), and three others who had all been members of the Waffen SS and convicted of various offences in post-war trials. They were spirited across the German border on the day of their escape where those still alive remain.

Beweging (NESB), as a national manifestation of the international fascist organization the European Social Movement, created by Per Engdahl in Malmö in 1951. It drew its support from the usual suspects, former SOPD adherents and ex-NSB or SS members, together with ideologues such as Arnold Meijer and the fascist priest Wouter Lutkie. However, its open political programme was designed to distance the movement from charges that it was just a reinvention of the NSB and SOPD. Much Nazi terminology was rephrased in an attempt to make it seem innocuous, but there were many elements of fascism in its programme, not least an espousal of corporatist ideas. In spite of this attempted cloaking, the authorities soon targeted the organization as merely a continuation of the banned NSB and its leaders were arrested. Initially limited to short prison terms, these penalties were then overturned by higher Amsterdam courts, on the grounds that the leader-principle and racism that were central to NSB ideology were nowhere present in that of the NESB. Referred back to courts in The Hague, the original sentences were reaffirmed, but the time taken meant that the defendants had already served their sentences. Although not a definitive ban on all fascist activity, the Dutch authorities' reaction to the NESB in the mid-1950s showed that there was no general tolerance for political movements that espoused ideas close to traditional fascism or National Socialism.

From then until 1963, there were no further open manifestations of fascism in politics, although organizations such as the Hulp aan invalide oud-Oostfronts-trijders, nabestaanden, politieke gevangenen e.a. (HINAG; Help for Former Eastern Front Soldiers, Relatives, Political Prisoners, etc.), ostensibly concerned solely with the welfare of former SS, NSB, and other fascist movements' members, continued to exist. The HINAG contained many former SOPD and NESB members, and there was a tension between those who were politically oriented and those purely concerned with social matters. Prompted by the political wing, the organization occasionally organized demonstrations or gatecrashed remembrance ceremonies in the later 1950s, but such activity was almost invariably confronted and dispersed by a large police presence. Some activists were peripherally involved in the creation of a federation of far right groups, the Nationaal Oppositie Unie (National Union of Opposition). This body consisted of very small parties, groupings, and even individuals, and professed not to be fascist. It gained only 0.34 per cent of the vote in the 1956 general elections. Again the traditional patterns of voter allegiance and abhorrence for radical right-wing alternatives prevented any form of breakthrough.

In the 1960s, men such as van Tienen continued their activities on the very margins of politics. Other groups emerged, such as the Noordbond (Northern League), which had links to the British fascist Colin Jordan and espoused the so-called 'Detmold Programme' that opposed 'coloureds, Jews, the clergy and the established democratic order'. Its politics were clear and its following limited, but the same could not be said of a rather different political phenomenon that came to prominence in the 1960s. This was the Boerenpartij (BP; Farmers' Party) created by Hendrik Koekoek. Established in 1958, the party had little success until the general election of 1963 when it garnered 2.1 per cent of the popular vote and three seats in the Dutch Second Chamber. The reasons for its success were complex but centred on the discontent among small farmers whose livelihoods were threatened by government policies—a factor that was highlighted in Koekoek's former home region where a number had refused to pay land taxes and had been evicted from their properties as a result. There was also a possibility that people with right-wing predilections finally saw a party that represented their interests and also had a political future. The party reached its peak in 1966–7 with 6.7 per cent of the vote in provincial elections and 8.8 per cent in the local elections. It also took more than 10 per cent of the vote in Amsterdam, thus showing that its appeal extended way beyond the ranks of discontented farmers. The general election of 1967 saw a 4.7 per cent poll, enough for a gain of four seats to a total of seven.

There is no doubt that the BP was ideologically on the far right, but its fascist credentials are more difficult to determine. Its nationalism and traditional peasant (*Bauerntum*) ideology marked it out as such, but any form of overt racism was missing from its pronouncements. Its success led to a scramble for candidates to fill its electoral lists, a process that led to the party's absorption of many figures with dubious political pasts. Even its long-standing members did not always stand close scrutiny. Hendrik Adams, who was appointed to a BP seat in the First Chamber in 1966, was soon forced to resign when it was revealed that he had written for the anti-Semitic journal *De Misthoorn* during the occupation and had threatened others with deportation. Koekoek tried to defend his nominee—playing down the journal articles and reasserting that Adams had never been a member of the NSB. What he failed to say was that he had been a member of the much more radical NSNAP! Further investigations unmasked other BP functionaries and representatives as former collaborators and members of NSB organizations. The BP supposedly purged itself in the months that followed but it lost support, and although Koekoek maintained a sufficient kernel of sympathy in his own locality to keep his seat in the Second Chamber, the focus of radical right and fascist politics moved elsewhere.

Opposition to foreigners, and specifically to *gastarbeiders*, began to be an issue from the early 1970s. Some resentment to immigration from the West Indian colonies had been evident since the later 1950s, but the increasing numbers of Surinamers together with *gastarbeiders* from Turkey, Morocco, and Yugoslavia in the major cities sparked increasing racial tension and an issue for far right politicians to exploit. The Partij Nieuw Rechts (PNR) led by Max Lewin attempted to gain a seat on Amsterdam City Council in 1974 under the slogan 'Amsterdam free of foreign taints'. At the same time, the Nederlandse Volk-Unie (NVU) stood in The Hague on a platform that 'The Hague should stay white and secure'. Lewin soon disappeared from public life, accused but not convicted of both being an East

German agent and planning a bomb attack on a metro station in the newly built social housing Amsterdam suburb of Bijlmermeer. Conversely, the NVU became the first in a series of extreme right-wing and ostensibly racist political parties that existed on the margins of Dutch political life beyond the end of the twentieth century. Although adopting or adapting many of the outward manifestations of former fascist organizations, these new formations were led by people too young to have had a Nazi past tainted by collaboration but were motivated by new causes and enthused by the success of the BP in highlighting a potential right-wing constituency.

The NVU was formed in March 1971 with the pan-Flemish activist Guus Looij as Secretary. He had contact with members of the Noordbond such as Jan Kruls and Joop Glimmerveen, and also with Florentine, the widow of Rost van Tonningen who acted as a sort of icon for far right groups. Initially Glimmerveen did not join the party as he thought it reactionary and a refuge for former NSB members, but he changed his mind later in the year, explaining that the NVU was the only party that concerned itself with the threats to the 'biological survival' of the Dutch people. In the interim, the NVU presented itself as a nationalist, pan-Netherlandish, and anti-communist movement. It sought to distance itself from earlier fascist movements by using the camouflage of having younger elements in the leadership while the older, and potentially less reputable, 'old fighters' stayed in the background. In spite of this, the movement was riven by organizational and ideological disputes. In 1972, Glimmerveen had become party propaganda chief and saw an opportunity for practical political action during racial tensions in parts of inner-city Rotterdam in August of that year by distributing pamphlets against the admission and continued residence of ethnic minorities in the Netherlands. By 1973, some of the founders of the NVU had been forced out and former NSB men such as Bernard Postma took centre stage. There was some debate about whether the party should stand in democratic elections, but its financial penury meant that it could not afford the deposits required for the 1974 provincial elections, and even local election nominations could not be funded. Glimmerveen was asked by elements within the party to stand in The Hague and agree to use his own money for the necessary deposit.

His campaign was based on extensive leafleting, highlighting the presence of immigrants from the Dutch West Indies in the city as employment and welfare parasites. Demands from mainstream parties for the NVU to be banned and the arrest of Glimmerveen himself on account of the contents of his election leaflets did not prevent him receiving nearly 4,000 votes, only 200 short of winning a seat on the council. In spite of his failure, he became a hero within the party and rapidly eclipsed Postma, becoming leader in the same year. The party ultimately avoided being banned because it had not financially supported Glimmerveen's campaign. It re-emerged in 1976 during riots in Schiedam, near Rotterdam, after a young Dutchman had been murdered by a Turk. The party moved in, spreading inflammatory racist leaflets, although its role in prompting the riots remains unproven. Increasingly the NVU adopted some traditional fascist trappings; Glimmerveen was now the 'leader', Mussert and Rost van Tonningen were seen as precursors and innocent of war crimes, and the party also adopted the runic script used by the SS. This increased NVU radicalism was reflected in the party's propaganda leading up to the 1977 general elections. Attempts by the left to persuade the government to ban it were unsuccessful—as was the party itself, polling just 33,343 votes nationally. Glimmerveen blamed this result on a lack of funds and manpower, and increasingly portrayed the NVU as a movement to save the 'white Germanic peoples'. Later he was also to publish an encomium to Adolf Hitler, praising him as a genial politician, great military leader, and economist. His followers meanwhile continued to voice racist opinions and slogans, most notably at a meeting at Soestduinen in 1979, for which three were subsequently arrested and condemned.

In the 1970s, the NVU became the focus for most fascist and National Socialist opinion in the Netherlands, exploiting existing racial tensions in inner-city areas and also playing heavily on white fears of further 'floods' of *gastarbeiders* and West Indian immigration. Its electoral success was minimal, although successive governments were shy of using the laws on treasonable political organizations against the NVU itself. An attempt to invoke the law in early 1978 misfired when a ban imposed by the Amsterdam courts was overturned by the High Court, but only after the party had been excluded from that year's local elections. Thus the authorities generally preferred to take action only against individuals. This line was probably prompted by worries that banning parties made the political culture look intolerant and undemocratic, and might also provide even more publicity for a movement that posed little direct political threat, but could nevertheless exploit and exacerbate local unrest.

To some degree this policy bore fruit as the party failed miserably in the 1981 general election, garnering only 10,522 votes. Glimmerveen resigned, only to rejoin the party later. In the interim, he was indicted by the courts for distributing racist and anti-Semitic literature, resulting in fines, and later a period in jail. His autocratic style, tolerating no opposition to his leadership, inevitably led to resignations and expulsions from the party. By 1980, it was estimated that the NVU had as many former members as actual members, and it was former members who were to establish the most notable political alternative to the NVU: the Centrumpartei (CP). Its founder, Frits Brookman, had been an NVU member for a short time, and had tried to create a separate political party in 1979, but this was undermined by extremists. His line was that the Dutch government was pursuing a form of apartheid, but one that discriminated against the (white) majority. Thus the influx of immigrants was creating a breakdown of society and posing a threat to Dutch culture. His new party was to created to oppose this trend, but within the rules of parliamentary democracy and human rights. Brookman was soon marginalized when forced to choose between his job and political activity by his employers, the Free University in Amsterdam. He was replaced as leader by Hans Janmaat, a former director of a furniture company and, at that time, a lecturer in social sciences, and someone untainted by an NVU past. Attempts to publicize the new party though the press led to its meetings being disrupted by the anti-fascist and anti-racist organizations set up to counter the NVU in the 1970s. In the elections of 1981, the party received only 0.1 per cent of the popular vote and there was much press debate whether parties such as the NVU and CP should be allowed to make political broadcasts on radio and television. As the NVU's star waned and Glimmerveen went his own way, the CP was able to stand in all eighteen electoral districts in the 1982 elections, obtain access to party political broadcasts, and ultimately gain 0.8 per cent of the poll (68,386 votes), mopping up most of the former NVU voters along the way. This total was enough to give Janmaat a seat in the Second Chamber.

This breakthrough for what was widely regarded as fascism was hotly debated in the Netherlands. Blame was laid on the tensions between white and non-white elements in the major cities, on the economic recession, and on the failures of the mainstream political parties. There was a mass demonstration when Janmaat took his parliamentary seat in The Hague and he was attacked in the street in late December 1982. A bomb at the Ajax football stadium the following January was initially blamed on one Ton Hoogduin, who had been Janmaat's bodyguard. The CP leader quickly distanced himself and his party from Hoogduin, although he was later to be cleared. This apparent brush with serious violence did the CP no harm and opinion surveys suggested that it was gaining popularity among a young (white) male constituency. Some four months later, six men were shot dead in a café in Delft by a Dutch-naturalized Turk who had been baited by one of them, saying that he might have Dutch nationality but he could never be a Hollander. The CP was able to use this killing, and its own increased public profile, to portray itself as a party of resistance to immigration whose support was growing. Social problems were to be met with more draconian laws and greater police powers, and the central issue of immigration was to be dealt with by a hermetic sealing of the country's borders. Anti-discrimination laws were to be swept away to stop the oppression of the Dutch people while ideas on strengthening family and milieu were also promoted.

The CP lost some elements from its activist elements when Glimmerveen rejoined the NVU, but the party achieved another remarkable result in local elections in Almere in 1983. This was a new commuter town built on reclaimed land near Amsterdam. Here the CP gained 9 per cent of the vote and two council seats, apparently receiving support mainly from white residents rehoused from the old quarters of Amsterdam. It was estimated that this percentage would translate into at least four parliamentary seats at a general election, a figure that might increase still further. There was further violence when the two councillors took their seats, only for one of them to renounce his CP membership a month later. Bernard Fresco, a self-styled 'Christian Jew', condemned the party as containing many former SS members, people who wanted to solve the problem of overpopulation with compulsory abortion and sterilization, but who were going to start with the foreigners. This attack was a major disaster for the CP as the condemnation was coming from one who had been inside the party machine, but it did not prevent a further breakthrough in Rotterdam in April when the CP won over 8 per cent of the vote in three wards and gained seven seats—and it would have been eight if the party had put up enough candidates. Its activists were again targeted and one was kidnapped and tied to a block of concrete daubed with the word 'racist'. He had to be freed by the fire brigade.

From 1984, the CP was riven by disputes. The arguments centred on the future direction of the party if it was to go on growing and become a 'fourth current' in Dutch politics. Some activists wanted the party to become even more radical in its stance, while others, like Janmaat, realized that a more obviously fascist stance would damage the party and result in a ban. There were also problems for many party supporters: at work, at home and among their families and friends. They had to decide whether to continue support for their party in spite of the obstacles placed in their way. The result was Janmaat being excluded from a new party executive and his creation of a new party, the Centrumdemocraten (CD). By the mid-1980s the politics of the extreme right consisted of Janmaat's CD that had taken some elements from the CP, a rump CP, the remains of the NVU, and a circle around Florentine Rost van Tonningen. All were committed to a strong nationalist stance with more-or-less racist overtones. All contained elements that advocated the use of violence, although for reasons of political expediency this was often played down. Likewise, the CP cloaked its links with old-style fascist groups, portraying former NSB, NESB, or NVU members merely as activists or advisers rather than members. However, the attempted respectability of all these right-wing political fractions was damaged by real or alleged links to avowed fascists and National Socialists from previous eras. Alongside these political groupings there was also a plethora of loosely defined youth movements—not necessarily linked to a specific party or leader, but nevertheless providing support and sometimes the main protagonists in direct actions against perceived enemies. These movements brought on a new generation of adherents to the cause such as Stewart Mordaunt and Nico Konst. It was also a member of one of these groups who carried out the brutal murder of an Antillean youth, Kerwin Duijnmeijer, in Amsterdam in 1983.

Although a revised version of the CP continued to win sufficient votes in local and municipal elections to return one or two councillors, a breakaway Centrumpartij '86 split its constituency. Janmaat also lost his seat in the Second Chamber in 1986, but regained it in 1989 with 0.9 per cent of the vote in the 1989 general election. There was less public protest at his election this time, and his success was seen as an echo of right-wing successes elsewhere in Europe; the Front National in France and the Republikaner in Germany to name but two. Domestically, he benefited from a lack of competition to his leadership and from support from former CP voters who had forgotten the mid-decade internal party bloodletting, but not the presence of immigrant minorities in their midst. After 1990, the CD held council seats in a number of major municipalities, as did the CP'86, with Stewart Mordaunt holding a seat in The Hague. As in previous times, closer investigation of some of the less well-known CD and CP'86 candidates revealed that they had extremist credentials.

It could be argued that all these radical right-wing movements that emerged in the 1970s and 1980s were essentially from the same fascist stable—and often the products of the same leadership cadres and memberships. Their public policies and statements were moderated and conditioned by the need to avoid judicial action against the parties and their leadership. In this tactic, the NVU and the outspoken Glimmerveen had been less successful than Janmaat and the CP/CD, although both attempted to balance on the same tightrope. Support came primarily from disaffected sections of the white populations in older inner-city areas of the major cities, the populations who saw themselves as most threatened by increasing levels of immigration through the last quarter of the twentieth century. Thus, during the 1990s, the CD and CP'86 (renamed the Nationale Volkspartij (NVP) in 1994) continued to garner a degree of electoral support although combined party membership was thought to number no more than 1,500 in the mid-1990s and activists to be limited to around 150 individuals. The impact of these parties holding council seats in many municipalities was stifled by internal political infighting and the fact that many of their representatives failed to attend meetings—or take up their seats at all.

Outside the ambit of the political parties, a number of extreme right fringe movements emerged. These include the Aktiefront Nationaal Socialisten (ANS) founded in 1995 by Eite Homan and the Jongeren Front Nederland '94 (JFN'94) led by Constant Kusters. Both were openly racist and anti-Semitic, and together their leaders persuaded a retired Glimmerveen to return to a revitalized NVU in the later 1990s, although they were to fall out again by 2000. The NVU attempted to strengthen its position through closer links with German and Belgian neo-Nazi groups and among certain disaffected sections of the youth population. This was done through the promotion of a particular form of 'skinhead' culture and through the music of neo-Nazi bands. Others were drawn in through the so-called 'gabber' house music. It may have had up to 10,000 adherents, of whom perhaps 10 per cent were overtly racist and a few drawn into extreme right-wing political activism.

These movements, together with the NVU and CD, survive to the present day, but their position on the extreme right of Dutch politics was undermined and then swamped by a completely different political movement that emerged from inner-city Rotterdam in the late 1990s. The Leefbaar Rotterdam (LR) movement arose from popular discontent about the sheer number of immigrants in the city and the stresses their presence placed on municipal, educational, and welfare provisions. Traditionally Rotterdam had been a stronghold for the social democratic Partij van de Arbeid (Labour), but the disaffection in the city that had been manifest for many years through limited support for the NVU and CD finally erupted when a more respectable alternative came on the scene. It came in the form of Leefbaar Nederland, a political party led by the charismatic and media-wise Pim Fortuyn.

His new movement benefited from popular disaffection with mainstream political parties and specifically from the political vacuum at the head of the Partij van de Arbeid created by the resignation of party leader Wim Kok. It was also able to exploit the general unease about increasing globalization and the threats thereby posed to many sections of Dutch society, and the feeling of crisis that followed the events of 11 September in the United States. Immigrants in the country were inevitably a major issue, and Fortuyn was outspoken in his need for a halt to further influxes because the Netherlands was now full. This posture harked back to the line taken by extremists like Glimmerveen and Janmaat, but Fortuyn was careful in how he explained the matter. Foreigners *per se* were not the problem, but their lack of assimilation into Dutch society was, and continued adherence to a 'backward' and reactionary Islamic culture by so many of the country's immigrants represented a threat to the Netherlands and its traditions. He even went so far as to call for the repeal of article 1 of the constitution that outlawed discrimination. This outspoken line saw his expulsion from Leefbaar Nederland, but he stood as a candidate for LR in the 2002 municipal elections, and his presence completely overturned the political landscape in the city when LR won 17 of the 45 council seats. For the spring general election that year he produced his own electoral list, the Lijst Pim Fortuyn (LPF), but was assassinated nine days before the poll. His assassin was a militant ecologist, Volkert van der Graaf, who claimed that he had shot Fortuyn because of his views on Islam. A combination of the political momentum built up by Fortuyn before the election coupled with an element of sympathy voting brought the LPF 26 parliamentary seats, making it the second largest party behind the Christian Democrats. Deprived of its leader the party nonetheless formed a new coalition government with the Christian Democrats under Jan Peter Balkenende, but its lack of organization and political experience soon led to fragmentation and the cabinet lasted only eighty-six days.

Can this latest manifestation of right-wing politics be described as fascist? There is no doubt that some support from the LPF came from the constituencies that had traditionally cast their votes for the NVU and CD, but these were nowhere near numerous enough to explain the massive electoral breakthrough that Fortuyn achieved. His message was far more subtle than overt racism or anti-immigrant, as he argued forcefully that race was not the issue, but assimilation. To reinforce the point, he nominated non-white candidates for local government positions and employed many in his party machine. His use of the media and of personality politics—and the fact that he effectively *was* the LPF—does have some overtones of fascism, as does the appeal to a form of Dutch cultural nationalism. His castigation of the decadence and misrule of the political classes and the bureaucratic mandarins in having promoted the multicultural experiment for their own ends could also have been taken from the fascist handbook. However, flamboyantly dressed and openly gay, the image he portrayed was far from that of a traditional dictator. Even his stance on immigration was prompted by the threat that multiculturalism posed to the many legislative gains that had been made in the Netherlands in relation to the emancipation of women and homosexuals. Thus his line was one of a liberal looking to protect existing freedoms from an increasing minority that refused to assimilate or be tolerant of the dominant, but clearly threatened, Dutch culture.

When fascism first appeared in Europe in the 1920s and 1930s, its appeal in the Netherlands was limited by existing allegiances based on ideology or confession, and by its image as a foreign or imported ideology. This seems to have been continued during the period 1940–5 when the increasing association of National Socialist movements with the German occupiers tended to lose them support from people who put Dutch interests first. The legacy of the war, including the tragic fate of Jews in the Netherlands, and the rebuilding of a post-war liberal-democratic political consensus effectively prevented any legal manifestations of fascism appearing. Welfare organizations for 'old fighters' were soon banned if they put their heads above the political parapet, and in any case they gained only minimal electoral support. New manifestations appeared in the 1960s with the first major examples of disaffection towards the consensus 'polder model' of Dutch politics, in the form of the Boerenpartij. Born of genuine rural discontent, it also garnered support from disaffected voters in the major cities. However, it was only in the 1970s that overtly racist parties begin to appear, bedecked with some of the trappings of their National Socialist antecedents. Their appeal remained limited and their press coverage probably far out of proportion to any real threat that they posed. Over time, they recruited a growing constituency from inner-city areas and from certain sections of disaffected young people, but suffered from continual arguments and fragmentation among the leaderships. Moreover, none of the aspiring mini-*Führers* could be described as particularly charismatic and they were largely denied access to the mainstream media to get their message across. Only with the arrival of Fortuyn could one argue that such a leader had emerged, but his ideology was far from the traditional fascism of the 1920s and 1930s, being centred on a form of media-based populism that highlighted a need for cultural nationalism. While Fortuyn did not live long enough to champion his ideas in coalition government, the subsequent four years have perhaps shown why fascism and radical politics have seldom made much of a long-term impact in the Netherlands. The fragmentation of the LPF after the murder of its leader was symptomatic of a problem that beset most radical right organizations—namely the propensity to quarrel and the unattractiveness of most of its leaders. Moreover, the actions of the Balkenende coalition in taking a much harder line on immigration and other social problems suggest that the political mainstream has responded to popular disaffection by stealing the ideological clothes of the protesters and incorporating them into its own legislative programmes. In this way consensus has been restored by a shift in government policy and in thinking. Whereas the multicultural model had been promoted, or at least assumed, by politicians anxious to solve problems associated with decolonization and labour shortage since the 1960s, this has now effectively been abandoned and replaced by a debate on how 'Dutchness' and Dutch culture should be defined in the future.

BIBLIOGRAPHY

BOUW, C., DONSELAAR, J. VAN, and NELISSEN, C. (eds), *De Nederlandse Volks-Unie: portret van een racistische splinterpartij* (Bussum: Het Wereldvenster, 1981).

DONSELAAR, J. VAN, 'Fout na de Oorlog: Fascist and Racist Organizations in the Netherlands 1950–1990' (Proefschrift, Rijksuniversiteit Leiden, 1991).

HANSEN, E., 'Fascism and Nazism in the Netherlands 1929–1939', *European Studies Review*, 11 (1981), 355–85.

HIRSCHFELD, G., *Nazi Rule and Dutch Collaboration: The Netherlands under German Occupation, 1940–1945* (Oxford: Berg, 1988).

HOLSTEYN, J. VAN, and MUDDE, C. (eds), *Extreem-Rechts in Nederland* (The Hague: SDU, 1998).

JONG, L. DE, *Het Koninkrijk der Nederlanden in de Tweede Wereldoorlog*, i: *Voorspel* (The Hague: Staatsuitgeverij, 1969).

KOSSMANN, E. A., *The Low Countries 1780–1940* (Oxford: Oxford University Press, 1978).

WARMBRUNN, W., *The Dutch under German Occupation, 1940–1945* (Stanford, CA: Stanford University Press, 1963).

CHAPTER 25

....

BELGIUM

....

BRUNO DE WEVER

I. INTRODUCTION

....

ON the eve of the First World War, Belgium boasted a long tradition of stable civil democracy.[1] Between the two wars, however, its government was challenged by fascist movements, which nevertheless did not succeed in destabilizing the country. In that respect, fascism in Belgium developed in a similar way to that in other West European democracies. It also had specific characteristics because of the nationality conflict between the (Dutch-speaking) Flemish and the (French-speaking) Walloons and the people of Brussels.

Belgian liberal democracy and its nation state came under the pressure of two movements that were at odds with Belgian society as it developed after the First World War. The two 'challengers' of the Belgian government got in each other's way and partially neutralized each other.

In the first place, there was a reactionary Catholic and French-speaking Belgian nationalist movement that could not resign itself to the increased power of anticlerical and left-wing political forces in general, and of the socialist labour movement in particular. In the 1920s, this movement came under the influence of Action Française and Italian Fascism. In the 1930s, it led to a right-wing populist movement that was successfully won over by the democratic government. During the Second World War, a hard core entered into collaboration with National Socialist occupying forces.

[1] The best general reading on Belgian political history is E. Witte, J. Craeybeckx, and A. Meynen, *Political History of Belgium from 1830 onwards* (Antwerp: Standaard Uitgeverij, 2000).

In the second place, there was a Flemish nationalist movement that was looking for confrontation with the Belgian state. In the 1930s, this movement was strongly influenced by German National Socialism and, during the Second World War, it collaborated closely with the Nazi occupiers.

II. Maurras and Mussolini in French-Speaking Belgium in the 1920s

The introduction of general plural suffrage (for men) in 1893–4 increased tenfold the number of Belgian voters. However, the plural voting right accorded owners of property and capital one or two additional votes. The result was that the Belgian Socialist Party (BWP) remained far from the majority it needed to change the system. The power of the Catholic Party, which was supported to a large extent by the conservative establishment, was not affected. On the eve of the First World War, massive strikes occurred for the introduction of the one man, one vote, system. During the First World War, the socialists joined the Belgian *union sacreé* in order to defend the fatherland against the German invader. The chairman of the party was included in a government of national unity. Already during the war the government agreed to introduce universal suffrage after the war, and meeting the main socialist demands such as the right to strike was considered as unavoidable. On Armistice Day King Albert I brought together the top politicians in his military headquarters at Loppem. The head of state announced the immediate introduction of the universal one man, one vote, voting right without the required constitutional revision having been approved.

The national elections (1919) brought a landslide. The BWP became as large as the Catholic Party, which lost its absolute majority after thirty years. This led to an existential crisis among Catholic conservative politicians, some of whom were never to stomach the '*coup d'état*' at Loppem. They thus placed themselves outside the new Belgian compromise democracy that was accepted by leading politicians from all parties.

The political frustration of the Catholic conservatives was based on nationalist rancour. Although 'poor little Belgium' emerged from the war victorious, at the negotiations in Versailles it received little compensation. A Comité de Politique Nationale arose, demanding annexations at the expense of Germany, the Netherlands, and Luxembourg. The most striking figure was the young Catholic lawyer Pierre Nothomb, with his call for a Belgian '*Renaissance nationale*', to be realized by a 'united party'. In 1924, Nothomb founded the Action Nationale, presenting itself as a right-wing authoritarian alternative to the Catholic Party.

Its anti-democratic and anti-parliamentary ideas were further expressed in the Brussels daily *Vingtième Siècle*, the weekly *Revue catholiques des idées et des faits*, and *Pour l'autorité*, a magazine that called itself the think-tank of the Catholic Party. Such journals openly sympathized with Mussolini and Italian fascism, but primarily they acknowledged the conservative royalism of Charles Maurras. This body of thought also attracted the French-speaking, Belgian nationalist veterans' organizations that wanted to continue the war against such 'internal enemies' as socialism and the Flemish movement.

The most important group was the Légion Nationale (1922), which was headed by lawyer and Mussolini-admirer Paul Hoornaert. Hoornaert worked with Nothomb until the latter switched to the Catholic Party in 1927, and the Action Nationale was dissolved. Hoornaert did not want to join a parliamentary party, expanding his militia on the Italian model to 7,000 members in the early 1930s. As Belgian nationalists, Hoornaert and his organization were very anti-German. They also condemned the Flemish movement, which they considered a German fifth column and a danger for the Belgian fatherland.

III. FLEMISH NATIONALISM IN THE 1920S BETWEEN DEMOCRACY AND AUTHORITARIAN TEMPTATION

When Belgium became an independent state in 1830, French was the only recognized language and was used by the elite throughout the country. A 'Flemish movement' developed, demanding equal rights and giving birth to a Flemish sub-nation. In 1914, the Flemish movement shared in the nationalist fervour and the indignation about the German invasion. However, the supposition that a thankful Belgian fatherland would honour the pro-Flemish lamentations soon faded in the face of harsh reality. In the army, many pro-Flemish soldiers faced 'Frenchification' from the active francophone elite. In response a Flemish nationalist Front Movement was founded demanding 'Home Rule' for Flanders.[2] German occupation did stimulate some collaboration from Flemish elements, and their 'disloyal' behaviour was recalled after the war as an excuse to block reform.

In 1919 the Frontpartij (Front Party), a Flemish nationalist group with 'Home Rule' as its main programme, came into being. Initially it placed its trust in the democratic government but that trust soon faded. The fact that the Front Party

---

[2] On Flemish nationalism in the First World War: S. De Schaepdrijver, *La Belgique et la Première Guerre Mondiale* (New York: Peter Lang, 2004).

acquired only limited electoral support (5.2 per cent in 1919; 6 per cent in 1925 of the Flemish electorate and so 3 per cent nationally) played a part, while Belgian governments at first refused to implement the 'Dutchification' of Flanders under pressure of the French-speaking conservatives. Yet a new social broadening of the Flemish movement could not prevent the estrangement of Flemish nationalism from democracy.

Joris Van Severen played a major part in this process.[3] Van Severen originated from a French-speaking environment in Flanders but, nevertheless, as a non-commissioned officer on the IJzer front, he was involved in pro-Flemish agitation in the army in 1916. His political commitment cost him disciplinary sanctions and degradation. In 1919 he was elected to parliament for the Front Party, then being impressed by the Bolshevik Revolution and professing a vague internationalism. But Van Severen was fundamentally influenced by French Catholic late romanticism and, from 1922, this stance evolved into Catholic integralism. Van Severen broke with the pluralist Front Party and in 1925 founded the Katholiek Vlaams Nationaal Verbond (Catholic Flemish National Union), focused on the doctrine of Maurras and enthusing about Mussolini and Gabriele D'Annunzio.

In this attitude, Van Severen was still relatively isolated from his party members. However, a number of Flemish-minded clergy joined him defining the Flemish people as totally Catholic. The weekly *Jong Dietschland* (1927–33) became the chief vehicle of this pro-fascist line.

In 1926 Van Severen moved in the direction of a pan-Dutch nationalism where the reunion of Flanders and the Netherlands (*Dietsland*) was formulated as the final aim of the Flemish movement. It did not matter that it was impossible to achieve this revolutionary goal via the parliamentary route. On the contrary, Van Severen proclaimed that his revolutionary policy should be led by an armed militia.

When he was not re-elected in 1929, he founded the Verbond van Dietse Nationaal Solidaristen (*Verdinaso*; Union of Pan Dutch National Solidarists) in 1931. It was a political group with a militia at its centre. Van Severen preached that politics depended on an ideologically educated and militarily organized group who blindly followed the leader's commands. As a matter of principle he rejected political parties and parliamentarianism because they divided the people. Parliament must be replaced by a corporate body. A pan-Dutch state was the national aim.

With these extreme views, Van Severen unleashed an ideological crisis in Flemish nationalism. His pan-Dutch nationalism and his version of a fascist New Order were applauded, but they were also contested. One prominent figure in the debate was the Flemish nationalist chief from Gent, Hendrik Elias, to be the Flemish

---

[3] The best synthesis on Van Severen and his political organizationsis R. Vanlandschoot, 'Verbond van Dietse Nationaal Solidaristen', in R. De Schryver and B. De Wever (eds), *Nieuwe Encyclopedie van de Vlaamse Beweging* (Tielt: Lannoo, 1998), 3192–204.

national socialist leader in the Second World War. Educated as a historian, Elias stayed in Rome from 1926 to 1927 at the Istituto Storico Belga (Belgian Historical Institute). There he learned for the moment that fascist dictatorship was a threat to human dignity.

His warnings did not prevent pro-fascist ideals from gaining support, especially among Catholic Flemish nationalist youth and school and university students. Very soon Verdinaso had several thousand members. Van Severen inspected his troops at martial rallies, modelled on those of the NSDAP at Nuremberg. Verdinaso also adopted the anti-Semitic rhetoric of National Socialism. Positive articles about National Socialism appeared in the Verdinaso press, although Van Severen himself kept a distance from *völkische* ideology, preferring to cite Maurras and Italian Fascism.

However, the *völkisch* nature of National Socialism with its Nordic German mythology was attractive to many young Flemish nationalists. The Flemish people were conceived as a transcendental phenomenon with its own immutable character-istics, and the *völkische* Flemish nationalists saw themselves as the new aristocracy who must lead the 'People' (with a capital 'p') in a battle of liberation against the decadent democracy of the misguided and individualist bourgeoisie on the one hand, and the anti-nationalist collectivism of the labour movement on the other. The 'People' were substituted for the sovereign nation and 'Freedom' (also with a capital 'f') for democracy. The increasing popularity of these national socialist ideas was facilitated because a number of Flemish nationalist collaborators who had emi-grated to Germany after the First World War had become active in the NSDAP. They now encouraged contacts and an influx of propaganda. The German *Flamenpolitik* (Flemish policy) from the war was endorsed by the Nazis and nationalists saluted it as an aide against French-speaking Belgium, seen as an appendage to decadent republican France.

When Hitler seized power in 1933, Flemish nationalists had the wind in their sails. Around that time, the economic crisis came to a head and many were convinced that the government could not deal with it. When the Flemish nationalists did badly in the national elections in 1932, many lost faith in the democratic system. It was a paradox that this happened when their movement had gained important parlia-mentary success, since, from 1930, major language laws recognized and safeguarded the Dutch-speaking character of Flanders. But extremists rejected such matters as a betrayal of the Flemish people. Flemish independence, and/or the longer-term political union of Flanders and the Netherlands, became the only acceptable aim.

In April 1933, the former Flemish nationalist member of parliament (1919–32) Staf De Clercq founded the Vlaams Nationaal Verbond (VNV; Flemish National League). It was a new Flemish nationalist party that ousted the Front Party, in disarray ideologically. VNV moved Flemish nationalism closer to the fascist new order.

IV. In the Shadow of Hitler
and Mussolini: VNV, Verdinaso,
and Léon Degrelle during the 1930s

The foundation charter of VNV broke with parliamentary democracy. Political parties and trade unions had to disappear and parliament was to be replaced by a corporative system. The VNV had an authoritarian leader and a Board of Leadership who ordered their followers to 'conscript' the Flemish people into the movement to educate them to Flemish and pan-Dutch nation awareness. The party organized a militia with 'political soldiers', who were represented in the propaganda as the core of the movement, and, from 1935, there was to be a strictly organized rally in martial style. The VNV thus displayed much similarity to Verdinaso but differed on one essential point. VNV participated in democracy, believing parliamentary action could be a propaganda tool and so concealing that VNV was a conglomerate of fascists and more moderate critics of the existing system. Leader Staf De Clercq's image emphasized his centrality to the movement rather than evoking 'enlightenment' in the way that Van Severen did. But VNV outshone Verdinaso precisely because of the hybrid nature of the movement and its leader. The regional Flemish nationalist party organizations from the Front Party and their mandatories joined. In 1935, the party already had 10,000 members. Radical youngsters found an attractive role model in Reimond Tollenaere, the propaganda leader appointed by De Clercq, who was just as enthusiastic about German National Socialism and wanted to model the VNV on it.

Van Severen and Verdinaso therefore confronted competition from VNV just as they were hit by the Belgian government's prohibition of militias in July 1934. These two factors accelerated Van Severen's ideological drift, with his seeking rapprochement with the Belgian state when announcing in 1934 that his aim was the restoration of the Burgundian Netherlands to which the Walloons belonged as romanized pan-Dutch. Verdinaso spread into Wallonia, talking about a national solidarist revolution for the whole country. Not the Belgian state but the democratic regime was the enemy. Now Verdinaso marched behind a Belgian flag and publicly revered King Leopold III. As a result of this new line, Van Severen was joined by some conservative Belgian Catholics but he lost his Flemish nationalist supporters, most of whom switched to the VNV.

The VNV did well in the national election of 1936. Compared with 1932, it doubled its members of parliament. Flemish nationalists gained 13.6 per cent of the regional electorate (7.1 per cent nationally). That tally was still far from a majority but it did convince the radical wing that De Clercq was using the right strategy on the road to seizing power, as Hitler had demonstrated in Germany, while the moderate wing was satisfied with their increased numbers. Soon, however, internal tensions precipitated a crisis.

The revelation of the national elections in 1936 was Léon Degrelle, who acquired 11.5 per cent of the votes with Rex, a party founded in 1935. Rex entered the Belgian parliament with 21 members (out of 202). Degrelle had not offered himself for election, but, with his rhetorical flair, he was undoubtedly the person who brought about the success. However, the deeper causes of Rex's prominence have to be looked for in divergent factors.

A first issue was the profound crisis that the Catholic Party was experiencing. Degrelle, who originated from a small Walloon town, belonged to the generation of young Catholics who, under the influence of Catholic Action (CA), dreamed of a Catholic revival of society. He studied law—a course he did not finish— at the Catholic University in Leuven. Mgr. Louis Picard, who, as founder of the Association Catholique de le Jeunesse Belge (ACJB; Belgian Catholic Youth Association), was one of the people who inspired CA in Belgium, appointed him head of Éditions Rex, a CA publishing company. In 1933 the dynamic Degrelle took full control over it, expanding it into becoming the political headquarters of a movement that denounced the failure of the Catholic Party and thus played on the deep dissension among Belgian Catholics. The roots of the crisis lay in the conservative groups' loss of power through the emergence of the Christian workers' movement and the Boerenbond (Farmers' Union). The Catholic Party was reduced to squabbling groups lacking a consensus about the party programme and leadership. It was mainly the church with its apparatus and moral authority that kept the party together. CA produced divergent and sometimes paradoxical effects in this context. On the one hand, it stimulated reconfessionalization; on the other, it ensured social broadening of the Catholic Party. In Flanders, CA stimulated the expansion of Christian Democratic mass organizations as a dam against socialism; in the more highly deconfessionalized Wallonia, CA ended up in such conservative organizations as the ACJB that opposed Christian Democracy. They were greatly inspired by the encyclical *Quadragesimo anno*, which they viewed as a plea for an authoritarian corporatism to replace parliamentary democracy.

A second factor was the economic crisis and its political ramifications. As a country dependent on exports, Belgium was harshly afflicted by the crash of 1929. The nadir came in 1934 with 800,000 unemployed, half not being insured. Belgian retail trade reflected decreased spending power, resulting in many bankruptcies. Tradesmen's associations sprang up making radical demands with populist arguments against the alleged 'money wall' of banks and high finance. When the Belgian government, composed of the three traditional parties (Catholics, liberals, and socialists), decided to devalue the currency by 28 per cent in 1935, this step fostered the conviction that the government was sparing the banks, but not the man in the street. The notion caught on everywhere, especially among radicalized Catholics, who used it to attack democracy. One of the most active critics was the conservative

Catholic politician Paul Crockaert. Degrelle enthusiastically backed his campaign against the 'banksters' and thus ended up in politics. On 1 May 1935, the 29-year-old neophyte held his first big meeting, thereby gaining the reputation of public orator and demagogue.

Degrelle exploited real or imagined financial scandals and in so doing aimed his most poisonous arrows at the chiefs of the Catholic Party, with the intention of taking the lead himself. However, it came to a breach, after which Degrelle founded Rex, his own party, which he took to the national elections in 1936 with an incoherent programme that was a mixture of Catholic moralism and Poujade-style public enticement. Its medley attracted many voters.

The elections resulted in defeat for the government parties. Particularly the Catholic Party took severe blows with a loss of 200,000 voters or 10 per cent of its electorate, so that the Belgian socialists became the biggest party. The gains on the right went completely to Rex and VNV. On the left, the Communist Party trebled its seats to nine, enhancing the fear that a leftist government was nigh, a nightmare increased by the installation of Léon Blum's Front Populaire (Popular Front) in France. Moreover, soon after the elections, there was a large strike to put pressure on the government to take social measures. Such events convinced many that a confrontation between 'left' and 'right' could no longer be avoided. News about the Spanish Civil War, which broke out in 1936, confirmed the picture.

Degrelle used this climate to deliver a fresh blow to the newly formed government, once again a tripartite alliance of the traditional parties. To the surprise of friend and foe it became known that Rex and VNV had concluded a secret agreement on 6 October 1936. Degrelle consciously leaked the news a few days after signing, because he wanted to heighten the political tension. Soon, he announced a 'march of 250,000 Rexists' to Brussels, with a grandiloquence that elevated him to being the Belgian Mussolini. The 'March' proved a false step, however.

Furthermore, the secret agreement with VNV had been a miscalculation. Degrelle had only been able to achieve it by making great concessions, including the regionalization of Belgium and the absorption of Rexist organizations in Flanders, where Rex had won 72,000 votes or 7 per cent. Degrelle accepted this loss in the conviction that a Rexist revolution would wipe out VNV with the other parties. Yet, it was a blunder, since the mainly French-speaking Rex voters thought that an agreement with anti-Belgian Flemish nationalists was incompatible with their Belgian patriotism. Furthermore, the government parties started an offensive against Rex. The demonstration in Brussels was prohibited and only a handful of Rexists followed Degrelle's instructions to muster, a failure that damaged Degrelle's image as tribune of the people and underlined that Rex was incapable of revolutionary non-parliamentary action.

Now Degrelle tried the parliamentary route. In early 1937 he ordered a Brussels Rexist MP to resign from parliament so that he himself could be the candidate and provoke a showdown. The government responded by pushing forward the Prime Minister, Van Zeeland, a Catholic with a technocratic image, as the opposing candidate from the three traditional parties. Degrelle was supported only by the VNV, but a number of Catholic newspapers adopted a neutral position and some conservative Catholics openly attacked Van Zeeland in parliament. In the last days of the campaign Degrelle made the mistake of boasting that he had the silent support of the church. The Archbishop of Brussels reacted promptly with a pastoral letter in which Rex was called 'a threat to the country and the Church'. Degrelle thus lost many Catholic voters, and his fate was sealed with his obtaining only 19 per cent of the votes against 76 per cent for Van Zeeland. Rex's ability to split Catholics and threaten the national democratic system was eliminated. In the 1939 elections Rex won only 4.4 per cent. Most of its supporters returned to the Catholic Party, while a rump evolved with Degrelle to open fascism.

Yet VNV still divided Catholics. On the Flemish side, the idea of formation of a front on the basis of a right-wing anti-democratic programme was closely connected with a movement within the Catholic Party that advocated the regionalization of Belgium. The weekly *Nieuw Vlaanderen* (New Flanders), where prominent Flemish-minded Catholics and professors from the Catholic University in Leuven cooperated, promoted a merger between a Flemish Catholic Party and VNV as a *Vlaamse Concentratie* (Flemish Concentration). Moderate leaders within VNV fell in with this approach.

The announcement of the agreement between Rex and the VNV in October 1936 was the direct spur for the regionalization of the Catholic Party. Immediately after the accord was announced, the movement broke into a Flemish and a French-speaking party. The Catholic Flemish People's Party (CFP)—as the Flemish element was to be called—immediately entered negotiations with FLN and achieved a deal at the end of 1936 which stated that a joint party would not be established on a confessional basis but agreed that members recognized the Catholic character of the Flemish people and 'the great value of the Catholic religion'. In the political field, a corporative regime was proposed in line with the papal encyclicals, while retaining an elected parliament for 'purely political' matters. As regards the national issue, a statute was requested for Flanders with retention of a Belgian federal state.

The accord, however, remained a dead letter, being immediately contested by the Catholic side and VNV. In the CFP, opposition arose from the Christian Democratic wing and the Christian trade unions on the one hand, and from the Church on the other. In VNV, the fascist faction rejected the accord as discreditable horse trading. Staf De Clercq put it most vividly: 'We must have the courage to be masters on our own. We are Flanders, comrades and that's it! That is right! We have the courage to be that alone and we also have the stubborn will to bring the others up to our standard, but not to lower our standard.'[4] This stance meant that along-term agreement between CFP and VNV was out of the question.

---

[4] Centre for Historical Research and Documentation War and Contemporary Society (Brussels), Documents of the Belgian Military Courts, 931, Speech of Staf De Clercq, 13 February 1937.

Given the failure of the Flemish Concentration, the fascist trend in VNV accelerated with the power of De Clercq enhanced. A cult was built around his personality
and the party programme prescribed that he was the personification of VNV. All
authority in the party came from him and the party leadership appointed by him.
'The leader thinks, the followers act', VNV propaganda proclaimed. To the outside
world, De Clercq played his part as authoritarian leader. Inside the movement, he
remained rather the mediator between the various wings in his party. At decisive
moments he lent support to the fascist element, favouring the expansion of a
uniformed militia with 'political soldiers'. On his orders, on 6 March 1938 several
hundred uniformed VNV members carried out a raid on Enghien, a small town on
the language border, where they brawled with French-speaking inhabitants. This
raid was also a political statement. De Clercq wanted to take the lead in the Flemish
movement through 'revolutionary actions'. Yet such events remained exceptional
because De Clercq was aware that a collision with the Belgian regime would destroy
VNV. Militants were told that they had to prepare for the impending revolution that
would result in the pan-Dutch people's state. They were imbued with the idea that
they were the elite of the 'real' Flanders and that their opponents in the other parties
were 'traitors to the People'. Particularly the socialists were excoriated as the lackeys
of communism and international 'Jewry'. From 1936, VNV propaganda contained
much anti-Semitism, without being explicitly racist.

In the 1939 elections, VNV won 15 per cent of the Flemish electorate (8.3 per cent
nationally). Unlike Rex, VNV therefore had slightly increased its support. However,
in the electoral contest, the party had blunted the sharpest edges of its programme.
It also put some popular independent candidates on the lists. In comparison with
Rex, VNV was better organized. The party could boast experienced cadres, old
hands in twenty years of Flemish nationalist political action. In 1939 it had 25,000
members, one-third of them being secret. So the party could take pride in having
supporters who remained hidden from the outside world. Flemish nationalism gave
the party a link with the Flemish movement as well and therefore with a broad
current of opinion in Flanders. In the 1938 local elections, joint lists with Catholics
were presented in several hundred communes. The rank and file retained hope in a
right-wing 'Flemish Concentration'.

Nationally, there was still talk of VNV as a Nazi fifth column but the relationship
between VNV and Germany was ambiguous. Officially the party supported the
end of the military alliance between Belgium and France in 1936, proclaiming that
no Flemish blood should be shed for French interests. In many senses, therefore,
VNV played into the hands of Nazi Germany. However, this line was backed by the
majority of the Belgian political elite and public opinion. Even when it dawned on
the public after the Czechoslovakia crisis that the threat of war came from Germany,
VNV propaganda continued to label France the major warmonger. The official
VNV viewpoint was: 'Un-frenchified, un-germanified. Whoever attacks us is the
enemy.'

In secret, De Clercq and some radical friends opened negotiations with agents of the Abwehr without the knowledge of more moderate party chiefs. De Clercq was forced into negotiations because the German secret service had acquired financial control of *Volk en Staat* (People and State), the only daily that was supposed to be a VNV periodical but in fact was headed by independent editors. *Volk en Staat* extolled National Socialism to such an extent that it endangered the official line. Especially the conflict between the Nazi regime and the Catholic Church was a sore point for many VNV sympathizers but *Volk en Staat* and radical Nazi-minded VNV leaders exploited the matter to their own ends being supported by the German Sicherheitsdienst. De Clercq convinced the Abwehr that a more moderate attitude would benefit VNV's credibility and that a strong VNV would be in Germany's interest. He declared that he was expanding a secret VNV organization in the Belgian army, which, in the event of war, would only obey his commands. Such an organization did exist, albeit in embryonic form. It is not certain whether the VNV leader consciously wanted to form a 'fifth column' and he probably preferred a Flemish nationalist Front Movement as in the First World War. But the fact that the members had to be prepared to execute any order from De Clercq, even desertion and sabotage, is significant and explains why Abwehr was interested. Belgian security forces were partially informed of these plans. In 1940, a publishing ban was imposed on *Volk en Staat* and various VNV leaders were pursued as elements dangerous to the state. During the occupation, De Clercq tried to cash in on his secret policy by claiming that the VNV had played a major role in the collapse of the Belgian army after the German invasion.

Léon Degrelle similarly sought contact with foreign fascist organizations. In 1936–7, he rejoiced in considerable financial support from Mussolini. Degrelle also went to Germany. In late September 1936, Degrelle had a discussion with Hitler without it leading to anything concrete. There were to be other contacts between Rexists and high Nazi officials. In early 1940, Degrelle asked Germany for financial support for the needy Rexist press. With its hyper-neutralist attitude, Rex played into the hands of the Nazis. Neither Degrelle himself nor the majority of his supporters was yet a pro-Nazi. But there could be at least the impression and therefore political opponents exploited the issue. Like VNV, Rex was deemed a German 'fifth column' in the periodicals of the traditional parties. It made impossible any cooperation between Rex and the hyper-Belgian nationalist Légion Nationale. Meanwhile, in its style and attitudes, Rex increasingly mimicked a fascist organization and thus drew further away from the Catholic electorate that had once given it such massive support.

Whereas in 1936 a quarter of the Belgian voters had voted for extremist parties, the three traditional parties were able to attract more than 80 per cent of the voters in the last elections before German occupation. In this regard there was no internal fascist threat for the Belgian regime. However, criticism of mass democracy and parliamentary government was also alive within the traditional parties. The

Catholic Party was especially marked by it, but in the Socialist Party, too, Hendrik De Man with his '*socialisme national*' sketched an 'authoritarian democracy'. The Belgian head of state, King Leopold III, who succeeded his prematurely deceased father Albert I in 1934, shared the opinion that democratic government could not cope with current problems. The king tried to play a greater part as head of the executive power over the parties, convinced that a more authoritarian state was a necessity. He probed the limits of his constitutionally defined power but remained a constitutional sovereign. The French-speaking and Belgian fascist groups Rex, Légion Nationale, and Verdinaso all made overtures to the king, but to no avail. The anti-Belgian Flemish nationalist VNV, by contrast, was not impeded by devotion to the Belgian Crown and the Belgian fatherland.

V. Flemish and Walloon National Socialists during the German Occupation, 1940–1944

When the Germans invaded on 10 May 1940, the police and security forces arrested thousands of Belgians and foreigners suspected of belonging to a 'fifth column'. Among those held were Degrelle and Van Severen. The two were taken to France where, on 20 May, Van Severen was murdered by French soldiers as an alleged German spy. Staf De Clercq was not arrested but his secret organization in the Belgian army was rounded up. The only acts of sabotage were committed by German secret agents and by Belgians in German service, some being members of minuscule pro-Nazi groups that had no political impact.

On 28 May 1940, the Belgian army capitulated on the orders of King Leopold III who, like his father at the IJzer front, was in supreme command. Since the king refused to follow his government to France in order to remain 'at the head of his troops' in the occupied country, a severe constitutional problem arose. As every-where else in occupied Europe, a curious situation developed in the months after the German victory, when the elites seriously reckoned with a Nazi final victory or a compromise peace. From that point of view, a modus vivendi with Berlin was sought. In Belgium this policy crystallized around King Leopold III, who again tried to play a part behind the scenes, although constitutionally it was impossible for him to govern. He sought contact with the occupier, meeting Hitler on 19 November 1940 after mediation by his sister Marie-José, who was married to the Italian Crown Prince. However, Leopold's schemes came to nothing since Hitler rejected royal political ambitions. Many Belgian politicians were equally disappointed. Hendrik

De Man, who, as chairman of the Belgian socialists, had announced the end of the democratic era on 28 June 1940, pushed things furthest. He disbanded his party trade union, aiming for a corporative transformation of society under the Belgian Crown. Like many others he was sidetracked because Hitler was not interested in retaining an independent Belgium, preferring annexation in the long term, although not yet saying so. For the time being, no statements were permitted on the political fate of Belgium. With this in mind Hitler installed a Military Government without a political mandate.[5]

The Belgian fascist groups held very varying positions in the first months of the occupation. Some were accepted as privileged partners of the occupier, while others were banned.

Because of the death of its leader, Verdinaso fragmented into divergent factions. One hoped for a place in an authoritarian Belgian regime led by King Leopold III. In July 1940 a short-lived agreement in that regard was concluded with the Légion Nationale. Another faction was involved in the birth of the Flemish SS, founded, under Nazi auspices, in August 1940 as a Greater German group. A third element negotiated with VNV and, in May 1941, the military government compelled it to be absorbed by the latter. Some members demurred with a minority evolving to armed resistance.

At the end of August 1940, the occupier banned the Légion Nationale. In June 1941, Hoornaert and part of his grassroots joined instead the Légion Belge, a far right-wing resistance group founded by former members of Rex. Hoornaert was arrested in 1942 and put in a German concentration camp, where he died of deprivation on 2 February 1944.

Léon Degrelle meanwhile was again restless.[6] The Rex leader saw himself in a prominent role in a Belgian government headed by the King, but with Degrelle as the strong man. On 9 July 1940, he founded the Formations de Combat (Combat Formations), a new militia. Many Rexists thought that their time had come. Degrelle negotiated with De Man and endeavoured in vain to talk with Leopold III. However, Degrelle did not get any support from the military government, which currently viewed him as a political charlatan and Rex as a 'clerical-fascist' movement. Moreover, Degrelle was hampered by one of the few political instructions that Hitler gave his soldiers. On 14 July 1940 he ordered that the Flemish had to be supported as much as possible, while the Walloons should not be given any privileges. This led to a new *Flamenpolitik* (Flemish policy) that turned VNV into the Germans' privileged partner.

[5] J. Gérard-Libois and J. Gotovitch, *L'An 40: la Belgique occupée* (Brussels: CRISP, 1971); J. Velaers and H. Van Goethem, *Leopold III: de Koning, het Land, de Oorlog* (Tielt: Lannoo, 1994).

[6] On Rex during the occupation: M. Conway, *Collaboration in Belgium* (New Haven: Yale University Press, 1993), 21–253; A. Colignon, 'Collaboration francophone: autopsie post portem', in J. Gotovitch and C. Kesteloot (eds), *Collaboration, répression: un passé qui résiste* (Brussels: Labor, 2002).

Staf De Clercq already had contact with Abwehr agents in the last days before the Belgian capitulation and, on 3 June 1940, he offered his party's cooperation to the military government. It was made clear to him that nothing should be decided yet concerning the future of Belgium and that therefore VNV had to surrender its pan-Dutch ambitions. For the same reason, VNV was not allowed to position itself as the Flemish National Socialist united party. Nevertheless, from September 1940 articles were published in the VNV press where National Socialism was propagated as the VNV ideological core. In particular, propaganda leader Reimond Tollenaere, who had admired National Socialism even before the war, made efforts to familiarize VNV members with Nazi ideology. It appeared that it was not difficult to convince them, since for many the pre-war ideology was being continued. Only the relationship with the faith and the Catholic Church was a tricky problem. De Clercq stated that Flemish National Socialism would be Christian, but at the same time he settled scores with 'political Catholicism'.

Anti-Semitism, of which the VNV had not been free even before the war, now acquired new legitimacy. The Jew had to be removed from the 'healthy people's body'. More novel was the statement that the Flemish people's body had to be safeguarded from Walloon blood. Simultaneously, the 'depopulated' Walloon area was claimed as *Lebensraum* for the Flemish people, who were blessed with many children. De Clercq was convinced that the '*Führer* of the German people, whom we recognize as the Leader of all Germans, will put an end to the fate that our people have been burdened with for 300 years: the draining of German blood into southern, Latin veins'.[7] In this way, the VNV leader gave a *völkische* content to Flemish nationalism. He also made VNV back the notion of the formation of a Greater German empire, of which Flanders would be an independent part. He had to remain silent about the pan-Dutch aim, but it lived on among many VNV militants. Within these outlines, in his first public speech under occupation, on 10 November 1940, De Clercq proclaimed unconditional cooperation with Germany, based on blind faith in Adolf Hitler.

The reasoning behind the VNV leader's enthusiasm lay in the foundation of the Flemish SS, a militia with black uniforms modelled on the German Algemeine-SS. The organization was patronized by *Reichsführer-SS* Heinrich Himmler, who wanted to use it to infiltrate the territory of the military government.[8] The Flemish SS presented itself as a Greater German movement that would bring *Heim ins Reich* (home into the empire) to Flanders. It opposed the 'provincial' and 'clerical' VNV. The group attracted some VNV and Verdinasco radicals and especially members from small Nazi groups that had sprung up before the war. Its base was weak but

[7] Centre for Historical Research and Documentation War and Contemporary Society (Brussels), Documents of the Belgian Military Courts, 943, Speech of Staf De Clercq, 23 February 1943.

[8] On the policy of the SS in Belgium see A. De Jonghe, 'De strijd Himmler-Reeder om de benoeming van een HSSPF (1942–1944)', *Bijdragen tot de geschiedenis van de Tweede Wereldoorlog*, 3–8 (1974–84).

the VNV leaders understood that the Flemish SS enjoyed high-level support. It was also understood by the military government, for whom the SS infiltration was a threat and who therefore vigorously continued cooperation with VNV by involving its supporters in the country's administration.

Thousands of VNV members manned Belgian government bodies from the highest to the lowest level. The party was thereby able to attract new sympathizers, so that its membership grew to 50,000 in 1941. The fact that VNV could avail itself of a pool of competent administrators was appreciated by the military occupation regime. The presence of VNV in local councils was important. In 1943, the party administered half of Flemish communes, a situation favoured by the appointment of VNV member Gerard Romsée as Secretary General of the Ministry of the Interior in April 1941. VNV members were also massively present in the new structures and organizations, along the same lines as the German regime, controlling the economy, employment, and provisioning. Thus VNV co-governed the Belgian state, which it wanted to destroy, and was an important executor of the unpopular occupation policy.

In May 1941 VNV renamed itself Eenheidsbeweging-VNV (Unity Movement—VNV), after it absorbed the Flemish segments of Rex, as well as the rump of Verdinaso, with the approval of the occupier. In propaganda the forced merger was represented as a forerunner of a Flemish National Socialist unity party which, with the shining example of the NSDAP in mind, would endow the Flemish with their own National Socialist state. The fact that increasingly Flemish people signalled that they did not like that future did not prompt reflection or adjustment.

In exchange for its new prominence, VNV had to support the German war effort. In April 1941, Reimond Tollenaere started a recruitment campaign for the Waffen SS, which did not prove very successful. Visceral war with the Soviet Union nonetheless entailed the foundation of an anti-Bolshevik Flemish Legion and of further paramilitary and military formations in Belgium.[9]

The conflict in the east also stirred Degrelle into new action. In autumn 1940, Degrelle had moved closer to the fascist model and had made it no secret that he wanted to win over the occupier. Energy was mainly put into the expansion of a Rex militia, the Formations de Combat, which at the end of 1940 numbered 4,000 militants in black uniforms. On New Year's Day 1941, Rex's preparedness to collaborate was symbolically settled when, in the party newspaper, Degrelle ended a pro-German article with 'Heil Hitler'. Just like VNV leader Staf De Clercq a month and a half before, Degrelle put his fate into the hands of the *Führer*. His followers found this choice harder to swallow than De Clercq's legions had. Once more many Rexists left the party. The assimilation of Rex-Flanders by the VNV, demanded by the occupier, had exposed how weak Degrelle's power was.

[9] On military collaboration in Belgium see B. De Wever, 'Military Collaboration in Belgium', in W. Benz, J. Houwink ten Cate, and G. Otto (eds), *Die Bürokratie der Okkupation: Strukturen der Herrschaft und Verwaltung im besetzten Europa* (Berlin: Metropol, 1998), 153–72.

With Barbarossa Degrelle received permission to establish a Walloon anti-Bolshevik legion. Thereafter, he staked everything on his military subservience. Degrelle joined the German army as a normal soldier and passed the interim leadership of Rex to Victor Matthijs. The latter was able to increase the followers of Rex to around 15,000 members in 1942, notably because Rexists were then made eligible for administrative positions. The input of Rexists on the eastern front, and in particular the propaganda exploitation of the military adventures of Degrelle himself, had increased the political credibility of Rex in the eyes of the German rulers. The relationship between Rex and Romsée also improved. But Rex found suitable candidates for government jobs with difficulty because the movement, unlike VNV, had few competent administrators in its ranks. Besides, because of the progress of the war, it became more difficult to find prepared candidates. Much more commonly than VNV members in Flanders Rexist authorities ran the risk of being murdered by the Resistance. From 1943, the party faced an exodus, with members by the end of the year numbering only 8,000, of whom less than a thousand were members of the Formations de Combats.

For Degrelle military action was all that counted, so that great pressure was put on young militants to commit themselves to military collaboration. Thus he himself was responsible for the further weakening of the Rexist position at home. Degrelle had united Rex's fate with his personal career, even at the cost of his last followers with any political weight.

As early as autumn 1942, Degrelle prepared an approach to the SS. He wanted to move the Walloon Legion from the Wehrmacht to the Waffen SS in order to gain more prestige. On 25 October 1942 at a Rexist meeting in Brussels, Matthijs pronounced that the Walloons were a German people. Some days later, Hitler, probably aware of such theoretics, called Degrelle 'der einzig wirklich brauchbare Belgier' (the only really accommodating Belgian). After he began talks with the SS, on 17 January 1943 Degrelle, in front of thousands of followers at the Brussels sports palace, announced that Wallonia was coming home to the German Reich. His latest twist did not convince many. Moderate Rexists now left the party. The few small Great German groups that existed in Wallonia at that time, such as Amis du Grand Reich Allemand (Friends of the Great-German Empire) and the Communauté Culturelle Wallonne (Walloon Cultural Community), could not compensate for the loss.

The collapse of Rex on the home front did not worry Degrelle. The conditions had been met to integrate 'his' Legion into the Waffen SS, with the establishment in mid-1943 of the SS-Sturmbrigade Wallonien. At the end of the year, the unit engaged in a spectacularly bloody escape from siege by the Red Army, a propaganda gift from heaven for Degrelle, who had taken part in the combat personally. On 20 February 1944, he received high military decoration from Hitler's hands and thus became the only important Belgian collaborator who could enjoy being received by the *Führer* himself. Degrelle, who had meanwhile been promoted

SS-Sturmbannführer (major), was allowed to march at the head of 'his' brigade in a parade through Brussels. By the unconditional commitment of himself and his movement to the German war effort, the *Chef* of the Rexists persuaded Hitler to consecrate him leader of the Walloon Greater German movement and *Volksteil*.

The VNV leader did not get such recognition. Since VNV had connected its fate with the will and therefore the decision of Hitler, it could only wait and urge for a clear endorsement of a Flemish state. However, it became increasingly clear that Berlin supported the Greater German movement.

The SS had decided in 1942 to launch the Duits-Vlaamse Arbeidsgemeenschap (DeVlag; German-Flemish Labour Community) as political competitor.[10] DeVlag had existed before occupation as a German-Flemish cultural association with hundreds of members, mainly active in literature and at universities. Under the impulse of the Flemish chairman, Jef Van de Wiele, and some German members who were active in the SS, DeVlag secretly became part of the SS complex in the spring of 1941. DeVlag acted as a political umbrella organization with the task of forming a German nationalist alternative to VNV. The Flemish SS continued to exist as the unofficial militia of DeVlag. The two organizations were headed by Himmler's personal representative in Brussels. Moreover, Gottlob Berger, head of the SS-Hauptamt, became *Präsident* of DeVlag, so that the bond with the SS was made official.

VNV, which initially lent support to the 'cultural' DeVlag, now forbade its executives (June 1943) and then its members (October) to remain in its ranks. VNV now defined itself as a dam against Germanization and as a defender of Flemish interests. That line led to great confusion. The defence of the Flemish interest actually consisted in enhanced subservience to the occupier and, in other words, to a greater zeal in destroying Flemish civil society and a fuller exploitation of the Flemish people for the German war effort. VNV members were put under pressure to report for military service because their commitment would be an expression of the desire for power by VNV and therefore, in National Socialist logic, become vital for safeguarding the Flemish state.

Very soon the paradoxes grew so great that the VNV lost any ability to expand. Whatever VNV leaders promised, 'Berlin' gave no political help. Hendrik Elias, who, after the death of De Clercq, became leader of the party, tried both negotiations and threats. In August 1943 he discontinued cooperation with the SS, but he did not leave any doubt that the VNV would retain its collaborative policy in all fields. At the same time, the battle between VNV and DeVlag was part of a greater struggle for power at a high level of the Third Reich between the army and the Party.

---

[10] On DeVlag see F. Seberechts, *Geschiedenis van de DeVlag: van cultuurbeweging tot politieke partij 1933–1945* (Gent: Perspectief Uitgaven, 1991).

In these circumstances, the Flemish nationalist collaboration slowly but surely became stuck in the political quicksand even if VNV still had 10,000 members on the eve of the liberation, generally executives and members of (para-)military formations. By then, VNV and DeVlag members had degenerated into a small, hated, and beleaguered minority on whom the guilt for the years of extreme wartime misery was pinned. Collaborators became increasingly embattled with civil society in Flanders. Many hundreds of militants or presumed followers were murdered by the Resistance. VNV members in administrative positions or collaborators in uniformed service were special targets for the 'terrorist' actions of the Resistance.

On 12 July 1944, Hitler belatedly installed a new civil administration, the Zivilverwaltung, in Belgium, split between a Reichsgau Flandern and a Reichsgau Wallonien under a German *Reichskommissar*. The Greater German organizations DeVlag and Rex were now officially recognized as expressions of the National Socialist unity of the Flemish and Walloons respectively. VNV was dissolved.

Soon after, in September 1944, the Allies arrived. Before and during the liberation, 15,000 Flemish and 10,000 Walloon collaborators and members of their families fled to the Reich with which they had merged their political fate. In autumn 1944, DeVlag and Rex each formed a so-called *Landsleiding* (Country Leadership) acting as governments in exile of the Flemish and Walloons respectively. In December 1944, Jef Van de Wiele and Léon Degrelle were separately received by the German Minister of Foreign Affairs, and in the German press it was announced that they were the leaders of the Flemish and Walloon 'liberation committees'.

Such an event lacked serious political significance because Belgium was safe from German recapture. With the outbreak of peace, the accomplices of the Nazi occupier were sentenced by military courts. Rex disappeared forever from the political scene. The party found no fertile ground in post-war Belgian society. For VNV the situation was somewhat different. Flemish nationalism soon flourished again and gave continuity to VNV, although the Flemish nationalist party that was refounded in 1954 unambiguously embraced parliamentary democracy. However, an undercurrent of post-war Flemish nationalism did not renounce VNV thought and is an explanation for the revival of right-wing Flemish nationalism during the 1980s and after. In the 2004 national elections, the extreme right-wing Vlaams Belang (Flemish Interest) won 24.1 per cent of the poll in Flanders.[11] Its key nowadays is xenophobia, but it accepts democratic procedure, so that it cannot be called (neo-)fascist. For the moment, those tangled elements who flirted with a Nazifascist new order between the wars have no clear heirs in Belgium.

---

[11] On Vlaams Belang see M. Swyngedouw, 'The Extreme Right in Belgium: Of a Non-existent Front National and an Omnipresent Vlaams Blok', in H. G. Betz and S. Immerfall (eds), *The New Politics of the Right: Neo-Populist Parties and Movements in Established Democracies* (New York: St Martin's Press, 1988), 59–75; L. Vos, 'The Extreme Right in Post War Belgium: From Nostalgia to Building for the Future', in S. U. Larsen and B. Hagtvet (eds), *Modern Europe after Fascism* (New York: Columbia University Press, 1998), 344–88.

BIBLIOGRAPHY

BOEHME, O., *De revolutie van rechts en intellectuelen in Vlaanderen tijdens het interbellum* (Leuven: Acco, 1999).

CONWAY, M., *Collaboration in Belgium: Léon Degrelle and the Rexist Movement 1940–1944* (New Haven: Yale University Press, 1993).

—— 'Building the Christian City: Catholics and Politics in Inter-war Francophone Belgium', *Past and Present*, 128 (1990).

DEFOORT, E., *Charles Maurras en de Action Française in België* (Nijmegen: Orion, 1978).

De l'avant à l'après-guerre: l'extrême droite en Belgique francophone (Brussels: De Boeck, 1994).

DE WEVER, B., *Greep naar de macht: Vlaams-nationalisme en Nieuwe Orde. Het VNV 1933–1945* (Tielt: Lannoo, 1994).

ÉTIENNE, J.-M., *Le Mouvement rexiste jusqu'en 1940* (Paris: Armand Collin, 1968).

GERARD, E., with the cooperation of Verleden, F., *De democratie gedroomd, begrensd en ondermijnd 1918–1939*, Nieuwe Geschiedenis van België 2 (Tielt: Lannoo, 2006).

VAN HAVER, G., *Katholieken in Vlaanderen tussen Demokratie en fascisme 1929–1940* (Berchem: EPO, 1983).

CHAPTER 26

....

BRITAIN AND ITS
EMPIRE

....

MARTIN PUGH

TRADITIONALLY fascism in Britain has been seen in fairly narrow terms as a phenomenon of the 1930s associated with Sir Oswald Mosley and the British Union of
Fascists (BUF). This approach to the subject made it easy to account for the fortunes
of fascism as a movement essentially marginal to British society and thus of limited
significance. It seemed doubtful whether Mosley, admittedly the one outstanding
leader thrown up by fascism, was ever capable of turning it into a serious contender
for power. Regarded as an opportunistic and unstable politician who rose rapidly
through the Conservative and Labour parties during the 1920s, he resigned too
hastily after serving as a junior minister in Ramsay MacDonald's government in
1929–30. A brief flirtation with the New Party led Mosley to humiliation at the
general election of 1931, but the experience accelerated his migration to fascism.
Using upper-class 'Biff Boys' recruited by the England rugby captain, Peter Howard,
and working-class 'stewards' led by Ted 'Kid' Lewis, a former welterweight boxing
champion from the East End, the New Party countered the violent attacks by Communist and Labour supporters who regarded Mosley as a traitor. 'Tom [Mosley]
says this forces us to be fascist' commented Mosley's associate Harold Nicolson MP.[1]

After a visit to Italy in January 1932 Mosley felt ready to commit himself to the
new course. He calculated that the National government was no more likely to solve
the problem of unemployment than its hapless predecessors; having seen both main

---

[1] H. Nicolson, *Diaries and Letters*, i: *1933–1939* (London: Weidenfeld and Nicolson, 1966),
21 September 1931.

parties at close hand he thought them ineffectual, unpatriotic, and intellectually bankrupt. In this situation, committing himself to the BUF was not such a risk; all over Europe parliamentary regimes were giving way to authoritarian ones, leaving Britain and France increasingly out of step. During the summer of 1932 Mosley drew up an impressive manifesto, *The Greater Britain*, prior to the launch of the BUF on 1 October. From the outset the BUF boasted a paramilitary organization. Mosley justified this on the grounds that without it he would be denied a platform and driven off the streets by the left; and in the longer run, as society descended towards chaos, the middle class would increasingly appreciate a movement organized to defend it from disorder and communism.

After a slow start the BUF began to grow rapidly when it attracted subsidies from Mussolini in 1933, enabling it to employ a large staff and publish several journals. It achieved a dramatic breakthrough during the first six months of 1934 when Lord Rothermere used his newspapers, the *Daily Mail* and the *Sunday Dispatch*, to support it and publicize its activities. An audience of 9,000 attended Mosley's Albert Hall rally in April. By June the organization claimed nearly 500 branches and around 40,000 members apparently largely drawn from Conservatives who felt disillusioned However, the bubble burst at the notorious Olympia Rally where 12,000 people, including large numbers of MPs and society figures, witnessed fascist methods at first hand. The violence meted out to hecklers by the blackshirt stewards provoked a wave of criticism by right-wing politicians and journals. 'At this stage in our political evolution we certainly have no need of private armies marching about in exotic costumes and under exotic names', pronounced the *Morning Post*, arguably the most right-wing national newspaper.[2] Olympia was thought to have opened people's eyes to the real character of the BUF and thus alienated 'respectable' opinion drawn to the movement by the *Daily Mail*'s campaign. Deeply rooted British beliefs in parliamentary democracy, respect for law, and freedom of speech now reasserted themselves, leaving the fascists permanently marginalized. The passage of the Public Order Act in 1936 completed the process by banning political uniforms and quasi-military organizations, giving the police more control over marches, and making it illegal for people attending public meetings to carry offensive weapons or to use abusive, insulting, or threatening language. During 1935–7 Mosley's movement compounded the reputation already earned for extremism and violence by concentrating on an anti-Semitic campaign in the East End of London which culminated in the battle of Cable Street in October 1936. This helped to discredit fascism by putting it in the context of continental fascism during the later 1930s when Jewish refugees were fleeing persecution from the Nazis. After 1939 the BUF's opposition to the war with Germany damned it in the eyes of almost all British people. In May 1940 Churchill's Coalition government introduced new regulations to detain over 700 fascists, including Mosley, though they were released in stages

---

[2] *Morning Post*, 3 May 1934.

during 1942–3. By that time Mosley and his movement had been so comprehensively discredited as to pose no real threat to the war effort.

The topic of British fascism rested at this point until the publication in 1975 of Robert Skidelsky's biography of Mosley forced scholars to take it more seriously. By examining the evolution of Mosley's ideas Skidelsky demonstrated that fascism involved far more than crude propaganda and one-track anti-Semitism. On the contrary, by the early 1930s he offered a programme at least comparable with any-thing put forward by the conventional parties in Britain and more considered than the proposals of either Mussolini or Hitler before coming into power. In particular, Mosley's combination of Keynesian policy for stimulating the economy and corpo-ratist proposals designed to protect workers from the ravages of capitalism made a constructive and compelling alternative solution for the problems of the depression to that of the conventional politicians. This was a crucial part of Mosley's appeal as a fascist. Moreover, insofar as Mosley fitted into the Keynesian framework, the more, by implication, he and his movement were part of the political mainstream of inter-war Britain rather than merely marginal and extremist.

Skidelsky's book also began to change explanations for fascism by charting the process that led a typical upper-class youth via the army and the First World War into conventional politics and eventually to fascism. It was otherwise tempting to dismiss support for fascism as an expression of individual psychology, as an irrational response by people of a certain mentality. This approach was clearly inadequate and implausible. The striking thing about Mosley was how long it took him to become a fascist after first entering parliament in 1918 until the formation of the BUF in 1932. It was not some imaginary fascist mentality but the experiences and pressures of wartime and post-war Britain that led him along the road to fascism; moreover, this was far from unusual, for many of his contemporaries travelled some way along the same path even if they did not all reach the same conclusion.

Subsequent studies of lesser-known fascists such as A. K. Chesterton and William Joyce have suggested a common explanatory framework. Men like Chesterton who had experience working in the empire for lengthy periods often developed extreme racist and xenophobic views which were not uncommon there; then on returning to Britain they were shocked to discover that the homeland had become a more liberal and democratic society during their absence. Feeling betrayed and marginalized they easily succumbed to conspiracy theses that portrayed Britain as the target of plots by German, Jewish, Irish, or Bolshevik elements attempting to destroy the empire and promote disruption at home. The war heightened such obsessions and seemed to offer proof in the shape of the Russian Revolution, followed by the publication of *The Protocols of the Elders of Zion* (1920), the Zinoviev Letter in 1924, and the General Strike in 1926. William Joyce's fascism developed from his early life in a loyalist community in Ireland at a time when the Liberal government in London was determined to grant Home Rule to the Irish Nationalists. Inevitably Joyce was outraged by the settlement of 1921 which partitioned Ireland and ended the

Union. The betrayal seemed proof of the moral decay afflicting the heart of British political life even among Conservative politicians. Like many other imperialists Joyce interpreted the loss of Ireland as the first step towards the dismemberment of the British empire. This was the mental framework for many British fascists between the wars—one they shared with large sections of British society.

Despite its impact Skidelsky's biography represented too great a challenge to conventional British assumptions, including British academic thinking, to be entirely acceptable. Critics thought he had been too sympathetic towards Mosley and his movement. Some felt he had exaggerated the Keynesian element in Mosley's thinking. Others argued that he had played down the anti-Semitism and portrayed fascists as the victims of violence rather than simply as the instigators of it. Although Skidelsky subsequently modified his original views, this did not detract from the importance of his book as a corrective to usual assumptions and as a means of opening up British fascism as a serious field of study.

For many years the chief restraint on scholars was the shortage of primary sources; in particular they were hindered by the withholding of official documents for fear of embarrassing well-connected people who had been associated with inter-war fascism. However, recent years have seen the release of quantities of material at the Public Record Office. Yet as many of these files originate with the Metropolitan Police and the Home Office they tend to reinforce the existing bias in assumptions about fascism in Britain. They focus on the paramilitary organization, on anti-Semitism, on urban fascism and the opposition to it, on the violence and the complaints made by MPs about it, and on the intelligence gathered by Special Branch and MI5 about internal splits and rivalries within the movement. Though very useful, this has helped to maintain a narrow picture of fascism as a law-and-order problem concentrated in a few big cities and hindered the appreciation of other aspects of the movement.

However, changing perceptions of the phenomenon of fascism in Britain owe less to the official papers than to a broader appreciation of the chronology of the movement. In effect, fascism enjoyed a much longer history in Britain both before 1914 and after 1918 than was once thought. Like other European countries Britain had a pre-fascist tradition; in fact many of the ideas later associated with fascism enjoyed wide circulation during the late Victorian and Edwardian period including anti-Semitism, fear about racial degeneracy, enthusiasm for eugenics, and obsessions about Britain as a victim of alien conspiracies.[3] The inter-war fascist critique of parliamentary democracy as an effete, corrupt system lacking legitimacy was articulated by the 'Radical Right' during the crises of the Edwardian period.

Such notions reached a climax during the First World War. Despite the triumphant outcome for Britain, some on the far right refused to be reassured, and,

---

[3] See for example, D. Stone, *Breeding Superman: Nietzsche, Race and Eugenics in Edwardian and Inter-war Britain* (Liverpool: Liverpool University Press, 2002).

as early as 1923, only months after fascists came to power in Italy, the first fascist organization had been launched. Despite the conventional emphasis in British historiography on the German Nazis, the contemporary perspective on fascism was far more influenced by the Italian example. This was partly because Mussolini's coup in 1922 marked the first check to what had looked like the inexorable march of bolshevism across Europe. Also, far from regarding fascism as something suited to the excitable Latin temperament, many on the right saw it as relevant to Britain; the problems being tackled by Mussolini—labour militancy, subversive forces, a corrupt parliamentary system—were all prevalent in Britain in the early 1920s. The impression that Mussolini had rejuvenated the 'Italian race' and restored national pride and unity made a heady appeal to those who felt disillusioned and alienated from the post-war democracy in Britain.[4]

In this context the emergence of the British Fascisti, subsequently British Fascists, under Rotha Lintorn-Orman in May 1923 was not so surprising. It drew upon a mixture of disgruntled peers and landowners, ex-military and naval officers, and people feeling politically marginalized or experiencing a declining income. In 1924 a breakaway group formed the National Fascisti, and in 1928 Arnold Leese established the Imperial Fascist League, a highly anti-Semitic organization with a more explicit fascist ideology than its predecessors. A more characteristically English expression of fascism appeared in 1930 in the shape of English Mistery, which gave rise to English Array in 1936. This collection is a reminder that fascism had put down an organizational base in Britain long before the appearance of Mosley's movement in 1932. The early fascist groups also enjoyed respectable connections with Conservative MPs, in the case of the British Fascists with Sir Patrick Hannon and in the case of English Mistery with Viscount Lymington. The British Establishment showed itself remarkably tolerant towards the paramilitary organization adopted by fascist groups during the 1920s; although military drilling was unquestionably illegal, the Home Office and the police made no attempt to enforce the law.[5] In some cases at least this reflected a widespread fear that society might well require some unofficial force to help restore order in the face of the alleged Soviet-inspired machinations such as the General Strike of 1926.

In recent years the traditional picture of fascism has also been extensively revised as a result of research into the character of the movement at local and regional level which has exploded the idea of a one-track fascist appeal or of a single type of fascist personality. In some ways the movement emerges from this work as highly opportunistic, exploiting issues of relevance to particular sections of society or to certain localities. It is well known that fascists disseminated anti-Semitic propaganda in areas such as Manchester, Leeds, and the East End where Jewish communities were

[4] M. Pugh, *'Hurrah for the Blackshirts!': Fascists and Fascism in Britain between the wars* (London: Cape, 2005), 39–43.
[5] Memorandum, 12 November, 1924, National Archives of Scotland: Gilmour Papers GD 383; PRO HO/144/22282, L.S.B. to Bovenden, 30 August 1930.

concentrated. But oral evidence has now revealed extensive activity in the textile districts of Lancashire and Yorkshire where fascists claimed to be able to recover thousands of jobs by imposing controls on output and exports from India, for example.

It seems clear that, as the country slowly recovered from the worst of the depression after 1934, the fascists targeted those regions, classes, and occupations that were not benefiting and felt a strong grievance towards the government. Agriculture, for example, proved to be susceptible to their message because so many landowners suffered from falling rents and land values and farmers were angry about collapsing prices and consequent bankruptcies. This is not eccentric when considered in the light of the farming districts in Germany, which had been the first to give support to the Nazis in the 1920s. It is easily overlooked that Mosley devoted much of his time to speeches in market towns all over England where he attracted huge crowds that responded enthusiastically to his attacks on City financiers and big business who made profits by flooding the country with imported food. A number of his leading BUF colleagues, including Jorian Jenks, Reynall Bellamy, and Robert Saunders, were recruited from the farming community. Where records of local organization survive, for Dorset for example, they show that fascist campaigns took place in rural and small-town England without the disorder associated with fascism in the big conurbations.[6] But this dimension still largely awaits its historians.

During 1937–9 the fascists also devoted much attention to the plight of small shopkeepers and to a lesser extent taxi drivers, barbers, clerks, and hotel employees suffering from competition and low incomes. They found a convenient scapegoat in the rapidly spreading multiples and chain stores, many of which were under foreign ownership and undercut corner-shop prices by bulk purchase and cheap foreign imports. According to Raven Thompson, the BUF's chief ideologist, 'shopkeepers have almost more to gain from corporate organization than any other section of the community'.[7] He argued that under the corporate state the number of stores would be regulated by issuing licences, big shops would be restricted to selling specific products, and businesses that failed to deal in British goods could be closed down.

In addition to recruiting from all social classes fascists also relied heavily on female participation, something not expected in view of their reputation for machismo. In this respect the British organizations seem to have made more compromises with women than their counterparts on the continent. Some of the leading women in the BUF had experience in Conservative organization while a few had even been suffragettes before 1914. The BUF pitched its appeal to them at two levels. Under the corporate state women would be represented in their conventional role as housewives and mothers; but their interest as workers would also be protected

---

[6] Robert Saunders Papers, A1, A2, A3, Sheffield University Library: Special Collections.
[7] *Action*, 4 June 1936.

by the system, for example, by guaranteeing them equal pay with men. This has been characterized not as feminism but as a feminist version of fascism.[8] At least a quarter, and perhaps as much as a third, of BUF membership was female. Their role became increasingly important later in the 1930s in the peace campaign and as doorstep canvassers in developing an electoral machine. Mosley boasted that 10 per cent of his parliamentary candidates were women, a higher proportion than in the other parties. Their prominence went some way to giving the movement a fresh and more respectable image.

One of the consequent effects of this research into the range and character of local support for fascism has been to cast doubt on the chronology of the movement's fortunes during the inter-war period. Admittedly, the lack of reliable figures for the membership of fascist organizations makes it difficult to generalize confidently. On the one hand there are what seem to be very inflated claims made by the early organizations in the 1920s, whose membership probably reached a peak around the General Strike in 1926. On the other hand, intelligence reports from 1934 onwards may indicate broad trends but are unlikely to give an accurate picture of support in the provinces. It is worth noting, for example, that in the summer of 1935 when the BUF is thought to have had only 4,000–5,000 members, sales of The Blackshirt stood at 22,000, while in the spring of 1936 The Blackshirt sold 23,000 and Action 26,000 copies.[9] This is a reminder that in the low periods fascist support was probably much wider than the formal membership of the BUF, and that the movement always had many passive members who are difficult to count because of their reluctance to identify themselves publicly.

Traditionally, BUF fortunes were believed to follow a simple pattern. A dramatic rise during January to June 1934 to around 40,000 or 50,000 members was followed by a sharp fall during 1934–5, triggered by reactions to the Olympia rally, from which it never really recovered. It now seems that the picture is more complicated. While Olympia shocked and alienated some people, it had the opposite effect on others. Britain enjoyed a long tradition of political violence and many Tory MPs openly defended the BUF's methods on the grounds that tough stewarding was the only way of ensuring freedom of speech for the right in the face of organized disruption by communists. To this extent the rally justified Mosley's claim that he alone possessed the organization needed to protect society from left-inspired chaos. Also, many young men found the prospect of violence and military training rather appealing. This interpretation was corroborated by Special Branch reports in the immediate aftermath of Olympia to the effect that hostile news-paper comments were misleading because the rally 'provided an unprecedented fillip to recruitment. For several days people of different classes queued up from

[8] See J. Gottlieb, *Feminine Fascism: Women in Britain's Fascist Movement 1923–1945* (London, I.B. Tauris, 2000).

[9] PRO HO/144/20146, Special Branch Reports, 20 January 1936, 3 March 1936.

morning to night at the National Headquarters [of the BUF] in Chelsea.'[10] The safest assumption is that there was, and continued to be, a considerable turnover of membership, and some of those who left in 1934 were probably reconnected via fascist front organizations designed to overcome the reservations of respectable people.

Subsequently the BUF managed to regain members in the East End of London largely through a vigorous anti-Semitic campaign, and a high proportion of total membership was concentrated in the area during 1935–6. The movement also re-gained momentum during 1938–9 as Mosley's peace campaign struck a chord with a country fearful of being dragged into another European war. Estimates put the membership at between 22,000 and 36,000 by the summer of 1939. This expansion probably involved further changes in composition. Observers of Mosley's rallies noted how he was recovering the 'respectable' support he had enjoyed in 1934, that is middle-class people who made his meetings resemble those held by the Con-servative and Liberal parties.[11] Conversely, he probably lost some of his working-class followers whose patriotic instincts reasserted themselves at the prospect of war with Germany and who felt embarrassed by association with pacifism. What seems certain is that fascism enjoyed another peak during the later 1930s even if it did not match that of 1934 by the time war broke out.

Recently scholars have begun to adopt fresh approaches by moving away from the empirical and narrative investigation of small fascist pressure groups, which tends to assume the inevitable 'failure' of fascism in Britain, partly by considering the cultural expressions of fascism and partly by analysing its role in the main political issues and crises of the inter-war period. The cultural approach includes fascist thinking about the cinema, theatre, music, masculinity, femininity, and rural life, all of which were seen to be relevant to contemporary fascist concerns about the demoralization and revival of the British race. They were especially anxious to stem the influence of America generally and Hollywood in particular on the younger generation; the domination of American cinema by Jewish interests was seen as posing an underlying threat to British ideas on race and empire. 'One of the duties of Fascism will be to recapture the British cinema for the British nation,' as Chesterton put it. To this end they hoped for a revival of interest in Shakespeare, regarding the Elizabethan era as the culmination of imperial greatness and cultural achievement, and thus as a proto-fascist period in British history.

If fascism is approached via the issues of the inter-war period the movement appears much less marginal not least because fascists framed their appeal in distinc-tively *British* terms. To some extent, of course, this was tactically necessary in order to deflect criticism of the movement as alien, especially in the later 1930s when links

---

[10] PRO HO/144/20142/108, Special Branch Report, 1 August 1934.
[11] PRO HO/144/21282, Special Branch Report, 16 July 1939.

with the Nazis became increasingly damaging and embarrassing. One Huddersfield fascist recalled that 'all our members present were taken aback and confused' in October 1936 when their evening drink was interrupted by the news that Mosley had married Diana Mitford in Goebbels's drawing room in Berlin.[12]

However, tactics are not a complete explanation. In many ways the thinking of British fascists reflected authentically British conditions and traditions. Chesterton, for example, placed fascism in a historical evolution from medieval times when the guilds and the feudal system had fostered a stable society and a community in which output, prices, and wages were regulated.[13] He believed that under fascism the corporate state would perform a similar function, safeguarding the interests of workers and consumers. According to the historian Sir Charles Petrie, 'the Feudal State was essentially a Corporate State in which the individual counted for very little and the community for a great deal'.[14] Fascists regarded the decline of feudalism as a disaster which had opened the way to divisions within society along class lines and the destruction of communities. They also held that medieval England enjoyed a real monarchy in which the king expected loyalty from his people and protected them in return; the king granted representation to interests and communities by allotting two MPs to specified boroughs and counties, not to mere numbers. All this had been swept away by the cult of the individual during the nineteenth century as England fell under the influence of liberalism and equality following the French Revolution.

From this perspective it was natural for fascists in English Mistery and English Array to see their movement as restoring the finest English traditions, especially medieval kingship, rather than introducing something novel. Until recently the relationship between fascism and monarchy in Britain has been neglected, but it was clearly a major element. Petrie argued that the experience of Italy in the 1920s demonstrated that fascism and monarchy went comfortably together; cooperation was natural because monarchy and fascism shared a common interest in the nation as a whole as opposed to the sectional interests represented by political parties: 'The case for a dictatorship in times of crisis can hardly be overstated.'[15] The problem was how to achieve one. According to Petrie, Victor Emmanuel had engineered the transition from a failing parliamentary democracy to a fascist system with minimal bloodshed by inviting Mussolini to form a government.

Such thinking was widely echoed by British fascists. Arnold Leese assumed that under fascism the Prime Minister would be appointed by the king, and when the need to replace him arose, the Fascist Grand Council would offer alternative names from which the king would choose. English Mistery held an almost mystical belief

---

[12] L. Grundy, *Don't Let Your Conscience Be Your Guide* (n.d), 43, Sheffield University Library: British Union Collection 5/3.

[13] *Action*, 13 August 1936; see also *Fascist Quarterly*, July 1935, 360–4; April 1939, 195–201.

[14] Sir C. Petrie, *Monarchy* (London: Bodley Head, 1933), 25–8.

[15] Ibid. 18; see also Pugh, '*Hurrah for the Blackshirts!*', 50, 239–42.

in monarchy. They claimed that the finest traditions of English kingship had been subverted by successive party politicians who had turned the king into a mere figurehead. Fascists believed that, if the king could be liberated, he would want to reverse unpatriotic policies such as the concessions to nationalist movements within the empire. Unfortunately George V appeared keen to stick to his constitutional role and remain above political controversy. Yet even he gave a tantalizing glimpse of royal power in 1931 following the collapse of Ramsay MacDonald's Labour government. For fascists this was a classic crisis of the inept parliamentary system. George V had boldly intervened to install a new National government and, in effect, to choose the prime minister.

Inevitably fascists looked with eager anticipation to the succession of the Prince of Wales who showed none of his father's respect for the constitution. He insisted on his right to intervene in foreign affairs to promote Anglo-German friendship, spoke tactlessly about the need for a dictatorship in Britain, and expressed his sympathy for the unemployed and his dissatisfaction with government policy when he visited the depressed regions. During 1936 the idea of reviving royal power received enthusiastic endorsement from a number of right-wing figures including the eccentric but wealthy Lady Lucy Houston who owned the *Saturday Review*. Following the death of George V in January 1936 Houston ran a series of shrill articles urging Britain's need for a benevolent dictator. 'We want to hail [Edward VIII] as our man of destiny who will free us from our perplexity', wrote Houston. 'Italy has her Mussolini; he is *her* man of Destiny.'[16] Consequently, when the abdication crisis broke in November and December, fascists were eager to join the king's party. Westminster was rife with speculation that following Baldwin's resignation there would be a royal coup. 'Are we to have a fascist monarchy?', one MP reportedly asked. Certainly Mosley expected to be invited to join a government formed by Churchill to support the king. Rank-and-file fascists regarded Edward VIII with great affection. 'With a member of the war generation and a kindred spirit on the Throne there would be a close understanding of our hopes and aspirations', wrote Reynall Bellamy.[17] Another BUF official, Jorian Jenks, explained that the king 'clearly believed in many of the things we believed in: in Britain and her Empire; in the need for real action to relieve the desperate poverty of the poor; in avoiding another war...and consequently in not picking another quarrel with Germany'.[18] The BUF quickly organized a countrywide campaign, chalking and painting three-feet-high slogans, 'STAND BY THE KING', on walls, roads, hoardings, and pavements. Thousands of people attended Mosley's rally in Victoria Park in Bethnal Green where he demanded: 'How would you like a Committee of Bishops and old skirts

---

[16] *Saturday Review*, 13 June 1936.

[17] R. Bellamy, in J. Christian (ed.), 'We Marched with Mosley' (n.d.), 170, Sheffield University Library: British Union Collection 5/5.

[18] J. Christian (ed.), *Mosley's Blackshirts: The Inside Story of the British Union of Fascists 1932–1940* (London: Sanctuary Press, 1986), 25.

in parliament to pick your girl for you?'[19] Mosley was undoubtedly tapping into a deep vein of pro-monarchist and anti-Establishment sentiment especially among working-class and lower middle-class people. This would have attracted a wider swathe of popular support into his camp and might also have brought Mosley himself into office; but the king's sudden decision to abdicate abruptly killed off this prospect. However, during the rest of the decade the BUF remained ready to organize a welcome for the Duke of Windsor when his much-heralded return to Britain materialized.

Even more than attachment to monarchy, the fascists' opposition to what they saw as a policy of 'scuttle' from Britain's imperial responsibilities placed them squarely in the mainstream of inter-war politics. For fascists the empire offered proof of the virile qualities of the British race but also a warning that they were being betrayed by spinelessness among the politicians of the Liberal–Conservative consensus. The imperial cause enabled fascists to combine patriotic, racial, and economic themes in a very satisfying way and to make an effective pitch for both Conservative and Labour support in some areas. During the 1920s several small and obscure groups broke away from the British Fascisti to form the British Empire Fascists, the Empire Fascist Movement, and the Empire Fascist League. In November 1933 Lieutenant Colonel Graham Seton Hutchinson founded the British Empire Fascist Party, an extremist organization that advocated the abolition of political parties, the introduction of a corporate state, and the suppression of nationalism in Ireland and India.[20] There was also a transfer of personnel from British fascism to colonial territories, notably to the 'White Highlands' of Kenya. This largely involved alienated aristocratic émigrés including Lord William Scott, a son of the Duke of Buccleuch, the Earl of Erroll, the Marquess of Graham, heir to the Duke of Montrose, and Viscount Lymington. In Africa they escaped the democratic conditions they so disliked at home and managed to use their limited resources to recreate a feudal lifestyle. Although they were too few and too scattered to sustain any significant organization, they maintained links between domestic British politics and the colonies. In 1934 the British Union of Fascists found it worthwhile to appoint Lord Erroll as its delegate from Kenya.[21] Lord William Scott was elected to parliament in 1935 and joined the BUF's front organization, January Club.[22] Later in the 1930s these men developed pronounced pro-Nazi sympathies; the Marquess of Graham and his brother, Lord Ronald Graham, joined the notorious Right Club in 1939 and worked for peace with Germany before and during the Second World War.[23]

[19] *Daily Express*, 5 December 1936.
[20] T. Linehan, *British Fascism 1918–1939: Parties, Ideology and Culture* (Manchester: Manchester University Press, 2000), 132–3.
[21] *The Blackshirt*, 29 June 1934.
[22] See Imperial War Museum: Luttman-Johnson Papers, Box 8, 10.
[23] R. Griffiths, *Patriotism Perverted: Captain Ramsay, the Right Club and British Anti-Semitism 1939–1940* (London: Constable, 1998), 118, 224–5.

However, although fascists hoped to develop the economic potential of empire and even to extend white control in Africa—hence their support for Mussolini's ambitions in Ethiopia—they were thwarted by three obstacles. First, the economic nationalism in Canada, Australia, and India made it impossible to use the empire simply as a source of food and raw materials for Britain and as a market for her manufactures. Second, they lacked political support, as became obvious from the consideration given to returning the territories Britain had recently obtained as mandates from Germany. Though the National government stopped short of returning them, its willingness to use colonies as weapons in the bigger game of international diplomacy was demoralizing. Thirdly, fascists were appalled but impotent in the face of concessions to nationalist demands in India. 'What folly to foist on India Western parliamentary institutions, which were never suitable to the East, at the very moment when they were breaking down at home', argued Mosley in the context of the 1935 Government of India Bill.[24] Although Mosley campaigned relentlessly in the depressed cotton districts of Lancashire where he proposed to recreate thousands of jobs by suppressing the Indian textile industry, there was no chance of the government taking up his ideas because of the provocation it would offer to the national movement. In India itself the official British community was, however reluctantly, increasingly committed to eventual self-government for Indians. The younger Indian Civil Service men increasingly displayed liberal sympathies, while the provincial governorships were filled by politicians appointed to ensure that the reform policy was implemented. Despite these problems the imperial cause enabled fascist propaganda to combine the patriotic, racial, and economic themes satisfactorily, and in so doing to extend their appeal to the supporters of both Conservative and Labour parties.

Although the aristocratic émigrés represented an influential metropolitan element in colonial society, a larger potential basis for an indigenous fascist movement existed in the poor, white farming communities suffering from falling agricultural prices, economic dislocation, and a consequent loss of confidence in conventional parties and liberal democracy. In Canada the depression fell heavily on farming in the prairie provinces and on the export of timber, pulp, and paper, undermining support for the Liberal and Conservative parties. During 1919–22 the United Farmer parties won elections in Ontario, Alberta, and Manitoba and held the balance of power in the House of Commons. They advocated occupational representation and regarded conventional parties as inherently corrupt, much as fascists in Britain did. In Quebec the economic discontent acquired a racial element because the French population resented the influx of British capital which threatened to integrate Canada into the world economy and destroy their traditional way of life. They found the idea of a corporate system under Catholic auspices much more attractive. Such sentiment was most effectively articulated by the Union Nationale under

[24] *Daily Mail*, 9 April 1934.

Maurice Duplessis, who won power in Quebec in 1936 and aspired to create a self-contained French state, though without complete separation from Canada. However, although the Union Nationale and the United Farmer movements enjoyed a certain amount of common ground with fascism and sympathized with General Franco and Benito Mussolini, they were never fully-fledged fascist parties. In effect, their emergence helped to absorb the discontent that might have been tapped by fascism.

During the 1920s and 1930s Australia also saw a good deal of complaint about the failure of democracy and second-rate political leaders and generated a corresponding need for discipline and effective leadership, even to the extent of dictatorship. Hence a fashionable demand to modernize the economy by applying science to industry during the 1920s, and the sympathetic interest in the work of Mussolini in 'making the desert bloom' by revitalizing rural economies. However, although some Australian intellectuals predicted that democracy would give way to strong leadership and a corporate state, the discontent was increasingly diverted away from an explicitly fascist movement towards the rising hostility among nationalists to links with the British empire. It was not until the mid-1950s that a grassroots movement based on the discontents of peasant proprietors emerged in the shape of the Democratic Labor Party, a breakaway from the Australian Labor Party. Essentially a pro-Catholic, pro-immigrant, and bitterly anti-communist movement, the DLP placed little importance on direct representation in parliament. It was not fascist, though its anti-democratic and anti-communist views enabled it to occupy the ground that a fully-fledged fascist party would have seized in Australia.

The centrality of issues such as empire and monarchy underlines how closely the British fascists were involved with the mainstream political system. On the one hand they adopted a militantly anti-Establishment line, but on the other they assiduously cultivated connections with it; Mosley, for all his contempt for the British Establishment, had no doubt of his ability to seduce enough of it for his purposes. This relationship was crucial to his short-term tactics and to his long-term strategy. The attention usually given to the paramilitary aspects of fascism has obscured the fact that Mosley never planned to obtain power by a coup. Rather, he expected to be invited into office during some crisis—just as Mussolini and Hitler had been. He boasted of the links his movement enjoyed in all the armed forces, especially in the RAF. Though a great deal remains to be discovered about these connections there is no doubt that some serving officers were fascists, the most senior being Air Commodore Sir J. A. Chamier, who joined the January Club (see p. 501) and organized Empire Air Days for the Air League.[25] In Britain as in other countries air power exercised a special fascination for fascists as a modern approach both to policing the empire and suppressing domestic revolt. As a result a number

---

[25] Hendon: RAF Museum, DC76/74/187, Air Ministry file for Sir J. A. Chamier, 23 October 1943; *The Aeroplane*, 30 May 1934.

of inter-war fascists shared a background in the Royal Flying Corps or as aviation pioneers and enthusiasts, including Mosley himself, L. T. C. Moore-Brabazon MP, Lord Semphill, and Charles Grey, the editor of *The Aeroplane.*

There is much more evidence about fascist connections within the Conservative Party and the House of Lords, although for many years this was obscured because the obituaries of inter-war politicians, and even their later entries in the *Dictionary of National Biography*, managed to omit any reference to their fascist history. It was, in fact, crucial to Mosley's strategy to cultivate these links because his entry into office when the parliamentary system eventually broke down was expected to be easier if the conventional politicians were already familiar with the idea of the corporate state. To this end in 1934 the BUF launched the January Club, one of several front organizations. Its secretary, Captain H. W. Luttman-Johnson, a Scots landowner and ex-cavalry officer, was well placed to present upper-class recruits with a respectable form of fascism that operated through dinners and lectures not through rabble-rousing and street fighting. Aiming to attract people who were 'in sympathy with the fascist movement' and 'believed that the present democratic system of government in this country must be changed', the January Club enrolled large numbers of Conservative MPs, peers, writers, and intellectuals as well as corporate members among leading British companies.[26]

As the Club was not a political party it minimized any embarrassment for members already involved in existing parties. Not that Conservative MPs were inhibited from speaking out in support of fascism in public. The Conservative Party had such an informal and decentralized approach to membership that many men and women found no difficulty in working within fascist and Conservative organizations simultaneously. Several MPs including J. T. C. Moore-Brabazon, Henry Drummond Wolff, Patrick Donner, Lord Lymington, and Lord Erskine were particularly closely connected to Mosley. It was important to him to have a number of parliamentarians ready to speak up for him when the time came to enter office. Meanwhile Mosley promoted this strategy by developing an electoral machine for the BUF from 1936 onwards, another aspect that has been largely neglected in accounts of the movement. Close advisers such as Major-General Fuller had been urging Mosley to abandon the vulgar image the BUF had acquired by tapping into its wider support as the National government lost credibility. The aim was to organize a trained agent, a candidate, propaganda, and women canvassers in each constituency. By the end of 1936 Mosley claimed to have 100 candidates in place. Some of their names— Viscountess Downe, Lady Pearson, Major-General Fuller, Admiral Powell—offered evidence of fascism as a respectable and patriotic movement, thereby making it unlikely that, despite regular surveillance by the intelligence services, any attempt would be made to suppress it. Even in 1940 none of these well-connected candidates was incarcerated, though their official role in fascism fully qualified them!

[26] *The Times,* 24 March 1934; Pugh, 'Hurrah for the Blackshirts!', 146–8; Imperial War Museum: Luttman-Johnson Papers, Box 1, 2.

While extensive research has created a broader and more credible picture of fascism in Britain, at least two aspects have remained controversial. Perhaps surprisingly, there is disagreement about the extent of anti-Semitism within the movement. The traditional view, which sees anti-Semitism as central, still commands wide support. Jews formed a fundamental element in the analysis of most interwar fascists who regarded them as an unpatriotic section of society, profiting from residence in Britain but, as investors in the industry and agriculture of competitors, responsible for flooding the market with cheap foreign goods. The BUF made Jews the target of its most sustained local campaign in the East End, and eventually it threatened to exclude them from parliament, deport them, and expropriate their property if they had been working against British interests. By the late 1930s when relations with Germany were deteriorating, fascists blamed the Jews for dragging Britain and the United States into war in order to seek revenge on Hitler.

However, some qualifications to this view are in order. Since anti-Semitism was rife in all parties and all classes between the wars, the prejudice expressed by Mosley was fairly routine. There is no evidence that he originally intended to make anti-Semitism a central part of BUF propaganda; but he claimed, with some reason, that Jews were so prominent in attacking the fascists that he was justified in responding. It is significant that many fascists, such as Arnold Leese of the Imperial Fascist League, regarded Mosley as rather soft towards the Jews, and the BUF attracted leading figures including Joyce, Chesterton, and Fuller whose obsessive anti-Semitism made Mosley appear almost moderate; as a result some of them left to form more extreme organizations like the Nordic League. There was a distinction between the fanatics who saw the Jewish question in *racial* terms, and those like Mosley who treated it more as a matter of tactics. As early as 1933 he recognized that Hitler had been mistaken in making violent attacks on Jews, and from time to time he issued instructions to his followers to tone down their rhetoric, with little effect it must be said.

Another dispute that says as much about the participants as about the issues involved concerns the ideological character of the BUF. Some contemporary critics always disparaged the organization as a left-wing version of fascism, perhaps influenced by Mosley's own history in the Labour Party. It is fair to say that he distinguished his ideas from the more reactionary expressions of fascism such as English Array. Mosley's economic strategy for tackling unemployment clearly involved large elements of state intervention, and he and his colleagues argued that workers and consumers would benefit from the regulation involved in the corporate state. The left-wing image was compounded by the violently anti-capitalist rhetoric adopted by fascists when blaming big business for bankrupting small shopkeepers and undermining British interests.[27]

[27] P. Coupland, 'Left-Wing Fascism in Theory and in Practice: The Case of the British Union of Fascists', *Twentieth Century British History*, 13 (2002).

However, Marxists find it hard to take the idea of a 'left-wing' fascism seriously. For them fascism arises as a symptom of the crisis of capitalism and its purpose is to save it rather than to overthrow it. It is fair to say that the hostility towards big business shown by continental fascist movements before they obtained power often gave way to a more compromising stance subsequently. On the other hand, the Marxist view is essentially too simplistic and rigid to accommodate the complexity of the empirical evidence for fascist ideas and support. During the 1930s the BUF attracted many recruits with a background in the Labour and Communist parties who were disillusioned with the inability of the left to respond to the depression and responded positively to Mosley's proposals. Rank-and-file members actually explained that what they liked about the BUF was the combination of socialism and patriotism it offered, something unavailable in the conventional parties. This element proved to be important in sustaining the movement. In the Blackburn branch Nellie Driver noted that 'Ex-Communists made the best active members. They were not nervous of street work or of opposition.'[28] Despite this sceptics claim that the BUF failed to win over the working class because it was too loyal to the trade unions and the Labour Party. However, such claims suffer from an obvious flaw. By the 1930s large numbers of workingmen had left the unions and only a minority were mobilized by the Labour Party even as voters let alone as members, leaving a huge untapped constituency for a populist movement. This is not to say that Mosley entirely succeeded, but as research into fascism in manufacturing districts proceeds it seems to suggest the viability of working-class fascism.

The question of the fascist legacy in British society has not provoked much disagreement. There is a strong case for saying the Second World War effectively put an end to fascism properly understood. For this there were three main reasons. First, the fascists had been damned as apologists for Nazi Germany; and although the accusations against them as fifth columnists had not been justified, they never managed to shake off their reputation. The execution of William Joyce for high treason in 1946 was seen as a reflection on the movement as a whole. Second, the Holocaust made such a lasting impact on the British conscience that anyone associated with anti-Semitism was regarded as beyond the pale. Third, the wartime success of the liberal state in rallying to defeat the enemy went a long way to discrediting the fascist analysis of the parliamentary system as effete and unpatriotic.

Yet post-war conditions were not entirely inimical to a fascist revival. Mosley could claim that his diagnosis that by going to war with Germany Britain would open Europe to the hegemony of the Soviet Union, seemed to a large extent to have been vindicated. By 1947 the British empire was being dismembered. Finally, a second great war had led the country once again into an era of high taxation and

---

[28] Nellie Driver, 'From the Shadows of Exile' (n.d.), 30, J. B. Priestley Library, University of Bradford: Nellie Driver MSS.

state intervention as the critics had warned. However, none of this made the impact that it had in the aftermath of 1918. With Ernest Bevin as Foreign Secretary no one could plausibly argue that the country was seriously succumbing to communism or subversion. As the domestic agenda had moved decisively to the left, full employment and social welfare had become priorities for both political parties. As a result fascists and their concerns appeared far more marginal and even irrelevant by comparison with the situation in the aftermath of the First World War.

Thus, although Mosley and Chesterton continued to be political active after 1945, they denied that they were fascists, and Chesterton even revised his anti-Semitic views. The Union Movement that Mosley founded in 1948 campaigned for imperial control of Africa, a united Europe, and an end to coloured immigration. But this did not amount to a full fascist programme; the movement found itself caught halfway between the conventional parties and the racist fringe. More extreme elements soon spawned a range of new groups including the National Party, the National Workers Movement, and Chesterton's League of Empire Loyalists which proved to be influential as a training ground for a new generation of leaders of the far right. They founded the White Defence League in 1956, the British National Party in 1960, the National Socialist Movement in 1962, and the National Front in 1967. It is, however, widely accepted that but for the issue of immigration none of these would have made any impact. Usually described as neo-fascist, these organizations claimed that Hitler had been right about the Jews and tried to cast doubt on the Holocaust. But they were notable chiefly for their internal feuding and for their failure to develop the kind of coherent or comprehensive programme that fascism had offered between the wars.

BIBLIOGRAPHY

BAKER, D., *The Ideology of Obsession: A. K.Chesterton and British Fascism* (London: I.B. Tauris, 1996).

BECKETT, F., *The Rebel Who Lost his Cause: The Tragedy of John Beckett M.P.* (London: London House, 1999).

COUPLAND, M., 'Left-Wing Fascism in Theory and in Practice: The Case of the British Union of Fascists', *Twentieth Century British History*, 13 (2002).

GOTTLIEB, J., *Feminine Fascism: Women in Britain's Fascist Movement 1923–1945* (London: I. B. Tauris, 2000).

——and LINEHAN, T. (eds), *The Culture of Fascism: Visions of the Far Right in Britain* (London: I. B. Tauris, 2004).

GRIFFITHS, R., *Fellow Travellers of the Right: British Enthusiasts for Nazi Germany 1933–1939* (Oxford: Oxford University Press, 1983).

LINEHAN, T., *East London for Mosley: The British Union of Fascists in East London and South-West Essex 1933–40* (London: Frank Cass, 1996).

——— *British Fascism 1918–1939: Parties, Ideology and Culture* (Manchester: Manchester University Press, 2000).

MARTLAND, P., *Lord Haw Haw: The English Voice of Nazi Germany* (London: The National Archives, 2003).

PUGH, M., '*Hurrah for the Blackshirts!*': *Fascists and Fascism in Britain between the Wars* (London: Cape, 2005).

RAWNSLEY, S., 'The Membership of the British Union of Fascists', in K. Lunn and R. Thurlow (eds), *British Fascism* (London: Croom Helm, 1980).

SKIDELSKY, R., *Oswald Mosley* (London: Macmillan, 1975).

STONE, D., *Breeding Superman: Nietzsche, Race and Eugenics in Edwardian and Inter-war Britain* (Liverpool: Liverpool University Press, 2002).

——— 'The English Mistery, the British Union of Fascists and the Dilemmas of British Fascism', *Journal of Modern History*, 75 (2003).

THURLOW, R., *Fascism in Britain: A History 1918–1985* (Oxford: Blackwell, 1987).

WEBBER, G. C., 'Patterns of Membership and Support for the British Union of Fascists', *Journal of Contemporary History*, 19 (1984).

CHAPTER 27

....

FRANCE

....

JOAN TUMBLETY

FRENCH scholars have been remarkably resistant to the idea that fascism ever had much purchase as a political force in France. This so-called 'consensus'[1] became established on the foundations provided by political historian René Rémond who in the 1950s first outlined a classificatory schema designed to encompass all French post-revolutionary right-wing political families. Rémond carved the rightist political landscape of nineteenth- and twentieth-century France into *trois droites*—the legitimists or monarchists who had always rejected the revolutionary inheritance; the economically liberal Orléanists who successfully reconciled conservatives to the Republic; and finally the Bonapartists who, in their fusion of authoritarianism and populism, were able to diffuse the political radicalism of the masses through the practice of a plebiscitary democracy which led the latter to accept the forces of order.[2] Rémond, convinced that the radicalism of European fascism made it distinct from and incompatible with traditional conservatism of any kind, argued that the anti-parliamentary leagues of the 1920s and 1930s constituted a new form of Bonapartism. Those elements on the political landscape which he was prepared to accept as fascist—the Faisceau of Georges Valois, the Francistes of Marcel Bucard, the Solidarité Française of Jean Renaud, and later the Parti Populaire Français (PPF) of Jacques Doriot—were dismissed as inconsequential fringe elements that failed to mobilize significant popular support or to threaten the Third Republican regime.

---

[1] W. D. Irvine, 'Fascism in France and the Strange Case of the Croix de Feu', *Journal of Modern History*, 63 (1991), 294.

[2] R. Rémond, *The Right Wing in France from 1815 to de Gaulle*, trans. J. M. Laux (2nd American edn, Philadelphia: University of Pennsylvania Press, 1969), 30.

Later francophone scholars such as Pierre Milza, Serge Berstein, Michel Winock, and Philippe Burrin, who have all made a distinctive contribution to the debate about fascism, fall largely within the wider interpretative framework initially supplied by Rémond. They argue for the marginality of French fascism, holding that the new rightist forces in the inter-war period espoused an authoritarian populism whose legalism and level of bourgeois support suggests an ideological affinity with conservatism rather than fascism. Those elements within the radical right whose fascism is admitted are at the same time dismissed as imitative of foreign models, or 'plagiarists', to echo the words of Rémond himself.[3] In the language of these scholars, France remained 'allergic' to—indeed 'immune' from—the fascist temptation.[4] Ultimately, the failure of any force on the radical right to seize power in a *coup d'état* between 1918 and 1945 is widely cited by such historians as proof that fascism failed to penetrate French minds in this period.

Yet I will argue that, whatever the authentic 'fascist' credentials of the various French movements which have begged classification by scholars of fascism, it was a configuration of contextual factors which kept them out of power rather than the intrinsic ideological weakness of fascism—or the radical right on the whole—as a political force. Even if the 'mobilising passions' (to use Robert Paxton's phrase[5]) which characterized inter-war European fascisms—racialism, anti-Marxism, a deep sense of national grievance—could not compete in France with the rival passions embodied in the democratic culture of the Rights of Man, fascism failed there because economic and political tensions did not cut as deeply as elsewhere in Europe. Crucially, the inter-war crisis of democracy did not unhinge traditional conservatives enough to make ruling elites abdicate some measure of power to the authoritarian populists to their right. Furthermore, the left was able to mobilize more support among the French populace, not only in the street battles of the period but also in the last pre-war elections which took place in 1936 and returned a leftist Popular Front to power. Ultimately, the significant levels of anxiety which this leftist victory provoked on the right were contained and diffused by the authoritarian premiership of Radical Édouard Daladier after April 1938.

Strikingly, even after the military defeat of 1940 and the collapse of the democratic Third Republic, the circumstances of German occupation did not lever French fascists into power. Instead, the conquering forces used the significant quasi-Briandist—and anti-communist—appeal of an illusory 'New European Order' to seduce *fascisant* activists and intellectuals into accepting the occupation of French soil and institutions. The Vichy regime itself arguably owed much more to the kind

---

[3] Ibid. 282.

[4] See S. Berstein, 'La France des années trente allergique au fascisme: à propos d'un livre de Zeev Sternhell', *Vingtième Siècle*, 2 (1984), 84–94. The so-called 'immunity thesis', which invoked the notion of French exceptionalism, was first given a name—and criticized—by French sociologist Michel Dobry in 1989.

[5] R. O. Paxton, *The Anatomy of Fascism* (London: Penguin, 2004), 41.

of clerical authoritarianism which animated Salazar's Portugal or Franco's Spain than to any model of fascism, however much the creation of the Milice (see below) served after 1943 to turn Vichy into a police state which used terror as a means of securing social order. There were fascist elements within the Vichy state but they were marginalized by traditional conservatives, and the German occupiers, for their part, preferred to work with compliant collaborators than with fascist dreamers.

No scholar disputes the variety of developments which flourished on the far right in France during the first half of the twentieth century. The question is how far any of them were fascist and why their advocates failed to seize power. This discussion will not attempt the folly of seeking to resolve long-standing definitional disputes but instead will reconstruct some of the conversations in which historians and other scholars have been engaged, convey the variety of illiberal populist positions that sought to mobilize support in this period, and articulate the nature of the inter-war crisis in French democracy which made the radical right so appealing to many.

I. The Roots of French Fascism: From the *Fin de Siècle* to the 1920s

Despite its reputation as the regime that divided the French least, the Third Republic provoked—from the 1880s to the 1930s—a series of illiberal, populist, and ultranationalist challenges to its parliamentary authority. Defeat in the Franco-Prussian War of 1870–1 and the subsequent loss of the provinces of Alsace and Lorraine nurtured a particularism and xenophobia which gained momentum amid the mass politics of the Third Republican era. Ironically, the latter provided a rationale for an illiberal attack on democratic modernity, while simultaneously providing the means of mobilizing popular support. On the one hand, the return of democratic elections and the legalization of trade unions angered those who would reject the egalitarian inheritance of 1789; while on the other, a mass press, facilitated by the liberal censorship laws of the early 1880s, served as a ready vehicle for popularizing and legitimizing even extreme political positions. The creation of the Ligue des Patriotes under Paul Déroulède in 1882, the rapid rise and fall of Boulangism in the late 1880s, and the establishment of the Catholic and anti-Semitic Action Française (AF) during the years of the Dreyfus Affair at the turn of the century all attest to the development of a populist and authoritarian right fostered amid the economic depression and increased immigration of the late nineteenth century. In a book first published in 1983, Israeli historian Zeev Sternhell argued that, far from being a weak force in France, fascism had been nourished there in precisely this climate of *fin de siècle* crisis. Indeed, Sternhell contested that *belle époque* France was the 'great ideological laboratory' of Europe and that proto-fascist ideas had flourished there before being exported to the rest of the continent.[6]

Yet, controversially, Sternhell also stressed the leftist origins of these impulses. His research emphasized such intellectuals as Georges Sorel and Maurice Barrès whose ideas represented a 'conjunction of elements of the nationalist, anti-liberal, and antibourgeois right and . . . the anti-democratic and anti-Marxist socialist and quasi-socialist left' in a way that was authoritarian, populist, and frequently anti-Semitic.[7] Much discursive energy has indeed been devoted to establishing whether fascism in France was 'more left than right, more socialist than capitalist, more revolutionary than conservative, more populist than elitist, more plebeian than bourgeois, and more traditionalist than modernist'.[8] The arguments are complicated by the fact that many of the activists whom historians generally place on the radical right refused the 'fascist' label (for example, the leaders of the Solidarité Française, the Croix de Feu, and even the PPF), and that many—if not all—of them have left a discursive trail that is flatly contradictory. Better, at any rate, to accept the paradoxical nature of fascism, to see it as at once reactionary and revolutionary, anti-capitalist and in effect protective of bourgeois interests, simultaneously modernist and anti-modern.[9]

What are the movements whose existence has so puzzled and exasperated scholars of fascism in France? In René Rémond's words, 'paramilitary movements sprang up like mushrooms after a storm' in the 1920s.[10] Their appearance was in part a response to developments on the left. Not only had the 1917 Bolshevik Revolution served to underline the potential of revolutionary socialism to topple regimes, but in France militant communists within the Socialist Party (the SFIO) formally split from that organization at the 1920 party congress held in Tours. Indeed, the newly formed Communist Party (PCF) initially won the majority of former SFIO members and the leftist victory at the 1924 legislative elections was interpreted as a danger signal on the parliamentary and extra-parliamentary right. In the mid-1920s several new movements on the radical right exerted their muscle in the streets and in the press, calling for a new and authoritarian kind of democracy. These groups, whose influence extended well beyond Paris, were neither as royalist nor as piously Catholic as the 'new right' of the *fin de siècle* and most did more to appeal specifically to workers—not very successfully—in an attempt to make a mass, cross-class movement. In general they craved a spiritual—rather than a materialist—revolution, and although an element of anti-capitalism was often

---

[6] Z. Sternhell, *Neither Right nor Left: Fascist Ideology in France*, trans. David Maisel (Berkeley and Los Angeles: University of California Press, 1986), 29.

[7] Ibid., pp. xvii–xviii.

[8] R. Soucy, *French Fascism: The Second Wave, 1933–1939* (New Haven: Yale University Press, 1995), 2.

[9] For example, see K. Passmore, *Fascism: A Very Short Introduction* (Oxford: Oxford University Press, 2002), 25.

[10] Rémond, *The Right Wing in France*, 273.

a part of their platform, they were hostile to the conventionally organized and Marxist left.

Yet the influence of *fin de siècle* ultranationalists persisted. The Action Française, generally regarded by historians as a form of reactionary integral nationalism rather than fascism, was still a presence in the press, in the Chamber, and on the streets during the inter-war period.[11] The movement's shock troops, the so-called Camelots du Roi, although small in number nevertheless attracted some of the more thuggish elements among the AF fraternity and exerted an aggressive paramilitary presence. The brutality of the Camelots' action, combined with the threat of Vatican condemnation over Maurras's unorthodox religious doctrines, alienated many of the movement's Catholic supporters. It must not be forgotten that, although arguably a declining force by the inter-war period with around 30,000 members at the time of its papal condemnation in 1926, the AF wielded considerable cultural influence over the French political elite in the first half of the twentieth century. Many of its sons—such as the *littérateurs* Robert Brasillach and Lucien Rebatet—evolved into self-proclaimed fascists by the end of the 1930s. The movement itself only managed to secure one deputy in the elections of 1919 which returned a conservative Bloc National to the Chamber, but as many as 5 per cent of deputies had a connection with it in 1924, and dozens of parliamentarians and other elites (in the armed forces, industry, and among the intelligentsia) can meaningfully be described as fellow-travellers for the entire inter-war period. That is how, despite its formal political marginalization, the AF was able to flavour the later Vichy regime.

Many adherents of the arguably fascist paramilitary leagues which sprang up after the success of the Cartel des Gauches in 1924 similarly had connections with the AF. Indeed, the fact that these groups competed in the same political space often led to conflict between them. The first of the new leagues, the Légion, had in fact grown out of the Ligue des Patriotes. Founded by war veteran Antoine Lédier in June 1924, this movement disavowed the royalism of the Maurrassians although it recruited from the same pool of potential supporters. Self-consciously inspired by the news of the fascist triumph in Italy, Lédier favoured an authoritarian overhaul of the French state where parliamentary democracy would be suspended and the economy run along corporatist lines. The Légion remained a resolutely middle-class affair in terms of its popular support—it had around 10,000 members by 1926, most of them in the provinces—and lacked the social radicalism of later incarnations on the radical right.

Another movement that clearly signposted its debt to Italian Fascism and which is generally accepted as fascist was the similarly short-lived Faisceau founded in 1925 by Georges Valois, a man who met Mussolini in 1924 and who subsequently

---

[11] Ernst Nolte's work is a significant exception. See his *Three Faces of Fascism: Action Française, Italian Fascism and National Socialism*, trans. L. Vennewitz (London: Weidenfeld & Nicolson, 1965).

benefited from the moral support of the Italian regime. After early connections with syndicalism, Valois had become a prominent member of the AF and founded the Cercle Proudhon in 1911 in an attempt to marry syndicalism with nationalism. His 'blue shirts' had garnered as many as 60,000 members by November 1926, often recruiting from within the ranks of the AF itself. The Faisceau was hostile to the Republic, was more interested than the AF in luring workers away from communism, and promised national reconciliation in place of class conflict. Unlike the traditionalist rhetoric of the AF, the Faisceau promised modernity, emphasizing the need for a corporatist revolution in social organization, and maintained—at the risk of alienating its principal financiers—an anti-capitalist rhetoric. In addition, unlike the AF, Valois shunned any connections with the Chamber. 'The Parliamentary State is about as useful as an ox-cart compared to an automobile,' he wrote in 1925.[12] Ironically, despite its acknowledged fascist credentials, the Faisceau proved much less willing to engage in street violence than the Camelots du Roi of the AF, for whom the Faisceau itself was often a target.[13] Neither did Valois's movement openly espouse anti-Semitism, despite the hostility which its leader had expressed towards Jews during his conversion to monarchism in the *belle époque*.

The success of Mussolini's blackshirts was generally welcomed by the conservative and radical right in France, although arguably more for the anti-communist attempt to restore order than for any promise of social and political revolution. In any case, rightists in France showed much more unabashed admiration for Mussolini's Italy than they were later to display towards a militarily expansionist Nazi Germany. One might argue that the leagues acknowledged their debt to the Italian Fascists in the same way that Mussolini himself referenced elements of French *fin de siècle* nationalist thinking—as an attempt to lend legitimacy to their position. Yet René Rémond saw such homage to Italian Fascism as proof of the derivative nature of the French extra-parliamentary right: '[t]o see a French fascism in the leagues', he wrote, 'is to take a scarecrow for a reality.'[14] Bruno Goyet has countered that the incorporation of an Italian Fascist 'gestural grammar' into the symbolic world of the radical right in France signified more than mere imitation. Such groups were seeking to set themselves apart from their immediate rivals in a crowded political space through what he terms a 'strategy of differentiation'.[15] Hence Valois sought to distinguish his Faisceau from the monarchist AF; and conversely the AF distanced itself from fascism so as to maintain its established political identity, to respond to Catholic fears about Italian Fascist attacks on religion, and arguably to dissociate

[12] G. Valois, in *Le Nouveau Siècle*, 13 December 1925, cited in E. Weber (ed.), *Varieties of Fascism: Doctrines of Revolution in the Twentieth Century* (Princeton: Van Nostrand, 1964), 184.

[13] A. Douglas, 'Violence and Fascism: The Case of the Faisceau', *Journal of Contemporary History*, 19 (1984), 689–712.

[14] Rémond, *The Right Wing in France*, 281.

[15] B. Goyet, 'La "March sur Rome": version orginale sous-titrée. La réception du fascisme en France dans les années 20', in M. Dobry (ed.), *Le Mythe de l'allergie française au fascisme* (Paris: Albin Michel, 2003), 69–105.

its violent Camelots du Roi from the tempting parallel with the Italian blackshirts. Similarly, Goyet argues that the Jeunesses Patriotes radicalized its programme by appealing to a widely shared admiration for Fascism when the Faisceau threatened to steal its membership. In any case, the relationship of the French leagues to Fascism was no doubt more than a function of ideology: it may well have reflected a disingenuous strategy for gaining and keeping popular support.

Historians—with the significant exception of Robert Soucy—have been less willing to believe that the Jeunesses Patriotes represented a fascist impulse of its own accord. It was nonetheless the principal beneficiary of the collapse of the Légion and the Faisceau between 1926 and 1928. One member inherited from the latter grouping was Marcel Bucard—also a member of the AF and Croix de Feu—who would become leader of the openly fascist Francistes in 1933. The JP, whose activists—like those of the Faisceau and the Francistes—also wore blue shirts, was formed in 1924 by the wealthy champagne producer, Barresian nationalist, and anti-communist Pierre Taittinger. It had its origins as the youth wing of the Ligue des Patriotes and indeed functioned, via a rather hierarchical military structure, as its paramilitary force. Like other movements on the radical right, the JP, despite its celebration of 'virility', encompassed a women's section and indeed advocated women's integral suffrage rights. This support for the female vote may seem surprising but was in fact far from unusual—Solidarité Française and the Croix de Feu were to espouse similar views. Their posture, however, was driven by assumptions about women's 'natural' right-wing tendencies rather than by any feminist impulse. Indeed, all such groups maintained a wholly masculinist world-view that was virulently hostile to the *femme moderne*. Both real and ideal women were largely reduced in these movements to a familial role, however much female 'fascist' activists themselves may have challenged that view in practice.[16]

Taittinger, in contrast to Valois, was a rightist deputy in the Chamber continuously between 1919 and 1940 and it is precisely his willingness to remain part of the parliamentary establishment that has led scholars in the 'consensus school' to reject the fascist credentials of this movement, despite the fact that after 1926 its militants self-consciously gave the fascist salute and often engaged in street violence.[17] By 1929 the JP had over 100,000 members and in 1928 it could boast twenty-seven members or close supporters in the French parliament. By the mid-1930s it claimed over seventy deputies as members. This willingness to collaborate with the political structures of the Third Republic is arguably what took the steam out of the movement by the end of the 1920s: only once the depression again radicalized rightist opinion did Taittinger reprise his anti-republican focus. In general, the stabilization of the franc and economic recovery in the late 1920s under the premiership of Poincaré ended this 'first wave' of French fascism.

[16] C. Koos and D. Sarnoff, 'France', in K. Passmore (ed.), *Women, Gender and Fascism in Europe, 1919–45* (Manchester: Manchester University Press, 2003), 169–88.
[17] The term is used in Soucy, *French Fascism: The Second Wave*, 6.

II. THE CRISIS OF THE 1930S

The so-called second wave of French fascism was nourished by the deeper economic and political crises of the 1930s. The economic depression started to bite in France after 1931 and the leftist majority returned by the 1932 elections unsettled the conservative and far right. Outside the Chamber, the socialist and communist left galvanized the support of the working classes and a leftist associative life thrived. In addition, increased immigration to France after Hitler's seizure of power in 1933 resulted in a sharp increase in the Jewish population of French cities which provoked an increasingly anti-Semitic response among rightist elements and in the press. When the legislative elections of 1936 returned a victory for the Popular Front alliance of communists, socialists, and radicals, anti-communism and a fear of 'national decline' became a veritable obsession for both traditional conservatives and the authoritarian populists to their right. In this climate, groups such as the JP found renewed strength for a time and new—albeit small—organizations like the Solidarité Française and the Francistes were formed. Bucard's Francistes could boast fewer than 2,000 members in the mid-1930s and the SF, despite a significant financial backing and a membership of up to 180,000 in February 1934, had fizzled out by the end of the year. The most significant elements on the radical right in the 1930s, however, were the Croix de Feu and PPF.

The so-called Stavisky riots of 1934 were both cause and effect of a resurgence of activity on the radical right and for many have constituted an iconic moment in the history of French fascism. As René Rémond himself puts it, '[n]othing has done so much to give currency to the idea of a fascist peril than this evening of Paris rioting'.[18] Indeed, it has always been a difficult task to distinguish these events from the mythology surrounding them. After weeks of consternation expressed in the national press about alleged governmental complicity in the illegal operations of the known fraudster Alexandre Stavisky, a Ukrainian Jewish émigré the radical right attempted to whip up enthusiasm for a charge against the Third Republic. The final straw for such groups had been new Prime Minister Édouard Daladier's dismissal of the league-friendly Paris prefect of police and on the morning of 6 February Action Française called for a demonstration against the Chamber of Deputies for that very evening, urging cries of 'A bas les voleurs!' to show the government that its supporters 'have had enough of the despicable regime'.[19] On that night, 40,000 demonstrators converged on the Place de la Concorde in central Paris and surrounded the Chamber of Deputies demanding the resignation of Daladier. The scale of physical conflict between demonstrators and police—provoked especially by AF, Solidarité Française, and JP militants—resulted in the bloodiest civil protest

---

[18] Rémond, *The Right Wing in France*, 283.

[19] *Action française*, 6 February 1934, cited in S. Berstein, *Le 6 février 1934* (Paris: Gallimard, 1975), 142.

in France since the Paris Commune of 1871. The events resulted in the immediate resignation of Daladier, whose government was replaced by the more authoritarian rule of Gaston Doumergue, a figure who was more accommodating of the extra-parliamentary right-wing leagues.

René Rémond is typical of most historians in asserting that the demonstrations—he prefers not to call them riots—are evidence not of the strength but of the weakness of French fascism. This consensus view of the 1934 riots has more recently been attacked as over-determinist. French sociologist Michel Dobry concedes, for example, that there was no overt plot to overthrow the regime and that the assault on the Palais Bourbon was uncoordinated, but he criticizes the flawed logic that has led historians to argue backwards from the outcome of the preservation of the Republic that fascism was an insignificant force in inter-war France. As Brian Jenkins puts it, '[i]t is almost as if Mussolini's "March on Rome" (October 1922) and Hitler's failed Munich *putsch* (November 1923) were seen as the template for the "fascist seizure of power" '.[20] In fact, these violent demonstrations effectively convinced the PCF that the Republic was in danger and that democratic parliamentarians were a lesser evil than the 'fascist' mob. Thus the night of 6 February 1934 prompted the beginnings of the anti-fascist Popular Front alliance that succeeded at the legislative elections of 1936. In the face of this leftist solidarity, the resurgent radical right, far from being neutralized by the advent of the conservative premiership of Gaston Doumergue, merely gained momentum.

Its most significant manifestation was the Croix de Feu. Founded in 1928 as a veterans' organization, the movement's membership was enlarged and its programme radicalized after Colonel François de La Rocque assumed leadership in 1931. The audacity of 6 February 1934 seemed to help recruitment: the Croix de Feu claimed only 35,000 members at the time of the riots but almost half a million on the eve of the elections in 1936 along with hundreds of regional offices. In fact the Croix de Feu was the fastest-growing political party on the right between 1934 and 1939. In an era when French political parties, especially rightist ones, did not recruit a large membership, it had as many as a million members in 1937. As historians are fond of noting, that gave it a larger popular base than the SFIO and PCF combined. The Croix de Feu enjoyed significant cross-class support in urban and rural France and it has been estimated that by 1939 the Parti Social Français (PSF)—the political party into which the Croix de Feu was transformed in 1936—had attracted the sympathy of around 3,000 mayors, 1,000 municipal councillors, and 12 deputies.

Historians have not been able to agree on whether this movement was fascist, and the 'consensus' opinion has been that the Croix de Feu—even more so its post-1936 incarnation the PSF—was a variant of traditional conservatism, however authoritarian. In the Rémondian paradigm, the Croix de Feu was not sufficiently

---

[20] B. Jenkins, 'The *Six février* and the "Survival" of the French Republic', *French History*, 20 (2006), 344.

radical, plebeian, or revolutionary to warrant the fascist label. La Rocque, unlike such ostensibly fascist leaders as Georges Valois or Jacques Doriot, had never been a revolutionary of the left, and his economic vision was not particularly collectivist. Yet La Rocque's movement desired a new elite that would replace republican democracy with a virile authoritarianism, was ferociously anti-Marxist and, in the late 1930s, expressed anti-Semitism despite its leader's claims to tolerance. Moreover it was a mass movement whose enormous membership was mobilized both in paramilitary rallies and through leisure organizations wherein the boundaries between mass culture and mass politics blurred. More seriously and successfully than any other movement on the radical right, the Croix de Feu mobilized female support in lively women's sections whose social action targeted working-class districts in a strategy for recruitment. Its paramilitary units, the so-called *dispos* who could be called upon to lead the counter-revolution at 'H-Hour', routinely engaged in political violence in a way that made the movement's claims to represent a force of order difficult to defend.[21] Historians like William Irvine, Robert Soucy, and Kevin Passmore have argued forcefully that the apparent legalism of the Croix de Feu, at least before 1937, is contradicted by many of its actions and may well have reflected political strategy rather than political conviction. They argue, too, that the conservative nature of Croix de Feu ideology and support does not necessarily disbar it from classification as fascist, since both Italian Fascism and German Nazism had a similar relationship with traditional conservatism.[22]

There has been no protracted dispute over the fascist credentials of the PPF, the movement founded by former communist Jacques Doriot shortly after the Popular Front victory in June 1936. Whereas in 1934 Doriot had preached collaboration between communists and socialists to combat fascism and capitalism (and was reprimanded by the PCF for espousing such rapprochement before it became official policy a matter of months later), by the end of 1936 he demanded class collaboration to defeat the anarchy of strikes and incipient communist revolution. Despite refusing the label 'fascist', by 1938 Doriot's movement was bitterly anti-Semitic and wanted to deprive recent immigrants of French citizenship. The PPF had a strong presence in Algeria, too, where, as for other movements on the radical right, its activism keenly exploited ethnic tensions and its anti-Semitism was more intense. In early 1938 the PPF reached the height of its popularity with some 100,000 members but its anti-communist appeal was diminished after the collapse of the Popular Front in April 1938.

Some historians have bypassed the search for definitional purity by focusing on the crisis in inter-war liberal democracy which made quasi-fascist political alternatives seem viable for a time both to political elites and to the general populace. Since 'these movements were all fishing in the same pool of ideas, and tapping the same

---

[21] K. Passmore, 'Boy Scouting for Grown-ups? Paramilitarism in the Croix de Feu and the Parti Social Français', *French Historical Studies*, 19 (1995), 527–57.
[22] Irvine, 'Fascism in France', 271–95.

veins of anti-democratic sentiment' anyway, what matters in the European context is the question of why that sentiment could successfully mobilize opinion in one set of circumstances and not in another.[23] In exploring such contextual factors, many historians have pointed out that the dividing line between the conservative and radical right was always somewhat porous.[24] If membership of the conservative Fédération Républicaine frequently overlapped with that of the monarchist Action Française or the more radical Jeunesses Patriotes or Croix de Feu, shared readership of their various newspapers was even more common. William Irvine suggests that amid a breakdown of 'conservative consensus' in the 1930s the appeal of the radical right increased for significant elements within conservative circles. FR leaders such as Louis Marin and Philippe Henriot, stricken with panic over the purchase achieved by communism and perturbed by the success of the Popular Front at the 1936 elections, reached out to radical populists in an attempt to build an anti-communist alliance with the power to mobilize the masses. In 1937 the FR, alongside Pierre Taittinger, acquiesced in PPF *chef* Jacques Doriot's desire for a 'Liberty Front' that would serve as an antidote to the leftist Front Populaire. Strikingly, what explains the FR's preference for seeking alliances with the radical PPF in this period (rather than with the more moderate PSF) is not so much ideological affinity but the fact that the restyled parliamentary party of Colonel de La Rocque posed a direct threat to FR electoral ambitions.[25] Thus, as in the 1920s, there was a sense in which widespread fear of communism helped to galvanize rightist support for a populist strike against the left, while the competition for political space effectively limited the ability of such groups to form a robust alliance.

At any rate, the radical right not only made its presence felt among political elites. The 1920s and 1930s were marked by a sectarian battle for urban streets and other public places where demonstrations and counter-demonstrations often resulted in physical violence. The kind of conflict engendered between rival newspaper vendors which had so characterized urban street life in the 1920s (members of the Faisceau and JP had carried canes to ward off attack) was exacerbated amid the deeper crises of the next decade. Père Lachaise cemetery in Paris, for example, was a contested commemorative site where communists frequently clashed with militants of the radical right. In May 1934 a ceremony organized by the capital's Italian community was attended by members of the Francistes, Croix de Feu, JP, and Solidarité Française, followers of the last provocatively giving the Roman salute. Indeed, fearing conflict, police attempted to make the SF members cover up their

[23] Jenkins, 'The *Six février*', 339.

[24] For example, M. Dobry, 'February 1934 and the Discovery of French Society's Allergy to the "Fascist Revolution"', in B. Jenkins (ed.), *France in the Era of Fascism: Essays on the French Authoritarian Right* (New York: Berghahn Books, 2005), 139. Ironically, even René Rémond admits that between 6 February 1934 and 1937 'a part of the classic right let itself be won over by the vocabulary, and taken in by the propaganda, of fascism'. Rémond, *The Right Wing in France*, 297–8.

[25] W. Irvine, *French Conservatism in Crisis: The Republican Federation of France in the 1930s* (Baton Rouge: Louisiana State University Press, 1979), 145.

blue shirts by putting on jackets. Eager to force a confrontation, both *L'Humanité* and an Italian anti-fascist publication had called on their supporters to arrive *en masse* at the cemetery to 'chase the fascists from the streets'.[26] In February 1936, just months before he became Prime Minister, the socialist Léon Blum was dragged from his car and beaten by royalist thugs attending the funeral procession for monarchist historian Jacques Bainville. As a result of this incident Charles Maurras, leader of the AF, was given an eight-month jail sentence for incitement to murder and Blum, once premier, issued a decree outlawing fascist leagues such as the Croix de Feu, Solidarité Française, JP, and the Francistes. Street violence did not end with this piece of legislation, however, and in March 1937 five people were killed in the northern Paris suburb of Clichy when a thousand leftists stormed a meeting of the Croix de Feu's new incarnation, the PSF. Furthermore, now driven underground, some elements turned openly to terrorism: the Comités Secrets d'Action Révolutionnaire (CSAR), sometimes known as the Cagoule and suspected by police of having as many as 6,000 members, murdered the Italian anti-fascist Rosselli brothers in June 1937 and staged bomb attacks which they often blamed on anarchists. This level of violence is indeed remarkable given how emphatically many scholars of French fascism have stressed that inter-war France was a 'stable democracy'.[27]

There were limits, however, to the fragility of the French state in this period. Tellingly, Henry Dorgères's peasant 'greenshirts', who were ready to suppress the unprecedented agricultural strikes of 1936 and 1937 in the north and north-west of the country, found that the regular police force—even under the Popular Front— needed no *squadristi*-style populist help in doing so themselves.[28] Indeed, willing to use force to restore order in the countryside, the French left had in addition helped to prevent the appeal of fascism there through its traditional support of smallholding peasant proprietorship.[29] There is much to support Robert Paxton's view that fascism failed in France because neither conservatives nor state authorities were sufficiently threatened for long enough by the political and economic crises of the decade seriously to appeal to it for support. In any case, Daladier's authoritarian rule after April 1938, with its greater recourse to decree laws, effectively ended both the Popular Front and the fears of communist insurgence that accompanied it. As a result, the ability of the 'fascists' to mobilize popular support was eroded. Although respectable politicians on the republican right had appealed to them for a time as anti-communist allies, neither the Croix de Feu nor the PPF, nor any of the other

---

[26] See police reports in the Paris Prefecture of Police archives, BA 2164, and *L'Humanité*, 19 May 1934.

[27] This irony is pointed out by Passmore, 'Boy Scouting for Grown-ups?', 529.

[28] R. O. Paxton, *French Peasant Fascism: Henry Dorgères's Greenshirts and the Crises of French Agriculture, 1929–1939* (Oxford: Oxford University Press, 1997), 90, 161–4.

[29] W. Brustein and M. Berntson, 'Inter-war Fascist Popularity in Europe and the Default of the Left', *European Sociological Review*, 15 (1999), 159–78.

movements on the radical right, ever came close to seizing power either by *coup d'état* or ballot box.

III. Vichy France, 1940–1944

It was military defeat by an external power rather than political subversion from within which brought down the Third Republic. On 22 June 1940, after six weeks of armed combat between the French and German armies, the recently appointed Prime Minister, Marshal Philippe Pétain, signed an armistice with the occupying German forces. On 10 July, Pétain was voted full constitutional powers by an over-whelming majority of serving French parliamentarians (the tally was 569 to 80), an act which allowed for unspecified revisions to the Third Republican constitution. At the same time, the authority and autonomy of this new *État Français* was delimited both by the original terms of the armistice and by the increasingly exploitative nature of occupation: France contributed more to the Nazi war economy than any other European nation under German rule.

The regime that was built on these compromised foundations and whose adopted seat was the resort town of Vichy functioned as a kind of court in which a small, appointed political elite surrounded Pétain as central decision maker.[30] The Vichy regime unleashed an authoritarian backlash against the ideals of republican-ism. The political virtues associated with the French Revolution—*liberté, égalité, fraternité*—were replaced with a communitarian slogan which had in fact been invented by the Croix de Feu in the 1930s—*famille, travail, patrie*. The regime's promises of national regeneration and reconciliation (that is, an end to the imag-ined divisions of 'class conflict' fomented by the left) were pursued under the aus-pices of a so-called 'National Revolution', a term formerly used by Action Française, the Faisceau, and the Croix de Feu. Indeed, the promise of spiritual renewal that the Vichy regime embodied amid the catastrophic circumstances of war led Action Française *chef* Charles Maurras to describe the defeat as a 'divine surprise'.

The emphasis on national reconciliation belied the regime's systematic policies of exclusion. From the summer of 1940 the regime sought to remove commu-nists, Jews, and Freemasons from public life by restricting their employment rights and in many cases forcing incarceration in the internment camps established for 'dangerous foreigners' under the late Third Republic. Anti-Jewish legislation was articulated independently of German demands, and the regime's systematic iden-tification and asset stripping of the Jewish population in France meant that when

[30] J. Jackson, *France: The Dark Years, 1940–1944* (Oxford: Oxford University Press, 2001), 145.

German pressure for deportations was applied from spring 1942 onwards Jewish men, women, and children were vulnerable to arrest.

The Vichy regime was thus anti-Semitic and anti-communist, illiberal and authoritarian. Furthermore, in the early 1970s American historian Robert Paxton definitively demonstrated the bankruptcy of any claim that Vichy ruled only by German *diktat*. Both in the nostalgic vision of its 'National Revolution' and in the accompanying exclusionary measures, the *État Français* was a regime rooted in the trajectory of indigenous French political developments, however infelicitous its origins. Yet few historians—even the ones who take issue with the 'immunity thesis'—have claimed that Vichy was fascist. In fact, the definitional dispute that has characterized studies of fascism in France often stops with the defeat of 1940. Historical debate on Vichy developed instead along a notionally separate axis, driven by the problem of collaboration rather than that of fascism.

Ironically, any confident disavowal of the fascist credentials of the Vichy regime rekindles the very notion of a fascist essence that many historians have long endeavoured to avoid. It seems circular logic indeed to discount the regime's borrowing of slogans from the inter-war radical—even fascist—right on the grounds that the language of such factions was widely shared by conservatives. In any case, the arguments used to deny that the Vichy regime was fascist centre on the distinctions in personnel that can be drawn between the overtly fascist-collaborationist journalists and activists in occupied Paris and the ruling elite of the regime in Vichy; the political pluralism of the Vichy regime evident in its rejection of a single party and its lack of totalitarian ambitions; its lack of interest in popular mobilization; and, for some scholars, the absence of any tendency towards military expansionism.[31] Despite the well-resourced popular cult of Pétain, there were no mass rallies as might be expected of a fascist regime, no liturgically expressed gratitude to the national saviour staged along paramilitary lines. If there are elements of Vichy rule and ideology that fit the fascist label, there is much about the regime that resists it.

The Vichy state was at the outset undeniably plural and pluralist. It was clear by the autumn of 1940 that neither Pétain nor his chief entourage were interested in the creation of a single party along fascist lines despite the inclusion of former members of the PPF such as Paul Marion among the Vichy elite. Indeed, Vichy's committees and national assembly (the largely impotent Conseil National created in 1941) operated throughout the entire period of occupation without any formal political party structure at all. Vichy's pluralism is perhaps demonstrated most obviously in its youth policy. Vichy propaganda, produced within the secretariat for youth under social Catholic Georges Lamirand, emphasized how the young—especially male

---

[31] For an astute and succinct discussion of these issues see J. Jackson, 'Vichy and Fascism', in E. Arnold (ed.), *The Development of the Radical Right in France: From Boulanger to Le Pen* (Basingstoke: Macmillan, 2000), 153–71.

youth—would play a crucial part in the country's spiritual regeneration. But the only official youth organization for boys that the regime created, the Compagnons de France, remained entirely voluntary and was forced to compete with a plethora of pre-existing independent youth organizations such as the scouts. Its membership dwindled from a high of 30,000 in the first few enthusiastic months of the regime, which represented a small fraction of the total membership (nearly 2 million) of youth movements in the non-occupied zone.[32] Despite the dreams of fascists like Paul Marion, Vichy failed to create a single youth movement along the lines of the Hitler Youth in Germany.

Furthermore, the individuals most likely to make a virtue of Franco-German cooperation and to seek a popular mobilization around Nazi-friendly ideology were far removed from the Vichy regime in Paris. Among them was Jacques Doriot whose PPF experienced a resurgence of popularity in the altered political—and financial—circumstances after defeat. Doriot, dressed in black and sweating profusely, regularly engaged large audiences of supporters with his vision of a re-formed France. After 1941 he was involved in recruiting volunteers for the collabora-tionist Légion des Volontaires Français (the anti-Bolshevik Legion) set up by a panel of ardent collaborationists and only reluctantly sanctioned by the Vichy regime. It sent thousands of French volunteers to fight in German uniform on the eastern front. At its height in 1942 the PPF—whose supporters were located primarily in Paris, Marseille, and North Africa—mustered perhaps 40,000 members and its newspaper, *L'Émancipation nationale*, sold in the tens of thousands.

Occupied Paris, with the lure of German contacts and money, provided fertile ground for other fascist-collaborationist initiatives, especially while the German armies were still triumphant. Perhaps the most significant was the Rassemblement National Populaire formed early in 1941 by Marcel Déat, a former neo-socialist whose nationalism had brought him to fascism. This organization, somewhat smaller in membership than Doriot's PPF, was created once Déat realized that his attempt in summer 1940 to win over Pétain to the fascist cause had failed. With a similar number of recruits, the Mouvement Social Révolutionnaire was founded in September 1940 by pre-war Cagoule (CSAR) activist Eugène Deloncle, a former naval engineer with a fondness for physical violence who was expelled from his own organization in May 1942 for the extremity of his thuggish behaviour. These groups supported and legitimized the anti-Semitism of the Nazi occupiers, and frequently criticized Vichy's 'National Revolution' in their press for dragging its feet in the quest to build a renewed France purged of such supposedly noxious elements as Jews and communists. In addition, a large collaborationist press existed in occupied Paris whose collective readership ran into the hundreds of thousands. Publications like *Je suis partout*, *La Gerbe*, and *Au pilori*, staffed mostly by survivors from the pre-war radical right, rationalized the Nazi presence, espoused a virulent anti-Semitism

---

[32] W. D. Halls, *The Youth of Vichy France* (Oxford: Clarendon Press, 1981), 147–8.

and anti-communism, and tried to convince a generally unwilling populace of the merits of the Nazi 'New European Order'. Ironically, while providing the context for this rightist resurgence, the very presence of the German forces amid a context of defeat robbed such elements of what would arguably have been their most powerful tool of mobilization: nationalism.[33]

The Vichy regime itself tended to represent collaboration as a necessary strategy rather than an inherent virtue, and its personnel differed from the radical revolutionaries based in Paris. In its early phase in particular the Vichy elite was dominated by political Catholics and provided the most military of all French administrations since 1832.[34] Thus the corridors of power were staffed by a combination of senior military personnel from the armed forces (for example, Foreign Minister and Deputy Premier Admiral Darlan and North Africa proconsul General Maxime Weygand), pre-war social Catholics such as Georges Lamirand and Paul de la Porte du Theil who were especially dominant in Vichy youth policy, and 'experts' such as the classicist Jérôme Carcopino in the Education Ministry. The influence of this latter group on policy between 1940 and 1944 has led historians to see Vichy as a regime that prefigures the 'technocratic' Gaullist Fifth Republic.[35] Indeed, outside Vichy's impotent Conseil National, former parliamentarians were thin on the ground: by the end of 1940 Laval was the only significant player left in Vichy's inner circle who had been involved in government under the Third Republic.[36]

Yet members of the radical right were not entirely absent, especially where the AF was concerned. Among Vichy's Maurrassians featured General Weygand and the figures of Raphael Alibert and Xavier Vallat who played crucial roles in developing Vichy policies of anti-Semitism. Furthermore, the industrialist Pierre Pucheu, who was Minister of Industrial Production for a time under Vichy, had been a prominent supporter of the PPF in the 1930s; and a figure close to Pétain, Minister of Information Paul Marion, had also been a *doriotiste*, as was Vichy ambassador to the Nazi authorities in Paris Fernand de Brinon. Thus it must be remembered that there was sometimes little ideological distance between Vichy political elites and the fascist-collaborationists who sought German approval in occupied Paris. It is nonetheless significant that Charles Maurras himself, along with PSF leader Colonel François de La Rocque, who both took refuge after the defeat in the so-called Vichy zone, maintained a distance from the regime itself, however much they admired the 'National Revolution'. Maurras's world-view was still informed by a lingering

---

[33] See M. Cointet-Labrousse, *Vichy et le fascisme: les hommes, les structures et les pouvoirs* (Brussels: Complexe, 1987), 248 and A. Chebel d'Appollonia, 'Collaborationist Fascism', in Arnold (ed.), *The Development of the Radical Right in France, 172–92.*

[34] Jackson, *France: The Dark Years*, 147.

[35] Yves Bouthillier, Minister of Finance, 1940–2, cited in ibid. 148.

[36] Ibid. 145; R. O. Paxton, *Vichy France: Old Guard and New Order, 1940–1944* (New York: Columbia University Press, 1972), 192.

Germanophobia and La Rocque, whose movement became known after 1940 as the Progrès Social Français, rebuffed invitations by fascists and ardent collaborationists to help in the construction of a single party. In fact, both François de La Rocque and former Faisceau chief Georges Valois were to be arrested towards the end of the occupation by the Gestapo for presumed acts of resistance. As Bertram Gordon has suggested, 'not all French fascists in 1940 became collaborators, but by 1944 all collaborationists had become fascists'.[37]

Indeed, things were to change somewhat throughout 1944. A combination of German pressure and the radicalization of the circumstances of occupation—not least the growing war against the Resistance—meant that 'ultras' such as fascist Marcel Déat and extremist Philippe Henriot became central figures in Vichy's last months, Déat as Minister of Labour and Henriot as an inflammatory Vichy radio propagandist who enrolled his own son in the SS.[38] But it was only after the final crumbling of the Vichy regime in August 1944 that the Germans looked seriously to Jacques Doriot as a potential leader for a collaborationist France in exile. Overtures were made to the PPF *chef* in the clearly desperate circumstances in which a number of collaborationist French activists joined the rump of German forces now taking refuge from the Allies in the south-west German town of Sigmaringen.

Historians such as Michèle Cointet-Labrousse, who argue that, while not fascist in inspiration, the Vichy regime developed fascist tendencies by 1944, usually cite the creation and use of the French militia—the Milice—as a key piece of evidence for such a transformation. From 1943, this paramilitary special police force was run by far right war veteran close to the PPF Joseph Darnand and funded—indeed eventually armed—by the German authorities. The Milice was at the vanguard of the war on the Resistance and in January 1944 its leader became the minister responsible for maintaining order with control of all French police forces.[39] In the words of Julian Jackson, this violently anti-communist and anti-Semitic body 'cultivated the image of a chivalric elite with something of the spirit of the Rumanian fascist movement the Legion of the Archangel Michael'.[40] It had as many as 30,000 members by the end of the occupation and engaged in extreme acts of political violence such as the assassination in summer 1944 of the Jewish former Republican deputies Jean Zay and Georges Mandel. In the opinion of Cointet-Labrousse this turn of events meant that, while fascism did not have a strong hold on the Vichy regime, by 1944 Vichy-era France had, under German pressure, turned into a police state with fascist attributes.[41]

---

[37] B. M. Gordon, *Collaborationism in France during the Second World War* (Ithaca, NY: Cornell University Press, 1980), 19, echoing a sentiment expressed by P. Ory, *Les Collaborateurs, 1940–1945* (Paris: Seuil, 1976), 270.

[38] Irvine, *French Conservatism in Crisis*, 223.   [39] Cointet-Labrousse, *Vichy et le fascisme*, 236.

[40] Jackson, 'Vichy and Fascism', 167.   [41] Cointet-Labrousse, *Vichy et le fascisme*, 245.

IV. Conclusion

The legal purges of collaborators staged after liberation in 1944 established a narrative of the occupation years which thereafter echoed in both Gaullist and communist circles. It held that ideologically driven collaborationism—or fascism—was a rare phenomenon. When in 1945 Jean-Paul Sartre deliberately misspelled Robert Brazillach's name in his pamphlet 'Qu'est-ce qu'un collaborateur?', his words had the effect of reducing the problem of Franco-German cooperation to facile admiration of the Third Reich and simultaneously denied the purchase of fascist ideas in France. As Alice Kaplan has argued, 'the gist of Sartre's argument is that the fascists are outsiders' rather than an organic part of French political culture.[42] Certainly, wartime collaboration and genocide sapped the legitimacy of any overtly fascist political option and the *trente glorieuses* of the post-war era made infertile economic soil for fascism outside a fringe of unrepentant collaborationists who styled themselves as martyrs of the 'Red Terror' of 1944.

However much early post-war scholars may have underestimated the appeal of the inter-war and Vichy-era radical right, the lack of a fascist *coup d'état* or regime in France is significant against the European context. The radical right in France did not lack conviction, ideas, or popular appeal, but it failed to convince enough political elites that it could resolve the crises of the inter-war period. It is likely that the 'Daladier moment' between April 1938 and March 1940 provided sufficient anti-communist and xenophobic reassurance to diffuse its mobilizing potential. As Michèle Cointet-Labrousse points out, in fact only a few rightists in France subscribed fully to the commonly cited view 'better Hitler than Blum'; for most, Daladier would do. Whatever the strength of inter-war fascism in France, its power was surpassed by the strength of traditional conservatism and by the resilience of the republican state.

BIBLIOGRAPHY

BURRIN, P., *La Dérive fasciste: Doriot, Déat, Bergery, 1933–1945* (Paris: Seuil, 1986).
DOBRY, M. (ed.), *Le Mythe de l'allergie française au fascisme* (Paris: Albin Michel, 2003).
IRVINE, W., *French Conservatism in Crisis: The Republican Federation of France in the 1930s* (Baton Rouge: Louisiana State University Press, 1979).
JENKINS, B. (ed.), *France in the Era of Fascism: Essays on the French Authoritarian Right* (New York: Berghahn Books, 2005).
MILZA, P., *Fascisme français: passé et présent* (Paris: Flammarion, 1987).

[42] A. Kaplan, *Reproductions of Banality: Fascism, Literature, and French Intellectual Life* (Minneapolis: University of Minnesota Press, 1986), 14.

PASSMORE, K., *From Liberation to Fascism: The Right in a French Province, 1928–1939* (Cambridge: Cambridge University Press, 1997).

RÉMOND, R., *Les Droites en France* (Paris: Aubier Montaigne, 1982); 4th edn. of *La Droite en France de 1815 à nos jours* (Paris: Aubier, 1954).

SOUCY, R., *French Fascism: The First Wave, 1924–1933* (New Haven: Yale University Press, 1986).

—— *French Fascism: The Second Wave, 1933–1939* (New Haven: Yale University Press, 1995).

STERNHELL, Z., *Neither Right nor Left: Fascist Ideology in France*, trans. D. Maisel (Berkeley and Los Angeles: University of California Press, 1986).

CHAPTER 28

....

JAPAN

....

RIKKI KERSTEN

I. THE QUAGMIRE OF PARTICULARISM

....

IN asking 'was Japan fascist' in the 1930s and 1940s, we enter into a conceptual
quagmire. Not only do we need to deal with the ongoing lack of resolution about
what fascism itself means, but we must also confront issues that challenge our
presumption of rationality and scientific objectivity when we engage in historical or
social scientific analysis of our world. If we can assume that fascism was more than a
phenomenon that arose between the wars in Italy, we must then ask whether political concepts can traverse particularistic territories and emerge not only unscathed,
but recognizable.

All of this is complicated further by the fact that this type of enquiry often seems
to be one way, from West to East. Was China 'communist'? Is Japan 'democratic'?
When our answer is the equivalent of 'well yes, but somehow different', we should be
alert to the implications. When we say 'China was communist' (or ironically, 'China
is capitalist'), but 'with Chinese characteristics', we are compromising the ability
conceptually to compare for reasons of culture, or even for reasons of identity. At
the same time, we often fail to apply this particularistic measure to the original
concept itself. The original is endowed with exclusive validity simply because it
came first.

In the study of fascism, many non-Asian writers see no difficulty in declaring
fascism to be a European phenomenon.[1] The study of fascism outside Europe then
becomes a predetermined hunt for absent attributes, for deficiencies, or, worse still,

---

[1] See for example M. Mann, *Fascists* (Cambridge: Cambridge University Press, 2004), 375, who
argues that fascism was specific to a certain period in European history.

attributes that are present but unmistakably 'cultural' in nature. In effect, Asian particularism is mobilized to deny conceptual legitimacy for fascism in an Asian context. For example, Paxton writes that Japan saw only a brief appearance by 'authentic fascists' in the late 1930s, but even then Japan lacked the essential attribute of a single mass-based party or movement: 'the Japanese variant of fascism was imposed by rulers in the absence of a single mass party or popular movement, and indeed in disregard of, or even in opposition to, the Japanese intellectuals who were influenced by European fascism'.[2] Stanley Payne for his part notes that Japan was 'too non-Western, to be receptive to genuine fascism'.[3] In this kind of approach, context is conflated with substance. If this is where our enquiry ends, it amounts to a form of intellectual colonialism.

While several scholars seek to constrain legitimate fascism in both a geographical and a temporal zone (namely Europe between the wars), others try to overcome this overly prescriptive approach. Roger Eatwell points out that 'there is no logical reason why other areas could not experience relatively similar socio-economic strains' that occurred in Europe after the First World War. For Eatwell, Payne not only ties fascism too closely to European historical experience, but fails to identify what is central and what is peripheral to an understanding of fascist ideology. He further indicates that, if culture and time are definitive, then fascism can only ever be valid in a western setting. This is indeed the crux of the issue in much non-Asian scholarship on generic fascism.[4] But as Larsen points out, particularism is a dual-edged sword. If it can condemn Japan as insufficiently European to properly be fascist, it can also label Germans as doomed by identity to be the carriers of 'the non-democratic norm'.[5] Mosse reminds us that precisely because 'all fascisms were nationalisms',[6] particularism has to have a place in the depiction and comprehension of fascism wherever it appears.

It is in the context of these kinds of problems that we encounter what we might call the adjectival escape clause, whereby fascism is attached to an adjective that shifts it outside the sphere of total legitimacy into a particularistic twilight zone. In Japan's case the term 'Emperor System Fascism' implies a kind of 'almost but not quite' variant of fascism. Likewise 'militarist fascism' achieves the same mantle of ambiguity when describing fascism in Japan. It was there, kind of, but then again, not really...

In addressing this problem of cultural context for fascist dynamics, Larsen states plainly that it is important to stress the 'national, contextual character' of fascism, including the Emperor System in Japan's case. Instead of culture, context for Larsen

---

[2] R. O. Paxton, *The Anatomy of Fascism* (New York; Vintage Books, 2005), 199.

[3] S. G. Payne, *A History of Fascism 1914–1945* (Madison: University of Wisconsin Press, 1995), 336.

[4] R. Eatwell in S. U. Larsen (ed.), *Fascism outside Europe* (Boulder, CO: Columbia University Press, 2001), 21, 25.

[5] Larsen (ed.), *Fascism outside Europe*, 708.

[6] G. L. Mosse (ed.), *International Fascism: New Thoughts and New Approaches* (London: Sage, 1979), 31.

denotes the way in which Japan responded to the global capitalist crisis 'by transforming the state into a totalitarian instrument for internal control and directing the state's coercive energies towards external expansion'. Whereas for Griffin the presence and role of the emperor represented a conservative and therefore insufficiently fascist (revolutionary) impetus,[7] for Larsen the emperor institution was window dressing for an identifiably fascist impulse.

History is littered with ambiguity and discomfort when relativism is seen to threaten the integrity of a concept. The *Historikerstreit* in 1980s Germany is one example.[8] Historians were troubled by the notion that the Holocaust could be 'relativized' by looking at it in comparative terms. In preserving the uniqueness of that evil, the conceptual integrity of genocide was interrogated. When Ernst Nolte tried to argue that the Holocaust was in fact not an 'original' phenomenon but a response or reaction to an earlier evil perpetrated by Russia, the howls of outrage resonated throughout German academe. Yet genocide studies have survived, if only because the world in which we live keeps giving us material to digest and explain.

When we turn to the matter of Japanese fascism, history intrudes in a similar vein, from within. The history of Japan's encounter with modernity (read 'Western modernity'), for instance in the 1850s, saw Japanese thinkers and politicians grapple with the hard question: what was the connection between being modern, powerful, and wealthy, and identity? Did Japan have to 'Europeanize' or 'Westernize' in order to achieve modernity? How important were religion, language, and culture to the modernization process? Japanese ruling elites were also mindful of the utility of seeming to be 'modern' in the sense of reflecting the image of the intrusive West back to them. Imitation was not only flattery, it was survival. The fact that Japanese asked the question is relevant to our examination of fascism in Japan.

At the risk of summarizing too much, Japanese in Meiji Japan (1868–1912) came to realize that socio-political and economic change occurred as an interactive exercise with culture. Culture was not so much a prerequisite for structural and institutional change as something that transformed, and was transformed by, those tangible and material dimensions. Moreover, institutions operated in the context of thought and culture, and could only do so if they resonated with that intangible realm. When Japanese in the Meiji era sought to imbue imported systems, processes, and structures with meaning, they did so in the knowledge that systems and cultures were necessarily interdependent. How then can we credibly search for a simple transplantation of European fascism in our retrospective quest for conceptual legitimacy for Japanese fascism?

---

[7] R. Griffin, *The Nature of Fascism* (London; Pinter, 1991), see especially 153–6.

[8] On the *Historikerstreit* see C. S. Maier, *The Unmasterable Past: History, Holocaust and German National Identity* (Cambridge, Mass.: Harvard University Press, 1997); E. Nolte, 'Between Myth and Revisionism? The Third Reich in the Perspective of the 1980s's', in H. W. Koch (ed.), *Aspects of the Third Reich* (London: Macmillan, 1985), 17–38; J. Habermas, *The New Conservatives: Cultural Criticism and the Historians' Debate* (Cambridge, MA: MIT Press, 1989).

Indeed, from late Meiji onwards culture would eventually become the object of a defensive attempt to 'protect' Japaneseness from Western emasculation. This would become an important aspect of the fascist transformation that occurred in inter-war Japan. It was in an atmosphere of anti-Western, pro-Japanese feeling that fascism entered the socio-political lexicon of modern Japan. It is interesting to note that one entity often singled out as an example of a fascist-like institution in Japan, the Shōwa Research Association, had 'anti-fascism' as one of its self-descriptors.[9] In this atmosphere, anti-fascism was synonymous with anti-western colonialism.

In raising the question of institutions versus dynamics, we touch on one way in which some scholars have tried to incorporate Japan into the fascist camp in conceptual terms. It was not institutions but functions, not attributes but dynamics, that some believe facilitate a fruitful understanding of what fascism meant in Japan. What Larsen called 'functional equivalence' was very much the approach taken by Japan's leading analyst of fascism, Maruyama Masao (1914–96).[10] We can appreciate the irony when we realize that Maruyama was often criticized by his peers for attempting to translate European concepts in a normative manner when interpreting the history of Japanese political thought. Maruyama has been accused of finding Japan 'wanting' compared to the West, of trying to force Japan into a western analytical mould. Maruyama's copious writings on Japanese fascism, and its comparison with that of Germany in particular, would set the markers for Japanese accounts of Japanese fascism thereafter. Our approach then is to examine Maruyama's writings on fascism to see whether we find his depiction of similar functions and dynamics in Japan and Europe convincing, despite the open acceptance on his part of cultural specificity as part of this exercise.

Another consideration when appraising approaches to fascism in Japan is the politicized nature of the historical context in which these approaches have been formulated. The pejorative power of the term 'fascist' is widely acknowledged, but this is more than a superficial blame game. Another dominant school of Japanese writing on Japan's fascism is informed by Marxism, whose troubled and ultimately ineffectual confrontation with fascism has served to undermine the credibility of post-war Japanese Marxists' argumentation concerning fascism. In post-war Japan Marxists had to endure the scepticism of those who recalled the mass political apostasy on the part of communists in the early 1930s. In the diaries of apostates and in subsequent commentaries on this personal political trauma, Japan's communists are seen to have subordinated internationalism to the inclusiveness of the Emperor System ideology. Marxist intellectuals have nonetheless led the charge in transcending particularistic arguments concerning fascism, in insisting that fascism arose as a result of a crisis in monopoly capitalism around the world after the First World War, with Japan as no exception. Barrington Moore, Gavan McCormack,

---

[9] See W. M. Fletcher, *The Search for a New Order: Intellectuals and Fascism in Prewar Japan* (Chapel Hill, NC: University of North Carolina Press, 1982), 96.

[10] Japanese names appear through this chapter with the family name first and given name second.

and Jon Halliday similarly attempt to squeeze Japan into this Marxian mould in a manner that does not exclude Japan's particular circumstance, but rather shows how this was ultimately incidental to the trend of global history. And yet, the persuasiveness of Japanese and non-Japanese Marxists' analysis of wartime fascism does depend on explaining why communism was so weak in the face of the Emperor System ideology. Particularism continues to intrude.

Utility and context arise again when we realize that the integrity of Japan's post-war democracy rests in part on how we differentiate post-war Japanese democracy from wartime Japanese fascism. If Japanese fascism is denoted by its Japaneseness, what does this mean for post-war democracy in Japan? For some, Japan needs to be depicted as part of the global madness of the past, so that its rosy post-fascist history can shine. An inclusive definition of democracy demands an inclusive definition of fascism. More complications niggle though, even here. Neo-nationalists in contemporary Japan such as Kobayashi Yoshinori and Fujioka Nobukatsu are evoking particularism in their quest for national pride in a continuous history, one that does not regard the 1930s as evil or any kind of aberration. Continuity of this kind threatens to tarnish the lustre of post-war Japanese democracy. It also places Japan firmly in the field of exceptionalism (which is exactly where neo-nationalists wish to see it). As with the Marxists, here we note that fascism is not really the issue at all, it is merely the cipher for some other fundamental concern.

The conundrum we face, one among many, is that particularism undermines the integrity of comparative history writing and political thought. At the same time, many Japanese writers, politicians, and activists have insisted on particularism as part of their view of their history. They have done so in the conviction that this does not exclude Japan from world history. We need to walk through this minefield of meta-analysis and parallel discourses to begin to understand how we might answer the question 'was Japan fascist?' We will begin by examining the circumstances of 1930s and 1940s Japan, mindful of the attribute-driven perspective that has dominated English-language writing on Japanese fascism so far. Then we will consider how scholars have wrestled with these questions, before turning to the maestro of Japanese writing on Japanese fascism, Maruyama Masao. We will consider him in the company of other Japanese writers on fascism, before drawing some tentative conclusions.

II. JAPAN BETWEEN THE WARS

Far from being out of sync with the world after the First World War, 1918 heralded Japan's arrival on the world stage. Japan sat at the table with the western victors at Versailles as an ally, and, thanks to Germany's defeat, emerged as an enhanced colonial power in Asia. Those heady days of Wilsonian idealism, self-determination, and the rise of mass participation in politics were just as wild and wonderful in Japan as they were in the rest of the world. Japan's Taishō democracy (1912–26) was formulated and implemented, however fleetingly, with full consciousness of the global nature of the democratic revolution. The Japanese left, in the company of a rejuvenated labour movement, was similarly galvanized by the Russian Revolutions of 1917. It seems a nonsense to imply that Japan was divorced from those trends that coursed through the fabric of Europe in the aftermath of the First World War. If this history is a prerequisite for fascism, Japan lived that history.

Intellectual activism of socialist and democratic hues was rampant in interwar Japan, to the dismay of those oligarchs who were trying to bed down the enormously ambitious nation-building exercise that had begun with the 1868 Meiji Restoration. The entry of the people into policy and politics was most unwelcome to the new elite of the Meiji era, and this impulse to contain the masses influenced the authoritarian structure of that nation building. Thus we saw the oligarchs promise a constitution to the people in 1881, with the Meiji Constitution itself promulgated in 1889 as a gift to the people from the emperor. This constitution logically positioned the emperor at the apex of spiritual and legal authority in Japan, while, at the same time, leaving space for political actors to rule without actually reigning. This structure was consistent with the philosophy of the Restoration itself, in that it phrased change in terms of tradition, and provided spiritual legitimacy to new power structures. While change was packaged with reference to the past, it should not be assumed that genuine transformation was thereby ruled out. We need to embrace the notion of radical conservatism properly to understand the symbolism and function of the imperial institution in Japanese politics after the Restoration.

It was as an ideology rather than as an institution that the Emperor was to feature in the madness that followed.[11] What would become known as the Emperor System was constructed as a series of ideological building blocks in the form of Imperial Rescripts which eventually transmogrified into the full-blown ideological tract *Kokutai no Hongi* (Cardinal Principles of our National Polity) in 1937.[12] The core notions embedded into the sphere of *kokutai* were: the divine origins of the imperial family; the essential racial and spiritual homogeneity of the Japanese; the notion of the emperor as the father of the nation; and a continuous ('unbroken') line of emperors from ancient times.

What may be taken as an unremarkable exercise in identity formation (most understandable in the context of rapid, socially destabilizing modernization, industrialization, and Westernization) morphed into a licence to invade and conquer when combined with an increasingly aggressive nationalism, and growing national

[11] For Meiji ideology see C. Gluck, *Japan's Modern Myths: Ideology in the Late Meiji Period* (Princeton: Princeton University Press, 1985).

[12] *Cardinal Principles of the National Entity of Japan (Kokutai no Hongi)*, trans. J. O. Gauntlett (Cambridge, MA: Harvard University Press, 1949).

insecurity in the midst of global economic and political crises as the 1920s slid into the 1930s. It was but a short hop to the sloganeering of the fascist era, featuring memorable phrases such as 'the family state' (*kazoku kokka*), the '(spiritual) community' (*kyōdōtai*), and 'the eight corners of the world under one roof' (*hakkō ichiu*). Add to this brew the instruments of repression in the shape of the Peace Preservation Law of 1925, and the enforcers of correct thinking in the Thought Police, and we have the makings of a proto-fascist system of domestic terror.

One thinker who wears the mantle as Japan's chief fascist ideologue was Kita Ikki (1883–1937). Kita forged a radical philosophy and programme that fused the sacred origins of the emperor with the imperative of expansion to produce the powerful logic of Japan's sacred mission in Asia. His most famous tract entitled *Fundamental Principles for the Reorganization of Japan* (1919) attracts the adjective 'fascist' because of its combination of these attributes of reform/revolution and expansion. For Kita, the emperor was an instrumental entity who would effect the unity of the people for the sake of fundamental reform within Japan, a reform that parliamentary democracy could never deliver. Without this type of radical reform at home, Kita believed that Japan could not implement its duty of leadership in the rest of Asia. This symbiotic relationship between domestic reform and expansion abroad was the hallmark of Japanese reformist (*kakushin*) thinking in these days of perceived national emergency, and was sufficiently inspiring to reformist elements in the military to propel them into an attempted *coup d'état* in 1936.

Kita situated his readers in the midst of crisis with his opening line: 'the great empire of Japan is at a national turning point as it confronts internal troubles and foreign danger...Truly, we are a small island isolated in the Eastern Sea.'[13] This Confucian formula of identifying a causal link between an external threat and internal disarray would become an almost indistinguishable tangle in the minds of reformists across the spectrum of institutions in inter-war Japan. For some, the transformation of Manchuria was the key to achieving real reform in Japan itself. For others, Japan's liberation of Asians from Western colonialism was an essential component of succeeding in the revolutionary Meiji mission at home. Frustrated with the pace and direction of political change after the Meiji Restoration, radical thinkers like Kita unleashed their vision of authoritarian, top-down 'reorganiza-tion'. It involved suspending parliament for three years, invoking martial law, and dramatically revising the institutional support systems and personnel surrounding the Emperor. It also entailed imposing the same 'reorganization' onto Korea, con-cluding the logic of absorption of one country, people, and race by the other.

Kita's subordinate objective was to deny legitimacy to the imported notion of democracy, which did not take Japan's *kokutai* (national polity) into account. 'Since the Meiji *ishin-kakumei* (restoration-revolution), Japan has been a modern

---

[13] Translation from B. Tankha, *Kita Ikki and the Making of Modern Japan* (Folkestone: Global Oriental, 2006), 167.

democracy with the emperor as the political centre. Why do we have these poor people who continue to think within the confines of literal translations of an imported idea "democracy"?',[14] he moaned. Kita wanted to restore the position of emperor to its Meiji origins, namely as 'the supreme commander above an equal citizenry'. The mission of Japan would become the destiny of world history itself, which would finally be released from a false and exclusive identification with European history. 'The Western–Eastern culture will be of Asian thought Japanized and universalized, which will enlighten the vulgar, so-called civilized peoples... The Japanese rising sun flag after defeating England, reviving Turkey, making India independent and China self-reliant will shed the light of Heaven on all the people of the world.'[15] Kita's manifesto, penned in exile in Shanghai, represented a tortured but heartfelt attempt to connect Japanese uniqueness with world history, creating a universalized version of Japaneseness. Fascist conceptions of reform and aggression were the glue that kept his formula more or less intact, even beyond his short lifetime.

Japanese between the wars were radicalized by economics as well as by ideas. As a late developer, Japan was extremely vulnerable to global shifts in power, finance, and trade. This vulnerability was exacerbated by the essentially lopsided nature of Japan's economic development, which saw sprawling urban centres and industrial combines coexist in the national economy with a backward and impoverished rural sector. Taken together, this lopsided modernity and the presence of a traditional symbol in the form of the emperor made Japanese Marxists question the progress of Japan's modernity/capitalism. Opinion divided between two main schools of thought, the Rōnō and Kōza factions.[16] In Japan and beyond, judgements concerning Japan's stage of historical development—or modernization—would have direct bearing on whether Japan was regarded as fascist (not to mention whether they thought Japan was ready for proletarian revolution). If fascism appeared as a sign of a capitalist system in its death throes, with the Second World War as the final paroxysm, then much depended also on whether Japan had experienced a proper bourgeois revolution, or whether Japan was still semi-feudal. This debate would have a strong influence on post-war Japanese assessments of inter-war and wartime fascism in Japan.

The ambiguities surrounding the Meiji state, and the dualistic nature of Japan's economy, led Kōza communists to determine that Japan had not yet experienced a full-fledged bourgeois-democratic revolution. In their view, the emperor institution and ideology operated as the linchpin of a hybrid system both politically and economically, and therefore needed to be abolished before Japan could move to the intermediate historical stage of bourgeois revolution (this would in the 1950s become known as Japan's 'incomplete modernization'). This became the platform

---

[14] B. Tankha, *Kita Ikki and the Making of Modern Japan* 171.   [15] Ibid. 229.
[16] For background on the Rōnō-Kōza debates see G. A. Hoston, *Marxism and the Crisis of Development in Prewar Japan* (Princeton: Princeton University Press, 1986), 179–222.

of the beleaguered Japanese Communist Party in 1922, ensuring that state repression would be swift as Japan moved from democracy towards authoritarianism in the late 1920s. For their part, the Rōnō intellectuals chose to see Japan in Taishō as properly democratic, and therefore, very much part of the universal move towards proletarian revolution. As Hoston states, 'the Rōnō-ha drew a distinction between the imperial institution, as a bourgeois monarchy relatively independent of the class conflict within the society, and the "emperor system" that the Kōza-ha had identified more strongly with feudal forces and with uniquely Japanese elements...for the Kōza-ha, the emperor was the determining element...for the Rōnō-ha, it was a mere appendage of the state apparatus'.[17]

The 1920s are often painted as schizophrenic, with the appearance of universal suffrage and party political cabinets alongside intensifying repression towards communists, socialists, labour, and, ultimately, liberals. The bogey of social unrest and the threat of political instability materialized as early as 1918 with the Rice Riots. The Great Kantō earthquake of 1923 unleashed a frenzied attack on anarchists and Koreans, revealing the simmering intolerance of authority toward these groups. Most observers agree that Japan's Taishō democracy did not evolve beyond the fledgling stage, and was ultimately unable to resist or counter the political incursions on the part of various 'transcendental' entities (such as the military and the emperor). Party political cabinets would not endure beyond 1932, and were replaced by military leaders who presided over an elected parliament.[18]

Japan shared with post-First World War Europe the fatal weakness of liberal democracy in the face of socio-economic instability. The irresponsibility built into the Meiji state structure evolved into what Maruyama called 'a system of irresponsibility', which saw entities such as the military (comprising feuding branches of army and navy that were each faction ridden) operate independently from parliament, with a direct line to the ultimate legitimizing symbol of the emperor. The 1930s featured a rise in mayhem from these disenchanted, unelected groups, with the attempted coup of 26 February 1936 on the part of young officers the epitome of violence at home.[19] Internationally, the army and eventually the navy struck out in a reckless manner in an attempt to secure Japan's interests in the region. The 1931 Manchurian Incident unleashed a wave of political assassinations at home, alongside a calculated mobilization of society and economy to prepare for what influential elements in the military, government, and bureaucracy thought was the inevitable course for Japan. The Asian component of the Second World War began with the Sino-Japanese War of 1937, though we should remember that Japan had annexed Korea as early as 1910.

Japan's quest for equality with the major powers had reached stalemate as early as the Triple Intervention of 1895, and the ideal had soured considerably by the time

---

[17] Hoston, *Marxism and the Crisis of Development*, 183.

[18] B.-A. Shillony, *Politics and Culture in Wartime Japan* (Oxford: Clarendon Press, 1981).

[19] See B.-A. Shillony, *Revolt in Japan: The Young Officers and the February 26, 1936 Incident* (Princeton: Princeton University Press, 1973).

of the London Naval Conference of 1930 when Japan was allocated a lesser entitlement of naval armament than the major Western Powers. This disenchantment with internationalism was counterbalanced, however, by the thrilling, motivational ideal of the frontier in Manchuria. Many activists both within and outside government viewed Manchuria as the crucible for political, economic, and industrial innovation, righting the wrongs of excessive Westernization, individualism, and estrangement from the revolutionary principles of the Restoration.[20] Japan's exit from the League of Nations in 1933 demonstrated the importance of Manchuria to the revolutionary programme of the 1930s.

In Japan in the 1930s economic insecurity teamed with resentment against the Western colonial Powers to produce a dominant nationalist movement, including the appearance of myriad small yet loud civilian rightist groups.[21] While they resembled in manner and deed the forces that would seize power in Germany and Italy, it was the loose association of military and bureaucrats who drove the radical agenda of a 'new order' in East Asia, and who articulated the programme of the Greater East Asia Co-Prosperity Sphere. As Japanese scholars have pointed out since 1945, there was never a need for any single entity to seize power, because they were able to operate freely within the Meiji constitutional structure of irresponsibility, under cover of an unchallengeable imperial symbol.

The masses were mobilized effectively through a combination of propaganda and fear, making the forging of a mass movement unnecessary. By 1937, Japan had what the majority of scholars in post-war Japan would call a fascist society, polity, and foreign policy, complete with an aggressive external agenda and a creed of spiritual superiority towards the West and racial superiority towards Asians. By 1940 all political parties had disbanded, to form an umbrella organization called the Imperial Rule Assistance Association. The authoritarian regimentation of Japanese society was thereby complete.

III. CONCEPTUALIZING JAPANESE FASCISM: MARUYAMA MASAO

Maruyama's conceptualization of what had happened in inter-war and wartime Japan would fundamentally and decisively influence post-war Japanese perspectives on fascism. Debates would be based on his philosophical terrain, phrased in his terms, and even those who disagreed with his interpretations and conclusions

---

[20] For a superb account of Manchuria in Japanese thinking see L. Young, *Japan's Total Empire: Manchuria and the Culture of Wartime Imperialism* (Berkeley and Los Angeles: University of California Press, 1998).

[21] On the civilian right see G. J. Kasza, 'Fascism from below? A Comparative Perspective on the Japanese Right, 1931–1936', *Journal of Contemporary History*, 19/4 (1984), 607–29.

would be forced to use his ideas as the point of departure for their disagreement. Some of Maruyama's work has been translated into English (with translations varying in quality), but it is sadly true that Maruyama's ideas, like those of his peers, have had little penetration into the world of ideas outside his country because of the language barrier. Japan specialists would be expected to know his work but, while Maruyama versed himself in the ideas and languages of Western philosophy and located his thought in a global context, his own ideas have not yet been rewarded with the same exposure. Here we will attempt to address his ideas in as much detail as possible, as understanding Japanese fascism without him is unthinkable.

The historical and political contexts in which Maruyama turned his attention to fascism would shape his interrogation of Japan's past as well as its present. His emphasis on psychological rather than economic factors, and his preoccupation with Japan's democratic proclivity, was a consequence of the charged political context of defeat. Another relevant factor influencing his approach was that he saw the need in this historical context of defeat and occupation to differentiate himself and the analysis of wartime Japan from the taint of formulaic Marxist explanations, which were themselves tarnished by the fatal inability of Marxists to resist the Emperor System during the war period. Maruyama wanted to understand the invisible dynamics of the Emperor System and how it impacted on society, with the explicit aim of underpinning Japan's post-defeat democracy. Maruyama exemplifies—and possibly was the first to articulate—the tendency after 1945 to regard fascism and fascist dynamics as the inversion, or opposite, of liberal democratic dynamics. Understanding fascism was for Maruyama an essential prerequisite for implementing democracy.

In 1945, after his repatriation from military duty in Hiroshima, Maruyama wrote a ground-breaking, confronting essay on ultranationalism entitled *Logic and Psychology of Ultranationalism*. Here he was primarily concerned with asking how Japanese had been deceived into 'embarking on a war against the rest of the world', and his analysis concentrated on the 'all-pervasive psychological coercion' of the Japanese people by the state. For him, this was evidence that Japan's modernity— and pre-war democracy—were incomplete. In focusing on the pathology of the Emperor System, Maruyama was setting the parameters for his approach to Japan's fascism. His concern with the 'interfusion of ethics and power' that flowed from the spiritual totalitarianism of the Emperor System ideology would feature in his reading of fascist dynamics as a cementation of society, and what he saw as the intrusion of the state into the private realm of morality, ethics, and value autonomy. His post-war intellectual agenda was set by his conviction that fascism had deprived individuals of their social and political autonomy and, therefore, the task for democracy post-war was to 'secure the internal freedom of the individual'.[22]

---

[22] All quotations in this paragraph are from Maruyama Masao, 'The Theory (sic) and Psychology of Ultranationalism', in *Thought and Behaviour in Modern Japanese Politics* (Oxford: Oxford University Press, 1969), 1–24.

A key aspect of Maruyama's understanding of the relationship between the Emperor System and the peculiarity of Japan's fascism rested not in the fact of the emperor's existence, but in the systemic expression of power within the Emperor System. Maruyama's depiction of 'the system of irresponsibility' was raised in several essays in the early post-war years. For instance, he wrote with biting sarcasm of the marked difference between German and Japanese fascist leaders on trial after the war. Whereas German leaders were rational and identified their actions with responsibility for those actions, Japanese military leaders blundered along driven by blind historical forces and *faits accomplis*, until they 'slithered into the depths of defeat'.[23]

This was a manifestation of what Maruyama called 'the maintenance of equilibrium through the transference of oppression' in his *Ultranationalism* essay. Put simply: power and responsibility were never co-located in an individual; instead, power and morality emanated from the ultimate locus of the Emperor, with responsibility being transferred downwards along the hierarchy. Thanks to the quarantining of the emperor as an individual through the transcendental political structure of the Meiji Constitution, the emperor could be right but never accountable. Thanks to the absolute moral authority borrowed from the emperor, individuals acting in his name could act with abandon, without reference to mundane notions of morality. The same paramount morality justified the policy of expansion into Asia, completing the fascist programme. Emperor System fascism then was not a peculiar type of fascism in itself; instead the Emperor System facilitated the expression of fascist dynamics in the form of a monolithic state and a society subsumed within it. The emperor was the justification for this system of irresponsibility; he was not the substance of fascism per se.

In Maruyama's view the presence of the Emperor was not the basis for Japanese exceptionalism with regard to fascism. However, Maruyama's Kōza-style perspective on Japan's incomplete modernity raised the issue of exceptionalism in another way, in that Japan could not be seen to have attained fascism in the same fashion that the Europeans did. To surmount this problem, Maruyama developed the notion of 'fascism from above' to describe Japan's path to fascism. In Maruyama's view, Japan developed 'fascism from below' in a manner similar to Europe between the 1931 Manchurian Incident and the attempted coup in 1936, but from then on Japan displayed 'fascism from above'. Maruyama described this transitional moment in 1936 as 'the great dividing line between fascism as a movement and fascism as a state structure'. According to Maruyama, this shift 'clearly determined that Japan's course towards fascism would not take the shape of a fascist revolution or coup d'etat as in Germany and Italy'.[24] If Japan was to be an exception to the European

---

[23] Maruyama Masao, 'Thought and Behaviour Patterns of Japan's Wartime Leaders', in *Thought and Behaviour*, 107.

[24] Maruyama Masao, 'The Ideology and Dynamics of Japanese Fascism', in *Thought and Behaviour*, 33.

norm, then Maruyama would phrase it in terms of top-down dynamics instead of cultural icons or symbols.

Maruyama identified several attitudinal features that fascist Japan shared with Fascist Italy and Nazi Germany. These included: a rejection of individualist liberalism; opposition to parliamentary politics; a positive view of foreign expansion; and glorification of the military, of racial myths and the national essence (in Japan's case, the *kokutai*). Provided that particularism did not attach to Japanese fascism in terms of its essential dynamics, Maruyama was also happy to articulate an array of distinguishing characteristics of fascism in its Japanese context. Significantly, these distinguishing aspects were for the most part not cultural but socio-economic in nature.

The first distinctive characteristic was the 'family state' (*kazoku kokka*) idea, whereby the emperor was the 'father of the nation' and the citizens of Japan were directly connected to the Emperor in spiritual terms. This all-encompassing notion 'defined the social context of Japanese fascism', according to Maruyama, and 'was connected with the failure of Japanese fascism as a mass movement'.[25] Japan's masses did not have to overturn existing authority, because in normative terms they were incorporated within that authority. In this way from 1936, after the suppression of the attempted coup, Japan's fascism 'ceased to take the form of radical uprisings but advanced steadily by legal means from within the governmental apparatus'.[26] This itinerary is why Maruyama emphasized in his writings on fascism the means by which the Japanese state and its institutions were fascistized from within.

Other features peculiar to Japan's fascism were accidents of economics and geography as well as history. Japan's rural poverty, particularly after 1929, led to the prominence of agrarianism in Japan's fascist ideology, especially in the 'fascism from below' era. Rural hardship radicalized the young officers in the military as well as the civilian rightists. Tellingly, this dimension of fascism in Japan was framed in anti-European terms, with industrialism characterized as a product of 'European' capitalism. Maruyama similarly identified the liberation of Asia from western colonialism as another anti-European sentiment that necessarily set Japan's fascism apart from those in Europe. Implicit references to Europe abound in Maruyama's scathing analysis of the pro-fascist intelligentsia in inter-war Japan, who according to him created a fascist ideology that was 'far inferior in quality and even more absurd in content' than that which occurred in Germany and Italy. But at no stage did Maruyama hold Europe up as a model or measure for Japan's historical experience and the political depiction of that experience.

While references to Europe litter Maruyama's works on fascism, his fundamental concern was always with Japan's post-war present rather than with the depiction of the fascist past for its own sake. What mattered to him was not that Japanese

---

[25] Ibid. 37.   [26] Ibid. 70.

fascism did not develop a mass base as European fascism did; instead it was his interpretation of this absence as evidence of the weakness of Japan's democracy in the pre-war period that bothered him. Likewise, the emergence of fascism from above after 1936 was not in itself of note as far as Maruyama was concerned. Rather, it was the fact that this type of authoritarian fascist dynamic represented evidence of a semi-feudal power structure that was essentially pre-modern in nature. His reading of modern Japanese history up to 1945 as an indictment of democracy and modernity was directed squarely at the immediate post-war pretence that Japan had a democratic tradition it could revive.

In deconstructing the fascist dynamic in Japan, Maruyama traced the evolution of a fascist impulse from the bowels of the Restoration itself. Japanese fascism was neither a creature of Europe nor a poorly indigenized version of its European original. It was rather a product of the radical fusing of tradition and revolution in the Meiji ideology of restorationism, in circumstances of thwarted modernity and democratization. This is underscored by the emergence in the 1930s of cries for a 'Shōwa Restoration' instead of an overturning of the imperial constitutional structure and regime, even in the midst of rightist violence and intimidation. It was in effect a call for a double restoration: to 'restore' the radical promise of 1868 by fulfilling the revolutionary potential of the Emperor System state. For Maruyama, the danger in assuming that fascism had been defeated by democracy in 1945 was that the persistence of fascist dynamics and structures would not be recognized for what it was. Fascism was for Maruyama a contemporary issue rather than a historical one; he believed neo-fascism remained possible even after the glorious triumph of democracy at war's end.

Later in the 1960s, Maruyama became more explicit about his conviction that fascism was not a creature of a specific place and time. He conceded that fascism could be defined either narrowly or broadly, with the narrow definition clinging to attributes (a single-party dictatorship; racial superiority; militarism; deification of a dictator; rejection of constitutionalism and parliamentarism; an authoritarian society), and a broader definition stemming from a Marxist reading of capitalism in crisis. Maruyama argued that the rate at which fascism developed in any given society depended on the revolutionary potential of the socio-political environment in each country, and the pace at which international conflict intensified around them. Rapid development of fascism would more likely lead to 'fascism from above' as in Japan, while a slower evolution would look more like the 'fascism from below' of Italy.

The most important point Maruyama made was that fascist processes and dynamics could arise anywhere:

it is dangerous to think in a fixed manner of fascism as something specific to a certain period in history or to a particular region. Therefore we should not just look at the system or social forms taken by monopoly capital or a right wing political party, but we should also look at the political function of fascism and the process by which it is universalized.[27]

Maruyama declared that the cementing of society into a monolith was for him the definitive expression of fascism as function. Fascism lives where self-directed, independent entities are annihilated, where alternative collectives are subsumed within a larger dominant one, and where uniformity and homogenization are the principal objectives of the fascist ethic. Maruyama saw this as the consistent spiritual tendency of fascism, the factor that identified a society and polity as essentially fascist.

IV. Japanese Writing on Japanese Fascism

Japanese academic writing on fascism in Japan is often dismissed as hopelessly entangled in the Marxist lexicon, lending monotonous predictability to analysis of modern politics and history. There is no question that Marxism has exerted a powerful influence on Japanese academe in the modern period, and that it continues to do so (though with diminishing dominance in contemporary Japan). Yet despite the straitjacket of the Kōza-Rōnō ideological divide within the Marxian camp, there has been remarkable accord on the question of whether Japan experienced fascism or not. This is in itself notable because of the trauma experienced by Japanese Marxism in the fascist period, which has injected further complexity into post-war writing on the inter-war era. In passing judgement on Japan's fascism, many Japanese scholars have been forced simultaneously to declare their hand on the question of Japan's modernity, and on the miserable fate of socialist revolution in their country. Very often, their answers were replete with personal implications, too, as scholars have had to explain their own wartime thought and behaviour. Despite all of this, the overwhelming majority of Japanese scholars agree that inter-war Japan, particularly between 1931 and 1937, was fascist.

When surveying a range of writers, we can observe a preoccupation with particularism and its implications for Japan. Many writers situate Emperor System fascism in a broader discussion of particularism per se, but more often than not with a view to including Japan in the fascist category. Tanaka Sōgorō for instance defined fascism in essentialist terms as a combination of internal repression and international

---

[27] Maruyama Masao, 'Nashonarizumu, gunkokushugi, fashizumu' (Nationalism, Militarism, Fascism), in *Gendai seiji no shisō to kōdō* (Thought and Behaviour in Modern Japanese Politics) (expanded edn, Tokyo: Miraisha, 1964), 296.

invasion. His concern was to ask whether, given that Japanese fascism used the past rather than the future as its primary reference point, this backward-looking reflex might disqualify Japan's fascism from legitimate comparison with those of Europe. But as far as the Emperor System was concerned, Tanaka regarded this as a mere instrument that achieved fascist integration at all levels. The consequent facilitation of institutional continuity, and of fascization from within, was peculiar to Japan but fascist all the same. The Emperor System was remarkable to Tanaka only in its sheer efficiency in mediating fascist dynamics. Tanaka represented particularism as something different from Europe, even anti-European, but never unfascist:

When poor imitations of Hitler came forward such as Kita Ikki they were soon eliminated, and the Emperor was allowed to shine above all; if Nazi-type institutions such as the Imperial Rule Assistance Association were conceived in a lukewarm manner they were subordinated to the Emperor System, and ultimately made it even more solid. Here is the locus of particularism in Emperor System fascism.[28]

Furuya Tetsuo was quite blunt in addressing the essentially anti-Western flavour of Japan's fascism. He denoted the preconditions for Japan's fascism as the environment created by the Washington system (whereby Japan was required unilaterally to disarm relative to the Western Powers), and the intolerable dominance of 'white man's imperialism' in Asia. He acknowledged that the process by which Japan was fascisized was different, and like Tanaka, Furuya presented Japan's fascism as more efficient than those of Europe, thanks to the integrative role of the Emperor System:

In Japan's case what was dramatically different was the fact that Japan's ruling institutions did not lose their capacity to suppress mass or revolutionary movements, they did not even have to use fascists to achieve their objective; instead they simply subjugated those movements and used their ongoing authority to incorporate them into the regime. This is what made Japan's case different . . . in other words, it was because the fascists did not require violence to achieve the suppression of a mass movement that fascist political parties were unable to destabilize the situation, and only ever managed to do so in a minor way right up to the very end.[29]

As Furuya and several other scholars indicate, Emperor System fascism was so efficient that it was able to incorporate even those who proclaimed themselves to be reformist (*kakushin*). Ironically, it was this smothering of real change by subsuming it within the mantra of traditionalism that both facilitated fascism, and prevented it from reaching the point of actually overturning the old regime. The *kokutai* ideology therefore both favoured fascism, and restricted its development.

Ishida Takeshi, a former student of Maruyama, comes closest to interrogating the utility of particularism in discussions concerning fascism in general, and fascism

---

[28] Tanaka Sōgorō, *Nihon Fashizumu shi* (History of Japanese Fascism) (Tokyo: Kawade Shobō Shinsha, 1961), 12–13.

[29] Furuya Tetsuo, 'Nihon fashizumu ron' (Theories of Japanese Fascism), in *Iwanami Kōza Nihon Rekishi*, 20 Kindai No. 7 (Tokyo: Iwanami Shoten, 1976), 84.

in Japan. He argues that insightful readings of fascism must incorporate both a particularist and a generic element in order properly to represent history. His own approach was to 'connect the particular tradition of Japan and the elements that Japan had in common in terms of world history in the "era of fascism", and in doing so, examine the subjective responses to those shared circumstances'.[30] Like Furuya, Ishida notes that the struggle in Japan was between tradition and reform (*kakushin*), and that ultimately even the self-styled reformers adopted the language and ideals of retrospection.

Only Itō Takashi stands out as a writer who refused to entertain the imperative of placing Japan in world history by emphasizing fascist dynamics and ideology over attributes. He declared that calling Japan 'fascist' was nothing more than an act of intellectual compensation on the part of scholars who for their own various reasons needed to make Japan's historical experience a relative one. Itō claimed that this approach was based on nothing more substantial than superimposing the notion of the Emperor System over the models represented by Germany and Italy, and lacked scholarly and historical integrity. He stated further that even the term 'Emperor System fascism' was dubious, because it originated with the 1932 Theses that had misconstrued and misread the nature of modern Japan entirely. Despite his overt differences from his peers, Ito shares with them the view that the dominant dynamics in inter-war Japan involved tension between two fundamental forces: restorationists (conservatives) and renovationists (progressives). Ito agrees with his colleagues that the conservatives won out in the end, with the restorationist paradigm prevailing.[31]

V. RESTORATION FASCISM

Japan's peculiar variant of fascism is presented by the majority of Japanese historians and political scientists as a means of differentiating Japan from Europe, but not as a means of excluding Japan from the category of fascist nations between the wars. Clearly many Japanese scholars are more concerned with fascist dynamics than with superficial indicators such as the signing of the Tripartite Pact in 1937. The imagery of the Second World War which placed Tōjō alongside Hitler and Mussolini in the rogues' gallery of enemies must be recognized as little more than signposting; putting Hirohito in the row starts to border on ignorance. Understanding what the emperor and the Emperor System meant to Japanese, and how these entities

---

[30] Ishida Takeshi, ' "Fashizumu-ki" Nihon ni okeru dentō to "kakushin" ' ('Reform' and Tradition in Japan in the 'Era of Fascism'), *Shisō* (January 1976), 3.
[31] Itō Takashi, 'Shōwa seiji shi kenkyū e no ichishikaku' (One Perspective on the Study of Shōwa Era History), *Shisō* (June 1976), 225.

structured and contributed to the incremental consolidation of a society and political structure that many regarded as fascist, is the real issue at hand. In engaging with this question, we also need to contemplate why it is that most Japanese in power in the 1930s did not consider themselves to be fascist, and even why they wished openly to be seen as anti-fascist. The desire to stand apart from Europe was a core element of Japan's fascist journey. At the same time, most Japanese commentators would agree after the fact, in the post-war world of democratization and national rehabilitation, that fascism was an apt descriptor for what had happened in Japan after 1931.

Many analysts of Japanese fascism have been captivated by the emperor and by the catchphrase 'Emperor System fascism'. Even those who do not accept the association of the emperor with fascism, such as Nakamura Kikuo, and who choose instead to quarantine the emperor from fascism by using 'militarism' to describe the 1930s in Japan, cannot do so without engaging with this particular denotation of fascism.[32] Yet when we examine the underlying concerns of Japanese scholars, it is neither exceptionalism nor particularism that preoccupies them. Instead, it is the counter-intuitive triumph of tradition over reform that comprises the phenomenon of restorationism in modern Japanese history which attracts the most attention. The pull of the past, the artifice of revolution packaged as conservatism, is the real puzzle. The pulse of Japanese fascism, indeed the actual function of the imperial institution and the Emperor System in Japan's fascist history, cannot be explained without reference to this intriguing mechanism. Perhaps we should take our cue from the voices of Japan past and present and replace 'Emperor System fascism' with the more accurate term 'Restoration Fascism'.

If we seek historical parallels between Europe and Japan in the form of attributes or temporal specificity, we pre-empt the quest for fascism in Japan with a search for absence, deficiency, or peculiarity. If we focus on the cultural packaging of politics in Japan in the 1930s, we serve the cause of orientalism, not political science or political history. Fascism studies have long been confounded by debates over substance, and attempts at comparative studies have foundered on the shoals of a stubborn resistance to relativizing this troubled concept.

The way in which we answer the question 'was Japan fascist' is important for many reasons. It is especially significant that we try to capture the many forms and manifestations of an idea and a phenomenon such as fascism, which can transcend borders yet penetrate the essence of identity itself. The nexus of particularism and universalism can be found here, in the shape-shifting forms of this political pariah. Japan was fascist, if fascism is seen primarily as a dynamic in society and politics that fuses collectives, smothers autonomy, and manufactures a national will to self-destruct and destroy. In these respects, Japan's fascism was like any other.

---

[32] Nakamura Kikuo, 'Tennōsei fashizumu wa atta ka' (Was There Such as Thing as Emperor System Fascism?), *Jiyū* (December 1965), 50–9.

BIBLIOGRAPHY

BIX, H. P., 'Rethinking "Emperor System Fascism": Ruptures and Continuities in Modern Japanese History', *Bulletin of Concerned Asian Scholars*, 14/2 (1982), 2–19.

BROOKER, P., *The Faces of Fraternalism: Nazi Germany, Fascist Italy, and Imperial Japan* (Oxford: Clarendon Press, 1991).

DUUS, P., and OKIMOTO, D. I., 'Fascism and the History of Prewar Japan: The Failure of a Concept', *Journal of Asian Studies*, 39/1 (1979), 65–76.

FLETCHER, W. M., *The Search for a New Order: Intellectuals and Fascism in Prewar Japan* (Chapel Hill, NC: University of North Carolina Press, 1982).

HOSTON, G. A., *Marxism and the Crisis of Development in Prewar Japan* (Princeton: Princeton University Press, 1986).

KASZA, G. J., 'Fascism from below? A Comparative Perspective on the Japanese Right 1931–1936', *Journal of Contemporary History*, 19/3 (1984), 607–29.

——'Fascism from above? Japan's Kakushin Right in Comparative Perspective', in S. U. Larsen (ed.), *Fascism outside Europe* (Boulder, Colo.: Columbia University Press, (2001), 183–232.

KERSTEN, R., *Democracy in Post-war Japan: Maruyama Masao and the Search for Autonomy* (London: Routledge, 1996).

LARSEN, S. U. (ed.), *Fascism outside Europe* (Boulder, CO: Columbia University Press, 2001).

McCORMACK, G., 'Nineteen-Thirties Japan: Fascism?', *Bulletin of Concerned Asian Scholars*, 14/2 (1982), 20–32.

MARUYAMA, M., *Thought and Behaviour in Modern Japanese Politics*, ed. I. Morris (Oxford: Oxford University Press, 1969).

MOORE, B., *Social Origins of Dictatorship and Democracy* (Harmondsworth: Penguin, 1966).

PAXTON, R. O., *The Anatomy of Fascism* (New York: Vintage Books, 2005).

WILSON, G. M., 'A New Look at the Problem of "Japanese Fascism"', *Comparative Studies in Society and History*, 10/4 (1967–8), 401–12.

PART V

REFLECTION AND LEGACIES

CHAPTER 29

COMPARISONS AND DEFINITIONS

ROBERT O. PAXTON

WHY did fascism take root and succeed in some parts of Europe and not in others? This question places us squarely in the domain of comparative history. The French historian Maurice Agulhon once observed that 'comparison does for history what experiment does for physics'.[1] To be sure, Agulhon's analogy is forced, because the historian, unlike the physicist, cannot manipulate his or her materials in order to design the perfect test of some hypothesis. But Agulhon was surely correct that comparison is one of the most powerful analytical tools available to historians.

But comparison must be used properly. I turn here for guidance to Marc Bloch, a master comparativist.[2] According to Bloch, comparison should be employed not in a search for similarities, which is likely to remain superficial, but in a search for differences. The most appropriate subject for historical comparison, Bloch maintained, is a process that is at work simultaneously in several different national settings, with differing outcomes. Comparison is likely to suggest which factors shaped these different results most powerfully, and which variables were 'indifferent' (Agulhon again). A classic example is Jürgen Kocka's study of the strikingly different political allegiances of white-collar worker organizations in Germany

[1] M. Agulhon, *La République au village* (Paris: Plon, 1970), 32. Cf. I. Kershaw and M. Lewin: 'comparison [offers] the nearest the historian can come to the laboratory experiment of the natural scientist': Kershaw and Lewin (eds), *Stalinism and Nazism: Dictatorships in Comparison* (Cambridge: Cambridge University Press, 1997), p. xi.

[2] M. Bloch, 'Pour une histoire comparée des sociétés européennes', in *Mélanges historiques* (Paris: Éditions de l'École des Hautes Études en Sciences Sociales 1983), 16 ff. (The original appeared in 1928.)

and the United States: authoritarian and nationalist in the former, democratic in the latter. While material conditions and problems were not dissimilar, Kocka found important historically developed differences in labour organization and class stratification. These included looser class identities and greater social mobility in the United States, the ethnic heterogeneity of the American workforce, and the generally egalitarian social climate and rhetoric of the United States.[3]

The development of fascism in Europe after 1919 presents a fruitful terrain for comparison. Every European nation, indeed all economically developed nations with some degree of political democracy, including the United States, Argentina, Brazil, and Japan, had some kind of fascist movement and at least a rudimentary fascist organization or two in the twenty years after 1919. In its earliest stages, therefore, the appearance of this kind of revolt against both liberalism and socialism in the name of a revived, unified, and purified nation does not give us much ground for comparison.

At further stages of development, however, the outcomes could be dramatically different. In Italy and Germany, fascist movements became major players and even achieved power. In the most solidly integrated and established Western European democracies, such as Britain and Scandinavia, fascist movements remained marginal. In some cases, such as France and Belgium, they became noisy and conspicuous but could approach power only after foreign conquest. A number of authoritarian regimes, including Franco's Spain, Salazar's Portugal, Antonescu's Romania, Horthy's Hungary, imperial Japan, and Vargas's Brazil, borrowed some trappings from fascism but excluded fascist parties from real power; some authoritarian rulers—Antonescu, Salazar, Vargas, and the leaders of imperial Japan—even crushed fascist movements.

Although such contrasting outcomes would seem to invite comparison, the comparative study of fascism is relatively rare. It is much more common to present parallel histories of the various fascist movements and regimes, one by one, than to make authentic comparisons.[4]

Comparison requires, of course, common elements to compare. In the case of fascism comparison is clouded by extensive differentiation among movements and regimes, and by abuse of the term as an epithet. Some have even concluded that the term 'fascism' is unworkable for serious social science, and should be abandoned. It may indeed be the case that fascism encompasses more variation than the other 'isms': fascists reject universal values as a matter of principle, denigrate human

---

[3] J. Kocka, *White Collar Workers in America, 1890–1940: A Social-Political History in International Perspective* (London: Sage Publications, 1980).

[4] For example, though there are some comparative observations in S. Payne, *A History of Fascism, 1912–1945* (Madison: University of Wisconsin Press, 1995), and E. Collotti, *Fascismo, fascismi* (Florence: Sansoni, 1989), comparison does not drive these useful surveys' exposition. Some works that claim to be comparative do not actually compare. R. Bessel (ed.), *Fascist Italy & Nazi Germany: Comparisons and Contrasts* (Cambridge: Cambridge University Press, 1996), for example, contains excellent but separate national chapters.

reason, sanctify national particularities, and show even less compunction than others in renouncing earlier promises in their quest for power. The Nazis' abandonment after power of advocacy on behalf of their first supporters—distressed artisans, lower civil servants, and family farmers—is a signal instance. Communism, too, took on profoundly different forms: think of Josef Stalin, Pol Pot, and Enrico Berlinguer. But no one suggests giving up the term on that account. In my view fascism fulfils easily the criteria of an appropriate subject for comparative study: a general phenomenon exists, and it was embodied differently in different national settings with differing degrees of success.

Despite their national variations, fascist movements and regimes share a sufficient number of common elements to sustain a general definition. Fascism might be defined as a form of political behaviour marked by obsessive preoccupation with community decline, humiliation, or victimhood and by compensatory cults of unity, energy, and purity, in which a mass-based party of committed nationalist militants, working in uneasy but effective collaboration with traditional elites, abandons democratic liberties and pursues with redemptive violence, and without ethical or legal restraints, goals of internal cleansing and external expansion.

Any definition of fascism, however, tends to give a misleadingly static image of a phenomenon that is mobile, adaptable, and dynamic. This is why I recently tried to analyse fascism in terms of a cycle of five stages of development, within each of which comparison can be illuminating.[5] For comparison works best, I believe, when it juxtaposes discrete processes within a larger historical phenomenon: for example, ways of enlisting support, ways of coming to power, or ways of exercising power. It is less helpful when addressed to vast generalizations—that is, to some general essence of fascism.

We must include Nazi Germany among the fascist states. This position is very widely rejected in Germany, and sometimes in Italy.[6] Wrongly so, in my opinion. The two leaders had no doubt about their political kinship. Hitler kept a bust of Mussolini in his study in the Brown House in Munich, and, as late as 1942, when most Nazi leaders dismissed Mussolini as a liability to the Axis, Hitler sent the *Duce* an affectionate letter on the twentieth anniversary of the Fascist March on Rome, referring to himself (Hitler) as Mussolini's disciple. More profoundly, Nazism and Italian Fascism shared the basic qualities listed above.

The differences between the German and Italian cases are very real, but they reflect the particularities of the two cultures and the specific circumstances in which the two movements succeeded, rather than incompatible inherent characteristics. The Italian *squadristi* employed violence more readily than the Nazis during the quest for power, while the ratio was reversed after power. Once in power, Mussolini put the state first while Hitler put the Nazi Party first, creating a greater potential for

---

[5] R. O. Paxton, *The Anatomy of Fascism* (New York: Alfred Knopf, 2004).
[6] The most influential Italian example is Renzo De Felice.

radicalization. The same political elements were in play in both regimes, however: charismatic leader, single party, absolute state, and residual civil society. The most important differences, of course, were Nazism's biological racism and its capacity for radicalization, although Italian Fascist imposition of a form of apartheid[7] in Africa and fascist laws for the defence of *la razza* should not be ignored. Mussolini was more violent, expansionist, and racist than his current historical reputation allows. In my opinion, the differences between Nazi Germany and Fascist Italy exist within a basic commonality. Indeed they are what make comparison worthwhile.

The proper study of fascism compares not only the movements but also their settings: the European societies in which fascism appeared and prospered, and the crises which gave fascist movements space to succeed. Classical fascism appeared in a quite particular context: troubled European democracies (often start-up democracies) confronted with the crises generated after 1917 by war, defeat, internal division, and incipient revolution. Much was new in the Europe of 1919 that made possible the invention of fascism. Fascism was, as Juan Linz famously demonstrated, a latecomer.[8] One should add that it was an unforeseen innovation, since popular mobilization had hitherto been linked to the left rather than to the right. Space was available to this new phenomenon only after a number of prior developments had prepared the way: the arrival of mass politics; the maturation of liberalism and even socialism to the point of becoming part of the Establishment, giving them sufficient leeway to reveal their shortcomings; the discredit of both parliamentary liberalism and parliamentary conservatism by their inability to cope with the crises of war and revolution after 1917. The First World War and the Bolshevik Revolution were indispensable preconditions: the war revealed the incapacity of classical liberal solutions (elections, the market, the school) no less than the classical conservative solutions (paternalism, religion, deference, a passive citizenry) to the problems posed by total war and its aftermath. And after Bolshevik success in Russia, non-socialists everywhere looked for an adequate riposte to revolution.

It is obvious that fascism enjoyed different degrees of success in different national settings, but understanding why poses problems of historical method and interpretation. Were these differences the result of contingent factors—the vagaries of the politics of the moment; leadership skills or lack of them on both sides; the intensity of crises—or did they stem from fundamental qualities of the state and society in question? And, if fundamental national qualities were the principal variable, were these the products of a recent past or of a long-term historical development?

---

[7] This term is used by Angelo Del Boca in 'Le leggi razziali nell'impero di Mussolini', in A. Del Boca, M. Legnani, and M. G. Rossi (eds), *Il regime fascista: storia e storiografia* (Bari: Laterza, 1995), 329–51.
[8] J. J. Linz, 'Some Notes toward a Comparative Study of Fascism in Sociological Historical Perspective', in W. Laqueur (ed.), *Fascism: A Reader's Guide* (Berkeley and Los Angeles: University of California Press, 1976), 4.

There have been several forms of long-term explanation for susceptibility to fascism. First came the argument, highly coloured by wartime propaganda, that German history took a particular course from Luther onward that led inexorably to Hitler.[9] Such works verged on propaganda in their acceptance of national stereotypes, and they were profoundly ahistorical in their assumption of immutability and inevitability. In a more scholarly form, this argument held that Germany diverged in the nineteenth century from a generalized Western European democratization process in a *Sonderweg* that included the failure of its bourgeois revolution, the tendency of German bourgeois to copy aristocratic values ('refeudalization'), and German liberalism's capitulation to nationalism under Bismarck.

Another influential long-term analysis, based upon political sociology, held that societies that had only partially modernized, where archaic economic interests and values survived to an important degree, were more susceptible to fascism than societies that had moved quickly and fully to modernization. Such complex, half-modernized societies (Germany was obviously the model) were vulnerable to the appeal of fascism in two ways: the victims of industrialization—independent artisans, small farmers—had survived in great numbers in such societies, and the spokesmen for pre-industrial values—aristocrats, anti-modernist publicists— remained numerous and influential enough to play upon these victims' grievances.[10]

Comparison weakens the force of this uneven modernization argument, for France is surely a sterling example of a dual economy and society where a large residual, defensive pre-industrial and pre-capitalist sector coexisted alongside considerable urban-industrial development. Or perhaps comparison requires us to broaden this hypothesis to include political culture: France did indeed produce important fascist publicists and numerous fascist or near-fascist groups, but their influence was limited not only by the power in France of the modern sector but also by the power of republican values. The *Sonderweg* approach, long influential, was substantially undermined in the 1980s by the observation of David Blackbourn and Geoff Eley[11] that it contained an implicit but unjustified assumption that British and French democracy, highly mythologized, constituted a norm from which Germany's deviation needed explaining.

---

[9] A classic early example was W. M. McGovern, *From Luther to Hitler: The History of Fascist-Nazi Political Philosophy* (Boston: Houghton-Mifflin, 1941). Such assumptions pervade W. L. Shirer's best-selling *The Rise and Fall of the Third Reich* (New York: Simon and Schuster, 1960).

[10] The founding text of this interpretation is T. Parsons, 'Democracy and Social Structure in Pre-Nazi Germany', in idem, *Essays in Sociological Theory* (rev. edn. Glencoe, IL: Free Press, 1954; 1st pub. 1942). For a modern reworking, see J. Kocka, 'Ursachen des Nationalsozialismus', *Aus Politik und Zeitgeschichte* (Beilage zur Wochenzeitung Das Parlament), 21 June 1980, 2–15. Geoff Ely criticized this approach, from a Marxist perspective, in 'What Produces Fascism: Preindustral Traditions or a Crisis of the Capitalist State?', *Politics and Society*, 12/2 (1983), 52–82.

[11] D. Blackbourn and G. Eley, *The Peculiarities of German History* (Oxford: Oxford University Press, 1984).

Long-term perspectives on preconditions for fascism are further burdened by intimations of inevitability. The most that one can legitimately conclude from a study of the long term, I believe, is that fascists enjoyed more 'potentials',[12] and their enemies and rivals fewer, in some European countries than in others. Relatively new and poorly integrated democracies, where conservatives felt incapable of surviving in mass politics, and nations whose historical traditions associated national glory with authoritarian rule were likely to offer less resistance to fascism than nations where conservatives had acquired confidence in their capacity to manage a mass electorate (as in Britain) and where national grandeur was associated with Jacobin patriotism (as in France). But the crucial decisions remained open until the last minute. Even in countries where democracy seemed likely to fail, as in Spain, there remained a choice between fascism and authoritarianism—about which more below.

That is why it is more rewarding, in my opinion, to concentrate on the short-term preconditions for fascism: the particular crises in which fascist movements found space to grow and, in some cases, reach power. A very impressive monographic literature treats the immediate preconditions for a fascist assumption of power. The most illuminating of these works start with the strains of total mobilization in the First World War, and the ensuing divisions and tensions in the social, economic, and political realms. Next they examine the progressive exhaustion of alternatives and the closing of options other than the fascist one, while recognizing that the final steps were matters of choice by the political leadership.[13] The fascist solution was by no means inevitable in Italy and Germany, and other solutions remained possible until the ultimate decision.

To be sure, the non-fascist options open to President Hindenburg and King Victor Emmanuel III were not limitless, and the two heads of state could not step out of character. The most obvious remaining possibility of governing Germany without Hitler was to continue presidential government under article 48, under either the existing chancellor (General Schleicher) or a different presidential appointee. This option meant accepting some unpleasant consequences: the prolongation of the political crisis, perhaps indefinitely, in the absence of a chancellor backed by a parliamentary majority; social unrest and the likelihood of continued expansion of the Communist vote; and probably a greater role in government for the army. The viability of this option would depend upon General Schleicher's success at drawing in some labour unions and other parts of the reformist left,

[12]   G. Ely, 'Conservative and Radical Nationalists in Germany: The Production of Fascist Potentials, 1912–1928', in M. Blinkhorn (ed.), *Fascists and Conservatives: The Radical Right and the Establishment in Twentieth Century Europe* (London: Unwin Hyman, 1990).

[13]   A. Lytttelton, *The Seizure of Power* (2nd edn, Princeton: Princeton University Press, 1987) is a model in the genre. For the short term in Germany see, most recently, H. A. Turner, Jr., *Hitler's Thirty Days to Power* (Reading, MA: Addison-Wesley, 1996).

as his mentor General Groener had done during the First World War, to reduce social polarization and revolutionary pressure. It is not too difficult to imagine a similar emergency government in Italy without Mussolini, supported by the king's willingness to sign an emergency powers decree, under a familiar conservative like Salandra or centrist like Giolitti, or even a non-political prime minister (perhaps the hard-nosed prefect of Bologna, Cesare Mori).

Both heads of state rejected an effort to control fascist violence through the adoption or continuance of emergency executive powers. They preferred to try to harness fascist electoral and street power to a new coalition that would be managed, they were convinced, by its conservative members.

The fragmentation and weakness of conservative and centre parties made a non-socialist government without fascist participation illusory in both Italy in 1922 and Germany in 1932. But why not include reformist socialists in a broad coalition that ranged from moderate left to moderate right and excluded the fascists—what Germans call a 'Great Coalition?' This option required the head of state to per-suade the centre and moderate right to abandon their quarantine of the moderate left, and to accept Social Democrats as governing partners. At the same time, the moderate left would have to accept participation in a socially and economically conservative government in order to preserve democratic institutions—a choice that the German Social Democrats had already made and were still ready to make, despite Communist denunciations, but that remained unacceptable to the Maxi-malists who still dominated the Italian Socialist Party. The Great Coalition option would have required vigorous arm twisting by the two heads of state, a role that nothing prepared them to play, and a conviction by party leaders of both left and right that fascism was worse than fraternizing with the class enemy. It was theoretically feasible but unlikely with the cast of characters on the stage at that moment.

The heads of state faced these choices, of course, only because the fascists had already achieved formidable levels of electoral and street power. Although Hitler never received a majority of the popular vote in any contested election (contrary to a tenacious legend), the Nazi Party had supplanted the Social Democrats as the largest party in Germany in July 1932. With 37 per cent of the vote they had to be taken seriously. The Italian Fascists' electoral power was comparatively modest. They won 35 seats in their one regular election, in May 1921, as part of Giolitti's National Coalition. Their *squadristi*, however, held de facto power in a number of north-eastern cities that they had occupied by force in 1921 and 1922. They thereby obliged the government to choose between repressing them by force or conceding to them some degree of governmental authority. In no other European country had fascist movements acquired so much leverage.

How the fascists established so massive a presence in these two societies is the heart of the matter. The commonest strategy of explanation is to spotlight the influence of anti-liberal intellectuals. The priority of intellectual preparation as a precondition for fascism is often only implicit, reflected in the nearly inevitable choice of fascist ideas and doctrine as the first chapter of almost any book on the subject. Comparison suggests some doubts on this score. For one thing, every modern state had its fascist thinkers and publicists and their sole existence does not explain much. Moreover, there is no clean fit between the saliency of fascist publicists and fascist success. France had many voluble and talented fascist intellectuals, but only defeat and occupation brought them close to power (and, even then, they were active mostly in Paris and not at Vichy until late in the occupation period). Ideological passions wax and wane, moreover. A European observer of 1900, informed that one European Great Power would be swept a generation later by a paroxysm of exterminationist anti-Semitism, would probably have picked Russia, or even anti-Dreyfusard France, rather than Germany as a plausible site for this development.

Not that we can dispense with the study of fascist ideas and doctrine. But we need to be clear about the role they played in fascist success. One could not have fascism without imagining it first. But I have argued elsewhere (to resounding criticism) that the relation of fascism to its doctrine is of a different nature from the relation of liberalism and socialism to their founding ideas. Fascists were openly contemptuous of human reason and intellectual enquiry. They appealed viscerally to their followers. And although they proclaimed their ideologies immutable, they violated and amended them without compunction. Fascists did best where a wave of popular disillusionment engulfed the previous leadership. Fascist imagery (both positive and negative) took root in the void of collapsed loyalties.

Other preconditions seem to me more immediately operative than the activity of fascist publicists. National defeat or humiliation is probably the most important single precondition, and fascists prospered by claiming to be the most uncompromising agents of renewal. Victor states could survive acute economic crisis without loss of legitimacy; Britain and the United States, for instance, had unemployment rates as high as Germany's in 1932. Comparison forbids us to trace a straight line between the severity of the Great Depression and fascist success. On a higher level of abstraction, it is difficult to perceive, as Marxists would have us do, that capitalism was having more difficulty perpetuating itself without new reinforcements in Italy and Germany than in, say, France.

The apparent imminence of Bolshevik revolution is the other most obvious precondition. Fascists' claim to be the best anti-communist bulwark was the other strong card that Hitler and Mussolini could play. Fear of communism and doubt that parliamentary democracy was tough enough to hold it off were quite likely the principal reasons for the acquiescence, or more, in fascism of much of the previously moderate centre and right.

The sociologist William Brustein has argued that the fascists won their following by making attractive social and economic promises, but his rational choice approach has been vehemently criticized.[14] Most authors prefer to emphasize the emotional seduction of fascism, its theatrical manipulation of public space, and the hegemony of its imagery. Fascist stagecraft did not work the same magic everywhere, however. The skill and talent of the fascist leaders had much to do with their success, but they are not a sufficient explanation, for some quite competent fascist chiefs—Oswald Mosley, for example—fared poorly.

A space had to become available. An important part of the story is the weakness and failure of traditional moderate and conservative parties, whose members haemorrhaged into fascism. Counter-intuitively, the vigour and health of a moderate parliamentary conservatism is emerging in recent work as one of the most important obstacles to the expansion of fascism.[15] Existing elites usually muddle through. Fascists did not so much overthrow them as profit by their discredit. Where either, or both, liberal democracy or constitutional conservatism failed, fascism could look like the only non-socialist alternative. Conversely, where either of these two more moderate alternatives was successful, as in Britain and France, fascism had little available space.

Payne argues that authoritarian regimes 'served more as a barrier against, than as an inducement for, fascism'.[16] One might seem little better than the other, but the distinction, as developed by Juan Linz, with Franco Spain in mind, is useful. Authoritarianism, in Linz's sense, governed through existing elites rather than through a single party; it preferred a passive citizenry to popular mobilization; and it distrusted foreign adventurism, valuing stability above expansion.[17]

The left's blunders deserve their place in any study of the preconditions for fascist success. After 1917 the left aroused fear out of all proportion to its capacity to do anything. The Communist–Social Democratic split made common action against fascism all but impossible. Communist strategists regarded a brief spell of fascist power as not entirely a bad thing, and dismissed as 'social fascism' the sacrifice of immediate social reform on the altar of saving democratic institutions.

A less obvious precondition that deserves attention is social division and insufficient social integration. It is sometimes claimed that new states were particularly susceptible to fascism because class conflict or regional separatism, or both, remained virulent in them. Fascism's claim to be the only force capable of overcoming such intractable divisions was certainly among its most persuasive arguments, and one that summoned up an authentically idealistic response. The astonishing chasm separating Social Democratic Germany from conservative Germany, and Italy's

---

[14] W. Brustein, *The Logic of Evil: The Social Origins of the Nazi Party, 1925–1933* (New Haven: Yale University Press, 1996).

[15] See K. Passmore, *From Liberalism to Fascism: The Right in a French Province, 1928–1939* (Cambridge: Cambridge University Press, 1997); R. Thurlow, 'The Failure of Fascism', in *The Failure of Political Extremism in Inter-war Britain*, University of Exeter Studies in History No. 21 (Exeter: University of Exeter Press, 1989).

[16] Payne, *History*, 312. He cites Spain, Portugal, Romania, and Poland.

[17] J. Linz, *Totalitarian and Authoritarian Regimes* (Boulder, CO: Lynn Rienner, 2000).

uncompleted Risorgimento, are justly notorious. But new states had no monopoly on class and regional divisions. Class division reached paroxysm in the France during the Popular Front of 1936, but national reintegration began under Daladier in 1938 and French far right parties grew in the late 1930s only if they soft-pedalled their most obvious fascist traits.[18] In Spain, where the sharpest class conflict and the most aggressive regional separatisms in Europe were supplemented by open war between religion and atheism, national reintegration could be achieved by a military authoritarianism that pre-empted fascism.

It has been tempting to link fascist success to some kind of psychological prepa-ration. Particularly today when the study of culture, sometimes uncritically de-scriptive, is at the centre of the historical profession, considerable interest attaches to male fantasies[19] or myths of decline, uncleanness, and disease overcome by violent redemption. An earlier generation wanted to apply Freud directly; Theodore Adorno was already delineating the authoritarian personality in the 1930s. But, again, even if we disregard the problems of psychoanalysing the dead, there is little here to explain what singles out Germany and Italy.

Without question fantasies of virility, violence, and domination played impor-tant roles in the emotional appeal of fascist movements and regimes. Some of the most enduringly helpful studies show the Nazis used values of hardness and camaraderie to condition police and paramilitary groups.[20] But why were fantasies of violence and domination attractive? They could acquire explanatory value for the rise of fascism and its arrival in power only if comparison were to show that they developed further in Germany and Italy than in Britain and France, and no one has had the temerity to suggest that, or the rashness to undertake such a measurement.

The relation of fascist success to religion needs to be evoked. Some have argued that the decline of religious values opens a space that can be occupied by pseudo-religions, political religions, like Nazism.[21] The principal weakness of this argument is the unlikelihood that Germans and Italians had become more detached from traditional religious faith by 1920 than the French or British.

Nevertheless, the persistence of the Catholic vote for the German Zentrum right up to the final election on 5 March 1933, alone among moderate parties, would seem to reinforce the view that Christian faith was an obstacle to fascist success. That case is weakened by the later willingness of the Zentrum to cast decisive votes for Hitler's

---

[18] Colonel François de La Rocque's Croix de Feu, and its post-ban sequel, the Parti Social Français, are the subject of a passionate debate. Did the PSF acquire millions of followers after 1936 because it remained fascist or because it moderated into a kind of proto-Gaullism? Kevin Passmore argues persuasively for a moderating tendency in 'Boyscoutism for Grownups? Paramilitarism in the *Croix de Feu* and the *Parti Social Français*', *French Historical Studies*, 19 (1995), 527–57.

[19] K. Theweleit, *Male Fantasies*, 2 vols (Minneapolis: University of Minnesota Press, 1987, 1989).

[20] H. Buchheim, ' "Hardness" and "Camaraderie" ', in H. Krausnick *et al.* (eds), *Anatomy of the SS State* (New York: Walker, 1965), 332–48.

[21] Among others, M. Burleigh, *The Third Reich: A New History* (New York: Hill and Wang, 2000), 255, and Payne, *History*, 490.

Enabling Act on 23 March 1933, and the willingness of the Vatican to conclude legitimizing concordats with both Hitler (1933) and Mussolini (1929), along with the enthusiasm of many German Protestants for the Nazis' 'positive Christianity'.[22] The anticlericalism of Hitler and Mussolini was personal and not integral to fascism, a point reinforced by the militant religiosity of some fascist movements—notably the Romanian Legion of the Archangel Michael and the Finnish Lapua. Fascists' quarrels with churches have had more to do with turf than with doctrine.

The chief obstacle to fascist recruitment turns out to be not faith as such but the resiliency of pre-existing socio-cultural attachments. Otto Kirchheimer's celebrated distinction among parties of mass integration and catch-all parties is helpful here. Parties of integration provide not simply a candidate at election time, but an entire way of life, complete with a view of the world and a panoply of publications, associations, and leisure-time activities. Such parties demand and receive full commitment. The superbly organized German Social Democrats, like the Zentrum, retained the sustained loyalty of most of their members to March 1933. Voters nurtured in the bosom of communities as enveloping as the Catholic parish or German organized labour were simply not 'available' for recruitment elsewhere. Proletarians with identical material interests who were in some way detached from the culture of German Social Democracy could be recruited, and were.[23]

In order to study fascist recruitment it is not sufficient to list the fascists' themes and describe their theatrical devices and suppose that every potential recruit reacted in the same way. We need to study the availability of potential recruits: whether as new voters; as Eley's 'potentials'; as outside other political, religious, or social attachment; or as prior voters for cadre parties that failed to exercise any profound cultural influence or generate enduring loyalty. The study of fascist recruitment demands the parallel and simultaneous study of how other loyalties evaporated and made more and more people 'available' for fascism.[24]

It seems strange in retrospect that fascist violence did not repel more potential recruits than it attracted. German and Italian citizens could remain indifferent to fascist violence if they were convinced that it was directed against others: Bolsheviks, Slavs, Jews, or other 'enemies of the people', even when, as in Hitler's

---

[22] R. Steigmann-Gall, *Holy Reich* (Cambridge: Cambridge University Press, 2003) makes clear the common ground provided by the religiosity of many (though not all) Nazi leaders and the nationalist strain within German Protestantism.

[23] A major achievement of recent scholarship has been to demonstrate the importance of proletarians within fascism. For voters, see T. Childers, *The Nazi Voter: The Social Foundations of Fascism in Germany, 1919–1933* (Chapel Hill, NC: University of North Carolina Press, 1983); idem, *The Formation of the Nazi Constituency* (London: Croom Helm, 1986); and J. Falter, *Hitlers Wähler* (Munich: C. H. Beck, 1991).

[24] L. E. Jones, *German Liberalism and the Dissolution of the Weimar Party System* (Chapel Hill, NC: University of North Carolina Press, 1988).

Night of the Long Knives, there were prominent 'collateral victims'.[25] The absence of an independent judiciary unwilling or unable to consider the claims of victims of fascist violence seems to me a major overlooked precondition of fascist success.

Fascist movements undergo extensive transformations during the process of acquiring power. For all but the most resolutely abstract theoreticians of fascism, the differences between movements out of power and those acquiring and exercising it constitute an important matter for comparison. I believe these differences are greater in the case of fascist movements and regimes than in, say, liberal or socialist movements and regimes. Fascist movements invest great effort in recruiting the entirety of a people, in a unifying way, rather than dividing a people as they claim traditional interest-group parties do. Before power, they go about this with much less care for consistency than later, when they are required to make concrete governing choices. In a word, they can be more anti-capitalist before power than after, given that all of them, in the cases known so far, have entered upon power in alliance with conservatives so desperate to preserve their rule that they are willing to share power with these uncouth newcomers, masters of the street and the microphone. After power, fascists can ignore some of their first faithful, and, in any event, they have a new device for unifying the people: war. Success against foreign enemies went a long way toward stilling domestic discontent in both Nazi Germany and Fascist Italy, though the corollary was that foreign defeat could quickly undermine the fascist chief's legitimacy.

The study of fascism does not end when a fascist chief acquires office, and when he transforms that power into dictatorship. How fascist dictators exercised their power is another fruitful matter for comparison. According to a very common interpretation, this is a simple subject: the dictator gave orders, and was obeyed. This intentionalist assumption is the foundation stone of all forms of totalitarian theory. Totalitarian theory is blind, however, to some of the most interesting questions about fascist regimes: how they persuaded or coerced social groups, institutions, and intellectuals to conform.

In place of a one-factor model of dictatorial power, I have proposed that we consider fascist regimes in their exercise of power in a much less monolithic and more conflictual way. Fascist regimes function in a never-ending state of tension and competition among four holders of power: the leader, party militants, the state apparatus, and civil society. No two fascist regimes work out these tensions in exactly the same way, but I believe that the same elements contend and compete within them all. I shall take up these four elements one by one.

The leader first, for his personal actions (and so far it has always been 'he') were at the centre of the story. There is no simple template for fascist leaders.

[25] See R. Gellately, *The Gestapo and German Society: Enforcing Racial Policy* (Oxford: Oxford University Press, 1990) and idem, *Backing Hitler* (Oxford: Oxford University Press, 2001); E. A. Johnson, *Nazi Terror: The Gestapo, Jews, and Ordinary Germans* (New York: Basic Books, 1999).

They have been surprisingly diverse in their social origins, political trajectories, and even personalities. It is tempting to follow the suggestion made by Ian Kershaw's superb biography of Hitler that what fascist leaders had in common was not so much qualities of their own as the projection upon them by a needy and adoring public of an image of a quasi-magical national redeemer.[26] In order to fulfil that proffered role, the leader had to have an unshakeable faith in his election to it—by fate, history, or a divinity—and his entitlement to go to any lengths and to take any risk to fulfil it.

It is apparent that the fascist leader's relation to his public is not like that of other kinds of leader, whether hereditary or elected. Max Weber's discussion of charismatic leadership still grasps best the particularity of fascist authority. It did not depend upon proofs of capacity, like bureaucratic leadership, or upon inherited entitlement. It bore some relation to divine ordination as in the priesthood (though Hitler and Mussolini were, for historical reasons, anticlerical). Like a priest, the fascist leader's efficacy in performing his mission does not depend on purely personal attributes—fascist leaders have not always looked the part—but a public faith that he incarnates the national destiny. Fascist leadership needed constant reconsecration by success, and hence could become brittle when the leader's magic stopped working. Mussolini discovered this in July 1943, but Hitler seemed immune to the penalties of failure.

Most studies of fascism focus on the leader with the fascination of a bird watching a snake. This convention does not improve our understanding, for while the fascist leader is indispensable, he does not rule alone. The common view that the leader does everything is the final triumph of fascist propaganda. Fascist leaders needed the help of elites and institutions in order to carry out their projects. It is a distortion to perceive the actions of fascist regimes as simple projections of the leader's will. Even fascist failures are not inevitably the leader's fault. We have already noted Oswald Mosley, a competent leader in an unpropitious setting. The setting may matter as much as the leader.

Fascist leaders inevitably had to contend with a party and its unruly militants. A 'party of integration' that claimed to speak for the whole nation, to energize and unite it, and to supplant a weak and corrupt liberal state is an essential character of fascism, as compared to traditional dictatorship or authoritarianism. But having unleashed the party for his own ascent, the fascist chief then had to discipline it when he assumed control of the state. The tense relationship between *Il Duce* and his *ras* is notorious. Hitler, too, faced repeated party rebellions, which he quelled at first with persuasion, and then with murder, as on the Night of the Long Knives. But the fascist leader could not totally suppress his party, for it gave him independence from traditional social powers. Leader and party remained locked in a state of constant tension.

---

[26] I. Kershaw, *Hitler, 1889–1936: Hubris* (New York: Norton, 1999), p. xxvi.

The role of the state apparatus in a fascist system of rule also needs to be under-stood as an unending negotiation. The fascist leaders, to be sure, held strong cards in their effort to harness the state apparatus to their projects. The functionaries were conditioned to obey the authorities in place. Moreover, many of them were gratified by a reassertion of national authority. On the other hand, fascist administrative practice flew in the face of bureaucratic rules of recruitment and advancement, and many a proud civil servant feared and resented the arrival of untrained party activists in key administrative positions, and the replacement of merit by party loyalty as the principal criterion for recruitment and advancement. Civil servants had some leverage, for the fascist regime could not function without at least the acquiescence of most of them.

There was no one necessary outcome to the negotiation between the fascist authority and the traditional state, and the Italian and German outcomes were quite different. Mussolini, probably because he feared and distrusted the *ras*, generally relied upon the state. Hitler gave his party far more leeway, though he never displaced the bureaucratic state. Crucially, the police became a party function in Nazi Germany. The Italian police, by contrast, was run by a career civil servant, the former prefect of Genoa, Arturo Bocchini, and the secret police, or OVRA, played a more limited role than military intelligence in enforcing Italian national security.[27]

Fascist regimes related to civil society in an even more complicated negotiation than that with the state. Civil society was simultaneously more diverse and more independent. Traditionally this relationship has been portrayed as *Gleichschaltung*, but that term seems to me to present the matter in a far too one-directional way. Civil society could have considerable leverage, and even the Nazis could not simply give orders. Some elements of civil society, such as the churches and the army, had powerful autonomous sources of independence. At the same time, both were willing to cooperate as long as their independence was recognized. In the end, even the Nazis were obliged to accept a certain realm of independence for powerful economic and social groups in what Wolfgang Schieder has called a *Herrschaft-skompromiss*, a compromise for rule.[28]

Collaborating social and economic groups did not have to be fully converted. It was enough for them to accept fascism as the least bad solution. Most German businessmen, we now know, had strong reservations about Hitler before 1933 and preferred Papen. Hitler, however, seemed to them preferable to any solution in-cluding socialists. Once Hitler was in office, although many businessmen would have preferred to continue to produce for world markets, they adapted to autarky

[27] See in general M. Franzinelli, *I tentacoli dell'OVRA* (2nd edn, Turin: Bollati Boringhieri, 1999).

[28] He devised the term for Fascist Italy. Kolloquien des Instituts für Zeitgechichte, *Der italienische faschismus: Probleme und Forschungstendenze* (Munich: Oldenbourg, 1983), 62. Massimo Legnani spoke similarly of a 'compromesso autoritario' in 'Sistema di potere fascista, blocco dominante, alleanze sociali', in Del Boca *et al.* (eds), *Il regime fascista*, 418 ff.

and found advantages in the destruction of independent labour organizations and in rearmament contracts. One needs to examine case by case the terms under which important social groups—doctors, lawyers, judges—collaborated with fascist rule.

Intellectuals deserve more space than we have here. Fascist success in obtaining the active support of outstanding intellectuals is remarkable, considering fascists' open contempt for them. Nationalism had already demonstrated its power among German intellectuals in 1914, and in Italy in 1915. In Italy, a measure of autonomy and awards of honours and places sufficed to achieve the acquiescence of many intellectuals. Ninety of the signers of Croce's 'Manifesto of the Anti-Fascist Intellectuals' of 1925 participated in the Fascist Encyclopedia of 1931. But Mussolini was willing to use force when necessary; some intellectuals like Carlo Levi were sent into *confino*; the most dangerous ones like the Rosselli brothers were murdered. Force or the threat of it was more palpable in Germany, and the Nazi regime demanded more than mere acquiescence. Nevertheless it was possible for an outstanding scientist like Max Planck to maintain some autonomy, and to assist some Jews. Technocratic intellectuals of international renown—like the German physicist Werner Heisenberg or the Italian demographer Corrado Gini—could find professional satisfaction in national revival. The number of non-Jewish intellectual exiles was small in both cases.

But *Gleichschaltung* was not simply a one-way street. Some individuals and groups could appropriate fascist authority for their own uses. Citizens could get rid of enemies or rivals by denouncing them to the police, to the point that police agencies instituted severe penalties for false denunciation. Italian Fascist rule did threaten some established powers, such as the family crime syndicates familiarly known as Mafia. Fathers and local bosses, however, especially in the Italian south, seem to have appropriated fascism to reinforce their traditional authority.

The fascist exercise of power, the result of competitive tensions among these four factors, was anything but unitary. The image of fascist power as a monolithic juggernaut, inspired by the high performance of the German armies under Nazism, is quite misleading. The polycratic image of fascist rule, proposed for Nazi Germany, is also appropriate for Mussolini's rule. But the competition between party and state for Hitler's favour clearly went much further than in Italy, and it remains today a plausible explanation for the Nazi regime's greater potential for radicalization. An inherent propensity for violence explains nothing, for Italian Fascism was more violent than Nazism during the period of gaining power. A much greater contributing factor was the existence of conquered territories, especially in the east, that Hitler allowed the party to run as fiefdoms without any countervailing bureaucratic or judicial power. Hitler's no man's land in former Poland was the incubator of the Final Solution and of much else that pushed the Nazi regime into the outer reaches of arbitrary violence.

How fascist regimes ended also merits comparison. Since fascist regimes need to stimulate ceaselessly mounting excitement in order to avoid lapsing into mere authoritarianism, fatal overreaching is a likely end for them. They are predisposed to attack until they have mobilized overwhelming counter-force against them. Hitler and Mussolini met very different ends, however, and this matter is not unrelated to the lesser penetration of Italian civil society by fascism. Obviously the presence of the Italian King was a potential pole of resistance, though Victor Emmanuel did nothing until Mussolini's incompetence had rallied the army against him. Hitler's opponents had almost no base to build upon.

Before concluding, some other comparisons are in order. Many commentators wish to pair Hitler with Stalin as the supreme evildoers, leaving aside the lesser Mussolini. If one concentrates on the techniques of coercion, Nazi Germany and Stalinist Russia can look rather similar.[29] A camp is a camp. But as soon as one examines the historical routes to power and the ways the two regimes related to the societies they ruled, profound differences appear. Hitler came to power with the complicity of traditional leaders and groups, and had to obtain at least their acquiescence in order to rule. Stalin reached power by establishing his personal dominance within a governing clique, and ruled a society radically simplified by revolution. Nazism had the ultimate aim of establishing the hegemony of a master race; Stalinism's ultimate aim was to establish a totally egalitarian society worldwide under Russian hegemony, by force if necessary. Stalin's victims may have been more numerous, but nothing in his regime—not even the displacement of suspect peoples like the Volga Germans—matched the systematic extinction of an entire people.

The totalitarianism concept makes for bad history in other ways: it reinforces the myth of the all-powerful ruler, ignores the rulers' complicated relations with social groups and civil society, and offers the elites a handy alibi.

The last issues to consider are whether one can legitimately speak of fascism after 1945, and outside Europe. Major scholars have thought not (e.g. Ernst Nolte, Renzo De Felice). Nevertheless, something that bears strong resemblances to fascism has existed since 1945, and outside Europe. Comparison between the classic fascisms and their post-war avatars reveal important differences. The post-war cases are all movements, of course, rather than regimes, and should be compared to pre-1945 movements and not to pre-1945 regimes.

Some elements are missing in the post-war European versions: aggressive expansionism and the glorification of war; anti-market economic nostrums such as autarky and corporatism; sweeping constitutional revisionism. The issue is complicated by the understandable reluctance of extreme nationalists to associate

---

[29] Scholarly, non-polemical discussions of this comparison include Kershaw and Lewin (eds), *Stalinism and Nazism* and H. Rousso (ed.), *Stalinisme et nazisme: histoire et mémoire comparée* (Brussels: Complexe, 1999).

themselves since 1945 with the more repugnant and the more suicidal aspects of classical fascism, even among its lineal descendants, such as the Italian Movimento Sociale Italiano. Even the most faithful disciples deny they are fascist.

Post-war circumstances differed even more fundamentally from inter-war circumstances than post-war movements differed from inter-war movements. Therefore evaluating post-war fascism demands even more attention to context than before.[30] After 1945, fascism was deeply discredited, and the crises that had opened the way after 1919 did not reappear. There was no depression on the scale of 1929. Democracies functioned relatively well in the ambient prosperity, and the political deadlocks of the inter-war period did not recur. Conservatives had learned better how to manage universal suffrage than in the early days of mass suffrage. European borders were more stable (with the significant exceptions of Belgium and Yugoslavia), since peoples had been moved to fit borders after 1945 rather than attempting to fit borders to peoples as in 1919. The defeat of Germany and Italy had been so total that revenge had little attraction. After 1989 the danger of socialist revolution diminished to the vanishing point. Almost none of the short-term preconditions of fascism were present in Europe after post-war reconstruction began to take hold.

The post-war leaders of extreme nationalist movements knew that circumstances were against them, and they did the best they could with the materials at hand in a generally prosperous and successful Europe. They tried to recruit the losers of 1945, such as Germans displaced from their Eastern European homes. They exploited the red scares of the 1970s. After unemployment and low economic growth became endemic in the 1980s, they built upon fear and resentment of immigrants. To a large degree the neo-fascist movements of recent decades have been one-issue movements that focused on the economic, social, and cultural threat of immigrants. Insofar as some of them have participated in government (in Italy and Austria) it is only after declaring themselves non-fascist or post-fascist and striving to enter the political mainstream.

I have no major objection to calling the more extreme forms of post-war European xenophobia and nationalism neo-fascist. At the very least they occupy the same position on the political spectrum, and attack the same enemies. Their opportunities are significantly less, and the absence of a pre-fascist crisis explains more than any quality inherent to the movements.

Now for fascism outside Europe. Labels exist to serve us, and we should design them for their usefulness. I think that the fascist concept is most useful when it is narrowly delimited. I would restrict it to states that have at least attempted to install parliamentary democracy and then have given it up when democracy appears inadequate to defend a threatened nation. That criterion excludes Third

---

[30] See the stimulating discussion in D. Prowe, ' "Classic" Fascism and the New Radical Right in Western Europe', *Comparative Politics*, 30/2 (1998), 212–34.

and even Second World dictatorships on a traditional model that lack the popular mobilization essential to fascism.

Nevertheless, some mass-based extreme forms of populist nationalism have existed outside Europe that closely resembled classical fascism. The issue is complicated by mimicry, for during the 1930s, when fascism was glamorous and successful, overt imitators emerged in the United States, South Africa, Japan, Argentina, and Brazil—a non-exhaustive list. American movements like William Pelley's Silver Shirts seem to me to correspond in every way to early-stage fascist movements in Europe. Brazilian and Argentine integralism explicitly copied Mussolini. In Japan, some intellectuals and young officers adopted explicitly fascist values from Europe that they thought would liberate Japan from the fetters of big business and permit it to embark on expansionist war under a strengthened Emperor.

None of these movements came anywhere near power on their own. The imperial Japanese cabinet suppressed Japan's indigenous fascist movement in 1932, while taking over some of its themes. Similarly, the dictator Getulio Vargas crushed Brazilian Integralism. Juan Perón pushed aside an earlier integralism in Argentina. These three regimes were often called fascist, particularly in Allied wartime propaganda. But their routes to power and their relationship with the states and societies they ruled differed profoundly.

At best these regimes might be called 'fascism from above'.[31] These dictators crushed authentic fascist movements, while adopting some of their doctrines and mobilizational styles. They did not rise to power on the upwelling of a party of mass integration, however, and their regimes did not have to contend with self-standing fascist parties and their prickly militants. Perón and Vargas were engaged in state building, not in reviving a damaged state in retreat from a failed liberalism. They did not unite their countries around aggressive expansionism.

Colonel Juan Perón has constituted the most ambiguous case. He had been Argentine military attaché in Rome, and Mussolini evidently impressed him. As Defence Minister (1942–4) he continued the Argentine army's traditional ties to Germany for training and weapons, and after 1946 he was close to Franco. In addition to the differences from classical fascism just mentioned, however, Perón's dictatorship had a significant tie to organized labour and attributed a powerful role to the dictator's mistress (later, wife), whom some considered the real power of the regime. Recent scholarship has tended to stress Peronism's indigenous character and to downplay its resemblances to fascist rule.

To conclude, while there have been unambiguously fascist movements outside Europe, it is difficult to find an unambiguously fascist regime there in the past. The future is another matter. As experiments with democracy spread worldwide, the opportunities for it to be found wanting in a crisis and to be replaced by one-party

---

[31] G. J. Kasza proposes a new category of dictatorships that crush local fascist movements and adopt some of their style in 'Fascism from Above? Japan's *Kakushin* Right in Comparative Perspective', in S. U. Larsen, *Fascism outside Europe* (Boulder, CO: Social Science Monographs, 2001), 182–232.

mass mobilizing regimes of national unification, purification, and expansion seem likely to broaden. Russia offers the greatest potential at the moment.

So we have not heard the last of fascism—perhaps of the word, but not of the thing.

BIBLIOGRAPHY

BURRIN, P., 'Politique et société: les structures du pouvoir dans l'Italie fasciste et l'Allemagne nazie', *Annales: économies, sociétés, civilisations*, 43/3 (1988).

COLLOTTI, E., 'Fascismo e nazionalsocialismo', in N. Tranfaglia (ed.), *Fascismo e capitalismo* (Milan: Feltrinelli, 1976), 137–58.

DEGRAND, A. J., *Fascist Italy and Nazi Germany: The 'Fascist' Style of Rule* (London: Routledge, 1995).

DIPPER, C. (ed.), *Faschismus und Fascismen im Vergleich: Wolfgang Schieder zum 60. Geburtstag* (Cologne: Vierow, 1998).

KASZA, G. J., 'Fascism from above? Japan's *Kakushin* Right in Comparative Perspective', in S. U. Larsen (ed.), *Fascism outside Europe* (Boulder, CO: Social Science Monographs, 2001), 182–232.

LEVY, C., 'Fascism, Nazism, and Conservatism: Issues for Comparativists', *Contemporary European History*, 8/1 (1999), 97–126.

LINZ, J. J., 'Some Notes toward a Comparative Study of Fascism in Sociological Historical Perspective', in W. Laqueur (ed.), *Fascism: A Reader's Guide* (Berkeley and Los Angeles: University of California Press, 1976).

NOLTE, E., *Three Faces of Fascism* (New York: Holt, Rinehart and Winston, 1963).

MANN, M., *Fascists* (Cambridge: Cambridge University Press, 2004).

PAXTON, R. O., *The Anatomy of Fascism* (New York: Knopf, 2004).

SCHIEDER, W. (ed.), *Fascismus als sozialer Bewegung: Deutschland und Italien im Vergleich* (Göttingen: Vandenhouck und Rupprecht, 1983).

—— 'La Germania di Hitler e l'Italia di Mussolini: il problema della formazione dei regimi fascisti', *Passato e presente*, 9 (1985), 39–65.

WIPPERMANN, W., *Europäischer Faschismus im Vergleich (1922–1982)* (Frankfurt am Main: Suhrkamp, 1983).

....

CHAPTER 30

MEMORY AND REPRESENTATIONS OF FASCISM IN GERMANY AND ITALY

....

NATHAN STOLTZFUS
R. J. B. BOSWORTH

I. THE GERMAN CASE

....

FOLLOWING the Second World War, countries around Europe crafted narratives claiming that they had virtuously resisted fascism. Italy, France, and Austria, as well as Germany, had to establish new political systems repudiating fascism, yet building on societies that had collaborated with or supported Nazi-fascist rule. The course of this drastic transformation of individual and social perspectives produced a mix of selective forgetting and remembering. To be sure, international opinion sometimes limited the degree of denial; historians and governments chose to remember or forget portions of national culpability based on calculations of what was most usable for immediate political purposes. On the other hand, memories of resistance, no matter how small, were expanded into national narratives.

The quickly emerging Cold War encouraged post-war Europe to subordinate concerns with righting past malevolence to investments in alliances within the new global antagonism. In perpetrator and collaborator countries, the rapid establishment of capitalist democracies and the repression of communism often conflicted with the prosecution of war criminals. Equally, the Cold War context proved opportune for countries—France and Italy are prime examples—to magnify the resistance of a fraction of the people into the history of the nation itself, while repressing memories of perpetration and collaboration.

While even its closest wartime ally and other pro-Nazi nations received an easy pass, as it were, in the examination of their pasts, Germany, with its greater degree of guilt, was subjected to international scrutiny that permitted it a lesser degree of denial. As a result, efforts by the West German Federal Republic (FRG) to come to terms with its past dwarf those of its collaborators and closest allies. During the 1950s, historians in the East German Democratic Republic (GDR), as well as in the FRG, were generally silent about the Nazi past. The GDR's founding ideology claimed that it was an anti-fascist state, comprised of communists who had resisted Nazism; this record exonerated the general populace while glorifying political leaders. Early in West Germany, however, foundations were laid for a democratic culture of openly discussed, conflicting interpretations.

For decades after the war, Germans were enjoined to learn from Nazi crimes, and in fact the FRG's greater efforts to come to terms with its fascist past have accompanied a robust democracy, with a less influential extreme right than in Italy (not to mention Austria). In Italy, the Social Movement (Movimento Sociale Italiano) was Europe's most successful extreme right party until the collapse of communism and it has not altogether renounced its legacy today, while Jorg Haiderlong remained a major player on the Austrian right. In contrast to West Germany, Italy, too, endured 'persistent and serious attempts of subversion of the democratic order by the extreme and conservative right within the very institutions of government'.[1] Compared with such fragility in democratic institutions, the FRG has featured widespread citizen watchfulness against extremism, represented by civilian-organized street protests that have shamed and sidelined public displays of neo-Nazism. Indeed, according to Timothy Garton Ash, 'human rights and civil liberties are today more jealously and effectively protected [by Germany] than (it pains me to say) in traditional homelands of liberty such as Britain and the United States'.[2]

For quite a while, such optimism had its challengers. German social philosopher Jürgen Habermas questioned whether the FRG's Cold War alliance afforded it the

---

[1] C. Levy, 'From Fascism to "Post-Fascists": Italian Roads to Modernity', in R. Bessel (ed.), *Fascist Italy and Nazi Germany: Comparisons and Contrasts* (Cambridge: Cambridge University Press, 1996), 165–96. Levy concluded that the extreme right has remained a political actor in Italian politics up to the present.

[2] T. G. Ash, 'The Stasi on our Minds', *New York Review of Books*, 54/9 (31 May 2007).

best path for maintaining traditional nationalist values. Still, over the decades, the majority popular German attitude has moved toward a Habermasian ideal, 'constitutional patriotism', a political culture of citizens actively exercising their civil rights rooted in constitutional principles.[3] Germany's indicators of a flourishing democracy, compared with those of Italy, raise the question whether Germans have succeeded due to greater efforts they made to come to terms with their wartime guilt and not because of more effective myths or fiercer efforts to deny. Henry Rousso's study of Europe's widespread selective memory presents a promising model for interpreting the impact of myths in the national experience. His classic study of the difficulty that the French and their government had in reconciling themselves with their nation's collaboration led him to conclude that unexpressed and thus unhealed wartime traumas lingered with detrimental effects on post-war social, political, and cultural life, through a series of phases.[4]

Although the FRG's path as penitent has been lonely, it, too, has been accompanied by weighty myths and denials. Common to East and West Germany was a historiography that used a story of resistance to portray the archetypal national experience. Given the GDR's claims that it was not a successor state of the 'Third Reich', East German historians had reason to forget that Nazism was a popularly based dictatorship. If the Socialist State allowed little room for GDR historians to deviate, the concordance between historians and the Adenauer administration in the FRG about Nazism and German resistance was long equally without friction.

Nazi Germany's allies and collaborators readily invented narratives claiming that resistance by small fractions were actually the stories of the people in general. However, despite its prominence in perpetration (not to mention the lack of resistance), Germany soon sponsored a resistance myth that made heroes of a small group of elite conspirators, depicted as a group of democratically minded military leaders heroically martyred for resisting totalitarianism. A companion myth that the army (Wehrmacht) under Hitler only performed honourably and heroically was backed in the FRG by a judiciary largely held over from the Nazi period. Once the initial widespread post-war view that the conspirators had been 'traitors' (as the Nazis had called them in 1944) dissipated, the myth about the 20 July 1944 plot to kill Hitler and the myth of an unblemished Wehrmacht supported each other. They were jointly sustained by selective remembering and forgetting. No matter how pleasing, this myth has long been faulted for its claim about the conspirators' political motives. Recent work has demonstrated that 'at the same time' that the military officers conspired to kill Hitler they were 'also participating in mass crimes',

---

[3] J. Habermas, 'Citizenship and National Identity: Some Reflections on the Future of Europe', *Praxis International*, 12/1 (1992), 1–19.

[4] H. Rousso, *The Vichy Syndrome: History and Memory in France since 1944* (Cambridge, MA: Harvard University Press, 1991; 1st edn. 1987).

while their definition of a just and necessary war in the east (if not the west) was not so different from that of the Nazis.[5]

Resistance recollections constitute one important measure of German memory of fascism as a whole because they bear so heavily on the overall narrative about fascism, including its most disturbing and distinguishing traits. Over the decades, other incidents of opposition beyond the July conspiracy have come to light, along with new categories for understanding oppositional behaviour. Yet the stability of interpretations of German resistance in the face of momentous changes in our understanding of the way Nazi power functioned is striking.

The idea of resistance as promulgated in the FRG fitted the idealized picture of the July plot, confining opposition to *Widerstand*, or centrally organized, politically motivated, efforts intended to overthrow the regime itself. Moreover, the history of resistance as a spectacular failure has served to exonerate the entire nation for not having resisted (begging the question whether they wished to resist). The heroic main figures in this 'German Resistance mythology' died in their 20 July 1944 effort to kill Hitler: if even military generals commanding great resources were martyred, the implication ran, ordinary people were right to go along with the Nazi regime as they waited for liberation from Hitler's tyranny by the Allies. Germans were Hitler's victims and did not resist, nor should we expect such supererogatory behaviour. The myth about 20 July continued to function as the basis of an increasingly established archetypal story of Germans during the Third Reich: resistance led to death, and dispensing with Nazism could focus on killing Hitler with little or no calculation about how to deal with the general opinion of the populace whom he had won over by carefully and continuously presenting himself as the *Führer* the people wanted.

During the first post-war decades this German resistance myth served the critical purpose of strengthening a popular opinion critical of Hitler rather than that which deemed the conspirators traitors. This purpose, however, has long been fulfilled and the continued lauding of 'the German resistance' has simultaneously carried starkly negative effects especially when it obscures the fact that most Germans were more interested in supporting Hitler than opposing him, even during Nazism's desperate demise.

Although the July plot should maintain its place as a model of resistance behaviour, its mythologized version has served Germany's persistent urge to normalize— that is, to possess a history no darker than that of the other major powers in modern history, and thereby win a future unencumbered by stigma and guilt. Yet, such normalization can readily entail evasions of the past and be beset by interpretations that cloud the present. It can foster and justify the recurring post-war desire among

---

[5] C. Gerlach, 'Men of 20 July and the War in the Soviet Union', in H. Heer and K. Naumann (eds), *War of Extermination: The German Military in World War II, 1941–1944* (New York: Berghahn, 2000), 127–45.

some Germans for a *Schlussstricht*, or a wish to be done with the accounting for Germany's crimes in the Second World War once and for all.

According to some analysts, Germany reached the peak in facing its war crimes and genocide during the 1980s and 1990s, switching instead in recent years toward the normalization of a *Schlussstricht*. At the same time it should be acknowledged that Germany's project of confronting the past would be more easily achieved in a context of European-wide efforts to do the same. For Germans the stakes are doubtless higher, and a more varied portrait of German behaviour during the Second World War may well provide a basis for better perceiving and pre-empting threats to their democracy in the future. But democracy is a Europe-wide phenomenon and will be best underpinned by a thorough and honest European reading of the past. In this regard, the most obvious comparison is always with Germany's closest ally, Italy, the Fascist dictatorship which, after all, offered Hitler many lessons on his own road to power and to war.

While general world opinion has long looked on the Italians as 'brava gente' (nice people), Germans have been painted, frequently enough, as outsiders unable to cross certain boundaries. Thus, in 1995, the victorious Allies denied Germany a place in commemorations of the fiftieth anniversary of the end of the Second World War. Finally integrated into official celebrations a decade later, Germany still faced worldwide anxieties. There was much hand wringing in the press about Germany's new-found freedom to wave its flag during the 2006 World Cup soccer play-offs; some who thought Germany had normalized enough for the moment let out a whoop of relief when Italy defeated Germany.

While the Nazi past provided the labels—Hitler, Auschwitz, the Gestapo—that signified 'unspeakable' evil, Allied opinion led the way in exonerating the Third Reich's allies and collaborators. The Moscow Declaration of 1 November 1943 already identified Austria as the victim of 'Hitlerite Germany', an identity highlighted in Austria's declaration of independence on 27 April 1945 and approved by the Allies when Austria achieved full sovereignty in 1955.[6] This judgement of a country that had fought the war and committed crimes as part of Germany with every indication of widespread popular support for Nazism indicated that a pass was available to others who were less implicated than the Austrians in a Nazi past.

Nonetheless, Germany's guilt did place it in a distinct position, as German philosopher Karl Jaspers's four categories indicated in 1946. Germany's behaviour fits Jasper's most serious category—criminality. For Germans, wrote Jaspers, 'our share is humility and moderation', even if wrongfully or unfairly reproached.[7] Furthermore, Germany's aggression and crimes were possible only because the Germans, and the Austrians as Germans, supported fascism in their country more

---

[6] D. Art, *The Politics of the Nazi Past in Germany and Austria* (Cambridge: Cambridge University Press, 2006), 105.

[7] K. Jaspers, *The Question of German Guilt* (New York: Fordham University Press, 2001; 1st edn. 1946), 117.

actively and more fanatically, relative to other perpetrators or collaborators. As the self-proclaimed 'master race', Germany attacked countries across the continent, which in turn fought in self-defence. None of Germany's European allies would have gone to war at that time had they not opportunistically or from a perceived need to take sides joined Germany's plunge into war and genocide. Although Austria, for example, brimmed with enthusiasm for German annexation in 1938, and provided war criminals and direct agents of genocide in disproportionate numbers, it could never have led the way to fascism, genocide, and war crimes that Germany charted. Tony Judt has maintained that acknowledgement of the Holocaust is the required 'entry ticket' of countries to Europe today and, in this regard, plainly Germany does indeed retain a primacy of guilt or responsibility.[8]

In the first post-war decades, the 'racial' impulse at the heart of Nazi war and genocide was largely overlooked in both Germanys. Since then, Germany has shifted to acknowledge this fundamental aspect of the Nazi regime. Still in the 1990s some found Germany's memory of Auschwitz gravely distorted, maintaining that this failure was due to an excessive and revisionist focus on the resistance of 20 July.[9] Throughout the post-war period, however, interpretations of resistance have held steady relative to increased acknowledgement of guilt and feelings of shame in Germany about the genocide of Jews.

Representations of the July plot meshed well with the earliest interpretations of Hitler's role, but these interpretations have long since undergone dramatic changes. The initial post-war paradigm for understanding the Nazi dictatorship viewed power as inherent in Hitler, with state and society governed according to his will. He held total power and so was 'the accident in the works' of an otherwise positive German story. This perspective was amended by social-structural models that inculpated Germany's bureaucracies and elites, and illuminated continuities from Germany's nineteenth century, delineating a so-called *Sonderweg* or special path behind the Nazi drive for domination of Europe. Later, an interpretative line evolving during the 1980s and 1990s argued that Hitler's power percolated up to him from popular consent and collaboration. Recent studies have gone on to indicate in fact that hundreds of thousands of Germans were perpetrators of Nazism's worst crimes, and not merely backers of a regime that carried out its deeds behind their backs.

This issue of the extent and durability of popular consent and collaboration that Nazism won and held has beleaguered interpretations in the FRG over the entire post-war period. While the GDR's official myth that the state consisted of communist resisters combined with state ideology easily to dispatch the matter, FRG historians from the beginning had to explain the 'German catastrophe' by

---

[8] T. Judt, *Postwar: A History of Europe since 1945* (London: Penguin, 2005), 803–4.

[9] F. Stern, 'Wolfsschanze versus Auschwitz: Widerstand als deutsches Alibi', *Zeitschrift für Geschichtswissenschaft*, 42/7 (1994), 645–50.

other means. Friedrich Meinecke focused on Hitler alone to explain fascism's arrival, calling Hindenburg's appointment of the *Führer* as chancellor an accident (*Zufall*).[10] Congruous with this perspective, the centrepiece of the July conspiracy to overthrow the regime was the assassination of Hitler. Yet even after Ian Kershaw's exploration of the Hitler Myth demonstrated that the *Führer*'s leadership depended on the people's reception of him as a leader, the July conspiracy suggesting a role for Hitler that ignored the place of the people in his exercise of power continued to dominate much official history.

Social-structural interpretations focused on the conservative elites and not just on Hindenburg to explain Hitler's 'seizure of power' in 1933. Not until decades after the war did historians begin to explain that popular acclaim had underpinned the Nazi movement's attractiveness to conservatives; its power as a mass movement was what forced compromises with conservative power holders. Conservatives gave fascists a hand because they themselves, like established bourgeois parties, were unwilling to appeal, or incapable of appealing, to the masses. Already in 1932 support for Nazism comprised a sufficient number to be called a social mainstream. The 20 July plot presented an eventual scenario—an apparent act of treason and a surge of support for existing authority—that seemed to confirm Hitler's good sense in rejecting repeated agitation within the SA for the Nazi Party to take power through a *coup d'état*.

Similarly important in assessing the significance of conservative assistance is the fact that, after he had dispensed with his partnership with conservatives by 1938, Hitler continued to view his 'racial' people as a partner in power. This was also the year when conservative, military-based, conspirators decided that they would not be able openly to kill or arrest Hitler because of his great popularity; imprisoning Hitler would not work since the people would demand the release of their leader.[11] Hitler had proved his special powers again and again to his mass movement— all against the backdrop of the Weimar Republic's failures and the circumstances following the First World War, to be sure. Backed by a succession of foreign policy triumphs, renewed national pride and self-esteem, and above all the restoration of order, his profile meant that the number of willing supporters of the Nazi-led government rose substantially through the 1930s. By the spring of 1939, 'the great majority of Germans could find some point of identification with Hitler and his achievements'. Similarly, it would be true that news of the plot to kill Hitler in July 1944 was followed by a surge in support for the *Führer*.[12] Hitler himself continued to view his racial people as his partner to the bitter end of his regime.

---

[10] F. Meinecke, *Die Deutsche Katastrophe: Betrachtungen und Erinnerungen* (Wiesbaden: Eberhard Brockhaus Verlag, 1947), 93, 104.

[11] See J. Fest, *Plotting Hitler's Death: The Story of German Resistance* (New York: Holt, 1997; 1st edn. 1994), 89, 91.

[12] I. Kershaw, *The 'Hitler Myth': Image and Reality in the Third Reich* (Oxford: Oxford University Press, 1987), 141, 216–19.

Nor were FRG historians unreflective of this situation. 'The great majority of German historians schooled in the Rankean tradition', including Gerhard Ritter and Meinecke, 'in international relations thought there was nothing wrong with Hitler until it was plain that he had lost the Second World War'.[13] Beyond the academy, post-war surveys of Germans indicated 'an enduring presence of Nazi attitudes', with positive images eroding slowly. By May 1964 those who considered the Nazi regime criminal still comprised only a slight majority.[14] Responding to such opinion as well as the Cold War, FRG Chancellor Konrad Adenauer negotiated the release of war criminals in return for the FRG's cooperation with the Western Alliance; most elite Nazi functionaries were quickly integrated into democratic Germany's reconstruction.

For a decade beginning in 1958, a succession of legal events confronted West Germans with a fuller representation of Nazi crimes. The Auschwitz Trial beginning in 1963 was prominent, although the Ulm Einsatzgruppen trial of 1958 had earlier stimulated public discussion of the murder of the Jews. Particularly ominous for the Wehrmacht Myth were revelations that the army had done a significant amount of mass shootings of Jews and communists; but the FRG judiciary quickly acquitted the implicated Wehrmacht unit.[15]

A determined FRG judiciary could have prosecuted numbers of Wehrmacht war criminals, but instead it preferred a whitewashed history of the army's war. The GDR held twenty trials of denouncers of Wehrmacht deserters, compared with one (who was acquitted) in the FRG. The GDR judiciary acquitted 17 per cent of Wehrmacht soldiers tried for classical war crimes, while the FRG acquitted 88 per cent and found just three Wehrmacht soldiers guilty. The GDR issued forty-nine sentences, all upheld by post-unification FRG courts.[16]

Despite plentiful records, including those used at the Ulm Trial, the FRG's conservative national historians, embodied in the Association of German Historians, promoted the Wehrmacht Myth. After the Second World War, Germany's professors had continued to teach national history in the same way that they always had done, omitting the Nazi period with the exception of literature on elite resistance. In the context of silence that these early years are known for, lessons on resistance were probably the most effective means of teaching not just German innocence but German honour. Fritz Fischer's thesis of 1961 suggesting continuities of German

[13] R. J. B. Bosworth, *Explaining Auschwitz and Hiroshima: History Writing and the Second World War 1945–1990* (New York: Routledge, 1994), 57–8.

[14] N. Thomas, *Protest Movements in 1960s West Germany: A Social History of Dissent and Democracy* (Oxford: Berg, 2003), 28; Kershaw, *Hitler Myth*, 264–7.

[15] C. F. Rüter, 'Die Ahndung von NS-Gewaltverbrechen im deutsch-deutschen Vergleich', in Die Linkspartei: PDS Fraktion im Landtag Sachsen-Anhalt (ed.), *Konferenz zum 60. Jahrestag der Befreiung vom Faschismus: Die juristische Aufarbeitung von NS-Verbrechen und deren Widerspiegelung in der Gedenkkultur* (Halberstadt: Druckerei Lüders, 2005), <http://www.linkspartei-pdslsa-lt.de/publikation/konf_reader_web.pdf> (2 August 2006), 65–82, 78 n. 54.

[16] Ibid. 72–3.

guilt from the nineteenth century to Nazism aroused a furore, attacking among other 'truths' the reigning interpretation that Hitler's rule broke radically with Germany's past. In 1962, as if to shore up the claim of Hitler's guilt and German innocence, Boards of Education from around the FRG 'imposed the theory of totalitarianism as a truth to be taught to every school-child'.[17]

Conservative nationalism continued to characterize the FRG's professional historians until the late 1960s encouraged newly open debate in universities, stimulated by a generation too young to be directly guilty themselves. The election to national office in the late 1960s of Willy Brandt, known not just as a Social Democrat but as a resister, who had fled the confines of Germany in war, also signalled a change in popular attitudes.

The 1960s saw the early development of diverse opinions and debates in the FRG that would come to full bloom by the 1980s. Serious challenges to the existing image of Hitler emerged. Hans-Ulrich Wehler and the Bielefeld school represented the strength of the social-structural perspectives for assessing continuities with the German past. The so-called functionalists challenged the view that Hitler's intentions governed state and society, as did Martin Broszat's concept of polycracy. The study of everyday life laid foundations for what would become the 'bottom-up' viewpoint on the regime's power and actions. The new concept of *Resistenz* began to break conceptualizations of civilian behaviour during the 'Third Reich' out of black and white constructions of resisters and victims.

Although not intended to embrace a separate category for identifying resistance,[18] *Resistenz* came to represent virtually all dissent and opposition other than that defined by *Widerstand*. Since there was not much German resistance, the expansive category of *Resistenz* underlined the futility of identifying resistance as something other than *Widerstand*, which was suited to focus attention on the July plot. A national day of tribute to that resistance was established, providing occasion each year for high-profile speakers and media coverage that continues to this day, while other instances of resistance can expect primarily local commemoration. These ceremonies take place at the German Resistance Memorial (Gedenkstätte deutscher Widerstand) and simultaneously at the Plötzensee Memorial, best known as the site of the gruesome execution of many of the 20 July conspirators, thus cementing the link between resistance and execution.

Through the decades, as studies uncovered more and more about popular acclaim for the thought and deeds of Hitler's dictatorship, interpretations of resistance remained entrenched. Few asked what limitations collective public opposition might have placed on the dictatorship, given that its converse, mass public support, had comprised the primary basis of Hitler's power. Class-based studies illustrated

---

[17] Bosworth, *Explaining Auschwitz and Hiroshima*, 62.

[18] I. Kershaw, *The Nazi Dictatorship: Problems and Perspectives of Interpretation* (4th edn. Oxford: Oxford University Press, 2000), 199.

by the 1970s and 1980s that Hitler had indeed curtailed even his rearmament programme to alleviate unrest among the working class. But arguments followed that
Hitler made these concessions only because he was particularly concerned about the
attitudes of the working class. This situation was interpreted to indicate that other
ordinary Germans acting collectively would not be able to evoke concessions (even
though cases of regime appeasement of groups beyond the working class continued
to surface).

In 1982 Michael Verhoeven's film *The White Rose* displayed resistance in the
context of overwhelming German complicity and the social struggle that resistance
demanded. Arriving at a high point in the publication of everyday history, it was a
portrait of ordinary Germans trying to change popular opinion rather than blow
up Hitler. Verhoeven's film illustrated denunciation, a key mechanism underlying
the Gestapo's work, and portrayed a Wehrmacht soldier shrugging off his part as a
perpetrator in mass murder as something someone else would have done anyway.
Verhoeven also brought to the screen images of noisy student dissent during the
January 1943 speech of a Nazi regional leader in Munich, which indicated that
collective open opposition might go unpunished. These ambiguous images, and a
last comment in the film that the Nazi judgements against the White Rose resisters
had not yet been set aside, induced the conservative German government for a time
to delay the movie's foreign distribution.

The fortieth anniversary of the Second World War's end and the ensuing
Historikerstreit yielded high-profile debates, but did nothing to dislodge the myths
of the German resistance. Christian Democrat Chancellor Helmut Kohl, himself
trained as a (conservative) historian, forcefully advanced the case for normalization
underpinned by improved visions of history as seen through the corrective lens
of two new history museums. Unburdened from stifling guilt, it seemed that,
under his aegis, German national pride and morale would rise again and Germany would become a more effective player in NATO and on the world stage.
Even President Richard von Weizsäcker, Christian Democrat son of a prominent
bureaucrat who had initially worked with the Nazis but representing the sensitively
responsible Germany compared with Kohl's fully normalized one, reiterated the
conservative national view about Hitler when asserting in his celebrated May 1985
speech that Hitler had made the 'entire people (*Volk*)' his 'tool' for persecuting
Jews.[19]

The *Historikerstreit* debates were waged on territory far removed from questions
about German popular responsibility. Historians showing the most concern about
German responsibility tended to use social-structural analyses to normalize the
Nazi period, but only within German and not international history. Commentary

[19] Bundespräsident R. von Weizsäcker, Speech to the German Parliament on the 40th Anniversary
of the End of the Second World War, 8 May 1985, <http://www.bundestag.de/geschichte/
parlhist/dokumente/doko8.html> (15 August 2006).

on the German resistance fell to their opposing conservative nationalists. Andreas Hillgruber sought a glorious past for the Wehrmacht without any special relationship to the July plot and through to the end of the war.[20]

Following the Cold War and German reunification, major debates concerned how Germans should express their wartime suffering, and were accompanied by renewed foreign angst about an alleged erosion of German concern about the Nazi past. While the GDR had commenced officially to acknowledge the resistance of the conspiracy to kill Hitler during the 1970s, acceptance of communist resistance by the officially established German Resistance Memorial in Berlin began a decade later amid considerable and continuing rancour.[21] Further indicating similarities of memory in the two Germanys, research shows that East German opinions evolved but, in that process, were influenced only weakly by the official line. After 1990, West Germans shared with East Germans the challenge of reconciling official and private memory. Half of Germans surveyed in 2002 said their relatives had disapproved of Nazism, while only 1 per cent thought their parents or grandparents had been 'involved directly in crimes'. Sixty-three per cent on the other hand mentioned the suffering of their ancestors during the war.[22] Thus, even today, Germans generally view their family past in consonance with those national conservative historians who have so long represented opposition as the majority narrative, and perpetrators as outsiders.

The history of the Wehrmacht remained a touchstone. The collapse of communism had prompted by the mid-1990s the holding of a 'Wehrmacht Exhibition', potentially devastating to the army's myth, but its impact remained partial. More recently, the publication of British Secret Intelligence Service records between 1942 and 1945 of the conversations of senior German military officers has struck a further blow.[23] Yet, even without the political impulsion of the Cold War, more than fifteen years on in the new Berlin Republic the judiciary has not proven more willing to prosecute, convict, or incarcerate Wehrmacht suspects. In 2006 a court reached the same conclusion about the massacre of Italians on Cephalonia in 1943 that it had come to in 1968, but with a more inflammatory rationale. The senior prosecutor in 2006 cited the 1939 Pact of Steel, concluding that Italian soldiers who resisted the German ultimatum to disarm following Mussolini's fall were roughly equivalent to German soldiers who deserted and sided with the enemy: turning from their

---

[20] C. S. Maier, *The Unmasterable Past: History, Holocaust, and German National Identity* (Cambridge, Mass.: Harvard University Press, 1988, 1997), 32.

[21] P. Steinbach, 'Teufel Hitler—Beelzebub Stalin? Zur Kontroverse um die Darstellung des Nationalkomitees Freies Deutschland in der ständigen Austellung "Widerstand gegen den Nationalsozialismus" in der Gedenkstätte Deutscher Widerstand', *Zeitschrift für Geschichtswissenschaft*, 42/7 (1994), 651–61.

[22] H. Welzer, S. Moller, and K. Tschuggnall, *Opa war kein Nazi: Nationalsozialismus und Holocaust im Familiengedächtnis. Zeit des Nationalsozialismus* (Frankfurt am Main: Fischer, 2002), 164, 246.

[23] S. Neitzel (ed.), *Tapping Hitler's Generals: Transcripts of Secret Conversations 1942–45*, introduction by I. Kershaw (London: Greenhill Books, 2007).

alliance they became 'fiercely fighting enemies and thus in the parlance of the military "traitors" '.[24]

Daniel Goldhagen's book, with its thesis about Germans as 'Hitler's willing executioners' primed by a visceral anti-Semitism, did provoke some easy expressions of guilt in 1990s Germany. But more challenging to the archetypal story presented by the myth of the 'German resistance' were histories of opposition by ordinary Germans that reached a broad audience for the first time. The nation's Jehovah's Witnesses, with more than a third of their 25,000 members imprisoned and 2,000 in camps, illustrated that terror and propaganda could not shape the behaviour of all 'racial' Germans, as did tens of thousands of intermarried Germans who refused to take the easy road out of untold miseries and uncertainties by simply leaving their Jewish spouses. The public protest of intermarried Germans is the most likely explanation for the rescue of some 2,000 German Jews from death. Furthermore, such behaviour indicated that a converse of publicly expressed collective support for Nazism had existed and that it had operated in a converse way to limit rather than enable the dictatorship.

As indicated by a number of protests, ordinary Germans under certain circumstances could undertake opposition, escape punishment for it, and achieve their limited aims, thereby curtailing the regime, although certainly without hobbling its capacity to rule. As if in response, but partially so, Marc Rothemund's 2005 film *Sophie Scholl: The Final Days*, rather than relaying one important story of ordinary Germans in details that effectively broaden the image of resistance, supports the identity-defining archetype established by the July plot. Opening with Scholl's capture as a reckless adolescent, the film relates her story as that of a helpless victim in Gestapo clutches, a predictable cat and mouse episode of torment leading to super-ordinary behaviour and execution. Resistance led to martyrdom, it seems, and selfishly drew family and friends into torment and execution. The standard portrait of the 20 July resistance and of the anti-Nazi aristocrats of the Kreisauer Kreis (Kreisau Circle) emphasizes that they were motivated by ethical, Christian impulses, and Rothemund's film frames repeated religious scenes and prayers, casting religion as Scholl's comforter. Scholl becomes increasingly saintly. The film claims grounding in newly discovered materials but portrays the Catholic Church only as a concerned caretaker of opposition, while Germans generally are represented as creatures in the wilderness who have forgotten their God. The words of one of Scholl's prayers to this effect are reminiscent of Kohl's controversial statement in 1985, which conservative nationalist historian Gerhard Ritter might have written in early post-war years, attributing Nazism to an 'accelerating disintegration of values and morals...the re-negation of God'.[25]

---

[24] Oberstaatsanwalt August Stern, Staatsanwaltschaft München I, Geschäftsnummer 115Js11161/06, 27 July 2006.
[25] Bosworth, *Explaining Auschwitz and Hiroshima*, 76.

While German histories have increased dramatically the assortment of behaviours treated as resistance, these additions have not challenged the archetypal story accompanying the resistance paradigm, which obscures the dimension of popular support and collaboration that is the *sine qua non* of fascism. The regime was sure to promote general support by brutal and public repression of assassination attempts, out of line as they were with opinion. On the other hand, public, collective, protests, which were as common as attempts on Hitler's life, show that Hitler preferred appeasing or at least not repressing these actions if they reflected general opinion. Yet public collective protest has been excluded from German portraits of resistance or, infrequently, interpreted to support the outdated archetype. In 2005, for example, a book on resistance dropped the Rosenstrasse Protest into a chapter entitled 'Resistance in SPD and KPD Circles during War', under the heading 'Trade Union Solidarity'. This casting of the 1943 life-risking protest by intermarried Germans in Berlin is as perplexing as its earlier inclusion under the rubric of German Jews 'Surviving in Hiding' by another well-known historian. The inaccurate placement of this protest leads to further inaccuracies, including the claim that the protest consisted in part of truancy from work, which was a mere by-product of the protest itself, as were belated, limited, and discreetly private church actions, which are credited here with a decisive role in the protest's outcome.[26]

Apologists for the long-standing myth of the 'German resistance' may have recognized that history does not support the overly heroic status that the myth has assigned the conspirators. Yet, they redouble efforts to shore up the July plot's dominant position and retain its archetypal implications. That is a pity because one obvious way for Germans to face the truths about the implications of popular acclaim for Hitler is to probe the converse of this behaviour in public collective displays of opposition. Democratic, modern Germany certainly is. However, before ascribing exemplary status to it in Europe, analysts must continue to worry about ongoing German distortions of the national past, even while they hail the honesty of much German history and some German memory.

II. The Italian Case

The story of the history and memory of Italy's dictatorship has parallels and contrasts with that of Germany. A toll of 'premature deaths' of around a million makes

---

[26] G. R. Ueberschär, *Für ein anderes Deutschland: Der deutsche Widerstand gegen den NS-Staat 1933–1945* (Frankfurt am Main: Fischer, 2005), 8. W. Benz (ed.), *Die Juden in Deutschland 1933–1945: Leben unter nationalsozialistischer Herrschaft* (Munich: C. H. Beck: 1988), 688. See A. Leugers, 'Widerstand gegen die Rosenstrasse', in *Theologie. Geschichte*, 1 (2006) <http://aps.sulb. uni-saarland.de/theologie.geschichte/inhalt/2006/11.html> (10 May 2007).

Mussolini's regime scarcely the equal of Hitler's or Stalin's in the sad history of twentieth-century political killing, and its murder of Italians, as distinct from peoples under its imperial rule, is far less than that of the Francoists in Spain. The initial fall of fascism in July 1943, and the division of the country from September 1943 to the war's end in April 1945 between Allied and Nazi armies, with collaborationist governments on each part trying ineffectually to embody the Italian nation, further deflect many Italians from wanting a reckoning with a bloody time of civil war of some description.[27] A minority have always used the Repubblica Sociale Italiana (RSI) as the touchstone of alleged fascist virtue and revolutionary commitment.[28] But, for the most part, the national war record ensures that non-Italians have not been too forceful in questioning their own cosy frequent assumptions about sunny *brava gente*, with their basic theory that Italians are too nice and too incompetent to be natural-born killers or fanatical 'fundamentalists'.

Henry Rousso's suggestion that the trauma of war most frequently encouraged forgetting rather than memory holds true in Italy, too. No doubt assisted by the Cold War, the prominent role in crusading against communism taken by Pope Pius XII, and the considerable electoral place of the Partito Comunista Italiano in national and local politics, Italian discourse in the 1950s did its best to shrug off the fascist past. Benedetto Croce, the great liberal philosopher and historian, led the way with his assertion that Mussolini's dictatorship had marked a 'parenthesis' in the otherwise positive course of Italian history; fascism, it seemed, was another 'accident in the works'.[29]

With any serious reckoning of its recent history held in abeyance, Italy enjoyed its 'economic miracle' and, while no longer burdened by being a Great Power, played a major role in the formation of a European Union and also expanded domestic freedoms in an unexampled fashion. By the onset of the 1970s, it seemed to have accepted a curious equation—politically the PCI was excluded from national government. Rather, every Prime Minister came from the centrist Christian Democrat party (DC). Somewhere not too far in the shadows, political and economic Italy kept wires open with the country's residual fascists, who expressed themselves most openly in the Movimento Sociale Italiano (the adjective 'sociale' signified a determination to carry forward the legacy of the RSI). In the cultural world, by contrast, and in the regional and local administrations especially in northern and central Italy, the DC could work with the PCI. In talking about the recent past, there was all but official endorsement of the so-called 'Myth of the Resistance', a classic

[27] The initiator of this debate was the anti-fascist work by C. Pavone, *Una guerra civile: saggio storico sulla moralità della Resistenza* (Turin: Bollati Boringhieri, 1991).

[28] For a recent study of how Fascists dealt with the immediate effects of defeat, see G. Parlato, *Fascisti senza Mussolini: le origini del neo-fascismo in Italia, 1943–1948* (Bologna: Il Mulino, 2006). Typical of the moment, Parlato plays up alleged fascist 'suffering' and coherence.

[29] For general historiographical background, see R. J. B. Bosworth, *The Italian Dictatorship: Problems and Perspectives in the Interpretation of Mussolini and Fascism* (London: Arnold, 1998).

'anti-fascist' story where the dictatorship was to be damned but also to be depicted as the product of Mussolini and his henchmen, a regime which perpetually lacked a 'genuine popular base'. Rather, from 1922 to 1943, and especially during the time of the partisans from 1943 to 1945, the Italian people had remained hostile to fascism and uncontaminated in the deepest sense by it. Put at its simplest, Italy, the border state of the liberal capitalist world, had developed a polity and an economy that were 'western' and a historical culture that was, at a minimum, deeply penetrated by the sort of 'anti-fascist' reading of the immediate past that had been installed in much of Eastern Europe.

The decade of the 1970s, however, shook both faces of this system. In 1976, the PCI went very close to being elected democratically to national government. The memoirs of Richard Gardner, Jimmy Carter's ambassador to Rome from 1977 to 1981, offer fine testimony to the bewilderment that such voting behaviour inspired in global halls of power and to the determination of the USA to keep the communists out. While Gardner was a worried observer in his embassy in the Via Veneto, in the spring of 1978 left-wing terrorists calling themselves Brigate Rosse (Red Brigades) kidnapped and then murdered the leading DC politician, Aldo Moro (Gardner feared the capture of Moro could be the signal for a general communist uprising).[30] Although the BR ideology had syncretic elements, it was posited on an application of history to the present. In the BR's deluded eyes, people like Moro and the rest of the governing caste, somewhere beneath their benign-sounding rhetoric, were evildoers. A terrorist act, the BR were sure, would strip the mask and show to an alerted public the fascist beast which had once again taken over Italy.

In fact, the brutality of the treatment of Moro ensured instead the evaporation of what had been quite a degree of sympathy for left terrorist aims and the fretting of the 'Myth of the Resistance'. The elections of 1976 turned out to be the apogee for the PCI and, by the end of the decade, the tellingly named line of Party Secretary Enrico Berlinguer, of a 'compromesso storico' (historic compromise), envisaging a grand coalition with the DC (and a complete exclusion of the MSI and any dallying with its version of history) in a replay of what had once been thought to have staffed resistance in 1943–5, had collapsed. The time of Thatcher, Reagan, and Kohl remained a little confused politically and culturally in Italy, if only because the great candidate of the 'West' as the needed new politician, Bettino Craxi, the anti-communist socialist, failed to make himself an Italian Mitterrand. Among academic historians, the sober and archivally driven work of Renzo De Felice in portraying Mussolini's rule continued inexorably, and its author was much promoted by American and local anti-communists. But De Felice's prose style was a model of tortuousness; his books may have been sold but they were seldom read, with the

---

[30] R. N. Gardner, *Mission Italy: On the Front Lines of the Cold War* (Lanham, MD: Rowman and Littlefield, 2005), 167.

exception being two interviews he gave in 1975 and 1995, where any panache was owed not to the historian but to his rightist interlocutors.[31]

At the moment of the fall of the Berlin Wall, any Italian memory of a generation of dictatorship therefore remained either obscured or confused. With Fukuyama's heralding the 'end of history', the final and complete triumph of the American version of liberal capitalism and an implied single reading thereafter of the past, present, and future, Italians were thrust into a world where most certainties of their post-war Republic withered away. Rapidly, every political party that had set out its electoral wares since 1945 fragmented or altered its prime purpose, name, and logo. Communists converted (in majority) into 'democrats', neo-fascists into post-fascists, the DC split right and left, and the socialists crumbled. By the new millennium, Italy's 'new' politicians included the media magnate Silvio Berlusconi, heading the party Forza Italia (Up, Italy) rallied by a football slogan and unreliably backed by Umberto Bossi and his Lega Nord (Northern League), seemingly threatening to undermine the united nation, by the 'post-fascist' Gianfranco Fini, presumably still fascist enough to favour a strong, central, state, and opposed by Francesco Rutelli, head of a movement called the Margherita (or Daisy) party.[32] Here, an onlooker might conclude, was bewilderment indeed and certainly historiographical currents continue to swirl through present-day Italy in a fashion that mocks the occasional foreign assertion that a consensus has been achieved in fascism studies.

One feature of the last decade has been the coming of Italian neo-fascists in from the cold. At the cost doubtless of a relabelling as post-fascists, those who want to find some positives in the history of the dictatorship remain active. From an initial insistence that an allegiance to the RSI could have an honourable side,[33] revisionism has extended to a rash of biographies where even the murderous Party Secretary of the 1930s, Achille Starace, can be called 'a war hero, a man of power no doubt but one of good nature, a loyal and fundamentally honest party boss, unreservedly generous in his service of the idea in which he believed'.[34] An English biographer has sought, with some confusion, to resurrect the reputation of the *Duce*, while

---

[31] R. De Felice, *Intervista sul fascismo*, ed. M. A. Ledeen (Bari: Laterza, 1975; rev. edn. 1997); idem, *Rosso e nero* (Milan: Baldini and Castoldi, 1995). For a more general study, highly friendly to its subject, see E. Gentile, *Renzo De Felice: lo storico e il personaggio* (Bari: Laterza, 2003).

[32] For an introduction to the 1990s and its dilemmas, see P. Ginsborg, *Italy and its Discontents 1980–2001* (London: Allen Lane, 2001).

[33] Among other accounts, see V. Costa, *L'ultimo federale: memorie della guerra civile 1943–1945* (Bologna: Il Mulino, 1997), repeating the theses that the last months of the war indeed constituted a 'civil war' in which realism more than fanaticism made the government of northern Italy the 'necessary republic' (repeating the title of the memoirs of the ex-RSI minister P. Pisenti, *Una repubblica necessaria (RSI)* (Rome: G. Volpi Editore, 1977)). Cf. C. Mazzantini, *I balilla andarono a Salò: l'armata degli adolescenti che pagò il conto della Storia* (Venice: Marsilio, 1995).

[34] R. Festorazzi, *Starace: il mastino della rivoluzione fascista* (Milan: Mursia, 2002), 10. For Starace's apparent war criminality in Ethiopia, cf. G. Bottai, *Diario 1935–1944*, ed. G. B. Guerri (Milan: Rizzoli, 1989), 102.

Berlusconi himself pronounced that Mussolini 'never killed anyone' and compared the punishment system of *confino*, visited on 11,000 Italians during the dictatorship, to a 'holiday camp'.[35]

The more measured approach, one that has echoed the tactics of sometime Foreign Minister and Deputy Prime Minister Fini (ostensibly Italy's ablest conservative politician), is rather that adopted by the distinguished liberal historian, but youthful fascist, Roberto Vivarelli. For Vivarelli, the son of a Siena squadrist and lawyer, his teenage commitment to fascism in 1944–5 was the result of family loyalty and devotion, and was entirely devoid of anti-Semitism or other Hitlerite flirtation: 'for me, the nation (*Patria*) and fascism were identical'.[36] The approach of James Gregor, the American political scientist who has found most merit and intellectual credibility in fascism, more drastically dates a successful regime to around 1937–8 and argues that 'wartime Fascism, . . . in alliance with Nazi Germany, had taken on emphatically alien features'.[37] In other words, an approach has developed which wants either to detach fascism from the killing of the Jews or is willing to regret Italian anti-Semitism but simultaneously sees little else to deplore in the history of Italy's 'long Second World War'.

The restriction of the story of this conflict to a 'war against the Jews' and only that is doubtless modish and, as Peter Novick has bravely noted,[38] is frequently accompanied by a search for a victimhood, which might not equal that of European Jewry but yet might have some comparison with it. So, in contemporary Italy, killing remains a touchy but telling issue. One special focus has been the shootings of innocent bystanders, whether in the Ardeatine caves massacre in March 1944[39] or the subsequent slaughter at Guardistallo near Livorno, in the Val di Chiana in the hinterland of Arezzo, or at Marabotto, above Bologna, as German troops retreated.[40] In these terrible events, with their parallels to the murders at Oradour near Limoges in France,[41] but also needing some context from the German sacking of an estimated 70,000 villages in all the Russias, the emphasis has usually been on a new honesty, one that can repair a 'divided memory'. The myth of resistance had hidden popular resentment of partisans who risked the lives of others in their combat with the Nazi-fascists and so visited terror and persecution on innocent

---

[35] N. Farrell, *Mussolini: A New Life* (London: Weidenfeld and Nicolson, 2003). For a detailed attempt to rebuke Berlusconi, see S. Corvisieri, *La villeggiatura di Mussolini: il confino da Bocchini a Berlusconi* (Milan: Baldini Castoldi Dalai, 2004).

[36] R. Vivarelli, *La fine di una stagione: memoria 1943–1945* (Bologna: Il Mulino, 2000).

[37] A. J. Gregor, *The Search for Neo-fascism: The Use and Abuse of a Political Science* (Cambridge: Cambridge University Press, 2006), 59.

[38] P. Novick, *The Holocaust in American Life* (Boston: Houghton Mifflin, 1998).

[39] A. Portelli, *The Order has been Carried Out: History, Memory, and Meaning of a Nazi Massacre in Rome* (New York: Palgrave Macmillan, 2003) with its over-blown claims.

[40] See, for example, G. Contini, *La memoria divisa* (Milan: Rizzoli, 1997); P. Pezzino, *Anatomia di un massacro: controversia sopra una strage tedesca* (Bologna: Il Mulino, 1997).

[41] S. Farmer, *Martyred Village: Commemorating the 1944 Massacre at Oradour-sur-Glane* (Berkeley and Los Angeles: University of California Press, 1999).

ordinary people hoping that, by keeping their heads down, they would ensure that the war would pass them by. As in Germany, there is no context here of the years of fascist rule or of the way so many Italians between the wars worked in lock step with Mussolini and his regime.

The survey of killing fields has been extended in two other directions, rather depending on current political preference. Mayhem did not automatically stop in Italy with the shooting of Mussolini.[42] Rather, for some months afterwards social instability permitted quite a bit of party and private vendetta in which more than 10,000 died, the majority fascists by some definition, with the region of the Emilia-Romagna, long thereafter to be the redoubt of the PCI, an epicentre. This killing has stimulated a lot of cheap moralizing, with commentators rarely placing the actions into their immediate or more long-term contexts. Here, 'memory' means deploring the past with evident contemporary political retribution sought on any lingering fans of the myth of the Resistance.[43]

For more critical analysts the focus instead is shifted to Italy's place during the war in a 'new world order'. In this regard, during the 1990s, an Italian victimhood was sketched among those who fell victim to Titoist forces (and their PCI friends and allies) in the *foibe* or caverns of the Carso above Trieste, or among those expelled from Istria and the rest of Dalmatia once those territories, gained in the First World War, were lost in the Second.[44] More salutary have been the efforts to acknowledge that Italians themselves were perpetrators in Greece and Yugoslavia, perhaps not quite so fanatically driven as their German allies but often bloody in their dealings with those they viewed as their national (rather than their racial[45]) inferiors.[46]

Here, then, have been some advances in historical honest dealing. Yet, Italians' reckoning with their nation's 'dark century' remains decidedly incomplete. It was typical of De Felice's massive 'biography' of Mussolini that, despite its assembly of more than 6,000 pages of 'facts', nowhere did the historian bother to estimate the number of Ethiopians killed by invading Italians in 1935–6 or during their shaky rule of that complex empire until their expulsion in 1941. Behind this detail lies

---

[42] For the deploring of the subsequent desecration of his body, see S. Luzzatto, *Il corpo del Duce: un cadavere tra immaginazione, storia e memoria* (Turin: Einaudi, 1998).

[43] For a recent review, see M. Storchi, 'Post-War Violence in Italy: A Struggle for Memory', *Modern Italy*, 12 (2007), 237–50.

[44] For even-handed general introduction, see G. Sluga, *The Problem of Trieste and the Italo-Yugoslav Border: Difference, Identity and Sovereignty in Twentieth-Century Europe* (New York: State University of New York Press, 2001).

[45] Fascist anti-Semitic practice remains an object of debate, with the historiography split between those who see an ability and desire to deflect Nazi fury (if for 'dishonourable' motives) and those anxious to locate anti-Semitic racism at the heart of Nazism. For examples, see J. Steinberg, *All or Nothing: The Axis and the Holocaust 1941–3* (London: Routledge, 1990); N. Caracciolo, *Uncertain Refuge: Italy and the Jews during the Holocaust* (Urbana: University of Illinois Press, 1995).

[46] The major study is by D. Rodogno, *Il nuovo ordine mediterraneo: le politiche di occupazione dell'Italia fascista in Europa (1940–1943)* (Turin: Bollati Boringhieri, 2003).

a graver structural issue (and the first adjective is well chosen). When the ghosts of the 'premature dead' of fascist governance parade, the blame for their cruel fate falls at least as much on 'Italy' as it does on fascism. If a tally of a million is reasonable, then half of them died in the Second World War that Mussolini entered in 1940, aggressively in the fascist manner and opportunistically in the style of 'Italy, the least of the Great Powers'. The other victims were in great majority killed in Italy's Mediterranean empire, murdered in other words because of the fascist dictatorship but also because the nation's 'best and brightest' wanted to shoulder the 'white man's burden' and did so because they were dreaming of becoming 'modern' Italians at least as much as because they had been both 'atomized' and fundamentalized by fascist 'totalitarianism' and its 'political religion'.

One terrible aspect of Italian colonial rule between the wars was the regime's willingness to use the period 'weapon of mass destruction', chemical weapons, to terrorize its indigenous enemies in both Libya and Ethiopia and despite the fact that Italy had signed the Geneva Convention banning such acts. It took a huge effort by the two anti-fascist historians of empire, Angelo Del Boca and Giorgio Rochat, to get post-war Italy to admit this history, and then the major account of the matter was published under the half-exculpatory title *Mussolini's Gas*.[47] To be sure the dictator had encouraged the bombing, following what was always his approach of urging the greatest brutality possible. But the actual perpetrators of chemical warfare were the generals of the royal Italian army, by most accounts at best a partially fascistized organization, and the bright young pilots of the air force, the nation's technologically cleverest and best. The real and still scarcely admitted cause of the post-war forgetting and obscuring of the matter was that this variety of warfare was Italian and not just fascist.[48] Post-Nazi Germans have indeed gone far to acknowledge the structures in their society, economy, culture, and polity that debouched into Nazism. Italians, like quite a few other Europeans, have been much more deficient in accepting the requirement rigorously to examine their past, both for its (often unconscious) virtues and its vices.

BIBLIOGRAPHY

Bosworth, R. J. B., *The Italian Dictatorship: Problems and Perspectives in the Interpretation of Mussolini and Fascism* (London: Arnold, 1998).

—— 'A Country Split in Two? Contemporary Italy and its Usable Pasts', *History Compass*, 4 (2006); web access at <10.1111/j.1478–0542.2006.00356.x>.

[47] A. Del Boca (ed.), *I gas di Mussolini: il fascismo e la guerra d'Etiopia* (Rome: Riunti, 1996).

[48] For evidence of the open discussion of the sense of chemical warfare, see R. J. B. Bosworth, *Mussolini's Italy: Life under the Dictatorship* (London: Allen Lane, 2005), 297–300.

FREI, N., *1945 und wir: Das Dritte Reich im Bewusstsein der Deutschen* (Munich: C. H. Beck, 2005).

GENTILE, E., *Fascismo: storia e interpretazione* (Bari: Laterza, 2005).

MICHALCZYK, J. (ed.), *Confront! Resistance in Nazi Germany* (New York: Peter Lang, 2005).

SABROW, M., JESSEN, R., and GROßE KRACHT, KLAUS (eds), *Zeitgeschichte als Streitgeschichte: Große Kontroversen nach 1945* (Munich: Beck, 2003).

SCHMÄDEKE, J., and STEINBACH, P. (eds), *Der Widerstand gegen den Nationalsozialismus: Die deutsche Gesellschaft und der Widerstand gegen Hitler* (Munich: Piper, 1986).

TUCHEL, J. (ed.), *Der vergessene Widerstand: Zu Realgeschichte und Wahrnehmung des Kampfes gegen die NS-Diktatur* (Göttingen: Wallstein Verlag, 2005).

VENTRESCA, R., 'Debating the Meaning of Fascism in Contemporary Italy', *Modern Italy*, 11 (2006).

WELZER, H., MOLLER, S., and TSCHUGGNALL, K., *Opa war kein Nazi: Nationalsozialismus und Holocaust im Familiengedächtnis. Zeit des Nationalsozialismus* (Frankfurt am Main: Fischer, 2002).

CHAPTER 31

NEO-FASCISM*

ANNA CENTO BULL

I. INTRODUCTION

THE term neo-fascism defines primarily those political and ideological groups and
parties which operated after 1945, especially in Europe, and were directly inspired by
the experience of the inter-war fascist and Nazi regimes in Germany, Italy, and other
European countries. These groups were often made up of remnants of fascist and
Nazi activists, who were not prepared to give up their political militancy or indeed
to renounce their ideologies despite military defeat. Whereas a large number of
people who supported these organizations were generically nostalgic of the past
and alienated from post-war liberal-democratic culture and institutions, many
held radical and uncompromising views, emphasizing the revolutionary nature
of fascism rather than its more 'reassuring' nationalist or statist version. To an
extent this division reflected the long-standing distinction between fascism as a
movement and fascism as a regime, as well as between fascism as revolution and
fascism as restoration, or indeed between a 'left' wing, advocating radical social
reforms, including some form of socialization of the means of production, and a
conservative wing, closer to business interests.

Immediately after the war, however, in most countries the goal of all neo-fascists
was to survive both physically and politically, and to this end they subordinated
their differences, working within the same organizations. A typical example is that
of the Italian Movimento Sociale Italiano (MSI), founded in 1946, which included
conservatives and radicals, nostalgics and revanchists. It was only in the second half
of the 1950s that splinter groups were created outside this party, in order to pursue

*The author wishes to thank Roger Eatwell for his useful comments on an earlier draft.

a violent and even terrorist path. Nevertheless, it would be wrong to emphasize these divisions, since even in Italy the break between the various wings was never clear-cut.

Since the emergence of a new global socio-economic and political order, new types of extreme right parties and movements have largely replaced the older nostalgic or radical groups, enjoying significant breakthroughs with the electorate in several countries. In Western Europe, these parties do not openly seek to overthrow democratic regimes or advocate violence; rather, they emphasize issues that are of concern to many contemporary voters, especially immigration and law and order. Conversely, in Eastern Europe, the extreme right revival took the form of violent ethnic ultranationalism, which may or may not have its roots in inter-war fascism or possess affinities with fascist ideology.

This situation promoted a renewed debate among scholars concerning the typology of these parties and the extent to which they represented a new phenomenon and a break with the fascist tradition, or whether they remained close to a fascist ideology, albeit cloaked under new guises. As part of this process, some scholars chose to draw a line under the historical experience of 'traditional' neo-fascism. Other scholars engaged in a process of redefining what constituted the 'fascist minimum', especially in terms of an ideological core, which would help distinguish a 'neo-fascist' family from other political organizations of the right. In so doing, they cast doubt on the ideological transformation undergone by many of the 'new' parties, emphasizing the continuity of neo-fascist themes from 1945 to the present.

Despite various attempts to achieve a systematic classification, there remain substantial disagreements concerning the nature of the extreme right today, not just in Europe but at a global level, and regarding the long-term legacy of both fascism and neo-fascism. It is also the case that the label of fascist is often attributed to a wide variety of phenomena, including, in recent times, Islamic fundamentalism (Islamofascism), or even Bush-fascism, with reference to the US Republican government. These definitions are highly controversial and the phenomena they refer to will not be taken into consideration in this chapter.

II. Analytical Approach

This chapter adopts a diachronic approach to neo-fascism, distinguishing between different historical-political stages and 'paying more attention to processes than to essences', as well as studying it 'contextually, spending at least as much time on the surrounding society and on fascism's allies and accomplices as on the fascist movements themselves'.[1] One of the reasons for this is that insufficient attention has

---

[1] R. O. Paxton, 'The Five Stages of Fascism', *Journal of Modern History*, 70 (1998), 10.

been paid in the literature to the role played by neo-fascist groups and their politics during the Cold War, when the world was dominated by the struggle between communism and anti-communism. As the heir to defeated regimes and the ideologies upon which these were based, what kind of political space, if any, was neo-fascism able to carve out for itself in the new bipolar international order? Did neo-fascism constitute a highly fragmented political area whose different components could only aspire to influence politics at a micro-level, perhaps occasionally at a national level, or did it manage to achieve a degree of international cohesion? If the latter, did neo-fascism gain some autonomy vis-à-vis the Communist International on the one hand, and the NATO alliance on the other, or did it settle for a (subordinate) alliance with one of the two blocs? Thanks largely to judicial material arising in Italy as a result of successive trials on the so-called 'Strategy of Tension', discussed below, we are now in a better position to understand some of the national and international processes at play during the Cold War and to locate within them neo-fascist activities and goals.

Another important date for understanding the evolution of neo-fascism in Western Europe is 1968, which spurred various extreme right intellectuals to modernize their ideas and make them more widely acceptable, ostensibly rejecting the old paradigms. The year 1968 and its aftermath also led some radical groups to adopt an 'existentialist', rather than ideological, stance, and to extend their sympathies to revolutionary and guerrilla movements worldwide. The collapse of authoritarian regimes in southern Europe between 1973 and 1975 further contributed to a rethinking of neo-fascist strategies and 'models'.

From the 1980s onwards, neo-fascism or, more accurately for some, the extreme right entered a new phase. As already discussed, a debate is still ongoing as regards the exact nature of the new breed of political movements and parties and whether they mark a break from or represent continuity with the past. Rather than adopting a specific approach, this chapter will briefly outline the main interpretations and assess their strengths and weaknesses, with reference to these movements' ideologies, policies, and electorates.

III. Defeated but Not Out: Neo-fascism after the Second World War

The starting point for understanding the nature and role of neo-fascism after 1945 is the objective and subjective condition in which the supporters of the defeated fascist and Nazi regimes found themselves at the end of the war, together with the way in which they were perceived and treated by the winners. Italy provides an excellent case study for an analysis of both losers and winners. There, the defining myth and ideological referent for neo-fascism was the Social Republic (1943–5), which represented the incarnation of the revolutionary, anti-capitalist, and 'socializing' wing of fascism, while also engaging in a brutal and vindictive war against fellow Italians, considered traitors to both the regime and the nation and abject cowards. After the war, the supporters and combatants of the Italian Social Republic found themselves in the condition of aliens, excluded from political activity, targeted for opprobrium and condemnation, and often also for acts of reprisal by the partisans. They therefore constituted 'Exiles in their Own Country' or 'The Excluded Pole', to use two popular expressions.[2] In response to their condition as political pariahs, they proudly adopted a deliberate process of self-exclusion, which fed upon their deep hatred and contempt for the new Italian democracy, a strong bitterness for losing the war, and a burning desire for revenge. To make matters worse, while they themselves were being ostracized, their arch-enemies, the Communists, were given posts of responsibility in the national government and were openly legitimized by the anti-fascist character attributed to the Italian nation.

In this context, the neo-fascists followed two different paths. On the one hand, they set up clandestine terrorist organizations, such as the FAR (Forze Armate Rivoluzionarie), founded in January 1946 by, among others, Giorgio Almirante, Clemente Graziani, Julius Evola, Pino Rauti, and Pino Romualdi. This organization was explicitly anti-democratic and revolutionary and was responsible, between 1945 and 1951, for various attacks against local sections of the left parties and trade unions, as well as partisans' associations. In 1951 many of its leaders were arrested and put on trial, but subsequently acquitted. In 1946, an amnesty for crimes committed during the period of the civil war was decreed by Palmiro Togliatti, leader of the Italian Communist Party (PCI) and the then Minister for Justice, in order to promote national reconciliation, put an end to violent reprisals, and perhaps also in acknowledgement of the impossibility of bringing all fascists to trial. As it was, 'the judiciary, and particularly the Court of Cassation, went much beyond this text, setting free fascist torturers who had been responsible for the most gruesome atrocities'.[3]

On the other hand, as one of the (possibly intended) consequences of the amnesty, the neo-fascists came out of clandestinity and formed, on 12 December 1946, the MSI. Many who had belonged to FAR, including Almirante and Romualdi, left it to join the new party as leaders. The MSI was divided internally between a radical wing which adopted as its ideological referent the Republic of Salò, a conservative and moderate wing which prioritized national interests, and a 'spiritualist',

---

[2] See M. Tarchi, *Esuli in patria: i fascisti nell'Italia repubblicana* (Parma: Guanda, 1995) and P. Ignazi, *Il polo escluso: profilo storico del Movimento Sociale Italiano* (Bologna: Il Mulino, 1998). On the attitudes of Italian neo-fascists towards the Republic of Salò and the Resistance, see F. Germinario, *L'altra memoria: l'Estrema destra, Salò e la Resistenza* (Turin: Bollati Boringhieri, 1999).

[3] F. Ferraresi, 'The Radical Right in Postwar Italy', *Politics and Society*, 16 (1988), 78.

Evolian wing. Beyond these considerable internal divisions, the party accepted the need to work within the democratic and parliamentary system.

The two main paths followed by neo-fascism in the early years after the war prefigured the later development within the movement of a parliamentary and an extra-parliamentary strategy, albeit with the existence of a considerable grey area between the two. This explains a series of splits from, but also mergers with, the MSI on the part of radical and young activists in subsequent years, especially the formation of Centro Studi Ordine Nuovo, set up by Pino Rauti in 1956, and Avanguardia Nazionale, set up by Stefano Delle Chiaie in 1959. In 1969 the bulk of Ordine Nuovo re-entered the MSI, seemingly as easily as it had left it, while Avanguardia Nazionale was disbanded in 1965, re-formed in 1970, and finally dissolved in 1974. In addition, the youth associations of the MSI had a critical attitude towards the 'parliamentary' path, thereby providing a bridge to the groups on the right of the party. In terms of ideology, there was also much common ground between the rank and file of the MSI and the radical splinter groups, thanks to the influence exercised by Evola's ideas, the attraction of Nazi symbolism, and the myths of the Waffen SS and Codreanu's Iron Guard.

Julius Evola (1897–1974) was without doubt the 'guru' of much of the young generation of Italian neo-fascists confronted with the dilemma of pursuing politics in a hostile environment. In his 1934 *Revolt against the Modern World*, Evola had theorized a critique against modernity which represented a phase of decadence and spiritual degradation, both in its democratic and in its communist guise, and promoted a mystical, esoteric adherence to pre-modern and non-Western civilizations, seen as incarnated, in modern times, in the Nazi rather than in the fascist regime. In his early post-war works, *Orientamenti* (1950) and *Men among the Ruins* (1953), Evola advocated a 'warrior spirit', as well as total intransigence and inner discipline, as the ideal attitudes of those who continued to fight while knowing that the battle was lost.[4]

Similarly to Italy, other European countries saw a resurgence of neo-fascism after the war, at first in a clandestine fashion, later also in a parliamentary guise, although nowhere were these groups successful in establishing a party of a size comparable to that of the MSI. In Germany, first the Deutsche Rechtspartei (DRP), founded in 1946, and then the much more radical Sozialistische Reichspartei (SRP), set up in 1949, represented attempts by former Nazi supporters and sympathizers to reconstitute a political party. The former split in 1949, while the latter, one of DRP's splinter groups, was banned by the Constitutional Court in 1952, leading to a

---

[4] On Evola's thought and his influence on neo-fascism, see T. Sheehan, 'Myth and Violence: The Fascism of Julius Evola and Alain de Benoist', *Social Research*, 48 (1981), 45–73; F. Ferraresi, 'Julius Evola: Tradition, Reaction and the Radical Right', *Archives européennes de sociologie*, 28 (1987), 107–51; R. Drake, *The Revolutionary Mystique and Terrorism in Contemporary Italy* (Bloomington, IN: Indiana University Press, 1989); M. Sedgwick, *Against the Modern World: Traditionalism and the Secret Intellectual History of the Twentieth Century* (Oxford: Oxford University Press, 2004).

fragmentation of this political area. In the 1960s, a new attempt was made with the formation of the Nationaldemokratische Partei Deutschlands (NPD), which gained some electoral success in *Land* elections but failed to gain representation in the national parliament, and declined steeply after 1969, to resurface in the 1980s. In Belgium, a few minor groups were formed in 1947–9 which had links with Léon Degrelle, leader of the ultra-Catholic and traditionalist Rexist movement in the 1930s, who had found refuge in Francoist Spain after the war. They never succeeded in reaching a respectable size until the emergence of the populist Vlaams Blok in the late 1970s.

In France, neo-fascists were even more ghettoized than in Italy, given wide public condemnation of their role as traitors and collaborators during the Vichy regime. A violent clandestine group, Jeune Nation, formed in 1949, was inspired more by Italian Fascism than by Nazism. It remained totally uninfluential until 1954, when the French defeat in Indochina gave it an opportunity to play the card of anti-communism and the defence of the west, while the Poujadist movement attracted many former Vichy supporters. Another small breakthrough came in 1961, when the Organisation Armée Secrète (OAS) was formed after it became clear that France was moving to a settlement in Algeria. This was a clandestine organization, made up of both authoritarian nationalists and neo-fascists, which resorted to terrorism to prevent Algeria's independence. One of its founders was Yves Guerin Serac, a traditionalist Catholic who went on to play an important role during the Cold War. Later, in 1972, the Front National was formed, but it was only in the 1980s that it enjoyed significant electoral success.

If Italian neo-fascism found a cult figure in Evola, French neo-fascism had its equivalent in Maurice Bardèche, author of *Qu'est-ce que le fascisme?* (1961) and director of the journal *Défense de l'Occident*. Bardèche's ideas revolved around a fascist European order and an authoritarian version of socialism, combined with racism and anti-Semitism. To combat bolshevism (his primary target) and liberalism, he advocated a moral revolution and a Spartan discipline, which would lead to the formation of a new elite, dedicated to war, sacrifice, and bravery.[5]

An important trait of both neo-fascism and neo-Nazism was historical revisionism, especially the denial of the Holocaust, coupled with more or less overt anti-Semitism. Another was the idea of a united Europe as a Third Force between the two rival imperialisms. This was partly a revival of a romantic Nazi vision of an anti-Bolshevik European order, which after the war found various permutations in propagandists like Bardèche, Evola, Mosley, and the dissident 'leftist' Nazi Otto Strasser, but also partly an acknowledgement that single-country nationalism was no longer adequate in the age of the superpowers. Consequently, at the international level, there were various attempts, from 1950 onwards, to re-establish an

[5] I. R. Barnes, 'Antisemitic Europe and the Third Way: The Ideas of Maurice Bardèche', *Patterns of Prejudice*, 34 (2000), 57–73; cf. his 'I am a Fascist Writer: Maurice Bardèche—Ideologist and Defender of French Fascism', *European Legacy*, 7 (2002), 195–209.

alliance between the different national groups and parties, the so-called 'Fascist' or 'Black' International.

Under the initiative of the MSI, two meetings took place in Rome (1950) and Malmö (1951), which established the European Social Movement. However, for many neo-fascists the new movement was not sufficiently radical or racist, so that a group of rebels, led by Gaston Armand Amaudruz, met in Zurich in September 1951 and founded the New European Order, an organization 'calling for a war against "mongoloid Bolshevism" and "negroid capitalism" ... in the support of the white man in his fight for racial survival and purification'.[6] Other organizations later came to the fore, including Jeune Europe and the Northern European Ring, each of which tended to represent a particular wing of neo-fascism, with none achieving a dominant role or promoting unification. The Fascist International, therefore, should more appropriately be conceived as an ensemble of different and autonomous, albeit overlapping, organizations.

In short, what the European situation shows is that the main characteristics of early neo-fascism were clandestinity, fragmentation, terrorist tactics, the idea of Europe as a Third Force, a cult of Nazi symbols and of the Waffen SS, bitter feelings of revenge and hatred, coupled with complete isolation due a general attitude of condemnation and stigmatization on the part of the public and the electorate. The only exception was Italy, where the MSI succeeded in establishing itself as a parliamentary force, although it attracted primarily the votes of a southern-based, nostalgic constituency, whose values were nationalist and conservative rather than fascist, and remained officially ostracized by the other parties. The overall picture was not promising in terms of neo-fascism achieving either a popular revival or a political role at the national and/or international levels. However, the Cold War created new political space for the groups that formed the neo-fascist galaxy, albeit in a subordinate position to one of the superpowers, that is, the USA. To complete the picture, therefore, it is necessary to analyse the attitude of the Allies towards many Nazi and fascist combatants, as well as towards the extreme right groups set up after the war.

IV. Neo-fascism, Anti-Communism, and the United States

Recently declassified CIA documents have shown what was for long suspected, that is, that US military and secret services shielded numerous Nazi and fascist

---

[6] K. P. Tauber, *Beyond Eagle and Swastika: German Nationalism since 1945* (Middletown, CT: Wesleyan University Press, 1967), 212.

criminals after the war, and enrolled them as soldiers and spies in the war against communism. In Germany, one of the Nazis in question was General Reinhard Gehlen, formerly the army's intelligence chief for the eastern front.[7] At the end of the war, Gehlen was effectively recruited by the CIA and was able to re-establish an intelligence network which made use of Nazis and known war criminals, and later was incorporated into the official West German secret service, BND. Gehlen also played a central role in the creation of Radio Free Europe in 1949, funded by the CIA as part of a psychological anti-communist campaign. Another recruiter was the former SS colonel Otto Skorzeny, responsible for rescuing Mussolini from the Gran Sasso in 1943, who created the ODESSA organization after the war to help Nazis escape from prosecution. Skorzeny also set up the Paladin mercenary group which was based in Spain and operated mainly in Africa until his death in 1975. While working for the CIA, these people remained faithful to their Nazi and racist ideals.

In Italy, the Americans, specifically James Jesus Angleton, Head of the Office of Strategic Services (OSS), rescued Prince Junio Valerio Borghese who notoriously had led the naval X Mas for the Republic of Salò and had been responsible for murdering and torturing scores of Italian partisans. Borghese was put on trial in 1947 and in 1949 was sentenced to twelve years in prison but was released by the court on the grounds that the amnesty allowed much of the sentence to be 'condoned'. He later went on to found a neo-fascist group known as the Fronte Nazionale. Again in Italy, the discovery, in 1994, of 695 judicial files on Nazi and fascist war crimes, which had been concealed in the late 1940s to prevent the culprits from being prosecuted, brought to light the connection between this episode and the 'exigencies' of the Cold War.[8] Finally, judicial and parliamentary documents have shown that two Italo-Americans named Leo Joseph Pagnotta and Joseph Luongo set up a web of intelligence personnel for the United States, co-opting ex-Nazi and ex-fascist officers. Allegedly Luongo in 1949 'had approached the Italian government to verify whether it was ready to use, in the event of "left wing uprisings", the collaboration of the FAR, a neo-fascist clandestine organisation for which the Americans had spent very considerable sums of money'.[9]

In Portugal, Aginter Press was set up by the Frenchman Guerin Serac, who had fled France to escape charges of treason and desertion. This was almost a continuation of the OAS, but with an international anti-communist mission. Aginter

---

[7] See *The CIA and Nazi War Criminals*, a National Security Archive website, providing access to released CIA information. Available at: <http://www.gwu.edu/~nsarchiv/NSAEBB/NSAEBB146/index.htm >.

[8] The discovery led to the formation of a Parliamentary Commission of Enquiry, set up with Law No. 107 of 15 May 2003, which in 2006 produced a majority and a minority report. See M. Franzinelli, *Le stragi nascoste: l'armadio della vergogna. Impunità e rimozioni dei crimini di guerra nazifascisti 1943–2001* (Milan: Mondadori, 2002).

[9] Commissione Parlamentare d'inchiesta sulle cause dell'occultamento di fascicoli relativi a crimini Nazifascisti, Document XXIII, No. 17-bis, *Relazione di Minoranza*, 24 January 2006, 207.

Press was also a cover for another international neo-fascist organisation, Ordre et Tradition, which had a paramilitary arm, known as Organization d'Action contre le Communisme International (OACI). Aginter Press remained active until 1974, recruiting and training mercenaries and terrorists in acts of sabotage, bomb attacks, and targeted killings. The organization was almost certainly funded by the CIA as well as the Salazar regime.

In Spain, where many Nazi combatants and collaborators escaped after the war, including the Croatian Ustasha leader Ante Pavelić, as well as Otto Skorzeny and Léon Degrelle, there was a dense network of local and international organizations. A local group was the Círculo Español de Amigos de Europa (CEDADE), set up in 1965, which had a Europeanist and increasingly neo-Nazi ideology. CEDADE was part of New European Order, the already mentioned international alliance created in 1951. In later years, Spain became the chosen destination for many Italian radical neo-fascists who had been charged with subversive violent activities, including Avanguardia Nazionale leader Stefano Delle Chiaie, a collaborator of Guerin Serac and Borghese and an admirer of Skorzeny.

At the international level, according to Italian historian and judicial consultant Aldo Giannuli, a convergence between Western conservative anti-communist organizations and the so-called 'Fascist International' took place only at the end of the 1950s.[10] It was thanks to decolonization and the formation of the OAS that a first rapprochement between conservative and authoritarian nationalists on the one hand and neo-fascists on the other became possible, leading to collaboration under the umbrella of the Aginter Press. Conversely, it was thanks to the World Anti-Communist League (WACL) that anti-communist organizations worldwide were brought together, seemingly blurring the divide between fascism and anti-fascism. WACL was formed in 1966 in South Korea but was predominantly US led and had 'chapters' in all parts of the world, including Western Europe. According to the Andersons, 'it is the one organization in which representatives of virtually every right-wing extremist movement that has practiced unconventional warfare are to be found. The League is the one constant in this netherworld; whether looking at Croation terrorists, Norwegian neo-Nazis, Japanese war criminals, or American ultra-rightists.'[11] The list of members provided by the authors included Giorgio Almirante, Stefano Delle Chiaie, Blas Pinar, leader of Fuerza Nueva, Jesus Palacio, leader of CEDADE, and various ex-SS officers, together with American and European military and intelligence representatives and ultra-conservative Christian politicians. Pino Rauti, the founder of Ordine Nuovo, was another contact of WACL.

---

[10] A. Giannuli, *Relazione di perizia* (Bari, 1997). Unpublished copy of the report courtesy of the author.

[11] S. Anderson and J. L. Anderson, *Inside the League: The Shocking Expose of how Terrorists, Nazis, and Latin American Death Squads have Infiltrated the World Anti-Communist League* (New York: Dodd Mead, 1986), p. x.

In short, a perceived need for an intelligence partnership with Nazis and fascists convinced the CIA after the war to overcome its initial reluctance and enlist the services as spies of many of their representatives. A similar strategy was pursued by eastern intelligence services, including the Stasi.[12] Later, however, the unfolding of the conflict between east and west made the neo-fascists acceptable partners of the latter bloc in the new 'dirty war', primarily in the role of mercenaries and terrorists. By contrast, the Communist bloc appears to have supported mainly extreme left terrorism, both in Western Europe and in the Third World. If this largely explains the attitude of the United States, what about the neo-fascists themselves? An important discriminant that emerged after the war, in fact, was the attitude that they should adopt towards the two superpowers, which is closely connected to issues of ideology, strategy, and tactics.

We need to distinguish between different positions in their ranks. The vast majority of neo-fascists rejected the bipolar logic: while they were vehemently anti-communist, they also deeply resented the Allies' victory and American imperialism, representing the triumph of capitalism and liberalism, to which they opposed socialization, a strong state, the intrinsic values of man, and the defence of an organic and authoritarian Western culture. In reality, however, neo-fascists often subordinated their ideological stance to strategic and pragmatic considerations and/or prioritized certain values at the expense of others, as can be seen in the Italian case. After the war, at an individual level many ex-fascists were driven by anti-capitalism and anti-Americanism to join the Communist Party, which welcomed them with seemingly few qualms. However, for the majority, fierce anti-communism, coupled with fear of reprisals by the Communist Party, whose chances of an electoral victory could not by any means be discounted, contributed to a more accommodating attitude towards the United States, as well as towards the military, police, and intelligence forces. There were also those, like Borghese, who had been rescued by the Americans and hence had personal reasons for agreeing to collaborate with them. This compromising attitude prevailed among neo-fascist organizations and was shared both by the moderate and the radical wings, as acknowledged by some of their representatives.[13] However, while the MSI, between 1951 and 1952, developed a policy of open acceptance of the western alliance, including NATO, radical neo-fascists continued steadfastly to adhere to an intransigent ideology combining anti-capitalism and anti-communism. For many radicals any compromise appears to have been palatable only at a secret level and particularly in the event that the communist threat and the need to roll back the enemy might open the way for an authoritarian 'solution'. It goes without saying that any alliance of this type was

---

[12] On the Stasi, see M. Dennis, *The Stasi: Myth and Reality* (Edinburgh: Pearson, 2003).

[13] See M. Brambilla, *Interrogatorio alle destre* (Milan: Rizzoli, 1995), especially the interviews with Rauti and Pisanò. N. Rao, *Neo-fascisti: la destra italiana da Salò a Fiuggi nel ricordo dei protagonisti* (Rome: Settimo Sigillo, 1999), 32–3; A. Streccioni, *A destra della Destra: dentro l'MSI, dai Far a Terza Posizione* (Rome: Settimo Sigillo, 2006).

conceived and carried out mainly by the leaders of the radical groups, with many rank-and-file activists left in the dark.

Having contextualized fascism after its defeat and especially when the Cold War started in earnest, the key question concerns the specific role carried out by neo-fascist organizations and their members in the fight against communism. To answer this question, we need to return to Italy and examine in some detail the development of a domestic version of an international line known as the 'Strategy of Tension', upon which recent judicial investigations and trials have thrown considerable new light.

V. Neo-fascism during the Cold War: An International 'Strategy of Tension'?

In the 1960s, with a partial thawing of East–West relations that was later to develop into open détente, anti-communist strategies worldwide started to diversify. Nowhere in Europe were the effects of the new course as apparent as in Italy, where Christian Democracy (DC), under the leadership of Aldo Moro, started negotiations with the Socialist Party, with a view to detaching it from its long-standing alliance with the Communists and making it into a partner in government. Obviously, given Italy's status as a dependent ally of the United States and a member of NATO, such an operation needed the consent of the Americans. The 'Opening to the Left' was finally sanctioned by the American President J. F. Kennedy and Pope John XXIII, and the Socialist Party was brought into government in 1963, after it had severed links with the Communist Party and officially recognized NATO.

While Aldo Moro's strategy represented an innovative way of containing communism, by isolating the PCI on the left and allowing a degree of change in an otherwise immobile political system, it was viewed as a fatal mistake by the more conservative and ultra-right forces in both Italy and the United States. In the late 1960s, growing student and worker unrest, increasing trade union influence, and undiminished support for the Communist Party confirmed many people's worst fears. In this context, a counter-strategy was conceived and implemented by an ad hoc coalition of forces, involving bombing campaigns aimed at killing innocent civilians and at creating an atmosphere of terror and disorder in the country, as well as various attempted *coups d'état*. The campaign developed in the summer and winter of 1969, with the worst attack in Milan, when a bomb exploded in a crowded bank in Piazza Fontana on 12 December 1969, killing seventeen people and injuring another eighty-eight. It escalated in the following years, culminating in two further massacres in 1974. Recent judicial trials have established, 'beyond any resonable doubt', that the neo-fascist group Ordine Nuovo was responsible for at least two bombing attacks, including the one in Piazza Fontana.[14]

As regards *coups d'état*, an aborted attempt took place on 7 December 1970, organized by Borghese's Fronte Nazionale, in collaboration with Avanguardia Nazionale (led by his friend Stefano Delle Chiaie), the Masonic Lodge Propaganda 2 (P2), and even the Mafia. The coup was apparently sanctioned by the CIA via Skorzeny and aimed at replacing the democratically elected government with an emergency administration of military and civilians.[15] Further plots took place between 1972 and 1974.

Known in Italy as the 'Strategy of Tension', the concerted campaign of bomb attacks and attempted coups appears to have represented the outcome of a domestic rapprochement between neo-fascist and conservative/military forces united in their dismay at Moro's policies and growing social disorder. The latter included sectors of the armed forces and intelligence services, as well as the more conservative wings of the Liberal, Social Democratic, and Christian Democratic parties and of the MSI itself. A key event in preparation for this strategy was a conference that took place on 3–5 May 1965 in Rome, organized by the Istituto Pollio, a body linked to the Italian military. The conference addressed the issue of unorthodox warfare, as part of both revolutionary insurgency and counter-revolutionary strategy (the real focus of the meeting). The list of participants included neo-fascist representatives like Rauti and Delle Chiaie, together with army generals, right-wing intellectuals, and business people. The composition of, and venue for, the meeting is itself revealing, as it shows that radical neo-fascists were rightful participants at a top military gathering where highly unorthodox means of combating communism were discussed.

According to an investigating magistrate for the Piazza Fontana attack, Guido Salvini, the role of Ordine Nuovo in the 'Strategy of Tension' was that of 'co-belligerent', rather than simply that of executors of someone else's plans, albeit its agenda was necessarily subordinate to those of other forces.[16] While radical neo-fascists participated in the campaign in the hope of forming an authoritarian government in which they would occupy positions of responsibility, their (more powerful) partners may well have entertained different goals, including a presidentialist system along the lines of the Gaullist Republic. Salvini's investigations

---

[14] For Piazza Fontana, see *Sentenza-ordinanza del Giudice Istruttore presso il Tribunale Civile e Penale di Milano, dr. Guido Salvini, nel procedimento penale nei confronti di Rognoni Giancarlo ed altri,* 18 March 1995, 3 February, 2 March, 18 March 1998. For another attack carried out in Milan in 1973, see *Sentenza-ordinanza del Giudice Istruttore presso il Tribunale Civile e Penale di Milano, dr. Antonio Lombardi, nel procedimento penale nei confronti di Maggi Carlo Maria ed altri,* 18 July 1998.

[15] For a reconstruction by a protagonist see A. Monti, *Il 'golpe Borghese' un golpe virtuale all'italiana* (Bologna: Lo Scarabeo, 2006). See also C. Arcuri, *Colpo di stato* (Milan: BUR, 2004). On Borghese, J. Greene and A. Massignani, *The Black Prince and the Sea Devils: The Story of Valerio Borghese and the Elite Units of the Decima Mas* (Cambridge, MA: Da Capo Press, 2004).

[16] *Sentenza-ordinanza,* 18 March 1998, by Salvini, 49–50.

have also unearthed links between domestic and international actors, pointing to an important role played by Guerin Serac and his Aginter Press, as well as to a benevolent attitude towards terrorism by the FTASE command in Verona, which was the equivalent of the NATO command in southern Europe.

The Italian case shows that a tactical collaboration between neo-fascist groups and conservative/military forces developed in parallel with an uncompromising, hard-line strategy which contemplated the use of violence as a legitimate, albeit unorthodox, means of combating communism (but also détente in all its manifestations). As such, the collaboration extended to all those parts of the world that were considered at risk of giving in to the enemy, including Latin America, where Operation Condor, a campaign of counter-insurgency involving assassinations of political opponents of authoritarian regimes, raged in the mid-1970s. Even in Australia, the 1960s saw the emergence of a strand of Nazi activism that was consistently used against the newly revitalized left and manipulated by the state with the connivance of its leaders.[17] In Europe, the strategy became visible in Greece in 1967, when the Colonels took power in the face of increasing support for the parties of the left; it peaked in the early 1970s, but later waned following the collapse of the Greek, Portuguese, and Spanish regimes, which deprived neo-fascists of both safe havens and political leadership.

Not surprisingly, many moved on to Latin American countries, where they placed their skills at the service of local dictatorships. A typical example is that of Delle Chiaie, who left Spain for Chile, from where he later went on to Argentina, Bolivia, and Venezuela, until he was finally arrested in Caracas in 1984.[18] As an Italian neo-fascist turned witness for the prosecution, Vincenzo Vinciguerra, recalled, groups made up of extreme right elements of various nationalities were often responsible for violent cover missions, 'with the consent of international intelligence services, especially those of the United States'.[19] The aim was to prevent investigators in individual countries from ascertaining the masterminds of these missions.

In conclusion, the role of international neo-fascism at the height of the Cold War appears to have been to a large extent that of a mercenary and terrorist force. Neo-fascists themselves strongly reject this label, preferring to portray their actions as having been inspired by Evola's teachings on the indomitable spirit of the 'warrior' fighting for his ideals against all adversities.[20] Others, like Vinciguerra, in retrospect accept this definition for much of post-war radical and 'revolutonary'

---

[17] J. Saleam, 'The Other Radicalism: An Inquiry into Contemporary Australian Extreme Right Ideology, Politics and Organization, 1975–1995', PhD thesis, <http://ses.library.usyd.edu.au/bitstream/2123/807/1/adt-NU20020222.14582202whole.pdf>.

[18] On Delle Chiaie's involvement in Operation Condor, see P. Mayorga, *Il Condor Nero: l'Internazionale fascista e i rapporti con il regime di Pinochet* (Milan: Sperling and Kupfer, 2003).

[19] Ibid. 130.

[20] A. Cento Bull, *Italian Neo-fascism: The Strategy of Tension and the Politics of Non-Reconciliation* (Oxford: Berghahn, 2007).

neo-fascism.[21] Whether they should be defined primarily as terrorists, revolutionary combatants, or co-belligerents, the majority of neo-fascists were unable to carve
out an autonomous political-military space for themselves and had to settle instead
for a subordinate position to the western bloc, within which they managed to retain
some, not inconsiderable, margins for manoeuvre. However, it would be wrong to
overestimate the threat that their intransigent, fiercely anti-democratic, and racist
ideology and their terrorism constituted for the liberal-democratic world, since it
was the latter that ultimately had the power to pull the plug on their activities. This
raises important issues of morality versus cynicism and ruthlessness in war (albeit
one of a cold variety), rather more than issues of 'threats to democracy'. Where
such threats turned out to be real, such as in Greece in 1967 and Chile in 1973, or
particularly menacing, as in the Italian case, the neo-fascists were part of a much
wider coalition of forces, which conferred upon them a degree of legitimacy and
the status of partner.

VI. Second-Generation Neo-fascists: AFTER 1968

The Cold War, however important, was not the only preoccupation of neo-fascists,
especially those brought up under the influence of the youth culture of the 1960s,
which seemed so antithetical to traditionalist ideas about the warrior spirit, hierarchy, discipline, and conservative sexual and family values. The year 1968 and its
aftermath also marked the emergence of new social movements and a new wave of
anti-capitalism, coupled with post-materialism, feminism, and environmentalism.
Inevitably, neo-fascism could not remain immune to the new ideas, especially when
it was clearly at risk of becoming an irrelevant and outdated ideology. This spurred
some of its thinkers to renovate and modernize their stock of ideas in two main
directions.

On the one hand, there were some short-lived attempts to revitalize a strand of
thought which sought to reconcile the extreme right with the extreme left, Hitler
and Mao united in a common fight against both imperialisms. This kind of 'Third
Way' had its roots in the inter-war period and a predecessor in the Belgian Jean-
François Thiriart (1922–92), who in 1960 founded Jeune Europe and later launched
an appeal for constructing a powerful unitary European nation. Initially this organization tended to support the OAS and European colonialism, but after 1965

---

[21] V. Vinciguerra, *Camerati addio: storia di un inganno, in cinquant'anni di egemonia statunitense in Italia* (Trapani: Edizioni di Avanguardia, 2000).

Thiriart developed a position of firm opposition to American imperialism coupled with support for anti-colonialist and revolutionary movements worldwide. Thiriart influenced, among others, the Italian Franco Freda, author of *La disintegrazione del sistema* (1969), where he attempted to combine Evola's ideas with an admiration for Maoist China.[22] In the late 1960s and 1970s, Nazi-Maoism inspired a particular strand of neo-fascist organizations, especially in Italy, starting with Lotta di Popolo, set up in Rome in 1969, followed years later by Terza Posizione (TP), a group influenced by both Evola and Freda, whose slogan was 'no longer on the right, or the centre, or the left' but indeed 'breaking the mould'. At another level, however, TP incarnated yet another trend within Italian radical neo-fascism known as 'armed spontaneity', which arose partly in imitation of the 'armed struggle' undertaken by various extreme left organizations, most notoriously the Red Brigades. 'Spontaneity' represented a youth rebellion against the state, the police, and the MSI, judged to have betrayed fascist revolutionary ideas, as well as against older-generation neo-fascists, deemed to have acted in connivance with state apparatuses. The phenomenon culminated in the formation of the Nuclei Armati Rivoluzionari (NAR), which was responsible for numerous killings between 1977 and 1981.[23]

If the NAR represented the last incarnation of the warrior ideal, at the opposite end we can locate the 'cultural' turn of the extreme right, especially influential in France, Germany, and Italy. In France, from 1968 onwards Alain De Benoist became one of the main thinkers of the European New Right, as well as a prominent representative of the Groupement de Recherche et d'Études sur la Civilisation Européenne (GRECE), an explicitly intellectual rather than political movement. Inspired by Gramsci's emphasis on the need for cultural hegemony, New Right thinking progressively replaced crude versions of biological racism with a more sophisticated 'communitarian-differentialist' ideology, upholding the right to difference and to identity, opposing globalization and homogenization as well as multiculturalism. In Italy, the main representative of the New Right was Marco Tarchi, who also attempted to rejuvenate and modernize neo-fascism in novel ways. Through the journal *La voce della fogna*, founded in 1974, he promoted debates on such unlikely topics as poetry, literature, pop and rock music, the environment, and feminism. Tarchi also launched annual meetings—the so-called Hobbit camps, inspired by Tolkien's trilogy—which were peaceful gatherings rather than paramilitary camps and attempted to amend the violent image Italian neo-fascism had by then acquired. In Germany, a group of intellectuals, influenced by De Benoist's ideas, set about 'rewriting history and undoing the post-war consensus and *raison*

---

[22] Franco Freda was tried for the Piazza Fontana massacre but found not guilty on the grounds of 'insufficient evidence', with a final verdict by the Court of Cassation on 27 January 1987. On the basis of fresh evidence, a new trial concluded in 2005 that Freda was indeed guilty of this massacre, even though he was no longer judicially liable.

[23] On the various phases of Italian neo-fascism, see F. Ferraresi, *Threats to Democracy: The Radical Right in Italy after the War* (Princeton: Princeton University Press, 1996).

d'être of the Bonn Republic'.[24] While New Right thinking was still in many ways linked to the usual suspects, not least Evola,[25] it clearly represented a growing realization that the world had entered a new historical phase and that old-style neo-fascism, so closely linked to pre-1968 and Cold War values, had run its course.

VII. THE EXTREME RIGHT TODAY: A NEW BEAST OR NEO-FASCISM IN A NEW GUISE?

Since the late 1970s, many right-wing and xenophobic movements have come to the fore, influenced both by the European and the American New Right, occasionally with discernible roots in, but often openly distancing themselves from, the fascist and neo-fascist past. Much recent debate among scholars has focused on reaching a new consensus on a definitional core of generic fascism, which would allow a clearer taxonomy of populist and extreme right movements across the world, distinguishing between 'proper' fascist and other spurious phenomena. Thus Griffin defined generic fascism as 'a genus of political ideology whose mythic core in its various permutations is a palingenetic form of populist ultra-nationalism'.[26] Eatwell, in turn, coined the definition of 'a holistic-national radical Third Way'.[27] These conclusions are especially useful in the current situation, where we find an eclectic plethora of groups and movements, ranging from the post-fascist Alleanza Nazionale to the liberal yet also anti-new-immigrant and anti-Muslim List Pym Fortuyn in the Netherlands to the ethno-regionalist xenophobic variety, such as the Lega Nord in Italy or the Vlaams Blok (now Vlaams Belang) in Flanders. What, if anything, do these movements and parties have in common? How much of a threat to democracy or, conversely, how much of a convergence towards accepting the liberal-democratic order do they represent? To what extent do the new definitions of generic fascism apply to these phenomena?

Scholarly opinion is inevitably divided regarding the new movements. According to Ignazi, the extreme right today includes two types of parties, those which

[24] M. Minkenberg, 'The New Right in France and Germany: Nouvelle Droite, Neue Rechte, and the New Right Radical Parties', in P. H. Merkl and L. Weinberg, *The Revival of Right-Wing Extremism in the Nineties* (London: Frank Cass, 1997), 73.

[25] See R. Griffin, 'Between Metapolitics and Apoliteía: The New Right's Strategy for Conserving the Fascist Vision in the "Interregnum"', *Modern and Contemporary France*, 8 (2000), 35–53 and 'Interregnum or Endgame? Radical Right Thought in the "Post-fascist" Era', *Journal of Political Ideologies*, 5 (2000), 163–78.

[26] R. Griffin, *The Nature of Fascism* (London: Pinter, 1991; paperback edn. London: Routledge, 1993), 26.

[27] R. Eatwell, *Fascism: A History* (New York: Penguin Books, 1996).

are heir to the fascist tradition and those which are anti-system yet also alien to such a tradition. The second type of parties, ranging from the Austrian Freedom Party to the Front National in France and the Progress Parties in Denmark and Norway, are generally more successful, as they 'offer an answer to those demands and needs created by post-industrialism and not satisfied by traditional parties: they do not revive the "palingenetic" myth of fascism'.[28] Ignazi therefore put the emphasis on the major changes which have characterized the transition from an industrial to a post-industrial society, including the decline of the working class and of traditional class-based parties, the collapse of the old ideologies, the growth of immigration, as well as shifts in values associated with post-materialism (but also a cultural backlash and a reaffirmation of socially conservative and intolerant values). Kitschelt preferred to distinguish between right-authoritarian parties, such as the French National Front, and populist anti-statist parties, such as the Freedom Party and the Lega Nord.[29] The latter successfully combined an anti-immigrants platform with support for free market policies.

The problem with these taxonomies is that they tend to capture the nature of these parties at a particular moment but do not take into account their development, as they can be highly opportunistic and freely change their policies. A typical example is that of the Lega Nord, which started as a centrist movement with no explicit fascist roots or symbols and gradually moved to the right, adopting European New Right ideas and adapting its ethno-regionalism to fit such ideas. Conversely, Alleanza Nazionale has evident roots in Italian Fascism and neo-fascism but has moved gradually away from those roots, openly denouncing fascism and embracing liberalism. To complicate matters, at the level of the rank and file of these parties, considerable nostalgic and emotional continuity with neo-fascism can be detected in Alleanza Nazionale, while there are no equivalent sentiments in the Lega Nord. In addition, as argued by Griffin, the irrelevance of a fascist ideology or roots for most of these parties, as for European New Right thinking, may have been overstated, so that they cannot neatly be separated on the basis of this criterion. In short, identifying the ideological core of a party is one thing, accounting for its dynamic trajectory is another, distinguishing between its leadership and rank and file is a third. In this context, Eatwell argued that a clear categorization of these parties is extremely difficult and that it might be more useful to consider their placement within a spectrum, since 'whilst there is a core doctrine, there are many varieties of extremism'.[30]

---

[28] P. Ignazi, 'The Extreme Right in Europe: A Survey', in P. H. Merkl and L. Weinberg, *The Revival of Right-Wing Extremism in the Nineties* (London: Frank Cass, 1997), 54.

[29] H. P. Kitschelt with A. McGann, *The Radical Right in Western Europe: A Comparative Analysis* (Ann Arbor: University of Michigan Press, 1995).

[30] R. Eatwell, 'The Rebirth of the Extreme Right in Western Europe?', *Parliamentary Affairs*, 53 (2000), 414.

Leaving aside the issue of classification, it is possible to argue that the extreme right in Western Europe today, as compared to the Cold War period, has been obliged to come to terms with the longevity of liberal democracy, thereby putting aside its revolutionary ideals. Violence has not necessarily been curbed, as evidenced by the fact that attacks against new migrants are often carried out by extreme right sympathizers, but it is no longer openly theorized. Conversely, in Eastern Europe, the collapse of communism has seen a revival of ethnic ultranationalism, which seemingly has closer roots in the inter-war authoritarian regimes, as well as points of contact with the heirs to the Communist parties. Anti-Semitism is still very prominent, while in Western Europe it has been put onto the back burner, whereas the anti-Muslim line has come to the fore.

To an extent the variety of forms taken by the extreme right since the 1980s is nothing new, given that this political area has always been characterized by eclecticism and internal divisions. In addition, every party and movement has to be analysed in its national context, as well as in the context of global socio-political change. With the end of the Cold War and the disappearance of the communist threat, the glue that kept together disparate groups has finally dissolved, replaced by the weaker adhesive of anti-immigration and xenophobia, as well as anti-Americanism. The end of the 'communist threat' led Kaplan and Weinberg to hypothesize a convergence between the extreme right in Western Europe and in the United States, around issues of race, culture, and post-industrialism, reflected in growing cooperation between groups and organizations across the Atlantic.[31] This would indicate that the absence of a strong common platform and a clear-cut enemy is not an impediment to continuing international collaboration.

VIII. Neo-fascist Legacy

There does not appear to be an obvious legacy of neo-fascism. The main legacy, that of an ideological core, pertains to fascism rather than neo-fascism, with the partial exception of the idea of an organic European culture and of Evola's 'interregnum'. According to Griffin, as we saw, the latter might explain the seeming acceptance of the democratic order by the European New Right, while in reality its intellectuals may still entertain enduring beliefs in a mythical return to an authoritarian golden age. Violent militancy and the warrior spirit, on the other hand, have been relegated to the fringes. In the age of unipolarity, anti-Americanism occupies

---

[31] J. Kaplan and L. Weinberg, *Emergence of a Euro-American Radical Right* (New Brunswick, NJ: Rutgers University Press, 1998).

centre stage, as well as anti-globalization and anti-immigration. While collaboration across national barriers is on the increase, not least thanks to the Internet, the new breed of extreme right parties no longer seem interested in resuscitating a 'Fascist International'.

If there is a legacy, it is a historical one concerning the unholy alliance of neo-fascism with sectors of the anti-communist conservative forces and intelligence services of western democracies, which is still partially shrouded in mystery. A truth recovery process has been set in motion but it is slow and unsatisfactory. US classified documents are being released reluctantly and patchily, not least because many of the protagonists in the countries affected by terrorism and *coups d'état* are still alive. In various countries, such as Italy and Chile, this historical legacy is closely linked to a judicial one. In Italy, there have notoriously been deliberate obstructions to the course of justice on the part of various state and political bodies in the trials concerning the bomb attacks linked to the 'Strategy of Tension'. This has caused a partial failure of the judicial process. In Chile, an amnesty law passed in 1978 under Pinochet covered crimes committed from 1973 to 1978. Since the end of the Pinochet regime in 1990, right-wing opposition parties have blocked efforts by congress to repeal the amnesty, and it has been only through ambiguities in the law that a number of the perpetrators of political killings, kidnappings, and torture have been prosecuted.

Arguably, therefore, an attitude of connivance persists to this day. The (remaining) neo-fascists are eager to erase this particular chapter of their political history as demeaning, as well as having an obvious interest in escaping justice for crimes of terrorism and violent subversion. Old and new democracies are equally at pains to avoid causing embarrassment to the political establishment or reopening old wounds among their populations. In this context, conspiracy theories, scandalous revelations, journalistic accounts, personal memoirs, and piecemeal declassified information continue to be released, while a comprehensive history of neo-fascism during the Cold War remains to be written.

BIBLIOGRAPHY

CHELES, L., FERGUSON, R., and VAUGHAN, M., *The Far Right in Western and Eastern Europe* (Harlow: Longman 1995).

EATWELL, R., *Fascism: A History* (New York: Penguin Books, 1996).

——and MUDDE, C. (eds), *Western Democracies and the New Extreme Right Challenge* (London: Routledge, 2004).

FERRARESI, F., *Threats to Democracy: The Radical Right in Italy after the War* (Princeton: Princeton University Press, 1996).

GREGOR, A. J., *The Search for Neo-fascism: The Use and Abuse of Social Science* (Cambridge: Cambridge University Press, 2006).

GRIFFIN, R., *The Nature of Fascism* (London: Pinter, 1991; paperback edn, London: Routledge, 1993).

——Loh, W., and UMLAND, A. (eds), *Fascism Past and Present, West and East: An International Debate on Concepts and Cases in the Comparative Study of the Extreme Right*, with an afterword by Walter Laqueur (Stuttgart: Ibidem-Verlag, 2006).

IGNAZI, P., *Il polo escluso: profilo del Movimento Sociale Italiano* (Bologna: Il Mulino, 1998).

——*Extreme-Right Parties in Western Europe* (Oxford: Oxford University Press, 2006).

LARSEN, S. U. (ed.), *Modern Europe after Fascism 1943–1980s* (Boulder, Colo.: Columbia University Press, 1998).

MERKL, P. H., and WEINBERG, L., *The Revival of Right-Wing Extremism in the Nineties* (London: Frank Cass, 1997).

INDEX

....